History Alive!®
World Connections

Chief Executive Officer
Bert Bower

Chief Operating Officer
Amy Larson

Director of Product Development
Maria Favata

Editorial Project Manager
Nancy Rogier

Production Manager
Jodi Forrest

Teachers' Curriculum Institute
PO Box 1327
Rancho Cordova, CA 95741

Customer Service: 800-497-6138
www.teachtci.com

ISBN 978-1-58371-948-0
1 2 3 4 5 6 7 8 9 10 -WC- 16 15 14 13 12

Manufactured by Webcrafters, Inc., Madison, WI
United States of America, May 2012, Job# 98443

Program Director
Bert Bower

Lead Creative Developer
Tracy Wells

Contributing Writers
David Fasulo
Brent Goff
David Holford

Curriculum Consultant
Liz Russell

Curriculum Developers
Bert Bower
Nancy Rogier
Nathan Wellborne
Tracy Wells

Teacher Consultants
Matt Moorman
Nathan Wellborne

Technology Consultants
Taru Jain
John Kelly
Marsha Russo

Scholars
Dr. Celine Dauverd
University of Colorado, Boulder

Dr. Bruce Grelle
California State University, Chico

Dr. Jeff Jones
University of North Carolina, Greensboro

Dr. Paula A. Michaels
University of Iowa

Dr. Douglas Peifer
Air War College

Dr. Marshal Poe
University of Iowa

Dr. Claire Sanders
Texas Christian University

Dr. Sarah Shields
University of North Carolina, Chapel Hill

Dr. Natalie Zacek
University of Manchester

Cartographer
Mapping Specialists
Madison, Wisconsin

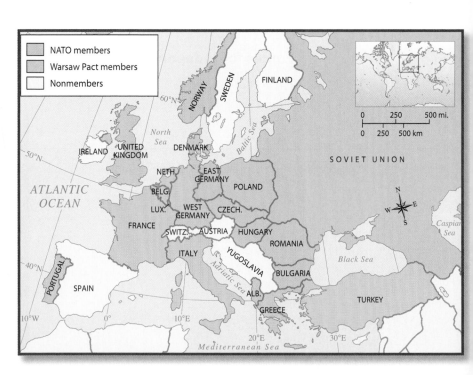

Maps

Illustrations, Graphs, and Tables

Selected Primary Source Quotations

Themes of World History

How can a thematic approach help us make sense of world history?

1.1 Introduction

What is world history? A simple way to define world history is to say that it is an account of the past on a world scale. World history, however, is anything but simple. Our world is vast. It is diversely populated. Human history goes back thousands of years. To manage such a deep and wide subject, historians take various approaches to the study of world history.

One approach is the traditional "Western heritage" model. It focuses on classical civilizations of the Mediterranean world—such as Greece and Rome—followed by the history of Europe and other Western nations. In this approach, other world regions—such as Asia, Africa, and Latin America—get little attention.

Another approach might be called the "different cultures" model. It maintains a Western focus but includes coverage of the rest of the world. The goal is to provide a foundation in Western civilization, while promoting understanding of other cultures. This approach treats the world as a collection of separate regions, however, with little to connect them.

History Alive! World Connections takes a third approach. It adopts a "big picture" view of world history, stepping back to see the world as an interconnected whole. It provides details about specific countries and regions, but presents those details in a larger, cross-regional and global context. While highlighting the world's diversity, it also makes connections and comparisons across cultures. It examines history from a global perspective, seeking to identify common patterns in historical events around the world.

One way historians identify patterns in world history is by applying themes to the study of the past. In this lesson, you will learn about the themes used in *History Alive! World Connections*. You will also learn about key concepts and ways of thinking that will help you organize information and enhance your understanding of world history.

History Alive! World Connections takes a "big picture" approach to the study of world history. "Era Overview" lessons look at an era in world history from a global and cross-regional perspective. Lessons that follow the Era Overview focus on specific regions and countries.

The UN lists Melaka as one of its world heritage sites. Formerly known as Malacca, the city developed under Malay, Portuguese, and Dutch influences.

evidence information in various forms used by historians to reconstruct the past

artifact a human-made object from the past

primary source a historical record or document produced by an eyewitness or other observer who lived during the time period in question

secondary source a record or document referring to past events but not produced at the time

1.2 How Historians Work

Historians seek to create accurate, meaningful accounts of the past. This task can present great challenges, especially when the history they recount lies in the distant past. To carry out their work, historians rely on certain methods and concepts to help them evaluate, organize, and interpret information.

The Process of History Writing   Historians typically begin their work with a question they hope to answer. One example might be, *How did the ancient Silk Road trade routes help spread religious ideas across Asia?*

The first step in answering that question is to gather **evidence,** information that helps in making statements or drawing conclusions about historical events. Evidence can come in many forms. It might be any one of the following:

- a document, such as a letter, a journal, or a map
- an **artifact,** or an object made by humans that reveals something about their lives or beliefs
- a drawing
- a piece of music
- information gathered from books or interviews with people

Historians refer to such evidence as sources. There are two basic types of sources. **Primary sources** are documents or other records of past events produced by people who experienced those events or who lived at the time. The journal of a Silk Road traveler would be a primary source. **Secondary sources** are documents created later, typically by scholars or other experts. A modern history of the Silk Road would be a secondary source.

Buildings created by people in the past that have survived to the present day can provide valuable evidence for historians. This picture shows the ruins of an ancient town in Mystras, Greece. What other types of nonwritten evidence do historians use?

Historians evaluate sources critically to assess their worth. Among other things, they examine sources for their **point of view**—the perspective or opinions a creator brings to a work. Point of view is not necessarily a bad thing, but historians must be aware of it when weighing the value of a source. If the point of view expressed in a source shows **bias**—a strong preference that might color the information—historians may reject the source as distorted and inaccurate.

Once evidence is gathered and evaluated, historians use it to reconstruct the past. They often begin by establishing a **chronology,** or sequence of events. Placing events in sequence helps determine cause and effect and reveals patterns over time. Historians also use evidence to analyze and interpret history. They seek to explain how and why things happened and to assess the significance of past events. Historians may bring their own point of view to their analysis of history. But careful historians try to ensure that the weight of the evidence supports their interpretation.

Key Concepts   Historians also rely on certain concepts to organize information and make sense of history. Two of the most important concepts concern perspectives on time and space.

Historians often divide history into periods of time. They may base these periods on a major turning point, such as the development of agriculture. Or they may base them on a unifying principle or theme, such as revolution. Dividing history into periods allows historians to present events in order. It also helps them make connections among events and highlight patterns in history. This process of dividing history into periods is known as **periodization**.

Three long periods often appear in world history courses. They are:

- ancient,
- medieval,
- and modern.

These periods generally reflect turning points in the history of Western civilization, such as the fall of Rome, the Renaissance, and the Industrial Revolution. They are less useful for other parts of the world, however.

In this text, historical periods are based on major eras in global history. Certain lessons reflect this "big picture" focus. For example, Lesson 4 looks at growing interactions among world regions after 300 C.E. Lesson 10 covers global expansion between 1400 and 1800. Lesson 14 examines revolutions in the 18th and 19th centuries.

A second key concept, known as **spatial frames,** concerns the different geographic perspectives that historians apply to world events.

These ancient Egyptian hieroglyphics are an example of a primary source which might be used by historians. They present a written record of the past produced by people who lived at the time. Writings from the past survive in many forms—on clay tablets, scrolls, or printed books, among others.

point of view a person's way of thinking about a subject

bias a personal preference or prejudice

chronology a sequence of events in time

periodization the division of history into periods of time

spatial frames different geographic perspectives that historians apply to world events

This is a Renaissance-era cathedral located in Florence, Italy. Historians can look at an event such as the Renaissance through different spatial frames. For example, a historian might study the beginnings of the Renaissance within the city of Florence. Or, they might zoom out to an interregional perspective to examine how Renaissance ideas spread throughout Europe.

interregional referring to a land area covering two or more regions

universal standards ideas or values, such as human rights, that are said to apply to all people

One way to understand this concept is to imagine that you are looking down on Earth from high above, watching human events with a powerful zoom lens. If you focus on a small area, you can see events taking place in a single nation. Zoom out a little and you will see events in the region where the nation is located. Zoom out a little more and you will get a larger, **interregional** view of events in two or more regions. If you keep zooming out, you will eventually get a global view. These different perspectives—national, regional, interregional, and global—are spatial frames.

By applying spatial frames to the study of history, historians can make comparisons and see larger patterns. For example, they might see that trade in a particular nation reflects economic trends in a larger regional, interregional, and global context.

Habits of Mind   When studying history, it can be useful to adopt certain ways of thinking. Historians refer to ways of thinking as "habits of mind." Three habits are particularly helpful in the study of world history.

The first habit is to look for global patterns over time and space. This means examining events at different times and in different places to see how they might be connected. It also means connecting local events to global trends. An example of this might be looking at how a war in one part of the world caused migration that influenced life in another place years later. Or it might be looking at how a development in one place, such as an invention, changed life around the world.

The second habit is to make comparisons within and among societies. An event or historical process may or may not have the same effect on all members of a society. It may also have similar or varying effects on other societies. Careful students of history look for similarities and differences in the ways societies respond to change. An example of this is comparing how societies around the world have adapted to industrialization.

The third habit is to assess **universal standards** in light of cultural differences. Examples of universal standards include the principles of democracy and human rights. Although claims for such standards may seem reasonable to many people, they may not be accepted everywhere. Careful students of history examine such claims in historical context, not suspending judgment but developing cultural awareness and understanding.

1.3 A Thematic Approach

Historians use themes to identify patterns in history. Many possible themes can apply to historical events. Two broad themes are continuity and change, that is, the way things have stayed the same or changed over time. Two other broad themes are integration and difference. *Integration* refers to ways in which the peoples of the world have been drawn together by historical factors. *Difference* concerns how they have remained distinct and diverse.

History Alive! World Connections highlights five themes in world history: cultural interaction, political structures, economic structures, social structures, and human-environment interaction. Studying history with these themes in mind will help you make connections among events and interpret the past.

cultural diffusion the spread of cultural traits from one society or place to another

Cultural Interaction   The way cultures interact is a key theme in world history. Throughout history, people of different cultures have exchanged ideas and adopted new beliefs and customs. This spread of cultural influences is known as **cultural diffusion**. At the same time, people have also rejected outside influences and come into conflict over new ideas. The study of how cultures have interacted and developed over time is crucial to our understanding of the world.

Various topics fit under the theme of cultural interaction. Some examples are:

- the growth and development of religions
- the formation and spread of other belief systems and philosophies
- the ideas of science and technology and how they move across cultures
- artistic influences in painting, music, architecture, literature, and other arts

Political Structures   A second key theme is the creation of political systems and forms of government. World history has often been presented as a series of one ruler or **government** after another. It is much more than that. Nevertheless, political structures are an important aspect of history and a key element in the growth of civilization. The way in which people have organized and governed themselves says a great deal about human society.

The triumphal arch is an example of the theme of cultural interaction in world history. The building of triumphal arches dates back to ancient Rome. Shown here is the Arc de Triomphe, the largest triumphal arch in the world.

This engraving depicts the execution by guillotine of King Louis XVI of France, during the French Revolution. The French Revolution is one example of a change in political structures, during which France transitioned from a monarchy to a republic.

Various topics fall under the theme of political structures. Here are some examples:

- forms of government
- the nature and growth of empires, large territories controlled by a single ruler or state
- the development of nations
- political revolts and revolutions
- regional or global organizations, such as the European Union and the United Nations

Economic Structures   The way in which societies organize their economies is another important theme. Economic motives lie at the heart of many human activities, from the quest for food to the pursuit of wealth. Economic factors have played a critical role in history, driving people and societies to innovate, explore, and expand. At the same time, economic interests have also been a source of great conflict.

This theme covers a wide range of topics. Some examples are:

- the birth of agriculture and the expansion of trade
- how labor is organized and used
- the rise of industry
- the development of economic theories that have had a major impact on people and events around the world

gender roles customs relating to the position of men and women in society

kinship family relationship, either by birth, marriage, or adoption

Social Structures   The organization of societies is also a key theme. In prehistoric times, people formed social groups to meet their need for food, shelter, and security. Over time, social groups banded together to form societies. Each society developed its own rules and customs to govern behavior and help it function. Although these structures varied from culture to culture, they also had many things in common. By examining and comparing social structures throughout history, we can get a better understanding of human life.

Among the topics covered by this theme are:

- **gender roles** and relations, including the place of women in society
- customs relating to family and **kinship**
- racial and ethnic differences and their impact on society
- division of society into social and economic classes

Human-Environment Interaction The interaction between humans and the environment is the fifth theme. The environment has been a key factor in human activity throughout history. The fact that people have to operate within the limits of the natural world has helped shape their actions. It has affected how and where people live and how they support themselves. At the same time, human actions have also changed the environment in many ways.

This theme covers topics such as:

- disease
- population growth
- migration
- patterns of human settlement

These factors can reflect or influence conditions in the environment. Another topic is the environmental impact of technology, a major concern today because of energy use and climate change. Throughout history, however—from the birth of farming to the creation of factories—the use of technology has affected the environment. By changing how we interact with the natural world, technology has had a major impact on the course of history.

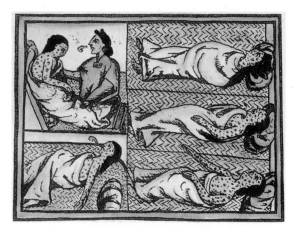

The spread of disease is one way in which history can be affected by the interaction between humans and their environment. This drawing depicts Aztec natives infected with smallpox which they contracted from the Spanish. Smallpox did not exist in the Americas before the arrival of the Spanish in the fifteenth century.

Summary

In this lesson, you learned about some of the methods, concepts, and themes used in the study of world history.

A "Big-Picture" Approach World history can be approached in various ways. The traditional approach focuses on the history of Western civilization. A second approach looks at the diversity of world regions. *History Alive! World Connections* takes a "big picture" approach that seeks to make connections among cultures and regions and identify patterns in history. It examines historical events in a cross-regional and global context.

How Historians Work Historians seek to answer questions about the past. They gather historical evidence and use it to reconstruct and interpret past events. They make use of key concepts, such as time periods and spatial frames, to help them organize information and make connections. They also apply certain habits of mind to analyze history. They look for links between events in different times and places and make comparisons within and among societies. They also evaluate universal standards in cultural and historical context.

A Thematic Approach Applying themes to the study of history can help reveal patterns in historical events. This text highlights five themes. It examines the interaction of cultures around the world. It looks at political, economic, and social structures throughout history. And it considers the nature and impact of human interaction with the environment.

Era Overview: Foundations of World History, Prehistory–300 C.E.

How did humans progress from bands of hunter-gatherers to the great civilizations of the ancient world?

2.1 Introduction

About 50,000 years ago, according to a widely held theory, our earliest ancestors began migrating out of Africa. Over many thousands of years, descendants of those physically modern humans spread through Asia, Australia, and Europe. They replaced existing populations of more primitive human beings. Thus, the theory goes, all modern humans originated in Africa.

Not all scientists agree on the origins of the human race. But they would all agree with one statement. In nearly every environment that they encountered, early modern humans thrived.

Around 10,000 years ago, humans began settling down. They turned to agriculture, raising crops and animals for food and clothing. Populations grew. Some 5,000 years later, the first cities arose, and with them the first civilizations. In time, a few civilizations developed into powerful empires. At each step in this progression, peoples of ancient times had basic features in common. They followed leaders, engaged in economic activities, and developed social structures.

Through their accomplishments, these ancient peoples laid the foundations of world history. Theirs is the story of how human beings colonized the continents and went on to develop more and more sophisticated societies that interacted with one another in a multitude of ways. As you will learn in this lesson, their story begins with humans as hunter-gatherers.

Themes

Cultural Interaction The move from hunting and gathering to more complex societies resulted in an enormous increase in the exchange of cultural knowledge.

Political Structures Political structures became more complex throughout ancient times, moving from small family units to expansive empires.

Economic Structures Ancient economies developed from a reliance on hunting and gathering to a reliance on agriculture supplemented by trade and commerce.

Social Structures The human social structure shifted from the basic equality of hunting and gathering groups to the hierarchy of complex state societies.

Human-Environment Interaction Human impact on the environment intensified as societies shifted from hunting and gathering to agriculture.

◀ This detail of an Assyrian sculpture shows cuneiform, an ancient form of writing.

2.2 Hunter-Gatherer Societies

The earliest human beings appeared on Earth an estimated 2.5 million years ago. For nearly that entire time, humans lived as **hunter-gatherers**. They hunted wild animals and gathered edible plants. It was a simple existence. Early modern humans, who had populated much of the globe by 30,000 years ago, continued the hunting-and-gathering way of life. They lived at a time when the last Ice Age was ending. Earth's climate was cycling through a series of warm and cold periods. Sea levels rose and fell. Across great areas of Earth's surface, different forms of vegetation came and went. Humans survived by adapting to this changing environment. Like the environment, the humans, too, changed over time.

Self-Sufficiency During the Stone Age   A few hunter-gatherer groups still exist today. They do not represent the great diversity of ancient hunting-and-gathering societies, but their way of life offers clues about early modern humans of the distant past. Those clues, along with evidence gathered by archaeologists, suggest that in a hunting-and-gathering economy the people were largely self-sufficient. They secured their own food supply and moved from place to place as needed to maintain it. They clothed themselves in the furs of animals that they had killed for food. They lived in caves, or they built shelters out of available materials, such as trees, brush, and animal hides. They crafted tools out of wood, bone, antlers, and stone.

Most of the materials used by ancient hunter-gatherers have disintegrated with the passage of time. The one that has survived the best is stone. When archaeologists dig at sites once inhabited by hunter-gatherers, nearly all of the tools and other artifacts that they find are made of stone. That explains the name given to the period between the emergence of stone tools and the later appearance of metal tools. Archaeologists call it the Stone Age. The Stone Age began some 2.5 million years ago. Archaeologists divide it into two major periods: the Paleolithic ("Old Stone") and the Neolithic ("New Stone").

Prehistoric people left behind cave art that gives clues about how they lived. This cave art from the Ennedi Plateau in Chad, Africa, shows people and the animals they may have hunted.

Stone Age Tools When archaeologists find stone tools, they use them to gain insight into the group that produced them. By studying an ancient people's tools, they can judge how advanced the community was. The earliest hunter-gatherers' "toolkit" included stone flakes—sharp pieces of stone that could be used like knives to butcher animals. To produce them, people hit a large stone with a fist-sized stone in order to flake off pieces.

After a number of flakes had been removed, what was left of the original stone had a jagged edge. This stone tool might have served as a chopper, useful in cutting wood, cracking nuts, or breaking open bones for their marrow. It might have been used as a digger, useful for gathering edible roots. Both types of tool could also be used as weapons for hunting or for fighting.

Knowledge of how to make tools was culturally transmitted. That is, it was passed from one generation to the next. In this way it became part of the hunter-gatherer band's **culture**—the shared beliefs, practices, and traditions of a group.

Through much of the Stone Age, tool-making techniques developed slowly. Archaeologists identify few differences in the design of tools made during that time. Near the end of the Paleolithic period, however, some dramatic changes took place. One advance was the development of composite tools, like the spear. It combined a sharp point with a wooden shaft, for thrusting or throwing. Other tools with a variety of specific uses began to appear. For the first time, hunter-gatherers began to use needles, often made of bone, to sew their clothing. Crude flakes were now worked into thinner blades and arrowheads.

The Quest for Food Hunter-gatherers relied for survival on the natural plant and animal resources found in their surroundings. They used their tools to gather, hunt, fish, and trap those resources. In the forested areas of Europe, for example, early modern humans gathered wild fruits, nuts, roots, and seeds. In meadows and on open plains, wild cereals grew along with wild peas, beans, and other plants. Game animals included rabbits, deer, and wild pigs.

To maintain a successful hunting-and-gathering economy, these early modern humans had to be mobile. That is, they had to be able to relocate often and quickly. Hunter-gatherers moved from one place to the next in an ongoing quest for food.

Much of their movement related to the seasonal migrations of the game animals that they hunted. They followed herds of deer and other animals as they moved from one grazing land to another. They trekked to coastal locations and rivers during the season when fish gathered there to produce and deposit eggs. They traveled to local lakes and marshes when it was time for migrating birds to stop there to feed.

This hand axe made from flint was discovered in France. It dates from the Paleolithic period. Designs for stone tools remained constant for much of the Stone Age.

culture the shared beliefs, practices, and traditions of a group

Hunting was a main source of food for early humans. Hunter-gatherers followed the herds of animals as they moved from place to place.

Gathering fruits, nuts, and other vegetative sources of food was also a seasonal affair. It, too, called for mobility.

Having to be able to move with the seasons had its limitations. Hunter-gatherers could not afford to gather possessions. They had no pack animals to help them carry loads of belongings from one place to another. They had to carry everything themselves. For this reason, they took only a few tools, weapons, and other goods with them.

Mobility was a key to the hunting-and-gathering way of life. Nonetheless, later hunter-gatherers maintained "central places"—sites within their territory to which they continually returned. These base camps were usually located in a resource-rich area, perhaps along a seacoast or lakeshore or near known supplies of food or fuel. There they slept, made their tools, cooked their meals, and took part in social activities.

Interactions Within and Between Groups   Hunter-gatherer bands consisted mainly of kin groups—people who claim a common ancestor. Bands typically ranged in size from 30 to 50 people. They shared food and otherwise worked together for common ends. Their economy was based on a division of labor. Men did the hunting and women did the gathering. Nonetheless, members of hunter-gatherer bands generally enjoyed equal status in the group. They had no real government—no one person had political power. But they did have leaders. These were probably elders who had the experience and personality necessary to gain the respect of the group.

Hunter-gatherers traveled far and wide to exploit available resources. The territory that they typically covered during a year might have ranged from 50 to 100 miles in diameter. Their seasonal movements sometimes led to contacts with other groups. They might have exchanged goods with those groups. But competition between groups could also lead to conflict over scarce resources. Tools might then become weapons.

Increased Social Complexity   At the end of the Paleolithic period, some hunter-gatherer communities were becoming more complex. They exhibited characteristics that set them apart from traditional hunting-and-gathering groups. Their populations were higher. Their base camps were larger and tended to become near-permanent settlements. They developed equipment for processing food and systems for storing and preserving it. Some hunter-gatherers may have sowed wild seeds to expand their source of plant food. The next step for these complex societies was to begin farming the land.

2.3 The Beginning of Agriculture

Complex hunter-gatherer societies appeared in regions that were rich in resources. Groups living in villages in such areas did not have to be particularly mobile. Nearly everything they needed for basic survival was available locally.

One such region existed in Southwest Asia, in the area known as the Fertile Crescent. This arc of land extended from the eastern Mediterranean across southern Anatolia (Turkey) and south to the Persian Gulf. Here, some 8,000–10,000 years ago, the first farmers appeared.

From Hunting and Gathering to Farming   The western area of the Fertile Crescent, near the Mediterranean Sea, offered a wealth of natural resources. Small hunter-gatherer societies settled there. They hunted mainly gazelles but also smaller mammals and birds. They gathered fruits, tubers, and seeds—especially the seeds of wild grasses.

Farther east in the Fertile Crescent, in the foothills of the Zagros Mountains, other hunter-gatherers had a more mobile way of life. There, wild goats, sheep, and cattle migrated in the spring from the lowlands into the highlands, following the ripening pattern of the wild grasses. The hunter-gatherers moved with them, hunting the animals and gathering the seeds of the grasses.

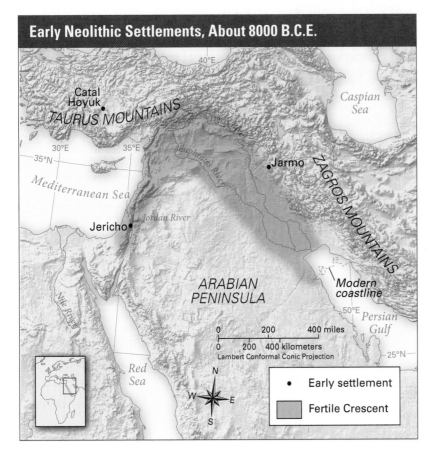

Early Neolithic Settlements, About 8000 B.C.E.

Many Neolithic settlements were located in the Fertile Crescent, where the land was fertile. Here, people built towns such as Jericho, Catal Hoyuk, and Jarmo.

Those grasses were the key ingredient in the momentous shift from hunting and gathering to farming. Farming involves both cultivating plants and raising animals. The first domesticated plants were grasses, in particular the large-grained cereals wheat and barley. The goats, sheep, and cattle that fed on wild grasses became the first domesticated animals (except for the dog, which had already been living with humans for thousands of years). Groups living in the Fertile Crescent also domesticated pigs.

Domestication is a biological process in which the physical characteristics of wild plants and animals change as a result of human intervention. The change likely happens over hundreds of years or more.

The following scenario suggests how hunter-gatherers might have begun domesticating wheat. Of two varieties of wild wheat, one dropped its ripened seeds when touched. That made it hard to harvest. Hunter-gatherers learned to collect only the variety that kept its seeds. That way, they could harvest the wheat by cutting the stalks and carrying them back to their village for processing. They saved and later sowed some of that same seed, intending to expand the resource in the wild. As a result, that one variety of seed began to dominate the local stands of wild wheat. Through this process, hunter-gatherers unintentionally changed the overall traits of the wheat in their territory.

Wheat was domesticated in the Fertile Crescent region. This made the development of agriculture possible, which resulted in the beginning of settled society.

domestication a biological process in which the physical characteristics of wild plants and animals change as a result of human intervention

sedentary settled; nonmigratory

In time, hunter-gatherers in the Fertile Crescent began to make these kinds of choices intentionally.

- They selected plants, as well as animals, that had favorable characteristics.
- By around 9,000 years ago, they were cultivating wheat—preparing the ground and then sowing and harvesting the seeds. They also grew barley, lentils, chickpeas, peas, and beans.
- They built structures for storing their food.
- Near their fields, they built houses, which together formed a farm village.
- They may have continued to hunt or to gather, but eventually, most came to rely on their domesticated plants and animals to provide for their basic needs.
- They were **sedentary**—they stayed in one place, in permanent, year-round settlements.
- They had become farmers.

Later, some groups moved away from the centers of farming to take up a herding way of life. On the grasslands of the Fertile Crescent, they lived with their herds of domesticated sheep, goats, and cattle. Periodically, they moved with the herds as the animals moved to fresh pastures. People who establish this kind of food-producing economy are called **pastoral nomads**. The nomadic herders of the Fertile Crescent likely preferred life in the wide-open spaces to life in the farm villages.

pastoral nomad member of a group whose economy revolves around its herd of domesticated animals, with which the group periodically moves to find new grazing land

cultural diffusion the spread of ideas, inventions, or other cultural elements from one society to another

Why Agriculture Arose   Increased knowledge of how to domesticate plants and animals is just one reason scholars give for why agriculture began when it did. They also note the development of new technology for gathering, processing, and storing foods. Another important factor is climate. The last Ice Age ended around 11,500 years ago. After that time, Earth's climate remained generally stable. In the Fertile Crescent and other places in which farming began, the climate turned favorably warm and rainy. Yet another reason for the rise of agriculture was population pressures. As populations increased, hunter-gatherers needed to expand their supply of food. Farming met this need.

The Spread of Agriculture   In 10,000 B.C.E., nearly every human was a hunter-gatherer. By 1 C.E., most were either farmers or herders. The shift from hunting and gathering to agriculture, once it had started in any location, took hundreds or thousands of years. During the transition, groups acquired needed resources through a mix of hunting, gathering, farming, and herding.

Agriculture first appeared in the Fertile Crescent around 9,000 years ago. Through **cultural diffusion**, it spread from there to Egypt, Europe, and India. Knowledge of agriculture might have been carried to those places by pastoral nomads, some of whom were also skilled farmers. These mobile peoples were free to travel far from their home

Agriculture was independently invented in China 8,000 years ago with the domestication of rice and millet. This photo shows terraced rice fields in modern-day China.

territory, wherever there was grass to feed their herds. Another way that agriculture spread was through the migration of farming peoples.

By 8,000 years ago, rice and millet were being domesticated in China. By 5,500 years ago, maize (corn) was being domesticated in the Americas, followed about a thousand years later by llamas. Agriculture appears to have arisen independently in these two places, as well as in sub-Saharan Africa and elsewhere.

The Impact of the Shift to Agriculture

The shift to agriculture ushered in the Neolithic period, or New Stone Age. Neolithic peoples developed new technologies to feed the ever-growing population. They crafted better stone tools, such as the stone-bladed plow for tilling the soil. They created pottery for storing food and decorated it with distinctive styles. In time, they invented the wheel, which served as a turntable for pottery-making and was a landmark improvement in transportation.

The expansion of agriculture changed people's relationship to the environment. Instead of drawing resources from an extensive territory, as hunter-gatherers did, farmers cultivated a small area intensively. In wooded regions, farmers cleared the ground through slash-and-burn methods. They chopped down trees and set fire to any remaining vegetation.

The rise of agriculture also had an important social impact. The population density—the number of people in a unit of area—rose as kin groups came together in farm villages. Humans, now sedentary, began to accumulate goods, sometimes in exchange for surplus crops. These included not just practical goods such as pots and grinding stones but also beads and bracelets made of imported shells and precious stones. Ownership of such luxury goods brought respect and signaled a family's wealth, as did the amount of land it farmed or the size of its herd.

Wealth gave individuals power. It set them apart from others. Instead of the equality that characterized hunter-gatherer societies, farming villages gradually became stratified. People were divided into status groups based largely on wealth.

The shift from hunting and gathering to agriculture is often called the Agricultural Revolution. Some scholars refer to it as the Neolithic Revolution to suggest that its impact went beyond farming. Whatever the name, this shift was, indeed, revolutionary. In the past, advances in human knowledge tended to remain within each isolated hunter-gatherer culture. Now technological and social innovations could be passed easily not only from one generation to the next but from one culture to another.

The ruins of the Neolithic village of Skara Brae are located on the coast of Scotland. The village consisted of ten round houses that were sunk into the ground as protection from harsh winter weather. Inventions of the Neolithic period such as pottery and improved stone tools have been found at Skara Brae. These new technologies made settled life possible.

2.4 The Rise of Civilizations

Settlements that arose during the Neolithic period grew in population and social complexity. Villages became towns. Over time, towns became cities. In a few of the world's river valleys, humans took the next step. Actually, they took an enormous jump. They developed the first civilizations.

Characteristics of a Civilization A **civilization** is a highly organized and complex society. This definition, however, is a bit too tame for historian Michael Cook. He declares that "the term *civilization* suggests that there is in fact some kind of quantum leap in complexity."

One "quantum leap" involved the development of writing. Before the rise of the first civilization, writing did not exist. The names of people, places, and events were not recorded. Humans had the necessary tools—sticks and brushes, inks and paints. But they needed something much more abstract. To acquire writing, a society had to find a way to represent spoken language with visual symbols. Each of the world's earliest civilizations managed to do this.

Ancient civilizations commonly shared several other characteristics besides writing. One was geography. Ancient civilizations arose in river valleys, where access to water and fertile soil made farming much more productive.

Another characteristic of ancient civilizations was large cities. Unlike agricultural villages, populated by related families, cities drew a wide mix of peoples from the surrounding region. Usually, the urban social system evolved into a **hierarchy**—a ranking of groups of people according to their importance, status, or power. One person, the king (or priest-king), held the top rank.

Most cities contained large public structures—palaces for kings and temples for priests—as well as markets for the exchange of goods. Rulers typically managed the economy, supporting state activities by taxing farmers, merchants, and artisans or by forcing people to labor for the state.

civilization a highly organized and complex society

hierarchy a ranking of groups of people according to their importance, status, or power

The invention of written language was one of the "quantum leaps" made by the first civilizations. This photograph depicts cuneiform, the wedge-shaped writing developed by the Sumerians.

The first civilizations rose in fertile river valleys. Shown here is the Indus River valley in present-day India.

Why Civilizations Arose   Each of the major early civilizations developed in a unique way. Scholars have found no single cause that explains why they arose. Instead, they cite a number of factors that worked together to bring about civilizations.

- **Access to Water** Complex states formed, in part, as a result of the success of agriculture. Irrigation played a key role in that success. The first civilizations developed in fertile river valleys, where farmers built canals and other structures to carry river water to their fields or to store floodwater. Ready access to water greatly improved crop yields—the amount of food that could be grown per acre. Plentiful food led to expanding populations. Settlements eventually became cities.

- **Government** As a settlement's population increased, its society changed in a number of ways. One way related to government. Some societies replaced rule by elders with rule by a central authority, the state. The state, run by the king and a multitude of trained officials, was better able to organize and coordinate the activities of the increasingly more complex society.

- **Defense** Growing communities competed with one another for resources. Competition could lead to conflict. For defensive purposes, large settlements built walls around themselves to ward off invaders. Kings sometimes gained power through their success in battle. But they took responsibility for the society's prosperity as well as its defense.

- **Specialized Jobs** With advances in agriculture, farmers were able to grow more than the society could consume, which meant that everyone did not have to be a farmer. Food surpluses supported those who chose to specialize, full-time, in other areas. They became artisans and warriors as well as priests and government officials.

- **Trade** Some became merchants, or traders. Growing settlements found that they could not produce all the resources that people needed or wanted. They engaged in long-distance trade both for necessities, such as raw materials, and for luxury goods. Having a steady supply of goods helped settlements grow, and thus trade was yet another factor in the rise of civilizations.

2.5 River Valley Civilizations

The earliest civilizations formed in river valleys, where rich soils encouraged high agricultural yields. That productivity, and the resulting surpluses, played an important role in the development of complex societies. Some 5,000 years after farmers first cultivated the soil of the Fertile Crescent, the region gave birth to the world's first civilization in Mesopotamia. From there, trade contacts may have spread the concept of civilization to Egypt and the Indus River Valley. As with agriculture, China appears to have developed its first river valley civilization independently.

city-state a political unit consisting of an independent city and the lands surrounding it

Mesopotamian Civilization   Around 3500 B.C.E., the world's first civilization arose in Mesopotamia. This region was located in the eastern part of the Fertile Crescent. Through this region flow two rivers, the Tigris and the Euphrates. *Mesopotamia* means "the land between the rivers."

Some 2,000 years earlier, farmers from the foothills of the Zagros Mountains began moving into the river valley. Little rain fell in the valley, but its soils were fertile. By diverting river water through canals to their fields, the farmers found that they could grow far more crops than they had been able to in the hills. Those crops included wheat, barley, and date palms. Use of the plow, animal power, and wheeled carts added to their success.

By 3000 B.C.E., several **city-states** had appeared in southern Mesopotamia in a region known as Sumer. These independent urban centers dominated the surrounding farmland and pasturelands.

Sumer's cities had formed around temples. The temple became the central agency that ran the city's affairs. Priest-kings and their officials managed the economy. The grain that farmers produced went into temple storehouses, from which it was redistributed to the people. The temple kept a portion of the crops to finance the building and maintenance of canals, temples, and city walls. Surplus crops also paid for weapons. The city-states of Sumer regularly fought one another over land and water.

The Sumerians invented a writing system known as cuneiform. Its picture-symbols were pressed into soft clay tablets using a tool that made a wedge-shaped mark. Cuneiform means "wedge-shaped." Sumerian officials first used cuneiform as a way

Sumerian cities centered around temples. This is an artist's interpretation of what the temple in the Sumerian city of Uruk may have looked like around 3000 B.C.E.

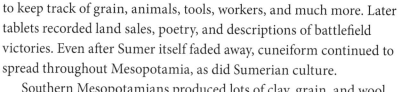

interregional involving or linking two or more regions

dynasty a series of rulers who come from the same family

This Egyptian stone carving depicts Hapi, the god of the Nile River. He wears a crown of lotus flowers. Ancient Egypt depended on the Nile River to provide water for agriculture. Here the figure of Hapi is surrounded by hieroglyphics, the system of writing developed by the ancient Egyptians.

to keep track of grain, animals, tools, workers, and much more. Later tablets recorded land sales, poetry, and descriptions of battlefield victories. Even after Sumer itself faded away, cuneiform continued to spread throughout Mesopotamia, as did Sumerian culture.

Southern Mesopotamians produced lots of clay, grain, and wool but not much else. They traded with other parts of the Fertile Crescent region for hardwood, stone, copper, gold, and semi-precious stones. They also engaged in **interregional** exchange to acquire luxury goods from places as distant as western Anatolia and the Indus River Valley. The main principles of civilization may have traveled along these and other trade routes, likely reaching Egypt in the mid-to-late 3000s B.C.E.

Egyptian Civilization Egypt, a desert country, has been called "the gift of the Nile." The Nile River flows south to north, arising in the highlands of eastern Africa and emptying into the Mediterranean Sea. In Neolithic times and beyond, the Nile overflowed its banks each summer. The floodwaters deposited fertile silt onto the adjoining lands.

Sometime after 5000 B.C.E., agriculture appeared in the Nile Valley, imported from the Fertile Crescent. Egyptian farmers grew the cereal grains barley and wheat, as well as flax, a plant whose fibers they wove into linen. They irrigated their crops from natural basins that retained some of the annual floodwaters. Farmers also raised cattle, goats, sheep, and pigs.

Increased production of food led to dramatic gains in population. By the late 3000s B.C.E., some farm villages had expanded into cities. Egyptian cities, unlike those in Sumer, did not become independent states, each with its own king. The main cities formed in the delta region, known as Lower Egypt, where the Nile split into branches that each emptied into the sea.

In the rest of this ancient land, known as Upper Egypt, several large bands of people competed for power. Around 3100 B.C.E., a leader named Menes took control of Upper Egypt and then conquered Lower Egypt, uniting the country for the first time. King Menes thus launched Egypt's first dynasty. A **dynasty** is a series of rulers who come from the same family.

By the time of Menes, priests had developed their own writing system, called hieroglyphics. Hieroglyph means "sacred carving." Scribes, specialists in the art of writing, used hieroglyphics to keep records and to communicate information. They carved the hieroglyphs on the stone walls of temples and tombs as well as on metal, wood, and clay. But they also wrote them with brush and ink on a paper-like material called papyrus, made from reeds.

Later Egyptian kings were commonly called pharaohs. The pharaoh was an **absolute monarch**—a ruler whose power is unlimited. By tradition, the pharaoh owned all of Egypt's land. As a result, through his palace officials—many of whom were scribes—he managed the economy as well as the government.

These massive stone pyramids were constructed at Giza in Egypt in the mid-2000s B.C.E. They were built using forced labor under the direction of the pharaohs, who were absolute monarchs.

Farmers paid part of their crops as taxes to officials. That surplus grain was then redistributed to non-farmers, with a portion reserved to pay for public-works projects. The government could also levy taxes in the form of forced labor in order to carry out those projects. For example, it recruited villagers and artisans to help build the massive stone pyramids of Giza in the mid-2000s B.C.E.

Indus Valley Civilization Sometime after 3000 B.C.E., in what is now Pakistan, a new civilization developed in and near the valley of the Indus River. The river arose in the high mountains of the Himalayas and flowed south through semiarid plains to the Arabian Sea, a part of the Indian Ocean. When it flooded each summer, the river deposited a layer of fertile silt that made for easy tilling of the soil.

That soil attracted farmers, who built villages and, in time, cities. The Indus River's floodplain extended far from the river. Because of extensive floodplain, the Indus Valley civilization spread over a larger area than that of Mesopotamia or Egypt.

The Indus often flooded deeply, so farmers built their settlements on high ground and surrounded them with barriers of stone or earth. They planted wheat and barley when the floodwaters receded. At some point they also began growing cotton. Some historians think that in the dry season they kept their crops watered through a network of irrigation canals. Farmers also domesticated cattle and other animals, likely including elephants.

absolute monarch a hereditary ruler whose power is unlimited

The Indus Valley culture developed a writing system, but scholars have had little success decoding it. For this reason, they know much less about the ancient Indus River region than they do about Mesopotamia or Egypt. Their descriptions of the civilization are based largely on their studies of the ruins of Indus Valley cities and other settlements.

The studies reveal that the Indus Valley civilization was home to around 100 villages and several walled cities. Two large cities, Harappa and Mohenjo-daro, dominated the region.

Harappa and Mohenjo-daro reflected the organization and complexity that is a key sign of a civilization. Each consisted of two sections—an elevated citadel, or fortress, and a lower residential area. Both were surrounded by walls. In the citadel, members of the ruling class likely conducted their political business and carried out religious rituals. In the residential city below, the people lived in brick houses linked by an orderly arrangement of streets. The finer homes had wells for water and bathrooms that drained into the city's main sewer system.

Within the lower city lived shopkeepers, merchants, scribes, and artisans. The artisans manufactured a variety of goods, including metal ornaments and weapons, fine ceramics, and cotton cloth. Woven cotton textiles and beads of semi-precious stone both served as popular goods for export. Indus Valley trade goods flowed northwest over the mountains to Iran and later also by boat across the Arabian Sea and through the Persian Gulf to Mesopotamia.

The ruins of Mohenjo-daro, one of the largest cities of the Indus Valley civilization. The elevated structure in the center was the citadel, and the lower buildings around it were residential areas.

Chinese Civilization   Two major river systems dominate China. Both flow generally west to east but in a weaving pattern that follows the contours of the landscape. The Huang He (huang heh), or Yellow River, is in the north. The Chang Jiang (chahng jyahng), or Yangtze River, is in the south. Chinese civilization arose in the valleys of both of these rivers at about the same time.

Early farmers were attracted to the fertile yellow soil, known as loess (less), that blankets the broad plain of the Yellow River. Yellow silt clouds the river, giving it its name. Farmers in the valley grew millet, a cereal grain, using dry farming rather than irrigation. To make up for lack of rain, they planted drought-resistant millet and learned ways to conserve soil moisture.

The agricultural settlements that appeared in the valley grew in population and complexity. By around 2000 B.C.E., several of them reflected key characteristics of civilization. Within large centers surrounded by defensive walls, artisans specialized in the making of ceramic pottery and the carving of jade, a semiprecious stone. They also worked copper and, later, bronze. Societies evolved a hierarchy, with a privileged minority at the top whose members could afford luxury goods obtained through long-distance trade.

The Shang (shahng) Dynasty came to power in the Yellow River Valley around 1600 B.C.E. The Shang may simply be one of several early Chinese civilizations. But it is China's first historical state. That is, the Shang were the first to record their dynasty's history using a formal writing system.

Their writing, or script, consisted of pictograms that stood for objects and ideas. That script appeared on bronze vessels, silk, and strips of bamboo linked with thread. It also appeared on what were called oracle bones. These cattle bones and tortoise shells served a special purpose. Shang diviners—persons who use magic to predict the future—first posed a question and then applied heat to the bones, causing cracks to form. The diviner then interpreted the cracks, with the goal of predicting the future.

A typical question concerned the health of the king or the success of warfare, hunting, or crops. On each oracle bone, they wrote the date and the question and, sometimes, the interpretation. Thus oracle bones comprise an important source of historical information about ancient China.

This tortoise shell oracle bone dates from the Shang dynasty in China. The writing on surviving oracle bones is an important source historians have about ancient China.

Civilization arose in a similar way to the south, in the Yangtze River Valley. Walled cities with hierarchical societies developed within an agricultural setting. However, farmers in this warmer and wetter region of China cultivated rice rather than millet, and they diverted water from the rivers as needed to irrigate their crops.

Chinese scholars refer to the several complex states that formed along the Yangtze as the Changjiang civilization. A key city in this civilization was Sanxingdui. In workshops outside the massive walls of this city, artisans crafted a variety of objects from clay, jade, ivory, turquoise, and bronze. The bronzes are particularly impressive. One, a statue of a man wearing a crown, stands more than 8 feet tall. Another, a sculpted tree with leaves, buds, and fruit—and a bird perched on each branch—rises 13 feet into the air.

The Parthenon, a temple dedicated to the goddess Athena, was built in the Greek city-state of Athens between 447 and 438 B.C.E. It still stands today and has become a symbol of ancient Athenian democracy.

empire a large political unit in which a number of different lands or peoples are governed by a single ruler

direct democracy rule by the people, carried out through direct participation in government

2.6 Ancient Empires

Ancient history is full of empires. In an **empire,** a single ruler governs a number of different lands or peoples.

Ancient empires typically developed when a powerful state conquered its weaker neighbors. Around 2350 B.C.E. in Mesopotamia, Sargon of Akkad formed the world's first empire. The Roman Empire, however, is likely the most famous ancient empire. Rome and another, earlier Mediterranean state, the Athenian Empire, experienced what is known as a classical age. The government, arts, and ideas generated by those civilizations had a lasting impact on world history and culture. Other classical ages occurred in China under the Han dynasty and in India under the Mauryan and Gupta dynasties.

The Athenian Empire Greece is a mountainous peninsula that juts southeast from the European continent into the Mediterranean Sea. In ancient times, many city-states arose on the Greek mainland and islands.

The Greeks called themselves Hellenes. They had the same ethnic background, shared the same customs, and spoke the same basic language. However, their city-states preferred to remain independent. Nevertheless, they came together politically when threatened by an outside power—or when forced to by a dominant city-state.

One such city-state was Athens. There, in 508 B.C.E, the world's first democracy appeared. The Athenians cherished their liberty, both personal and political, and they designed a government that would protect it. Theirs was a **direct democracy**—citizens participated directly in the rule of their state. Women, foreigners, and slaves were excluded from citizenship. Everyone else over age 20 had a right to vote in the people's assembly and to make speeches there concerning public policy. They could also elect magistrates, the officials who carried out decisions made in the assembly.

Pericles, a general and a leader of the Athenian democracy, offered this insight into his city-state's government:

> *Our constitution does not copy the laws of neighboring states; we are rather a pattern to others than imitators ourselves. Its administration favors the many instead of the few; this is why it is called a democracy. If we look to the laws, they afford equal justice to all . . . .*
>
> —Pericles, "Funeral Oration," 430 B.C.E.

Warfare threatened Athens, and its democratic freedoms, throughout the classical age. In 490 B.C.E., the Persian Empire of Southwest Asia invaded Greece, but the Athenian army fought them off. Ten years later the Persians sailed across the Aegean Sea and attacked once more. They were again defeated, this time by a group of city-states led by Athens and long-time rival Sparta. The Athenian navy, which ruled the seas around Greece, played a key role in the victory.

In 478 B.C.E., Athens formed an alliance with a number of island and coastal city-states around the Aegean Sea. Their goal was to defend against further Persian invasions and to attack Persian strongholds in the region. Athens, with its powerful navy, took charge. It decided which states would provide ships or money to support what historians call the Delian League.

Eventually, the Delian League had some 200 members, with Athens in firm control. By the 440s B.C.E., the contributions of most city-states took the form of tribute—payment made as a sign of submission—sent to Athens's treasury. What had started as an alliance had become an Athenian Empire.

Athens continued to expand its empire. In response, Sparta put together its own alliance of Greek city-states. In 431 B.C.E., Sparta attacked Athens. Thus began the Peloponnesian War. By the time it ended in 404, the Athenian navy had been smashed and Sparta had taken command in Greece.

In the following century, Athens made a strong recovery and even restored its empire. But the end of its power came in 338, when an army from the kingdom of Macedonia, a northern neighbor, conquered all of Greece. The Greek culture did not disappear, however. A Macedonian king, Alexander the Great, overran the Persian Empire, capturing lands stretching from Egypt east to India. He founded new cities in those lands. Greek and Macedonian settlers in those cities spread Hellenism—Greek language, customs, and philosophy—through much of Alexander's empire.

The Roman Empire Greek city-states continued to function until, in the 100s B.C.E., they were crushed by a new Mediterranean powerhouse. The Rome Empire began as a city-state in the middle of the Italian peninsula. It grew steadily through military aggression, and it would keep expanding for about 400 years. Rome's conquest of the Mediterranean region made it an empire, although the Romans still thought of their country as a republic. A **republic** is a system of government in which the people rule through representatives.

republic a system of government in which the people rule through representatives who govern according to law

At its largest, the Roman Empire extended over the entire Mediterranean region and large parts of the Middle East and Europe.

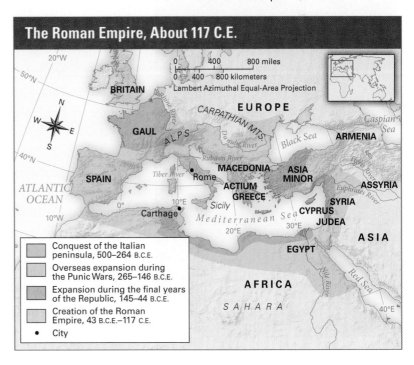

The Roman Empire, About 117 C.E.

0 400 800 miles
0 400 800 kilometers
Lambert Azimuthal Equal-Area Projection

BRITAIN
EUROPE
CARPATHIAN MTS
GAUL
ALPS
Danube River
Black Sea
ARMENIA
Caspian Sea
Rubicon River
MACEDONIA
ASIA MINOR
ASSYRIA
SPAIN
Tiber River
Rome
ACTIUM
GREECE
Euphrates River
SYRIA
ATLANTIC OCEAN
Sicily
CYPRUS
JUDEA
Carthage
Mediterranean Sea
ASIA
EGYPT
AFRICA
Nile River
Red Sea
SAHARA

Conquest of the Italian peninsula, 500–264 B.C.E.
Overseas expansion during the Punic Wars, 265–146 B.C.E.
Expansion during the final years of the Republic, 145–44 B.C.E.
Creation of the Roman Empire, 43 B.C.E.–117 C.E.
● City

Romans had founded the republic after dethroning their king in 509 B.C.E. They resolved to govern the Roman Republic according to laws. Around 450 B.C.E., to ensure the rights of all citizens in the courts, the Romans compiled their first set of written laws, the Twelve Tables.

Rome's republican system had three main parts—popular assemblies, magistrates, and the Senate. In assemblies, male citizens voted on laws and elected magistrates to carry out the laws. The magistrates at first selected the members of the Senate, who wrote legislation and handled foreign affairs.

Later the Senate, grown much more powerful, severed its link with the magistrates and assemblies. However, in later years the Senate surrendered much of its authority to the emperor.

For much of the late Republican period, Rome was an empire. The military deeply influenced Roman society. All citizens were expected to serve as soldiers. The state's leaders came largely from the military. Rome's main foreign policy was to expand its borders through conquest.

Rome was continually at war. Major conflicts included the three Punic Wars, which started in 264 B.C.E. and ended in 146 B.C.E. with the complete destruction of the North African city-state of Carthage. This was followed by wars of expansion in Anatolia, Syria, Gaul (France), and Britain, by battles along the frontier with Germanic peoples, and by several slave revolts and civil wars. One civil war ended when a rebellious Julius Caesar defeated Pompey the Great. Caesar then made himself sole ruler of Rome. After Caesar's assassination in 44 B.C.E., his great-nephew Octavian stepped into the power vacuum.

This is a statue of Octavian. He became the first official Roman emperor in 27 B.C.E. and assumed the title of Augustus ("majestic"). He is depicted here with idealized features in a style influenced by Greek sculpture.

In 27 B.C.E., Octavian became the first official emperor. He assumed the title Augustus, which means "majestic." Under Augustus and the next 15 or so emperors, the Mediterranean region enjoyed a time of relative calm known as the "Pax Romana," or "Roman Peace." The Romans, great road builders, extended their network of roads into conquered territories. This made the movement of troops to Roman colonies easier. It also encouraged trade and the diffusion of Roman culture and ideas throughout the empire. Rome also extended citizenship rights to conquered peoples, which helped integrate them into Roman society and government.

Tranquil times ended in the late 100s C.E., when the empire was battered by periods of civil war and military rebellion. A series of short-lived emperors added to the instability. In the late 200s, Emperor Diocletian split the empire into eastern and western halves. The "Roman Peace" was shattered for good in the 300s, when migrating Germanic peoples crossed the frontier and began to take over Roman lands. In 476, these peoples brought the Western Roman Empire to an end.

The Han Dynasty   The Han came to power in 206 B.C.E., after a civil war toppled the Qin (chin) dynasty. Just 15 years earlier the Qin had united all of China under a single emperor. The Han ruled for two centuries, lost control from 9 until about 25 C.E., and then ruled for another two centuries. During the earlier period of rule, called the Western Han, the capital was at Chang'an (chahn-ahn). The later period is called the Eastern Han, when the capital was moved eastward to Luoyang (lwaw-yahng), on the Yellow River.

The Qin had unified China after a long period of warfare among rival states. One goal of the Han government was to keep China stable. To do this, the Han needed loyal and capable officials to administer the government, especially in the outlying provinces. The Han established centers for the training of scholar-officials based on the teachings of Confucius, a philosopher born in the mid-500s B.C.E. Those teachings emphasized proper behavior and the maintenance of traditional ways and values.

The Han army drove the fearsome Huns away from their border with the help of the Great Wall and the newly-invented crossbow. The Han dynasty brought around 400 years of security and progress to China.

Another goal was to enlarge the empire. The Han army, equipped with the newly invented crossbow, gained new territory in several directions. To the north they pushed the fearsome Xiongnu (SHE-OONG-noo) people, also known as the Huns, away from the Great Wall that hugged China's border. To the northeast the Han colonized part of the Korean peninsula. To the south they took possession of coastal lands well into Vietnam. To the west they gained control of caravan routes that passed through Central Asia.

As a result of the westward expansion, the Han opened up inter-regional trade starting around 100 B.C.E. They exported mainly silk, some of which reached as far west as Rome. The trade routes across Asia became known as the Silk Road. The Silk Road also carried goods and ideas eastward into China, including Buddhism, a religion that arrived from India during the time of the Eastern Han dynasty.

During the Han period, China's population grew. The government sought to increase food production by encouraging farmers to move out of the densely populated Yellow River Valley. To help them resettle in northern border lands, the Han provided farmers with land and houses. Other farmers migrated south to take up rice farming in the less-populated Yangtze River Valley, where the government built irrigation works. Advances in iron-making also boosted agriculture. Farmers could till the soil more effectively using iron rather than wood or stone blades on their plows.

The Han dynasty brought China some 400 years of security and progress. Han China nearly matched the Roman Empire in size. Under the Han, the Confucian ideal took hold and became a permanent anchor for Chinese society. Today, when the Chinese refer to traditional Chinese culture, they mean the way of life that developed under the Han dynasty.

The Mauryan Empire and Gupta Empire

Historians have long described the era of the Gupta (GOOP-tuh) Empire (320–535 C.E.) as India's classical age. But many also see the earlier Mauryan (MOOR-yuhn) Empire (321–185 B.C.E.) as a key period in India's history. Leaders of both empires united much of South Asia from their homeland in the Ganges River Valley of northern India.

The most admired leader of the Mauryan Empire was its third king, Ashoka (uh-SHOKE-uh). Ashoka set out to expand the empire, but a massacre stopped him. The slaughter, by his troops, of many thousands of people from the east coast kingdom of Kalinga had a profound effect on Ashoka. He converted to Buddhism, a religion of peace, and vowed to conquer not through military force but through the moral teachings of dharma (DAHR-muh).

Ashoka sent Buddhist missionaries throughout the empire and also into Southeast Asia and Central Asia. He instituted religious tolerance in India, supporting Buddhist as well as non-Buddhist groups. Ashoka also issued edicts expressing his philosophy. These decrees were carved into stone pillars. Through these and other actions and policies, Asoka worked to unify the many different peoples of his empire.

This is an example of a pillar erected by Ashoka, the third king of the Mauryan Empire. Ashoka's pillars were inscribed with his edicts, which expressed his Buddhist philosophy.

After Ashoka's reign, the Mauryan Empire gradually fell apart. The rulers of the next great Indian state, the Gupta Empire, maintained Ashoka's policy of religious tolerance. They did not, however, follow Ashoka's lead when it came to conquest. They relied on military force to gain territory. The Gupta army, made up of horse-mounted archers, an elephant corps, and foot soldiers, had great success in battle.

Agriculture and interregional trade also helped the Guptas build an empire that enjoyed peace and prosperity. The state appears to have assisted farmers by providing irrigation works, although it did take part of the farmers' crops as taxes. By this time, the secret of growing silk had reached India from China, and silk weaving was flourishing. As the Western Roman Empire declined, Gupta traders sold costly silk cloth to the Eastern Roman, or Byzantine, Empire. They also increased trade with Southeast Asia.

Gupta emperors spent some of their wealth in support of the arts and sciences. At least one emperor maintained several scholars at his court. Religious art was widespread. Images of the Buddha appeared in various formats, including copper sculpture and colorful painted murals. Religious literature also enjoyed popularity, as did a variety of non-religious drama and poetry. Gupta mathematicians in the 400s were aware of the concept of zero and employed the decimal system. By the end of that century, Indian astronomers had calculated pi and had determined that Earth rotates on its axis and revolves around the Sun.

Summary

In this lesson, you learned about the development of hunting and gathering societies, the beginnings of agriculture, and the rise of ancient civilizations.

Cultural Interaction Most cultural knowledge accumulated by hunter-gatherers stayed within the group. Farmers and herders had more interaction with outsiders. Knowledge of agriculture appeared first in the Fertile Crescent and spread from there to Egypt, Europe, and the Indus River Valley. The main principles of civilization spread in a similar way, although civilizations also arose in several places independently. Complex societies exchanged elements of their cultures, often along trade routes. In this way Buddhism spread from India to China.

Political Structures Political structures grew progressively more complex during ancient times. Elders served as leaders of hunter-gatherer groups and farm villages. Civilizations often turned to priest-kings for leadership and a set of officials to carry out government policy. Strong states arose, and some, through conquest of neighboring lands, became empires.

Economic Structures The earliest humans survived by hunting animals and gathering plants. The development of agriculture, marked by the domestication of food plants and animals, led to an increase in the production of food. Surplus crops allowed some members of society to pursue non-farming activities, including trade. Agriculture remained the basis for the economies of even the largest states and empires. Trade brought them needed goods as well as luxury items.

Social Structures Hunter-gatherer and ancient village societies were made up of kin groups, or related families, in which all members had fairly equal status. Generally, the men did the hunting and the women did the gathering. Cities drew their much larger populations from a variety of different groups within the surrounding region. In such complex states, societies evolved hierarchies, often based on differences in economic status.

Human-Environment Interaction Mobility was a key characteristic of hunter-gatherers. They moved from place to place to maintain access to the animals and plants that gave them food, clothing, and shelter. Farmers stayed in one place and tended to settle in resource-rich areas. They cleared land near their villages for planting crops. The first civilizations rose in river valleys, where fertile soils and irrigation water helped them raise plenty of food. Improved tools, such as the plow, also boosted food production.

World Religions

How have religions influenced human society?

3.1 Introduction

By 500 B.C.E., the roots of the world's great religious traditions were emerging in the Middle East, India, and China. Judaism was well established in the Middle East, and later Christianity and Islam developed there. Hinduism and Buddhism arose in India. And China developed Confucianism, a philosophy that became a state religion.

All these religions are unique, but they also have key elements in common. They all set down basic ethical principles to guide human actions. They use sacred texts to teach moral values, often through stories or parables. They offer a universal message that appealed to people in different places and with diverse cultural backgrounds.

This broad appeal and emphasis on ethics made the new faiths different from earlier religions. Previously, most religions had been local, based on the worship of gods and spirits associated with particular places. They involved rituals, such as animal sacrifice, that were designed to appease the gods and win their favor. People looked to the gods to help them in their daily lives, to bring prosperity and protect them from their enemies.

In contrast, universal religions look beyond this world and its practical needs. They offer the hope of a better life and access to a higher truth. Because these religions are "portable"—because they can be practiced anywhere—they were able to spread to other parts of the world. In this way, they became world religions.

In this lesson, you will read about the six major world religions. You will learn about their origins, basic beliefs, and practices. You will also see how they spread beyond their lands of origin to influence human society around the world.

Themes

Cultural Interaction Religions spread cultural ideas and also changed as they expanded around the world. Their interaction with other cultures and belief systems was sometimes peaceful and sometimes not.

Political Structures World religions influenced rulers and political systems. Some religious institutions exercised great power.

Economic Structures Some religious institutions amassed great wealth. An emphasis on charity helped people in need.

Social Structures Religions influenced social systems such as families and schools. In some cases, they reinforced social classes. In others, they helped break down class barriers.

The city of Jerusalem has holy sites belonging to three world religions— Judaism, Christianity, and Islam.

monotheism belief in one God

covenant a sacred agreement

Torah Judaism's most sacred text, consisting of the first five books of the Hebrew Bible

3.2 Judaism, Christianity, and Islam

The world religions that arose in the Middle East—Judaism, Christianity, and Islam—share some common traits. The most important is **monotheism,** the belief in a single, all-powerful God. They also believe in prophets, holy people who revealed the word of God. One important prophet in these religions is Abraham, known as the father of the Jewish people.

Judaism: Origins and Development   The early history of Judaism is shrouded in the mists of time. Most scholars believe, however, that Abraham was a real person who was born some 4,000 years ago in Mesopotamia. According to Jewish scripture, God visited Abraham one day and made a sacred agreement, or **covenant,** with him. Abraham promised that he and his descendants would follow God's teachings and God promised to love them. Abraham's descendants were known as the Israelites, sometimes called the Hebrews. They were the ancestors of the Jewish people.

According to the **Torah,** Abraham and his family moved to Canaan, later called the Land of Israel, a region of land along the eastern coast of the Mediterranean Sea. His descendants later formed the twelve tribes of Israel. The tribes traveled to Egypt to escape a famine. The Torah says that they were enslaved by the Egyptians for generations and that God performed miracles to free them. On the return from Egypt, the prophet Moses had a vision of God while praying at

Military defeat at the hands of the Babylonians and the Romans contributed to the exile of most Jews from their ancient homeland. By 200 C.E., Jewish communities could be found settled throughout the area of the Roman Empire, in the Middle East, Europe, and Africa.

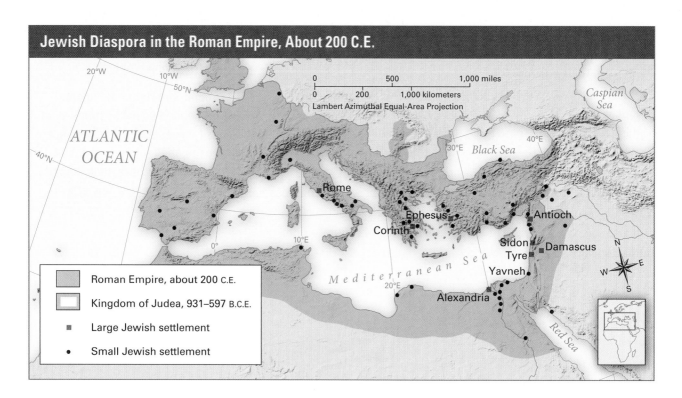

Jewish Diaspora in the Roman Empire, About 200 C.E.

Mount Sinai. There, according to scripture, Moses revealed God's laws on stone tablets. These laws, which included the Ten Commandments, would form the basis of Judaism.

The Israelites settled again in Canaan, which they regarded as their "promised land." By 1000 B.C.E., they established the Kingdom of Israel, led by kings who united the tribes of Israel. The second of these rulers, King David, made the city of Jerusalem the capital of the kingdom. His son, King Solomon, built the Temple, the most sacred place in Judaism, there.

When Solomon died, in about 930 B.C.E., the Kingdom of Israel separated into two kingdoms, Israel and Judah. Both were later invaded and conquered. The kingdom of Israel was conquered in 722 B.C.E. by the Assyrians. In 597 B.C.E., the Babylonians invaded Judah and attacked Jerusalem, then the capital of Judah. Jerusalem fell to the Babylonians in 586 B.C.E. Most of the people of Judah, now known as Jews, were forced into exile. The Babylonian Exile was the start of the **Jewish Diaspora** (die-AS-pur-ruh). From this time on, the Jewish people were dispersed across the Middle East and beyond. Other invaders, including the Romans, later occupied their land and caused more Jews to leave. Nevertheless, the Jewish religion survived. Jews both within the Land of Israel and throughout the Diaspora maintained strong connections to their homeland, stressing its importance and facing toward Jerusalem in their daily prayers.

Jewish religious leaders called *rabbis*, which literally means "teachers," were crucial to the survival of Judaism. They preserved Jewish teachings and discussed ways to apply these teachings to new situations that Jews encountered. The early rabbis recorded Jewish traditions. This record eventually became the Talmud, which together with the Hebrew Bible forms the foundation of Jewish religious practice and ethical values. It includes some of Judaism's most famous quotes, such as "What is hateful to you, do not do to your neighbor: that is the whole Torah; all the rest of it is commentary; go and study it."

Jewish Diaspora the spread of the Jewish people outside their homeland, beginning about 586 B.C.E.

polytheism the worship of multiple gods

This engraving shows King Solomon overseeing the building of the First Temple, which was completed around 957 B.C.E. The temple served as a center of worship and national identity for ancient Israel. The First Temple was destroyed by the Babylonians in 586 B.C.E. The Second Temple was rebuilt in its place, although it too was eventually destroyed. Today, the site of the Second Temple, in Jerusalem, is still the most sacred site in Judaism.

The Beliefs of Judaism The central teachings of Judaism are contained in the Torah, which makes up the first five books of the Hebrew Bible. The Torah contains the Ten Commandments, along with other teachings handed down by God to Moses.

The first commandment is central to Judaism. It says, "You shall have no other gods before Me." This law reminds Jews of their promise to worship only one God. Judaism transmitted the idea of monotheism to the rest of the world. It contrasted with the **polytheism,** or worship of many gods, which was typical of other religions at the time.

Another commandment requires Jews to set aside a holy day each week, called the Sabbath, for rest and prayer. This requirement later became a custom among Christians, too.

Other commandments in the Torah lay down moral values. One says, "Honor your father and mother." Others forbid stealing, lying, or murdering. The Torah says that Jews have a responsibility to live by God's moral teachings and make them known to the world.

Judaism also stresses the importance of equality and social justice. It teaches that God considers all people equal and says that people should be treated fairly. One passage says, "You shall open wide your hand to your brother, to the needy and to the poor." Caring for less fortunate people in society is a basic value in Judaism.

The Spread and Influence of Judaism   The troubles faced by the Jews as a result of the Diaspora threatened their survival as a people. Cut off from their roots in Israel, they had to find ways to maintain their traditions in foreign lands. For example, praying together in synagogues became a central feature of Judaism. At times, the Jews faced great persecution for their customs and beliefs.

Nevertheless, Jewish migration from Israel also helped spread the ideas of Judaism. Over the centuries, Jews settled in many parts of the Middle East, Europe, and Africa. They also made their way to Asia and, eventually, to the Americas. Although Judaism was not adopted widely among other cultures or peoples, Jews built strong communities around the world that helped preserve their culture and religion. They continued religious practices, such as studying the Torah and observing the Sabbath, that helped keep Judaism alive.

The teachings of Judaism have had a great impact on the world. The principle of monotheism influenced two other great religious traditions, Christianity and Islam. Judaism's moral teachings and its idea of a weekly day of rest were also important influences. The emphasis on ethical conduct influenced the development of law in many lands. Jewish ideas of justice and equality also helped nurture the concept of democratic freedoms.

As a result of the Jewish Diaspora, many Jews settled in Eastern Europe. A prosperous Jewish community developed in the Czech city of Pilsner, where the Great Synagogue, shown here, was built in the 19th century.

Christianity: Origins and Development   The second world religion to emerge in the Middle East was Christianity. The birthplace of Christianity was a territory at the eastern end of the Mediterranean Sea. The Romans called it Judea. It had once been a part of the ancient Kingdom of Israel. The first Christians were Jews and maintained many Jewish beliefs. They worshiped one God, valued taking care of the needy, recognized Abraham as a prophet, and believed the Hebrew Bible was holy. But Christianity soon developed its own doctrine and a much larger following.

The origins of Christianity lay in the life and teachings of Jesus, considered by Christians to be the Son of God. The story of Jesus is based largely on accounts in the New Testament of the Christian Bible. Born in the Roman province of Judea about 6 B.C.E., Jesus was a Jewish teacher. When he was around 30 years old, he left home to travel across Judea and teach the word of God.

Jesus taught that God was merciful and loving and that people should love God and their neighbors. He said that those who lived according to God's will would be forgiven their sins and relieved of suffering. The Christian Bible says that Jesus healed the sick and performed other miracles. In the process, he gained many followers. Among them were twelve special disciples known as the **apostles,** who were given the task of spreading Jesus' message.

Soon, some people began calling Jesus the Messiah, or "anointed one," chosen by God to save humankind. He later became known as Christ, the Greek term for *Messiah*. The Roman authorities who ruled Judea saw Jesus as a troublemaker, however. They feared that he might spark a rebellion among the Jews. They arrested him and sentenced him to death.

The New Testament of the Christian Bible tells that around 30 C.E. Jesus was put to death by crucifixion, a common form of execution used by the Romans. According to the New Testament, friends placed his body in tomb. The New Testament says that three days later Jesus rose from the dead and then appeared to his disciples. Christians call this event the **Resurrection**.

For Christians, the Resurrection proved that Jesus was a holy savior. They said that anyone who recognized him as the Messiah would enter the Kingdom of God. Although the Romans often persecuted Christians, Christianity gradually spread throughout the empire. Paul, who was named an apostle after Jesus' death, played a key role by bringing non-Jews into the faith.

Eventually Christianity became the official religion of the Roman Empire. Over time, the Roman Catholic Church became rich and powerful. The Christian faith later divided into Catholic, Orthodox, and Protestant branches. But Christianity as a whole continued to expand.

The New Testament tells that Jesus was executed by the Romans, who ruled the province of Judea where Jesus lived. He was put to death by crucifixion, a method of execution the Romans commonly used. Because of Jesus' death on the cross, the cross has become an important Christian symbol.

apostles   the twelve followers of Jesus, designated to spread his message

Resurrection   in Christian belief, Jesus' rise from the dead

One of the central beliefs of Christianity is that Jesus rose from the dead. To Christians, this is a miracle known as the Resurrection. According to Christian belief, Jesus ascended to heaven 40 days after he was resurrected. This fresco depicts the resurrected Jesus ascending to heaven as his disciples look on.

The Beliefs of Christianity   The Christian holy book is the Bible. It consists of two parts. The Old Testament is the Hebrew Bible, which Christians recognize as the word of God. The New Testament is a collection of stories and teachings written by various people who knew Jesus or played key roles in the early Christian church. The New Testament contains the Gospels, which are accounts of Jesus' life and teachings.

Christian doctrine is complex, with many different interpretations. But several key ideas are found among almost all Christians. One of these is the Trinity. According to Christian teaching, God consists of three beings in one—Father, Son, and Holy Spirit—in a union known as the Trinity. Christians believe that God the father is the creator of the universe. They believe that God the son is Jesus, known to his followers as Jesus Christ. And they believe that the Holy Spirit is God's presence and power at work in the world today.

Christianity also teaches about the Resurrection and salvation. They believe that Jesus rose from the dead and lives in heaven. They also believe that God can save people from sin and grant then everlasting life after death. This belief is called salvation. Many Christians believe that salvation depends on God's grace, which is God's gift of love and divine assistance which absolves people of their sins. This gift is said to be open to all who believe in Jesus and ask for God's forgiveness.

Christians practice their faith by trying to follow Christ's moral teachings and by observing certain customs and rituals. Many go to church on Sunday to worship and pray. They may also perform sacred rituals called sacraments. One sacrament is baptism, which makes a person a member of the Christian church. Another is Holy Communion, the symbolic sharing of bread and wine. This ritual mirrors the Last Supper, the final meal the New Testament says that Jesus had with his disciples. Christians also take part in holidays and festivals, such as Christmas and Easter, which celebrate the birth and Resurrection of Jesus.

The Spread and Influence of Christianity   By the first century C.E., Christianity had spread to many parts of the Roman Empire. In later centuries, it also gained followers in Persia, China, and India. Christian missionaries carried the faith to Africa and the Americas. Today, Christianity is the most widely practiced religion in the world, with some two billion followers worldwide.

The spread of Christianity was not always peaceful, however. Although millions of people converted to the new religion, others resisted. Conversion was sometimes accomplished by force. Christians and Muslims, in particular, clashed over their religious beliefs. In many cases, Christianity also adapted to local cultures. In Latin America, for example, Christian beliefs blended with native traditions, producing a faith that was more meaningful to the local population.

Christianity was spread to Latin America by European missionaries. As in other parts of the world, in Latin America Christian practices and beliefs were adapted to indigenous cultures. This photo shows an Easter Week procession in Oaxaca, Mexico.

Over the centuries, Christianity has had a great impact on culture and society. As with Judaism, Christian ethics have influenced codes of law in many countries. Christian charity has helped millions of poor and suffering people. The power of Christian belief and institutions has also influenced politics and government. Throughout history, many rulers have depended on the support of Christian churches to gain and hold power.

Islam: Origins and Development   Islam emerged in the Middle East in the 600s C.E., centuries after Judaism and Christianity. It grew rapidly, however, and soon became one of the world's major religions.

Islam was taught by Muhammad, who was born in Mecca, in Arabia, in around 570 C.E. At the time, Mecca was an important trade center and pilgrimage site. A shrine in the heart of Mecca, called the Ka'bah, was filled with statues of local gods and spirits.

Muhammad became a successful and respected merchant. As the years passed, however, he was increasingly drawn to spiritual matters. One day in about 610 C.E., according to Islamic teachings, Muhammad was meditating in a cave when an angel appeared before him and revealed the word of Allah, or God. The angel told him he had been chosen as Allah's prophet, or messenger.

Around 613 C.E., Muhammad began to preach in Mecca. He called on Arabs to worship the one, true God. In Arabic, the word *Islam* means "to submit." Muhammad's followers became known as Muslims, meaning "those who submit to God."

Many local leaders saw Islam as a threat to their power and prestige, however, and began to persecute the Muslims. In 622, Muhammad and his followers left Mecca and traveled to the city of Medina.

The Expansion of Islam, 632–750

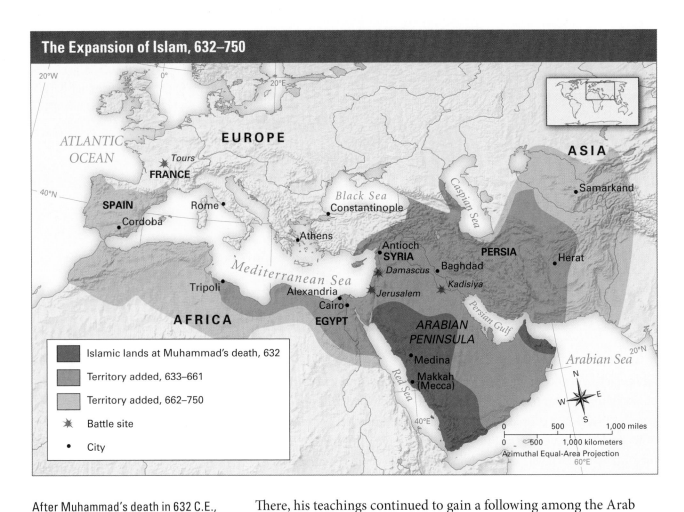

After Muhammad's death in 632 C.E., Muslim leaders and their armies continued to spread Islam throughout the lands they conquered. Muslim armies did not usually force the peoples they conquered to convert to Islam, but over time most people in these lands converted to the new faith.

Qur'an the holy book of Islam

Sunnah the example set by Muhammad for how Muslims should live

There, his teachings continued to gain a following among the Arab tribes. By 630, the Muslims were strong enough to retake Mecca and establish Islam as the dominant faith of Arabia. They destroyed the statues of gods in the Ka'bah and turned it into a holy shrine of Islam.

Muhammad died in 632. But the Muslim leaders who followed continued to win converts and expand the religion. By 750, Islam had moved beyond Arabia to become the main religion of the Middle East and North Africa. It also spread to Spain, Central Asia, and India.

The Beliefs of Islam Muslims recognize the Jewish and Christian prophets, including Abraham, Moses, and Jesus. But they regard Muhammad as the last and greatest prophet who revealed the complete message of God. They believe that the **Qur'an,** the Muslim holy book, contains the word of God as revealed to Muhammad.

Muslims also revere the **Sunnah,** the example Muhammad set for how Muslims should live. The Sunnah is recorded in a collection of stories called *Hadith,* which describe Muhammad's actions and teachings.

The required acts of worship for Muslims are called the Five Pillars of Islam. The first pillar is the profession of faith: "There is no god but God and Muhammad is his prophet." This pillar emphasizes the duty Muslims have to worship one God only.

The second pillar is daily prayer. Muslims are expected to pray five times a day: at dawn, noon, mid-afternoon, sunset, and after nightfall. They kneel before God and recite verses from the Qur'an. Prayer does not have to take place at a mosque, or place of worship, but can be performed anywhere.

The third pillar is charity. Muhammad told the wealthy to share their riches with the less fortunate. Muslims are supposed to give at least 2.5 percent of their surplus wealth every year to the needy. The Qur'an says: "You will never attain righteousness until you give freely of what you love."

The fifth pillar of Islam encourages all Muslims to make a pilgrimage to Mecca, known as the Hajj, once in their lives. Here, pilgrims on Hajj encircle the holy shrine called the Ka'bah at the Great Mosque, in Mecca. About two million Muslims perform the Hajj each year.

The fourth pillar is fasting. The Qur'an instructs Muslims to abstain from food or drink during daylight hours for the entire month of Ramadan, the ninth month of the Muslim calendar. Fasting is meant to encourage self-control and clear the mind so that it can be filled with the spirit of faith.

The fifth pillar is the pilgrimage to Mecca, known as the Hajj, which takes place in the twelfth month of the year. This pilgrimage promotes fellowship and equality among believers. The Hajj is not required, but all Muslims are encouraged to undertake it at least once in their lifetime.

The Spread and Influence of Islam Islam continued to extend its influence over the next several centuries. It spread east across South Asia to the islands of Indonesia. It moved north into Turkey and the Balkans region of Europe. It also expanded rapidly along the east coast of Africa and into the African interior, south of the Sahara.

Islam was a missionary religion, seeking to win converts, particularly in areas where polytheism prevailed. Muslims sometimes waged "holy war," clashing with followers of other religions, including Christians. But they also respected Christians and Jews as people of faith and often lived alongside them in peace.

Today, with over a billion followers, Islam is the second largest religion in the world. More than a religion, however, it is a way of life. In Muslim lands, Islam has had a profound impact on culture, society, and politics. Shari'ah, Islamic law based on the Qur'an and Sunnah, provides guidance on all aspects of life, from clothing and food to education and finance. Shari'ah also forms the basis of legal codes in many Muslim countries.

caste a hereditary social class in Hindu society

3.3 Hinduism and Buddhism

Ancient India gave birth to two major world religions, Hinduism and Buddhism. Both had common roots in the Vedas, a collection of religious hymns, poems, and prayers composed in the Sanskrit language thousands of years ago.

Hinduism: Origins and Development   The origins of Hinduism go back to the second millennium B.C.E. The religion had no clear starting point or founder, however. It developed over the centuries by drawing from India's many religious and cultural traditions. It incorporated ideas from the ancient Indus River civilization and from a nomadic people called the Aryans, who entered India from Central Asia sometime during the 1000s B.C.E.

Modern-day Hinduism is a very complex religion. Many beliefs, forms of worship, and deities, or gods, exist side by side, and often differ from place to place. The Vedas, to which Hinduism traces its early roots, remain sacred to many Hindus today.

Most scholars believe that the Aryans brought the first Vedas with them to India. Like most ancient peoples, the Aryans worshipped many gods. They used the Vedas—a form of sacred oral literature—to address the gods and sing their praise. They also performed elaborate rituals that were meant to please the gods and keep the universe in balance. The priests who carried out these rituals exercised great power and influence. As Vedic religion spread across India, it blended with local beliefs and customs. Over time, it evolved into what we now call Hinduism.

Vedic religion divided society into four social classes. The highest class was the Brahmins, or priests. These class divisions persist in modern India. Here, a group of Brahmin women gather in Pushkar, India.

Vedic religion called for the division of society into four main social classes. The top class was the Brahmins, or priests. Next came the Kshatriyas (KSHA-tree-uhs), the rulers and warriors. The third class was the Vaishyas (VIESH-yuhs), the herders and merchants. At the bottom were the Shudras (SHOO-druhs), the servants, farmers, and laborers. This basic social structure would eventually develop into the much larger **caste** system of India, which includes thousands of sub-groups within these four main classes.

Sometime after 1000 B.C.E., religious seekers in India began to take Vedic religion in a new direction. They sought a more personal faith that did not require complicated rituals and the intervention of priests. They used meditation and other forms of spiritual practice to achieve a deeper, more mystical religious experience. These ideas—expressed in a new set of texts called the *Upanishads*—became an important element of Hinduism.

In addition, two epic poems, the *Mahabharata* and the *Ramayana*, also appeared around this time. They told stories about Hindu gods, kings, and heroes. They conveyed religious and philosophical ideas and provided a model for Hindu life. These new works joined the Vedas and *Upanishads* as part of the body of sacred Hindu literature.

The Beliefs of Hinduism   The Hindu belief system is highly complex. It does not conform to a uniform set of ideas or practices. Nevertheless, certain basic elements are common to most schools of Hindu thought.

One element is polytheism. Hindus believe in multiple gods and goddesses that control different aspects of the universe. Some people devote themselves to a particular god or goddess, saying prayers and leaving offerings in the hope of gaining divine help. Many Hindus believe that the various gods and goddesses are forms of a single, supreme, and divine force called Brahman. The goal of many Hindus is to unite their soul, or *atman*, with Brahman.

Hinduism is polytheistic, and Hindus worship multiple gods and goddesses. This temple in Singapore is richly decorated with sculptures of many Hindu deities.

Hindus believe that time moves in a great circle, like a giant wheel. Events repeat themselves, just as the seasons do. Birth, life, and death are part of this cycle. When people die, their soul is said to be reborn in a different body. This cycle of rebirth, called reincarnation, is a key feature of Hindu belief.

Two other basic elements are dharma and karma. **Dharma** stands for law, duty, and obligation. Every Hindu has a dharma that reflects his or her caste in Indian society. People follow their dharma by performing their duties and living in an honorable way. Living honorably includes observing common social values, such as nonviolence and charity toward others.

Karma refers to a person's actions and the consequence of their actions. The law of karma says that people who live properly will have good karma and be reborn to a higher caste. Those who fail to live a proper life will have bad karma and be reborn to a lower caste, perhaps even as animals.

The ultimate goal of Hindu belief is to escape reincarnation entirely. Devout Hindus believe that by living a spiritual life, they can free themselves from karma and attain *moksha*, or release, thus merging their soul with Brahman and ending the cycle of rebirth.

dharma a belief found in Hinduism and other Indian traditions that a person has a duty or obligation to live an honorable life

karma a belief found in Hinduism and other Indian traditions that the good and evil done in a past life determines the nature of that person's next life

The Spread and Influence of Hinduism   Unlike Christianity and Islam, Hinduism did not spread far beyond its land of origin. Although its values are universal in many ways, Hinduism is strongly linked to Indian culture.

Nevertheless, through trade and migration, Hindu beliefs and customs did spread to many parts of Southeast Asia. There they blended with local traditions and ways of life. Today, there are around 900 million followers of Hinduism, most of them in South Asia.

Hindu beliefs are deeply woven into Indian society. So are Hindu festivals and the devotion to Hindu gods. Many Indians make religious pilgrimages to holy sites, such as Varanasi, where they purify themselves in the waters of the Ganges River. At the same time, certain Hindu ideas and practices, such as yoga, have also gained a following around the world.

Buddhism: Origins and Development   Buddhism embraced the ideas of karma and reincarnation. But it did not emphasize complex rituals, the caste system, or polytheism. Instead, it focused on the search for enlightenment, or pure wisdom.

Buddhism arose from the teachings of Siddhartha Gautama (si-DAHR-tuh GOW-tuh-muh), who became the Buddha, or "enlightened one." Siddhartha lived from about 563 to 483 B.C.E. According to tradition, he was born into a ruling family in northern India. As a youth, he enjoyed the privileged life of a prince. When he was 29 years old, however, he stepped outside his palace and saw the pain and suffering of the world. He was shocked by the reality of poverty, disease, and death. Soon after, he left his comfortable life to wander across India in search of a greater truth.

Like many Indian mystics at the time, Siddhartha sought to achieve a higher consciousness through meditation and ascetic practices. (To be ascetic means to give up worldly pleasures.) According to Buddhist tradition, Siddhartha fasted to the point of starvation. After several years, however, he had still not attained the release he was seeking. He concluded that the path to truth could not be found in either the life of a prince or an ascetic. He decided to seek a "middle way" to enlightenment between the extremes of pleasure and pain.

Buddhist tradition says that Siddhartha sat down under a large fig tree—known as a bodhi tree—and began to meditate. This went on for many days. Then one night, he reached a new level of consciousness. He envisioned his past lives and the effects of karma. He shed his desires and became enlightened. By morning, he had attained **nirvana**—a state of happiness and peace—and had become the Buddha.

Although he had attained his goal and could now rest, Siddhartha felt a duty to help others. He began to teach his ideas and soon gained a following. Gradually, Buddhism began to spread across northern India.

Buddhist tradition holds that Siddhartha Gautama achieved nirvana while meditating under a bodhi tree. He became known as the Buddha, or "enlightened one." Statues of the meditating Buddha are a common feature of Buddhist ritual.

nirvana an ideal state of happiness and peace, attained through enlightenment

The Beliefs of Buddhism The basic teachings of Buddhism are known as the Four Noble Truths. These principles form the core of Buddhist thought.

The first Noble Truth says, "Suffering is present in all things, and nothing lasts forever." Disease, loss, and death are inevitable. Ignoring or denying this truth only leads to more suffering. A Buddhist should recognize this reality and offer kindness and compassion to those who suffer.

The second truth says, "The cause of suffering is desire." This means that the desire for pleasure, power, or possessions gives rise to suffering. Emotional attachment is another form of desire.

The third truth says, "Removing desire removes suffering." Buddhism teaches that the only way to end suffering is to eliminate desire.

The fourth truth says, "The way to remove desire is to follow the Eightfold Path." The Eightfold Path is a set of guidelines to achieve enlightenment. These are the eight guidelines:

1. Right understanding: Deeply understand the Four Noble Truths.
2. Right purpose: Live a life of selflessness, love, and nonviolence.
3. Right speech: Be careful and truthful in what you say.
4. Right action: Do not kill, steal, lie, or hurt others.
5. Right livelihood: Earn a living in ways that do no harm.
6. Right effort: Promote good actions and prevent evil actions.
7. Right mindfulness: Be aware of but not attached to your emotions, thoughts, or feelings.
8. Right concentration: Focus your mind with practices such as meditation.

At the heart of Buddhist teachings is the idea that all things change. Even when one finds pleasure in life, it does not last forever, and one suffers when it is gone. The Eightfold Path offers a way to end suffering and find peace. This path follows the "middle way."

The Spread and Influence of Buddhism At first, Buddhist ideas spread slowly among religious seekers in India. In the 200s B.C.E., however, the Emperor Ashoka helped popularize Buddhism. Buddhist missionaries and traders carried the faith across South Asia and beyond. Although Hinduism remained dominant in India, Buddhism became the leading faith of Southeast Asia, Central Asia, and China. From China, it spread to Korea and Japan.

Buddhists have established monasteries throughout the world. Buddhist monks renounce worldly possessions and dedicate their lives to contemplation. They live according to Buddhist principles, and strive to fulfill the teachings of the Four Noble Truths and the Eightfold Path.

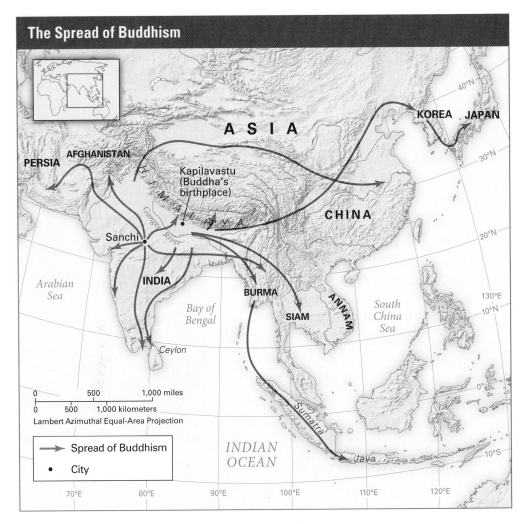

The Spread of Buddhism

KOREA JAPAN

A S I A

PERSIA AFGHANISTAN

Kapilavastu
(Buddha's
birthplace)

CHINA

Sanchi

Arabian
Sea

INDIA

BURMA

Bay of
Bengal

SIAM

ANNAM

South
China
Sea

Ceylon

0   500   1,000 miles
0   500   1,000 kilometers
Lambert Azimuthal Equal-Area Projection

Sumatra

INDIAN
OCEAN

Java

→ Spread of Buddhism
•   City

Buddhism began in northern India and spread throughout southern Asia. Ashoka, king of the Mauryan Empire in present-day India, spread Buddhism in his empire and beyond its borders. Buddhist missionaries and traders also helped expand the religion.

As it expanded, Buddhism took on new forms by adapting to local customs and traditions. It divided into two major branches, Theravada and Mahayana. Theravada thrived in southern Asia and represented a more traditional style of Buddhism. Mahayana, which developed in northern Asia, embraced newer ideas. One form of Chinese Buddhism evolved in Japan to become Zen Buddhism, a form that emphasized meditation.

Buddhism had a great impact wherever it went. Buddhists opened monasteries to promote the study and spread of Buddhist thought, which in turn influenced society and government. Many monasteries became wealthy and powerful through large donations of money and land. Faced with this growing power, Chinese rulers cracked down on the Buddhist faith in 845 C.E. But Buddhism continued to grow in other parts of Asia.

Today, Buddhism is the fourth largest religion in the world, with 350 million followers. Buddhist teachings on nonviolence and respect for the natural world have influenced social and political movements worldwide.

3.4 Confucianism

While Buddhism was emerging in India, Confucianism was taking root in China. In many ways, Confucianism was less a religion than a philosophy and way of life. Nevertheless, it became an official faith with a devout following among the Chinese people.

Confucianism: Origins and Development   Confucianism is based on the teachings of Kongfuzi, whose Western name was Confucius (kuhn-FYOO-shus). Confucius lived from around 551 to 479 B.C.E., during the same era as the Buddha. Like the Buddha, he became a great teacher whose ideas influenced the lives of millions of people.

Confucius was born in the small state of Lu, in eastern China. At the time, China was in turmoil. The central government had lost control and civil wars ravaged the land. For many Chinese, this was a sign that their ruler had lost the **Mandate of Heaven**. According to this belief, a ruler held power with the support of heavenly spirits. If the ruler governed poorly, heaven withdrew its support and the ruler lost power.

As a young man, Confucius applied himself to learning, focusing on the classics of Chinese literature and philosophy. He believed that a revival of traditional Chinese culture would help restore order in society and promote harmony between earth and heaven.

Confucius became a famous teacher with a devoted following of student disciples. His main goal, however, was to influence government. He held several minor positions in the state of Lu, but he gained little backing for his ideas. During his fifties, he left Lu and wandered from state to state, seeking a wise ruler who would put his teachings into practice.

After 13 years and many hardships, Confucius returned home in disappointment. He continued to study and teach until his death, at age 73. Although he had failed to win official support during his lifetime, however, his ideas steadily gained favor after his death. Over the centuries, they had a profound impact on Chinese life.

The Beliefs of Confucianism   The ancient Chinese worshiped many gods and spirits, including the spirits of their dead ancestors, who were said to look down from heaven. Confucius honored these beliefs. He said that his teachings came from heaven. But his focus was on human society and life on earth. As he put it, "If we are not yet able to understand life and to serve humanity, how can we understand death and serve spirits?"

Confucius was a famous philosopher and teacher whose ideas about a well-ordered society spread throughout China. This statue of Confucius stands at a temple dedicated to the philosopher in Shanghai, China.

Mandate of Heaven the Chinese belief that a ruler's power stemmed from divine authority

Confucius honored traditional Chinese religious beliefs, such as ancestor worship. In many ways, ancestor worship reinforced the basic Confucian value of respect for one's parents and elders, known as filial piety. Such practices continue to this day. One example of this is Tomb-sweeping Day, when families visit the graves of deceased relatives.

filial piety respect shown by children to their parents

ideology a set of basic ideas, beliefs, and values that form the basis of a social, economic, or political philosophy or program

Confucius believed that building a better, more harmonious society would bring humans closer to heaven. To do this, he said, people should follow ethical guidelines to improve their relations with others. The main guideline was to live a life of virtue. The most important virtue was *ren*, which means "benevolence" or "humanity." Confucius urged people to treat others as they would like to be treated themselves, with respect and kindness. "What you do not want done to yourself," he said, "do not do to others."

According to Confucianism, there are five basic relationships in society: between parent and child, husband and wife, older sibling and younger sibling, friend and friend, and ruler and subject. The most important relationship is between parent and child. Confucius said that **filial piety**—respect of children for their parents—was critical to the social order. He said that people should respect and obey those with higher social status, particularly their elders. In return, people in authority, such as parents and rulers, should set a good example. They should be kind, honest, wise, and faithful.

Despite this emphasis on social categories, Confucius urged respect for all people, regardless of social class. He stood up for the rights of the common people and accepted students from all walks of life, rich or poor. He called for universal education to benefit all of society.

The Spread and Influence of Confucianism   After Confucius's death, his disciples collected his teachings in book called the *Analects*, which helped spread his ideas throughout China. Other scholars advanced the principles of Confucianism.

Chinese rulers later adopted Confucianism as a state **ideology**—a basic set of ideas, beliefs, and values. Knowledge of the Confucian classics became the basis of the state civil service exam. Confucian ethics became enmeshed in Chinese culture. School children memorized his sayings, and temples were erected in his memory. Some Chinese even worshipped Confucius as a god. In effect, Confucianism became a state religion.

Confucian ideas also spread to other parts of Asia. Korea, Japan, and Southeast Asia were all strongly influenced by Confucianism. Today, Confucian ethics remain an important part of Asian culture.

3.5 The Impact of World Religions

The growth and spread of world religions had a great impact on society. Many effects were specific to particular cultures or regions, such as the influence of the Hindu caste system on India and Confucian ethics on China. But other effects were more global in nature. These broad effects cut across cultural lines to influence human society in general.

Global Effects on Society World religions helped shape society and culture in various ways. One key factor was the creation of large communities of people with shared beliefs. Before the rise of universal religions, most people had worshiped local gods in small communities. Because the new, universal religions had broad appeal and could be practiced anywhere, they produced much larger communities of believers.

These communities were linked by common belief systems and ethical values that helped people live together. They also brought economic and political benefits to their members. For example, Muslim traders did business with other Muslims in distant lands. They built large trade networks based on religious ties. Jewish communities provided strength and support, which helped Jews maintain their identity despite discrimination and periods of oppression. Early Christians helped each other survive in the face of Roman persecution.

World religions gave strength to people undergoing hardship and difficulties. They gave meaning to daily life and offered the hope of a better afterlife. Believers gained spiritual peace from prayer, meditation, and other religious practices. People in need also got aid and support from religious institutions. An emphasis on charity and caring brought comfort to the poor and afflicted in society.

The spread of world religions has created communities of people with shared beliefs and values across the world. For example, the Catholic Church, just one branch of Christianity, has 1.1 billion members spread around the world. Here Pope Benedict XVI greets Catholics on a visit to the African country of Benin.

The Blue Mosque, built in Istanbul in the 17th century, is just one example of the human creativity that religion has inspired. The ornate interior is decorated with natural motifs and verses from the Qur'an, all made of small mosaic tiles.

World religions also influenced social and political structures. Rulers and religious leaders often worked together to uphold the existing social and political order. Religious establishments supported rulers in return for official backing and protection. Churches often counseled believers to accept their place in society. They told them that faith and patience in this life would bring rewards in heaven.

At the same time, religious ideas also prompted social and political change. People sometimes rebelled against rulers who failed to uphold moral laws. Religious ethics also gave rise to legal codes that applied to everyone, regardless of social class. The Judeo-Christian idea that everyone was equal in the eyes of God supported the principle of democratic equality. Women, who were often portrayed as inferior to men, even gained some rights through religion. Islam, for example, guaranteed women's property and inheritance rights. Christian monasteries provided a refuge for women.

Religion also had a strong impact on art and culture. It helped spread cultural ideas and values around the world. Many great works of art—from cathedrals and temples to paintings and music—were inspired by religious faith. Religion also promoted literacy by encouraging people to read sacred texts. In this way, it expanded education and learning. In addition, religion influenced many cultural celebrations, holidays, and festivals. These events often merged religious beliefs with local customs and traditions.

Cultural and Religious Interactions As world religions expanded, they came into contact with diverse peoples and cultures. In the process, they adapted and changed. As Buddhism spread across Asia, for example, it absorbed many local customs. Regional variations of Buddhism developed in China, Tibet, Japan, and Southeast Asia. In

some places, Buddhists continued to worship ancient, pre-Buddhist spirits. Shrines to these spirits even existed inside Buddhist temples.

Christianity also evolved as it spread across the Roman Empire. It blended Greek, Roman, and Germanic customs with its Jewish heritage. The celebration of Christmas, for example, combined Christian and pre-Christian beliefs. Christmas day was set on the date of an ancient feast day and celebration of the sun.

As they expanded, world religions also came into contact with each other. Sometimes the result was conflict. During the Crusades, Christians and Muslims fought over control of the eastern Mediterranean, especially the city of Jerusalem, which both saw as holy. Muslims also attacked Hindus as idol-worshipers during their conquest of India. Often, however, world religions coexisted. Muslims, Christians, and Jews lived together in the Muslim Empire. Buddhist and Confucian ideas mixed in China. Hinduism and Buddhism mingled in Southeast Asia.

As world religions expanded they sometimes came into conflict. One example of this is the Crusades, when Christian armies attempted to reclaim Jerusalem and the eastern Mediterranean from Muslims. The Crusades began in the 11th century and were the Christian response to centuries of Muslim wars of expansion.

Summary

In this lesson, you read about the six major world religions: Judaism, Christianity, Islam, Hinduism, Buddhism, and Confucianism. You learned about their origins and basic beliefs. You also learned how they spread to different parts of the world and influenced human society.

Cultural Interaction Religions spread new ideas and values as they expanded. They also adapted to local customs and beliefs. Religions also interacted, in both peaceful and violent ways. Religious beliefs and practices blended in many parts of the world.

Political Structures Religion and government often worked hand in hand. Religions influenced political systems by lending support to governments and rulers. Some religious institutions exercised great power in their own right. At times, religious believers also challenged rulers and rebelled against political authority. Religious ethics provided a basis for laws in many countries. Religions sometimes provoked conflict, violence, and wars, and other times they inspired cooperation, benevolence, and the quest for peace and justice.

Economic Structures Religions exercised economic power as well. The Catholic Church and Buddhist monasteries amassed great wealth and large land holdings. Religions also provided help to the poor and others in need. Charity toward others was a basic religious value. Religions have typically challenged the idea that the accumulation of wealth and possessions will by itself lead to human happiness.

Social Structures Religions helped support the social order by urging compliance with authority and the social class system. But religions also undermined class distinctions by emphasizing the basic equality of all believers. Religious ethics sometimes upheld the rights of women and the poor and other times preserved patterns of discrimination and oppression.

Era Overview: Expanding Interactions, 300–1500 C.E.

Why did the first empires decline, and how did new empires rise to take their place?

4.1 Introduction

In 629 C.E., a Chinese Buddhist named Xuanzang (shoo-wen-zahng) set out on a long journey to India. His goal was to spread Buddhist learning and form closer ties between India and China. He traveled by land, heading west on the Silk Road across Central Asia before turning south to India. All told, he would cover more than 10,000 miles on his remarkable journey.

Xuanzang encountered many dangers along the way. He got lost in the Gobi Desert and nearly died of thirst. Snow and freezing conditions in the Tian Shan Mountains killed many members of his party. Bandits attacked and robbed him. But he also met with great kindness and hospitality. His writings about the people and places he visited provide a valuable historical record of the time.

In India, Xuanzang studied with Buddhist monks and visited sacred Buddhist sites. He settled for a time in northern India, which he described as a peaceful land governed by a wise and generous ruler, King Harsha.

In 645, after 16 years abroad, Xuanzang returned to China. There he became a renowned Buddhist scholar. With his help, China developed closer relations with India. At the time, China was gaining strength under the Tang (tahng) dynasty. India, in contrast, was growing weaker. Just two years after Xuanzang's return, King Harsha died and his kingdom fell apart. India remained divided for centuries to come.

During the period from 300 to 1500 C.E., the world changed in many ways. Kingdoms and empires rose and fell, and new ones took their place. Meanwhile, different parts of the world became more connected through trade and the exchange of ideas. In this lesson, you will read about key developments during this period of expanding interactions.

In 629 C.E., Xuanzang began a remarkable 10,000 mile journey from China to India.

Themes

Cultural Interaction The growth of empires and trade routes increased contacts among peoples. Ideas, customs, and beliefs spread more easily around the world.

Political Structures Empires rose and fell, including the great civilizations of the classical world. The Muslim and Mongol empires ruled vast territories.

Economic Structures Trade networks expanded during this period. States and empires grew wealthy from increased trade and commerce.

Social Structures The collapse of classical civilizations changed society in Rome, China, and India. But new social structures soon emerged.

Human-Environment Interaction The world population fell as a result of disease and other factors. This trend began to reverse, however, with increased food production.

These painted terracotta warriors date from the Han dynasty period. In the late Han period, the dynasty was forced to invest a lot of money into their army to defend China's borders from nomadic tribes. The increased tax burden caused unrest and contributed to the downfall of the Han dynasty.

millennium a period of 1,000 years

epidemic an outbreak of disease that spreads rapidly

4.2 Crisis in the Classical World

Early in the first **millennium** C.E., a series of crises shook the classical civilizations of China, Rome, and India. The Han, Roman, and Gupta empires had flourished for hundreds of years. They had dominated their separate worlds and produced great cultural achievements. By 550 C.E., however, they had all collapsed.

The Han Decline   The first to fail was the Han Empire. The Han dynasty had ruled China for four hundred years. It created a system of strong, centralized rule and expanded China's borders. Agriculture, trade, and commerce grew. It was a time of peace and increased prosperity.

In 220 C.E., however, the Han dynasty fell. The causes of that collapse were complex and went back many years. Political factors played an important part. In 9 C.E., Han rule had been interrupted by the overthrow of a young emperor. The Han later regained the throne, but various factions in government began to struggle for power. Over time, these internal struggles undermined Han control.

Other factors played a role, too. One key factor was pressure on China's borders by nomadic tribes from Central Asia. These tribes had long threatened northern China. Faced with this constant danger, China spent heavily on military defense. Much of the cost was financed by higher taxes on Chinese peasants. Unable to pay their taxes, many peasants had to sell their land to wealthy landowners. The gap between rich and poor grew, and peasant revolts broke out. In addition, deadly diseases such as smallpox—brought to China along the Silk Road from other parts of the world—sparked **epidemics** that ravaged the population.

All these factors caused instability in China and weakened the Han dynasty. Regional warlords began to challenge Han power. Bandits roamed the land. In 220, the last Han emperor gave up the throne. China broke into warring kingdoms for nearly four centuries.

The Fall of Rome   Two centuries later, the Roman Empire collapsed. Rome suffered from many of the same problems that troubled the Han, including attacks from nomadic tribes. Like the Han, Rome declined over a period of many years.

Political problems were one factor. Rome never developed a reliable system for choosing its leaders. By the 200s C.E., most Roman emperors were generals who seized power by force. They depended on their soldiers for support, and few stayed in power for long. Twenty-six emperors ruled Rome in the last half of the third century. All but one was killed or committed suicide.

Other problems were economic and social in nature. To support the empire and its defense, Rome raised taxes to levels that were too high for most poor farmers to bear. Many left their farms and fled to the cities. But there were not enough jobs to support these migrants. Poverty and social problems increased. Diseases also swept across the empire, killing as much as one fourth of the population. Farming and trade suffered, and tax revenues plummeted. The price of food and other goods shot up. This inflation fueled anger and social unrest.

The Roman Empire's enormous size had always made it difficult to govern. To solve this problem, the emperor Diocletian split the empire into eastern and western halves. In 324, Emperor Constantine transferred the capital to the eastern city of Byzantium, which became Constantinople.

In the meantime, Germanic tribes continued to attack the western empire. Invaders entered Rome and sacked the city twice, once in 410 and again in 455. Rome was teetering on the brink of collapse. In 476, a Germanic leader overthrew the last western emperor. The eastern empire, later known as the Byzantine Empire, survived for another thousand years. But it never regained the strength or glory of the Roman Empire at its height.

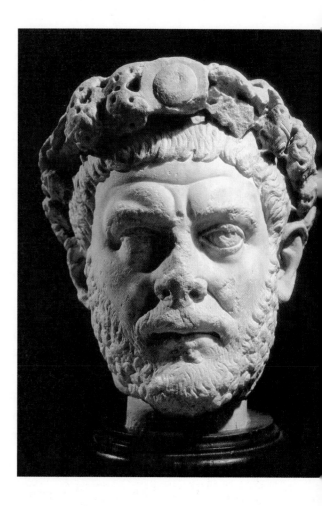

The emperor Diocletian split the Roman Empire into eastern and western halves in an attempt to make the vast territory easier to govern. The western half fell to Germanic tribes in 467, while the eastern half survived for over a thousand years in the form of the Byzantine Empire.

The End of Gupta Rule The Gupta Empire was the third classical civilization to fall. The Gupta kings ruled northern India for more than two centuries, beginning around 320 C.E. Although they created a strong central government, they gave local rulers a good deal of **autonomy**. During the Gupta era, the economy prospered and Indian civilization entered a golden age.

Compared with the fall of the Han dynasty and imperial Rome, the reason for the Gupta collapse was simple: foreign invasion. For years, a nomadic group known as the White Huns had threatened India from the northwest. The Gupta Empire was shielded from these attacks by two barriers, one geographic and the other political. The first barrier was the towering Hindu Kush and Himalayan mountain ranges to the north. The other was the military strength of the Persian state to the west.

Around 450, however, that protection broke down. The White Huns crossed the mountains and invaded India. Gupta forces repelled the invaders at first. But the cost of this defense drained the empire's resources. When the invaders returned, they overran northern India. By 550, the Gupta age was over. Except for a brief period in the 600s, under King Harsha, India was divided into small kingdoms for the next six centuries.

autonomy self-government; independence

This Persian stone relief carving from the 200s C.E. shows the Roman Emperor Valarian bowing before the Sassanian king Shapur I after he was taken as a prisoner of war. The Sassanian Empire of Persia was one of the strongest surviving states after the collapse of the classical Han, Roman, and Gupta Empires.

Afro-Eurasia the vast region made up of Africa, Europe, and Asia

Orthodox Christianity the religion of the Eastern Orthodox Church, which split from Catholicism during the Byzantine Empire

Mesoamerica a region of pre-Columbian culture stretching from central Mexico through northern Central America

Civilizations on the Rise   The collapse of classical empires had a significant impact across much of **Afro-Eurasia,** the vast region made up of Africa, Europe, and Asia. For centuries, large portions of North Africa, Europe, and Asia had enjoyed peace and stability under imperial rule. The security those empires provided helped promote trade and the exchange of ideas across the continents. Now that system had collapsed. Other strong states survived, however. New empires eventually emerged.

One of the strongest surviving states was the Sassanian Empire of Persia. The Sassanians, who ruled from 226 to 651 C.E., controlled a large territory that extended from the Roman Empire in the west to Gupta India in the east. Sassanian rule relied on a strong warrior culture and a thriving economy based on agriculture and trade. The Sassanians spent much of their wealth on wars with the Roman and Byzantine empires. But they also developed large cities and a flourishing culture.

In China, several centuries passed before another dynasty, the Sui (sway), united the country in 589. But it was the Tang dynasty that really revived Chinese power. The Tang took control in 618 and ruled for 300 years. They were followed by another great dynasty, the Song (soong), which ruled for another three centuries. Under the Tang and Song, China enjoyed a long period of prosperity and cultural achievement.

In Europe, the fall of Rome led to a long period of decline, often referred to as the Dark Ages. Cities crumbled. The economy shrank and the population fell. But new political structures gradually emerged, and order began to return. Around 800 C.E., a powerful leader named Charlemagne united parts of central and western Europe in a kingdom known as the Holy Roman Empire. By 1000, farming and trade were on the rise, and the population began to grow. During this period, traders and missionaries from the Byzantine Empire introduced their customs and beliefs into Russia and eastern Europe. As a result, many people there converted to **Orthodox Christianity**.

States and empires also developed in Africa and the Americas. In East Africa, the kingdom of Axum built a prosperous trading empire that ruled the coast and highlands of what is now Ethiopia between 100 and 600 C.E. In southern Africa, the kingdom of Zimbabwe grew rich by trading in gold and other products. And in West Africa, the kingdoms of Ghana, Mali, and Songhai also gained wealth and power through the gold trade.

In the Americas, great civilizations arose on both continents. In **Mesoamerica**—a region comprising parts of modern Mexico and Central America—the Olmecs, Maya, Aztecs, and other peoples created powerful states with large cities and prosperous trade networks. In South America, the Incas built a great empire that stretched for thousands of miles along the Andes Mountains. In North America, the Pueblo Indians and other peoples created sophisticated cultures based on farming and trade.

4.3 The Muslim Empire

In the 600s, another great empire emerged, this time in Southwest Asia. Starting from the Arabian Peninsula, Muslim conquerors quickly gained control over a vast territory. Over the next few centuries, the Muslim Empire spread Islamic culture and beliefs across three continents.

Origins of the Empire The origins of the Muslim Empire lie in the teachings of Muhammad, the founder of Islam. Muhammad had his spiritual revelation—his message from God—in around 610 C.E. He began preaching in his hometown of Mecca and soon gained a following. But other Arabs rejected his message and forced him and his followers to flee the city. From his new base in the town of Medina, Muhammad continued to preach and gain support among Arab tribes. Finally, by 630, his forces were able to retake Mecca. Two years later, Muhammad died.

At that point, the Muslim community picked Abu Bakr, Muhammad's father-in-law, as their new leader. He became the first **caliph,** or Muslim ruler. Three more caliphs followed in succession: Umar, Uthman, and Ali. These men established the caliphate, or Muslim state. The caliphate combined both political and religious authority.

During the rule of the first four caliphs, from 632 to 661, Arab armies conquered the rest of Arabia and then moved into the Middle East and North Africa. They took Persia from the Sassanians and Egypt from the Byzantine Empire. Their success hinged on two main factors. One was their fervent belief that God was on their side. The other was their mastery of the camel for desert transport and warfare. They also benefited from weakness in the Byzantine and Persian empires, which had been fighting each other for years and suffered from internal problems.

In 661, a new caliph—a member of the Umayyad family—took power. He moved the capital to Damascus, Syria, and established a dynasty. The Umayyads continued to expand the empire, moving deeper into North Africa and capturing Spain. They also took lands in northwestern India and defeated Chinese forces in Central Asia. Only crucial defeats in France and at Constantinople blocked their advance into Europe.

The first four caliphs, Abu Bakr, Umar, Uthman, and Ali, are depicted in this Italian engraving. Under the first four caliphs, Muslim armies conquered much of the Middle East and North Africa.

caliph a spiritual and political leader of the Muslims

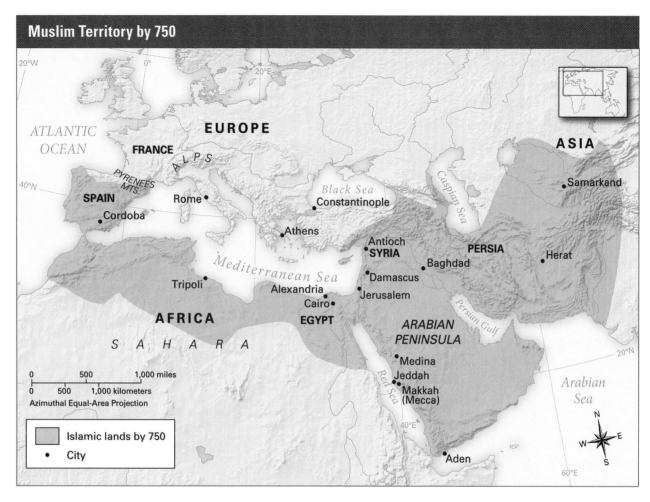

Muslim Territory by 750

By 750 Muslim leaders had spread Islam and Muslim rule across the entire Middle East and as far west as Spain. However, defeats in France and Constantinople prevented their conquest of Europe.

Shi'a a minority branch of Islam that maintains loyalty to the caliph Ali and his descendants

Sunni the majority branch of Islam, which accepted the rule of the Umayyad and Abbasid caliphates

Sufis a mystical form of Islam in which believers seek direct personal experience of God, often through prayer and meditation

In 750, the Umayyads were overthrown by another dynasty, the Abbasids. Under the Abbasid caliphate, the capital was moved further east, to Baghdad. The Abbasids ruled for 500 years, until 1258, overseeing a golden age of Muslim culture. They had lost most of their power by the mid-900s, however. By that time, separate dynasties ruled different parts of the Muslim world, including Spain, North Africa, and Persia.

A serious split also occurred among the Muslim faithful. Some Muslims had never accepted Umayyad or Abbasid rule. These Muslims, known as **Shi'a,** remained loyal to the fourth caliph, Ali, and his descendants. The majority of Muslims, known as **Sunni,** accepted the Umayyad and Abbasid rulers. Over time, the split between Shi'a and Sunni Muslims led to separate branches of Islam.

Another group, the **Sufis,** also emerged at this time. They were Muslim mystics who rejected the worldly nature of the Umayyad and Abbasid caliphates. They lived simply and sought a direct experience of God. As Muslim holy men, the Sufis later played an important role in the spread of Islam.

Despite these differences, by 900 the Muslims had created an empire that stretched across much of Afro-Eurasia, from Spain in the west to India and Central Asia in the east. They regarded this empire as **Dar al-Islam**—"the House of Islam"—a realm under Muslim rule where Islam would prevail. Over the next several centuries, Islamic influence would continue to grow, extending further into Africa, Europe, and Asia.

Dar al-Islam lands under Muslim rule, where Islam can be practiced freely

Muslim Society and Economy   The Muslim Empire absorbed many different cultures and peoples. It included Arabs, Christians, Jews, Persians, Indians, Turks, North African Berbers, and Black Africans, among others. As a result, Muslim society was highly diverse.

In general, Muslim rulers respected Christians and Jews as "People of the Book"—that is, believers in God—and allowed them to practice their faith. But non-Muslims were subject to a special tax, along with other restrictions. Although second-class citizens, they were usually allowed to live in peace and manage their own affairs.

Eventually, though, most people in the Muslim world converted to Islam. Many also learned Arabic, the language of the Islamic holy book, the Qur'an. A common religion and common language helped unite people throughout the empire. Over time, many Muslims came to identify themselves as Arabs because of their language and faith.

Social structures in the Muslim world varied considerably depending on local traditions. In the Muslim heartland of Southwest Asia, however, a common system of social classes had developed by the 900s. At the top of this system were Arabs or Muslims by birth. Next came converts to Islam. The third class was made up of people who practiced other religions, including Christians and Jews. At the bottom were slaves, typically people captured in war. As in most other cultures at the time, women were generally considered inferior to men. They did enjoy certain rights, though, including the right to own property. For the most part, women's work revolved around the home and family.

Arabic, the language of the Qur'an, spread across the Muslim world. People across the empire came to share a common language and religion, and began to identify themselves as Arabs.

In this illustration from a 1237 Arab manuscript, Muslim merchants transport goods by ship. Muslim merchants used sea routes to trade throughout Europe, Africa, and Asia.

Agriculture and commerce formed the economic foundations of the Muslim world. Trade, in particular, was a key activity. Arab merchants had long taken part in overland trade across Southwest Asia. Muhammad had himself been a trader early in life. As a result, Muslims had a positive attitude toward commerce. They took advantage of the various trade routes that linked Muslim lands with the rest of Afro-Eurasia. They traded goods ranging from West African gold and Arabian honey to Indian spices and Chinese silks.

Muslim traders relied on camel caravans to travel long distances across harsh desert lands. But they also made use of ships and sea routes to sail between Europe, Africa, and Asia. Along with these means of transport, other key factors helped promote trade in the Muslim Empire. These factors included a common language, a common set of laws, and a common currency. In addition, Muslim rulers offered guarantees for the safe conduct of trade and commerce.

Agriculture was also important in the Muslim world, though arid conditions limited farming in many places. One notable exception was Spain. There, Muslims developed extensive irrigation systems and grew crops such as sugar and citrus fruits, imported from South Asia.

Economic prosperity led to the growth of urban areas across the Muslim world. Cities such as Córdoba, Fez, Cairo, and Baghdad became important centers of trade, commerce, and culture. One visitor to Baghdad around 1000 C.E. described the glories of the Abbasid capital:

> *The city of Baghdad formed two vast semi-circles on the right and left banks of the Tigris [River]. . . . The numerous suburbs, covered with parks, gardens, villas, and beautiful promenades, and plentifully supplied with rich bazaars [markets], and finely built mosques and baths, stretched for a considerable distance on both sides of the river. . . . [M]arble steps led down to the water's edge, and the scene on the river was animated by thousands of gondolas, decked with little flags, dancing like sunbeams on the water.*
>
> —Yakut, *Geographical Encyclopedia*

The Culture of Islam   Life in Baghdad and other Muslim cities reflected the great achievements of Islamic civilization. This culture drew on a variety of influences. The beliefs of Islam and the traditions of Arabia played a central role. But Muslim culture also absorbed ideas and styles from classical Greece and Rome, Persia, India, and China.

Architecture flourished in the Muslim world. Architects built beautiful mosques, or Muslim houses of worship, with large domes and tall minarets, or towers. They designed ornate palaces and decorated them with colorful tiles and complex carvings in geometric and floral patterns. They also laid out elaborate gardens, filled with lush greenery and watered by fountains. The Alhambra—a royal palace and fortress in Granada, Spain—is a good example of the magnificence of Muslim architecture.

Art and literature were also important in Islamic civilization. The art of handwriting, called calligraphy, was a fine art in the Muslim world. So was the creation of textiles and rugs with intricate designs. Although Islam discouraged depictions of the human figure, Muslim artists in Persia and India painted exquisite miniatures of people and animals in natural settings. Writers crafted wonderful stories, such as the tales in *A Thousand and One Nights,* also known as *Arabian Nights.* Other writers, such as the Persian Sufi poet Rumi, wrote beautiful poems.

Muslims also advanced scholarship and learning in many fields. Libraries and universities, such as the famed al-Azhar in Cairo, thrived in the Muslim world. Muslim scholars translated and preserved ancient Greek classics, including the writings of Aristotle and Plato. The work of Muslim philosophers such as Ibn Sina (i-bin SEE-na), known as Avicenna in Europe, had great influence on later European thinkers.

Muslim scholars made important advances in mathematics, astronomy, and medicine. They adopted math concepts from India, including the use of zero and the system of Arabic numerals still in use today. They also developed algebra and applied it to the study of astronomy. In medicine, Muslim specialists treated diseases, performed surgery, and wrote books that became standard medical texts in Europe.

Muslims also developed key technologies in irrigation and navigation. They built canals, dams, and waterwheels. They borrowed and adapted the triangular sail from ancient Greece and the magnetic compass from China. They also refined the art of papermaking, another Chinese invention. In these and many other ways, Islamic civilization made great advances.

A view of a courtyard in the Alhambra, a palace and fortress constructed in the 1300s in Granada, when Spain was under Islamic rule. The columns, arches, and intricate carved stone decorations exemplify the Islamic architecture of the Medieval period.

4.4 The Mongol World

By the mid-900s, the Muslim Empire had fractured. An Umayyad prince governed Spain, while a Shi'a dynasty called the Fatimids ruled Egypt. The Abbasid caliphs still reigned in Baghdad, but they were controlled by a Persian dynasty to the east. Later, in 1055, Turkish nomads known as Seljuks conquered the Persians and gained control over the Abbasid caliphate. Muslim civilization would continue to flourish for several centuries, but the Muslim Empire was over.

One final blow remained, however. In 1258, Mongol conquerors stormed into Baghdad and killed the last Abbasid ruler. A new empire had been born.

The Mongol Empire   The Mongols were a group of nomadic tribes from the plains of Central Asia. For centuries they had lived as herders in the grasslands north of China. They slept in felt tents, called yurts, and survived on meat and milk from their animals. They also raided and fought with other tribes.

In 1206, a Mongol leader, or **khan,** managed to unite the Mongol tribes into a powerful fighting force. His name was Temujin, but he took the title of Genghis Khan, or "Universal Ruler." Under his leadership, the Mongols began a campaign of conquest that would create the largest empire the world had ever known.

Genghis first turned his army south, toward China. After several years of fighting, he had taken a large portion of northern China. He then moved west, capturing the lands of Central Asia and gaining control over the Silk Road. Crossing the Himalayas, he also occupied parts of modern-day Pakistan.

Several factors contributed to Genghis's success.

- First, the Mongols were fierce warriors and excellent horsemen. They could ride far and fast, and even sleep while riding.
- They were also well trained and highly disciplined. Genghis organized his troops on the decimal system, dividing them into groups of 10, 100, 1000, and 10,000.
- Genghis was a skilled military strategist who knew how to deceive his enemies. At times he would appear to retreat, only to draw his enemy into a trap.
- Genghis could also be ruthless. If a city rebelled after being conquered, he would return and raze it to the ground, leaving no survivors. His reputation for brutality caused some enemies to surrender without a fight.

khan Mongol tribal leader

In 1206 the Mongol leader Genghis Kahn united the tribes of Central Asia into a single army of fierce warriors on horseback. In the center of this illustration you can see Genghis Kahn charging into battle with his weapon raised.

In 1227, Genghis died. Power then passed to his son and grandsons, who continued the conquests. The Mongols took the rest of China, all of Russia, and most of Southwest Asia. Their westward advance was finally halted at the gates of Vienna and the shores of the Mediterranean. By 1260, Mongol lands extended across Eurasia, from China to Europe. In half a century, the Mongols had created an empire more than twice as large as the Muslim Empire, and six times larger than Rome at its height.

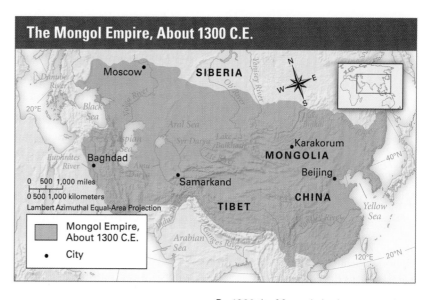

The Mongol Empire, About 1300 C.E.

By 1300 the Mongols had conquered lands extending from China to Europe and encompassing an area six times larger than the Roman Empire.

Mongol Rule Because the Mongols were nomads, they had no real experience with governing. They did have a strong moral code, however, which they enforced through their own legal system. Among other things, this code forbade theft, lying, betrayal, and defiance of authority. The penalty for violating this code could be death.

The Mongols could also be flexible. They allowed conquered peoples to maintain their own customs and traditions. In many cases, they adopted local customs themselves. They practiced religious tolerance. One of Genghis's grandsons reportedly said, "We believe in one God. . . . But just as God has given different digits [fingers] to the palm, so He has given different religions to men."

In 1265, the Mongol Empire split into four parts, called khanates. The largest and most important of these, the Khanate of the Great Kahn, included China and the Mongol homeland. Its ruler, Kublai Khan (KOOH-bly KAHN), united China and ruled like a Chinese emperor. He also maintained ties with the other khanates and kept the empire connected.

During this period, a huge network of exchange developed across the Mongol world and beyond. This network relied on the **Pax Mongolica,** the peace and security that prevailed under Mongol rule. The Mongols expanded trade routes and built a courier system to speed communication throughout the empire. As a result, trade increased dramatically across Afro-Eurasia. A growing volume of goods flowed along the Silk Road, from China to Europe and Africa. Ideas and inventions traveled, too. Paper and gunpowder—two Chinese inventions already adopted in the Muslim world—made their way to Europe during this period.

Pax Mongolica the state of peace that existed in Eurasia under Mongol rule

In this European illustration, Kublai Kahn receives the Venetian trader Marco Polo at his court. Marco Polo stayed at the Mongol leader's opulent royal court for a time in the late 1200s and served as an adviser to the Kahn.

bubonic plague a deadly bacteria responsible for the Black Death of the 1300s; transmitted by fleas living on infected rats

Of course, people also made the journey. The most famous traveler on the Silk Road, the Venetian trader Marco Polo, became an adviser to Kublai Khan and later wrote about the marvels of the khan's royal court. Among the innovations he noted was paper money, which the Mongols used to promote trade. This new currency, Polo said, could be used to "buy anything, including pearls, precious stones, gold, or silver." The Mongols also issued a kind of passport and credit card for travel throughout the empire. This document indicated the traveler's importance and the level of service that person should receive along the way.

Under the Mongols, travelers could journey the length of Asia, from China to Europe, with little concern for their safety. As a Chinese writer noted at the time, "The land within the Four Seas [Asia] had become the territory of one family, civilization had spread everywhere, and no more barriers existed."

The Mongol Collapse   The Mongol Empire lasted for around a century. Then, like all giant empires, it collapsed. Political disunity among the khanates was one problem. Another was the tendency of the Mongols to adopt the customs and culture of the people they ruled. Over time, they lost the warrior spirit that had driven their conquests.

The main cause of the collapse, however, was disease. Like Han China and imperial Rome, the Mongol Empire was stricken by a deadly illness that spread along trade routes. The disease was **bubonic plague,** also known as the Black Death. It began in the 1330s in China, where it killed as much as half of the population in just twenty years. From there it spread west along the Silk Road, killing millions more. It devastated the populations of Southwest Asia and Europe, where at least a quarter of the people died. The plague was most deadly in cities, where people lived close together. But it also ravaged the countryside.

The Black Death brought down the Mongol Empire. It reduced populations and disrupted trade and commerce. Movement along the trade routes slowed to a trickle. As a result, links between the four parts of the empire were broken. Each khanate faced mounting pressures. Two were overthrown quickly: the Persian khanate in 1335 and the Chinese khanate in 1368. The Mongols who ruled Russia—known as the Golden Horde—broke into smaller groups that declined in power over the next few centuries.

Only in Central Asia did Mongol rulers remain in power. In the late 1300s, a warrior known as Timur Lang, or Timur the Lame, took control. Attempting to revive the Mongol Empire, he expanded into Southwest Asia, seizing lands from India to the Mediterranean. He was a brutal ruler, however, who governed through terror. In the early 1500s, his descendants would conquer India and establish the Mughal Empire.

4.5 Expanding Networks of Exchange

During the centuries from 300 to 1500, the various regions of the world became increasingly connected. People, ideas, and goods began to move more freely within regions and around the world. Religions also spread beyond their lands of origin to become established in new places.

Trade Networks   Several major trade networks flourished during this era. The largest network connected the various parts of Asia with each other and with Africa and the Mediterranean. The Silk Road was the major land route in this network. It carried an enormous amount of trade over the centuries, particularly during the time of the Han and Mongol empires. The use of camel caravans—an Arab innovation—enhanced overland travel through desert regions.

This medieval European illustration shows merchants transporting merchandise on the Silk Road, the major land route between Europe and Asia. The use of camels, as shown here, made overland travel through desert regions easier.

Sea routes were also important. Merchant ships sailed from Korea, Japan, and China through the South China Sea to the ports of Southeast Asia and India. They crossed the Indian Ocean, the Arabian Sea, and the Persian Gulf to the shores of Southwest Asia and East Africa. They also moved up the Red Sea to link with trade routes in the Mediterranean.

A second major trade network crossed Europe. Although the fall of Rome disrupted trade for centuries, by the year 1000 merchants were starting to revive European trade. The Vikings—a warrior people from Scandinavia—helped launch this network in the 800s by expanding along sea and river routes. They crossed the Baltic and North seas and traveled around Spain into the Mediterranean. They also moved down the rivers of Russia to the Black and Caspian seas. They traded furs, lumber, salt, glass, horses, woolens, and many other goods. They also brought slaves from Britain and the Slavic lands of eastern Europe to trade in the Muslim world.

A third major trade network linked Africa's Mediterranean coast with the lands south of the Sahara Desert. This network, called the trans-Saharan trade route, was based on the exchange of two valuable products: salt and gold. Traders carried salt from the northern desert and traded it for gold from south of the desert. This trade supplied two-thirds of the world's gold and supported the powerful kingdoms of Ghana, Mali, and Songhai.

Other, smaller trade networks existed in the Americas and the South Pacific. In the Americas, a loose trading system spanned the continents but centered on the high civilizations of Mesoamerica and the South American Andes. In the South Pacific, the island groups of Polynesia, Melanesia, and Micronesia were conducting sea trade by the 1400s.

World Religions Exchange networks and the growth of empires also helped spread religious beliefs across Afro-Eurasia. As a result, the major faiths—Buddhism, Hinduism, Judaism, Christianity, and Islam—became **world religions**. Traders and missionaries carried Buddhism throughout Asia. Hinduism traveled with Indian traders to Southeast Asia. Islam spread over a large region from West Africa to Central Asia. It also gained a foothold in India and Southeast Asia. Christianity spread across Europe and Russia, and also took root in Egypt and Ethiopia. Judaism became established in communities stretching from western Europe to Central Asia and beyond.

These religions expanded during a period of change and upheaval throughout Afro-Eurasia. Their promise of salvation or spiritual peace offered comfort to people unsettled by urban life and the rise and fall of empires. In many cases, the religions interacted peacefully. In the Muslim world, for example, Jews, Christians, and Muslims often lived side by side, with little conflict.

Religious tensions and conflicts did develop, however. Muslims showed little tolerance for Hinduism, with its belief in many gods. When Muslim conquerors invaded India, they tried to convert Hindus to Islam. Tensions also developed between the two branches of the Christian faith: Roman Catholicism and Orthodox Christianity. In 1054, the two churches split officially.

The biggest conflicts, however, occurred between Christian and Muslim armies. In 1095, the Catholic Church launched the **Crusades** in an effort to oust Muslims from the holy lands of the Eastern Mediterranean. Christian armies also sought to retake Spain from the Muslims. By 1250, they had recaptured most of the Iberian Peninsula.

Exchanging Knowledge Ideas and technologies also moved through exchange networks. It would be impossible to list all the ideas spread during this era. But such a list would include writing systems and discoveries in math, astronomy, and medicine. It would also include technologies in such areas as irrigation, navigation, printing, and papermaking.

The system of Arabic numerals is one example. The Muslims adopted this system from India and later passed it along to Europe. Arabic numerals were much more practical than the Roman numerals used in Europe at the time. Based on the decimal system, they allowed for the development of modern math.

One important technology that spread widely at this time was the camel saddle. Devised in Arabia, this invention made camels useful for transport in desert areas. This, in turn, had a great impact on overland travel and the development of trade in Afro-Eurasia.

The Catholic Church launched the Crusades in 1095. The goal of the Crusades was to drive Muslims from the holy lands of the Eastern Mediterranean. This European manuscript from the 1200s shows Muslim and Christian armies charging into battle.

Environmental Factors The growth of exchange networks also had environmental effects, including the spread of disease. Populations suffered from devastating plagues that were transmitted along trade routes. Deadly diseases like smallpox, measles, and the bubonic plague helped cause the collapse of the Han, Roman, and Mongolian empires. As networks expanded, so did the danger of infectious disease.

As a result, the world population fluctuated greatly. It fell from an estimated 257 million in 200 C.E. to 206 million in 700 C.E. By 1000 C.E., the population had recovered and was growing rapidly. But the plague of the 1300s caused another sharp decline. By 1500, the population was rising again.

Increased prosperity from trade and agriculture boosted the world population. But this prosperity had environmental consequences. Farmers cut down forests to raise more rice and wheat, causing deforestation in some areas. Expanded cultivation also produced soil erosion and flooding, as soils ran off into rivers and raised water levels. This problem was evident in China's Huang He River valley, the nation's breadbasket. There, frequent flooding over the years caused terrible destruction and loss of life. As a result, the Huang He was known as "China's Sorrow."

The growth of trade networks increased the spread of disease. For example, the bubonic plague spread along trade routes across Eurasia, devastating many different societies as it went.

Summary

In this lesson, you read about major developments in the world between 300 and 1500 C.E. During this period, the growth of empires and exchange networks increased connections among the regions and peoples of the world.

Cultural Interaction Contact and interaction among cultures expanded with the growth of empires. The Muslim Empire brought many different peoples together and forged a culture that reflected many influences. The Mongol Empire promoted the exchange of ideas and customs across Afro-Eurasia. World religions spread widely during this period.

Political Structures Classical empires fell, but new states arose to take their place. The Muslim and Mongol empires ruled vast territories and created new political structures. They could not hold their empires together, however, and fractured into separate states.

Economic Structures Agriculture and trade were the main economic activities. Trade expanded with the growth of trade routes and new forms of transport. Growing prosperity helped strengthen the Muslim and Mongol empires. The disruption of trade, however, led to the Mongol collapse.

Social Structures Societies suffered with the collapse of civilizations in China, Rome, and India. Europe, in particular, entered an age of disorder with the end of the Roman Empire. The rise of Islam imposed new social structures on large portions of Afro-Eurasia.

Human Environment Interaction Expanded agriculture and trade had environmental effects. Diseases followed trade routes, killing millions and reducing the world population. Rising food production helped populations recover but led to deforestation, erosion, and floods in some areas.

The Decline of Feudalism

How did events in Europe contribute to the decline of feudalism and the rise of democratic thought?

5.1 Introduction

In this lesson, you will explore key events that contributed to the decline of feudalism. This decline took place in Europe from the 12th through the 15th centuries.

There were many causes for the breakdown of the feudal system. In this lesson, you will focus on three: political changes in England, a terrible disease, and a long series of wars.

In England, several political changes in the 12th and 13th centuries helped to weaken feudalism. A famous document known as *Magna Carta*, or Great Charter, dates from this time. Magna Carta was a written legal agreement that limited the king's power and strengthened the rights of nobles. As feudalism declined, Magna Carta took on a much broader meaning and contributed to ideas about individual rights and liberties in England.

The terrible disease was the bubonic plague, or Black Death. The plague swept across Asia in the 1300s and reached Europe in the late 1340s. Over the next two centuries, this terrifying disease killed millions in Europe. It struck all kinds of people—rich and poor, young and old, town dwellers and country folk. Almost everyone who caught the plague died within days. In some places, whole communities were wiped out. The deaths of so many people led to sweeping economic and social changes.

Lastly, between 1337 and 1453, France and England fought a series of battles known as the Hundred Years' War. This conflict changed the way wars were fought and shifted power away from feudal lords to monarchs and the common people.

How did such different events contribute to the decline of feudalism? In this lesson, you will find out.

Themes

Cultural Interaction Feudal culture declined as new military technology reduced the importance of castles and feudal lords.

Political Structures Reforms in England and the Hundred Years' War weakened the nobility and strengthened the power of both the monarchy and the common people.

Economic Structures The plague caused trade and commerce to slow, and the feudal model of agricultural production was undermined as peasants gained greater opportunities.

Social Structures The hierarchical structures of feudal society were challenged by war and disease as the common people gained influence throughout this period.

Human-Environment Interaction The bubonic plague spread from Asia to western Europe and caused mass death along the way.

The bubonic plague made death an ever-present part of life in Medieval Europe. In this image, the white Horseman of Death, a traditional Christian symbol, is followed by an army of the dead.

Magna Carta a written legal agreement signed in 1215 that limited the English monarch's power

5.2 Political Developments in England

There were many reasons for the decline of feudalism in Europe. In one country, England, political developments during the 12th and 13th centuries helped to weaken feudalism. The story begins with King Henry II, who reigned from 1154 to 1189.

Henry II's Legal Reforms   Henry made legal reform a central concern of his reign. For example, he insisted that a jury formally accuse a person of a serious crime. Cases were then tried before a royal judge. In theory, people could no longer simply be jailed or executed for no legal reason. There also had to be a court trial. These reforms strengthened the power of royal courts at the expense of feudal lords.

Henry's effort to strengthen royal authority led to a serious conflict with the Catholic Church. In the year 1164, Henry issued the Constitutions of Clarendon, a document that he said spelled out the king's traditional rights. Among them was the right to try clergy accused of serious crimes in royal courts, rather than in Church courts.

Henry's action led to a long, bitter quarrel with his friend, Thomas Becket, the archbishop of Canterbury. In 1170, four knights, perhaps seeking the king's favor, killed Becket in front of the main altar of Canterbury Cathedral. The cathedral and Becket's tomb soon became a popular destination for pilgrimages. In 1173, the Catholic Church proclaimed him a saint. Still, most of the Constitutions of Clarendon remained in force.

King John's acceptance of Magna Carta has been illustrated and painted many times. He is often, as he is here, incorrectly shown signing his name with a pen. In fact, he stamped his royal seal on the document to show his agreement.

King John and Magna Carta

In 1199, Henry's youngest son, John, became king of England. John soon made powerful enemies by losing most of the lands the English had controlled in France. He also taxed his barons heavily and ignored their traditional rights, arresting opponents at will. In addition, John quarreled with the Catholic Church and collected large amounts of money from its properties.

In June 1215, angry nobles forced a meeting with King John in a meadow called Runnymede, beside the River Thames, outside of London. There, they insisted that John put his seal on a document called **Magna Carta**, which means "Great Charter" in Latin.

Magna Carta was an agreement between the nobles and the monarch. The nobles agreed that the monarch could continue to rule. For his part, King John agreed to observe common law and the traditional rights of the nobles and the Church. For example, he promised to consult the nobles and the Church archbishops and bishops before imposing special taxes. He also agreed that "no free man" could be jailed except by the lawful judgment of his peers or by the law of the land. This idea eventually developed into a key part of English common law known as **habeas corpus** (HAY-be-us KOR-pus).

In many ways, Magna Carta only protected the rights and privileges of nobles. However, as time passed, the English people came to regard it as one of the foundations of their rights and liberties.

King Edward I and the Model Parliament   In 1295, Edward I, King John's grandson, took a major step toward including more people in government. Edward called together a governing body called the **Model Parliament**. It included commoners and lower-ranking clergy, as well as high-level Church officials and nobles.

The Impact of Political Developments in England   These political changes contributed to the decline of feudalism in two ways. Some of the changes strengthened royal authority at the expense of the nobles. Others weakened feudalism by eventually shifting some power to the common people.

Magna Carta established the idea of rights and liberties that even a monarch cannot violate. It also affirmed that monarchs should rule with the advice of the governed. Henry II's legal reforms strengthened English common law and the role of judges and juries. Finally, Edward I's Model Parliament gave a voice in government to common people, as well as to nobles. All these ideas formed the basis for the development of modern democratic institutions.

5.3 The Bubonic Plague

You have learned how political developments in England helped to weaken feudalism in that country. Another reason for the decline of feudalism was the **bubonic plague,** which affected all of Europe. The bubonic plague first struck Europe from 1346 to 1351. It returned in waves that occurred about every decade into the 15th century, leaving major changes in its wake.

Historians think the plague began in Central Asia, possibly in China, and spread throughout China, India, the Middle East, and then Europe. The disease traveled from Central Asia to the Black Sea along the Silk Road (the main trade route between Asia and the Mediterranean Sea). It probably was carried to Italy on a ship. It then spread north and west, throughout the continent of Europe and to England.

This 14th-century illustration shows King Edward I attending his Parliament. The King of Scots is seated to his right; the Prince of Wales is seated to his left.

habeas corpus the legal concept that an accused person cannot be jailed indefinitely without being charged with a crime

Model Parliament a governing body created by King Edward I that included some commoners, Church officials, and nobles

bubonic plague a deadly contagious disease caused by bacteria and spread by fleas; also called the Black Death

The Black Death   Symptoms, or signs, of the plague included fever, vomiting, fierce coughing and sneezing fits, and egg-sized swellings or bumps, called *buboes*. The term "Black Death" probably came from these black-and-blue swellings that appeared on the skin of victims.

The dirty conditions in which people lived contributed significantly to the spread of the bubonic plague. The bacteria that cause the disease are carried by fleas that feed on the blood of infected rodents, such as rats. When the rats die, the fleas jump to other animals and people. During the Middle Ages, it was not unusual for people to go for many months without a change of clothing or a bath. Rats, covered with fleas, often roamed the floors of homes looking for food. City streets were filled with human waste, dead animals, and trash.

At the time, though, no one knew where the disease came from or how it spread. Terrified people falsely blamed the plague on everything from the positions of the planets to lepers and to Jews.

Persecution of the Jews did not begin with the plague. Prejudice against Jews had led the English government to order all Jews to leave the country in 1290. In France, the same thing happened in 1306 and again in 1394. But fear of the plague made matters worse. During the Black Death, many German cities ordered Jews to leave.

The Impact of the Plague   The plague took a terrible toll on the populations of Asia and Europe. China's population was reduced by nearly half between 1200 and 1393, probably because of the plague and famine. Travelers reported that dead bodies covered the ground in Central Asia and India.

Some historians estimate that 24 million Europeans died of the plague—about a third of the population. The deaths of so many people speeded changes in Europe's economic and social structure, which contributed to the decline of feudalism.

The bubonic plague, or Black Death, most likely originated in Asia. In the 14th century, this disease killed about one-third of the population of Europe and brought about major political and social change.

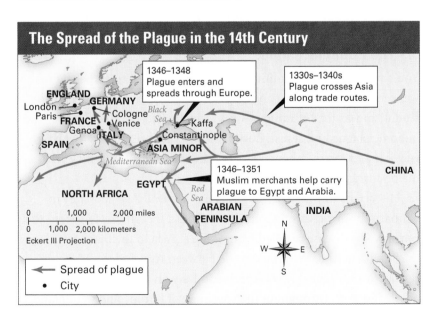

The Spread of the Plague in the 14th Century

1346–1348
Plague enters and spreads through Europe.

1330s–1340s
Plague crosses Asia along trade routes.

ENGLAND
London
Paris
GERMANY
Cologne
Black Sea
FRANCE
Venice
Genoa
ITALY
Kaffa
Constantinople
SPAIN
ASIA MINOR
Mediterranean Sea
CHINA

1346–1351
Muslim merchants help carry plague to Egypt and Arabia.

NORTH AFRICA
EGYPT
Red Sea
ARABIAN PENINSULA
INDIA

0   1,000   2,000 miles
0   1,000   2,000 kilometers
Eckert III Projection

N
W   E
S

⟵ Spread of plague
•   City

Trade and commerce slowed almost to a halt during the plague years. As Europe began to recover, the economy needed to be rebuilt. But it wouldn't be rebuilt in the same way, with feudal lords holding most of the power.

After the plague, there was a shift in power from nobles to the common people. One reason for this was a desperate need for workers because so many people had died. The workers who were left could, therefore, demand more money and more rights. In addition, many peasants and some serfs abandoned feudal manors and moved to towns and cities, seeking better opportunities. This led to a weakening of the manor system and a loss of power for feudal lords.

After the plague, a number of peasant rebellions broke out. When nobles tried to return things to how they had been, resentment exploded across Europe. There were peasant revolts in France, Flanders, England, Germany, Spain, and Italy.

The most famous of these revolts was the English Peasants' War in 1381. The English rebels succeeded in entering London and presenting their demands to the king, Richard II. The leader of the rebellion was killed, however, and after his death, the revolt lost momentum. Still, in most of Europe, the time was coming when serfdom would end.

This skeleton appears on a gravestone dating from the Middle Ages. When the plague hit Europe people were surrounded by the dead and the dying, and this was reflected in the objects they created.

5.4 The Hundred Years' War

Between 1337 and 1453, England and France fought a series of battles for control over lands in France. Known as the **Hundred Years' War,** this long conflict contributed to the erosion of feudalism in England and in France.

English monarchs had long claimed lands in France. This was because earlier English kings had actually been feudal lords over these French fiefs. French kings now disputed these claims. When Philip VI of France declared that the French fiefs of England's King Edward III were part of Philip's own realm, war broke out in France.

Early English Successes   Despite often being outnumbered, the English won most of the early battles of the war. What happened at the Battle of Crécy (KRAY-see) shows why.

Two quite different armies faced each other at the French village of Crécy in 1346. The French had a feudal army that relied on horse-mounted knights. French knights wore heavy armor, and they could hardly move when they were not on horseback. Their weapons were swords and lances. Some of the infantry, or foot soldiers, used cross-bows, which were effective only at short ranges.

> **Hundred Years' War** a series of battles fought between France and England from 1337 to 1453

Joan of Arc inspired the people of France to fight. To this day she is honored for her heroism. This statue of Joan of Arc, created in the 19th century, stands in the city of Paris.

heretic a person who holds beliefs that are contrary to a set of religious teachings

In contrast, the English army was made up of lightly armored knights, foot soldiers, and archers armed with longbows. Some soldiers were recruited from the common people and paid to fight.

The longbow had many advantages over the crossbow. Larger arrows could be fired more quickly. The arrows flew farther, faster, and more accurately, and could pierce the armor of the time. At Crécy, the longbow helped the English defeat the much larger French force.

The French Fight Back   The French slowly chipped away at the territory the English had won in the early years of the war. In 1415, after a long truce, English King Henry V again invaded France. This time, the English met with stronger resistance. One reason was that the French were now using more modern tactics. The French king was recruiting his army from commoners, paying them with money collected by taxes, just as the English did.

Another reason for increased French resistance was a new sense of national identity and unity. In part, the French were inspired by a 17-year-old peasant girl, known today as Joan of Arc. Joan claimed that she heard the voices of saints urging her to save France. Putting on a suit of armor, she went to fight.

In 1429, Joan led a French army to victory in the Battle of Orléans (OR-lay-uhn). The next year, the "Maid of Orléans" was captured by English allies. The English pushed certain Church leaders to accuse Joan of being a witch and a **heretic** and to burn her at the stake.

Joan of Arc's heroism changed the way many French men and women felt about their king and nation. Twenty-two years after Joan's death, the French finally drove the English out of France. Almost 500 years later, the Roman Catholic Church made Joan a saint.

The Impact of the Hundred Years' War   The Hundred Years' War contributed to the decline of feudalism by helping to shift power from feudal lords to monarchs and to common people. During the struggle, monarchs on both sides had collected taxes and raised large professional armies. As a result, kings no longer relied as much on nobles to supply knights for the army.

In addition, changes in military technology made the nobles' knights and castles less useful. The longbow proved to be an effective weapon against mounted knights. Castles also became less important as armies learned to use gunpowder to shoot iron balls from cannons and blast holes in castle walls.

The new feeling of nationalism also shifted power away from lords. Previously, many English and French peasants felt more loyalty to their local lords than to their monarch. The war created a new sense of national unity and patriotism on both sides.

In both France and England, commoners and peasants bore the heaviest burden of the war. They were forced to fight and to pay higher and more frequent taxes. Those who survived the war, however, were needed as soldiers and workers. For this reason, the common people emerged from the conflict with greater influence and power.

At the Battle of Crécy, the English army's lighter armor and longbows triumphed over the French knights' heavy armor and crossbow.

Summary

In this lesson you learned about the decline of feudalism in Europe in the 12th to 15th centuries. The major causes of this decline included political changes in England, disease, and wars.

Cultural Interaction The culture of feudalism, which centered on noble knights and castles, declined in this period. The spread of new military technologies such as the longbow and cannon made the armored knight and fortified castle less important. The disaster of the plague influenced culture, causing some to celebrate life in the face of mass death. Others had the opposite reaction and fixated on death and the afterlife, which was reflected in art.

Political Structures In England the signing of Magna Carta and other political reforms laid the foundations for more democratic forms of government. The Hundred Years' War between France and England shifted power away from feudal lords to both the monarchy and the common people. It also increased feelings of nationalism, as people began to identify more with the king than with their local lord.

Economic Structures The feudal system of agriculture and land ownership declined in this period. The plague caused trade and commerce to slow. Due to the death of one third of the population of Europe from the plague, labor shortages occurred. This created greater economic opportunities for peasants, and they demanded increased wages.

Social Structures The hierarchical social structure of feudalism was destabilized as a result of the plague, which affected all social classes equally. When the plague passed and feudal lords attempted to reestablish their authority, peasant rebellions occurred as commoners refused to accept the old social order. The common people also gained greater power as a result of the Hundred Years' War.

Human-Environment Interaction The bubonic plague spread over trade routes from Asia to western Europe and killed one third of the population of Europe. Its spread was aided by the fact that most people lived in unhygienic conditions at this time, especially in the cities. In the wake of the plague many peasants left their manors for greater opportunities in the cities.

The Byzantine Empire

How did the Byzantine Empire develop and form its own distinctive church?

6.1 Introduction

In this lesson, you will learn about the Byzantine Empire. This great empire lay in two continents, Europe and Asia. It lasted from about 500 to 1453 C.E., when it was conquered by the Ottoman Turks.

At first, the Byzantine Empire was the continuation of the Roman Empire in the east. In 330 C.E., the Roman emperor Constantine moved his capital from Rome to the city of Byzantium. This city was an old Greek trading colony on the eastern edge of Europe. Constantine called his capital New Rome, but it soon became known as Constantinople, which is Greek for "Constantine's City."

Later, control of the huge original empire was divided between two emperors—one based in Rome and one based in Constantinople. After the fall of Rome, the eastern empire continued for another 1,000 years. We call this the Byzantine Empire, after Byzantium, the original name of its capital city.

East and west remained connected for a time through a shared Christian faith. But the Church in the east developed in its own unique ways. It became known as the Eastern Orthodox Church. Over time, Byzantine emperors and Church officials came into conflict with the pope in Rome. The conflict eventually led to a permanent split between the Eastern Orthodox Church and the Roman Catholic Church.

In this lesson, you will learn about the Byzantine Empire, one of its greatest emperors, and its distinctive church. Let's begin by exploring the empire's capital—the fabulous city of Constantinople.

Themes

Cultural Interaction The Eastern Orthodox Church played a central role in daily life in the Byzantine Empire and inspired distinctive and magnificent art and architecture.

Political Structures The Byzantine state combined religion and government—the emperor also had supreme authority over the Eastern Orthodox Church and was considered God's representative on earth.

Economic Structures The Byzantine Empire prospered through trade and Constantinople became the wealthiest city in the Mediterranean region.

Social Structures Although a small minority became fabulously wealthy through trade, most people in the Byzantine Empire lived in poverty.

Human-Environment Interaction Constantinople prospered in part due to its strategic location at the crossroads between Europe and Asia.

◀ This modern drawing re-creates the city of Constantinople during the Byzantine Empire.

Constantinople the city on the eastern edge of Europe, which Constantine made the capital of the Roman Empire in 330 C.E.

Byzantine Empire the name for the eastern Roman Empire, located at the crossroads of Europe and Asia; it lasted from about 500 to 1453 C.E.

6.2 Constantinople

Constantinople was more than 800 miles to the east of Rome. Why did Constantine choose this site to be the capital of the Roman Empire?

One reason was that the site was easy to defend. It was surrounded on three sides by water. The Byzantines fashioned a chain across the city's harbor to guard against seafaring intruders. Miles of walls, fortified by watchtowers, and gates discouraged invasion by land and by sea.

Constantinople also stood at the crossroads of Europe and Asia, and the many sea and overland trade routes linking east and west. During the **Byzantine Empire,** this special location helped to make the city, and some of its citizens, very wealthy. For more than 700 years, Constantinople was the richest and the most elegant city in the Mediterranean region. Ivory, silk, furs, perfumes, and other luxury items flowed through its markets. A French soldier who saw the city in 1204 exclaimed, "One could not believe there was so rich a city in all the world."

At its height, Constantinople was home to around one million people. The city's language and culture were Greek, but traders and visitors spoke many languages. Ships crowded the city's harbor, loaded with goods. The city streets, some narrow and twisting, some grand and broad, teemed with camel and mule trains.

Life in Constantinople was more comfortable than in Western Europe. The city boasted a sewer system, which was quite rare in medieval times. Social services were provided by hospitals, homes for the elderly, and orphanages.

The eastern Roman Empire, later called the Byzantine Empire, ruled much of the Mediterranean world for several hundred years.

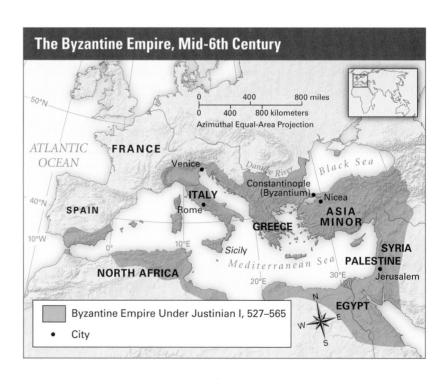

The Byzantine Empire, Mid-6th Century

ATLANTIC OCEAN

FRANCE

Venice

Danube River

Black Sea

Constantinople (Byzantium)

Nicea

ITALY

Rome

SPAIN

ASIA MINOR

GREECE

Sicily

Mediterranean Sea

SYRIA

PALESTINE

NORTH AFRICA

Jerusalem

EGYPT

50°N

40°N

10°W

0°

10°E

20°E

30°E

0   400   800 miles
0   400   800 kilometers
Azimuthal Equal-Area Projection

Byzantine Empire Under Justinian I, 527–565
• City

Despite the luxuries enjoyed by the rich, many people lived in poverty. The emperor gave bread to those who could not find work. In exchange, the unemployed performed such tasks as sweeping the streets and weeding public gardens.

Almost everyone attended the exciting chariot races at a stadium called the Hippodrome. Two chariot teams, one wearing blue and the other green, were fierce rivals. In Constantinople and other cities, many people belonged to opposing groups called the Blues and Greens after the chariot teams. At times the rivalry between Blues and Greens erupted in deadly street fighting. But in 532, the two groups united in a rebellion that destroyed much of Constantinople. You will find out what happened in the next section.

6.3 The Reign of Justinian I

One of the greatest Byzantine emperors was Justinian I, whose long reign lasted from 527 to 565. But Justinian's reign nearly came to an abrupt end much sooner. In January 532, the emperor and his beautiful wife, Theodora, were attending chariot races at the Hippodrome. In the past, Blues and Greens among the spectators had often fought with each other. This time, however, both groups were upset over the arrests of some of their members. To Justinian's horror, they united in denouncing him. Fighting broke out, spilled into the streets, and escalated into a full-scale rebellion.

During a revolt in Constantinople, the empress Theodora (third from the left) encouraged her husband, Justinian I, to stay and fight for his city.

The rioting continued for a week while Justinian and Theodora hid in the palace. Much of the city was in flames. Justinian's advisors wanted him to flee the city. Theodora, however, urged him to stay and fight. With her encouragement, Justinian put down the revolt. According to the official court historian, Procopius (pro-KOH-pee-us), 30,000 people were killed in the fighting. The city of Constantinople lay in ruins.

Justinian was determined to rebuild the city on a grand scale. He put huge sums of money into public works. Soon, Constantinople had new bridges, public baths, parks, roads, and hospitals. The emperor also built many grand churches, including the magnificent Hagia Sophia (AH-ee-yah SOH-fee-uh). Its name is Greek for "Holy Wisdom." Today, this great structure is one of the most famous buildings in the world.

Besides rebuilding Constantinople, Justinian tried to reclaim some of the Roman Empire's lost territory. He launched military campaigns that, for a time, took back parts of North Africa, Italy, and Spain.

Justinian is most famous, however, for creating a systematic body of law. Under his direction, a committee studied the thousands of laws the Byzantines had inherited from the Roman Empire. They revised outdated and confusing laws. They also made improvements, such as extending women's property rights. The result of their work is known as Justinian's Code. It became the basis for many legal codes in the western world.

Procopius, the court historian, wrote glowing accounts of Justinian's achievements. But he also wrote the *Secret History*, in which he called the emperor "a treacherous enemy, insane for murder and plunder." Throughout Byzantine history, distrust and divisions often plagued the imperial court. Justinian's court was no exception.

6.4 The Eastern Orthodox Church

To the Byzantines, Christianity was more than a religion. It was the very foundation of their empire.

When Constantine built his new capital, he intended it to be the religious center of the empire, as well as the seat of government. Constantine himself tried to settle religious disputes by assembling a council of bishops.

Over time, the Byzantine Church separated from the Church in Rome and became known as the **Eastern Orthodox Church**. The word *orthodox* means "in agreement with right belief." The leaders of the medieval Eastern Orthodox Church thought that their church was based on a set of beliefs that they could trace back to Jesus Christ and to the work of bishops in early Christian councils.

Eastern Orthodox Church
a Christian religion that developed out of early Christianity in the Byzantine Empire

Hagia Sophia was built between the years 532 and 537. Its architectural features inspired the design of many later Orthodox churches.

The Role of the Eastern Orthodox Church in the Empire

Religion and government were more closely linked in the Byzantine Empire than in the west. The Byzantines viewed the emperor not just as the head of the government but as the living representative of God and Jesus Christ. This meant that church and state were combined into one all-powerful body.

The state religion also united people in a common belief. The Eastern Orthodox Church played a central role in daily life. Most people attended church regularly. Religious sacraments gave shape to every stage of the journey from birth to death. Monasteries and convents cared for the poor and the sick. These institutions were supported by wealthy people and became quite powerful. Let's look at some of the practices of Eastern Orthodoxy.

Church Hierarchy   Like Roman Catholic clergy, Orthodox clergy were ranked in order of importance. In Byzantine times, the emperor had supreme authority in the Church. He selected the **patriarch** of Constantinople, who ranked just below him in matters of religion.

Unlike the pope in the west, the patriarch did not claim strong authority over other patriarchs and bishops. Instead, he was "first among equals." The patriarch of Constantinople (modern Istanbul, Turkey) still holds this honor.

A feature of Eastern Orthodox churches is an image of Christ the Pantocrator, like this one, watching over Orthodox worshippers from the dome above.

Orthodox priests served under patriarchs and other bishops. Unlike Roman Catholic priests, who were not allowed to marry, many Orthodox priests were married. Bishops, however, could rise only from the ranks of unmarried clergy.

Liturgy and Prayer   The Orthodox Church service corresponding to the Roman Catholic mass was the Divine Liturgy. Both the clergy and worshippers sang or chanted the liturgy, or form of public worship. The liturgy was conducted in Greek or in the local language.

Orthodox Christians also prayed to saints. Two saints were particularly important. Saint Basil promoted charity and reformed the liturgy. Saint Cyril helped create the Cyrillic (sih-RIL-ik) alphabet, which allowed scholars to translate the Bible for people in Eastern Europe.

> **patriarch** in the Eastern Orthodox Church, the bishop of an important city

Architecture and Art   Christian faith inspired magnificent architecture and artwork in the Byzantine Empire. With its square base and high dome, the cathedral Hagia Sophia served as a model for many Orthodox churches. The architecture of the church also reflects Orthodox views. The simple base represents the earthly world. Upon it rests the "dome of heaven." Rich decorations on the inside were meant to remind worshippers of what it would be like to enter God's kingdom.

Building on the Greek love of art, the Orthodox Church used many images in its services and prayers. Byzantine artists created beautiful icons, which were usually painted on small wooden panels. Artists also fashioned sacred images as mosaics and painted them in murals.

An image of Christ as the *Pantocrator*, or ruler of all, gazed down from the domes of all Orthodox churches. Most churches also displayed an icon of Jesus's mother, Mary (called the *Theotokos*, or godbearer) and the Christ child over the altar.

Many Byzantines believed that sacred pictures brought them closer to God. But later, icons also became a source of violent disagreement.

Byzantine emperor Leo III banned the use of religious images, or icons, in 730 C.E. The ban was lifted in 843. This mosaic of Jesus in Hagia Sophia escaped destruction because it was created after the ban was lifted.

6.5 Conflict Between East and West

Medieval Europe and the Byzantine Empire were united in a single faith, Christianity. Over the centuries, however, cultural, political, and religious differences brought the two parts of the old Roman Empire into conflict.

The two regions had been quite different even in the days of the early Roman emperors. The eastern half of the empire had many cities, much trade, and great wealth. The western half was mostly rural and agricultural, and not nearly as wealthy.

Other differences became more pronounced after the fall of Rome. Byzantine culture was largely shaped by its Greek heritage. The west was influenced by Frankish and Germanic cultures. In the city of Constantinople, people spoke Greek. In the west, Latin was the language of scholars, diplomats, and the Church.

Perhaps most important was the conflict that developed between the churches of east and west. After the fall of Rome, popes gradually emerged as powerful figures in western Europe. The popes claimed supreme religious authority over all Christians. The emperors and patriarchs of the east did not claim that power.

Other differences added to the conflict. Let's look at three major disagreements and how they led to a split in the Christian Church.

Iconoclasm The first major disagreement concerned religious icons. Many Christians in medieval times used images of Jesus, Mary, and the saints in worship and prayer. Some Christians in the east, however, believed that people were wrongly worshipping the icons as if they were divine. In 730 C.E., Byzantine emperor Leo III banned the use of religious images in all Christian churches and homes.

This policy of *iconoclasm* ("icon smashing") led to the destruction of much religious art. Throughout Christian lands, people cried out in protest. In Rome, Roman Church leaders were angry because Leo's order applied to parts of Italy that were under Byzantine control. Pope Gregory III even excommunicated the emperor.

The Byzantine Empire lifted its ban on icons in 843. But the dispute over iconoclasm had caused a major split between the east and west. It also helped drive popes in Rome to look for support and protection against enemies.

The Crowning of a Holy Roman Emperor Another major disagreement occurred in 800 C.E. At the time, Empress Irene was the ruler of the Byzantine Empire. Because she was a woman, Pope Leo

III did not view her as true or strong enough to govern. He wanted the protection of a strong leader to help defend the Church in the west.

Instead, Leo decided to crown Charlemagne, the king of the Franks, as Holy Roman emperor. The pope's action outraged the Byzantines, who felt that their empress was the rightful ruler of the remains of the Roman Empire.

The Final Break   Matters between east and west came to a head in 1054. The patriarch of Constantinople, Cerularius, wanted to reassert Byzantine control of the Church. He closed all churches that worshipped with western rites. Pope Leo IX was furious. He sent Cardinal Humbert to Constantinople. The cardinal marched up to the altar of Hagia Sophia. In front of everyone, he laid down a bull (a proclamation by the pope) excommunicating Cerularius.

Cerularius responded by excommunicating the cardinal. This was only a symbolic act, for the patriarch did not have that power. But it showed that the split, or schism, between east and west was complete. Despite future attempts to heal the division, the Eastern Orthodox Church and the Roman Catholic Church were now separate churches.

The division between the Eastern Orthodox and Roman Catholic churches lasted until 1964. In that year, Patriarch Athenagoras (left) and Pope Paul VI (right) met in Jerusalem and made a formal statement that undid the excommunications of 1054.

Summary

In this lesson you learned about the founding of the Byzantine Empire and the Eastern Orthodox Church.

Cultural Interaction The largely Greek culture of the Byzantine Empire was influenced by the European and Asian cultures it encountered through trade. The Eastern Orthodox Church had a tremendous influence on everyday life and inspired magnificent art forms—domed churches like the Hagia Sophia, painted icons and mosaics. In the 700s, however, conflict arose with the western church over the use of icons.

Political Structures Church and state were combined in the Byzantine Empire. The emperor was also the head of the Eastern Church and was viewed as the representative of God on earth. In the 500s the emperor Justinian reformed the laws of the empire by creating a systematic body of law, known as Justinian's Code. It became a foundation for the law of the western world.

Economic Structures Extensive trade made the Byzantine Empire wealthy. Luxury goods such as ivory, silk, furs, and perfumes were especially important. The Byzantine Empire at this time was relatively wealthy and urban compared to western Europe, which was much poorer and more rural.

Social Structures A small minority in the Byzantine Empire became fabulously wealthy from trade, but a majority remained poor. In Constantinople hospitals, homes for the elderly, and orphanages provided social services for the poor.

Human-Environment Interaction Constantinople became a wealthy and prosperous city in part due to its central location at the crossroads of trading routes between Europe and Asia.

The Political Development of Imperial China

Which method of selecting officials led to the best leaders for China?

7.1 Introduction

Welcome to imperial China. Historians divide Chinese history into periods ruled by dynasties, or ruling families. In this lesson, you will learn about China's political development under several dynasties from 220 to 1644 C.E.

China was first unified under an emperor in the 3rd century B.C.E. From the beginning, emperors needed help to rule. Emperor Han Wu Di, for example, once sent out this announcement:

Heroes Wanted! A Proclamation

Exceptional work demands exceptional men. . . . We therefore command the various district officials to search for men of brilliant and exceptional talents, to be our generals, our ministers, and our envoys to distant states.

Over time, Chinese emperors tried several ways of finding qualified people to administer their government. One method was to rely on the class of wealthy families. Emperors like Han Wu Di, however, preferred to choose officials for their merit, or worth. During the Han dynasty, candidates for government jobs had to prove their knowledge and ability by passing strict tests. As a result, a class of scholar-officials evolved. Under later emperors, this system developed into a rule by officials of proven merit.

In the 13th century C.E., a nomadic people called the Mongols built a great empire in Asia. Toward the end of the century, the Mongols took over China. Under Mongol emperors, government officials in China were foreigners. Some officials were Mongol friends and relatives of the emperor. Others were trusted people from other lands.

How did these approaches to government affect China? Which method won out? In this lesson, you will explore these questions.

Themes

Cultural Interaction The government and society of imperial China was strongly influenced by the philosophy of Confucianism.

Political Structures China was ruled by hereditary imperial dynasties. All dynasties ruled using large bureaucracies of government officials, although methods for choosing officials varied.

Economic Structures Because Confucian philosophy looked down on merchants, business and trade were not encouraged in imperial China.

Social Structures During some dynastic periods the aristocracy governed China while in others civil service examinations allowed for increased social mobility.

The Chinese held exams for hiring scholar-officials to help the emperor rule.

emperor the political leader of a territory containing several countries or groups of people

imperial belonging or related to an emperor

dynasty a line of rulers descended from one family

7.2 The Government of Imperial China

In 221 B.C.E., Prince Zheng (JUNG), the head of the state of Qin (CHIN), became the first Chinese ruler to claim the title of **emperor**. He took the name Qin Shihuangdi (CHIN shee-HWANG-dee), which means "First Emperor of Qin." From that time on, China usually had an **imperial** form of government headed by an emperor or, sometimes, an empress.

China's Imperial Dynasties   Chinese emperors named a relative—often a son—to become emperor after their deaths. In this way they established a **dynasty,** or line of rulers from the same family.

From ancient times, Chinese rulers based their right to govern on the Mandate of Heaven. According to this idea, Heaven had chosen a particular dynasty to rule. The Chinese believed that Heaven supported the dynasty for as long as an emperor ruled well. Natural disasters such as floods, famines, plagues, and earthquakes were taken as signs that Heaven was displeased. If an emperor ruled badly and lost the Mandate of Heaven, the people could overthrow him.

The table below lists the imperial dynasties that ruled China between 221 B.C.E. and 1644 C.E. In this unit, you will focus on the dynasties that followed the Han dynasty.

China's Imperial Dynasties

Dynasty	Time Period	Known for
Qin dynasty	221–206 B.C.E.	unification of China under an emperor
Han dynasty	206 B.C.E.–220 C.E.	a golden age for a united China
Six dynasties	220–581 C.E.	a period of chaos and division
Sui dynasty	589–618 C.E.E	reunification of China
Tang dynasty	618–907 C.E.	economic development and growth; many inventions and discoveries
Five dynasties in the north Ten Kingdoms in the south	907–960 C.E. 907–970 C.E.	a period of chaos and division
Song dynasty	960–1279 C.E.	economic development and growth; many inventions and discoveries
Yuan dynasty (the Mongols)	1279–1368 C.E.	control of China by foreigners
Ming dynasty	1368–1644 C.E.	opening up of China to foreign influences at the start of the dynasty; closing down of China by the end of the dynasty

China's Breakup and Reunification

The Han dynasty of ancient China held power for more than 400 years. This was a golden age of expansion and prosperity for China. In 220 C.E., however, the Han rulers lost their grip on power. A long period of disunity and conflict followed. This period ended when the Sui and Tang dynasties reunified China.

What happened to bring about the end of Han rule? Like earlier emperors, the Han governed China with the help of a large **bureaucracy** of government officials. As long as the bureaucracy was skilled, honest, and hard working, China prospered. By 220, however, corrupt, or dishonest, relatives and servants of the emperor had seized control of the government.

Warriors on horseback fought for Chinese emperors as they struggled to maintain control of the empire against warlords and invaders. These sculptures of a warrior and his horse were created during the Qin dynasty.

The result was disastrous. High taxes sent many families into poverty. Workers were forced to labor for long periods of time on public projects. Bandits attacked farmers in the countryside. This led **warlords** to oppose the emperor and fight against one another. The government grew weak and could not protect farmers.

Small farmers also suffered because they had to pay taxes and give half of everything they produced to their landlords. As they fell into debt, they had to give up their own land to large landowners and work for them, instead.

At last, the farmers rebelled. They believed that the Han dynasty had lost the Mandate of Heaven. No new dynasty took over from the Han. Instead, China broke apart into separate kingdoms, just as Europe did after the fall of Rome. Nomadic invaders ruled the north. Several short-lived dynasties ruled the south.

In 589, the northern state of Sui (SWAY) conquered the south and reunified China. The Sui dynasty created a new central government and ruled for 29 years. By 617, however, heavy taxes led to unrest and a struggle for power.

In 618, a general named Li Yuan declared himself emperor and established the Tang dynasty. Tang rulers built on the accomplishments of the Sui dynasty. They strengthened the central government and increased Tang influence over outlying areas.

Under the Tang, a unified China enjoyed a period of wealth and power that lasted nearly 300 years. Let's look now at how Tang rulers approached problems of government.

bureaucracy a highly complex body of workers with many levels of authority

warlord a military leader operating outside the control of the government

aristocracy a ruling class of noble families

civil service examination a test given to qualify candidates for positions in the government

7.3 Aristocracy: The Tang Dynasty

Like earlier emperors, Tang rulers relied on a large bureaucracy. Officials collected taxes and oversaw building and irrigation projects. They managed the army and enforced the laws. But how could emperors be sure that they chose the best people for these positions?

Earlier emperors answered this question in different ways. Before the Han dynasty, emperors chose members of the **aristocracy** to help them govern. These people were born into noble families of wealthy and powerful landowners. But simply being wealthy did not make a person talented and knowledgeable.

To improve the bureaucracy, Han emperors created **civil service examinations**. Candidates took long tests to qualify for office. The tests had questions on Chinese classics, poetry, and legal and administrative issues. Mainly, they were based on the works of Confucius (kon-FEW-shus), China's great philosopher and teacher. This began the system under which a class of scholar-officials ran the government.

Later, Tang emperors also used civil service exams to fill some government positions. Early in the dynasty, however, emperors chose aristocrats for most high-level jobs. Some officials were hired because their fathers or grandfathers had held high government rank. Some were hired because of personal recommendations. Often, aristocrats gained positions by marrying into the imperial family.

Even the civil service exams favored aristocrats. The tests were supposedly open to all except for certain groups, such as merchants, actors, and beggars. In theory, any man could attend the university where students prepared for the exams. In reality, however, only the wealthy could afford tutors, books, and time to study. As a result, aristocrats held almost all offices in the early part of the Tang dynasty.

Civil service exams to choose China's government officials were based largely on the teachings of Confucius, a Chinese thinker and teacher who lived from 551 to 479 B.C.E.

Peasant rebellions and battles between generals ended the Tang dynasty in 907. Once again, China split apart. Five military dynasties followed one another to power in the north. The south broke up into independent kingdoms.

Beginning in 960, the Song (SOONG) dynasty rose. Gradually, Song emperors reunified the country. As you will see, they built on the civil service system to reform how government officials were chosen.

During the Song dynasty, scholar-officials performed many tasks. Here scholars organize ancient manuscripts.

7.4 Meritocracy: The Song Dynasty

Under Song emperors, the idea of scholar-officials reached its height. The Song relied on civil service exams and opened them up to far more candidates. In this way, they created a **meritocracy**.

The exams were influenced by a new school of thought known as neo-Confucianism. This new teaching blended the teachings of Confucius with elements of Buddhism and Daoism (two traditional religions in China).

A Confucian scholar, Zhu Xi (JU SHEE), commented on classic Chinese writings. In 1190, his work was published as the *Four Books*. This work became the basis of study for all civil service exams.

Confucius taught that people must act properly in five important relationships: ruler and subject, father and son, older sibling and younger sibling, husband and wife, and friend and friend. Except for friends, one person in each relationship is above the other. Those above should be kind to those below. Those below should respect and obey those above. In particular, subjects must be loyal to their rulers. Song emperors and scholars believed that officials who had studied Confucius would be rational, moral, and able to maintain order.

Under the Song, people from lower classes gained the ability to become scholar-officials. They could attend the new state-supported schools and go on to the university. If they passed a local test, they could take the imperial exam in the capital. On those exams, they wrote essays and poems in a certain style. They answered questions about political and social problems based on Confucian ideas.

The exams were set up to prevent cheating. Candidates were locked in a small room for several days. A second person copied each paper so that the examiners wouldn't know whose work they were reading.

Only a small proportion of candidates passed the difficult exams. Those who failed could take the tests again in the future. Those who passed had to wait a few years before their first appointment. When it came, it was for a job far from their hometown, so that they could not play favorites among family and friends. At the end of three years, officials could move up in rank.

Despite the challenges, people were happy to get such respected jobs. As government officials, they also enjoyed certain privileges, such as being excused from taxes and military service.

meritocracy rule by officials of proven merit

7.5 Government by Foreigners: The Period of Mongol Rule

In the 13th century, the Mongols conquered almost all of Asia. In 1276, they captured China's imperial capital. Three years later, the last Song emperor died fleeing from the invaders.

The Mongol leader, Kublai Khan (KOOH-bly KAHN), took the title of emperor of China. He called his dynasty the Yuan dynasty. For nearly 100 years, from 1279 to 1368, China was under Mongol rule.

Under the Mongols, Chinese society was divided into four classes. The Mongols were at the top. Next came foreigners who were their friends. These people included Tibetans, Persians, Turks, and Central Asians. Many of them were Muslims. The third class was made up of the northern Chinese, who were more accustomed to the Mongols than were the southerners. The southern Chinese came last.

Kublai Khan ended the system of civil service exams. He did not believe that Confucian learning was needed for government jobs, and he did not want to rely on Chinese people to run his government. To fill important positions, he chose other Mongols whom he felt he could trust. Some of these people were his relatives.

But there weren't enough Mongols to fill every job. Besides, many were illiterate, or unable to read and write. Kublai and later Mongol emperors needed people who could handle the paperwork of a complex government. They were forced to appoint trusted foreigners to government positions, even some Europeans. Chinese scholars were appointed only as teachers and minor officials. Other Chinese worked as clerks, and some of them rose to important positions.

Without the examination system, however, there was a shortage of capable administrators. In 1315, the Mongols restored the exam system. Even then, they set limits on who could take the exam, favoring Mongol and other non-Chinese candidates.

The Mongols were a dynamic group of nomads who conquered huge areas of Asia, including China.

As time went on, fighting among Mongol leaders weakened the government of China. So did the greed and corruption of officials. The Mongols had also made many enemies among the native Chinese. In the 1350s and 1360s, rebels rose up against them. In 1368, the Mongol dynasty collapsed, and the Chinese reestablished their own government under the Ming dynasty. The Ming ruled China for nearly 300 years.

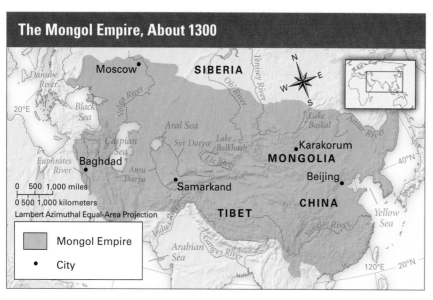

The Mongol Empire, About 1300

Moscow
SIBERIA
Danube River
20°E
Black Sea
Volga River
Ob' River
Yenisey River
Aral Sea
Lake Baikal
Amur River
Caspian Sea
Syr Darya
Lake Balkhash
Karakorum
MONGOLIA
Euphrates River
Baghdad
Ile River
Amu Darya
40°N
Beijing
Samarkand
CHINA
TIBET
Yellow Sea
Indus River
Arabian Sea
Ganges River
Yangtze River
120°E
20°N

0   500   1,000 miles
0   500   1,000 kilometers
Lambert Azimuthal Equal-Area Projection

Mongol Empire
• City

7.6 The Revival of the Civil Service System

Under Ming emperors, civil service exams were again used to fill government positions. This system lasted into the 20th century.

In many ways, the exam system served China well. It provided a well-organized government. The education of its scholar-officials emphasized moral behavior, justice, kindness, loyalty to the emperor, proper conduct, and the importance of family. These values helped to unify Chinese culture.

The civil service system gave poor men who were ambitious and hard working the chance to be government officials. At the same time, it ensured that officials were trained and talented, not merely rich or related to the emperor.

Yet China's civil service system may also have stood in the way of progress. The exams did not test understanding of science, mathematics, or engineering. People with such knowledge were therefore kept out of the government. Confucian scholars also had little respect for merchants, business, and trade. Confucians had often considered merchants to be the lowest class in society because they bought and sold things rather than producing useful items themselves. Under the Ming, this outlook dominated, and trade and business were not encouraged. In addition, the bureaucracy became set in its ways. Its inability to adapt contributed to the fall of the Ming in 1644.

The Forbidden City was a large palace compound constructed in the early 15th century in Beijing, which was the capital city during the Ming dynasty. It served as the residence for the emperor and as the center of government.

Summary

In this lesson, you have learned how China was governed between 220 and 1644 C.E.

Cultural Interaction The culture of imperial China was strongly influenced by Confucianism. Confucianism emphasized respect for authority and the importance of a well-ordered society. Civil service exams chose government officials based on their knowledge of classic Confucian texts.

Political Structures China was ruled by hereditary imperial dynasties. It was believed that a dynasty's authority came from divine favoritism, known as the Mandate of Heaven. Dynasties governed China using large bureaucracies of government officials, although different dynasties chose these officials using different methods. During the Yuan dynasty China was under foreign rule and was part of the larger Mongol Empire.

Economic Structures Confucius taught that merchants were the lowest class in society because they produced no actual goods. As a result, business and trade were looked down upon in imperial China and were not encouraged.

Social Structures During the Tang dynasty China was governed by the aristocracy. During the Song and Ming dynasties social mobility increased. The civil service exam allowed poor but ambitious men the chance to rise into the class of government officials. Under the Yuan dynasty, Mongol rulers divided society into four distinct classes, with Mongols at the top and native Chinese at the bottom.

Ghana: A West African Trading Empire

To what extent did trans-Saharan trade lead to Ghana's wealth and success?

8.1 Introduction

The early West African societies of Ghana, Mali, and Songhai all created empires that gained much of their wealth from trade. In this lesson, you will learn more about the role of trade as you explore Ghana, the first of West Africa's empires.

The kingdom of Ghana lasted from sometime before 500 C.E. until its final collapse in the 1200s. It arose in the semidesert Sahel and eventually spread over the valley between the Senegal and Niger rivers. To the south was forest. To the north lay the Sahara. Today, this region is part of modern nations Mali and Mauritania (maw-reh-TAIN-ee-uh). The modern country of Ghana takes its name from the old kingdom, but it is located far to the south.

The earliest writings about the kingdom of Ghana come from Arab scholars. These scholars recorded information they had gathered from travelers to Ghana. By the time they began writing about Ghana in the 9th century, it was already a flourishing empire.

Historians do not know for certain how Ghana developed into an empire. Possibly, a group of warriors used iron weapons to defeat their neighbors. In fact, the word *ghana* means "war chief." We do know that control of trade, particularly the gold trade, made the king of Ghana and his people very wealthy. West Africans still sing songs about the majesty of ancient Ghana.

In this lesson, you will first learn about Ghana's government and military. Then you will learn how Ghana's people acquired wealth by participating in trans-Saharan trade. You will examine how trade led to Ghana's wealth and success. Finally, you will find out how Ghana declined and a new empire, Mali, arose in West Africa.

Themes

Cultural Interaction Trade brought the cultures of West Africa and North Africa into contact, often with the mediation of Muslim merchants.

Political Structures Ghana was ruled by a powerful king who served as a military, judicial, and religious leader.

Economic Structures The power and wealth of Ghana was based on taxation of the trans-Saharan trade of gold and salt.

Human-Environment Interaction Salt and gold were natural resources that generated enormous trade and wealth in Ghana. The kingdom of Ghana declined when other natural resources grew scarce.

◀ Camel caravans carried goods across the Sahara to and from medieval Ghana.

Ghana a medieval civilization and empire in West Africa

matrilineal a family line traced through the mother

8.2 Ghana's Government and Military

Arab scholars described **Ghana** as a fabled "land of gold." Their accounts paint a picture of a rich kingdom with a strong government and a large and powerful army.

The King and His Government   Ghana was ruled by a powerful king. The king was the head of the army and had the final say in matters of justice. He also led the people in religious worship.

Ghana's king acquired great wealth through control of the gold trade. Gold was especially plentiful in areas to the south of Ghana. As you will see, Ghana's government collected taxes on the gold that passed through the kingdom.

To preserve his wealth, the king tightly controlled the supply of gold. All the gold nuggets, or chunks, found in the kingdom had to be given to the king. Ordinary people could have only gold dust. One of the king's gold nuggets is said to have weighed almost forty pounds. According to legend, another was large enough to be used as a hitching post for his horse.

Each day, the king held court with his people. The king arrived at court to the beating of royal drums. He was splendidly dressed in colorful robes, gold jewelry, and a cap decorated with gold. His people showed their respect for him by kneeling and throwing dust on their heads as he approached.

Once at court, the king conducted the business of his empire and heard the people's concerns. One Arab historian described the scene at the court like this:

> Behind the king stand ten pages [young servants] holding shields and swords decorated with gold and on his right are the sons of the vassal kings of his empire wearing splendid garments and their hair plaited [braided] with gold. The governor of the city sits on the ground before the king and around are ministers seated likewise. At the door . . . are dogs of excellent pedigree [ancestry] who hardly ever leave the place where the king is, guarding him. Round their necks, they wear collars of gold and silver.

A large group of officials was paid from the kingdom's wealth to help the king govern. These officials were probably in charge of different parts of Ghana's society, such as the armed forces, industry, tax collection, and foreigners. The king appointed governors to rule some parts of his empire, such as the capital city and some conquered areas.

When the king died, his son did not inherit the throne. The royal inheritance was **matrilineal,** which means that it was traced through women's bloodlines rather than men's. Therefore, in Ghana, the son of the king's sister was the heir to the throne.

Ghana's kings wore caps like this one, decorated with gold.

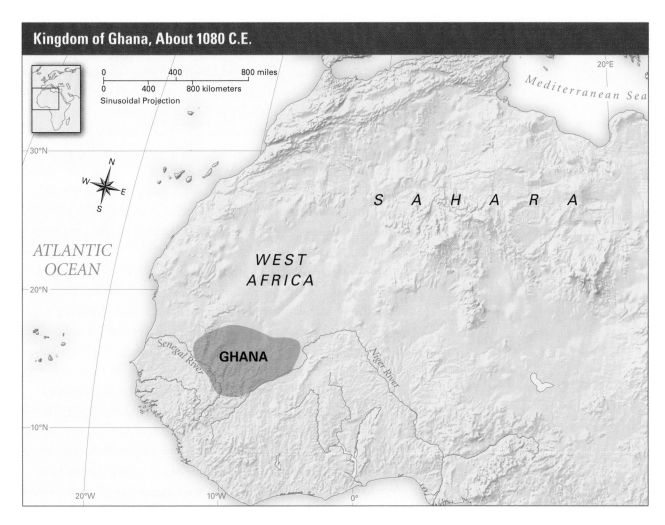

0   400   800 miles
0   400   800 kilometers
Sinusoidal Projection

Mediterranean Sea

20°E

30°N

N
W   E
S

ATLANTIC
OCEAN

SAHARA

WEST
AFRICA

20°N

Senegal River

GHANA

Niger River

10°N

20°W   10°W   0°

Ghana's Military   Ghana's military included a regular army, reserve forces, and elite soldiers. The regular army was made up of several thousand career soldiers. They kept the borders secure, put down minor revolts, and maintained peace and order. These soldiers wore knee-length cotton pants, sleeveless tunics (long shirts), sandals, and headdresses adorned with feathers. The color of a soldier's tunic and the number of feathers in his headdress indicated his rank. The soldiers used weapons such as spears, daggers, swords, battle clubs, and bows and arrows. They were well paid and highly respected.

During wartime, the king called up additional reserve forces and the troops of other governors under his rule. Every man in the empire was required to complete military training so that he would be ready to serve when called. Stories tell of a king who could call up an army of 200,000 warriors. This number no doubt grew as the story was passed on, but the king certainly could summon a sizable army.

Special groups of soldiers were selected for their courage, honesty, and intelligence. These soldiers served the king as bodyguards, escorts, and military advisors.

Its location at the crossroads of major trade routes south of the Sahara and along the rivers brought medieval Ghana great wealth and power.

8.3 Trade: The Source of Ghana's Wealth

Ghana was located between two areas that wanted to trade—North Africa and West Africa. Traders from North Africa crossed the Sahara with salt, copper, and cowrie shells—a type of seashell that was used as money. The merchants traded these and other goods for kola nuts, hides, leather goods, ivory, slaves, and gold from the southern forests of West Africa. Then they returned to North Africa, bringing the goods from the south to markets at home.

Ghana's location allowed it to control this **trans-Saharan trade**. Traders going to and from the south had to pass through Ghana. Each time, they paid heavy taxes on their goods. These taxes helped to make Ghana rich.

The History of Trans-Saharan Trade   Trans-Saharan trade has a long history. Archeologists have found evidence that North Africans brought back gold from the southern forests of West Africa as long ago as 400 to 500 B.C.E. Travel across the Sahara, however, was especially challenging for these early peoples.

Centuries later, two factors led to the growth of trans-Saharan trade. The first was the introduction of the camel to the Sahara. The second was the spread of Islam.

Camels were first brought to the Sahara by Arab traders around 300 C.E. These animals are well suited for desert travel. A camel can drink up to twenty-five gallons of water at a time. As a result, it can travel several days in the desert without stopping. Also, camels have double rows of eyelashes and hairy ear openings that help keep out blowing sand.

The introduction of camels allowed traders to establish caravan routes across the Sahara. By the 4th century C.E., large amounts of gold were being made into Roman coins in North Africa. It is likely that that gold came from West Africa.

Trade expanded even more because of the spread of Islam. In the 7th century, Muslims invaded Ghana's empire. Besides wanting to convert West Africans to Islam, Muslims hoped to control trade in West Africa. Ghana turned back the invaders, but many Muslims settled in West African towns and became merchants.

Control of the trans-Saharan trade made Ghana wealthy and powerful. By the year 1000 C.E., Ghana's empire dominated the trade routes between North and West Africa.

The Journey South   The traders who traveled to West Africa faced a long, difficult journey. The trans-Saharan caravan routes began in North Africa along the northwestern border of the Sahara. From there they stretched across the desert, passed through Ghana, and continued south to the Gulf of Guinea and east to present-day Chad.

trans-Saharan trade trade between peoples north and south of the Sahara

Camels were especially suited for transporting goods across the Sahara.

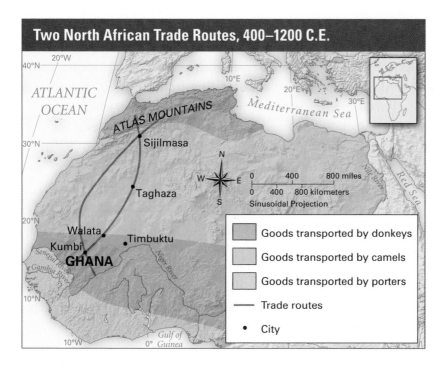

Two North African Trade Routes, 400–1200 C.E.

ATLANTIC OCEAN

ATLAS MOUNTAINS

Mediterranean Sea

Nile River

Red Sea

Sijilmasa

Taghaza

Walata

Kumbi

Timbuktu

GHANA

Senegal River

Gambia River

Niger River

Gulf of Guinea

0   400   800 miles

0   400   800 kilometers

Sinusoidal Projection

Goods transported by donkeys

Goods transported by camels

Goods transported by porters

Trade routes

City

Differences in geography led to different methods of transport along the trade routes between North and West Africa.

In 1352, a Muslim historian and traveler named Ibn Battuta (ib-ehn bat-TOO-tah) crossed the Sahara with a trade caravan. Battuta's account of his trip shows what the traders' journeys were like.

Battuta's caravan began at the oasis city of Sijilmasa (see-jeel-MAH-sah), on the northern edge of the Sahara, in the foothills of the Atlas Mountains. Donkeys carried goods from Europe, Arabia, and Egypt to Sijilmasa from the Mediterranean coast. Then camel caravans took the goods south.

Battuta and his caravan stayed in Sijilmasa for a few months, waiting for the rainy season to end. When the watering places were full and there was grass for the animals to eat, the traders set out. The caravan traveled from oasis to oasis. Each day, the traders walked until the afternoon, when the sun was high in the sky. Then they rested until the sun went down.

Walking across the Sahara was challenging and dangerous. Caravans sometimes lost their way, and some traders died in the desert. During one stretch of Battuta's trip, the travelers could not find water, so they slaughtered some of their camels and drank the water stored in the animals' stomachs.

On its way through the desert, the caravan stopped at Taghaza, a village where salt mines were located. There, it took on a load of salt. When the traders reached the town of Walata, at the edge of the desert, they transferred their salt and other goods from the camels to donkeys and to porters, people who carry goods for a living. Then they continued south, passing through Ghana on their way to markets on the Gulf of Guinea, near the southern forests. The entire journey took about two months.

8.4 The Gold-Salt Trade

Many items were traded between North Africa and West Africa, but the two goods that were most in demand were gold and salt. The North Africans wanted gold, which came from the forest region south of Ghana. The people in the forests wanted salt, which came from the Sahara. Ghana made most of its money from the taxes it charged on the gold-salt trade that passed through its lands.

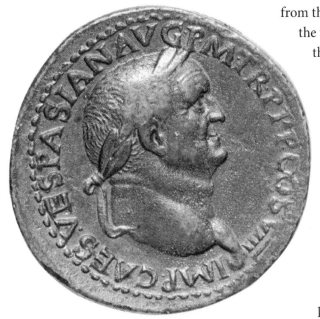

The Romans and people in Muslim lands used West African gold to make their coins.

Wangara: The Secret Source of Gold

Gold has long been a source of wealth in much of the world. In the time of Ghana's empire, people in Muslim lands and in Italy made coins from gold. Muslims also needed gold to purchase silk and porcelain from China, which would accept only gold in exchange.

In an area known as Wangara, gold was plentiful. Wangara was located near the forests south of Ghana, but no one except the people of Wangara knew its exact location. The Wangarans kept the locations of their gold mines secret. According to ancient stories, merchants occasionally captured a gold miner and tried to force him to reveal the location of Wangara. The miners would give up their lives rather than reveal the secret.

In one story, after the capture of a miner, the Wangarans stopped trading for three years. They wanted to make sure no one had discovered Wangara's location. To this day, no one knows for certain exactly where Wangara's mines were located.

Taghaza: A Village Built with Salt
To West Africans, salt was more precious than gold. Their culture had little use for gold, except as an item for trade. But they craved salt, and for good reason. Salt is an important part of a person's diet. When people and animals perspire, or sweat, they lose salt in their perspiration. People who live in hot climates, like West Africa, perspire a lot and must replace the salt they lose. West Africans also needed salt to keep their food from spoiling and to give to their cattle. In addition, people liked the taste.

West Africans had no local source of salt. They had to obtain it from Taghaza and other places in the Sahara.

Salt was produced in two ways in the Sahara. One method was through evaporation. Water was poured into holes in the salty earth. The water slowly drew out the salt and then evaporated in the sun. The salt that remained was scooped out and packed into blocks. The second way to get salt was through mining. At Taghaza, salt deposits were found about three feet below the surface of the earth. Miners, enslaved by Arab merchants, reached the salt by digging trenches and tunnels. Then they cut it out in large blocks.

Taghaza would not have existed without salt. It was a dismal place, without crops or vegetation. People lived there for one purpose only: to mine and sell salt. Even the houses and mosque were built of salt blocks. Trade caravans passed through Taghaza on their way through the Sahara. There, they picked up salt to sell in Ghana and the southern forests. Because no food was produced in Taghaza, the miners had to rely on caravans to bring food, such as camel meat, dates, and a type of grain, called millet. If the caravans didn't come, the miners starved.

In some parts of Africa, salt is made by the evaporation of water in areas called salt flats, such as this one. The salt is then dug out in large blocks.

Ghana's System of Taxes

Traders paid taxes to Ghana on all the goods they carried through the empire. Goods were taxed both when traders entered Ghana and when they left. Ghana charged one-sixth of an ounce of gold for each load of salt that came into the kingdom from the north. It then charged one-third of an ounce of gold for each load the traders took out of the kingdom to the south. The traders also paid taxes for carrying other types of goods. For every load of copper, they were charged five-eighths of an ounce of gold. They paid a little more than one ounce of gold per load of general merchandise.

The taxes enriched Ghana's treasury. They also helped pay for armies that protected the kingdom and allowed the king to conquer other territories. Traders benefited as well, because Ghana secured the trade routes against bandits who might rob the caravans.

8.5 The Exchange of Goods

When trade caravans entered Ghana, they brought their goods to the great marketplace in the capital city of Kumbi. From there, they headed to the southern forests to trade with the Wangarans.

Kumbi had the busiest market in West Africa. Many local crafts-people sold their goods there. Ironsmiths sold weapons and tools. Goldsmiths and coppersmiths sold jewelry. Weavers sold cloth, and leatherworkers sold leather goods. There were blue blouses from Spain and robes from Morocco, in North Africa. People could also buy cattle, sheep, honey, wheat, raisins, dried fruit, ivory, pearls, and slaves. All goods, including slaves, were paid for with gold dust.

Even today, salt is an important trade item in West Africa.

Kumbi had one of the largest slave markets in West Africa. The slaves were captured by raiders along the southern border of Ghana. Many were bought at Kumbi by Arab merchants, who took them across the Sahara and sold them to North Africans and Europeans.

Trade with the Wangarans took place along a river in the southern forests. Traders carried out their business using a system of silent barter, or trade. The caravans arrived bringing wool, silk, cotton, dates, figs, grains, leather, and salt. They spread out their goods along the river. The traders beat on a drum to announce that they were making an offer to trade. Then they walked several miles away from the site.

When the Wangarans heard the drum, they traveled to the site by boat. They put some gold dust next to the goods, beat a drum, and left. Later, the traders returned. If the amount of gold dust was acceptable, they took it and left. If not, they went away again and waited for the Wangarans to return and leave more gold dust. The groups bargained back and forth in this way without ever meeting in person.

This system of silent barter had two advantages. First, it allowed people who spoke different languages to trade. Second, it allowed the Wangarans to protect the secret location of their gold mines.

8.6 The Decline of Ghana and the Rise of Mali

Ghana's empire reached its height around the year 1000 C.E. War and the loss of natural resources led to the West African empire's downfall, and the rise of a new power.

In the second half of the 11th century, Muslim warriors known as Almoravids began attacking Ghana's empire. In 1076, they captured the capital city of Kumbi. Ghana's king regained power in 1087, but the old empire had broken apart.

The loss of natural resources further weakened Ghana. The growing population had put great stress on scarce resources, such as trees and water. Trees were cut down to provide charcoal for iron-smelting furnaces. Water became so scarce that farmers could no longer grow crops and keep flocks. People were forced to leave in search of better conditions. The empire came to an end in 1203, when a rival kingdom took over Kumbi.

The end of Ghana's empire opened the way to the rise of a new power, Mali. Around 1240, a group of West Africans called the Mande conquered Kumbi. Their homeland of Mali was south of Kumbi, closer to the Niger River. The Mande built an empire that reached from the Atlantic Ocean to beyond the Niger River, and from the southern forest to the salt and copper mines of the Sahara.

Like Ghana, Mali gained much of its wealth from the control of trade, particularly in gold. Its leaders had accepted Islam, and under their rule, the Muslim faith went on to become even more influential in West Africa.

Natural resources, such as water and trees, are still scarce in areas like the Sahel.

Summary

Trade played a key role in the growth of kingdoms and empires in West Africa. The first of these was Ghana.

Cultural Interaction The spread of Islam resulted in increased trade as Muslim traders settled in North African towns. Trade between North Africa and West Africa brought increased cultural contact. In Wangara a system of silent barter was developed, which allowed people who spoke different languages to trade with each other.

Political Structures Ghana was ruled by a powerful king who served as the military and religious leader and had final say in judicial matters. Government officials in charge of different aspects of government helped to govern. Ghana used its great wealth to build up its army, conquer other peoples, and build an empire.

Economic Structures Ghana became wealthy and powerful by taxing the trade that came through its kingdom. Gold from Wangara and salt from the Sahara region were especially important commodities. Ghana's wealth paid for armies who secured trade routes, which made travel and trade safer and easier for merchants.

Human-Environment Interactions Ghana's wealth was based on exploitation of natural resources. Gold was mined in West Africa and salt was produced in the Sahara, and these commodities were transported across Ghana. The introduction of camels as pack animals in this period allowed traders to cross the dry Sahara more easily than they had before. Ghana's decline was brought about by the depletion of natural resources in their environment. Trees and water became scarce as the population grew, and people were forced to migrate to other areas.

Achievements of the Mayas, Aztecs, and Incas

*What were the significant achievements
of the Mayas, Aztecs, and Incas?*

9.1 Introduction

There were three great peoples of the early Americas: the Mayas, the Aztecs, and the Incas. In this lesson, you will study the cultures of these peoples and explore their unique achievements.

The history of these civilizations stretches from very ancient times to just a few centuries ago. Mayan civilization dates back to 2000 B.C.E. It reached its height in what is called the Classic period, from about 300 to 900 C.E. The Aztecs and the Incas built their empires in the two centuries before the Spanish arrived in the 1500s.

Scholars have learned about these cultures in various ways. They have studied artifacts found at the sites of old settlements. They have read accounts left by Spanish soldiers and priests. And they have observed traditions that can still be found among the descendants of the Mayas, Aztecs, and Incas.

The more we learn about these cultures, the more we can appreciate what was special about each of them. The Mayas, for example, made striking advances in writing, astronomy, and architecture. Both the Mayas and the Aztecs created highly accurate calendars. The Aztecs adapted earlier pyramid designs to build massive stone temples. The Incas showed great skill in engineering and in managing their huge empire.

In this lesson, you will study these and other achievements of the Mayas, the Aztecs, and the Incas. You will focus on three main areas of culture: science and technology, arts and architecture, and language and writing.

Themes

Cultural Interaction The Mayas, Aztecs, and Incas made impressive cultural achievements in the areas of science and technology, arts and architecture, and language and writing.

Human-Environment Interaction The peoples of Mesoamerica adapted their environment to suit their needs by building artificial islands, causeways, terraces and roads.

This Mayan pyramid, known as the Magician Pyramid, was located in the ancient city of Uxmal, in present day Mexico.

This Mayan arch served as the entrance to a sanctuary dedicated to the goddess Ixchel. Mayan builders developed a construction method where an arch was shaped like an inverted staircase.

9.2 Achievements of the Mayas

Many of the greatest achievements of the Mayas date from the Classic period (about 300 to 900 C.E.). Hundreds of years later, their ideas and practices continued to influence other Mesoamerican groups, including the Aztecs.

Science and Technology   The Mayas made important breakthroughs in astronomy and mathematics. Throughout Mayan lands, priests studied the sky from observatories. They were able to track the movements of stars and planets with great accuracy. The Mayas used their observations to calculate the **solar year**. The Mayan figure for their year of 365.2420 days is amazingly precise.

solar year the time it takes Earth to travel once around the sun

These calculations allowed the Mayas to create their solar calendar of 365 days. They also had a sacred 260-day calendar. Every 52 years, the first date in both calendars fell on the same day. This gave the Mayas a longer unit of time that they called a Calendar Round. For the ancient Mayas, this 52-year period was something like what a century is to us.

Mayan astronomy and calendar-making depended on a deep understanding of mathematics. In some ways, the Mayan number system was like ours. The Mayas used place values for numbers, just as we do. However, instead of being based on the number 10, their system was based on 20. So instead of place values for 1s, 10s, and 100s, the Mayas had place values for 1s, 20s, 400s (20 times 20), and so on.

The Mayas also recognized the need for zero—a discovery made by few other early civilizations. In the Mayan system for writing numbers, a dot stood for one, a bar for five, and a shell symbol for zero. To add and subtract, people lined up two numbers and then combined or took away dots and bars.

Arts and Architecture The Mayas were equally gifted in the arts. They painted, using colors mixed from minerals and plants. We can see the artistry of Mayan painters in the Bonampak murals, which were found in Chiapas, Mexico. The murals show nobles and priests, as well as battle scenes, ceremonies, and sacrifice rituals.

The Mayas also constructed upright stone slabs called **steles** (STEE-leez), which they often placed in front of temples. Most steles stood between 5 and 12 feet tall, although some rose as high as 30 feet. Steles usually had three-dimensional carvings of gods and rulers. Sometimes, the Mayas inscribed them with dates and hieroglyphics in honor of significant events.

Another important art was weaving. We know from steles and paintings that the Mayas wove colorful fabric in complex patterns. Women made embroidered tunics called *huipiles* and fashioned lengths of cloth for trade. Mayan women still use similar techniques today. They still make their huipiles in traditional designs. People from different towns can be distinguished by the colors and patterns of their garments.

In architecture, the Mayas built temple-pyramids from hand-cut limestone bricks. An unusual feature of Mayan buildings was a type of arch called a corbel vault. Builders stacked stones so that they gradually angled in toward each other to form a triangular archway. At the top of the arch, where the stones almost touched, one stone joined the two sides. The archway always had nine stone layers, representing the nine layers of the underworld (the place where souls were thought to go after death).

Language and Writing The Mayas developed the most complex system of writing in the ancient Americas. They used hieroglyphics, or picture symbols, to represent sounds, words, and ideas. Hieroglyphic inscriptions have been found on stoneware and other artifacts dating from possibly as early as 300 B.C.E.

Over time, the Mayas created hundreds of **glyphs**. Eventually, scribes could write down anything in the spoken language. They often wrote about rulers, history, myths and gods, and astronomy.

Not all Mayan groups shared the same language. Instead, they spoke related **dialects**. Today, about four million Mesoamericans still speak one of thirty or so Mayan dialects.

Weaving is a traditional Mayan art passed down through generations of women.

stele a vertical stone slab or pillar with carvings or inscriptions

glyph a symbol for a word, idea, or sound in a hieroglyphic system of writing

dialect a regional variety of a language

9.3 Achievements of the Aztecs

The Aztecs adapted many ideas from earlier groups, including their calendars and temple-pyramids. But the Aztecs improved on these ideas and made them their own.

Science and Technology   One of the Aztecs' most remarkable technological achievements was the construction of their island city, Tenochtitlán. The Aztecs enlarged the area of the city by creating artificial islands called *chinampas*. Today, flower farmers in Xochimilco, near Mexico City, still use chinampas. Tourists enjoy taking boat trips to see these "floating gardens."

Just as impressive as the chinampas were the three causeways that connected Tenochtitlán to the mainland. The causeways were often crowded with people traveling in and out of the capital. During the rainy season, when the waters of the lake rose, the causeways also served as dikes.

To manage time, the Aztecs adapted the Mayan solar and sacred calendars. The 365-day solar calendar was especially useful for farming, since it tracked the seasons. Priests used the sacred 260-day calendar to predict events and to determine "lucky" days for such things as planting crops and going to war.

One of the most famous Aztec artifacts is a calendar called the Sun Stone. Dedicated to the god of the sun, this beautifully carved stone is nearly twelve feet wide and weighs almost twenty-five tons. The center shows the face of the sun god. Today, the Sun Stone is a well-known symbol of Mexico.

Adapted from the Mayan calendar, the Sun Stone calendar shows the face of the Aztec sun god. It includes a 365-day agricultural calendar and a 260-day sacred calendar.

Arts and Architecture The Aztecs practiced a number of arts, including poetry, music, dance, and sculpture. Poets wrote verses to sing the praises of the gods, to tell stories, and to celebrate the natural world. Poetry was highly valued. Aztec poets sung their poems or recited them to music. Sometimes, actors performed them, creating a dramatic show with dialogue and costumes.

Music and dance were important features of Aztec ceremonies and holidays. People dressed up for these special occasions. Women wore beautiful blouses over their skirts. Men painted their faces, greased their hair, and wore feathered headdresses. The dancers formed large circles and moved to the beat of drums and the sound of rattle bells. The dances had religious meaning, and the dancers had to perform every step correctly. Sometimes, thousands of people danced at one time. Even the emperor occasionally joined in.

The Aztecs were also gifted painters and sculptors. Painters used brilliant colors to create scenes showing gods and religious ceremonies. Sculptors fashioned stone statues and relief sculptures on temple walls. They also carved small, lifelike figures of people and animals from rock and semiprecious stones, such as jade. In technical craft and beauty, their work surpassed that of earlier Mesoamerican cultures.

In architecture, the Aztecs are best remembered today for their massive stone temples. The Aztecs were unique in building double stairways, like those of the Great Temple in Tenochtitlán. The staircases led to two temples, one for the sun god and one for the god of rain. Smaller pyramids nearby had their own temples, where sacrificial fires burned before huge statues of the gods.

Traditional Aztec dance and ceremonies are still performed in Mexico today.

Language and Writing Spoken language was raised to an art in Aztec society. Almost any occasion called for dramatic and often flowery speeches. The rich vocabulary of the Aztec language, Nahuatl, allowed speakers to create new words and describe abstract concepts.

The Aztec system of writing used both glyphs and **pictographs**. A pictograph is a drawing that depicts a word, phrase, or name, rather than symbolizes it. For example, the Aztec pictograph for war was a symbol of a shield and a club. The Aztecs did not have enough pictographs and glyphs to express everything that could be spoken in their language. Instead, scribes used writing to list data or to outline events. Priests used these writings to spark their memories when relating stories from the past.

> **pictograph** a drawing that stands for a word, phrase, or name

9.4 Achievements of the Incas

Like the Aztecs, the Incas often borrowed and improved upon ideas from other cultures. But the Incas faced a unique challenge in managing the largest empire in the Americas. Maintaining tight control over such a huge area was one of their most impressive accomplishments.

Terraces anchored with stones can still be seen in the ruins of the Incan city of Machu Picchu.

suspension bridge a bridge held up by cables anchored at each end

trephination a type of surgery in which a hole is made in the skull

Science and Technology The Incas' greatest technological skill was engineering. The best example is their amazing system of roads.

The Incas built roads across the length and width of their empire. To create routes through steep mountain ranges, they carved staircases and gouged tunnels out of rock. They also built **suspension bridges** over rivers. Thick rope cables were anchored at stone towers on either side of the river. Two cables served as rails, while three others held a walkway.

In agriculture, the Incas showed their technological skill by vastly enlarging the system of terraces already in use by earlier Andean farmers. The Incas anchored their step-like terraces with stones and improved the drainage systems in the fields. On some terraces, they planted different crops at elevations where the plants would grow best.

To irrigate the crops, the Incas built canals that brought water to the top of a hillside of terraces. From there, the water ran down, level by level. People in South America still grow crops on Incan terraces.

The Incas also made remarkable advances in medicine. Incan priests, who were in charge of healing, practiced a type of surgery called **trephination**. Usually, the patient was an injured warrior. Priests cut into the patient's skull to remove bone fragments that were pressing against the brain. As drastic as this sounds, many people survived the operation and recovered full health.

Arts and Architecture Making textiles for clothing was one of the most important Incan arts. The quality and design of a person's clothes were a sign of status. The delicate cloth worn by Incan nobles often featured bright colors and bold geometric patterns. Incan women also made feather tunics, or long shirts, weaving feathers from jungle birds right into the cloth.

Fashioning objects out of gold was another important art. The Incas prized gold, which they called the "sweat of the sun." Gold covered almost every inch inside the Temple of the Sun in the Incan capital city of Cuzco. Incan goldsmiths also fashioned masks, sculptures, knives, and jewelry.

Music was a major part of Incan life. The Incas played flutes, seashell horns, rattles, drums, and panpipes. Scholars believe that the modern music of the Andes region preserves elements of Incan music.

In architecture, the Incas are known for their huge, durable stone buildings. The massive stones of Incan structures fit together so tightly that a knife blade could not be slipped between them. Incan buildings were sturdy, too—many remain standing today.

Peruvian musicians today use instruments similar to some of those used by the Incas, such as these flutes, panpipes, and drums.

Language and Writing   The Incas made their language, Quechua (KECH-wah), the official language of the empire. As a result, Quechua spread far and wide. About ten million people in South America still speak it.

The Incas did not have a written language. Instead, they developed an ingenious substitute: the knotted sets of strings called *quipus*. The Incas used quipus as memory aids when sending messages and recording information.

Summary

In this chapter, you explored the cultural achievements of the Mayas, Aztecs, and Incas. All three Mesoamerican peoples accomplished advances in science and technology, arts and architecture, and language and writing.

Cultural Interaction   The cultural achievements of the Mayan Classical period had a lasting impact on later Mesoamerican cultures. The Mayas were able to develop a very accurate solar calendar with their knowledge of astronomy and math. The Aztecs later adopted a calendar based on the Mayan system and created the famous Sun Stone calendar. The Mayas and Aztecs both painted elaborate, colorful murals. The Aztecs also followed the Mayan example in constructing large stone temple-pyramids. The Incas constructed huge stone buildings as well. The Mayas and Incas were both known for weaving elaborate, colorful fabrics.

Human-Environment Interaction   The peoples of Mesoamerica engineered their environment to best suit their needs. In Tenochtitlán the Aztecs constructed artificial islands to enlarge the area of their city. They also constructed causeways connecting the island city of Tenochtitlán to the mainland that served as bridges and dikes. The Incas adapted to their mountainous terrain by creating terraced farms. They also created an elaborate system of roads throughout their large empire.

ruled with absolute power. In the late 1500s, a British diplomat described the cruel force exercised by Czar Ivan IV, commonly known as Ivan the Terrible:

> *To show his sovereignty over the lives of his subjects, the late emperor Ivan Vasilevich, in his walk or progresses, if he misliked the face or person of any man whom he met by the way, or that looked upon him, would command his head to be struck off. Which was presently done, and the head cast before him.*
>
> —Ambassador Giles Fletcher,
> quoted in *The European Emergence*

Cannon fire helped the Ottoman Turks conquer Constantinople in 1453. The fall of the city marked the end of the Byzantine Empire, the eastern half of the Roman Empire that had survived for a thousand years after the fall of Rome.

In Persia, the Safavid Empire arose during this era. Between 1501 and 1722, the rulers of the Safavid Empire used gunpowder weaponry to control the lands between the Ottoman Empire to the west and India to the east. Unlike the Ottomans, who were Sunni Muslims, the Safavids were followers of Shi'a Islam. Under their greatest ruler, Shah Abbas, they built a strong, centralized state. They promoted the arts and built a splendid capital at Isfahan.

During the same period, Muslim invaders from Central Asia took power in India and established the Mughal Empire, which lasted from 1526 to 1707. The Mughals defeated much larger Indian armies by using firearms and cannons. Eventually they gained control over most of the Indian subcontinent. They established an effective government and grew rich from the trade in cotton cloth and spices. Under their rule, the economy and culture of India flourished.

East Asian states also increased their power during this era. In China, the Ming dynasty ruled until 1644, when it fell to Manchu invaders from the north. The Manchus formed the Qing dynasty and expanded the Chinese empire. They maintained China's economic prosperity, while restricting European access to Chinese trade. Between 1400 and 1800, the Chinese population more than quadrupled, to around 330 million, or one third of the world's population. During this period, the Chinese traded with the Americas. New foods brought to China provided more calories than foods from Europe, causing a population boom.

In the 1500s, Japan also built a centralized state under strong military rulers, called shoguns. The shoguns used guns to defeat local lords and unify the country. They founded the Tokugawa Shogunate, which brought more than two centuries of peace and stability to Japan. The Tokugawa rulers maintained tight control and isolated Japan from most foreign contact.

Commercial Revolution the rapid expansion of trade and commerce that transformed Europe, starting in the 16th century

capitalism an economic system in which all resources are privately owned and markets determine how those resources are distributed

secular non-religious, related to concerns of the world

Emerging European Dominance   Despite their success, most of the gunpowder empires had declined by the late 1700s. The Safavid Empire had collapsed, and the Ottoman and Mughal empires were failing. Even Qing China was showing signs of weakness. Asia remained prosperous, with the largest economies and populations in the world. But Asia's power was beginning to fade.

In contrast, Europe was getting stronger. Several interrelated factors help account for Europe's rising power by the late 18th century. A major factor was the **Commercial Revolution**. This was the rapid expansion of business, fueled by overseas trade and colonization. European colonial powers, particularly Spain and Portugal, exploited the resources and markets of their overseas colonies. Other countries, such as Britain and Holland, devised new methods of business and banking. These changes gave rise to **capitalism**, an economic system based on private enterprise. As commercial activity spread throughout Europe, living standards rose and wealth increased. This new wealth, in turn, enhanced the military and political power of European states.

Europe was in a good position to benefit from the Commercial Revolution. Its states and societies were younger than those of Asia, and its social, political, and economic structures were more flexible. As commerce increased, merchants and bankers took on more power in society and politics. The rise of capitalism began to affect work patterns, social classes, and many other aspects of European life.

Ideas and culture were changing too. During this era, new ways of looking at the world swept across Europe. These ideas ranged from new religious beliefs to the **secular** principles of science. All these factors—economic, political, social, and cultural—helped propel Europe's rise to power.

The Commercial Revolution helped European nations gain dominance on the world stage. European colonial powers exploited the resources and markets of their overseas colonies. Shown here are warehouses of European companies in Canton, China, in the early 1800s. Canton is now known as the city of Guangzhou (gwahng-joh).

10.4 Atlantic Empires

Europe's expansion across the Atlantic was a key element of the first global age. By founding American colonies, western European countries built empires and created new networks of exchange that had a deep impact on the rest of the world.

Colonization of the Americas   Spain and Portugal formed the first American colonies. Spanish colonization began in the Caribbean, or West Indies, in the late 1400s. From there, Spain went on to occupy large portions of North and South America. Portugal colonized Brazil in the early 1500s. A century later, the British, French, and Dutch all claimed colonies in the West Indies. They also colonized the east coast of North America, occupying lands that would later become the United States and Canada.

The colonization of Spanish America began with the Spanish conquest. Small armies of Spanish **conquistadors** defeated the Aztec and Inca empires and brought millions of Indians under their control. They destroyed great civilizations whose roots went back thousands of years. In their place, Spain established a colonial empire that stretched from the American Southwest to the southern tip of South America.

Spain tried to maintain tight control over its American empire. A system of royal officials managed the colonies under direct orders from the crown. Spain was far away, however, so local officials often governed as they saw fit. In 1552, one colonist in Guatemala wrote to the king, "Oh sacred Majesty, how just and good are the royal orders you send to this province, and how officials mold them here and do what they wish!"

The social structure of the Spanish colonies was based largely on race. White colonists—born either in Europe or the Americas—made up the top social class. They enjoyed the most power and privileges. Next came the **mestizos,** or mixed-race descendants of Europeans and Indians. At the bottom were native Indians and, later, black Africans.

The Catholic Church also played an important role in colonial society. The church and crown were closely linked, and most Spaniards were devout Catholics. The spread of Catholic beliefs was a prime motive of the Spanish conquest. One conquistador wrote that he had come "to serve God and his Majesty, to give light to those who were in darkness, and to grow rich, as all men desire to do."

Francisco Pizarro led his army through the Andes to conquer the Inca empire in Peru in 1530. Pizarro and his men were among the Spanish conquistadors who helped Spain build a colonial empire from the American southwest to the tip of South America.

conquistadors Spanish conquerors of the Americas

mestizos persons of mixed European and Native American ancestry

Economies of Silver   Silver mining became the main economic activity in the Spanish colonies. The Spanish forced Indians to labor in the mines. Thousands of tons of silver were shipped from the Americas. The richest deposits were at Potosí, in modern-day Bolivia. By 1600, Potosí was producing half the world's silver and had become one of the world's largest cities.

Silver from the Americas had an enormous impact on the world economy. Minted into coins, it dramatically increased Europe's money supply. Suddenly there was much more money available for trade and investment. Much of this silver ended up in China, where it was exchanged for Chinese silks and other valuable goods. Wealth from silver financed European monarchies and increased personal fortunes. It stimulated the rise of capitalism. But this flood of money also caused **inflation,** or rising prices. Countries that invested wisely, such as Britain and Holland, prospered despite inflation. But other countries, including Spain, found that sudden wealth could do more harm than good. Rather than investing in agriculture and industry, they spent their money and warfare, leaving them deeper in debt.

Agriculture was less important than mining in the colonies, at least until the development of the plantation system. The Spanish crown granted large estates to some colonists, stripping the land from Indian communities. These landed estates, called *haciendas,* supplied food to growing colonial cities and reinforced the power of wealthy families. But they were not a major economic enterprise.

Plantations were another story, however. These large estates grew crops for export, including sugar, cacao, tobacco, indigo, and cotton. Sugar was the first plantation crop. Columbus brought sugarcane to the West Indies, but it was in Brazil that sugar production really took off. By the early 1600s, Brazil was the world's leading sugar producer. French and British colonies in the West Indies later caught up and surpassed Brazil. During the 18th century, all these colonial producers made huge fortunes supplying sugar to the world market.

> **inflation** rising prices, usually caused by an increase in the money supply

An engraving made in 1643 shows Potosí, in present-day Bolivia, and the hill famous for its deposits of silver.

A Continental Exchange   Sugarcane was just one of a host of plants and animals brought to the Americas by European colonizers. In turn, Europeans took many American foods back to the Old World. The exchange between the hemispheres is known as the **Columbian Exchange**. It had a major impact on the world's cultures and environment. Without the Columbian Exchange, the Americas would not have had grains like wheat, rice, and oats. It would not have had onions, bananas, grapes, coffee, or citrus fruits. Nor would it have had livestock like horses, cattle, pigs, and sheep.

For its part, Europe would not have had foods such as potatoes, corn, beans, tomatoes, peppers, peanuts, squash, and chocolate. These crops had major nutritional benefits. Potatoes and corn, in particular, helped Europeans eat better and live longer. As a result, their populations increased.

Africa and Asia also benefited from the Columbian Exchange. Cassava, or manioc, a root crop native to Brazil, thrived in the poor soils of Africa and nourished millions of Africans. Other crops, including sweet potatoes and chili peppers, became staple foods across Africa and Asia. In fact, more than a third of the crops grown in China today originally came from the Americas.

The Columbian Exchange had negative effects, too. Some Old World plants grew out of control in the Americas. For example, clover, spinach, mint, and artichoke grew like weeds, choking out native species. Rats brought over on European ships became a plague across the Americas. Worst of all, many Old World diseases spread like wildfire, with deadly effects on Indian populations.

Death and Slavery   Native Americans had no immunity to diseases that people of Europe and Asia had been contracting for thousands of years. They had never been exposed to smallpox, measles, influenza, and other illnesses common to the Old World. When these diseases arrived in the Americas, their impact was devastating. Indians began dying in horrifying numbers. One eyewitness in Peru noted deaths "by scores and hundreds. . . . Villages were depopulated. Corpses

Columbian Exchange the transfer of plants, animals, and diseases between the eastern and western hemispheres

Potatoes were one of the foods that spread from the Americas, probably the Andes region, during the Columbian Exchange. The potato remains an important food crop today.

were scattered over the fields or piled up in the houses or huts." Smallpox was especially deadly, as one Spaniard observed in the late 1500s:

> *Large bumps spread on people, some were entirely covered.*
> *. . . [Victims] could no longer walk about, but lay in their*
> *dwellings and sleeping places, no longer able to move or stir. . . .*
> *[M]any just starved to death; starvation reigned, and no one*
> *took care of others any longer.*

—Bernardino de Sahagún,
General History of the Things of New Spain

Scholars estimate that during the 16th century Old World diseases killed at least 50 percent of the native population, amounting to tens of millions of people. Many died even before making contact with Europeans, as viruses spread from one community to another. It was, in the words of one scholar, "the greatest destruction of lives in human history." Historians call this tragedy the **Great Dying**.

The spread of deadly disease made the European conquest of the Americas much easier. It weakened Indian resistance and opened up the land for European settlement. It also deprived the colonizers of Indian workers and harmed colonial economies. To remedy this problem, the colonies began to import black slaves from Africa. Spain brought the first African slaves to the West Indies in 1502. But the Atlantic slave trade really began with Portuguese shipments of slaves to Brazil in the mid-1500s. A century later, African slaves were working on plantations across the Americas.

Slavery had existed since ancient times. The Sumerians, Greeks, Romans, and Arabs had all used slaves. Most slaves in the ancient world were debtors or prisoners of war, however. States and kingdoms in Africa had long traded slaves. When the Portuguese arrived on the African coast in the early 1400s, they began buying slaves from African traders, too. Eventually, the British, French, and Dutch got involved. By the 1800s, more than ten million African slaves had been shipped to the Americas. Around one in six died en route.

The slave trade had a major impact on Africa. It uprooted millions of Africans and tore African societies apart. It also strengthened African states and warlords involved in the slave trade and introduced European goods, including guns, into many parts of Africa.

The slave trade had an even greater impact on the Americas. It supported plantation economies rooted in violence and brutality, leaving a legacy of racism and inequality that persists to this day. It also brought millions of Africans to the hemisphere and spread African culture to the New World. In the process, it transformed the social and cultural landscape of the Americas.

Great Dying the devastation of American Indian populations by diseases brought over from Europe

An illustration from a 16th-century Spanish history text shows Aztecs infected by smallpox contracted from the Spanish. During the 16th century, diseases from Europe killed at least 50 percent of the native population of the Americas.

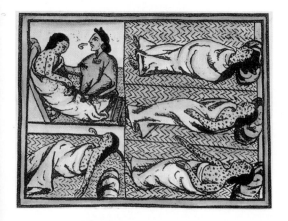

10.5 The Movement of Religion and Ideas

The world of ideas expanded along with the growing connections brought on by exploration, empire building, and trade. As regions became more connected, ideas and religious beliefs spread more rapidly from place to place. This movement of ideas and religion also helped transform the world.

Spreading Faith in the Americas

Several major religions extended their global reach during this period. Christianity was a prime example. The colonization of the Americas brought two large continents into the Christian world. In Spanish America, Catholic priests converted millions of American Indians to Christianity. In most cases, Indians blended Christian teachings with their own traditional beliefs. The British and French also brought Christianity to their North American colonies.

At the same time, Catholic missionaries traveled to Africa and Asia. The Portuguese established missions along the coasts of Africa and India, in the East Indies, and in East Asia. Spaniards brought the Catholic faith to the Philippines. They also expelled Jews and Muslims from Spain, making that country uniformly Catholic. Portugal also forced Jews and Muslims to convert or leave soon after Spain began this policy.

The Catholic Church built many missions in Spanish America to convert American Indians to Christianity. This is Mission Concepción in what is now San Antonio, Texas.

Islam expanded during this period, too. The Ottomans carried Islam into southeastern Europe, while the Mughals did the same across much of India. Muslim traders and missionaries took Islam to the East Indies and Southeast Asia. They also continued to spread their faith across Africa.

A new religion called Sikhism also developed in India. This religion combined elements of Islam and Hinduism. It spread rapidly in northern India, adding another element to India's rich spiritual tradition.

In Asia, Buddhism gained a wider following. Mongols in Central Asia began converting to Tibetan Buddhism in the late 1500s. Buddhism also gained strength in China, Japan, Korea, and Southeast Asia.

About 1450, Johannes Gutenberg revolutionized printing technology by inventing a printing press that used large quantities of moveable metal type and that could produce hundreds of pages of printed material in a single day. Here, a pressman makes a copy of Martin Luther's 1517 treatise against the Catholic Church.

humanism a Renaissance philosophy emphasizing the worth of the individual and balancing religious faith with secular learning

Reformation a reform movement of the 16th and 17th centuries that split the Catholic Church and gave birth to the Protestant religion

Counter-Reformation the movement to revive Catholicism in response to the Reformation

New Ideas in Europe   During this era, new ideas and ways of thinking also arose in Europe. Artists and thinkers of the Renaissance revived classical art and culture and helped shape new views of the world. They promoted **humanism,** a belief in the value of the individual. They combined religious faith with a secular interest in human society and the natural world.

By encouraging new ways of thinking, the Renaissance helped pave the way for the **Reformation**. This religious movement split the Catholic Church and gave birth to Protestant religion. It began in 1517 with the actions of Martin Luther, a German monk and teacher. Luther believed that the church had grown corrupt. He called for reform and a more personal approach to faith. His views, spread by the printing press, sparked cries for religious change across Europe. Religious wars broke out and ravaged much of the continent. But the Reformation resulted in the creation of new Protestant faiths.

The printing press was crucial to the Reformation, and to the spread of ideas in general. The Chinese were the first culture to invent paper and develop a way of printing from carved woodblocks. Moveable type made from clay was first developed in China in the 11th century. More significant to the advance of printing technology, Koreans developed moveable type made from metal in the 1200s. In 1377, the Koreans printed a text for Buddhists that today is the world's oldest known book printed with moveable metal type. German metalworker Johannes Gutenberg advanced printing technology in Europe another 200 years later. In about 1450, Gutenberg invented a printing press that used moveable metal type and that could turn out 300 pages in a single day. Gutenberg's press made printing faster and more efficient.

The Catholic Church responded to the Reformation with its own reform movement, the **Counter-Reformation**. This movement sought to revive and strengthen Catholicism. As part of this effort, the church expanded its missionary work and funded new art and architecture to glorify the Catholic faith.

Meanwhile, another major shift was taking place in the world of ideas. By the 1600s, scholars and thinkers inspired by the Renaissance and the discoveries of the global age had begun to study the natural world in new ways. They applied the power of reason to the observation of nature. This new approach to learning is known as the **Scientific Revolution**. Early scientists made key advances in astronomy, physics, biology, medicine, and many other fields. The methods and discoveries of science would have a profound impact on the world.

In the 1700s, European thinkers also turned their attention to the workings of society and government. They applied scientific principles to the study of human affairs, hoping to bring about a new age of reason. This school of thought was known as the **Enlightenment**.

Some European monarchs were drawn to the Enlightenment and tried to govern according to its principles. They wanted to modernize their societies and promote economic progress. For the most part, however, the Enlightenment undermined the rule of kings. It promoted the idea of democratic rights and freedoms. In the end, these ideas would give rise to reform movements and revolutions around the world.

Scientific Revolution a shift in thinking about the study of nature that began in the mid-1500s and moved beyond religious teachings

Enlightenment an 18th-century movement that sought to apply scientific methods to the study of society and its problems

Summary

In this lesson, you learned about the first global era, from 1400 to 1800. During this period, the world expanded and changed in many ways.

Cultural Interaction Voyages of exploration brought the world closer together and promoted the spread of ideas and beliefs. Christianity and Islam extended their reach, while new currents of thought in Europe began to alter views of nature and society. New technologies arose, advancing travel, communication, and warfare.

Political Structures European monarchs built strong states and ruled with absolute power. Gunpowder empires in Asia also expanded. Through overseas conquests, European countries built their own empires in the Americas, extending their power across the Atlantic.

Economic Structures Trade networks expanded, producing a global economy. As commerce increased, the ideas of capitalism began to develop. The slave trade also grew, fueling the plantation system and placing millions of Africans in bondage.

Social Structures Social classes in Europe began to change with the development of capitalism. New social systems also developed in the American colonies. The expansion of slavery produced a legacy of racism and inequality. But it also brought African cultural influences to the New World and enriched American societies.

Human-Environment Interaction European colonization of the Americas prompted migration across the Atlantic. It also caused the transfer of plants, animals, and diseases between the hemispheres. These changes had important effects on the global environment.

Le siege du grant turc auec ij deses principaulx coteilles
Le siege du capiteme ginal de la turquie

Expanding Empires Outside Europe

What made empires outside Europe rise and decline?

11.1 Introduction

On April 6, 1453, the Ottoman Turks began their attack on the city of Constantinople. They bombarded the Byzantine capital with artillery, blasting away at the city's walls. Yet for weeks the Byzantine defenders held on.

Constantinople's defenses were the strongest in the world. An extensive system of moats, walls, and towers repelled enemy forces. Over the centuries, many attacking armies—including the Ottomans—had tried but failed to capture the city.

This time, however, things were different. The Byzantine Empire was near collapse. It controlled only Constantinople and a few nearby ports and islands. The Ottomans, in contrast, were on the rise. They had conquered the lands of Anatolia to the south and the Balkans to the north. They had the Byzantines surrounded. They also had them outnumbered. A Byzantine force of just 7,000 troops faced an Ottoman army of 100,000. Furthermore, Constantinople's walls had not been built to withstand cannon fire.

After nearly two months of siege, the end came suddenly. On the morning of May 29, the Ottomans broke through the walls and captured the city. Constantinople was in Islamic hands.

The fall of Constantinople had a major effect on Europe and Asia. The city had once halted the Muslim advance into Europe. Now that obstacle was gone. A new, Muslim empire controlled the Eastern Mediterranean and its trade routes to Asia. The Ottoman rise also underscored the growing importance of gunpowder weapons in the formation of powerful states and empires.

In this lesson, you will read about five great empires of Eurasia, beginning with the Ottoman Empire. You will learn how they rose to power and why they eventually declined.

11

Themes

Cultural Interaction Large empires brought together diverse peoples across Eurasia. Some cultures adapted, while others resisted change.

Political Structures Rulers built strong, centralized states to maintain control over large territories.

Economic Structures Trade and commerce brought increased wealth, but agriculture remained the chief economic activity.

Social Structures Class systems brought order to societies but also imposed rigid social differences.

◄ A 15th-century French illustration of the Ottoman siege of Constantinople in 1453

11.2 The Ottoman Empire

After the capture of Constantinople, the Ottomans went on to build one of the largest empires in history. At its height in the 1600s, the Ottoman Empire controlled Southwest Asia, coastal North Africa, and large parts of Europe.

Origins and Expansion   The Ottomans were a Muslim tribal group that emerged in northwestern Anatolia in the late 1200s. They traced their origins to Turkish nomads who had migrated from Central Asia centuries before. They took their name from Osman, a powerful warrior chief who united various tribes and began a campaign of conquest in 1299.

By the early 1300s, the Ottomans were expanding into Byzantine territory. They took the towns and cities south of Constantinople, then crossed into Europe. By 1400, they had captured much of the Balkan Peninsula. They suffered a setback when Timur Lang, the last of the Mongol conquerors, seized a large part of Anatolia in 1402. But they rebounded, and in 1453 took Constantinople. They renamed it Istanbul and made it their capital.

The Ottoman sultan, or ruler, who captured Constantinople was Mehmet II, also known as the Conqueror. Under Mehmet and his

The Ottomans created a vast, wealthy, and prosperous empire, and became the leaders of the Muslim world. They ruled over a wide variety of diverse societies and cultures.

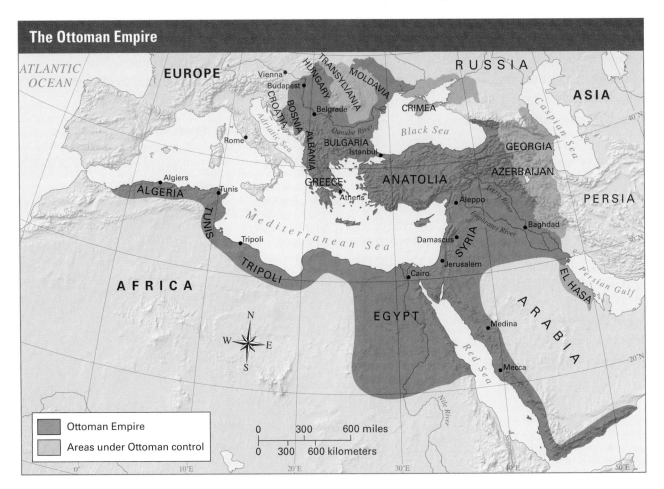

The Ottoman Empire

Ottoman Empire

Areas under Ottoman control

successors, the Ottomans continued to expand the empire. They took the rest of the Balkans, including Greece, and the lands around the Black Sea. They occupied Mesopotamia and portions of Arabia, Palestine and Syria, Egypt, and North Africa. They seized Hungary in 1526 and almost captured Vienna. Many of these conquests took place under their greatest sultan, Suleyman I. Known as Suleyman the Magnificent, he ruled from 1520 to 1566.

By the mid-1600s, the Ottomans ruled an empire nearly the size of ancient Rome. They controlled rich agricultural lands and prosperous trading cities, which brought great wealth to the empire. They also occupied the holy cities of Mecca and Medina, giving them claim to leadership of the Muslim world. They had achieved their conquests by building a powerful military, which made effective use of field cannons and armed infantry. And they maintained their empire by creating a strong, efficient government.

Suleyman the Magnificent was an Ottoman sultan who ruled from 1520 to 1566. In this miniature painting, he is shown on horseback surrounded by his army. How does this depiction of the sultan reflect the organization of Ottoman society?

Organization of the Empire The Ottoman state was highly centralized. All power flowed from the sultan, who governed as an absolute ruler. For six centuries, the royal family of Osman kept the throne, passing it down through male members of the family. There was no clear line of succession, however. The sultan's heirs had to fight for power. So when one of them gained the throne, he typically had his brothers and other male relatives killed or imprisoned to prevent challenges to his rule.

The sultan sat at the top of a large political structure. Directly beneath him was the grand vizier, the chief minister in charge of the government. The grand vizier met with other ministers and military leaders in a governing council called the divan. Beneath these high officials lay a large bureaucracy of lesser officials who served the government at all levels. A network of provincial governors managed the conquered territories and linked them to the central government in Istanbul.

The Ottoman bureaucracy was a merit-based system. Most officials gained office based on their abilities, not their social position. Such a system is called a **meritocracy**. Other states, notably China, developed similar systems. In the Ottoman state, however, many of the top officials were captives. These captives, most of them Christians, were taken from conquered lands in Anatolia and the Balkans. They were brought to Istanbul, where they were converted to Islam and trained for a life in government service.

meritocracy a system in which advancement is based on individual ability or achievement and not on birth rights

To ensure a steady supply of captives for government service, the Ottomans levied a tax called the *devshirme*. This tax required conquered regions to provide a regular allotment of children to serve the sultan. Many of the boys were trained for military service. They became part of an elite fighting force called the **janissaries**. Because of their training and allegiance to the state, the janissaries were renowned as the best soldiers in the world.

The brightest and most capable captives, however, were groomed for government office. The most successful became ministers, judges, and governors. One famous example was Ibrahim Pasha, the son of a Greek fisherman who was sold into slavery and entered the household of Suleyman the Magnificent. He later married the sultan's sister and became the grand vizier, second in power only to the sultan.

The Ottomans divided society into two broad classes: the rulers and the ruled. The rulers were members of the military and governing class, which included both Muslims and non-Muslims. They did not pay taxes. The people being ruled included taxpaying commoners, such as farmers, artisans, and merchants.

janissary slave soldier in the Ottoman Empire, usually Christian

The two men in elaborate dress in this 1513 illustration were Ottoman janissaries. The janissaries were an elite fighting force that was originally composed of young captives who had been trained by the Ottomans for a life of military service. The janissaries were highly respected for their military skill. They became a powerful political force within the Ottoman Empire.

A Diverse Society

Ottoman society was ethnically diverse, with large numbers of Greeks, Serbs, Bulgarians, Romanians, Armenians, Turks, and Arabs. The Ottomans were generally tolerant of different cultures and religions. They allowed Orthodox Christians and Jews to practice their faith, subject to certain restrictions and special taxes. Although second-class citizens, non-Muslim groups were organized in separate communities that were given the right to manage their own religious affairs.

The Ottomans were less tolerant of Shi'a Muslims. As Sunnis, they saw the Shi'a as a challenge to their authority and often persecuted them. They also waged long and vicious wars with the Safavid Empire of Persia. The Safavids were a Shi'a state that bordered the Ottomans to the east.

Under Suleyman, the Ottomans developed a strong legal code. This code was based on Shari'a, or Islamic law. But the code also included non-Islamic provisions for situations that were not covered by Shari'a. Suleyman's law code provided a uniform legal system regardless of people's social and religious origins. For that reason, he was also known as the Lawgiver.

A Gradual Decline   Suleyman's reign was the high point of the Ottoman Empire. After his death in 1566, Ottoman power gradually declined.

One early blow occurred in 1571 at the Battle of Lepanto. This naval battle off the coast of Greece pitted the Ottoman navy against a combined European fleet. The Europeans dealt the Ottomans a stinging defeat, their first major loss in battle. The Ottomans recovered and even conquered more lands. But they were dealt another harsh blow in 1683, when they again failed to take Vienna, the capital of Austria's Hapsburg Empire. By this time, the Ottoman's image of invincibility had been shattered.

In addition, a series of increasingly weak and corrupt sultans led the Ottoman Empire in its final centuries. One reason for this weakness may have been the Ottoman policy of imprisoning possible heirs to the throne, which included the sons of the reigning sultan. As prisoners, these contenders to the throne did not receive the education or training they needed to rule the empire. Those who eventually rose to power mismanaged the empire, and the central government lost power and authority.

The Ottomans also suffered from economic problems. By the 1600s, European countries had developed new sea trade routes to Asia that bypassed the traditional land routes across Ottoman territory. This reduced the amount of revenue the Ottomans could earn from trade. An influx of silver from the new American colonies also lowered the value of the Ottoman currency and caused inflation.

The Ottoman rulers took steps to modernize in the late 1700s. The sultans and their ministers adopted reforms in an effort to strengthen the economy and government. But by this time the empire was shrinking. At the same time, Europe was growing more powerful. The Ottoman Empire survived until the early 1900s, but was finally dissolved in 1923, after World War I.

Mustafa II, Sultan from 1664 to 1703, presided over the unsuccessful Ottoman siege of Vienna in 1683. This defeat checked Ottoman westward expansion. It also helped shatter the Ottoman Empire's image of military invincibility. This painting of Mustafa II was done by a German artist.

This painting from Mughal India shows a mythical meeting between Timur, a 14th-century Mongol ruler, and Babur, the 16th-century founder of the Mughal Empire. In this imaginary scene, Timur hands Babur the imperial crown. What point might the painting be trying to make?

11.3 Mughal India

In the 1500s, a new empire arose in India under the Mughal dynasty. Like the Ottomans, the Mughals were Muslim Turks with ethnic roots in Central Asia. They, too, built a large empire with the aid of gunpowder weapons and an efficient, centralized government.

Founding the Empire   The founder of the Mughal dynasty was Babur, a descendant of the Mongol leaders Timur and Genghis Khan. Mughal was the Persian word for "Mongol." As a young man, Babur moved south from Central Asia to conquer Afghanistan. But he had his eyes set on India.

For three hundred years, a group of Muslim states known as the Delhi Sultanate had ruled most of northern India. In 1526, Babur invaded India. Near Delhi, he confronted the army of Sultan Ibrahim. The sultan had 100,000 troops against Babur's 12,000. But Babur's soldiers were well trained and equipped with artillery and muskets. Babur later wrote:

> *I put my foot in the stirrup of resolution and my hands on the reins of confidence in God, and marched against Sultan Ibrahim. . . . The sun had mounted spear-high when the onset began, and the battle lasted until midday, when the enemy was completely broken and routed.*
>
> —Babur, *Memoirs*

Babur went on to conquer most of northern India. In 1530 he died, leaving the throne to his son Humayun. His son was a poor ruler, however, and lost most of the empire. When Humayun died in 1556, he left only a small kingdom around Delhi to his son Akbar.

A Golden Age   Akbar was just 13 years old when he took power. He was a brilliant leader who soon revived the Mughal Empire. Akbar ushered in a golden age of Indian civilization that lasted for more than two centuries.

Akbar continued to expand the empire. Over his 40-year reign, he conquered more than half the Indian subcontinent. But his greater skill was in governing. He divided India into provinces and districts and established an efficient system of administration. He also reformed the tax system to reduce taxes on peasant farmers.

Akbar ruled as an Indian, not as a foreign conqueror. He knew that his rule could only succeed with the support of India's diverse population. He promoted tolerance by allowing his subjects—whether Sunni or Shi'a Muslims, Hindus, or Sikhs—to worship as they pleased. He eliminated unfair taxes on Hindus and appointed Hindu leaders to high positions in government. In addition, he invited Hindu, Muslim, and Christian scholars to his court and even hired a Jesuit tutor for his son. Despite his tolerance, however, he was ruthless in putting down opposition. When a Hindu prince defied his authority in 1568, he sacked the prince's city and massacred its defenders.

Art and culture flourished under Akbar's rule. The Mughal Empire brought together cultural traditions from the Indian, Persian, and Arab worlds. Persian was the official court language. It blended with local tongues to form Hindi, the main language of modern India, and Urdu, the official language of Pakistan.

Akbar valued learning and promoted the arts. Poetry and painting, particularly miniature painting, flourished in Mughal India. Mughal architects mixed Islamic and Indian styles to create buildings with great domes, arches, and minarets. These buildings were beautifully decorated with carvings, mosaics, and other intricate designs.

Akbar died in 1605, leaving behind a strong and orderly empire. The rulers that followed over the next century maintained the empire, though with less skill.

Shah Jahan ruled for three decades, from 1628 to 1658. He is best known for his lavish court life and the construction of the Taj Mahal. Built in memory of his wife, this building—with its marble dome and splendid gardens—is one of the world's architectural treasures.

The next ruler, Aurangzeb (AWR-uhng-zehb), held power for five decades, until 1707. He was a fervent Muslim who abandoned Akbar's policy of tolerance toward Hindus. He removed Hindu officials from government and reinstated the much-hated taxes on Hindus. At the same time, he carried out a long and bloody military campaign that brought most of southern India into the Mughal Empire. Under his rule, the empire reached its greatest size.

Trade and Interaction   The success of Mughal rule depended on the vast wealth and resources of the Indian subcontinent. During the Mughal era, India's economy was larger than that of any European nation. It supported a population of some 150 million people, much larger than Europe's. Abundant farmlands, particularly in the Ganges River plain of northern India, produced large harvests of rice, sugar, and other crops. Industries made a wide range of goods, from cotton cloth to gold jewelry.

The Taj Mahal (background) was constructed by Shah Jahan, who ruled from 1628 to 1652. It was built in memory of his wife, Mumtaz Mahal, who is shown in the portrait. The building is one example of the flourishing of art and culture that occurred in the Mughal Empire.

Much of the wealth of the Mughal Empire came from widespread trade with regions including China, Africa, and Europe. This illustration from a 17th-century manuscript shows an encampment of Mughal merchants selling grain.

Trade and commerce were critical to the Indian economy. For centuries, India's position on sea routes across the Indian Ocean had spurred the growth of trade. These trade routes connected India with China and the Spice Islands to the east, and with Southwest Asia, Africa, and Europe to the west. This maritime trade brought great wealth to India.

Along these trade routes, Mughal merchants and Sufi missionaries also spread Indo-Muslim culture and the Islamic faith. During the Mughal era, many people in Southeast Asia—particularly Indonesia—converted to Islam. Indonesia is a largely Muslim country today as a result of this exchange.

During this era, European traders also came to India, drawn by its many riches. The Portuguese had arrived in the early 1500s. By the 1600s, the French, Dutch, British, and Danish had also established trading stations on Indian shores. They exchanged silver from the Americas for cotton cloth, spices, and other Indian trade goods.

The Mughal Decline   By the 1700s, European influence in India was growing. Meanwhile, Mughal power was in decline. Aurangzeb's focus on conquest had distracted attention from other critical needs and depleted the royal treasury. His harsh policies toward Hindus had also turned many Indians against Mughal rule. "Your subjects are trampled underfoot," one Indian wrote. "Every province of your empire is impoverished." Rebellions broke out, and various regions separated from the Mughal state. The empire began to unravel.

A series of weak Mughal rulers was unable to reverse the decline. By the late 1700s, Britain had taken advantage of this weakness and gained effective control over large parts of India. The Mughal ruler became a figurehead, with no real power. Mughal rule officially lasted until 1857. But by the early 1800s, India was essentially a British colony.

11.4 China Under the Ming and Qing

During the era of Ottoman and Mughal rule, two dynasties governed China, the Ming and the Qing (ching). Both dynasties took power during times of upheaval. To restore order, they established strong, centralized rule and revived traditional Chinese values, including Confucian ideals.

The Ming Revival   In the mid-1300s, China was in turmoil. The Mongol Yuan dynasty was still in power, but disease and natural disasters had weakened the Mongol grip. Bandits and rebels roamed the countryside. In 1368, a Chinese rebel army overthrew the Mongols. The rebel leader, Zhu Yuanzhang (JOO yuwen-JAHNG), took power and established the Ming dynasty. In Chinese, the word Ming means "brilliant."

The new Ming emperor set out to restore traditional Chinese rule. He revived the state examination system, used to select officials for the **civil service**. This system of tests was based on the Chinese classics, especially the works of the philosopher Confucius. Under Ming rule, Confucian scholars were again elevated in Chinese society. Classical art and literature were held up as models for artistic expression.

> **civil service** the bureaucracy of government officials
>
> **despot** an absolute ruler

The emperor also reformed the tax system and distributed land to Chinese peasants. Under the Ming, agriculture prospered. New crops such as potatoes and corn, brought from the Americas in the 1500s, increased the food supply. As a result, the Chinese population doubled during the first two centuries of Ming rule. Trade and commerce also increased, though Ming rulers—in traditional Confucian style— favored agriculture over business.

During his 30-year reign, Zhu Yuanzhang brought peace and stability to China. But he was also a **despot** who ruled with an iron hand. Fearing threats to his power, he had thousands of officials executed for suspected wrongdoing. He described his actions this way: "In the morning I punish a few; by evening others commit the same crime. . . . Day and night I cannot rest. . . . To be a ruler is indeed difficult."

The Ming Emperor Yong Le built a new capital at Beijing. He also built the imperial palace at the city's center, known as the Forbidden City. The palace's ornate decoration and huge scale symbolized the power of the Ming dynasty.

Ming Expansion   In 1403, the emperor's son, Yong Le (yoong LAW), took power. He continued to strengthen the Chinese state. He rebuilt the Great Wall, an ancient defense against nomadic invaders from the north. He also built a new capital at Beijing. The city was enclosed by high walls and featured a great palace—called the Forbidden City—at its heart. In its grand design, the new capital symbolized the power of the Chinese empire.

The Ming emperor Yong Le sponsored the voyages of Admiral Zheng He to Southeast Asia, India, Arabia, and Africa between 1405 and 1433. These voyages were very successful, but still the Ming government decided to end sea travel in the 1430s. Why?

Route of Zheng He

(Map showing route of Zheng He across Africa, Arabia, Persia, India, and Asia, with cities including Beijing, Nanking, Hangchow, Canton, Saigon, Malacca, Calicut, Jidda, Ormuz, and Mogadishu. Labels for ASIA, PERSIA, ARABIA, INDIA, AFRICA, CHINA, INDIAN OCEAN, and PACIFIC OCEAN.)

Legend:
— Route of Zheng He
• City

Eckert III Projection

tribute payment or respect offered by a less powerful state to a more powerful state

Mandate of Heaven the Chinese idea that the right to rule came from divine approval

Yong Le also expanded China's influence overseas. He sponsored a series of great ocean voyages under the command of Admiral Zheng He (JEHNG HUH). Between 1405 and 1433, Zheng He led a large fleet on seven voyages to Southeast Asia, India, Arabia, and Africa. He met with foreign rulers and brought back exotic goods, including zebras and giraffes. The main purpose of the voyages was to increase the flow of **tribute** to China. For the Ming, the tribute system demonstrated Chinese power. It bolstered their age-old belief that China, which they called the "Middle Kingdom," was the center of the world.

Although the Ming voyages were a great success, the government ended sea travel in the 1430s. The expeditions were expensive, and China decided to focus attention on the defense of its northern border. The decision also reflected the conservative Chinese view that other cultures were inferior and had little to offer China. Increasingly, the Ming rulers looked inward and isolated China from the rest of the world.

The Qing Dynasty Ming rule lasted for nearly three centuries. By the early 1600s, however, the Ming dynasty had grown weak and corrupt. Famine and rebellions ravaged the country. In Chinese terms, the Ming had lost the **Mandate of Heaven,** the traditional right to govern. In 1644, Manchu invaders from the north stormed into China and seized power with the aid of gunpowder weapons. They formed a new dynasty, the Qing (ching), which means "pure."

The Manchus came from Manchuria, a region just north of Korea. Although the Chinese saw them as foreign barbarians, the Manchus had long been influenced by Chinese culture and had adopted many Chinese customs. At first they met strong resistance to their rule. Over the next few decades, however, they brought all of China under their control.

To remain in power, the Manchus adopted policies that were both tough and generous. On the one hand, they forced Chinese men to submit to their rule by wearing their hair in the Manchu style, with a shaved forehead and pigtail in the back. They also kept control of the military by reserving the top positions for Manchus.

At the same time, the Manchus showed respect for Chinese traditions. They preserved the structure of Ming government and ruled according to Confucian principles. They supported the state exam system and allowed Chinese officials to hold high positions in government. They upheld the values of classical Chinese culture. In this way, the Manchus gradually won acceptance from the Chinese people.

The Qing dynasty also benefited from having two outstanding emperors. The first, Kangxi (kahng-shee), ruled from 1661 to 1722. His grandson, Qianlong (chyahn-lung), gained the throne in 1735 and held power just as long. Both men were wise and capable rulers. They expanded the boundaries of the empire and brought peace and prosperity to China. Qing China became the largest and richest empire in the world.

Isolation and Decline   As in the past, most of China's wealth came from agriculture. But trade and commerce also played an important role. Like good Confucian rulers, the Qing officially discouraged trade, while allowing it in limited form. They restricted European traders to the port of Canton, in southern China, and showed little interest in European goods. In 1793, Emperor Qianlong wrote to King George III of England: "Our Celestial Empire possesses all things in abundance. We have no need for barbarian products." Nevertheless, the Qing agreed to exchange Chinese goods—including silk and tea—for silver from the Americas.

As a result, China's economy continued to grow, and so did its population. Between 1650 and 1800, the population rose from 140 million to 350 million, more than a third of humanity. China could not sustain such growth forever, though. In the 1800s, it began to experience food shortages and famine. Once again, rebellions broke out and the dynasty faltered.

In some ways, China's success under Qing rule also contained the seeds of its decline. For centuries, China had relied on its traditions to ensure stability, prosperity, and power. But as global interaction increased and the world began to change, this conservative approach hindered progress. China rejected new ideas in science, technology, and economics that might have brought increased productivity and wealth. Instead, it fell back on its old ways. This reluctance to change left China vulnerable to the growing power of Europe. The Qing dynasty lasted until 1911, but as a result of its policies by the late 1800s it was increasingly dominated by Western powers.

Although the Qing were Manchu invaders, they continued many Chinese Confucian traditions. For example, they maintained the state examination system by which people had traditionally acquired government appointments. This painting from the Qing era shows aspiring government officials, seated at desks, taking the civil service examination.

This detail from a folding screen depicts Lord Tokugawa's army attacking Osaka Castle in 1615 to eliminate a rival leader. Tokugawa rule had been established through military dominance in the late 1500s. However, the Tokugawa still had to work to control rival warlords, or daimyo, throughout the country.

11.5 Tokugawa Japan

While the Ming dynasty ruled China, another strong dynasty—the Tokugawa—took power in Japan. In the 1600s, the Tokugawa (toh-koo-GAH-wah) unified Japan and brought a long period of peace and stability to the country.

A Feudal System   For centuries, Japan had been a feudal society, much like medieval Europe. Local lords, known as **daimyo** (DIE-mee), controlled large landed estates. They relied on armies of **samurai** warriors to defend their land and settle disputes with other lords.

At the top of this feudal structure was the emperor, who claimed descent from a mythical sun goddess. But real power rested in the hands of the **shogun,** a military leader who ruled on behalf of the emperor and demanded the allegiance of the daimyo. In theory, the daimyo respected the shogun's authority, but the system was unstable. Because power was decentralized and allegiance based on military strength, a lord who grew strong enough might challenge the shogun and seize power himself.

In the late 1400s, civil war broke out when a series of weak shoguns lost control of the state. For the next century, the daimyo, backed by their samurai armies, battled each other for power. This period of warfare was known as the Age of the Warring States.

Finally, in the late 1500s, two powerful daimyo gained the upper hand. Using muskets and field artillery, they defeated their rivals and took power. But it was a third lord, Tokugawa Ieyasu (toh-koo-GAH-wah ee-yeh-YAH-soo), who finally ended the wars and united Japan. In 1603, he became shogun. He created a dynasty and a government that ruled Japan for the next 250 years.

daimyo feudal lords in Japan

samurai Japanese warriors

shogun military ruler in feudal Japan

Tokugawa Rule   To ensure stability, the Tokugawa rulers formed a strong, centralized government. They established controls on the daimyo and on Japanese society that allowed them to govern effectively. Scholars have referred to the Tokugawa system as centralized feudalism.

To curb the power of the daimyo, the Tokugawa rulers created a secret police force to root out opposition. They banned the use of firearms and the construction of new castles. They also restricted the movement of samurai and forced the daimyo and their families to live as virtual hostages in Edo, the capital city now known as Tokyo. This arrangement placed a great financial burden on the daimyo while curbing their power and helped ensure their loyalty.

The Tokugawa also established a rigid social structure, consisting of four social classes. At the top was the warrior class of lords and samurai, which made up around 5 percent of the population. Next came farmers, considered the most productive part of society. Artisans made up the third social class. At the bottom were merchants. An elaborate code of etiquette laid out rules for the dress and behavior of each class.

In principle, social mobility was rare in Japan. This rigid structure was designed to ensure social order and respect for authority. In this way, it helped reinforce Tokugawa rule.

Chinese Influence   The social system of Japan reflected Confucian values from China. As an island nation, Japan had never been conquered by China. But it was still heavily influenced by Chinese civilization.

As early as 500 C.E., Chinese culture was making its mark on Japan. Along with Confucian thought, the Japanese borrowed their writing system and early political structures from China. They absorbed Chinese influences in art and literature. They also adopted Buddhism from China. Over time, however, the Japanese blended Chinese customs with their own traditions to form a unique Japanese culture.

During the Tokugawa era, various art forms flourished in Japan. **Kabuki** is a form of theater that combines elaborate costumes, music, and dance. It became popular in Japanese cities. Visual artists created beautiful woodblock prints showing scenes from urban and rural life. Writers and poets explored new forms of literature, including short verse called **haiku** (HI-koo).

kabuki a style of Japanese theater

haiku short Japanese verse of 17 syllables

In a modern staging, this actress wears the elaborate costume and makeup characteristic of Kabuki theater. Kabuki productions also feature music and dance. The art form became very popular in the urban centers of Tokugawa Japan. Today Kabuki is performed with both male and female actors, but in the Tokugawa era, women did not participate, and men performed both male and female parts.

The Jesuit missionary St. Francis Xavier arrived in Japan in 1549, as depicted in this 16th-century Japanese painting. The Tokugawa were initially open to foreign influence, and St. Francis Xavier established five small Catholic communities in Japan. However, the Tokugawa were disturbed when their fellow Japanese began converting to Christianity, and the missionaries were expelled.

A Policy of Isolation   Not long before the Tokugawa took power, European traders and missionaries had arrived in Japan. At first, the Tokugawa rulers remained open to foreign influence. They took an interest in Western goods and welcomed new ideas in science, map-making, and shipbuilding. They even allowed Catholics to set up missions. They became alarmed, however, when Japanese began to convert to Catholicism. Religious intolerance spread in the form of expelling the missionaries and cracking down on Christian converts.

This xenophobia, or fear of foreigners, started to affect commercial exchange when the government also began to restrict trade. By 1638, it had expelled most European traders, limiting trade to just one port. Only the Dutch were allowed to visit, once or twice a year. The government also prohibited Japanese from traveling abroad and outlawed the building of large ships.

For the next two centuries, Japan was effectively isolated from the rest of the world. This policy of isolation was beneficial in that it helped the Tokugawa rulers preserve Japanese traditions and maintain control. But the negative impact was that it also prevented Japan from gaining useful knowledge from abroad. Like China under the Qing, Japan did not benefit from developing ideas in science, technology, and other fields that would have helped the country develop.

Ultimately, this lack of progress left Japan vulnerable to foreign powers. In the mid-1800s, American warships forced Japan to open up to foreign trade. Not long after, the Tokugawa government came to an end. Japan had entered a new era.

11.6 The Russian Empire

In the 1500s, Russia formed a powerful state and began to expand its territory. Over the next few centuries, it built a great empire that stretched across Eurasia. Unlike China or Japan, however, Russia made efforts to modernize by adopting Western ideas.

czar a Russian emperor

boyars Russia's landowning nobility

The Rise of Russia The origins of the Russian state go back to the late 1400s and the rise of Prince Ivan III of Moscow. At the time, the Mongols still controlled Russia, but they were divided and their power was waning. They allowed Russian princes to govern their own cities in return for tribute payments. They also allowed Russians to practice their Orthodox Christian faith, which helped bolster Russian identity under Mongol rule.

Ivan III—also known as Ivan the Great—came to power in 1462. Seeing that the Mongols were in decline, he began to conquer lands around Moscow and build up his strength. By 1480, he had thrown off Mongol control. He continued his conquests over the next two decades, tripling the size of Moscow's territory and making it the dominant power in Russia. He began to call himself **czar,** the Russian form of "caesar." He saw Russia as the "Third Rome": the heir to the Roman and Byzantine empires and the defender of Christianity.

Ivan the Great's successors continued to expand the Russian state. The most powerful of the early czars was his grandson, Ivan IV, who gained the throne as a child in 1533. During his reign of nearly 50 years, Ivan IV took three steps to strengthen the central government and modernize Russia. First, he conquered Mongol lands to the south and east, incorporating them into Russian territory. Second, he instituted reforms, including a uniform code of laws, to make the state more efficient. Third, he fought feudalism and took steps to curb the power of the **boyars,** Russia's landed nobility.

Ivan is best remembered, however, as a cruel tyrant who terrorized Russian society. Mid-way through his reign, he became obsessed with threats to his rule. He persecuted the boyars by attacking them and seizing their lands. He created a secret police force and had thousands of people arrested, tortured, and killed. These actions earned him the nickname Ivan the Terrible.

St. Peter's Basilica in Moscow, constructed under Ivan the Terrible, is a beautiful example of Russian architecture. This impressive building is located at the center of the city and its construction reflects the Russian Empire's consolidation of power around Moscow.

Rule of the Romanovs   After Ivan's death in 1584, his son Fyodor became czar. Fyodor was a weak ruler, however, who failed to mend the divisions caused by his father. In the early 1600s, after Fyodor's death, Russia was engulfed in a 15-year period of civil war known as the Time of Troubles.

In 1613, however, a new czar, Michael Romanov, came to power. Gradually, Russia began to recover from the social divisions Ivan had created. The Romanov family would rule Russia for the next 300 years.

Under the Romanovs, Russia continued to expand its empire. It moved east, taking in the lands of Siberia—a huge portion of the Asian continent—and extending Russia's borders to the Pacific Ocean. Siberia was rich in resources, including furs. During the 1600s, Russian colonizers settled in Siberia and established a lucrative fur trade.

The Modernizing Czars   The Romanovs continued to reform and modernize the Russian state. The leaders in this effort were Peter I, also known as Peter the Great, and Catherine the Great who mark the golden age of Russia's enlightenment.

When Peter took power in 1682, Russia was still largely isolated from Europe. But Peter was determined to open Russia up to the West. He took a long journey through England and France to absorb new ideas. He visited factories, hospitals, and museums, and even worked for a time in a shipyard. He returned home with plans to transform Russia into a modern nation.

Peter sought to gain access to a coastline on the Baltic Sea, which he successfully acquired via war with Sweden. The territory gained from Sweden would become "Russia's window into the West." There he built a modern new capital named after himself—St. Petersburg—based on European designs. He brought in European advisers and specialists, set up schools to teach technical subjects, and established an academy of sciences to promote new learning. Under his rule, Russia built factories and roads and established a professional army and civil service on the European model. The government required officials to dress in the Western style and to shave off their beards.

Russia's modernizing efforts continued under another emperor, Catherine II, who ruled from 1762 to 1796. She was also

Peter the Great, who ruled from 1682 to 1725, worked to modernize and westernize his empire. In this painting of Peter the Great's court, you can see the western style of dress Peter encouraged. Previously government officials had dressed in a more uniquely Russian style, wearing robes and long beards, quite a contrast from the new style above.

known as Catherine the Great. Like Peter the Great, Catherine also founded schools and supported the arts and sciences. She promoted Enlightenment principles of justice and good government. But like her predecessors, she was an absolute ruler who governed with an iron fist, allowing few freedoms and forcing Jews into a limited area called the Pale of Settlement.

The End of Monarchy   By the time of Catherine's reign, Russia faced a looming crisis that would eventually bring down the czars. For more than a century, Russia's **serf** population had been grow-ing. In 1800, around half of all Russian peasants—around 20 million people—were tied to the soil like peasants in western Europe had been prior to the 14th century. They had no rights and lived in terrible pov-erty. When they revolted, as they sometimes did, their uprisings were brutally repressed.

serf a peasant farmer bound to the land with no political representation of social rights

Thus, while Russia was taking steps to modernize, its social system was still mired in the past. Russia was the last European country to outlaw serfdom, in 1861, and by then it was too late. In 1917, a revolution erupted and brought an end to the Russian monarchy as a result. The Romanov attempt to modernize Russia had been too concentrated on science and technological developments and ignored socio-political developments. This unbalance brought about the last of the European revolutions.

Summary

In this lesson, you learned about five powerful empires that ruled in Eurasia during the period from 1400 to 1800. These empires gained power with the aid of gunpowder weapons and main-tained control over large territories.

Cultural Interaction The Eurasian empires incorporated many different peoples and cultures. Some, like the Ottomans and Mughals, reflected diverse cultural influences. Others, like the Chinese and Japanese, held fast to their own traditions and resisted cultural change. The Russians modernized by opening up to the West.

Political Structures All five empires built strong, centralized states to govern their territory. They created official bureaucracies and codes of law to make government more effective. Nevertheless, most rulers—such as the Ottoman sultans and the Russian czars—held absolute power.

Economic Structures Trade and commerce became increasingly important across Eurasia, especially in the Ottoman and Mughal empires. Trade grew in China, too, though without official support. In the Confucian style, both China and Japan favored agriculture over commerce.

Social Structures Eurasian states imposed class structures designed to maintain social and political order. But rigid social systems, such as those in Japan and Russia, left empires unprepared for change.

Transformations in Europe

***What ideas transformed Europe
in the early modern era?***

12.1 Introduction

In 1455, the German metalworker Johannes Gutenberg launched a revolution in ideas. Using a printing press, he published Europe's first printed book—the Gutenberg Bible. Previously, books in Europe had been copied by hand, a laborious task that made them expensive and relatively rare. After Gutenberg, books could be produced cheaply and in great quantities. The printing press brought dramatic changes to Europe, and later to the world.

Gutenberg did not invent printing. By 700 C.E., the Chinese were using carved wooden blocks to print books on paper. From there, the technology spread to Korea, Japan, and the Muslim world. The Chinese later invented movable type, using a separate clay block for each character, but this process was not efficient for the thousands of characters in Chinese writing. The Koreans produced moveable metal type in the 1200s, but faced similar problems as the Chinese. Gutenberg's innovation was to make durable metal type for the much smaller European alphabet and combine it with an effective printing press of his own design. The combination worked brilliantly.

Gutenberg's press caused an explosion in book publishing. By 1500, hundreds of printing houses across Europe had produced some 30,000 titles—around 20 million books in all—in more than a dozen languages. This print revolution helped spread ideas and knowledge across Europe. It promoted literacy and education. It also helped energize four important cultural and intellectual movements of early modern Europe: the Renaissance, Reformation, Scientific Revolution, and Enlightenment.

Themes

Cultural Interaction New ideas and religious beliefs spread across Europe with the aid of the printing press. Artists, scientists, and thinkers shared knowledge and advanced learning.

Political Structures Political conditions helped give rise to cultural movements. Those movements, in turn, influenced political structures.

Economic Structures Wealth and prosperity in Europe nurtured the Renaissance. Ideas generated during the Scientific Revolution and Enlightenment had important economic effects.

Social Structures The ideas of the Renaissance, Reformation, and Enlightenment helped transform European society.

Johannes Gutenberg's movable type printing press revolutionized the way ideas were spread throughout Europe. It played an important role in spreading the ideas of the Renaissance, Reformation, Scientific Revolution, and Enlightenment.

12.2 The Renaissance

In 1550, the Italian artist Giorgio Vasari wrote a book, *The Lives of the Artists*. In it, he praised the revival of classical Greek and Roman culture occurring in Italy at the time. Vasari contrasted this cultural flowering with the "darkness" of the Middle Ages after the fall of Rome. Historians would later refer to this age of cultural revival as the **Renaissance,** a French word meaning "rebirth."

Roots of the Renaissance Historians generally date the Renaissance to the period from 1300 to 1600. In fact, the Renaissance did not start or end at a particular time. Nor did it represent a clear break with the past. Many of the changes that took place during this period had their roots in the late Middle Ages.

By 1300, Europe was moving out of the feudal age. Increased trade and commerce were generating new wealth, prosperity, and urban growth. Universities in Paris, Oxford, and other cities had emerged as centers of higher learning. National monarchies and city-states were gaining more power. The Catholic Church was still a dominant force, but it was losing some of its control over cultural and political life.

During the 1300s, wars and the bubonic plague—the Black Death— caused great turmoil in Europe. These events devastated whole regions and populations and shrank the labor force. But they also helped destroy feudalism and create new possibilities for change. One of those changes was the growth of urban workshops that made use of new, laborsaving devices. The skilled artisans who worked in these small industries produced a wide range of luxury goods and machinery. From this artisan class came many of the craft workers, artists, architects, and other creative individuals who powered the Renaissance.

Italian Origins The Renaissance began in Italy, where conditions were ideal for a cultural resurgence. In 1300, much of Italy was controlled by city-states, such as Rome, Venice, Florence, and Milan. These city-states had grown rich from trade and commerce. Wealthy Italian merchants and bankers had money to spend on luxuries and works of art.

City-state rulers also sought to compete with their rivals by bringing artistic glory to their cities. Rich patrons of the arts, such as the ruling Medici (MED-ih-chee) family of Florence, offered financial support to writers and artists. Education also became more important, as the demands of business and government called for more literate people versed in accounting and law.

Other factors played a part, too. Italy had long been engaged in trade across the Mediterranean. This foreign contact gave Italians a greater awareness of the world. The Italian people were also surrounded by the remains of classical Rome. This heritage helped stimulate interest

Paradoxically, the horrors of the plague paved the way for the cultural flowering of the Renaissance. This German allegorical print depicts a sick man being touched by the "demon of the plague."

in the past. This interest was enhanced by contacts with the Byzantine Empire, where much classical scholarship was preserved. During the 1300s and 1400s, many Byzantine scholars moved to Italy to escape the growing threat of the Ottoman Empire. They brought a large body of knowledge with them.

Although Renaissance thinkers sought to revive classical culture, this culture had never really disappeared in Europe. The Catholic Church had preserved the works of Plato, Aristotle, and other ancient philosophers, but it interpreted their work from a Christian perspective. What the Renaissance thinkers did was return to the original sources and read them in a new, non-religious light.

In reviving classical thought, the artists and writers of the Renaissance were guided by **humanism**. This philosophy balanced religious faith with a **secular** point of view. It emphasized the dignity and worth of the individual. As humanists, the Renaissance thinkers studied classical art and literature for their insights into human life, rather than spiritual matters.

The city of Florence was a center of Renaissance cultural achievement. One reason for this was the patronage of the Medici, a wealthy banking family. The cathedral, which still dominates the skyline of Florence, above, was designed by the architect Filippo Brunelleschi, who was sponsored by the Medici.

Renaissance Writers   The first great writer of the Italian Renaissance was Dante Alighieri (ahl-ee-GARE-ee). His greatest work, *The Divine Comedy*, is an epic poem that describes the author's imaginary journey through the afterlife. Dante was the first well-known author to write in both classical Latin and the Italian **vernacular,** or native language. He promoted the use of Italian to make learning more available to a wider audience.

Two great humanists followed in Dante's footsteps. Francesco Petrarca—known as Petrarch—wrote lyrical poetry, also in Italian. He scoured libraries across Europe for classical works and brought them to wider attention. A second great writer was Giovanni Boccaccio (boh-KAH-chee-oh). His most famous work, *The Decameron*, tells the story of ten young people who flee Florence to escape the plague. While away, they tell stories to pass the time. The book appealed to many Italian readers, though the church did not like its liberal approach to the younger generation.

Another writer, Niccolò Machiavelli (mahk-ee-uh-VEL-ee), wrote books with political themes. His best-known work, *The Prince*, offered highly practical advice to rulers. For example, he wrote that a ruler should always be ready for war. "Once princes have given more thought to personal pleasures than to arms," he wrote, "they have lost their domain." He also wrote that it is more important for a ruler to be feared than to be loved. Although Machiavelli's advice may seem harsh for a Renaissance humanist, his realistic approach matched the secular spirit of the time.

humanism a Renaissance philosophy emphasizing the worth of the individual and balancing religious faith with secular learning

secular non-religious; worldly

vernacular the native language of a people, region, or country

perspective a painting or drawing technique that gives the appearance of depth on a flat surface

Renaissance Art The Italian Renaissance also produced an extraordinary outpouring of art. Renaissance painters mastered the art of **perspective,** giving visual depth to their work. Sculptors working in stone revived the realism of classical Greek sculpture. Three of the greatest Italian artists were Leonardo da Vinci (duh VIN-chee), Michelangelo (MY-kul-AN-juh-loh), and Raphael (RAF-ee-ul).

Leonardo was a true "Renaissance man," a person who is skilled at many different things. He was a painter, sculptor, architect, and engineer. He is perhaps most famous for his painting the *Mona Lisa*, a portrait of a woman with a mysterious smile. But he also made thousands of drawings of human anatomy, plants and animals, mechanical devices, and weapons. He even designed a flying machine, centuries before airplanes were invented.

Michelangelo was a brilliant artist who depicted the human body in astonishing detail. His greatest masterpiece is the painting on the ceiling of the Sistine Chapel in Rome, which shows scenes from the Bible. His stone sculptures *La Pietà* and *David* are also remarkable for their realism.

Michelangelo was commissioned by Pope Julius II to paint the ceiling of the Sistine Chapel in the Vatican. His paintings were remarkable for their realistic depictions of the human body. The realism of Italian Renaissance art is one way in which it differs from the art of the Middle Ages.

Raphael emphasized balance and composition in his paintings. One of his greatest works, the *School of Athens*, shows philosophers from ancient Greece alongside artists and thinkers of the Renaissance. It reflects the humanist devotion to classical ideals.

The Northern Renaissance By the mid-1400s, the Renaissance was spreading to other parts of Europe, particularly northern Europe. Cities in Germany, France, Great Britain, Holland, and Flanders (modern-day Belgium) were beginning to grow and prosper after decades of disease and warfare. These cities became fertile ground for Renaissance ideas, spread through the new medium of the printing press. Northern writers and artists also traveled to Italy to study, and Italians came north. As a result, Renaissance art and humanism took hold in northern Europe.

Northern humanists maintained their Christian faith, but they also wrote works critical of the church and society. The greatest of the Christian humanists was the Dutch writer Desiderius Erasmus. In his most famous work, *The Praise of Folly*, written in 1509, Erasmus criticized corruption and abuses in the Catholic Church.

A few years later, in 1516, the Englishman Sir Thomas More published his famous book *Utopia*. This visionary work describes an ideal society governed by reason, rather than the power of kings or popes, where all property is shared and people enjoy equal rights.

The greatest writer of the Northern Renaissance was William Shakespeare, who lived from 1564 to 1616. The themes of classical culture and humanism are evident in many of his plays, including *Julius Caesar.* Shakespeare's interest in the ways of the world and his love of vernacular English mark him as a true Renaissance man.

Great artists of the period included Albrecht Dürer (DYUR-ur), Jan van Eyck (yahn van YK), and Pieter Bruegel (BROY-guhl). Dürer was a German artist who studied in Italy and mastered the use of perspective. Van Eyck and Bruegel were both Flemish painters. Van Eyck advanced the Flemish technique of oil painting, which gave his work a rich, luminous quality. Bruegel is famous for his scenes of Flemish peasant life.

This 19th-century print depicts William Shakespeare kneeling before Queen Elizabeth I, who served as his patron. The Elizabethan age saw a great flowering of English culture.

The Renaissance and Religion   At times, the values expressed in Renaissance art and literature provoked tensions with the Catholic Church. The church had long regarded itself as the guardian and interpreter of knowledge and culture. But that position was challenged by the secular philosophy of humanism, which advanced the classical Greek idea that "man is the measure of all things." Humanist philosophy suggested that individuals could understand the world for themselves and even question church teachings. It implied that individuals were free to make their own moral and ethical choices. These ideas undermined church authority.

Nevertheless, most Renaissance thinkers remained faithful Christians. Although they might embrace humanism and criticize church practices, they did not question the basic tenets of Christian religion. In fact, humanist thinkers like Erasmus promoted the search for a deeper spiritual experience. This quest for a more meaningful faith would lead to a major transformation of Christianity during the 1500s.

Jan Hus was a Czech preacher who attacked the corruption of the Catholic Church. He was burnt at the stake for heresy in 1415, depicted above. His ideas are often seen as paving the way for the Protestant Reformation.

Reformation a reform movement of the 1500s that split the Catholic Church and gave birth to the Protestant religion

indulgence an official church pardon that relieved Catholics from punishment for sins

heresy holding religious beliefs that contradict the teachings of the church

excommunication expulsion from a church or religious community

12.3 The Reformation

In October 1517, a Catholic scholar in Germany named Martin Luther wrote a letter to the archbishop of Mainz. In the letter, he criticized church corruption and called for reforms. Luther's views were spread in printed pamphlets and soon sparked a religious revolt. Many protesters left the Catholic Church and formed new Christian religious movements. This became known as the **Reformation**.

Problems in the Church   For centuries, the Catholic Church had commanded the loyalty and faith of most Europeans. But over time, problems had arisen within the church. Although priests took a vow of poverty, the pope and other high officials lived in wealth and luxury. Some Catholic clergy had wives and children, despite their vows of celibacy. Local priests were often poorly educated. Many were illiterate and barely understood the Bible. The church also engaged in corrupt practices, including selling church positions and charging for services. The church even sold pardons, known as **indulgences,** which released sinners from punishment.

Critics had called attention to these problems in the past. In the late 1300s, Oxford professor John Wycliffe criticized the wealth and immorality of church officials. Another critic, the Czech preacher Jan Hus, called for an end to church corruption. In 1415, Hus was burned at the stake for **heresy**. Christian humanists like Erasmus and More had also mocked superstitions and false doctrines taught by the church.

Luther echoed these concerns, but he did not mean to start a revolt. Instead, he hoped to prompt a debate within the church. His initial complaint was over the selling of indulgences. But his real aim was to restore purity to the church. He believed that rituals like confession and praying to the saints did not bring salvation, as the church claimed. He argued that salvation came from faith alone, and that the Bible was the only source of religious truth. "One thing, and only one thing, is necessary for Christian life," he wrote. "That one thing is the holy Word of God." Luther argued that believers did not need priests to show them the truth. He said that any Christian could read the Bible and understand God's message.

A Protestant Revolution   Luther's ideas did not sit well with church leaders. They regarded his views as heresy and a threat to church authority. In 1520, Pope Leo X demanded that Luther retract his teachings, on pain of **excommunication**. Luther refused and was expelled from the church. He soon went into hiding to avoid punishment.

But he continued to write and publish his work, which was printed and circulated throughout Europe.

Luther and his followers formed the Lutheran Church, a new branch of Christianity. Lutheran ministers simplified church services and rituals and preached in German rather than Latin. Many Germans abandoned Catholicism in favor of the new Lutheran faith.

At the time, Germany was part of the Holy Roman Empire, a state that also included parts of France, Italy, and central Europe. The German territories enjoyed considerable self-rule within the empire, however. Some of their ruling princes defied the emperor, Charles V, and sided with Luther. They became known as **Protestants** for their protests against the Catholic Church.

Meanwhile, other Protestant groups arose in different parts of Europe. Switzerland was a major focus of reform activity. In Zurich, Huldrych Zwingli (HUL-drick ZVING-lee), a Catholic priest inspired by Luther's ideas, founded a new religious **denomination**. His Reformed Church emphasized Bible study and banned all images and music from church services.

In Geneva, the reformer John Calvin founded an even stricter denomination. Calvin emphasized the values of thrift, hard work, and the rejection of worldly pleasures. Members who did not uphold these values were excommunicated. Calvin also stressed the notion of predestination. This is the idea that some people are chosen by God for salvation. Calvin's church gained followers throughout Europe—in France, the Netherlands, Germany, and England. His ideas later had a major impact on religion in British North America.

England also underwent its own Reformation. In 1534, King Henry VIII formed the Church of England, also called the Anglican Church. Henry broke with the Catholic Church because it refused to grant him a divorce from his wife, but also because he wanted to claim power over the church—and its wealth—in England.

The spread of Protestant religion provoked conflicts across Europe. In Germany, Protestant and Catholic states fought a series of bitter wars that lasted for a century, until the mid-1600s. Religious wars and persecutions also ravaged France, the Netherlands, and other countries. Only Italy, Spain, and Portugal remained outside Protestant influence. Eventually, it became custom that the ruler of each state would choose the religion of his people. This led to the migrations of many believers to more hospitable lands.

In 1520 Pope Leo X issued a bull, or official decree, demanding that Martin Luther renounce his ideas. Luther would not, and was excommunicated from the Catholic Church. In this illustration, Luther demonstrates his defiance by burning the papal bull.

Protestant a Christian who separated from the Catholic Church during the Reformation; today, any member of a Christian church founded on the principles of the Reformation

denomination a religious group or movement within a larger religion sharing a common interpretation of that religion

The Catholic Church of the Counter-Reformation period built churches in a new lavish and ornate style. The Brazilian church above, with its elaborate gilded decoration, exemplifies the style of this period. This style contrasted sharply with the austere Protestant church architecture of the period.

Counter-Reformation a movement to revive and defend Catholicism in response to the Reformation

Scientific Revolution a shift in thinking about the study of the natural world that began in the 1500s and departed from traditional religious teachings

The Catholic Response   To meet the challenges of the Reformation, the Catholic Church began its own campaign of reform and renewal. This movement is known as the **Counter-Reformation**.

The church took a number of steps to defend Catholicism. In 1545, it began a series of meetings known as the Council of Trent. This council defined Catholic doctrine and called for needed reforms. One reform was to end the sale of indulgences. Another was to improve education for priests. The council also imposed more rigid discipline on Catholics, making church attendance mandatory and banning certain books. These and other changes helped establish more order and unity in the church.

The church also sought to increase its membership through renewed missionary activity and a more personal style of worship. It founded a new religious order, the Jesuits, to win Catholic converts in Europe and overseas. It also built lavish new churches, filled with magnificent art to inspire the faithful. This splendid style was designed to appeal to the emotions. It offered a stark contrast to the simple, severe quality of Protestant religion.

The Counter-Reformation helped revive the Catholic Church. Nevertheless, by the 1600s the Reformation had changed the face of Europe. The continent was no longer united around the Catholic religion. Rulers claimed more freedom from religious authority. Europeans were also more educated and literate, thanks to the Protestant emphasis on Bible study and the effects of the printing press. Although Europe remained highly religious, these changes encouraged secular trends in European society.

12.4 The Scientific Revolution

The changes that took place in European society during the Renaissance and Reformation also helped prompt new ways of looking at the natural world. Beginning in the 1500s, scientists—then called natural philosophers—used their powers of reasoning and observation to understand the laws of nature. This movement became known as the **Scientific Revolution**. It would transform life in Europe, and eventually around the world.

The Origins of Modern Science   Before 1500, most Europeans relied on two main sources of knowledge about the natural world. One was the Bible and religious teachings. The other was the work of classical philosophers such as Aristotle. But the Renaissance and Reformation undermined traditional authority and encouraged independent thought. Some people began to look beyond religion and the classics for answers to questions about nature and the universe. This questioning spirit encouraged the growth of science.

Other factors also played a part. Universities gave scholars the opportunity to pursue studies in science and math. Overseas trade and exploration brought new knowledge from China, India, and the Muslim world. The discovery of the Americas exploded old notions of world geography and exposed Europeans to new peoples, plants, and animals. Sea voyages also sparked interest in astronomy, navigation, and mapmaking. European states increasingly supported research and technology in these fields. All these developments were aided by the printing press, which helped spread information and promote new learning.

The Scientific Revolution did not happen suddenly or bring change overnight. It was a gradual process with roots in the Middle Ages and the Renaissance. It really began to take off during the period from the mid-1500s to the late 1700s. In many ways, the revolution still continues today.

Understanding the Universe   The first major breakthroughs in science came in the field of astronomy. Since the days of ancient Greece, most people had believed that Earth was the center of the universe. This view is known as the **geocentric theory**. According to Aristotle, the sun, planets, and stars all revolved around Earth in circular orbits. The Greek astronomer Ptolemy expanded on this theory in the 2nd century C.E. The church also supported the idea of an Earth-centered universe.

In 1543, however, the Polish astronomer Nicolaus Copernicus offered another theory. He determined that Earth and the other planets revolve around the sun. His **heliocentric theory** described the solar system more accurately. But his work was largely ignored at the time.

Nevertheless, by the early 1600s other scientists were building on the work of Copernicus. The German astronomer Johannes Kepler used math to calculate the movement of the planets. He determined that they travel in elliptical orbits, rather than circles. The Italian scientist Galileo Galilei (gal-uh-LEE-oh gal-uh-LAY) observed the sky directly with a new invention, the telescope. His observations supported the heliocentric theory. In response, the Catholic Church charged Galileo with heresy and forced him to retract his views. But his ideas continued to spread.

During the Scientific Revolution, natural philosophers investigated the world using reason and observation. One of the most famous scientific experiments of all time, pictured above, involved Galileo observing falling bodies dropped from the tower of Pisa.

geocentric theory   the idea that Earth is the center of the solar system or universe

heliocentric theory   the idea that the sun is the center of the solar system, with Earth and the other planets revolving around it

The next major advance in understanding the universe came from the English physicist Isaac Newton. In 1687, Newton published the *Principia*, or *Principles,* a book that explained the laws of gravity and motion. Newton's work had an enormous impact. People began to see the universe as a well-designed machine, much like a clock, that works on mechanical principles. Although the mechanical universe contradicted church teachings, most early scientists, including Newton, were not opposed to religion. In fact, many regarded the laws of nature as another example of the miracle of creation.

The Scientific Method A key outcome of the Scientific Revolution was the development of the **scientific method**. This method is based on careful observation and testing of data. It forms the basis of scientific investigation.

The method involves several steps. It begins with a problem or question based on observation. The scientist then forms a hypothesis, or assumption, to answer the question. The hypothesis is tested in an experiment, and the results are recorded. The scientist then analyzes the results to determine whether the hypothesis is correct or not.

Two early scientists had a critical influence on the development of the scientific method. One was René Descartes (reh-NAY dey-KAHRT), a French philosopher skilled at mathematics and logic. Descartes believed that human reason could be used to solve complex problems. The other figure was Francis Bacon, an Englishman who emphasized the value of experimentation. Bacon also believed that science should have practical benefits. "The true and lawful end of the sciences," he wrote, "is that human life be enriched by new discoveries and powers." This idea would promote the growth of technology, with all its economic and environmental effects.

The Expanding Sciences As the Scientific Revolution continued, other scientists made key discoveries in various fields. In many cases, they took advantage of new inventions, such as the microscope and thermometer, to aid their discoveries.

Some of the most important advances occurred in the fields of biology, medicine, and chemistry. The Swedish biologist Carl Linnaeus developed a system for classifying plants and animals by scientific type. The English physician William Harvey discovered how blood circulates through the body. The French chemist Antoine Lavoisier explained the chemical process that creates fire.

These pioneering scientists helped establish the foundations of modern science. Their work provided the basis for other scientific advances and new technologies that would transform the world. At the same time, the ideas of science also inspired new ways of thinking about human society, based on the principles of reason and progress.

scientific method a method of investigation involving observation and theory to test scientific assumptions

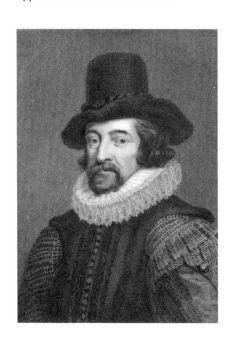

Francis Bacon was an English philosopher who had a major influence on the development of the scientific method. He believed that science and technology should be used in practical applications for human benefit.

12.5 The Enlightenment

In the mid-1600s, European thinkers began to apply scientific principles to the study of society and government. They believed that reason was the key to human progress and that scientific methods could be used to solve social problems. This intellectual movement, which reached its peak in the 1700s, was called the **Enlightenment**.

Sources of Enlightenment Thought   The Enlightenment was a direct outgrowth of the Scientific Revolution. Enlightenment thinkers were inspired by science and its goal of understanding the laws of nature. They believed that human society also functioned under natural laws. They hoped to use the power of reason to understand and improve society. As a result, this period is sometimes called the Age of Reason.

The Renaissance and Reformation also influenced the Enlightenment. Enlightenment thinkers adopted the Renaissance ideas of individualism and secular thought. From the Reformation, they took the habit of questioning authority. They were skeptical of received knowledge and insisted on discovering truth for themselves. They followed the example of Descartes, who wrote, "The first rule was that I would not accept anything as true which I did not clearly know to be true."

From classical Greece and Rome, Enlightenment thinkers also got the idea that people should have a say in their government. Those who supported this idea took inspiration from the democracy of ancient Athens and the republic of ancient Rome.

Thinkers across Europe embraced Enlightenment ideals, especially in Britain and France. Although these thinkers generally shared a devotion to the ideas of reason and progress, they did not always agree. The Enlightenment was a diverse movement, with many points of view.

The British Enlightenment   The first major thinkers of the Enlightenment were from Great Britain. Two of the most important were Thomas Hobbes and John Locke. Hobbes wrote his most important book, *Leviathan*, in 1651. In it, he argued that people were naturally selfish and needed strong rulers to keep order. He believed that absolute monarchy was the best form of government.

John Locke held very different views from Hobbes. He favored constitutional monarchy, a form of government in which laws limit a monarch's power. Locke argued that the basis of government was a **social contract** in which people agree to be ruled in return for protection of their **natural rights**. These rights include the right to life, liberty, and property. If a government failed to protect natural rights, Locke said, the people had a right to overthrow it. Locke's ideas had a major impact on political thought, especially in France and in England's North American colonies.

Rene Descartes was a French Enlightenment philosopher who questioned all knowledge that was not based on his own reason. He famously declared, "I think therefore I am," by which he meant that the fundamental fact of man's existence could only be based on his ability to reason.

Enlightenment an intellectual movement of the 18th century that applied scientific methods to the study of society and government

social contract an agreement in which people give power to a government in return for its protections

natural rights rights that belong to people "by nature," simply because they are human beings

The success of the Enlightenment was based on the spread of ideas. Enlightenment ideas were spread through books and through salons, shown here. Salons were meetings for intellectual discussions that were often hosted by a wealthy patron. They were especially important to the French Enlightenment.

Another key figure in the British Enlightenment was the Scottish philosopher Adam Smith. His book *The Wealth of Nations* laid the foundations for modern economics. Smith believed that a free market, based on competition and self-interest, would benefit society as a whole. But he also argued that a successful economic system must help the poor. As he wrote: "No society can surely be flourishing and happy, of which the far greater part of the members are poor and miserable."

Some Enlightenment thinkers also addressed the rights of women and children. For example, in 1792 the English author Mary Wollstonecraft voiced early feminist ideas in her book *Vindication of the Rights of Women*.

French Philosophers   In the 1700s, the center of the Enlightenment shifted to France. In Paris, the *philosophes*—a French word for Enlightenment thinkers—gathered for lively discussions in private homes, called salons.

Among the most famous *philosophes* were the Baron de Montesquieu (MON-tuh-skyoo), Voltaire, and Jean-Jacques Rousseau (roo-SO). All three had an important influence on the founding ideals of the United States.

Montesquieu's most famous book was *The Spirit of the Laws*. In it, he made the case for a three-part system of government, with a **separation of powers** among executive, legislative, and judicial branches.

Voltaire—whose given name was Francois-Marie Arouet—was a brilliant writer and thinker who advocated religious tolerance. He criticized religious persecution and supported freedom of speech.

Rousseau believed that people are corrupted by society and that they can find a purer life in harmony with nature. But he also recognized that government was necessary and argued for a political system based on the will of the people. He wrote: "The people, being subject to the laws, ought to be their author; the conditions of society ought to be regulated solely by those who come together to form it."

separation of powers
the division of powers among branches of government

The Impact of the Enlightenment   The Enlightenment had various effects. One was to encourage new ways of thinking among some political leaders. Monarchs like Russia's Catherine the Great embraced reform ideas in education and social welfare. They became known as enlightened monarchs, though their reforms were often half-hearted.

More importantly, the Enlightenment gave rise to new political ideals. The ideas of liberty, natural rights, and republican government spread throughout Europe and the Americas. They encouraged the American and French revolutions of the late 1700s. They also helped spark independence movements in Latin America in the early 1800s.

The Enlightenment also promoted an optimistic faith in the future. Enlightenment thinkers believed that society could be understood and improved. Many thought that social and political progress were inevitable. These ideas carried forward into the modern era.

This period also encouraged the trend toward secular attitudes in society. It emphasized reason over religion in the search for knowledge. It also promoted the principles of religious toleration and respect for the individual. These too were key legacies of the Enlightenment.

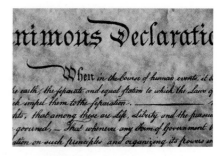

The Enlightenment gave rise to the political ideals that inspired the American Declaration of Independence. Its famous statement of the right to "life, liberty, and the pursuit of happiness" was adopted from the political philosophy of John Locke.

Summary

In this lesson, you read about four key movements in Europe: the Renaissance, Reformation, Scientific Revolution, and Enlightenment. Together, they helped transform European society in the early modern era.

Cultural Interaction   Each movement spread new ideas and beliefs. The Renaissance revived classical learning and promoted secular attitudes. New styles of art and literature emerged. The Reformation challenged Catholic beliefs and produced new Christian faiths. The Scientific Revolution used the power of reason to discover natural laws. In the process, it altered views of nature and the universe. The Enlightenment applied scientific principles to the study of society. It encouraged belief in human progress.

Political Structures   City-state politics in Italy helped give birth to the Renaissance. The Reformation sparked religious wars and reduced the power of the Catholic Church. The Enlightenment promoted new political ideals that sparked reform and revolution in Europe and the Americas.

Economic Structures   Growing prosperity provided the economic foundations for the Renaissance. The methods and discoveries of the Scientific Revolution led to the growth of technology. Enlightenment ideas gave rise to the modern science of economics.

Social Structures   The Renaissance, Reformation, and Enlightenment all had effects on European society. The emphasis on individual worth and secular thought helped loosen social restrictions. The challenge to the authority of the Catholic Church also shook up society.

MAPPA
TOTIUS MUNDI
Adornata juxta Obfervationes
Dñn Academiæ Regalis Scientiarum
et nonnullorum aliorum, fecundum annotationes recentifsimas.
Per G. de L'Isle Geographum Parisiis.
Proftat nunc in Officina
TOBIÆ CONRADI LOTTER
Geogr. et Chalcogr.
AUG. VIND.

ANNOTATIO
Autor reddit ratione
in fua nova Introductione
in Geographiam de mutationibg
quas fecit in hac Mappa, ficut etiam
de cæteris, quas in lucem
edidit.

Toward a Global Economy

What factors led to European dominance in the emergence of the first global age?

13.1 Introduction

Portugal, a small European country bordering the vast Atlantic Ocean, sent sailors south in the early 1400s to explore the western coast of Africa. Part of their mission was to find West Africa's fabled "River of Gold." The Portuguese believed that this river was the source of the gold that trading caravans had, for centuries, carried north across the Sahara.

In the early 1400s, sailing the seas was a dangerous business. Sailors had to be tough. But even the toughest Portuguese sailor might have trembled to hear the words "Cape Bojador" (boh-juh-DOHR). This piece of land bulging out into the Atlantic presented a psychological barrier, a barrier of fear. Rumors hinted at the many hazards that lay beyond the cape. Perhaps, some sailors thought, it marked the edge of the world.

Finally, in 1434, a captain named Gil Eannes dared to sail past Cape Bojador into the unknown waters to the south. He found out why sailors feared to venture past the cape. At that point, a powerful ocean current drove ships to the south. The winds, too, blew southward. To sail north, back to Portugal, ships had to veer well out into the Atlantic to avoid the current. The knowledge and experience gained by sailing in the open ocean led to improvements in ship design and navigational tools. These advances would allow Portuguese sailors to make longer exploratory voyages.

Portuguese sailors eventually found enough gold to make their exploration a commercial success. By the end of the 1400s, they had sailed around the southern tip of Africa to India and other lands bordering the Indian Ocean. They called that region the Indies. They knew it as the source of spices and other goods prized by Europeans. Reaching the Indies marked an important stage on the road toward a global economy.

Themes

Cultural Interaction European exploration in the Americas and Asia resulted in the interchange of previously unknown goods throughout the world. Europeans spread their customs and religion, often forcibly, to the peoples they encountered.

Political Structures Europe saw the rise of sovereign nation-states and the creation of overseas empires.

Economic Structures European overseas colonies supported a mercantilist economic system and aided in the accumulation of capital.

Social Structures European settlers in Latin America created a stratified society with those born in Europe at the top.

Human-Environment Interaction Europeans colonized the Americas and forced enslaved Africans to migrate as well. They brought diseases with them that killed many Native Americans.

By the early 1700s, Europeans had enough knowledge about the world to create this detailed world map.

13.2 Economic and Political Changes in Europe

Portugal's ocean voyaging came less than a century after a catastrophic event. In the mid-1300s, a disease called the Black Death swept through Europe. This killer plague sharply decreased populations and damaged economies. Although the Black Death returned periodically, by 1400 Europe had begun a healthy recovery. Two key changes marked this revival. Together, they would help Europeans dominate the first global age of world history.

Trade Connects Southern and Northern Europe   The first change was economic. Trading centers in southern and northern Europe, over time, established strong ties with one another.

These two regions had separate patterns of trade. In the south, Italian city-states such as Venice and Genoa grew rich from Mediterranean trade with Muslims from the Middle East. This trade brought them luxury goods, including silk from China, ivory from East Africa, and pepper and other spices from India. In the north, a powerful association of trading cities known as the Hanseatic League developed a secure and profitable commercial network. Its products were mainly bulk goods, such as grains, wool, wood, fish, and iron. Hanseatic merchants also traded furs, beeswax, honey, and amber.

Earlier, in medieval times, merchants from south and north would have come together to trade goods mainly at fairs. Fairs were regional markets set up from time to time in a central location. As economic activity increased, Europe's merchants sought more regular trade. By 1400, direct trade had largely replaced commercial fairs, as merchant ships carried goods back and forth between European port cities in the north and south. Direct trade helped unify Europe economically.

Italian city-states became rich in the Middle Ages from Mediterranean trade. In the 1300s, they also increased their direct trade with northern Europe. This painting depicts the large market in Naples, Italy, in the early 1700s.

National States Arise The second change was political. Through the 1400s and 1500s, unified **nation-states** slowly emerged. In Spain, Portugal, England, the Netherlands, and France, kings secured their political authority by seizing power from local nobles and the Catholic Church. These newly formed nation-states were **sovereign** and territorial. That is, they were self-governing and independent, and they ruled over a specific geographical area.

All five of these states had ports on the Atlantic Ocean. That put them in a good position to take advantage of future long-distance trading opportunities. It also meant that they would compete with one another to advance their own fortunes.

Economic competition among European nation-states gave Europe an advantage over other regions of the world. For one thing, it led to innovation. For example, each state sought to build stronger and faster sailing ships to outdo its rivals. Those rivals would quickly copy—and try to improve upon—any such innovation.

Competition also led governments to seek partnerships with businesses. States needed the resources of merchants, bankers, and investors to succeed with ventures overseas. A sovereign national state could help mobilize those resources in a number of ways. It could create a national market for the exchange of goods. It could standardize weights and measures. It could enact laws to protect private property. The state could also ensure the safety of merchants traveling within its boundaries. European states did all these things.

Competition among European states took military as well as economic form. England and France had fought off and on from the mid-1300s to the mid-1400s. After this Hundred Years' War, they remained bitter enemies. Warfare pitted Catholic states against Protestant states during the Reformation for another 80 years, starting in the 1560s.

During this time, European states underwent a military revolution. They built up large and powerful armies and navies and supplied them with top-quality weapons. Larger cannons appeared not only on the battlefield but also on ships. This military buildup took money—lots of money. European states raised massive amounts of **revenue** through taxation and borrowing. To collect and distribute revenue and otherwise administer the state's affairs, complex **bureaucracies** arose. Those bureaucracies also managed the voyages of exploration that several nation-states undertook. Like the revival of Europe, those explorations would have economic and military aspects.

nation-state a politically independent state whose people have a common culture and nationality

sovereign self-governing and independent

revenue income used to fund a nation's expenses

bureaucracy a complex system of officials and workers who manage the activities of a government

Competition among European nation-states led to technological innovations in weaponry. Nation-states began to fortify their navies with powerful weapons, such as cannons.

13.3 Europeans Look Outward

As early as the 1400s, economic competition led some European states to begin looking outward, beyond their shores. They had trade in mind. They knew that trade could bring wealth, and with wealth came power. The first of those states was Portugal.

The explorers who sailed south from Portugal along the western coast of Africa hoped to find gold, and they did. But some leaders and thinkers in Portugal, and in its neighbor, Spain, had a longer-term goal. They wanted to bypass the Muslim and Italian traders who controlled the luxury goods arriving in the Mediterranean from Asia.

Portugal led the Age of Exploration. Its rulers first sent explorers along the coast of Africa. Later, European explorers voyaged across the Atlantic and Pacific Oceans. The crew of one Portuguese expedition sailed completely around the world.

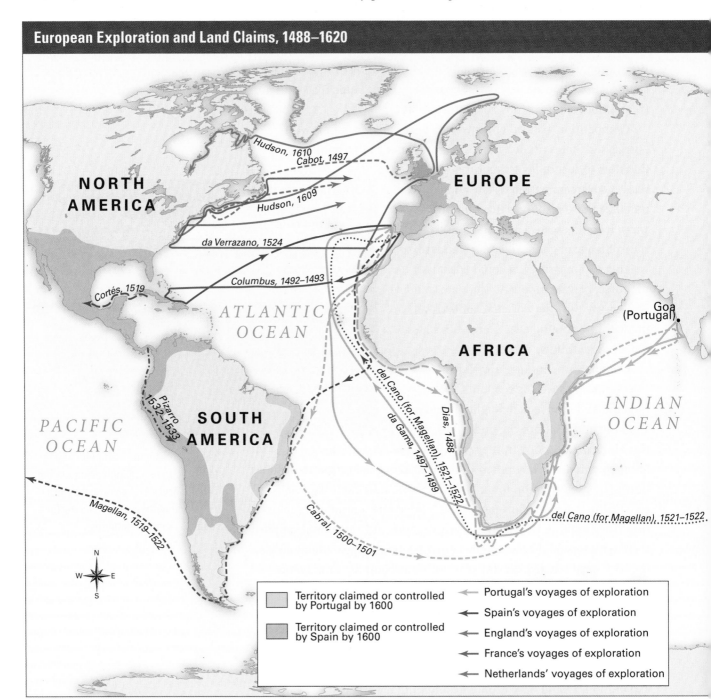

European Exploration and Land Claims, 1488–1620

NORTH AMERICA

EUROPE

AFRICA

SOUTH AMERICA

ATLANTIC OCEAN

PACIFIC OCEAN

INDIAN OCEAN

Goa (Portugal)

Hudson, 1610
Cabot, 1497
Hudson, 1609
da Verrazano, 1524
Columbus, 1492–1493
Cortés, 1519
Pizarro, 1532–1533
Magellan, 1519–1522
del Cano (for Magellan), 1521–1522
da Gama, 1497–1499
Dias, 1488
Cabral, 1500–1501
del Cano (for Magellan), 1521–1522

N W E S

▢ Territory claimed or controlled by Portugal by 1600	← Portugal's voyages of exploration
▦ Territory claimed or controlled by Spain by 1600	← Spain's voyages of exploration
	← England's voyages of exploration
	← France's voyages of exploration
	← Netherlands' voyages of exploration

They wanted direct access to that Asian trade. More to the point, they wanted the profit from that trade.

Reasons for Exploration   The pursuit of profit was the main reason for all European exploration. Two related motives, competitiveness and the craving for Asian goods, also played important roles. Other factors, too, pushed European states to explore and expand. A new type of ship, the caravel, made it possible to sail against winds and currents and survive long voyages across stormy seas. Curiosity about the unknown world and an adventurous spirit also motivated Europeans.

A desire to spread Christianity was one factor that motivated European exploration. The Jesuit religious order played a central role in foreign missionary work. Here, a Jesuit missionary accompanying a Spanish expedition forcibly converts a Native American to Christianity.

Religion was yet another prime factor. Europeans wished to bring Christianity to non-Christians. They believed that doing so would save those people's souls. Christians were also concerned about the growing power of another religion, Islam. They had tried, and failed, to weaken that power through the Crusades, the religious wars of the late Middle Ages. By the mid-1400s, a powerful Muslim empire led by the Ottoman Turks threatened to overrun Europe. The Ottomans would soon control all overland trade moving west into the Mediterranean Sea. By bypassing the Mediterranean gateway controlled by Muslims, Christian states in Europe could strike a blow against their enemy.

Portuguese Ships Reach India
Portuguese explorers had royal support. One of the king's sons personally sponsored the early explorations of the African coast. His name was Henrique, but he became known as Prince Henry the Navigator. He did not join any voyages of discovery. He did, however, help launch a steady stream of explorers who would eventually open a sea route to India.

ASIA

PACIFIC OCEAN

Magellan died, 1521

Magellan, 1519–1522

•Malacca (Portugal)

AUSTRALIA

After sailing past West Africa's Cape Bojador in 1434, the Portuguese kept exploring southward. Along the coast, they traded for gold, and they also looked for slaves. At first, the Portuguese raided villages in order to capture and carry off Africans, but violent African resistance to raiding limited the practice. By 1450, the Portuguese had begun actively bartering for slaves. Muslim merchants and local African rulers would gather captives taken in raids in the interior. They would trade them to the Portuguese, usually for cloth but also for grain, silver, and horses.

Profits from the gold and slave trades financed further voyages and the establishment of trading posts and forts at regular intervals. In this way, the Portuguese worked their way slowly down the western coast of Africa. It was not until 1488 that the first Portuguese sailor, Bartolomeu Dias, sailed around southernmost Africa and into the Indian Ocean. In 1498, Portugal's Vasco da Gama reached India, establishing what would become a well-traveled route from Europe to the riches of Asia. On a voyage to India two years later, a fleet of ships under Pedro Cabral swept far to the west while rounding Africa—and ended up in Brazil. Portugal claimed that land.

Early Exploration of the Americas   Several years before Da Gama reached India, an Italian sailor named Christopher Columbus had a bold idea. He knew that the world was round. Instead of sailing east to get to the Indies, he decided to sail west, directly across the Atlantic Ocean. Based on some faulty thinking, he believed that Asia was a lot closer to Europe than it actually was. He wrote, "Between the edge of Spain and the beginning of India, the sea is short and can be crossed in a matter of a few days." Columbus persuaded Spain's monarchs, Isabella and Ferdinand, to fund a voyage westward. Like the Portuguese, they wanted access to the silks and spices of the Indies without having to enrich the Muslims who controlled the trade routes from Asia to the Mediterranean.

This Italian postage stamp celebrated the 500th anniversary of the first voyage of Christopher Columbus.

In 1492, Columbus made his first voyage to the Americas. He left Spain in August with three ships— the *Niña,* the *Pinta,* and the *Santa Maria.* Showing his skill as a sailor, he headed south to the Canary Islands, where he picked up the trade winds that blew westward across the Atlantic. On October 12, Columbus reached an island in the Bahamas, which he called San Salvador. He later sailed to Cuba and Hispaniola. Columbus called the native peoples Indians, because he believed that he had reached the Indies. He would maintain that belief through three additional voyages.

Spain claimed the right to trade and settle in the lands Columbus had found. The pope, who was Spanish, supported their claim. He granted them control of "all islands and mainland found and to be found . . . towards the south and west." This vague language alarmed the Portuguese, who wanted to protect their rights in Africa and along the sea route around Africa. In 1494, the two countries negotiated the **Treaty of Tordesillas** (tawr-day-SEEL-yahs). This agreement drew an imaginary line from the North Pole, through the mid-Atlantic Ocean, across Brazil, to the South Pole. This "line of demarcation" gave Spain all rights to lands west of the line and gave Portugal all rights to lands east of the line.

The Italian merchant and sailor Amerigo Vespucci made two trips across the Atlantic, in 1499 for Spain and in 1501 for Portugal. After his second voyage, which took him to Brazil, he wrote a number of letters about what he saw. In them, he described the western lands as a "new world." A mapmaker in 1507 split the lands into two continents, and he named the southern one "America" after Vespucci. The name stuck and was gradually applied to both continents.

Spanish Conquests in the Americas

Spain continued to send explorers to the Americas. In 1513, Juan Ponce de León landed on the shores of Florida. The same year, Vasco Núñez de Balboa crossed a narrow strip of land—the Isthmus of Panama—and came upon a vast sea. It was the Pacific Ocean.

To this point, the mission of Spanish explorers was trade and discovery. That changed with the expedition commanded by Hernán Cortés.

Cortés had conquest in mind when he landed in Mexico in 1519. He and his small army of **conquistadors,** or conquerors, marched inland with their crossbows, gunpowder weapons, and horses. They fought some Native American groups and forged alliances with others.

Cortés learned of the dominant Aztec Empire, centered in the city of Tenochtitlán. He set out for the city, aiming to conquer the Aztecs. After a series of negotiations, bloody battles, and retreats, the Spaniards and their Indian allies made a final assault on the city in May 1521. Three months later, they had achieved victory, at a cost of more than 100,000 Aztec lives.

A similar fate awaited another great civilization, the Incas of Peru. Weakened by civil war, the Incas fell to Spanish conquistador Francisco Pizarro. In 1532, with a small force of foot-soldiers and cavalry, Pizarro captured the Inca ruler. The Spaniards later destroyed the Inca capital at Cuzco. They looted the city and carried away huge amounts of gold and silver.

Treaty of Tordesillas agreement that split all not-yet-explored lands between Spain and Portugal

conquistador Spanish conqueror of the Americas

Francisco Pizarro was a Spanish conquistador who conquered the Inca civilization of Peru. He was able to do this with a very small force of men by taking the Inca emperor, Atahualpa, hostage. This illustration shows Pizarro leading his exhibition through the Andes mountains.

Ferdinand Magellan captained an expedition that would become the first to circumnavigate the Earth. Magellan sailed from Spain with five ships and 270 men, but only one ship and 17 original crew members made it all the way around the world and back to Spain. Magellan himself was killed in the Philippines.

Further Voyages of Exploration   Spain had a lengthy head start over its competitors in claiming territory in the Americas. But England, France, and the Netherlands all took an interest in this "new world." Their early explorations focused on North America.

The king of England sent John Cabot, an Italian navigator, west across the ocean in 1497. In the North Atlantic off the coast of Canada, Cabot found an abundance of fish, a resource that would attract fishermen from England, Spain, Portugal, and France. But Cabot failed in his mission to find a route through the Americas to Asia—what came to be known as the Northwest Passage.

The French mariner Jacques Cartier also sought in vain for a way around the American land barrier. In 1535, he sailed up the Saint Lawrence River as far as present-day Montreal. Based on Cartier's explorations, France would later claim Canada.

The English navigator Henry Hudson, sailing for the Netherlands in 1609, explored the Hudson River, thinking it could be the Northwest Passage. Sailing for England the next year, he searched the shores of Hudson Bay. But again he failed to find a way through the continent.

Meanwhile, the Spanish mariner Ferdinand Magellan had set out in 1519 to find a southern route around the Americas to Asia. He succeeded in sailing from the Atlantic around the southern tip of South America and into the Pacific. Magellan reached the Philippine islands in 1521, where he died in an attack by native peoples. The remaining members of his crew continued the voyage westward through the Indian Ocean, around Africa, and back to Spain, thus becoming the first to **circumnavigate**—sail completely around—the globe.

circumnavigate travel completely around

13.4 The Atlantic World

European exploration, conquest, and colonization of the Americas affected all four continents bordering the Atlantic Ocean. It resulted in a distinct Atlantic world, in which European states used the peoples and resources of the Americas and Africa to boost their economies. Throughout the Americas, native peoples and Africans suffered under the dominating Europeans.

American Colonies   In the 1500s and 1600s, Spain expanded throughout what we today call Latin America. The Spanish Empire included the West Indies (the islands of the Caribbean Sea), Mexico, Central America, and South America except for Brazil. Spain focused on extracting resources from its colonies.

One important resource was silver. From the mid-1500s onward, mining—of silver and also gold—became a major industry in Mexico and in Peru. These precious metals had to be extracted from the earth by hand. For this difficult, dangerous work, the Spanish turned to the native peoples, forcing them to labor in the mines. Toiling long hours, Indian laborers dug out the metal ore and then carried heavy baskets of it to the surface.

The amount of silver that Spain took from American mines far outweighed the amount of gold. That silver brought the nation great wealth—and great power. King Philip IV of Spain declared, "In silver lies the security and strength of my monarchy."

Spain used some of its enormous supply of silver to buy imported goods, such as grains from the Baltic and spices from Asia. It also shipped some to its colony in the Philippines, where it was used to buy manufactured products and Asian luxury goods. Much of the rest of Spain's silver went to pay for the series of wars that it fought in the 1500s and 1600s.

The Spanish forced natives to perform grueling and dangerous work mining precious metals in the New World. Millions of laborers in Spanish gold and silver mines died from overwork and exposure to the elements.

A second key resource extracted from Spanish America was sugar. Sugarcane thrived in the soil and climate of the West Indies, and the worldwide demand for sugar kept increasing. As a result, Spanish growers established a number of sugar plantations on the islands. As in the mining industry, Indians served as forced labor—as slaves—on these plantations.

During the same period, the Portuguese colonized Brazil. They based their early economy on brazilwood, which they cut and shipped to Europe. This wood was a source of red dye (and of the colony's name). Starting in the late 1500s, the Portuguese made far greater profits from sugar. Like the Spanish, the Portuguese in Brazil relied mainly on the native population to perform the grueling work necessary to harvest and process sugarcane. By 1600, Brazil produced more sugar than anyplace else in the world. In 1695, a huge gold strike in an inland region of Brazil boosted the colony's economy further.

Spanish and Portuguese success did not go unnoticed by other European states. In the late 1500s, the English and the Dutch (people of the Netherlands) established a presence in the Americas. First they followed the Spanish into the Caribbean, looking for profitable ventures. There, Dutch and English pirates attacked Spanish ships and made off with silver and other precious cargo. Later they set up bases in the Caribbean islands to support their attacks on shipping. The French did the same.

In time, these three northwestern European states established sugar plantations on land that they had claimed. By the mid-1600s they were competing with Spain on two levels. They were exporting agricultural products, including sugar, to Europe, and they were also providing Spain's American colonies with most of their manufactured goods. At the same time, the French, English, and Dutch also had colonies of their own on the mainland of North America—in coastal Canada, Virginia, New York, and New England.

Many Indians, forced to work in the mines and on the sugar plantations, died from accidents and from overwork. But many more died from disease. In fact, all over the Americas the native people were dying of diseases carried to their lands by explorers and settlers. Because they had been isolated from the rest of the world, the Indians of the Americas were never exposed to smallpox, measles, and other diseases. They had no resistance to them. In what historians call the **Great Dying,** these diseases killed many millions of Indians, perhaps half of all Indians in the Americas at the time of Columbus's arrival.

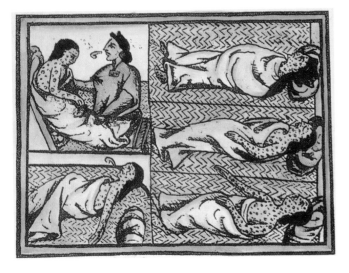

Smallpox, which was brought to Mexico by the Spaniards, ravaged the native Aztec population. This 16th-century illustration shows victims of a smallpox epidemic being treated by an Aztec medicine man.

Great Dying the devastation of American Indian populations by diseases brought over from Europe

The Trans-Atlantic Slave System

As a result of the Great Dying, the Europeans needed more labor for their plantations. At first the British (as they were known after England merged with Scotland in 1707) tried using indentured labor, as did the French. In the system of **indentured servitude,** a person agreed to work for a period of time, often four to seven years, in return for passage to the Americas, food, and a place to live.

Indentured servants from Britain found the work on West Indies sugar plantations to be brutal. Many of them died. They had a similar experience on the tobacco and rice plantations in Britain's North American colonies.

African people provided the labor on sugar plantations in the New World. Here, African slaves plant sugarcane while being supervised by a white overseer.

Since 1500, the Portuguese had been shipping a limited number of enslaved Africans to the Caribbean. Africans seemed better able to survive as laborers than American Indians. They could do the exhausting and dangerous work, and they had a greater immunity to disease. For these reasons, European mine and plantation owners began to import many more enslaved Africans. Between around 1600 and 1650, more than 250,000 Africans were forced to migrate to the Spanish colonies. Another 150,000 went to Brazil.

For many years the Portuguese controlled trade along coastal Africa. Later, the English, French, and Dutch also established trading posts on the Atlantic coast. From there European merchants built relationships with African rulers willing to trade slaves. Together they set up a system for enslaving Africans and shipping them from Africa to the Americas.

The Africans and the Europeans had a fairly equal role in this trans-Atlantic slave system. Africans managed the gathering of slaves. Slavery was already widespread in African society, and trading in slaves across the Sahara had been going on for centuries. Some slaves were kidnapped in raids by African slavers. Others were made slaves by some legal judgment or to repay a debt. But most slaves were taken captive in war.

As European demand for slaves increased in the late 1600s, a few states in the interior of Africa began to focus on finding and delivering slaves. The production of slaves became their main economic activity. Coastal African states tended to serve as **middlemen** in the slave trade. They established trade routes from the interior to the coast and handled the exchange with European traders.

indentured servitude a system by which a person agreed to work for a period of time in return for being transported to the Americas

middleman a person who provides a service that links two people or groups

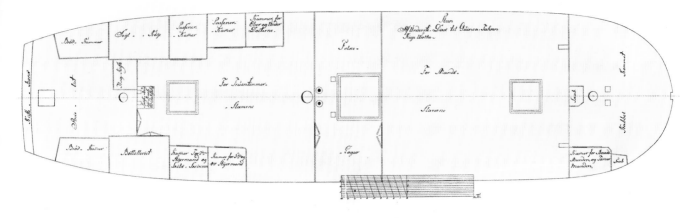

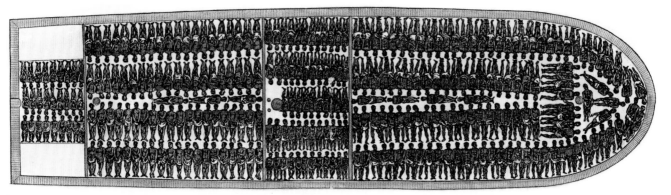

This deck plan shows how enslaved Africans were forcibly held on slave ships in the 1700s. People were crowded together to make room for as many slaves as possible. Merchants expected that many would inevitably die on the journey.

triangular trade a colonial pattern of trade that involved the transport of slaves from Africa to the Americas, sugar and other products from the Americas to Europe, and manufactured goods from Europe to Africa

European ships carried the enslaved Africans across the Atlantic. The voyage is known as the Middle Passage. It was the middle part of the slave's overall journey—and perhaps the most horrifying. The slave ship's crew packed their cargo of Africans into the hold. Often they had no room to stand or stretch. To prevent revolts, male slaves were often chained in place. The food was limited and of poor quality, and conditions were unsanitary. Disease spread quickly. Many of the Africans died on the voyage, which could take from three weeks to three months.

Before 1650, Portuguese ships transported most of the enslaved Africans heading to the Americas. The majority went to mainland Spanish America. After 1650, northern European slave traders took over much of the business, and their main destination shifted to sugar plantations in Brazil and the West Indies. Later, Britain would dominate the highly profitable slave trade, transporting slaves throughout the Americas, including to plantations in their North American colonies. In the 1700s alone, some 6 million enslaved Africans were forced to migrate to the Americas.

The transport of enslaved Africans to the Americas was just the first "side" of what is known as the **triangular trade**. In American ports, the merchants traded their slaves for sugar, silver, tobacco, and other products of the mines and plantations. Then, the shipping of those raw materials to Europe formed the second side of the triangle.

In Europe, they picked up manufactured goods such as textiles and weapons, as well as raw metal, rum, and tobacco. The third side of the triangle was the voyage to Africa to trade those goods for slaves.

The Columbian Exchange The trade between Europe and the Americas had consequences beyond just boosting European economies. It launched the **Columbian Exchange,** a two-way distribution of plants and animals named after Columbus. Until the arrival of Columbus, the peoples of the Americas were isolated from the rest of the world. That isolation meant that they had no immunity to European diseases. But it also meant that many of their plants and animals were unique to the Americas.

Europeans took a special interest in American food plants. These included maize (corn), potatoes, beans, squashes, pumpkins, peanuts, avocadoes, tomatoes, chili peppers, and cocoa. Merchants carried these to Europe and, from there, to Africa and Asia. Over time, these plants helped increase food production and improve the diets of people around the world.

The Columbian Exchange also brought new plants and animals into the "new world" from the "old world." Peaches, oranges, bananas, sugarcane, coffee, oats, and wheat all became important crops in the Americas. Europeans also introduced beasts of burden and new sources of protein in the form of horses, cattle, pigs, goats, and sheep. European agriculture and the grazing needs of horses, cattle, and sheep had a great impact on the natural environment. Much land was converted from forest to farm and pasture.

Some historians include people, along with their customs and ideas, in the Columbian Exchange. Around 1.4 million Europeans and more than five times that many Africans had migrated to the Americas by 1800.

In Latin America the intermixing of Europeans, Africans, and Indians created a distinctive colonial society. That society was stratified, or formed into classes, according to place of origin, race, skin color, and other factors. At the top of the social pyramid stood those born in Europe. The lower classes included Indians, Africans, and people of mixed blood.

A different kind of class structure evolved in colonial North America. Its basis was economic, with white merchants and planters at the top of the social hierarchy. Within the colonies, Indians and Africans had little, if any, social prestige or political power.

Columbian Exchange the transfer of plants, animals, and diseases between the eastern and western hemispheres

These tortillas and salsa are made from ingredients that were part of the Columbian Exchange.

13.5 Europeans in the Indies

As earlier chapters explained, the collapse of Mongol rule in Asia, starting in the 1300s, led to the rise of large, centrally governed states. In the centuries that followed, Muslim empires stretched from India across Southwest Asia and North Africa. China moved westward into Central Asia. Russia expanded eastward. These powerful states, with much to gain from trade, helped keep Asia's overland trade routes secure.

During the same period, European states pioneered the sea route around Africa and then steadily extended oceanic trade throughout the Indian Ocean and east to China. Overland routes funneled trade goods to dozens of European trading posts planted along the coast. For the first time in history, Europe, Africa, Asia, and the Americas were directly connected by a global trading network.

Beginning in the 1700s, the Chinese government confined all trade with Europeans to the southern port city of Canton. European merchants built large warehouses by the Canton harbor, shown here in a Chinese painting from the 1700s. Europeans coveted luxury goods from China, such as the fine painted porcelain which was produced in the region around Canton.

Portugal Gains Access to Asian Maritime Trade

The great powers of Asia focused on expanding their land-based empires. They did take part in maritime, or sea-based, trade, but they claimed no political right of ownership over the seas. Europeans were more possessive. In 1499, Vasco da Gama laid claim to the entire Indian Ocean for Portugal. The Portuguese set about building a trading empire, based on territorial rights granted them in the Treaty of Tordesillas.

Portugal's main goal was to sail to the Indies, trade for spices and other luxury goods, and sail back home. There was just one problem. The Asians did not need or want most European goods. Instead of exchanging products, Europeans would have to pay for Asian goods with money—mainly silver.

One option was to take part in the intra-Asian trade. Some merchants began carrying foods and other ordinary goods from one part of the Indies to another, making a profit on each trade. Over time, they built up cargoes that could be exchanged for fine spices (black pepper, ginger, cinnamon, nutmeg, mace, and cloves), Indian textiles, Chinese porcelain, and other Asian goods highly prized by Europeans.

To conduct trade, Portuguese merchants needed land bases. They often used force to get them. By the 1500s, European long-distance cargo ships came equipped with cannons. The Portuguese used those guns to attack and take control of key coastal towns. In this way, they captured Goa in India, Hormuz in the Persian Gulf, and Malacca on the Malay Peninsula. Malacca was the center of the East Indian spice trade. It also controlled the narrow Strait of Malacca. This led from the Indian Ocean to the Pacific and thus served as the eastern gateway to China and Japan.

The Portuguese used their naval advantage to dominate shipping in the Indian Ocean. They overpowered Asian merchant vessels and stole their cargoes. They blocked access to traditional shipping routes, too. One such route carried spices and other luxury goods through the Red Sea and across Egypt to the Mediterranean. The Portuguese never established a complete monopoly of the coastal trade, because Asian merchants fought back. Some armed their ships. Others changed their trade routes. Over time, however, the Portuguese gained control of a large part of the intra-Asian trade.

The European Model of Expansion   By the mid-1500s, the Portuguese had established an effective model of expansion into Asian trade. The model had three basic parts.

1. The Portuguese relied on their superior ships, armed with gunpowder weapons, to establish land bases and achieve control of the seas.
2. At their land bases they established trading posts, called factories. These commercial centers managed Portuguese trade and finances in the region.
3. Finally, they built fortresses to protect their factories and the small colonies that arose nearby.

By 1600, the Portuguese had a string of more than 50 fortified coastal trading posts from East Africa all the way to Japan. To this time, the only other European state competing with Portugal in Asia was Spain, which controlled the Philippines. Soon, however, Portugal had a lot more company in the Indies. In the 1600s, the Dutch and the English, by applying the same model of expansion, would nearly eliminate Portugal from the Asian trade.

Competing for the Asian Trade   The English, in 1600, and the Dutch, in 1602, each formed an East India Company to carry out long-distance trade with Asia. The government of England gave the English East India Company, and only that company, the right to trade in Asia. The government of the Netherlands authorized its Dutch East India Company not only to conduct trade but also to carry out political negotiations and to engage in warfare. The Dutch would fight to limit the success of the English in the Indies and to eliminate the Portuguese from the region.

Like the Portuguese, the Dutch took a military approach to creating a trading empire in the Indies. They hired experienced naval officers to help establish and maintain their outposts. Negotiations with local Asian officials went much more smoothly when a ship bristling with cannons anchored just offshore. The Dutch East India Company set up factories in India and Japan and points in between, but they focused their efforts on the East Indies.

These copper coins were issued by the British East India Company, which was given sole right to trade in Asia by the English government. The company traded in India and the Persian Gulf, where these Arabic-inscribed coins might have been used.

By the end of the 1700s, the British had become the dominant trading power in Asia. Chinese tea was one of their most important trade goods. In this image, dockworkers unload tea in London.

In the East Indies the Dutch hoped to monopolize the spice trade by taking control of the Spice Islands, now part of eastern Indonesia. There, most of the world's supply of nutmeg, mace, and cloves grew. First the Dutch wrested control of the islands from the Portuguese. Then they used force and threats of force to compel local leaders to cooperate. In one group of islands, they slaughtered the native people and took over the production of their nutmeg and mace, bringing in enslaved Africans to cultivate the trees that yielded the spices. Then, in 1641, they seized Malacca from the Portuguese.

The English East India Company, at least at first, took a less violent approach to the Asian trade. Its traders sought permission before locating a factory on foreign territory. Kept out of the East Indies by the Dutch, the English focused on trade with India. There they negotiated for trading rights with the Mughal Empire and local Indian officials.

English merchants followed a fairly standard trading procedure. They used silver to buy Indian textiles and then traded the textiles in the East Indies for pepper and other spices, which they shipped to England. They also carried Indian cotton and indigo, a plant that yielded a blue dye, to Europe.

Some 200 years after the Portuguese arrived in the Indies, European merchants were still confined to coastal trading posts and various islands. In 1757, however, the British took control of the Indian territory of Bengal after Mughal power collapsed. In the years that followed, Britain would gain control of all of India and absorb it into its colonial empire.

The India trade brought the British great wealth, helping them expand into other parts of Asia. Economic power gave them military power—the ability to build ships, equip them with weapons, and engage them in warfare with their competitors. The British ousted the Portuguese from ports such as Hormuz and battled the Dutch off and on throughout the 1600s.

In the 1700s, European demand for spices fell, severely reducing the Dutch East India Company's profits. The demand for Indian textiles, Chinese tea, and other goods rose. The British were well-positioned to profit from trading in those goods. After the French general Napoleon Bonaparte conquered the Netherlands in 1795, the British took over most Dutch outposts in the Indies. Great Britain now dominated the Asian trade.

mercantilism an economic philosophy that favored self-sufficiency, called for stockpiling gold and silver, encouraged exports, and discouraged imports

13.6 Transformation of European Economies

In the first global age, the European states that engaged in long-distance trade created new economic strategies. Those strategies represented early stages in the growth of modern capitalism. The Spanish, Portuguese, Dutch, English, and French merchants who shipped goods among Europe, the Americas, Africa, and Asia were merchant capitalists. They accumulated capital, or wealth, through trade. Trade made countries wealthier, too, and stronger. For this reason, governments established merchant-friendly policies.

John Locke was an influential English philosopher and political thinker in the 1600s. His ideas influenced the writing of the U.S. Constitution. He also supported the economic philosophy known as mercantilism.

Mercantilism   The philosophy behind those policies came to be known as **mercantilism**. Mercantilism evolved out of the intense economic competition among European states. A major focus of that competition involved trying to build stockpiles of bullion—gold and silver. English thinker John Locke offered this observation on the role of bullion:

> *Riches do not consist in having more Gold and Silver, but in having more in proportion, than the rest of the World, or than our Neighbours, . . . who, sharing the Gold and Silver of the World in a less proportion, want [lack] the means of Plenty and Power, and so are Poorer.*
> —John Locke, from
> *Lowering of Interest*, 1691

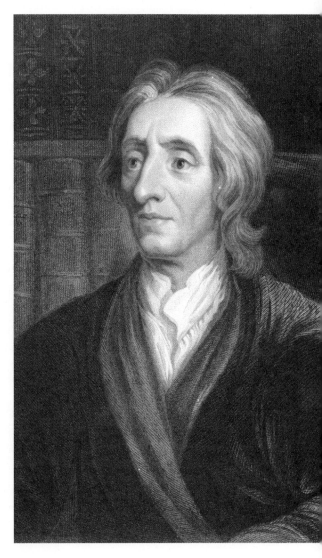

Mercantilists aimed to make their country richer and more powerful at the expense of other countries. To increase national wealth, governments allied themselves with businesses. They founded colonies to supply industries with raw materials and provide a market for finished goods—the goal being self-sufficiency. This goal also called for exporting as much as possible while importing as little as possible. Exports of goods brought gold and silver into a country. Imports sent gold and silver to other countries. To discourage imports, states placed taxes on them.

In the Atlantic world, Spain and Portugal paid huge amounts of silver and gold for manufactured goods. This trade made Dutch, English, and French mercantilists happy. Trade with Asia frustrated them, because it drained bullion out of their treasuries. From 1600 to 1800, the nations of western Europe shipped some 21,000 tons of bullion, mainly silver, to Asia.

Capitalism   Mercantilism is often viewed as an early form of capitalism. Like mercantilism, it is a difficult concept to define. In its ideal form, **capitalism** is an economic system in which all resources are privately owned and markets determine how those resources are distributed.

During the mercantilist age, with the steady expansion of trade, several important features of capitalism appeared. One was the profit motive. European states began looking outward in hopes of making profits from foreign commerce. Another was the accumulation of capital. By applying mercantilist principles, those states built up their stocks of gold and silver. A third feature was financial innovation. The Europeans improved credit techniques, finding more efficient ways of making capital available to business.

Bank loans funded **entrepreneurs,** people willing to take the risks of starting and running a business. Entrepreneurs launched the East India Companies. The English and Dutch East India Companies were both founded as joint-stock companies. They raised capital by selling stock, or shares of ownership in the company. The owners held the stock jointly.

This new form of business organization was a forerunner of the modern corporation. The East India Companies were run, not by their investors, but by elected directors. They had access to the large amounts of capital needed to fund costly long-distance trading voyages. A round-trip to Asia could take three years. The East India Companies could afford to wait that long. When such a voyage was successful, all the owners profited.

capitalism an economic system in which all resources are privately owned and markets determine how those resources are distributed

entrepreneur a person willing to take the risks involved in starting or running a business

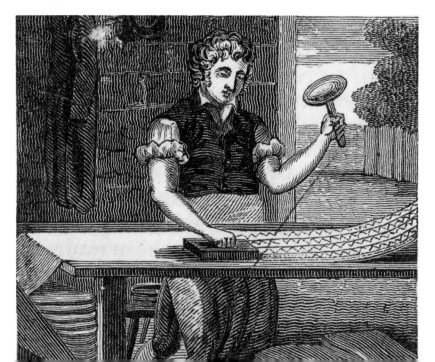

Calico cloth was cheap cotton cloth imported from the Indian city of Calcutta, from which it got its name. Here an English printer decorates plain calico cloth by hand. Some calico cloth was printed in India before it was exported.

Major Shift in Demand Black pepper remained a highly sought-after item of foreign trade well into the 1600s. European consumption of rare spices, indigo, and fine Chinese silks also stayed high. In the late 1600s and early 1700s, however, consumer demand shifted away from luxury goods. Europeans imported greater amounts of sugar and tobacco from the Americas, tea and textiles from Asia. The combination of imported sugar from the West Indies and tea and porcelain from China gave rise to a new tradition—the tea party.

The shift in demand may best be reflected in the flood of cotton textiles from India, including cheap calico cloth. Not all of the cotton fabric stayed in Europe. Merchants re-exported much of it to the Americas, Africa, and the Middle East. The growing worldwide demand for cotton cloth had consequences beyond boosting Asian imports. Competition for this market helped trigger a revolution in the way goods were manufactured. England's textile industry, bolstered by the mechanization of spinning and weaving, would be the driving force in that Industrial Revolution.

Summary

In this lesson, you read about factors and events that led to Europe's dominance in the first global age.

Cultural Interaction European colonizers imposed their customs and religion on the native peoples of the Americas and on the enslaved Africans forced to migrate to the Americas. The Columbian Exchange involved the distribution of previously unknown foods across the continents. Trade with Asia introduced European consumers to new products, such as tea.

Political Structures Sovereign nation-states rose in Europe as kings maintained power over local nobles and the Church. Through conquest and trade, several nation-states established empires.

Economic Structures Europeans followed a mercantilist philosophy, which encouraged exports and discouraged imports. A state operating under a mercantilist system obtained resources from its colonies. Those colonies also served as markets for the state's manufactured goods. Europe's increased profits from foreign trade led to the accumulation of capital, or wealth. The amassing of wealth was a key factor in the expansion of capitalism that took place during the first global age.

Social Structures European settlement in Latin America brought about a stratification of society. People born in Europe occupied the highest social class.

Human-Environment Interaction Europeans migrated to and colonized the Americas. The diseases that they brought with them killed a large number of the native peoples. They forced millions of enslaved Africans to cross the Atlantic to work on plantations and in mines. Europeans cut down forests in the Americas in order to cultivate crops. They greatly expanded pasture land in order to feed the cattle, horses, and other domesticated animals that were new to the Americas. Europeans also extracted resources from the land through the mining of gold and silver.

Era Overview: An Age of Global Revolutions, 1700s–1914

What forces drove the revolutions of the 1700s, 1800s, and early 1900s?

14.1 Introduction

In 1776, a group of 13 British colonies launched the American Revolution by publishing the Declaration of Independence. It was a historic event. The Americans chose to "dissolve the political bands" that had tied them to Great Britain and secure their own rights to "Life, Liberty and the pursuit of Happiness." This decision paved the way for political revolutions in France and throughout Latin America.

Another historically noteworthy, though less earth-shattering, publication appeared that same year in Great Britain. It was a book called *The Wealth of Nations* by Adam Smith. This book marked the beginning of economics as a social science. In it Smith formulated economic laws that, he believed, guided the decisions of individuals as they took part in the exchange of goods. Those laws focused on the economic importance of free competition among individuals who were all pursuing their own self-interest.

Smith's laws were put to the test in the century that followed as several countries shifted the basis of their economy from agriculture to industry. This radical change, known as the Industrial Revolution, had already begun in Britain by the time Smith published his book. It would later spread to other Western European nations, the United States, Japan, and Russia.

Smith had no real notion of the future impact of **industrialization**. This conversion to large-scale manufacturing would change not just the workplace but society at large. It would also help fuel a new era of empire building. Industrialized nations had the wealth and power— military as well as economic—to engage in intense competition with one another to claim new territory in Asia and Africa.

Themes

Cultural Interaction Imperialism in Western, industrialized states led to the introduction of new technologies and belief systems into Africa and Asia.

Political Structures Revolutions of the late 1700s and early 1800s overturned existing political structures and encouraged a wave of nationalism across Europe and beyond.

Economic Structures The Industrial Revolution shifted the focus of Western economies from agriculture to industry and encouraged the rise of industrial capitalism.

Social Structures The Industrial Revolution brought great social changes with it, from a shift in where and how people worked to the rise of a wage-earning working class.

Human-Environment Interaction During the 1800s, industrial centers attracted migrants not only from rural areas but also from other countries.

◄ The American Declaration of Independence was signed in Independence Hall in Philadelphia.

political revolution a seizure of government by people intent on replacing the existing political system

14.2 Political Revolutions

Through much of history, monarchs ruled with the support of other members of society's privileged classes. Most of the world's peoples accepted that state of affairs—even some of the Enlightenment thinkers who put forward radical ideas about government and people's natural rights. Starting in the late 1700s, however, radical ideas became reality. Political revolutions began to replace rule by a monarch with rule "by the people." Of these, the American Revolution was the first.

The American Revolution   A political revolution is a seizure of government by people intent on replacing the existing political system. It is something that comes about over time, as various forces gradually build to an explosion. In the case of the American colonies, the path to revolution began in 1763, at the end of another conflict, the French and Indian War.

Before then, Britain had given its 13 North American colonies substantial freedom. The king and Parliament had other things to worry about, namely defending against its rivals France and Spain. The French and Indian War, known in Europe as the Seven Years' War, was just the latest in a series of costly international conflicts. Britain's victory in that war ousted France from North America and gave British leaders time to focus on problems with their Atlantic coast colonies.

One issue involved control. The Americans enjoyed considerable self-government and economic freedom. Britain moved to exert tighter central authority over the colonies. Another issue involved money. The French and Indian War had drained Britain's treasury. To pay for the ongoing defense of the colonies, the British levied a series of taxes on Americans. Many colonists, having no direct link to Parliament, decried this "taxation without representation." Mounting resistance to British policies ultimately led to the revolution.

This painting depicts the American Revolutionary War battle at Bunker Hill, which took place in 1775. Political revolutions influenced by the American Revolution would occur throughout the world in the years to come.

The Americans had no reason to believe that they could defeat Britain, the strongest military power in the world. They endured several humiliating routs before victories at Trenton and Saratoga raised their spirits. The latter victory persuaded France to support General George Washington and his Continental Army with troops, supplies, and warships. The Spanish and Dutch also helped by keeping British naval forces busy in Europe. The British surrender at Yorktown came after a French blockade of the Virginia coast helped American ground troops trap Britain's main army.

The Declaration of Independence listed numerous reasons for American separation from Britain. But they all came down to issues of freedom and liberty. As Patrick Henry famously said, "Give me liberty or give me death!" The desire for freedom and liberty also played an important role in the Federal Convention that followed the war, in 1787.

The resulting United States Constitution, and the Bill of Rights attached to it, created a novel form of government. It was a democracy based on principles of **republicanism**—separation of powers and representation of the people through their elected officials. Republicanism would also emerge as a driving force of the French Revolution.

republicanism belief in a form of government marked by separation of powers and representation of the people through elected officials

liberalism a political ideology favoring individual political and economic freedom, with limits on state power

The French Revolution   A French officer, the Marquis de Lafayette, led the American army that trapped the British near Yorktown. After returning to France, he played a key role in the French Revolution. That revolution began in 1789, triggered by a financial crisis. Mounting debt resulting from continual warfare, including support for the American Revolution, threatened to bankrupt France.

To resolve the crisis, the king called a rare meeting of the Estates-General, a representative assembly consisting of the three French "estates," or classes. During the meeting, the common people, known as the Third Estate, took over. These educated, working-class representatives demanded political, economic, and social rights denied them by the two privileged classes—the nobles and the clergy.

Some nobles, such as Lafayette, worked with the Third Estate. Lafayette drafted the Declaration of the Rights of Man and the Citizen, a core statement of French revolutionary principles. Like the founding political documents of the United States, this Declaration reflected a liberal philosophy. **Liberalism** favors individual political and economic freedom as well as equality. The demands of the Third Estate echoed through the streets of Paris and soon took the form of a people's uprising. Violence spread to the countryside, where peasants attacked their landlords and destroyed property.

Mob violence played a central role in the French Revolution. Ordinary people in both Paris and the French countryside took up arms either for or against the revolution.

coup d'état a sudden violent overthrow of government; translated as "a blow against the state"

France's neighbors feared that their own citizens might rise up and overturn their privileged classes. They also feared the French army, and with good reason. In 1792, French forces attacked Austria and then invaded Italy. By the end of the next year, France had enlisted more than a million new soldiers.

In 1799, the army's leader, Napoleon Bonaparte, took part in a **coup d'état** that effectively ended the French Revolution. But warfare did not cease. After crowning himself emperor, Napoleon led a French army of conquest that dominated much of Europe by 1806.

The French Revolution had taken a very different track from the American Revolution. Its leaders went from establishing a limited constitutional monarchy to executing the king and creating a republic. At least 15,000 more enemies of the revolution, including several of its former leaders, were executed during a Reign of Terror from 1793 to 1794. The revolution was a radical attack on old institutions aimed at bringing about a new and better society. It altered people's ideas of what a political revolution could do. It also inspired other peoples to seek political liberty by overthrowing absolute rulers and societal restraints.

Toussaint L'Ouverture and his men were defeated by the French at the Ravine aux Couleuvres, as seen here. However, L'Ouverture eventually succeeded in leading the slave colony of San Domingue in revolt against the French. As a result, the slaves were freed, and the republic of Haiti was created in 1804.

Latin American Independence Movements In 1791, inspired by the French Revolution, slaves in the French colony of Saint-Domingue revolted. Saint-Domingue was a sugar- and coffee-producing colony on the Caribbean island of Hispaniola. A free black man, Toussaint L'Ouverture, joined the rebels in what became known as the Haitian Revolution. He helped lead them to victory and independence from France. Their struggle, which lasted until 1804, greatly altered the social order in the former colony, which they renamed Haiti.

Napoleon's invasion of Portugal in 1807 and Spain in 1808 sparked unrest in much of the rest of Latin America. With ties to their home country severed, some Spanish colonists began devising their own, separate governments. Conflict broke out between patriots, who sought independence, and royalists, who opposed splitting with Spain.

The patriots tended to be Creoles, American-born descendants of Spanish settlers. They read Enlightenment authors and were inspired by the ideals of liberty and republicanism that came out of the American Revolution. The royalists were mainly *peninsulares,* or Spanish-born colonists whose natural loyalty was to Spain.

Creole resistance to Spanish power went back to the late 1700s. Spain had then taken steps to regain control of Spanish America, much as the British had tried to reassert their authority over their North American colonies. They created new administrative units and placed *peninsulares,* not Creoles, in charge. They levied new taxes and took over parts of the economy. The Creoles resented these and other Spanish policies aimed at centralizing control.

The struggle for independence began in earnest in Buenos Aires, a city in present-day Argentina, when Creoles took political control and held on to it. That same year in Venezuela, patriots forced the Spanish governor to leave. But royalist forces fought back. Over the next several years, control of Venezuela moved back and forth between the opposing sides.

During the same period, two patriot armies developed in South America. Venezuelan Simón Bolívar led the Army of the North, which relied at first on Haitian weapons and money and foreign troops. José Francisco de San Martín led the southern army, the Army of the Andes. Region by region, the patriot armies overcame royalist resistance.

In Mexico, the independence movement began in 1810 with an explosion of violence against authority. Loyalist forces regained control by capturing and executing the revolution's leaders. In 1821, after a shift in Spain toward liberalism, royalists and rebels worked together to produce a declaration of independence. By 1826, the independence movement had succeeded in wresting all of Spanish America from Spain, with the exception of two islands, Cuba and Puerto Rico.

Brazil achieved independence from Portugal without a violent upheaval. Social tensions existed, but between the dominant white people and the vastly larger population of enslaved Africans. The whites, fearing a slave revolt like the one in Haiti, relied on Portugal for protection. They stayed loyal in spite of policies that they disliked. In 1808, forced out of their homeland by Napoleon, the exiled Portuguese royal family settled in Brazil along with 10,000 or more supporters. They made Brazil the administrative center of the Portuguese empire. When the emperor returned to Portugal, he left his son behind to govern Brazil. In 1822, the new ruler declared Brazil independent.

Simón Bolívar was a hero of the Latin American independence movement. As the leader of the Army of the North, he overcame royalist forces region by region. Like many leaders of the revolutions in Latin America, Bolívar was a Creole, or someone of Spanish descent born in the colonies.

nationalism pride and devotion to one's nation; also, the idea that a people with a common language, culture, and history should have its own nation-state

14.3 Nationalism and Nation-States

The peoples of the new Latin American states showed great pride in their country. Pride is one common aspect of **nationalism**. People's loyalty to their family or local leader expands into something bigger, encompassing an entire nation. In France, Napoleon had tapped that spirit of nationalism to form a massive volunteer army. As the army overran much of Europe, nationalism spread with it. In some places, it arose in the form of an "us-against-them" response to foreign invasion. In other places, it resulted from admiration of the French system.

Nationalism had two main effects. It stimulated the breakup of multinational empires. It also helped create nation-states by unifying people of the same ethnic origin living in separate states.

The Revolutions of 1848 A concerted effort by a group of European states stopped Napoleon in 1815 and restored France's monarchy. Nevertheless, republicanism survived. It made a strong comeback in the Revolutions of 1848. These uprisings resulted from growing demands across Europe for political liberalization and social and economic reform.

One of the first revolts occurred in Paris, France. There the government used military force to stifle street protests. Its inability to end the demonstrations or suppress the violence weakened leaders' authority. Around that time, protests broke out in other major cities in Austria, Germany, and Italy. Revolution threatened to engulf Europe. To avoid that, several monarchs hastily promised reforms. Some leaders stepped down, and new constitutions were created. No great political shifts came directly out of the Revolutions of 1848. The uprisings, however, gave a boost to nationalist movements that, in time, produced several new nation-states.

In France, the Revolution of 1848 forced the abdication of King Louis Philippe, who had ruled since 1830 (the Bourbon monarchy had been restored in 1815). This is a scene depicting the storming of the throne room in the Tuileries Palace.

Italy Napoleon had invaded Italy in 1796. At the time, the Italian peninsula contained a mix of independent states and states ruled by Spain, Austria, and the Roman Catholic pope. The French invasion set off efforts to overthrow absolute rule. Napoleon wanted to centralize his rule of Italy as a unified republic. He told Italians, "You have only particular laws and you need general laws. Your people have only local customs and it is necessary that you acquire national habits." In 1815, however, France lost its claim on Italy.

During the Revolutions of 1848, nationalists in Italy were still fighting for greater freedoms and political unity. In the years that followed, the Kingdom of Sardinia took the lead. With France as an ally, it waged a successful war against Austria. Sardinia won some territory as a result. It then began annexing additional states in north and central Italy. In each state, citizens were allowed to vote whether or not to accept the Sardinian takeover. Sardinia also supported a successful armed invasion of southern Italy. Nationalists finally achieved unification in 1861 with the formation of the Kingdom of Italy. Sardinia's ruler became Italy's king.

The Kingdom of Sardinia took the lead in unifying Italy. Some of the Italian states were allowed to vote on unification. This drawing shows the Kingdom of the Two Sicilies voting to join Sardinia. A united Kingdom of Italy was achieved in 1861.

Germany As in Italy, the French Revolution had a strong impact on the process of German unification. Napoleon had destroyed the Holy Roman Empire when he conquered much of Europe. After Napoleon's defeat, a gathering of European states at the Congress of Vienna in 1815 replaced the empire with a German Confederation of 39 states. Nationalists worked to unify those states.

The demands of industrialization played a role in unifying Germany. In 1834, German states joined together in an economic alliance. This took Germans farther down the path to political unification. However, they did not actually achieve it until a series of wars led to the formation of the German Empire in 1871.

After the Meiji Restoration, Japan sought to industrialize using western powers as a model. Emperor Meiji himself adopted some European customs, such as his clothing style shown in this painting.

Meiji Japan From 1197 to 1867, Japan was a dual state. It had two rulers. The emperor possessed only ceremonial power. Japan's true ruler was the dominant warlord, or shogun. Under the shogunate, the country had largely avoided contact with Westerners (Europeans and North Americans). But starting in the 1850s, Western powers began insisting on opening relations with Japan. The shogunate was too weak, militarily and economically, to resist Western pressure. In 1868, an army led by allies of the emperor ended the reign of the last shogun. The emperor once again took power in what is called the Meiji (MAY-gee) Restoration.

constitutionalism a political theory calling for government according to fundamental laws and principles

concession a special economic privilege granted to a foreign power

The Meiji government realized that only by matching Western advances could Japan survive in the modern world. To unify the country, Meiji leaders looked to **constitutionalism,** which calls for governing according to fundamental laws and principles. They also sought to industrialize Japan, using Western powers as a model. The resulting Meiji reforms strengthened Japan and helped modernize it.

Russia   Napoleon's invasion of the Russian Empire in 1812 inspired a nationalistic response. It also helped spread Western ideas, such as liberalism, into Russia. But significant change did not come until the 1860s. At that time the czar—Russia's all-powerful leader—instituted basic social and economic reforms. He insisted, however, on keeping his monopoly on political power.

That monopoly was severely tested by the Russian Revolution of 1905. Peasants and workers, along with discontented members of the middle and upper classes, tried to topple a weak and incompetent czar. More political reforms followed, but the basic power structure remained unchanged.

China   In the mid-1800s, China tried to limit its trade with the West. Yet China was weak. Western powers used their military superiority to force China to trade more openly. In 1895, as a result of war with a resurgent Japan, China lost control of Korea. Japan also extracted economic **concessions** from China. Western powers took this opportunity to seize strategic ports and other territory. The carving up of China had begun.

Foreign bullying of China helped create nationalist feelings among the Chinese. They wanted the foreigners out of their country. That came to include the ruling Qing (ching) dynasty. The Chinese saw themselves as Han people, or descendants of the Han dynasty. The Qing dynasty, however, was founded by Manchus who had invaded some 250 years earlier. It was easy to blame this alien dynasty for the weakness of the Chinese state.

In addition, strong support existed among urban, educated Chinese for a republican form of government. These and other factors came together to trigger the Chinese Republican Revolution of 1911–1912. The resulting republic, however, would fall victim to internal power struggles and further foreign intervention in the years that followed.

The Boxer Rebellion of 1900 was an outgrowth of Chinese nationalist feelings. During the Boxer Rebellion, peasants targeted Christians and Western missionaries in an effort to drive foreign influences out of China. In this drawing, Boxer rebels are shown destroying western telegraph poles.

14.4 Industrial Revolution

Humans settled down as farmers starting around 8,000 B.C.E. That shift to farming is called the First Agricultural Revolution. In the late 1700s C.E., another huge transformation began. Known as the Industrial Revolution, it changed how work was done. In the process it changed entire societies. Until that time farming and manufacturing made use of muscle power. The revolutionary aspect of industrialization was the switch to machine power. Machines did work much more quickly and efficiently than humans or animals.

Early Industry in Britain The Industrial Revolution began in Great Britain in the 1760s. Why there? One of the big reasons was coal. Britain had a lot of this fossil fuel. Coal was crucial to the efficient production of iron and, later, steel. Just as important, coal became the main source of energy used by industry.

Britain also had gifted inventors and bold entrepreneurs. New fiber-spinning and weaving technologies, including the spinning jenny and the water frame, speeded up textile production. Entrepreneurs built bigger textile machines and linked them together in a central location—a factory. They powered the early factories with flowing stream water. The water turned a large wheel, which spun a crankshaft, which activated the machinery. Later another British invention, the steam engine, replaced waterpower in many places.

Indirectly, coal mining had led to the development of the steam engine. Coal mines, dug deep into the ground, tended to fill with water. Pumps powered by steam engines kept the mines from flooding. The first efficient steam engine, designed by James Watt, appeared in the 1760s. By the 1780s, improved models were driving the machinery in textile factories. The steam engine, by putting coal's potential energy to work, became the key invention of the Industrial Revolution.

Scholars cite several other reasons for Britain's early industrialization. One is political. Britain's government was based on liberalism. It gave its citizens the freedom and security to pursue new ways of doing things. It also backed overseas trading ventures. The success of those ventures infused the economy with **capital**. Capital can be money. It can also take other forms, such as the factories and machinery used to produce goods.

Another reason behind the rise of British industry is rapid population growth, which supplied labor for factories and consumers for factory goods. Yet another is transportation. To ship raw materials and finished goods, Britain built a system of canals and later a network of railroads.

Here a steam engine, the structure on the right, helps draw coal from a mine in Staffordshire, England in the 1850s. What do you notice about the different parts of the steam engine? What was the role of coal in the Industrial Revolution? Why was the steam engine important?

capital wealth in the form of money or of resources that are used to produce other goods

For all its advantages, Britain did not industrialize in isolation. The Industrial Revolution was a global phenomenon. Britain's interactions with Asia, Africa, and the Americas made its industrialization possible. Take the cotton textile industry, for example. Cotton did not grow in Britain. During this period Britain imported raw cotton from the West Indies, India, and Egypt. But the American South, where enslaved Africans provided the labor, was Britain's largest supplier by far. By 1800, British merchants had access to overseas markets as far away as China. There they traded their cotton cloth and other machine-made goods for sizable profits.

Industrialization Spreads   Britain provided the model for how to industrialize. From Britain, industrial technologies and processes spread first, in the 1820s, to northwestern Europe and the northeastern United States. Where coal supplies were limited, as in France and New England, waterpower ran factories. By the 1880s, industrialization had begun in Russia, Japan, and parts of central Europe, as well as in several British colonies.

In 1880, Britain remained the world's top economic power. By 1900, Britain, Germany, and the United States together produced two-thirds of all the world's manufactured goods. On the eve of World War I, in 1914, the United States had developed into the world's leading industrial power, followed by Germany and Britain.

All three of these countries, as well as France and Japan, built extensive rail networks. Railroads, with their coal-fired steam locomotives, proved to be a key driver of the Industrial Revolution. Their speed made it possible to ship products rapidly and cheaply over long distances.

As it industrialized, the United Kingdom developed a railroad network. This photograph from 1899 shows the Corris Railway in Wales. In what ways were railroads important to the Industrial Revolution?

This helped companies develop a national market for their manufactured goods. Railroads also helped factories grow. Factory managers could rely on railroads to deliver equipment and supplies in a timely manner. Railroads themselves consumed great amounts of coal and steel, thus helping those industries thrive. They also employed huge numbers of workers. In addition, the enormous amounts of capital needed to start and maintain a railroad encouraged innovations in financing and promoted the rise of big business.

Industrial Capitalism   In the era leading up to the Industrial Revolution, European merchants prospered. They oversaw the manufacture, by hand, of a variety of goods. They traded those goods throughout the world. Over the years these merchants amassed the business skills and the capital needed to support the rise of industry. Some searched for new and more efficient ways to make products—and profit. In the process these merchant capitalists became industrial capitalists.

For industry to flourish, societies needed a means of concentrating large amounts of capital. Early in the period, the joint-stock company served this purpose. It raised capital by selling stock, or shares of ownership in the company. Since the 16th century, these companies had been involved in trade. Now they began to appear in industries such as mining and railroads.

In a joint-stock company investors held the stock jointly. All investors shared the profits—and any losses. In fact, if a joint-stock company went bankrupt, any of the investors could be forced by law to cover its debts. To encourage investment, states began passing laws limiting investors' liability, or legal responsibility. Thus, in the mid-1800s, a new and robust business form, the corporation, was born. This innovation spread quickly through Europe and became a cornerstone of capitalism.

Capitalism has a variety of meanings. Basically, it is an economic system in which all resources are privately owned. Markets determine how those resources are distributed. Modern capitalism arose with industry. In a strictly industrial context, the meaning might focus on owners and workers. It can be viewed as a system in which a fairly small number of capitalists own the means of production—such as the factories and equipment. They employ a much larger number of wage laborers to produce goods. The employers, or owners, sell the goods and reap the profits.

Corporations allowed for large concentrations of capital that made possible the funding of expensive business enterprises, such as factories. Corporations encouraged investment because they limited the liability of investors should a business go bankrupt.

capitalism an economic system in which all resources are privately owned and markets determine how those resources are distributed

socialism an economic system in which the government owns the resources and distributes them in a way that meets social needs

Karl Marx.

Karl Marx observed the increasing gap between rich and poor that was developing in industrialized Europe. This led him to formulate his theory of class struggle. He believed that industrialization would inevitably create the oppressive conditions that would lead to the revolt of the working class.

Economic inequality between the owning class and the working class appeared to be a built-in aspect of capitalism. Some people argued that the great wealth generated by the Industrial Revolution should be shared by all members of society. This theory, known as **socialism,** aimed to replace private ownership of the means of production with public ownership. The German philosopher Karl Marx explored the historical struggle between the social classes. Marx denounced capitalism and predicted that a worker revolution would one day replace it with a classless, socialist system.

Industrial laborers were often poorly paid and forced to work long hours in unhealthful, dangerous conditions. Yet, in general, they preferred reform to revolution. They joined political parties that campaigned for social improvements. They also banded together to form labor unions. Labor unions sought to improve workers' wages and working conditions. Yet the world's workers never rose up against the capitalist system as Marx had predicted.

Consequences for Societies Worldwide Wherever industrialization took hold, economies grew. New technologies and methods greatly increased productivity and lowered costs. Societies, too, changed in fundamental ways. The Industrial Revolution—over time—transformed how people worked, where they worked, where they lived, and more.

Traditionally, manufacturing took place in home workshops. Rural households—men, women, and children—worked together to spin thread, weave cloth, and make tools and other goods. Merchants provided raw materials to these skilled artisans and paid them for their work. This "domestic system" declined with the rise of industry.

Industrialists completely changed the method of organizing production. They gathered their workers together in factories. Workers, and machinery, had to be near the power source—flowing water or steam engine. They also increased specialization. Jobs that one person had handled in a home or shop were now subdivided into multiple tasks.

This improved efficiency but made the work more boring. It also took much of the skill out of the work. Instead of weaving fabric by hand on a loom, textile factory workers merely tended their machine. Unless there was a breakdown, they never even had to touch the cloth. Industrialization also took some of the pleasure out of work. There was little time to relax or daydream in a fast-paced factory.

In the early years of the Industrial Revolution, women regularly worked in light industries such as textiles. In Western countries, however, many were later displaced from their manufacturing jobs in favor of men. They often ended up taking in laundry at home or working as domestic servants. However, in countries such as Russia and Japan, which industrialized later, the need for cheap labor meant that women filled the factories.

Children had always worked, especially on the farm. At first, few people took issue with child labor in factories. Children were expected to help support their family. Owners hired them in part because they worked for less pay than adults. Also, their size was a benefit. It allowed them to slip inside a power loom to fix a broken thread while the machine was still running. It also made it easier for them to work in the narrow tunnels of coal mines. As the 1800s progressed, reformers began to push for laws limiting child labor. By 1900, in the West and in Japan, education had become most children's main occupation.

During this time, agriculture made greater use of factory-made tools and machinery. As a result, fewer workers were needed to produce food. Industrialization thus encouraged mass migration "from field to factory." The jobs were in the factory towns. The Industrial Revolution also boosted global migration, as people moved to countries with growing industries. Urbanization increased, as factory towns quickly grew into cities.

Factories ran mainly on coal. The environmental consequences of the burning of coal included heavily polluted air. Waste from factories fouled nearby waters as well. Charles Dickens described the atmosphere of a mid-1800s English factory town this way:

> *It was a town of machinery and tall chimneys, out of which interminable serpents of smoke trailed themselves for ever and ever, and never got uncoiled. It had a black canal in it, and a river that ran purple with ill-smelling dye.*
> —Charles Dickens, *Hard Times,* Chapter V

At the beginning of the Industrial Revolution, children were expected to work to help support their families. Children's small hands were considered to be better at handling the small parts of complicated machinery, such as this spinning frame. As the 19th century progressed, however, legislation was passed in Europe and the United States to limit child labor.

The new imperialism of the late 18th and 19th centuries was concerned with finding markets for the consumer goods produced by industrialization. This is one aspect that made it different from the old-style imperialism of the 15th through 17th centuries. In this late 18th-century Chinese painting, European trading ships sail up to warehouses in the port of Canton.

imperialism a policy in which a state takes political and economic control of areas beyond its borders

14.5 Imperialism

In the late 1800s, several industrialized states expanded their territory. They were by no means the first powerful states to do so. The Roman, Athenian, Ottoman, Gupta, Han, and many other states had all practiced **imperialism**. They had taken control of land, resources, and peoples beyond their borders. So had Portugal, Spain, Great Britain, France, and the Netherlands starting in the 1500s. During this pre-industrial period, these European powers had ruled the seas. They had conquered and colonized the Americas and had opened coastal trading posts across the rest of the world. Three centuries later, in the midst of the Industrial Revolution, another imperialist expansion began. A slightly different set of global powers hungrily gobbled up territory, mainly in Africa and Asia. The colonies that they established, however, served a different purpose from the earlier ones.

The New Imperialism In the pre-industrial period, European imperialist powers developed a mercantile economic system. They relied on their colonies for slaves, precious metals, and consumer goods such as spices and sugar. Europeans obtained what they wanted by trading with the native peoples or colonists. This old-style colonialism often involved warfare. European powers used force to acquire colonies. They also competed militarily with one another to hold on to their colonies. In time, however, many colonies in the Americas fought to gain their freedom. Their political revolutions curbed the imperial ambitions of European states for a while.

Those ambitions returned full force in the late 1800s. With industrialization in full swing, Western powers scoured the world for raw materials to keep their factories going. They also sought sources of food for the workers who labored in those factories. At the same time, they pursued markets for their machine-made products. New colonies fulfilled some—though by no means all—of those needs.

Times had changed, however. Now, if a colony was unable to supply enough of a resource, the dominant state would often just take over the production process. In this way, Western powers introduced modern industrial practices into their colonies. These colonizers typically extended their dominance beyond the economy, however. They built roads and railways, mines and factories, schools and hospitals. They trained police and set up Western-style legal systems. They imposed their own leaders, language, and culture. In short, they practiced a modern form of imperialism.

Besides their role as a supplier of resources, colonies served other purposes as well. One was strategic. Imperialist powers expanded into places that gave them a geographic or economic edge on their rivals. Britain, for example, had come to rely on India as a market for its textiles. British forces took control of territory along the sea route to India to keep that commerce secure.

Colonies also served as a source of national prestige. By adding territory, a weak government could boost its political standing at home. All in all, the new imperialism served the European states well. By 1914, they would occupy or control most of the world.

The Suez Canal through Egypt cut a significant amount of time off the trading route between Britain and India. When Britain's access to the canal was threatened in 1881, it responded by occupying Egypt. This image shows a ceremony for the opening of the canal in 1869.

The Scramble for Africa   Europeans' imperialism seemed to contradict their liberalism. It had nothing to do with freedom and equality. One way that they justified imperialism was to argue that it brought progress to so-called "backward" peoples. Europeans argued that they had a moral duty to introduce others to the knowledge, wealth, and Christian values of Western civilization. Many thought that their global dominance could be explained as biological superiority to other races. Scholars have pointed out the racism inherent in such views. The Western attitude toward Africa is a prime example.

Starting in the late 1400s, European states had traded along the African coast, mainly for slaves. By the late 1800s, nearly all of the world's major states had abolished slavery. The coastal trade with Africa had largely vanished, although Africans themselves continued to practice slavery.

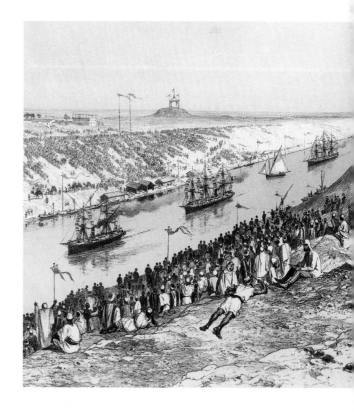

European interest in Africa was rekindled in 1869, with the opening of the Suez Canal. This waterway through Egypt linked the Mediterranean and Red seas. It greatly cut the travel time between Britain and India. When a rebellion in Egypt threatened to close the canal in 1881, Britain occupied the country. This action unleashed a "scramble for Africa." The major European powers all began claiming territory in Africa.

When the dust settled, nearly the entire continent was in European hands. The British held on to Egypt and took much of the rest of northeast Africa. They also controlled lands from South Africa north to Rhodesia. The French occupied nearly all of West Africa. Germany, Italy, and Portugal each grabbed several sizable chunks of territory. Spain claimed smaller areas on the western coast. The scramble left Belgium with just one region along the Congo River basin in the center of the continent. But that region was huge. Its mineral wealth would make it one of the few African possessions that yielded a profit.

Imperial Powers in Asia   Since the early 1600s, the British East India Company had been acquiring territory in India. When the government took charge of the colony, in 1858, all of India came under British rule. There the modernizing effect of imperialism was clear. The British introduced new technology and greatly expanded access to education. At the same time, it exploited India's people and resources for its own benefit. Karl Marx noted the paradox in British imperial policy. He wrote:

> *England has to fulfill a double mission in India: one destructive, the other regenerating— the annihilation of old Asiatic society, and the laying of the material foundations of Western society in Asia.*
>
> —Karl Marx, "The Future Results of the British Rule in India," 1853

From India, Britain extended its control westward into Persia. There it competed for dominance with Russia, which had steadily expanded southward through Central Asia during the 1800s. Russia also looked eastward, toward an ever-weakening China. In 1891, Russia began building its Trans-Siberian Railroad. It would run from Moscow east to the Pacific coast. The Chinese conceded, or granted, to Russia an area of land in Manchuria for its railway. This concession gave Russia control of that chunk of northern China.

In 1911, King George V and Queen Mary of England traveled to India as part of the celebration of King George V's coronation. In addition to King of England, George V was also granted the title Emperor of India. The British called India "the jewel in the crown" because it was their largest and most valuable colony.

Of all the lands on the Asian continent, the greatest object of imperial interest was China. Starting in the mid-1800s, Britain, France, and Germany competed for access to China's markets and its huge population of consumers. These Western powers all demanded, and obtained, more open trade.

Then, in the 1890s, Japan entered the competition. Its Meiji government had transformed and strengthened its economy and military and was ready to expand. In 1894, Japan and China went to war over control of the Korean peninsula. The Japanese won. Their victory encouraged the Western powers to demand even more concessions from China.

China had traditionally exerted its influence over much of Southeast Asia. But Western powers had long challenged China in the region. By 1890, the French had conquered Indochina and the British held Burma, Singapore, and parts of Malaya. To the east, in the Pacific Ocean, Western powers annexed many islands. Britain, Germany, and a new imperialist power—the United States—vied for control of strategic island ports.

Summary

In this lesson, you read about the political and economic revolutions that transformed the world in the 1700s, 1800s, and early 1900s.

Cultural Interaction In the late 1800s, Western powers expanded beyond their borders. Under a policy of imperialism, they interacted culturally with Africa and Asia. They introduced new technologies to their colonies. They improved transportation, education, and access to medical care. However, attitudes toward native cultures were often based on racist ideas.

Political Structures Enlightenment ideas about government provided a philosophical basis for the revolutions of the late 1700s and early 1800s. Those revolutions replaced existing political structures with more democratic forms of government. They also triggered a series of nationalist uprisings that let to the formation of new nation-states and the breakup of multinational empires.

Economic Structures The Industrial Revolution transformed economies, first in Europe and the United States and later in Japan and elsewhere. It largely replaced muscle power with machine power. The huge expense of building factories and railroads encouraged the rise of industrial capitalism.

Social Structures Industrialization greatly altered society. Manufacturing moved from the rural home or shop to the urban factory, a life-changing experience for the workers who moved with it. Agricultural laborers also moved to the city to work in factories. Laborers became part of a working class, in contrast to the owning class who built and ran the factories and other large enterprises.

Human-Environment Interaction The steam engine that powered textile factories, railroads, and other industries ran on coal, which led to a huge expansion of mining and a huge increase in pollution. Industries required a large number of laborers. People in need of work migrated not only "from field to factory" within an industrializing country but also from other countries.

Political Revolutions and Their Legacies

How were political revolutions during the 1700s and 1800s similar and different?

15.1 Introduction

As the year 1775 came to a close, British colonists in North America faced a crucial question. Should they work out their differences with Great Britain, or should they declare their independence?

In January 1776, a publication appeared that helped Americans answer that question. The 50-page pamphlet, titled *Common Sense,* made a strong case for independence: "Every thing that is right or natural pleads for separation. The blood of the slain, the weeping voice of nature cries, 'TIS TIME TO PART."

Thomas Paine, the pamphlet's author, grew up a student of the Enlightenment. Political thinkers of the Enlightenment used reason to identify people's rights and freedoms. One thinker, John Locke, wrote that it was proper to overthrow a government that violated people's natural rights. This was a radical idea—one that Paine believed firmly and expressed persuasively. Six months after *Common Sense* came out, the Americans declared independence. Their political revolution had officially begun.

Paine's writings influenced other revolutions as well. He strongly defended the French Revolution in his book *Rights of Man.* It helped make Paine a hero to the French, who elected him to their National Assembly. Revolutionaries in Latin America, too, admired Paine. At least one of them, Francisco de Miranda, met with Paine well before Spain's colonies rebelled.

The influence of Paine's work played a part in the political revolutions of the 1700s and 1800s. But major events in history have many causes. At the root of this era's political upheavals lay a set of Enlightenment ideas. Though radical, these ideas, which were spread via the writings and actions of Paine and others, made sense to people across the globe. They helped generate an era of democratic revolution whose impact can still be felt today.

Themes

Cultural Interaction Enlightenment ideas circulated around the world, helping support political uprisings in the Americas, Europe, and Asia.

Political Structures Revolutions of the late 1700s replaced monarchies with representative political systems. Democratic movements inspired similar changes in political structures elsewhere in the world.

Economic Structures The spread of liberalism encouraged economic freedom and the protection of private property.

Social Structures Tensions among social classes helped trigger some political revolutions.

This cartoon depicts Thomas Paine valiantly fighting against the injustices of his day by penning words of revolution to the masses.

The American Revolution had a profound impact on the nations of Europe. This 1784 German print illustrating the Boston Tea Party is just one example of the ways in which America's example was popularized overseas. In this depiction you can see revolutionaries dressed as Indians dumping tea into the ocean, as people look on.

15.2 The American Revolution

The American Revolution began with musket shots exchanged between British army regulars and a colonial militia at the Battles of Lexington and Concord in April 1775. By war's end, some 4,400 Americans had been killed in battle. Another 18,000 or more had died off the battlefield, mainly from disease. The British death toll was about the same.

The Path to War   The trouble started right after the French and Indian War, a nine-year struggle that ended in 1763. The British defeated the French and their Native American allies, but at great cost. The victory ended the French threat in North America. But the Indian threat remained. Americans, especially pioneers on the western frontier, demanded protection from Indian attacks. The British expected their colonies to help pay for their own defense.

To raise revenue, the British passed the Stamp Act in 1765. It required colonists to pay a tax, represented by a stamp, on everyday goods such as newspapers and playing cards. The tax outraged colonists. A secret organization known as the Sons of Liberty arose in several cities to organize protests against the Stamp Act. Before this time the colonies acted, for the most part, as distinct and separate units. Opposition to the Stamp Act was beginning to unite the colonies.

The violence of some protests, including threats against tax collectors, led Parliament to repeal the Stamp Act in 1766. But other new taxes followed. Colonists again reacted with demonstrations. They boycotted, or refused to buy, goods that carried a tax. In one protest in December 1773, colonists dressed as Indians dumped a load of tea from a British ship into Boston Harbor rather than pay the tax on it. Britain denounced this Boston Tea Party and took steps to punish the colony. The Coercive Acts, known in the colonies as the "Intolerable Acts," closed the port of Boston. They also increased the power of the royal governor at the expense of local leaders.

As the Intolerable Acts showed, the British had more in mind than just raising tax revenue. They also wanted to exert more control over their colonies. Almost from the beginning, the English settlers had enjoyed a modest level of political freedom. Elected representatives served in colonial assemblies. The assemblies had key lawmaking powers. Nonetheless, most colonies also had royal governors appointed by the British monarch. In theory those governors had the power to say when the assemblies would meet, veto laws passed by the assemblies, and choose key officials. But in reality the colonies largely governed themselves.

After passage of the Intolerable Acts, those political freedoms now seemed in jeopardy. Colonists feared that Britain would tighten its control of all the colonies. Their alarm increased when Parliament passed the Quebec Act. This act expanded the province of Quebec southward to the Ohio River. Colonists would be kept from settling in this fertile region.

Colonial leaders decided to join together to form a single governing body to present their complaints to the British. By forming a united front, they hoped to have more power to negotiate. From September to October 1774, the First Continental Congress met in Philadelphia. The Congress consisted of a mix of moderates and radicals. The moderates wanted to compromise with the British to avoid a showdown. The radicals hoped to persuade the British to restore the freedoms that they had come to cherish. If not, they were ready to separate completely from Britain.

The Fight for Independence   Weeks before the Second Continental Congress convened in May 1775, the Battles of Lexington and Concord took place. The American Revolution had begun. Soon the radicals took charge, insisting on breaking free from Britain.

With the help of persuasive writings such as Paine's *Common Sense* and Thomas Jefferson's *Summary View of the Rights of British America*, the movement for independence swept up many colonists—although not all. A significant number of Loyalists, especially in parts of New York, New Jersey, and the Carolinas, opposed the Patriots. They would continue to support Britain throughout the Revolutionary War.

The members of Congress chose George Washington to command the Continental Army. Washington had earned their respect by his leadership of British troops during the French and Indian War. From the fall of 1775 to the spring of 1776, Patriot forces took the offensive. They invaded and later retreated from Canada. They pushed the British out of Boston.

In June 1776, the Continental Congress appointed a committee to prepare a document declaring the colonies' independence. Jefferson wrote the first draft. After some debate and revisions, the members of Congress signed the Declaration of Independence on July 4, 1776. Benjamin Franklin knew that this document was also a declaration of war. As he signed it he noted, "We must all hang together or assuredly we will all hang separately."

It did not take long for the British to respond. By September, armed with about 32,000 troops and a huge fleet of warships, they had taken New York City. Washington and his army fled. The British followed, chasing them into New Jersey. To escape, the Continental Army had to cross the Delaware River into Pennsylvania.

George Washington was already a war hero of the French and Indian War when he was chosen to lead the Continental Army. Washington would eventually lead the Patriot forces to an unlikely military victory over the British.

Just when the Patriot cause looked bleakest, Washington pulled off a daring move. On Christmas night, 1776, he led his army back across the ice-choked river to attack the British at Trenton, New Jersey. Before they left, he boosted his troops' spirits with words recently written by Thomas Paine:

> *These are the times that try men's souls. The summer soldier and the sunshine patriot will, in this crisis, shrink from the service of their country; but he that stands it now, deserves the love and thanks of man and woman.*
>
> —Thomas Paine, *The American Crisis,*
> No. 1, December 23, 1776

Washington's men decisively defeated the British force at Trenton. Ten days later, they won another victory at Princeton. Washington showed that he was a superb strategist. But he knew that he owed much of his success to foreign powers. France, along with two other British enemies, Spain and Holland, had been secretly sending vital supplies to the Continental Army.

The French were willing to do more, but they needed proof that the Americans could indeed win the war. That proof came with the Battle of Saratoga, in upstate New York. By winning there, the Americans stopped the British from taking control of the Hudson River Valley, which would have isolated New England from the rest of the country. After that victory, France started to take an active role in the war. Thus Saratoga was a turning point in the revolution.

This 19th-century print depicts the British General Burgoyne surrendering his sword to General George Washington after the Battle of Saratoga. The victory at Saratoga helped win the support of the French, who were convinced that the Patriots actually had a chance of winning the war.

Many bloody battles followed. The war shifted away from the northern colonies as the British took control of much of the South. Eventually, with the help of French troops and ships, the Continental Army trapped the main British army at Yorktown, in Virginia. The surrender of that army in October 1782 marked the end of major hostilities. The Americans had won their independence.

Treaty of Paris   The official end of the Revolutionary War came in 1783 when American and British delegates signed the Treaty of Paris. In the peace treaty, Great Britain acknowledged the independence of the United States. It also accepted the expansion of the new nation from the Great Lakes south to Florida and westward to the Mississippi River. For its part, the United States agreed to recommend that states restore to Loyalists their rights and liberties and any property that might have been taken away during the war.

The Constitution of the United States, which begins with the famous phrase, "We the People," was only created after the failure of the Articles of Confederation. The Constitution was written by a convention of leaders in 1787, and its creation involved a lot of debate and compromise.

Constitution and Bill of Rights   Thomas Paine had come up with the name for the new country—the United States of America. Just how "united" those states would be, however, was unclear. But its first constitution offered some clues.

In 1781, the states had ratified, or approved, the Articles of Confederation. This written constitution spelled out the role of the central government and its relationship to the states. After their experience with British tyranny, Americans were in no mood to invest much power in a central government. The Articles did give Congress certain powers. But to carry out those powers, it needed support and money from the states, and the states did not willingly provide either.

Basically, the states were to be considered **sovereign**. Each had the ability to create laws, resolve disputes, and otherwise make and carry out policies without interference by other states or the central government.

sovereign self-governing and independent

In general, the Articles of Confederation proved to be a failure. It left the central government too weak to resolve nationwide economic problems or maintain order. A number of leaders called for a convention to fix the Articles. The Constitutional Convention met in Philadelphia in May 1787. The 55 delegates decided quickly that instead of trying to fix the Articles of Confederation, they would replace it. By the end of that long, hot summer, the people of the United States had a brand new Constitution, one that has continued to serve the country to this day.

The process of creating the Constitution involved a great deal of debate and compromise. One major issue concerned competition between large and small states. The large states wanted representation in Congress to be based on population. The small states wanted each state to have an equal number of representatives both in the House of Representatives and the Senate. This issue was finally settled through the Great Compromise. A state's representation in the House would be based on its population. Each state would have an equal number of senators.

A related issue involved the counting of slaves in determining a state's population—and thus the number of its representatives in the House. Southern states wanted each slave to be counted. Northern states objected. The compromise was to count each slave as three-fifths of a person.

rule of law the idea that all citizens, even the most powerful, are subject to the law

The Constitution laid out a plan of government based on the separation of powers. It allotted powers to three branches—the executive, legislative, and judicial. Each branch could check, or restrain, the power of the other two. The Constitution also served as the supreme law of the land. It helped ensure that the rule of law would prevail. **Rule of law** means that the law applies to everyone. Nobody—not even the president, the highest official in the land—is above the law.

The states ratified the Constitution in 1788. Three years later, they approved a Bill of Rights, intended to protect individuals' civil liberties. In this way, the Constitution completed the American political revolution. It replaced the monarchical political system with a totally new structure of government—a representative democracy.

15.3 Revolutions in France, Italy, and Germany

The American Revolution changed the political system, but it did not really alter people's day-to-day lives. The French Revolution, on the other hand, led to a major social upheaval. A radical assault on France's traditional institutions—the monarchy, the Church, feudalism—the revolution thoroughly transformed French society.

Social Divisions and Financial Problems The French people in the 1700s were sharply divided socially. The nobles and the clergy, or officials of the Roman Catholic Church, represented the top two estates, or legal categories. To be a noble or a member of the clergy, a person had to meet specific legal requirements. Everyone else, from merchants to peasants, belonged to the Third Estate. This commoner class made up some 95 percent of the population.

Most French peasants lived in crushing poverty. This 1788 French engraving depicts King Louis XVI handing out alms to the needy. However, charity was not enough to alleviate the suffering of the peasantry, and it could not prevent bitter feelings towards the nobility and clergy.

The commoners, for the most part, accepted the three-tiered society. However, many of them resented certain feudal privileges granted to the landowning nobles and clergy. Noble landlords had an exclusive right to carry weapons, hunt, and demand work from the peasants. They could levy taxes but were themselves exempt from most taxes. Of the third estate, merchants and government officials paid a limited amount in taxes. The tax burden fell largely on the peasants, most of whom were poor.

For France, the 1700s was a century of continual warfare. To pay for their military ventures, including support of the colonists in the American Revolution, French kings had to borrow more and more money. By 1788, King Louis XVI faced severe financial problems. In fact, France hovered on the verge of bankruptcy.

Louis considered a set of reforms for resolving the economic crisis. They included raising taxes. The peasants, however, could not afford to pay any more than they already did. Meager harvests, rising consumer prices, and high unemployment had already taken a terrible toll on the poor. Yet the rich were protected from new taxes by their exemptions and traditional rights.

To move forward with reforms, the king decided that he needed the approval of the Estates-General. This assembly of representatives from all three estates had not met since 1614. However, the king's decision to summon the Estates-General proved disastrous. It gave the commoners access to power. They used that power in ways that led, through a complex series of events, to a political revolution.

A Radical Revolution On May 5, 1789, the Estates-General met at Versailles, the king's palace, some 10 miles outside Paris. Delegates to the meeting brought lists of grievances to discuss with the group. Many also brought their Enlightenment ideas about liberty and about government based on natural laws. Most representatives of the Third Estate had legal backgrounds. On June 17, they declared themselves to be a National Assembly, with the power to govern France. They started designing a constitution.

The king took steps to stop the Assembly from meeting, which roused the people of Paris. On July 14, a mob destroyed the Bastille, a fortress and prison that symbolized royal power. The revolution had moved into the streets. In the weeks that followed, it also spread to the countryside. Most peasants, out of fear, remained on the sidelines. But some took this opportunity to destroy their landlords' property, especially documents that showed how much they owed their masters in feudal dues.

As these outbursts of violence suggest, the French Revolution had no sharply defined goal, such as independence. Instead, it was a broad-based war on privilege, powered by Enlightenment ideas. The course of the revolution resembled a roller-coaster ride. It had several stages, as dominant groups came and went.

The National Assembly kept control only for a few years. But by 1791, it had transformed France. It had adopted the Declaration of the Rights of Man and Citizen, a document that defined the individual and collective rights of all three estates as equal and universal. It had turned the country into a constitutional monarchy. It had forced the French Catholic Church to cut its ties with Rome. It had abolished feudalism, the system of privileges held by the nobles and clergy. All French citizens were now equal under the law. As the Declaration of the Rights of Man and of the Citizen—the preamble to the constitution—stated, "Men are born free and remain equal in rights."

As the French Revolution spread from Paris to the countryside, some peasants lashed out against the privileges of the elite. In this image, French peasants destroy the feudal documents that recorded how much they owed their landlords.

On October 5, 1789, French women of the third estate organized a march on the palace of Versailles. This was an exception however. Most women did not participate in the revolution. Many women remained loyal to conservative forces such as the Catholic Church.

As for women, they were largely left out of the revolution. The men "reasoned" that women were, "by nature," unfit to take a political role. The feminist Olympia de Gouge reacted by drafting a Declaration of the Rights of Woman and of the Citizen. There she wrote, "Woman is born free and lives equal to man in her rights."

Some women did join the French Revolution. They took part in protests and joined political clubs. Others actively opposed the revolution. Many of these defended priests, who were often mistreated, and tried to ward off attacks on the Catholic Church.

After 1791, the French Revolution took a turn toward violence. Fearing a foreign plot to undermine its progress, France declared war on Austria and Prussia in 1792. It also replaced the National Assembly with a body known as the Convention, which would govern until 1796.

Extremist politicians gained control of this new assembly. They encouraged a thirst for blood among the people, and their rule became a Reign of Terror. In 1793, they beheaded King Louis XVI and his wife Marie Antoinette and replaced the monarchy with a republic. Their quest for absolute unity and loyalty led to the deaths of tens of thousands more citizens in the next year and a half. Many were executed, as the king had been, by guillotine. Many more were killed in clashes with opponents of the revolution throughout the country.

Moderates in the Convention took charge in 1794. They executed the main agent of the Terror, Maximilien Robespierre. If this did not mark the end of the French Revolution, it came five years later with the rise to power of a shrewd and power-hungry French general, Napoleon Bonaparte.

Napoleon Takes Control   In 1799 Napoleon, a skilled army commander, seized control of France in a coup d'état, bringing an end to representative government. Napoleon ruled as a dictator. Yet he also retained—in theory if not always in practice—many of the gains of the revolution, including citizens' equality, individual liberty, and protection of property rights. In 1804, he put forward a law code that safeguarded these ideals. It became known as the Napoleonic Code.

That same year, Napoleon crowned himself emperor of France. But he did so with the support of the French people, who voted in favor of restoring the monarchy. Thus he upheld, at least outwardly, the ideal of **popular sovereignty**—that the people are the source of all political power.

Soon after Napoleon took power, he defeated Austrian forces in Italy and Germany, ending a long-standing threat to France. But he was not done. To add to his empire, Napoleon led campaigns across Europe. French forces defeated Austria in 1805 and Prussia in 1806. In 1807, Napoleon's armies invaded Portugal in the west and Russia in the east. The French emperor thus extended his control and influence over much of the continent.

Napoleon also spread revolutionary French ideas and institutions. One of them, popular sovereignty, held that a people should govern itself. Even after Napoleon's reign ended, in 1815, the French Revolution continued to inspire Europeans who valued liberty and equality. They challenged the authority of monarchies, seeking to replace them with republics. They took part in nationalist movements. Nationalists saw the value of living in a nation-state, in which one unified people governs itself. For example, inhabitants of Italy and Germany, both of which were divided into many small city-states and principalities, began to identify themselves as Italians and Germans.

Italian Unification   Italy in the 1800s consisted of a mix of states ruled by various princes and the pope. The Austrian Empire controlled a large region in the northeast and dominated other states. The main thrust of the unification movement was to gain independence from Austria, a struggle known as the Risorgimento ("Resurrection" or "Rising Again").

popular sovereignty the doctrine that the people are the source of all political power wielded by the state

Although Napoleon seized power in a military coup, he claimed to rule according to the will of the people. How did Napoleon justify his claim that he was continuing to uphold popular sovereignty?

liberal favoring individual political and economic freedom, with limits on state power

conservative favoring the maintenance of existing institutions and traditional values

In 1848, popular uprisings rocked major cities across much of Europe. In Italy, Giuseppe Mazzini and other republican reformers took over several states and announced the formation of a republic. Austrian and French armies, however, quickly moved in to extinguish the revolution.

After 1848, the Kingdom of Sardinia in northern Italy led the unification movement. It was the only constitutional monarchy in Italy. Its king, Victor Emanuel II, and its prime minister, Camillo di Cavour, worked on a plan to oust Austria from Italy. In 1859, Sardinia secretly allied itself with France. It then provoked Austria, which threatened to take military action. France stepped in and, after three battles, secured a settlement with Austria—without consulting Cavour.

The settlement left Austria in charge of the Italian state of Venetia. It also allowed rulers of states in central Italy to maintain their control. Sardinia moved to annex those states. It succeeded, but only after allowing their inhabitants to vote on the annexation. In 1860, the fighter and revolutionary Giuseppe Garibaldi led his army of red-shirted volunteers into southern Italy. He conquered Naples and Sicily and later turned them over to Sardinia. Nearly all of Italy was now unified. In 1861, the first Italian parliament proclaimed Victor Emanuel II the king of Italy. Complete unification came nine years later, after Venetia and Rome had been annexed.

German Unification German nationalists, too, sought greater unity after the 1848 revolutions. They included a **liberal** middle class of business and factory owners—the bourgeoisie—who saw the need for a national market. Economic unity, however, would come only with political unity.

As in Italy, the Austrian Empire had long dominated the various German states. But Austria was growing weak. Prussia, the largest and strongest German state, took a leading role in the unification movement. In 1866, after defeating Austria in war, Prussia grew even larger and more powerful. It now controlled two-thirds of Germany's population and territory. In 1867, Prussia unified this territory as the North German Confederation.

Prussia's prime minister, Otto von Bismarck, was the architect of Prussia's expansion. Although **conservative,** he adopted the goal of national unification, in part to ensure that Prussia would dominate Germany. To meet this goal, Bismarck needed a way to persuade the southern German states to unite with the northern states. He achieved this result by provoking France into a war. The southern states, their intense anti-French feelings aroused, joined with the North German Confederation in 1871. Together, they defeated France in the Franco-Prussian War and established a unified German Empire.

Otto von Bismarck was the conservative and militaristic leader who led the movement for German national unification. He accomplished his goals using the military might of his home state of Prussia.

15.4 Revolutions in Latin America

Columbus's voyage west across the Atlantic Ocean in 1492 initiated European interest in the Americas. In the years that followed, Spain claimed most of Latin America. Portugal acquired Brazil. There they established colonies, from which they extracted resources that brought them great wealth. They held on to those colonies for some three centuries, until a string of revolutions rocked the entire region.

Haiti In 1791, inspired by the French Revolution, slaves in the French colony of Saint-Domingue revolted. In this sugar- and coffee-producing colony on the Caribbean island of Hispaniola, slaves far outnumbered the dominant whites. A third class included freed people of color and mulattos, or people of mixed black and European ancestry. This class lacked social and political equality with the whites.

A free black, Toussaint L'Ouverture, joined the rebels and helped lead what became known as the Haitian Revolution. It was a combined slave rebellion and anti-colonial uprising. By 1800, L'Ouverture and his army had eliminated their opponents and taken control of the colony. After Napoleon gained power in France, he sent a French force to the colony to suppress the revolt. Mulattos joined with black leaders to defeat the French troops in 1804, declaring their independence from France and massacring thousands of French colonial administrators and their families. They founded the first black republic in modern history, which they renamed Haiti.

Toussaint L'Ouverture led a successful rebellion in the French slave colony of Saint-Domingue and helped found the republic of Haiti, the first black-ruled republic in modern history.

Revolution in the Spanish Colonies Social tensions within Spanish America's multiracial societies also played a role in the drama that unfolded there. After the Haitian Revolution, whites feared that rebellions might arise among the lower classes of Indians, enslaved Africans, and people of mixed blood. The minority white population dominated politically. It consisted of Creoles and *peninsulares*. Creoles were American-born descendants of Spanish colonists. *Peninsulares* were Spanish-born settlers. No major slave rebellions took place. But a series of Creole-led revolutions resulted in the founding of new nations throughout Spanish America.

Creoles had once played a leading political role as colonial officials. But in the late 1700s, Spain's leaders decided to exert greater control over their colonies. They introduced reforms that took the right to rule their own areas away from the Creoles. From then on, Spain entrusted important political and military positions to the *peninsulares* and generally snubbed the Creoles.

In 1808, French forces under Napoleon invaded and occupied Spain, severing the link between Spain and its colonies. Many Creoles saw this as an opportunity to restore their position in colonial society—both political and economic. The more radical among them, influenced by Enlightenment ideas and motivated by the American Revolution, sought to free themselves from Spanish rule. Wherever these liberal-minded patriots could gain control, they set up local councils to govern themselves.

The *peninsulares,* too, established councils. But these Spanish citizens were not revolutionaries or liberals. They were royalists—they, along with a significant number of Creoles, remained loyal to the Spanish king. They fully expected Spain to restore its control of the colonies one day.

These differing visions collided throughout Spanish America as the revolutionary movement grew. Spain had divided its colonial territory into regions, called viceroyalties. New Granada occupied northwestern South America. Río de la Plata, present-day Argentina, was located in the south. Peru lay between them. New Spain included Mexico and most of Central America, as well as Spain's Caribbean colonies. The story of the revolutions in Spanish America varied from one viceroyalty to another.

San Martín in Río de la Plata   The first solid achievement for the Creole patriots occurred in Buenos Aires. They established self-rule in this southeast coastal city and maintained it in spite of several assaults by royalists. Buenos Aires became a base for spreading the revolution throughout the southern part of South America. In 1816, patriot groups within the viceroyalty joined together to form the United Provinces of the Río de la Plata and declared their independence from Spain. They chose Buenos Aires as the new country's capital.

The patriots realized that their country could not be secure until the Spanish had been driven from power throughout the continent. The viceroyalty of Peru, a key royalist stronghold, had to be conquered. In 1817, patriot leader José de San Martín formed and trained an army in Río de la Plata. It included blacks, mulattos, and mestizos—people of mixed Indian and European ancestry. He led this 4,000-man army across the Andes on a bold mission against royalist forces in Peru.

First, Martín's Army of the Andes marched into Chile, south of Peru. In 1814, a Peruvian army had stamped out the revolutionary movement in this province. San Martín restored the Chilean patriots to power in 1818 by defeating the royalist forces.

In September 1820, San Martín and his army headed north, by sea, to Peru. By July of the next year, the Army of the Andes had carried the revolution all the way to Lima, Peru's capital. The royalist army fled into the mountains. In July 1821, San Martín declared Peru independent.

Jose de San Martín was a patriot leader who successfully led an army against royalist forces in Peru. His patriot army included Creoles, blacks, mulattos and mestizos, who fought against the privileged peninsulares class.

The patriots had succeeded in taking control of the towns, but a powerful royalist army still had support in the countryside. To plan his next move, San Martín decided to consult with another great patriot commander, Simón Bolívar.

Bolívar in New Granada   Bolívar, a wealthy Creole, had led the revolution in New Granada. That revolution began in his home state of Venezuela. He and his small Army of the North supported independence movements there and elsewhere in the viceroyalty. For his success in freeing various regions, he received the title "The Liberator."

However, the road to independence was not easy. Bolívar suffered many defeats along the way, and the rule of key cities often shifted back and forth between patriot and royalist forces. Patriots in Caracas, Venezuela, for example, twice established a republic only to later lose control. The second republic was overturned in 1815 by a large army sent from Spain. That army forced Bolívar to flee to Jamaica. From there he sailed to Haiti, which provided him the resources needed to continue the fight for independence.

Still, the Army of the North made little headway in New Granada until 1819. By then, Bolívar had changed his strategy. He and his army had relocated to the Venezuelan countryside to escape Spanish forces. They engaged in **guerrilla warfare,** living off the land and making quick, hit-and-run strikes against the enemy. Bolívar's army now consisted of not only Creoles but also a number of British and Irish troops and, for the first time, mulattos. In addition, Bolívar had help from an unlikely source, the *llaneros*. He persuaded these horse-riding cattle herders of the plains to switch sides after being poorly treated as mounted soldiers in the royalist army.

In the spring of 1819, Bolívar led his diverse army on a long and perilous march west across the Andes into present-day Colombia. There he launched a surprise attack on the Spanish force. It was the first in a series of patriot victories that, by May 1822, had brought independence to New Granada.

Resistance to Revolution in Peru and Mexico   In July 1822, Bolívar and San Martín met in Ecuador. There San Martín decided to step aside and let Bolívar take the lead in the effort to liberate Peru. Bolívar and his army accomplished this task in a series of battles starting in August 1824. By April 1825, he had tracked down and defeated the remaining royalist forces in the region then called Upper Peru. The nation formed from Upper Peru would rename itself Bolivia in honor of their Liberator.

Simón Bolívar was a wealthy Creole patriot who led the Army of the North to victory against the Spanish in the region of New Granada. Bolívar's army included Creoles, British and Irish troops, mulattos, and *llanero* cattle herders.

guerrilla warfare an approach to warfare that relies on mobility, hit-and-run tactics, and the element of surprise to harass a larger, stronger opponent

This engraving depicts the Battle of Boyacá, which occurred on August 7, 1819 in Colombia. Simón Bolívar and his army succeeded in forcing a majority of the Spanish forces to surrender. By 1822, after a series of patriot victories, the region of New Granada won independence from Spain.

Mexico, like Peru, remained staunchly loyal to Spain. *Peninsulares* there ran the government and blocked attempts by Creoles to introduce liberal reforms. In 1810, a radical Creole priest, Miguel Hidalgo, called for independence. He inspired a nationalist uprising of Indians and mestizos across the Mexican countryside. Their goal was to force the Spanish out of Mexico. Hidalgo's followers killed many *peninsulares* and destroyed much property. The independence movement threatened to become a social revolution. Fearing that, many Creoles joined Mexico's royalist army.

The army finally overpowered the rebel forces and executed Hidalgo and his successor, José María Morelos. But the movement for independence did not die. In 1821, in an unexpected turnabout, Creole soldiers conducted a successful coup d'état against their Spanish officers. They achieved independence and the promise of a constitutional monarchy. But their leader, the former royalist Agustín de Iturbide, declared himself emperor. His reign lasted less than a year, as Mexicans from across the political spectrum opposed him.

Mexico remained unstable in the years that followed, as political, economic, and social ills plagued the country. This was the case in many of the nations to which the revolutions of Latin America gave birth. Liberals and conservatives continued to clash. Military strongmen—known as *caudillos*—vied for control at the local, provincial, and national levels. They promised order but often used oppressive measures to secure it. Economies wrecked by revolution could not bring about the prosperity that people hoped for. Also, hostility among the various social classes persisted.

Brazil Napoleon's invasion of Portugal in 1807 did not set off a major uprising in Brazil, a Portuguese colony. It did, however, cause a reversal in the relationship between the mother country and the colony. The French army's conquest of Portugal forced the nation's royal family to flee to Brazil. They arrived in the city of Rio de Janeiro in March 1808, along with thousands of members of their court.

The Portuguese ruler enacted economic reforms that pleased Brazil's privileged class and helped keep liberal-minded Brazilians in check. Brazil quickly became the political center of the Portuguese empire. When the king finally returned to Portugal in 1821, he put his son, Dom Pedro, in charge of the colony. The following year, faced with growing calls for political reform by republicans, Dom Pedro declared Brazil's independence.

15.5 Revolutions in East Asia

The late 1800s found two East Asian countries, China and Japan, moving in opposite directions. China, the traditional East Asian powerhouse, was steadily declining. Japan, on the other hand, was enjoying an economic and military revival. Japan owed its rise to a revolutionary restoration of the monarchy. China's political upheaval would come later, in the form of a republican revolution.

Meiji Japan   In 1853, Japan received a "wake-up call" from the United States. It came in the form of a squadron of four warships, two powered by steam and two by the wind. The ships, commanded by Matthew Perry, arrived unannounced in a Japanese harbor. Their mission was to open Japan to trade and diplomatic relations. Perry completed his mission the following year, when Japan signed a treaty that allowed an American diplomat to reside in Japan and opened the door to trade. Other European powers began demanding similar privileges.

Perry's success revealed to the Japanese just how weak their country had become. The shogun—the dominant warlord and supreme ruler of Japan—lacked the military might to resist American demands. He could no longer preserve Japan's traditional isolation from the West (Europe and North America). That isolation may have helped keep Japan stable and peaceful, but it also prevented the country from moving forward into the modern age.

The shogun came under increasing pressure. Many Japanese blamed him for the unprecedented presence of "barbarian" diplomats and traders on Japanese soil. They also held him responsible for the woeful state of the Japanese military, especially its outmoded weaponry. During the shogunate, Japan's emperor had remained a figurehead, with only ceremonial power. Support for restoring imperial rule began to grow.

In 1867, rising contempt for the shogun boiled over into rebellion. The uprising succeeded in part because members of the main rebel group had learned how to make and use modern weapons. In 1868, the Meiji emperor officially ended the shogunate and took control of Japan. The return of power to the emperor, however, was just the start of a political revolution known as the Meiji Restoration.

Meiji reformers took steps to strengthen Japan, using the West as a model. They wrote a constitution and set up a representative government. They abolished the feudal system, shifting power from local lords to the central government. The reformers introduced Western technology, improved education, and modernized the economy.

In 1853, four American warships commanded by Commodore Perry arrived in Japan. The mission succeeded in obtaining trading privileges from the traditionally isolationist Japanese. Many Japanese saw this as a sign of the weakness of their country. In this image Commodore Perry is received by Japanese imperial representatives.

This 1858 print from a British newspaper shows a battle during the Opium Wars. British forces proved too powerful for the Chinese, and they conceded access to trading ports to the British.

Qing China Since ancient times China had thought of itself as the center of the universe—the Middle Kingdom. Outsiders were "barbarians." In the 1800s, however, China's great civilization fell into decline. Foreign threats helped trigger internal clashes that threatened to tear the country apart.

A non-Chinese people, the Manchus, gained the Mandate of Heaven—the divine right to rule—in 1644. They formed the Qing (ching) dynasty, which maintained peace for nearly two centuries. During this time, China allowed European Christian missionaries to bring their religion into China. It also engaged in foreign trade through a single port, Guangzhou.

At Guangzhou, foreign merchants bought Chinese tea, silks, and porcelains. But China neither needed nor wanted much that the Europeans could offer—except opium. The British brought this drug, grown in its colony in India, to China while Chinese smugglers then sneaked it into the country. In 1840, after China cracked down on the opium trade, the British sent warships to China. In the Opium Wars that followed, the British navy proved too powerful for the poorly armed Chinese forces. In 1842, Britain secured a treaty with China that opened several Chinese ports to trade. Soon other European powers demanded and gained access to these treaty ports.

The inability of the alien Qing dynasty to restrain foreign powers or to improve economic conditions led to an uprising known as the Taiping Rebellion. The Taiping movement, which arose in the south, was loosely based on Christian teachings. It called for the redistribution of land to the peasants, equality of the sexes, and other social changes that threatened to undermine Chinese tradition. Starting in 1853, thousands of peasants joined the rebellion and marched, as an army, northward.

The rebels captured several cities along the way, including the former capital of Nanjing, and added many more people to their cause. Fanatics in battle, they slaughtered all who opposed them. After more than a decade of fighting, the Manchus—with help from Europeans and their advanced arms—ended the rebellion. Tens of thousands of Taiping rebels were killed in the retaking of Nanjing in 1864.

Another peasant movement, this time in northern China, arose from a group calling itself the Righteous Harmonious Fists. Westerners called them the Boxers. The goal of what became known as the Boxer Rebellion was to rid China of foreigners, especially Christian missionaries and their converts. The Qing government, frustrated by years of European abuse, encouraged the movement. Peasants, suffering from a long drought, swelled the Boxer ranks, and in June 1900, they marched on the capital, Beijing. Western troops moved in to protect their diplomats, and when the Qing threw its support behind the Boxers, eight foreign powers sent in a much larger military force. This small army ended the siege of the capital. Later, the Qing reversed course, helping the foreign powers end the rebellion.

After the Boxer Rebellion, the Manchus instituted some reforms. They supplied China's army with modern weapons. They built railroads and boosted industry. They also promised to move toward a constitutional government. For some Chinese, they did not move fast enough.

Led by a U.S.-educated physician named Sun Yat-sen, a group of radical nationalists made plans to end the Qing dynasty and install a republican government. In 1911, an uprising started that came to be known as the Chinese Republican Revolution. Some provincial officials and army commanders joined the revolution, which quickly toppled the Qing government. In January 1912, Sun Yat-sen won election as president of the newly formed republic. A month later, China's last emperor stepped down. The Qing had lost the Mandate of Heaven.

The Boxer Rebellion was defeated by a combined force of eight foreign powers. In the print above, British and Japanese forces engage with the Boxer rebels.

Summary

In this lesson, you read about the political revolutions that occurred throughout the world in the 1700s and 1800s. Many of these revolutions were influenced by the democratic ideals of the Enlightenment.

Cultural Interaction Political revolutionaries in the Americas, Europe, and Asia based many of their actions on ideas formulated in Europe during the Enlightenment. Those ideas later appeared in the constitutions put in place by newly formed nations.

Political Structures The revolutions that took place from the late 1700s to the early 1900s sought to replace monarchies with more representative political systems. The French Revolution encouraged the spread of nationalism and, along with the American Revolution, inspired political upheavals elsewhere.

Economic Structures Liberal ideas, which called for individual economic freedom and the protection of private property, appealed to business interests and helped bring about revolutionary political change in the West. In the mid-1800s, the desire by Western powers to trade with China and Japan put pressure on those countries to modernize their economies.

Social Structures Tensions among social classes in France played a key causal role in the French Revolution, and the revolution itself transformed French society. The social structure in Haiti was also changed, by a slave rebellion that turned into a political revolution. During the revolutions in Spanish America, white society split along class lines.

The Industrial Revolution

What was so revolutionary about the Industrial Revolution?

16.1 Introduction

In the 1700s, metalworkers used large amounts of coal, which burned with the intense heat needed for making iron. Coal suppliers, however, had a problem. Coal mines, dug deep in the ground, tended to fill with water. A British inventor named Thomas Newcomen designed an engine to pump water out of the mines. His engine burned wood or coal to boil water and produce steam. It converted the steam's heat energy into mechanical energy to drive the pump. The Newcomen engine worked, but not very efficiently.

In 1763, James Watt had the job of repairing a Newcomen engine. Watt made scientific instruments for a living, and he had an inventor's mind. He knew he could make an engine that did not waste so much of the potential energy of the fuel. The solution eluded him for months. But then, one day, while strolling through his hometown of Glasgow, Scotland, the answer suddenly came to him. Watt set to work right away building a model, and in 1769 he won a patent for his much more efficient steam engine.

Watt spent the next two decades perfecting his steam engine. By 1790, he had turned his steam engine into a sturdy, practical, powerful machine. It would be put to use not only in coal mines but also in steamboats, locomotives, and factories. The steam engine would power the **Industrial Revolution**.

Many scholars are reluctant to call this period of industrialization a "revolution." It took place over too long a period, they say, and affected the whole world. Yet the changes brought on by this shift from muscle power to machine power were enormous, and revolutionary in their scope. This chapter explores the Industrial Revolution, starting where it all began: Great Britain.

Themes

Economic Structures As a result of the Industrial Revolution, economies shifted from a focus on agriculture and manual labor to a focus on industry and mechanization.

Social Structures The pool of low-paid industrial laborers formed the core of a new social group, the working class.

Human-Environment Interaction Industrialization drew migrants from rural areas and from distant lands to cities and newly urbanized factory towns.

This historical steam engine-powered train still operates on a preserved railway in Britain.

16.2 Great Britain Leads the Way

The Industrial Revolution, led by Great Britain, completely transformed how work was done. By the mid-1800s, British manufactures far exceeded those of any other country. Industrialization happened so quickly in Great Britain that it earned the nickname "workshop of the world." Why did the revolution start in this small, European island nation?

Factors of Industrialization Great Britain became the first nation to industrialize because it had all of the necessary factors:

1. **Political Stability** Britain had a stable government that supported individual political freedom, property rights, and equality of opportunity. These traits encouraged entrepreneurs to take risks in pursuit of profit.

2. **Labor** Britain had plenty of people available for work. British farmers produced so much food that many of its people were freed to do different kinds of work. Many of those people went to work in industry.

3. **Raw Materials** Britain had plentiful supplies of the raw materials needed in industry, such as coal for fuel or wool for textiles.

4. **Banking System** Britain's banks provided loans to entrepreneurs to finance large projects, such as factories, railroads, and coal mines.

5. **Transportation System** Britain had a network of navigable rivers and seaside ports. It built a nationwide system of canals. Later, it developed a railroad network, making the transportation of goods and raw materials cheaper and faster than ever before.

As textile making became mechanized, it required larger and more expensive equipment. This eventually shifted the site of fabric production from individual homes to factories.

Innovation in Textiles The first industry to be transformed in Great Britain was textile production. Before industrialization, every step of cloth making had to be done by hand. The raw fiber, like wool and cotton, had to be cleaned and untangled. The fibers had to be twisted into thread. Then the threads had to be woven into cloth. Each step was laborious and time-consuming. Skilled artisans used simple tools and equipment to make cloth in their own homes.

In the mid-1700s, English inventors created machines to speed up the cloth-making process. In 1733, John Kay invented the flying shuttle to automate the weaving process. Now weaving was faster, but spinners could not spin thread fast enough to keep up. James Hargreaves invented the spinning jenny in 1764 to allow one person to spin dozens of threads at the same time.

But threads produced on a spinning jenny often broke. Richard Arkwright solved this problem in 1769 with his water frame, an invention capable of producing stronger thread. The water frame was powered by a waterwheel turned by a fast-flowing river.

These machines were too large and expensive for ordinary workers to use in their own homes. Owners of textile businesses began building factories where they could install multiple machines to make textiles faster than ever before. Now workers would come to the factories to make fabric.

Resources   Great Britain had plenty of rivers, and its earliest factories took advantage of the water power they provided. Eventually steam engines replaced water wheels, and they needed coal to fuel them—and Britain had an abundant supply of coal. Now factories could be built away from rivers, in more places than ever before.

Great Britain also had a steady supply of fiber. Britain had a long tradition of raising sheep for wool, and wool production more than doubled between 1700 and 1850. British textile merchants also imported cotton from Great Britain's colonies in India and the Americas, and later, the United States.

By the time Great Britain industrialized, it had already built an extensive network of canals. Canals were a relatively cheap and quick way to transport goods.

Transportation   Great Britain also had a good transportation network. Britain had many navigable rivers and seaports that had long made coastal trade possible. By the 1770s it had built a system of well-maintained toll roads. Moving goods by road was slow, however, so Britain created a nationwide network of canals. Goods and raw materials could travel faster and more cheaply along canals.

Eventually, the steam engine was applied to transportation, resulting in the development of the steam locomotive and the development of railroads.

Soon, steam locomotives crisscrossed the country on a complex network of rails. By 1852, Great Britain had built some 7,000 miles of track. Railroads carried heavy loads of food and freight quickly and reliably, helping create a national market for goods. The economy boomed as manufacturers could create a product in one location and sell it anywhere in the nation.

16.3 The Revolution Spreads

Industrialization steadily improved Great Britain's economy. It increased the amount of goods produced and greatly raised worker **productivity,** or the amount of goods each worker, on average, produced. Wealth generated by industrialization enhanced the standard of living for many people. It also made more tax revenue available to the government. Competing nations took notice and sought to develop their own industries. Generally, they adopted the elements of the British model that suited their circumstances.

productivity the amount of goods or services that result for each unit of required resources used (output per unit of input)

Belgium   Belgium, located across the English Channel from Great Britain, was the second country to take part in the Industrial Revolution. Belgium borrowed techniques and technology from the British, but its industrialization followed a different pattern. The people of Belgium had long been known for their woolen textile industry. By 1820, they had begun to mechanize that industry. But the traditional hand weaving of complex designs persisted into the mid-1800s. Belgium's textile industry grew, but not as fast as Great Britain's.

Belgium's industrialization focused more on its abundant reserves of coal and iron ore. Exports of coal brought in valuable revenue, and the coal itself fueled the iron-making process. Belgium used the iron to produce machinery, locomotives, ships, and weapons. Later, Belgium developed a thriving steel industry.

France   France, with the help of British equipment, entrepreneurs, and engineers, also began to industrialize in the 1820s. It established numerous textile mills for the production of cotton cloth. Other factories produced machinery, including steam engines. France later had to import coal from Great Britain and from Belgium, because it lacked significant reserves of its own. As a result, France's factories relied more on waterpower than steam power.

Belgium was the second country to industrialize. Belgium used its abundant coal reserves to make iron, which was then used to produce machinery, locomotives such as the one seen here, ships, and weapons.

The United States   As in France, early industry in the United States depended on waterpower, abundant in New England. Cotton textile mills mushroomed in New England in the 1820s. The mills modeled their technology and organization on those of British factories. Like the British, New Englanders' raw cotton came from the American South.

New England factories also made metalwork. They used specialized equipment to produce metal parts for machinery and for guns. They owed their success to the earlier work of Eli Whitney and Simeon North, who established a method of manufacturing **interchangeable parts**. These inventors devised machine tools that could cut, plane, and drill part after part to nearly the exact same size and shape. The use of interchangeable parts allowed the rapid assembly of machines or other complex devices in a factory, based on a series of simple operations.

Further innovations sparked the Industrial Revolution in the United States. One was the cotton gin, another accomplishment of Eli Whitney. His machine for cleaning cotton led to a vast Southern expansion of cotton production—and slavery. The **Bessemer process,** an inexpensive way to convert iron into higher quality steel, greatly increased steel production. Cheap steel helped the heavy industries of the American Midwest to expand. They used the region's plentiful iron ore and coal to build steel plants and factories that produced machinery and railroad rails—and the steel girders that, in the 1880s, made possible the first true skyscrapers.

The heart of any factory was its machinery, and machinery has moving parts that interact. Without lubrication, that machinery would overheat and eventually grind to a halt. Through much of the 1800s, workers lubricated their machines with whale oil. In the 1850s, scientists developed a new and less expensive lubricant—coal oil.

interchangeable parts parts that can be swapped for one another in the assembling of a product, because they have been precisely cut and shaped to be identical

Bessemer process a relatively inexpensive method for converting iron to steel by using a blast of air to remove carbon from molten iron

The American Eli Whitney invented the cotton gin (short for cotton engine) in 1793. Here two slaves are shown operating a cotton gin, which mechanically separated the cotton fiber from the seed.

Then, in 1859, an entrepreneur in Pennsylvania drilled the world's first commercially successful oil well. Products that can be made from oil include gasoline and kerosene. Kerosene soon became industry's lubricant of choice. Oil, also known as petroleum, slowly began to replace coal as the basic energy source of the Industrial Revolution. Gasoline fueled the automobile, which was powered by a ground-breaking invention, the internal-combustion engine.

Germany Germany began industrializing fairly late, in part because it consisted of a number of independent states for most of the 1800s. In 1834, however, many of those states joined in creating a free-trade zone. Germany soon established itself as a leader in heavy industry, especially metalwork. Using its abundant coal and iron ore, Germany produced the rails needed to establish an efficient railway system.

Railroads and their support industries, including steel-making, remained the leading sectors of the German economy through the 1800s. Late in the century, the chemical, electrical equipment, and weapons industries also prospered. By 1914, Germany was second only to the United States as an industrial power.

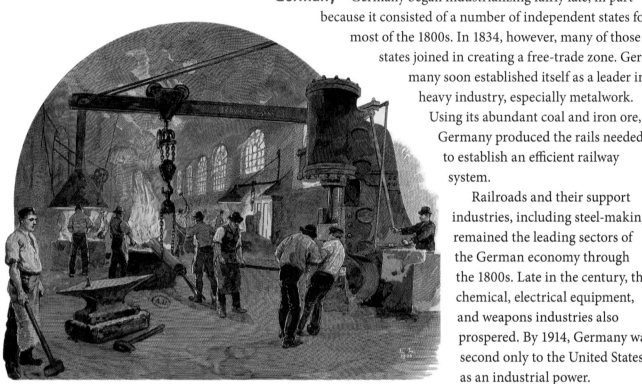

This illustration depicts the metal works in Kiel, Germany. Although Germany began slowly, it industrialized rapidly in the second half of the nineteenth century, focusing especially on heavy industry.

Japan Industrialized Western states used their wealth to build up a strong merchant fleet and navy. They sailed across the world in search of trade. Until the mid-1800s, Japan had kept itself isolated from outsiders. Now the increased contact by Westerners helped push the Japanese into a political revolution. The Japanese ousted the shogun, or strongest warlord, from power and restored their emperor to the throne, in what is called the Meiji Restoration.

The new government followed a course of modernization, using the West as a model. This included industrializing. The Japanese mechanized the silk-weaving industry and built railroads and ships. Japan quickly gained a position of economic dominance in East Asia. From its colonies and through concessions forced from China, Japan extracted needed resources, such as coal, and found markets for its industrial products.

16.4 Economic Transformation

The industrialization that got its start in Great Britain was a slow revolution. It took decades to blossom. Wherever it spread, the Industrial Revolution transformed the economy. Ways of crafting goods changed. Ways of growing crops changed. New financial and business structures developed.

The Domestic System   Long before the Industrial Revolution, some people made their living at craftwork. Skilled artisans, both in towns and in rural areas, produced goods needed locally. These included tools, pots and pans, glassware, furniture, and much more. One sign of a shift toward a new form of production was the growth of cottage industry, also known as the **domestic system**.

In the domestic system, cottage workers produced goods in home workshops. They made goods not for local use but for national and international markets. Typical cottage workers lived in the countryside, farmed for most of the year, and in the off-season made cloth. They provided the cheap labor needed at the time to meet the demands of a competitive textiles market.

The production of wool cloth usually followed a certain process. A textile merchant, based in a town, bought wool from a sheep farmer. He delivered this raw material, along with instructions about what he needed, to a household in the countryside. Family members carded the wool, spun it, and wove it into cloth on a hand loom. The merchant paid them for their work and took the cloth to another workshop, where skilled workers dyed the cloth and otherwise completed the processing. The merchant then retrieved the finished fabric, which was ready for market.

The Factory System   The domestic system naturally gave way to the **factory system**. Instead of traveling from cottage to cottage, some cloth merchants decided that they could save themselves time and better meet rising demand by gathering workers together in a single factory. The merchants provided their workers with spinning wheels and looms and whatever other equipment they needed. In time, many other goods besides textiles were made in factories.

The factory system had several advantages over the domestic system. In a factory, merchant-entrepreneurs could supervise their workers. They could also take advantage of innovations in technology and new sources of energy, especially the steam engine. In short, they could make the revolutionary shift from muscle power to machine power.

domestic system a pre-industrial system of manufacturing in which workers crafted products in their homes using raw materials supplied by merchants

factory system an industrial system of manufacturing in which workers, raw materials, and machinery are gathered under the same roof

Workers in factories performed a single, specialized task all day long. This picture was taken in a wool-combing factory in Bradford, England, in the late 19th century.

In addition, factory owners developed new ways of organizing work. They saw that when individual skilled workers carried out all the tasks to make a product, each worker needed a variety of different tools, but most of the tools sat idle much of the time. In the factory system, unskilled or semi-skilled workers specialized in just one of the tasks needed to make a product. Each worker did only that task, all day long, and they learned to do it rapidly.

The factory and the shift to simplification were two key aspects of what became known as **mass production**. Another was the use of interchangeable parts. Factory workers could sit at their station with a pile of standardized parts in front of them and know that the parts were all the same and that any one of them would fit properly.

The desire to speed up the manufacturing process even more led to the use of the moving assembly line. An assembly line carried a product on a conveyer belt or track from one station to the next. Workers added one new part at each station. Starting in 1913, Henry Ford of the United States built his Model-T automobile using an assembly line. He was the first to apply assembly-line principles to large-scale manufacturing. The practice soon spread to other industries.

All of these changes increased efficiency and productivity. They also lowered the cost to produce many goods. Lower costs meant lower prices for consumers. By the late 1800s, incomes were rising, especially among the middle class in industrialized countries. This helped strengthen consumer demand for manufactured goods.

A Revolution in Agriculture The mechanization that took place in industry also helped transform agriculture. No longer did farmers have to harvest their grain with hand tools. In the 1830s, the American inventor Cyrus McCormick developed a horse-drawn mechanical reaper that could cut and collect the grain. In the years that followed, a variety of other machines appeared to help farmers plant, harvest, and process crops. Through mechanization, farmers could expand their production while cutting back on the amount of labor needed to produce food.

> **mass production** the high-volume, low-cost manufacture of identical items through the use of specialization and interchangeable parts

One of the results of the Industrial Revolution was the mechanization of agriculture. Here a variety of machines are being used to harvest wheat.

Besides using new machinery, farmers used new agricultural methods. They improved the soil with chemical fertilizers and cover crops. Cover crops, such as clover, add nutrients to the soil when plowed under. Farmers also worked to control pests, increase irrigation, and breed superior livestock. The agricultural revolution helped expand the population by making more healthful food available, and it helped farmers produce enough food to feed the growing population.

The agricultural revolution coincided with a changing perspective on land rights. Traditionally, peasants had raised crops and grazed animals on so-called common lands. But technically, the land was private property. Peasants who farmed the land paid dues to the landowner.

Starting in the 1500s in England, landowners revoked the traditional peasant right to farm on common land and enclosed their land with fences or hedges, as seen here. The enclosure movement left many peasants landless, and they became an available workforce for early factories.

During the 1500s in England and continuing there and elsewhere into the 1800s, landowners took back the rights to their land. Historians call this the **enclosure** movement. Landowners, often under force of law, enclosed their land with hedges or fences to mark its boundaries.

One reason for enclosure was economic. Large landowners realized that they could earn more from growing cash crops such as grain, or raising sheep for the growing textile industry, than they could from renting the land to peasants. The enclosure movement had several important consequences. Many peasants were left with no land to cultivate. The same was true for many smallholders—farmers owning smaller amounts of land. Because of economic downturns or the expense of fencing in their land, they sold their plots to wealthier landowners. On their estates, many large landowners established commercial farms.

Some peasants and former smallholders stayed on the land as wage laborers. Others turned to manufacturing in their homes and later in independent shops or small factories. But many became landless and unemployed—or, at best, seasonally employed—workers. As countries began to industrialize, these former farmers provided a ready workforce for the early factories as they migrated to urban areas in search of work.

The enclosure movement had moral and legal effects as well. It helped develop the notion that making a profit from one's land—even if that meant ending traditional land rights of peasants—was acceptable. It also marked the appearance of capitalist agriculture, or the large-scale growing of crops and raising of animals for profit. Through the years, this commercialization of agriculture led to the establishment of a legal system that would support the rise of industrial **capitalism**.

enclosure the repossession and fencing-in by landowners of formerly common lands, often for the purpose of commercial farming

capitalism an economic system, based on the premise of self-interest, in which all resources are privately owned and markets determine how those resources are distributed

One result of industrialization was that powerful corporations, such as John Rockefeller's Standard Oil, came to control entire industries. This American cartoon from 1905 criticizes big business. It shows a "corporate vulture" controlling government with the power of its wealth.

monopoly complete control by one firm of the production and/or the supply of a good

Financing Industry   Without capitalism, there might not have been an Industrial Revolution. As the saying goes, it takes money to make money. Wealthy individuals, or capitalists, saw the potential profits to be made by investing in factories and machinery. Their money helped boost industrialization. A broader pool of investor-owners developed with the rise of corporations. A corporation could accumulate great amounts of investment capital. The more money that capitalists had to invest in businesses, the larger the businesses could grow. This allowed for the formation and expansion of the huge enterprises that came to dominate the Industrial Revolution.

The banking system also played a key role in industrialization. Through loans to industrialists and manufacturers, private banks directed customers' savings into projects such as the building of railroads and factories and the mining of coal. They encouraged the formation of capital in its physical form—the buildings, machines, tools, and equipment used to manufacture goods. Also, governments set up national banks to improve domestic and international trade. Together, private and national banks provided financial backing that stimulated the growth of industry.

Big Business   Industry grew, along with the companies that thrived in the competitive, capitalist world. They won a greater share of the profits available from selling in a national market. Their wealth allowed them to buy up smaller competitors, merge with them, or drive them out of business. By the late 1800s, big business dominated industrial economies.

In the United States, several firms and the industrialists who ran them gained enormous wealth and power. In the oil business, John D. Rockefeller established a **monopoly** with his Standard Oil Company. Andrew Carnegie built his Carnegie Steel Company into the world's largest corporation. Powerful companies ruled other economies as well. France had its Parisian Gas Company and Great Britain its Midland Railway. In Japan, big business consisted of firms known as zaibatsus. Through investment, they controlled many of Japan's industries and banks.

Big businesses were able to gather enough capital to meet the needs of a growing consumer market. They built huge factories and filled them with hundreds of workers. They mass-produced goods at lower prices to meet rising consumer demand—and increase their own profits. A growing assortment of shops and stores sold the many new products that appeared. They included the sewing machine, typewriter, telephone, phonograph, light bulb, bicycle, dishwasher, radio, vacuum cleaner, and washing machine.

16.5 Social and Political Consequences

The Industrial Revolution was, first and foremost, an economic phenomenon. But it can be termed a revolution in part because it also transformed the social and political spheres. Industrialization changed the structure of people's day-to-day lives. Moreover, industrialization led to the rise of big government.

Industrial Labor   In the domestic system, the making of cloth was often a family business. Father, mother, and children all had roles in the various processes needed to turn raw fiber into fabric. Families worked together in the familiar environment of their home. Family members could work at their own speed and take breaks when they wanted. They could eat meals together and manage the household together. The spinning or weaving or dying was part of their daily domestic routine. Furthermore, they had a personal, and socially equal, relationship with the merchant who directed their work.

Before industrialization, people performed work at home and families worked together. This engraving illustrates how embroidery would have been produced in the domestic system.

Laboring in a factory was far different. The main goal there was productivity, and employers strived to get the most out of every worker. The key was discipline. Factory laborers had to follow orders and obey the rules or they could be fined. Workers were expected to show up at the workplace six days a week, on time, and to put in a full day—typically 12 hours for much of the 1800s. By 1900, workers were punching time clocks to mark their arrival and departure times to the minute.

In the home workshop, families chatted or sang as they worked. Not so in the factory. Employers insisted that factory employees focus completely on their work. In the late 1800s, employers began hiring efficiency experts. These industrial engineers devised specific instructions for how workers should do each job, down to such details as the best way to move their hands. The goal was always to speed up production. Employer and employee now had an impersonal relationship. Beyond that, employees now occupied a separate—and lower—social group, the working class.

More and more, workers were treated like the machines that they ran. A British writer, John Byles, characterized factory work this way:

> *Night and day, the indefatigable [untiring] and ponderous piston stamps. Night and day, relays of human flesh struggle to keep up with its remorseless and unwearied march.*
>
> —Sir John Barnard Byles, *Sophisms of Free-Trade and Popular Political Economy Examined*, 1872

Women and Children   In cottage industry, women and children performed vital tasks in the home workshop. At the start of the Industrial Revolution, women and children continued to take part in the manufacture of goods. Factory owners could rely on them to perform the unskilled labor, but they could pay them a lower wage than men.

The New England textile industry, in its early years, hired many women to run the machines that spun and wove cloth. Most female mill workers were young and unmarried. They were known as "factory girls." When Russia and Japan industrialized later in the century, they needed cheap labor to compete with Western textiles. That meant that women filled many of the jobs in textile factories.

Nevertheless, many women were put out of work during the shift from the domestic system to the factory system. Some managed to find work outside the home, often as household servants or teachers. Some started a laundry service in their own home.

By around 1900, Western societies had generally come to the conclusion that industrial labor was primarily the province of men. Only 20 percent or so of women continued to work in manufacturing. Of these, many labored in sweatshops—small factories, typically in the garment industry, where wages were low and conditions unhealthy.

Children, too, helped in the manufacture of cloth, working in textile factories in Great Britain, the United States, France, Belgium, and elsewhere. They also labored in other industrial sectors, such as coal mining. Like women, they worked for a low wage. Yet the incomes of many families were so low that they depended on the earnings of all of their members—including the children. Toward the end of the 1800s, the education of children gained importance, and governments began regulating child labor. First, children's working hours were cut back. Later, laws prohibited factories from hiring children.

In this illustration, women and children work to sift coal. At the start of the Industrial Revolution, many women and children worked in factories. By 1900, however, people viewed industrial labor as only appropriate for men.

Urbanization   Before the Industrial Revolution, manufacturing took place largely in the countryside, in home workshops. Towns served mainly as centers of government and commerce. With industrialization, the town became the main location of manufacturing. Factories attracted a steady stream of workers from the countryside, where the agricultural revolution had reduced the need for farm labor. These migrants settled near the factories, greatly expanding the population of existing towns and cities or creating towns where none had previously existed.

Industrialization also encouraged mass migration from one country to another. Throughout the 1800s, the United States was a major destination for immigrants. Some traveled across the Pacific Ocean from China and Japan. Most, however, came from Europe—even from industrializing countries such as Germany, where too many people competed for too few jobs. The growing United States offered factory work, but it also lured immigrant farmers to its wide-open spaces out West.

The explosion in the number of factories and the flood of migrants to factory towns resulted in rapid **urbanization**. Within those newly urbanized centers, living conditions were often appalling. Unlike today, government regulation, or legal restriction, of industry was practically nonexistent. Outdoors, smoke belching from factories polluted the air. Chemicals and other industrial wastes fouled rivers, lakes, and coastal waters. So did raw sewage from rapidly expanding towns and cities.

Indoors, living conditions in urban areas were just as bad. Filthy, overcrowded apartment houses encouraged the spread of communicable diseases such as cholera, smallpox, and typhoid fever. Yet few government programs for dealing with public-health issues existed until the second half of the 1800s. Urban death rates soared.

This 19th century engraving shows a slum area of London known as the Devil's Acre. As migrants flocked to cities to work in factories, cities became overcrowded and dirty.

urbanization the process of turning a rural area or village into a town or city

Labor Unions   For many industrial laborers, conditions at work were no less harsh than those they experienced at home. They often spent their 12-hour work day in a dark, damp, dirty factory amid the deafening whine and clank of machinery. Factories were dangerous too, with few of the safety precautions that we take for granted today. Pay was another issue. To make a living, merchants have goods to sell. Farmers have crops. Workers, however, have only their labor. Yet employers sought to keep wages as low as possible.

The quest for profits drove the industrialists who ran the factories. They could increase profits by keeping expenses low. Thus it made sense—from a purely economic viewpoint—for them to pay as little as possible in wages and spend as little as possible in improving working conditions. For most of the 1800s, government did not fight for workers' rights. For this, workers had to turn to labor unions.

labor union an organization formed by workers to represent them in negotiations with employers concerning employment issues

strike an agreement among workers to stop working in order to force an employer to improve wages, hours, benefits, or working conditions

A **labor union**, also known as a trade union, is an organization formed by workers to negotiate with employers to resolve work-related issues. During the era of industrialization, those issues usually involved wages, hours, and working conditions. By the late 1800s, strong unions in Europe and the United States had begun to make economic gains for workers, often through strikes or the threat of strikes. A **strike** is an agreement among workers to stop working until the employer meets their demands. Strikes could turn violent, with workers battling police or private guards hired by companies to try to break the strike to force employees back to work.

By 1900, through strikes as well as through changes in the law, most workers in the West worked fewer hours. Although hours still varied from one industry to another, the 10-hour workday and 6-day work-week became the standard. Still, many issues remained, and workers continued to rely on labor unions to resolve them well into the 1900s.

From Laissez-Faire to Regulation   Through the first century or more of the Industrial Revolution, industries grew without government intervention. Western governments largely heeded the economic laws set down by Adam Smith in his book *The Wealth of Nations,* published in 1776. Smith famously wrote, "It is not from the benevolence of the butcher, the brewer, or the baker, that we expect our dinner, but from their regard to their own interest." In other words, because producers seek profit, they create food and other goods. Government, Smith maintained, should not interfere in this process.

Smith's economic laws lay at the heart of a doctrine known as laissez-faire (les-ay FAIR), a French term that loosely translates as "leave it alone." Western industrialists did not want the government interfering with the economy. Their economic strength gave them political power. As a result, the government largely left them and the economy alone. Government's laissez-faire policies were rooted in a key element of liberalism—the right to private property.

In this 1843 cartoon, the luxurious lifestyle of industrial capitalists is contrasted with the often appalling working conditions of everyday laborers. Labor unions tried to improve these conditions.

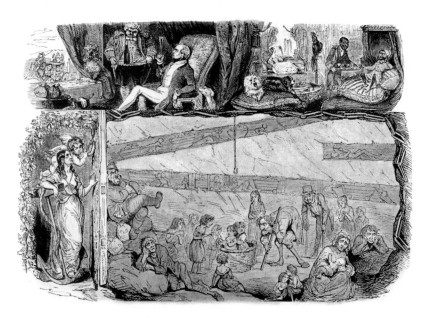

In the late 1800s, however, the rise of big business led government, especially in the United States, to rethink its position on laissez-faire. Corporations were joining together in various combinations—pools, mergers, trusts, cartels—to gain control of markets. These activities hurt consumers because by gaining control of markets, corporations could set prices artificially high and keep competitors from entering the market. The U.S. Congress gradually took steps to restore fairness and competition through laws and regulations. In time, big government would curb the excesses of big business.

A Worldwide Trend Until the 1900s, industrialization was limited to a handful of Western countries, as well as Russia and Japan. But the desire for profits and the general wish to improve living standards led to a widespread push for industry. Also, as more and more peoples throughout the world have demanded a voice in government, liberal democracy has spread across the globe. Capitalism, with its doctrine of private property, has been closely tied to democratic government.

Another phenomenon owed its success, at least partly, to the Industrial Revolution. Nations that industrialized often used their newfound wealth to strengthen their military. In the late 1800s, some of those nations exercised their power by establishing colonies in foreign lands. On that basis, they formed or expanded empires. Their imperialism is the subject of the next chapter.

ADAM SMITH 1723-1790

Adam Smith believed that the government should not interfere in the economy, an idea known as laissez-faire economics. Laissez-faire policy dominated the early period of industrialization. Today Adam Smith's portrait appears on the British 20 pound bill, pictured here.

Summary

In this lesson, you read about the Industrial Revolution, which began in Great Britain and spread to countries throughout the world. Industrialization fundamentally transformed the way people worked and lived.

Economic Structures The Industrial Revolution transformed economies by mechanizing manufacturing and agriculture and shifting from the domestic system of producing goods to the factory system. The need for a means of financing industrialization led to the rise of industrial capitalism.

Social Structures In cottage industry family members worked together to produce goods at their own pace. Factory work called for much more discipline. It also distanced employers from employees, whose unskilled labor and low wages marked them as members of the working class. In the West, women and children were steadily pushed out of factory work.

Human-Environment Interaction New technology, such as the steam engine, made the factory system practical. Factory work attracted migrants from rural areas and from other countries. As a result, the urban population increased greatly, as did air and water pollution and deadly diseases, which spread quickly through overcrowded apartment houses.

Imperialism Throughout the World

How did a few nations come to control so much of the globe?

17.1 Introduction

In September 1898, a British-led army steadily approached Omdurman, a city in the Sudan just west of the Nile River. The British planned to capture the city and thus take command of the entire Nile Valley before their rivals, the French, could do so. Britain had gained control of Egypt in 1882. This expedition would extend Britain's rule more deeply into the African continent.

An army of Mahdists opposed the mixed British and Egyptian force. The Mahdists, Sudanese followers of the Muslim religious leader al-Mahdi, greatly outnumbered their opponents. Yet they had nowhere near their technical skill or firepower. The campaign to conquer the Sudan showcased British industrial might. British engineers had built a 383-mile-long railway across the desert to transport troops and supplies. Their steam-powered gunboats controlled the Nile River. Their modern rifles and machine-guns could fire a barrage of bullets a distance of 1,500 yards or more.

Many Mahdists carried rifles, but they were older, less effective models. Most fought with spears or swords. During the battle, British artillery shells and bullets mercilessly cut down the Mahdist warriors as they charged across the sandy plain. Thousands of them died. Winston Churchill, a British soldier at Omdurman, later wrote that the slaughter was "a matter of machinery." He called his fellow troops "soldiers of scientific war."

Industrialization, with its advances in military science and technology, was a key factor in the British victory at the Battle of Omdurman. By 1914, Britain and a handful of other industrialized European nations would control most of Earth's surface—both land and sea. Along with Japan and the United States, they comprised the world's main imperialist powers.

> **Themes**
>
> **Cultural Interaction** Western imperialist powers introduced new technologies, political ideals, and religious beliefs into Asia and Africa.
>
> **Economic Structures** The age of industry helped trigger the new imperialism, through which Western powers sought new sources of raw materials and new markets for their exports.
>
> **Social Structures** Conquests led Europeans to see themselves as superior to conquered Asian and African peoples.

◀ This 1897 lithograph commemorates the triumphs of the British military in the Sudan and Crimea.

imperialism a policy in which a state takes political and economic control of areas beyond its borders

17.2 The New Imperialism

Starting around 1500, European states practiced **imperialism** by establishing coastal outposts and colonies in Africa, the Americas, and Asia. Their purpose was to support overseas trade. Independence revolutions and the ending of the slave trade severely eroded the imperial system. By the early 1800s, the extent of Western empires had decreased considerably. However, later in the century, a new form of imperialism appeared. A different set of imperialist powers once again sought to expand by exerting control over lands, resources, and peoples beyond their borders.

Renewed Expansion   The new imperialism varied from the old style. Typically, under the old imperialism, a European merchant ship would sail to a colonial port, where it picked up a load of slaves or spices or other goods. Often, with demand being low for Europeans' products, they paid in silver—a "cash-and-carry" arrangement. By around 1800, this mercantile economic system had faded away. Later, a new system evolved. Europeans still took control of foreign lands. But the resulting colonies served not only as sources of raw materials and food but also as markets for machine-made products.

What gave rise to this new imperialism? The answer is not clear-cut. Trade still played a part. But it was no longer the key driving force. The European expansion of the last quarter of the 1800s appears to have come about in a haphazard, unplanned manner. Historians cite a complex mix of possible economic, political, and social factors to explain the rise of new imperialism.

This photo shows enormous racks of drying cowhides. Argentina exported these hides to industrialized nations to be made into manufactured leather goods. A key factor motivating the imperialism of industrialized nations in the 19th century was their need for raw materials.

Industrialization One factor that nearly all historians agree on is industrialization. As French statesman Jules Ferry wrote in 1890, "Colonial policy is the daughter of industrial policy." Nations that mechanized their manufacturing sector became more productive. As a result they needed an increasing supply of natural resources—such as cotton, wool, timber, ore, dyes, and petroleum—to feed their growing industries. And those industries needed larger markets for their manufactured goods. By dominating lands overseas, a country could help fulfill both needs.

Industrialization also increased nations' wealth and power. That gave them a huge advantage in warfare against less developed countries, as the Battle of Omdurman showed. Advances in military technology included rifles that shot farther and more accurately and steam-powered warships that served as platforms for artillery. Some scholars argue that such military advantages led naturally to imperialism. Industrialized European states, they say, expanded because they could.

Political and Socio-Economic Motives Western powers also had political reasons for engaging in imperialism. In the 1800s, competition among those powers was as fierce as ever. Control of key locations or resources could give a country a strategic edge over rival states.

Imperialism also gave political leaders an edge at home by helping them unify public opinion. Social and economic issues—poverty, labor strikes, business downturns—multiplied as countries industrialized. That led to political fragmentation as various interest groups arose to push for reforms. The ability to dominate other lands enhanced a country's status and prestige, giving its citizens a sense of national superiority that encouraged unity. Thus the popularity of an imperialist foreign policy helped politicians overcome political differences and gain support for their domestic policies.

Imperialism was popular in Western nations. The acquisition of overseas colonies increased a nation's power and prestige, and citizens took pride in their country's conquests. This illustration shows Londoners celebrating news of a British victory in the second Boer War in South Africa in 1900.

racist based on prejudices related to racial differences

"White Man's Burden" Feelings of superiority also had a cultural aspect. Europeans saw themselves as a culturally advanced people with a mission, or duty, to civilize more "backward" peoples. This led Christian missionaries to travel to foreign lands to bring their religion and culture to those they considered less fortunate. British poet Rudyard Kipling called this the "White Man's burden":

> Take up the White Man's burden—
> Send forth the best ye breed—
> Go, bind your sons to exile
> To serve your captives' need;
> To wait, in heavy harness,
> On fluttered folk and wild—
> Your new-caught, sullen peoples
> Half devil and half child.
> —Rudyard Kipling, "White Man's Burden," 1899

In the late 1800s, Western peoples knew that they had far outstripped others in creating new technology. That led them to believe that they were not only culturally but also biologically superior to the races of peoples in Africa and Asia that they dominated. This **racist** viewpoint helped them justify their imperialism and the way they treated people in their colonies.

Western nations believed imperialism was morally justified. They saw themselves as conquering "barbarism" by spreading civilization to "backward" peoples. In this cartoon, the bearers of "civilization" face off against "barbarism."

17.3 Colonies and Spheres of Influence in Asia

In Asia in the late 1800s, European states held colonies in a number of prime locations. Where colonies were not practical, they established spheres of influence. A **sphere of influence** is an area within which the political and economic interests of one nation are favored over other nations. Britain, with its large and powerful navy, led the domination of the continent. Its imperialist ventures centered on South Asia.

sphere of influence an area within which the political and economic interests of one nation are more important than those of other nations

South Asia The story of imperialism in South Asia is the story of the British in India. Until 1858, the British East India Company had administered colonial India. The Company's control ended after the Great Rebellion, sometimes called the Indian Mutiny.

The Great Rebellion broke out in 1857 among soldiers of the British-led Indian army. British distribution of cartridges greased with animal fat triggered the rebellion. Before loading a cartridge into their gun, soldiers had to bite off the end of it. Indian soldiers found this extremely offensive culturally. Their Hindu and Muslim religions both forbade oral contact with animal fat. However, the Great Rebellion actually reflected pent-up hostility toward the British, who had, over the years, not only challenged Indians' religious beliefs but also dominated their political and economic lives.

The Great Rebellion broke out in India in 1857. It was an expression of pent-up Indian hostility toward the British. In this image, you can see the damage done to the Umbrella Palace in Lucknow, India, after the rebels had laid siege to the British there.

The British squelched the rebellion, but it caused them to alter their Indian foreign policy. The colony came under the direct control of Parliament, a period known as the British Raj. British rule grew more authoritarian. A former British official in India, Sir James Stephen, offered a reason for taking a harsh approach to governing. "It will never," he wrote in 1883, "be safe for the British Government to forget for a moment that it is founded not on consent but on conquest."

The Great Rebellion shocked the British. They had misjudged the extent of Indian resentment. Afterward, the British cut back on efforts to turn members of India's upper classes into Europeans. They did train Indians for government jobs in the Indian Civil Service. But they were kept from rising to policy-making positions, which were held by the 1,000 or so British members of the Civil Service. Britain continued to manage much of the Indian economy, introducing some industrial technology into a society based on farming. India's population rose, but so did the incidence of famine.

This political cartoon from 1898 shows the countries of Great Britain, Germany, Russia, France, and Japan carving out spheres of influence in China. China looks on, powerless to stop it.

hegemony indirect social, political, or economic influence exerted by a dominant state

Central and Southwest Asia British defense of its Indian colony included attempts to check the expansion of Russia. Since the 1500s, Russia had steadily advanced southward from its original homeland surrounding Moscow. By 1885, Russia extended its control of Central Asia to the northern borders of Persia (Iran) and Afghanistan, India's neighbors to the west. Its influence on those countries deepened.

Britain deemed Russia's advances a threat to the future of India. During this period, it invaded both Persia and Afghanistan to keep Russia from dominating. In 1907, Britain and Russia ended up splitting Persia into commercial spheres of interest. Afghanistan became a buffer between Russia and India.

East Asia Europe's imperialist powers competed intensely in East Asia. For them, the biggest prize was China. China had begun industrializing in the 1860s, using the West as a model. It failed, however, to develop a strong manufacturing base. With the world's largest population, China offered the Europeans an enormous market for their products.

China's weak military could not resist European advances. Britain, France, Germany, and Russia all demanded and received concessions from the weak Chinese government. They carved out spheres of influence over key ports and large chunks of Chinese territory. Britain held sway over the fertile Yangtze River valley. France gained **hegemony** over a large region in the south. Germany forced China to yield control of a smaller region on the northern coast. Russia's sphere of influence lay to the north of the Korean peninsula.

In the 1890s, Japan joined in the China land grab. Like China, Japan had once been one of the West's commercial targets. But the country had grown much stronger since 1868. At that time the Meiji Restoration had restored Japan's emperor to power. It had also started a period of modernization based on Western ways. A popular slogan, "A rich country, strong army," reflected the country's newfound imperialist ambitions.

Japan, a small, mountainous island nation, envied China's expansive farmlands. It also saw China as a possible source of coal and iron ore, which Japan needed in order to compete in an industrializing world. China had plentiful reserves of those minerals. So did China's neighbor Korea, a country that China had traditionally ruled.

In 1894, Japan went to war with China over control of Korea. Despite being seen as the underdog, Japan won the nine-month-long Sino-Japanese War. (*Sino* stands for "Chinese.") As a result, China had to recognize Korea's independence. It also had to pay Japan's war costs and give Japan the island of Formosa (present-day Taiwan) and the Liaodong Peninsula in Manchuria.

In 1814, Britain took control of the Cape Colony. In the years that followed, several thousand British settlers arrived. By then a number of its earlier settlers, known as Boers or Afrikaners, had migrated away from the coast in search of land to farm. Their quest for land and slave labor brought the Boers into continual conflict with indigenous, or native, African peoples.

The Boers also clashed with their new British overlords, who tried to restrain their expansion. Then, in 1834, the British abolished slavery. As a result, from 1835 to 1837, many Boers left the colony altogether in what historians call the Great Trek. Those Boers eventually established three republics—Natal, the Transvaal, and the Orange Free State. The British annexed Natal but recognized the other Boer republics' independence. However, ongoing tensions between the British and the Boers later led to two wars, in 1881 and 1899. The treaty ending the second Boer War also brought an end to the Boer republics.

Unlike most of the rest of the continent, South Africa was blessed with enormous mineral wealth. In the 1860s, settlers discovered diamonds. The diamond fields attracted thousands of prospectors, including immigrants from Europe and the United States. Railway construction, trade, and employment all boomed.

Then, in 1886, South Africans struck gold. This set off an industrial explosion. Much of the gold was located deep underground. Large enterprises formed to acquire land, using capital raised in New York and London. Commercial mining companies went to work, using steam-powered machinery to do the digging. They bought South African coal to fuel their machines and to run the steam locomotives that serviced the goldfields. They hired tens of thousands of workers. South Africa's economy surged.

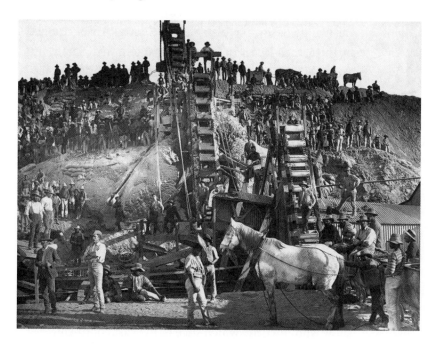

This photo shows a South African diamond mine in operation. South Africa's mineral wealth attracted prospectors and immigrants from Europe and the United States. South Africa had the largest number of white settlers on the continent.

While Britain established a thriving, if troubled, colony in South Africa, France was also making inroads into the continent. By 1850, the French colony of Algeria, in North Africa, had attracted several thousand settlers from France. They came as traders, government officials, and farmers. Native Algerians violently resisted French expansion. To protect its colonists, France had to maintain a large army in Algeria.

By 1880, Britain and France had invested a lot of time and money in Africa. In the next 30 years, other European powers would do the same. Their rush to establish colonies became known as the scramble for Africa.

The Scramble for Africa   Instability in Egypt helped trigger the scramble for Africa. Egypt fell deeply into debt in the 1870s, in part because of the expense of building the Suez Canal. The canal, which ran through Egypt, was completed in 1869. It linked the Mediterranean and Red seas. For the British, the canal brought their most valuable colony, India, much closer. Compared with a voyage around Africa, sailing by way of the Suez Canal chopped some 4,500 miles off the trip.

France and Britain worked to keep Egypt stable. Both countries had invested heavily in the country. But they also recognized the Suez Canal's strategic importance as the gateway to India and East Asia. By 1880, they had taken financial control of the country. Their intervention in Egypt set off protests by Egyptian nationalists who, in 1882, led an uprising. In part to protect their access to the canal, the British put down the rebellion and occupied Egypt.

France invaded and occupied Tunisia in 1881, and it became a French protectorate. This 1899 view of Tunis, the capital city, shows the Porte Française gate and the European-style boulevards which the French constructed. During this era, large communities of Europeans lived in the city, making up a substantial portion of its population.

France decided not to join Britain in the assault on Egypt. But it undertook its own expansion, from Algeria east into Tunisia. Then, in 1884, Germany laid claim to the western coastal region of South Africa and three other substantial areas. Belgium quickly followed by claiming the Congo Basin, a huge region in Central Africa drained by the Congo River. In the years that followed, Spain, Portugal, and Italy all asserted their rights to various territories.

The scramble for Africa had started, and with it came multiple disputes. Europeans met at the Berlin West Africa Conference of 1884–1885 to try to iron out their differences. The stated goal of the conference was to open the interior of Africa to free trade and, in the process, bring civilization to the native peoples. The "interior" referred mainly to the vast Congo River basin, a million square miles of Central Africa. The formal conference achieved written agreement on this goal. In informal negotiations, members of the conference resolved other disputes. Then and later, diplomats signed treaties and had maps of Africa drawn to show who "owned" which slice of the vast continent.

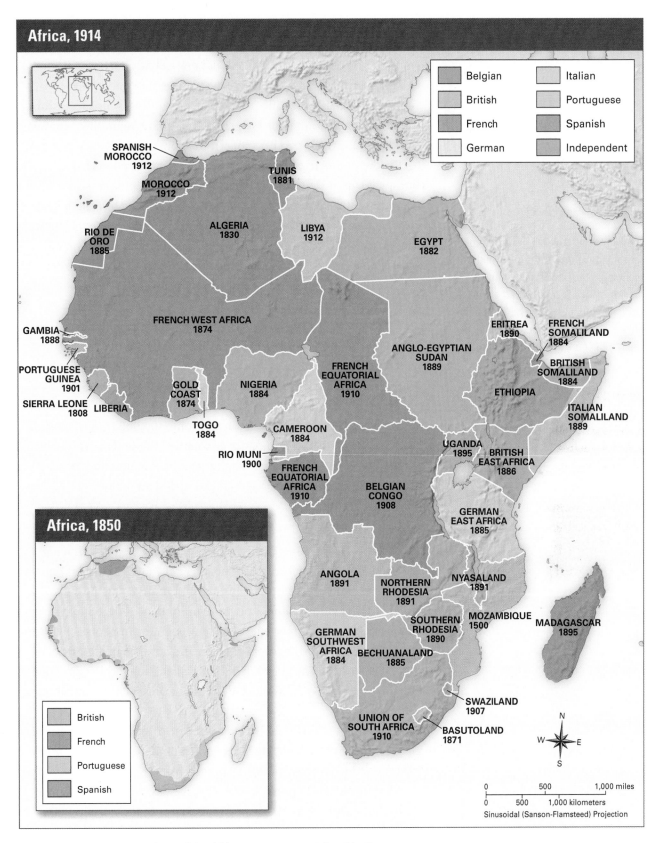

Africa, 1914

Belgian	Italian
British	Portuguese
French	Spanish
German	Independent

SPANISH MOROCCO 1912

MOROCCO 1912

TUNIS 1881

RIO DE ORO 1885

ALGERIA 1830

LIBYA 1912

EGYPT 1882

FRENCH WEST AFRICA 1874

GAMBIA 1888

PORTUGUESE GUINEA 1901

SIERRA LEONE 1808

LIBERIA

GOLD COAST 1874

TOGO 1884

NIGERIA 1884

CAMEROON 1884

RIO MUNI 1900

FRENCH EQUATORIAL AFRICA 1910

FRENCH EQUATORIAL AFRICA 1910

ANGLO-EGYPTIAN SUDAN 1889

ERITREA 1890

FRENCH SOMALILAND 1884

BRITISH SOMALILAND 1884

ETHIOPIA

ITALIAN SOMALILAND 1889

UGANDA 1895

BRITISH EAST AFRICA 1886

BELGIAN CONGO 1908

GERMAN EAST AFRICA 1885

ANGOLA 1891

NORTHERN RHODESIA 1891

NYASALAND 1891

MOZAMBIQUE 1500

MADAGASCAR 1895

GERMAN SOUTHWEST AFRICA 1884

BECHUANALAND 1885

SOUTHERN RHODESIA 1890

SWAZILAND 1907

UNION OF SOUTH AFRICA 1910

BASUTOLAND 1871

Africa, 1850

British	
French	
Portuguese	
Spanish	

N
W E
S

0	500	1,000 miles
0	500	1,000 kilometers

Sinusoidal (Sanson-Flamsteed) Projection

▲ In 1850, only small sections of the African coast were claimed by European powers. By 1914, the African continent was almost completely divided into European colonial possessions.

Again and again, imperialist forces in Africa were able to put down popular rebellions with their superior weaponry. This image shows American soldiers manning a Maxim machine gun, the most advanced weapon at the time. British colonial soldiers had a popular saying: "Whatever else, we have got/ the Maxim gun, and they have not."

Resistance to Imperialism   Claiming a territory on paper was easy. Actually taking physical control of that territory was not so simple. Sometimes, African elites cooperated with European occupiers. But nearly everywhere, native peoples resisted imperialist expansion. Much of that resistance was violent—and largely unsuccessful. As the Sudanese found out at the Battle of Omdurman, sheer courage could not effectively combat modern weaponry.

Throughout Africa this point was proven over and over again. Europeans used superior firearms to put down popular resistance. Uprisings by the Ashanti people in Gold Coast, the Ndebele in Rhodesia, and the Zulu in Natal all ended fairly quickly. Some rebellions, though unsuccessful, lasted much longer. In West Africa, a Mande tribe led by Samory Touré fought against French occupation from 1883 to 1898. In East Africa, the Tutsi and Hutu resisted the Germans and British from 1911 to 1917.

One major African resistance campaign did meet with success. It involved Ethiopia and Italy. Menelik, Ethiopia's emperor, had modernized his country, which included acquiring up-to-date weapons for his sizeable military. When Italy sent 18,000 soldiers to take control of Ethiopia, Menelik declared war. On March 1, 1896, at the Battle of Adowa, the emperor sent out a force of some 100,000 troops, most of them well-armed. They quickly overwhelmed the Italian army, which suffered heavy losses. Italy gave up its goal of conquest and, instead, accepted Ethiopia as a sovereign and independent nation.

17.5 Western Influence in Latin America

Western powers dominated countries and territories by occupying them and ruling them directly. Scholars refer to this as formal imperialism. In contrast, informal imperialism is marked by indirect rule. The dominant country exerts pressure or influence without physical conquest. Informal imperialism is often economic in nature, but it can also include force or the threat of force, and cultural imperialism, or influence. The informal version of imperialism, often called hegemony, was the type most often wielded by Western powers in Latin America.

Independent Politically but Not Economically   By 1830, nearly all of Latin America had gained its political independence. Yet many issues remained unresolved. They ranged from the clash of liberal and conservative ideals to power struggles waged by military strongmen.

In that volatile atmosphere, even resource-rich nations in Latin America failed to industrialize. They remained largely dependent on Britain, France, and other Western countries for manufactured goods. Political turmoil and economic dependence opened these Latin American states to imperialism, both formal and informal.

Western Economic Control   Through most of the 1800s, Britain remained the most highly industrialized nation on Earth. As such, it needed easy access to raw materials as well as markets for its goods. In its own economic interest, therefore, it favored the removal of all barriers to trade. As applied to Latin America, scholars call this "free-trade imperialism." It involved both trade and **capital**.

Britain viewed the Latin American revolutions as a way to strengthen its commercial ties with the region. The economies of the new Latin American countries produced mainly raw materials. They depended on industrializing nations, especially Britain, to buy those goods. Argentina, for example, based its economy on the export of meat, hides, and grain into the early 1900s.

British capital added to the control that Britain exercised over Latin America. British investors saw potential profit in expanding the ability of countries such as Brazil, Argentina, and Uruguay to export their raw materials and foodstuffs. British business people migrated to Latin America to oversee these investments, which included the raising of sheep and cattle and the building of facilities to transport goods. British banks financed the capital expansions through loans. Managing those loans gave the banks further influence over Latin American economies.

As they industrialized, France and the United States duplicated Britain's approach to Latin America. French and American businesses and banks invested in Latin America and provided loans for capital expansion. The United States, however, also got politically involved in the region.

capital the tools, machines, and buildings used to produce goods and services

Monroe Doctrine a U.S. foreign policy focused on keeping European powers from controlling any Latin American nation

Roosevelt Corollary an extension of the Monroe Doctrine declaring that the United States would police unstable Latin American debtor nations; also known as the Big Stick Policy

In this political cartoon from 1901, the United States, represented by a strutting rooster, patrols the yard while the birds in the "European coop" are boarded in by a plank labeled "Monroe Doctrine." The Monroe Doctrine declared that European powers should not interfere in Latin America.

United States Foreign Policy

During the 1800s, the United States came to view Latin America as its personal sphere of influence. In 1823 President James Monroe put forward the **Monroe Doctrine,** which banned the nations of Europe from further colonizing Latin America.

In 1904, President Theodore Roosevelt extended the Monroe Doctrine in an address to Congress that became known as the **Roosevelt Corollary**.

Roosevelt noted that the Monroe Doctrine was designed to prevent European meddling in the Americas. Yet he pointed out that nearly a century later many countries in Latin America were still too weak to defend themselves.

Roosevelt stated that the United States therefore must use "international police power" to preserve peace and order in the hemisphere and protect American interests. The Roosevelt Corollary implied two things. Europe had no reason to interfere in Latin America, and the United States was now powerful enough to police the entire region.

Western Aggression Much of Western imperialism in Latin America was informal, but not all. In spite of the Monroe Doctrine, Britain and France continued to practice imperialism in the region. Britain established or formalized its control of British Guiana in 1831, the Falkland Islands in 1833, British Honduras in 1859, and Jamaica in 1866.

France tried to conquer Mexico in 1862. Mexico's failure to pay its debts to European banks had led Britain and France to send a naval force there in 1861 as a threat. France ended up occupying the country and installing its own emperor. Mexican resistance and pressure from the United States forced France out in 1867.

In 1898, the United States itself engaged in formal imperialism. After winning the Spanish-American War, it occupied Cuba and seized Puerto Rico. Later, under the pretext of ensuring stability, the United States intervened militarily in Nicaragua, Haiti, and the Dominican Republic. It also helped Panama break away from Colombia in order for the United States to acquire the right to build the Panama Canal.

HIS NEIGHBORLY SUGGESTION.

UNCLE SAM. — Now, young man, while I'm digging here, I'd like a long period of depression in the Revolution Business.

The construction of the Panama Canal provided the United States with trading opportunities and, more importantly, control in Latin America. This cartoon shows America, as a tall and commanding Uncle Sam, warning smaller and weaker Central America to stay out of trouble while America builds in the region.

17.6 Impact of Imperialism

By 1900, powerful Western states controlled half the continent of Asia. They ruled some nine tenths of Africa. Their influence extended over a quarter of the Americas. The actions of these imperialist powers had a complex mix of positive and negative effects on colonized peoples.

Imperialism killed people, especially in Africa. European armies used force—often brutal—to secure and hold on to territory. One example is the rebellion by the Herero and Nama people in German South West Africa. In 1904, the rebels killed about a hundred traders and farmers. The German response was to try to exterminate the two African groups. Only a quarter of the original population of 100,000 Herero and Nama survived the slaughter that followed.

At the same time, imperialism had some humanitarian consequences. Through the 1800s, European societies developed a sense that slavery was morally wrong. It went against their ideals of liberty and equality. By 1888, all Western nations had abolished slavery. They used their wealth and superior military power to try to root out this evil not just in their colonies, but everywhere. As a result, slavery declined markedly in Africa, the Philippines, Indonesia, and elsewhere.

Many other aspects of Western society found their way into distant colonies, in a process known as Westernization. The imperialists imposed their own legal systems, taxes, and political administration. They introduced Western education, medicine, technology, languages, and dress. They worked to convert native peoples to Christianity.

Colonizers also improved their colonies' **infrastructure**. This supported their key economic goal—expansion of a colony's exports. Europeans built railroads to transport goods from plantations and mines to the nearest port. There they constructed warehouses to hold the goods and harbor facilities to serve the cargo ships that carried the goods. However, they stopped short of encouraging their colonies to industrialize. In general, colonized lands continued to serve solely as sources of raw materials and a few consumer goods well into the twentieth century.

In the 19th century many Christians moved to their country's colonies to spread their faith. They felt they were performing a moral duty by "uplifting" the "savages" of the world. The spread of Christianity contributed to the process of Westernization. In this image, English missionaries teach native children in New Guinea.

> **infrastructure** large-scale transportation, communication, and other systems that support economic activity

Summary

In this lesson, you read about the second era of European imperialism, during the 19th and early 20th centuries. In this period, a few European nations with great military and industrial power took control of much of the world.

Cultural Interaction Western imperialist powers used their advanced military technologies, such as the machine-gun and the steam-powered gunboat, to conquer new territories. They introduced their culture—including education, language, political ideals such as equality and liberty, and the Christian religion—into Asia and Africa.

Economic Structures Industrialization helped trigger the new imperialism, through which capitalistic Western powers sought raw materials for their factories and markets for their machine-made goods. The colonized lands themselves failed to industrialize during the imperialist period.

Social Structures Racist attitudes supported Europeans' notion that they were culturally and even biologically superior to the Asian and African peoples that they dominated.

Era Overview: Global Crisis and Achievement, 1900–1945

How did the global balance of power change between 1900 and 1945, and why?

18.1 Introduction

The crowd lined the route of the motorcade, eager for a glimpse of their next emperor as he passed by. Archduke Franz Ferdinand, heir to the throne of the Austro-Hungarian Empire, was visiting Sarajevo in Bosnia-Herzegovina (BAWZ-nee-uh hurt-suh-go-VEE-nuh), a province in the empire with a large Serbian population. But not everyone gathered that morning of June 28, 1914 had come to cheer the archduke. Seven young men spread along the route had come to assassinate him. Among them was 19-year-old Gavrilo Princip (gah-VREE-low PREEN-sip). Princip viewed the archduke's death as key to freeing the province from Austria-Hungry, to join the neighboring nation of Serbia.

With a pistol hidden in his coat, Princip stood at the curb and waited his chance. He heard a loud boom a short distance away. Another of the assassins had thrown a grenade. But it had bounced off the archduke's car and exploded in the street. The car sped past Princip's position, headed to safety at Sarajevo's city hall.

Believing the mission had failed, Princip walked to a nearby deli to buy lunch. When he left the deli, incredibly, he saw the archduke's car directly in front of him. Ferdinand was headed to the hospital to visit those wounded in the grenade attack. The driver had taken a wrong turn and had stopped to turn around. Princip ran forward, pulled out his gun, and started firing. Both the archduke and his wife Sophie were hit.

"It is nothing. It is nothing," Ferdinand insisted when asked if he was hurt. But it was not nothing. In fact, it was quite something, indeed. Within minutes both the archduke and Sophie were dead, and within weeks their deaths plunged Europe into war.

Themes

Cultural Interactions The rise and spread of communism and fascism resulted in political unrest and increased international tensions.

Political Systems Conflict arose as nations sought to expand or protect their empires and as subject peoples sought to be free.

Economic Systems Nations sought control over areas that could provide raw materials for their industries and markets for their goods.

Human-Environment Interaction Two major wars brought great destruction to large areas of the world.

The assassination of Franz Ferdinand ignited tensions in Europe that started World War I.

18.2 The Turn-of-the Century World

The rivalries, jealousies, and tensions that Ferdinand's assassination ignited into World War I in August 1914 had been developing for many years. Austria-Hungary, Russia, Germany, France, and the Ottoman Empire (centered in present-day Turkey) competed for land and influence in Europe, and along with Great Britain, for colonies and control over much of Africa and Asia.

Similar tensions also existed elsewhere. To the west, the United States was seeking to become the dominant nation in the Americas. In the east, Japan had abandoned its traditional policy of isolation and was seeking land and power in mainland Asia. China was struggling with the **spheres of influence** the European powers and Japan had carved out in that large but weak and divided nation.

sphere of influence an area within which the political and economic interests of one nation are more important than those of other nations

protectorate a relationship in which the protection and partial control of one nation is held by another, more powerful nation

A World of Empires The popular nineteenth-century expression that "the sun never sets on the British Empire" was still true at the dawn of the twentieth. With territories on every continent, Great Britain controlled one-fifth of the world and a quarter of its population. Great Britain and France ruled most of Africa. Along with Russia, Great Britain had vast holdings in Asia, where the French and Dutch were also important colonial powers. This division of the world left little opportunity for two ambitious and rapidly industrializing nations—Germany and Japan.

Germany, which did not become a unified nation until 1871, finished a distant third to Great Britain and France in the scramble for colonies. This outcome did not sit well with ambitious German leaders. "To stand dreamily to one side while other people split up the pie, we cannot and we will not do that," proclaimed German foreign secretary Bernhard von Bulow in 1899. "If the English speak of a 'Greater Britain;' if the French speak of a 'Nouvelle [New] France;' if the Russians open up Asia; then we, too, have the right to a greater Germany."

Russia's vast empire spread from its border with Germany east to the Pacific Ocean. Russia's Trans-Siberian Railroad, completed in 1904, was the first to link Europe and Asia. It also fueled Russian dreams for expanding trade, landholding, and influence in East Asia. In the early 1900s, Russia seized Chinese Manchuria and established a **protectorate** over Mongolia, which had declared independence from China.

The Emergence of Japan and the United States Russia's move on Manchuria brought conflict with Japan, which also desired the resource-rich region. In 1904 Russia and Japan went to war over Manchuria and Korea—another area of rivalry between the two nations. The war went badly for Russia and ended in 1905 when the United States, with German and British support, forced a settlement. Manchuria was returned to China and Russia agreed to respect Japan's control over Korea, which became a Japanese colony in 1910.

Port Arthur in Manchuria was the site of the longest and most violent battle of the Russo-Japanese War. Japan emerged victorious but neither power was happy with the ultimate outcome of the war.

Neither Russia nor Japan was happy with the war's outcome. Russia's military defeat, coupled with the loss of Manchuria, added to the unrest that led to revolution in 1905 and eventually to the communist Bolshevik Revolution of 1917. The frustration of Japan's ambitions in Manchuria created resentment and tensions that contributed to the coming of World War II.

For the United States, settling the Russo-Japanese War marked its emergence as a major player on the world stage. Like Germany and Japan, the United States came late to the quest for empire. Also like those nations, its expansion overseas was linked to a need for resources and markets for its growing industries. However, unlike German and Japanese **imperialism,** U.S. actions were not driven by a desire for land. Although the United States annexed Hawaii and seized the Philippines from Spain in the 1890s, American attention focused on U.S. business investments in Latin America.

Like the Americans, European companies invested in Latin American mines, railroads, plantations, and other businesses. However, political instability sometimes put such investments at risk. In 1904, the United States announced that it would take charge in any Latin American nation that could not properly manage its affairs. It took such action in several nations between 1904 and 1916. The policy blocked European powers from increased control in Latin America to protect their investments and made the United States the major power in the region. It also caused much resentment in Latin America.

imperialism the policy of extending a nation's power and influence by gaining control over territory through political or military means

economic imperialism the domination of one nation by another nation—and companies within it—that is economically more powerful

Nationalism was a central factor in many of the conflicts that arose in the first half of the 20th century. This army recruiting poster from World War I appealed to British nationalism to stir up support for the war.

RALLY ROUND THE FLAG

"WE MUST HAVE MORE MEN"

Nationalism and Imperialism

The idea that they were not capable of managing their own nations offended the pride of Latin American peoples. U.S. and European **economic imperialism** benefitted development in Latin America. But it also aroused a spirit of nationalism, as it did in China at about the same time. Chinese nationalism led to the Boxer Rebellion of 1900. A group of anti-Western Chinese known as the Boxers rose up against the European presence there. The European powers, the United States, and Japan all sent troops to end the uprising. The result was increased foreign control and a further weakening of China's rulers.

Nationalism was a powerful force throughout the turn-of-the century world. One of its basic principles is that people of the same culture should rule themselves and have their own nation. Nationalism also involves intense love for one's country and, sometimes, the idea that the country and its culture are superior to others. These beliefs and their expression help explain much of the history of this period. They also are responsible for many developments and events of the later twentieth century.

Nationalism was a driving force behind German unification. The nationalist belief in cultural superiority was a factor in British, French, and other European imperialism in Africa and Asia. At the same time, however, nationalism also helps explain the unrest that developed in European empires. Between 1900 and 1914, African peoples revolted against the rule of every European colonial power. In Asia, Indian nationalism fueled a movement for self-rule in the British Empire in the late 1800s—and later for independence. In the early 1900s, nationalist groups called for violent resistance to British rule in Burma and French rule in Vietnam. In the Philippines, American troops crushed a long-running war for independence in 1901. And it was Serbian nationalism in 1914 that inspired the assassination of Archduke Ferdinand and sent all of Europe to war.

18.3 Empires in Europe

As the struggle for colonies and control played out in Africa and Asia, the European nations of Germany, France, Russia, and Austria-Hungary also sought land, security, and power within Europe. One result of this effort was a shifting series of alliances among them.

The Alliance System Germany and France competed for a region on their border called Alsace-Lorraine. Austria-Hungary and Russia both desired land and influence in the Balkans. To protect themselves against their rivals, Germany and Austria-Hungary signed a defense agreement in 1879. Italy later joined this agreement to form what was known as the Triple Alliance.

The Triple Alliance threatened to isolate France in Western Europe. At the same time, Russia feared rival Austria-Hungary's alliance with Germany. So Russia and France signed a treaty in 1894. This agreement threatened Germany on both its eastern and western borders. The situation grew even more tense in the early 1900s when Britain, fearing Germany's growing industrial might, joined Russia and France to form the Triple Entente. *Entente* is a French term meaning "agreement" or "understanding."

This cartoon from 1888 portrays Germany, Austria-Hungary, and Italy, the members of the Triple Alliance, as the three Fates, controlling the destiny of Europe. The Triple Alliance was a defense agreement the three powers signed to protect themselves against their rivals.

Europe's Balance of Power The alliance system was one result of a shift in the balance of power that was underway in Europe. Austria-Hungary was battling rising nationalism from ethnic groups within its borders and was trying to avoid decline. Russia, humiliated by Japan in Asia and also challenged by nationalism and other unrest, faced a similar challenge. The Ottoman Empire, once a powerful force in Eastern Europe, was already in serious trouble. Nationalism sparked Serbia, Romania, and Bulgaria to declare independence. Austria-Hungary gained control of Bosnia-Herzegovina and Britain, France, and Italy seized Ottoman territory in North Africa.

As these old empires weakened, Germany was on the rise. With a smaller overseas empire than Britain and France, Germany used its industries to build a strong military and its power in Europe instead. Germany's increasing power alarmed Russia and France. The British viewed Germany's naval buildup as another threat. Not only was Britain an island nation, but its navy's control of the high seas was vital to protecting its world-wide empire. These concerns helped to unite Britain, Russia, and France in the Triple Entente.

Clashing Empires   The borders, interests, and ambitions of the Russian, Austro-Hungarian, and Ottoman empires came together on Europe's Balkan Peninsula. Russia had long sought expansion into the region, wanting to gain access to a warm-water port. This goal caused Russia to support the Serbian and other nationalist revolts against Turkish rule.

Austria-Hungary also wanted to weaken the Ottoman hold in the Balkans. However, it felt threatened by Russia's actions. Not only did it oppose Russian influence in the region, it wanted the Balkans for itself. In addition, Austria-Hungary feared that new, independent nations in the region would stir nationalist unrest among those ethnic groups in its own empire.

Meanwhile, the Ottoman Empire faced its own problems with nationalism. In the early 1900s, a group of Turkish nationalists called the Young Turks took control of the government. The Young Turks launched reforms to strengthen Turkish culture across the empire. This action stirred nationalism and unrest in its Arab and Christian populations.

Austria-Hungary took advantage of these events to officially make Bosnia-Herzegovina part of its empire in 1908. In 1912, Russia encouraged Serbia and the other independent Balkan nations to declare war on Turkey. The war cost the Ottomans almost all that remained of their empire in Europe. Much of this land went to Serbia, doubling its size. But Serbia remained landlocked, with no outlet to the sea. Plus it had visions of an even larger nation that included all Serbians in the Balkans. To fulfill this vision and give itself a border on the sea, Serbia turned its attention to Austria-Hungary's new province of Bosnia-Herzegovina.

This cartoon comments on the land grab that resulted from war between Turkey and independent Balkan nations in 1912. As the Ottoman Empire (here depicted as Santa Claus leaving a bag of toys) crumbled, different powers in the region scrambled for their territory. Much of the land went to Serbia.

18.4 World War I and Its Consequences

Austria-Hungary blamed Serbia for the assassination of Archduke Ferdinand in June 1914. It saw a chance to use the horrible event to end Serbian ambitions and nationalism in the region. Backed by the promise of German support, Austria-Hungary made a series of demands on Serbia. Serb leaders agreed to most of these demands. But Austria-Hungary declared war on Serbia anyway.

militarism the predominance of the armed forces in making and carrying out the policies of a nation; the glorification of military preparedness and armed strength

The World Goes to War The archduke's death ignited war in the Balkans. Larger forces were responsible for turning this regional conflict into a world war. They are the now-familiar forces of nationalism, imperialism, **militarism,** and the alliance system.

The tensions between Austria-Hungary and Serbia were fueled by each side's nationalism and desire for increased territory and influence. Nationalism and imperialism caused Russia to support Serbia. Russians and Serbs are both Slavic peoples. In addition, Russia hoped that siding with Serbia would increase its influence in the Balkans and perhaps even gain territory there.

The bloodstained coat worn by Archduke Franz Ferdinand when he was slain by Gavrilo Princip in 1914 stands as mute evidence of the trigger that set off World War I.

To support Serbia, Russia began massing troops along its border with Austria-Hungary. Germany responded by declaring war on Russia on August 1, 1914. Within days, Russia's allies France and Britain had joined the conflict. Both had been building their militaries for years in response to Germany's arms buildup and they were prepared for war. Japan also declared war on Germany, hoping to gain control of German possessions in Asia.

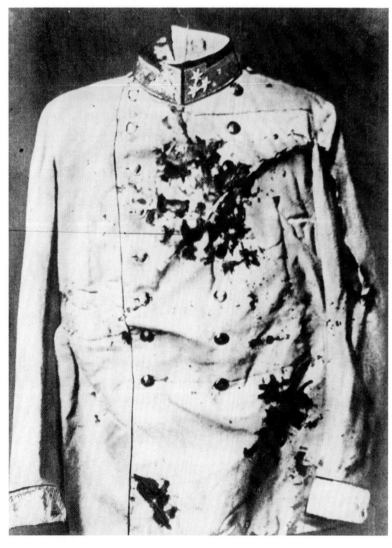

Because of their central location in Europe, Germany and Austria-Hungry were called the Central Powers. Russia and its allies became the Allied Powers. The Ottoman Empire's long rivalry with Russia over the Balkans and the Black Sea brought it into the war as another Central Power. Meanwhile, lured by promises of Austrian territory, Italy abandoned the Triple Alliance and joined the Allies in 1915. The conflict became a true world war when the United States entered it in 1917 on the side of the Allies.

At the beginning of World War I, French and British troops met the invading German army in northern France. The opposing armies dug defensive trenches and faced off in brutal fighting that lasted for three years and killed more than 7 million soldiers.

Fighting World War I The outbreak of war stirred national pride across Europe. Both sides predicted a short war and were confident of victory. No one expected the long, bloody conflict that followed.

German forces quickly invaded France with the intent of defeating France first and avoiding a two front war. But British and French troops stopped the German forces. The opposing armies then dug a network of defensive trenches across northern France, along what became known as the Western Front. The industrialization of the late nineteenth century had given both sides highly effective weapons, such as long-range artillery and machine guns. For three years, each side tried to push the other back, out of its trenches. The loss of life was horrific. More than 1.7 million soldiers were killed in one year alone.

The fighting was also brutal on the war's Eastern Front, as German troops pushed deep into Russia. Heavy Russian losses helped cause the government's collapse in 1917 and the formation of the communist Bolshevik government. The Bolsheviks made peace with Germany and pulled Russia out of the war in March 1918.

Other fighting took place in Africa, Asia, and the Middle East. But it was the fighting in Western Europe that decided the outcome of World War I. By mid-1918, American troops and supplies arriving in Europe finally tipped the balance on the Western Front. Allied forces began pushing the German army back, leading to a cease-fire in November 1918. Germany's formal surrender came when the Treaty of Paris was finalized in 1919.

Outcomes of World War I The first world war destroyed the old order in central and eastern Europe and in the Middle East. Austria-Hungary and the Ottoman Empire were broken up. Nine new countries were created from Austria-Hungary and from land taken from Germany and Russia. What remained of the Russian Empire became the Union of Soviet Socialist Republics (USSR or Soviet Union) under communist rule.

In the Middle East, Turkey overthrew its Ottoman ruler and became a republic. The rest of the Ottoman Empire was divided into Arab nations that were put under British and French control. Britain and France, along with Japan and other Allied nations, took over all of Germany's colonies in China, Africa, and the Pacific, as required by the Treaty of Paris.

The Allies' punishment of Germany went far beyond taking its land and colonies. The Treaty of Versailles, the peace treaty with Germany, reduced its military to a size that made it almost powerless. In addition, Germany was forbidden to keep troops in the Rhineland, a region along its border with France. The ban left Germany unable to protect this important industrial region. Finally, Germany was forced to admit that it had started the war and to pay $33 billion for war damages. This harsh and humiliating treaty damaged Germany's national pride and left Germans bitter about its terms.

This picture shows European leaders negotiating the Treaty of Versailles, which ended the war with Germany. The treaty forced Germany to accept blame for the war and pay enormous sums of money as reparations.

Postwar Problems   World War I was very costly, both in money spent to fight it and in the high loss of life. Countries in which fighting took place, such as France, also had to deal with great destruction and the cost of rebuilding damaged areas. France, Britain, and Germany had huge war debts, and almost all of Europe suffered from inflation, high unemployment, and other economic problems resulting from the war. In addition, Germany, Poland, and the nations created from the breakup of Austria-Hungary were trying to form democratic governments. In some of these nations, people turned to **authoritarian** leaders in hopes of restoring political and economic order. The new democratic nations of Hungary and Poland, for example, quickly became **dictatorships**.

The Rise of Dictators   Italy and Germany were among the nations that adopted extreme solutions to their problems after World War I. Anti-communist leader Benito Mussolini took advantage of Italy's unrest to come to power in 1922. Mussolini led a political movement that he called **fascism**. Fascism is an extreme form of nationalism that puts the nation above all else. It accepts the use of force and the denial of rights and freedoms in order to make the people serve the good of the nation. Control usually rests in one all-powerful leader.

Mussolini used the peoples' desire for political and economic stability to gain control of Italy's democratic government for his Fascist Party. Once in control, he abolished elections and banned all other political parties. He also ended all civil rights in Italy, including freedom of speech, freedom of assembly, and trial by jury. By the late 1920s Italy had become a police state. In return, Mussolini promised that he would restore to Italy the power and glory of ancient Rome.

authoritarian relating to or favoring a concentration of power in a leader or leaders who are not responsible to the people and which calls for blind submission to authority

dictatorship a nation or government in which total control is in the hands of one all-powerful ruler

fascism a political philosophy or system marked by strong central authority and that places the nation, and often a race, above individual rights and freedoms

Adolf Hitler (center) and Benito Mussolini (right) became dictators of Germany and Italy, respectively. In Italy, Mussolini was known as *Il Duce*, or "The Leader." Hitler's title was *Der Führer*. It meant the same thing.

Germany followed a similar course. In 1921, Adolf Hitler became head of a small German political party called the National Socialist German Workers Party. The party is commonly known in English as the Nazi Party. The Nazi Party was extremely nationalistic, anti-democratic, anti-socialist, and anticommunist. By promising to protect the nation from communism, it gradually gained voter support and influence in Germany's new, democratic government.

Hitler's attacks on Germany's treatment by the Allies after World War I added to the party's popularity. He promised to undo the war's results, regain Germany's lost territory and colonies, and restore Germany as a great military power. His fiery speeches appealed to the patriotism of many Germans who felt bitter and humiliated by the Treaty of Versailles.

Hitler's rise to power was also aided by the Great Depression that struck the United States in the early 1930s. As the Great Depression spread worldwide, its effects increased Germany's postwar economic problems and pushed more voters to the Nazi Party. In 1933, Germany's president named Hitler to head the government. Hitler quickly convinced Germany's parliament to give him emergency powers to put down an alleged communist revolt. He then used these powers to become a dictator and, like Mussolini, turned his nation into a police state. Freedom of the press and opposition political parties were banned.

In the Soviet Union, dictatorship emerged from a different source—communism. The Soviet Union had only one political party in the 1920s—the Communist Party. A power struggle developed for leadership of the party in 1924. By 1928, Joseph Stalin had emerged as head of the Communist Party and leader of the Soviet Union. Stalin gradually increased his control by using a network of spies and secret police to eliminate party members and others suspected of opposing his rule. By the early 1930s, the Soviet Union had become a totalitarian dictatorship. Totalitarianism is a system in which the government totally controls all aspects of a society, including the economy. Meanwhile, the Soviet Union continued to support communist revolution in Europe and Asia.

Nowhere did communism and fascism clash more violently than in Spain. Like several other European nations, Spain became a military dictatorship in the 1920s. In 1931, the dictatorship fell and a democratic republic was formed. When elections put a communist-led government in power in 1936, fascist elements in the army revolted. Civil war followed. The Soviet Union sent military aid to supporters of the government, while Germany and Italy aided the rebels, who called themselves Nationalists.

By 1939, the Nationalists had gained control of Spain. Their leader General Francisco Franco set up a dictatorship similar to the fascist governments of Italy and Germany.

Nationalism and Unrest in Asia and Africa   A civil war also took place in China. Weakened by decades of European imperialism, by the end of World War I China barely existed as a nation. Chinese nationalists had overthrown the emperor and formed a republic. However, most governing power was held by regional warlords. In 1926 Chiang Kaishek (chang ky-SHEK), head of China's Nationalist Party, began a military campaign to unite China. Aid from the Soviet Union helped Chiang defeat the warlords. Then he turned against the communists and expelled them from his Nationalist movement. This action launched a long civil war that ended in a communist victory in 1949 and the creation of China's current communist government.

Like China, Japan introduced western-style democracy. However, the Allies' treatment of Japan after the war humiliated and angered many Japanese. By blocking Japan's desire to be the greatest power in Asia, the western nations strengthened the military's influence in Japan's government. The suffering that resulted from the Great Depression also turned many Japanese against the West, further strengthening Japanese nationalism and militarism. By the mid 1930s the military was in control of Japan's government.

Nationalism grew stronger throughout Asia in the 1920s and 1930s. In Southeast Asia, a young Vietnamese communist known as Ho Chi Minh (hoe-chee-MIN) helped launch a sometimes-violent movement to free Indochina from French rule. To the west, Mohandas Gandhi (Moe-HAHN-dahs GAHN-dee) began a nonviolent campaign for India's independence from Great Britain. Still farther west, Arab unrest led Britain and France to recognize the independence of Jordan (1923), Syria (1930), and Iraq (1932). However, British or French troops remained in all three nations.

Britain and France kept a tight hold on their colonies in Africa. Although Britain granted Egypt independence in 1922, British troops continued to occupy that nation, in part to protect the vital Suez Canal which connected the Red Sea and the Mediterranean. Elsewhere, Britain and France tried to weaken African nationalism by giving more power to tribal leaders and increasing Africans' role in colonial governments. However, by the late 1930s independence movements existed in Nigeria, Kenya, and several other African colonies. Such calls for independence would increase after World War II.

Chiang Kaishek was the leader of China's Nationalist government from 1928 to 1949. He fought to unite a fractured China under a single government. However, it was the Communists who would eventually unite China, after they defeated Chiang's Nationalist army in 1949.

18.5 A Second World War

Most historians believe that the Treaty of Versailles after World War I, combined with the effects of worldwide depression in the 1930s, created conditions that set the stage for World War II. By the late 1930s, tensions in Europe were as high as they had been before World War I. In Asia, Japan was once again on the move to enlarge its empire and establish itself as a great power.

In this photo Hitler and the British Prime Minister Neville Chamberlain shake hands at the Munich Conference. Britain and France thought the agreement they made with Hitler at Munich could avoid war, but Hitler violated its terms and continued to demand more land for Germany.

appeasement the policy of giving in to the demands of a potential enemy in order to avoid conflict

Aggression and Appeasement In 1931, Japan seized Manchuria, the region it was forced to return to China in 1905, following the Russo-Japanese War. China complained to the League of Nations, an international peacekeeping organization set up by the Treaty of Versailles. When the League condemned Japan's actions, Japan withdrew from the organization. The League of Nations did not have its own military force. No nation proved willing to use force to help, and in 1937 Japanese troops launched new attacks to conquer all of China.

The great powers' failure to respond to Japan's aggression encouraged Mussolini to act on his promise to expand Italy's empire. In 1935 Italian forces attacked and soon conquered Ethiopia, one of the few independent nations in Africa. Again, the League of Nations condemned this act of aggression. But also again, no other nation rose to oppose it. The major powers—France, Great Britain, and the United States— were too involved with their own problems, many of which resulted from the Great Depression. In addition, people in all three nations remembered the horrors of World War I. They were not willing to risk a new war to save Ethiopia.

Like Mussolini, Adolf Hitler was also encouraged by the Allies' unwillingness to act. In 1933, Hitler announced plans to rearm Germany in defiance of the Treaty of Versailles. Three years later, in another violation of the treaty, he moved German troops into the Rhineland. He also made alliances with Italy and Japan. When Britain and France did not respond, Hitler pushed forward with even greater plans. In 1938 he annexed neighboring Austria. Then he demanded a German-speaking region of Czechoslovakia called the Sudetenland. At last, Britain and France protested.

British and French leaders met with Hitler in Munich, Germany, in September 1938. At the Munich Conference, they agreed to allow Germany to take the Sudetenland. Hitler assured them that this was his last demand for territory. By adopting this policy of **appeasement**, Britain and France thought they were avoiding war. However, six months later, Hitler seized the rest of Czechoslovakia. Then he demanded territory from Poland.

This stark black and white photo shows railroad tracks leading to the entrance of Auschwitz, Nazi Germany's largest concentration camp and extermination camp. Historians estimate that between 1.1 and 1.5 million people died at Auschwitz. Ninety percent of them were Jews.

Finally convinced that appeasement had failed, Britain and France pledged to defend Poland. But by now Hitler had little fear that they would actually go to war. Just in case, however, in August 1939 he signed an agreement with Soviet leader Stalin. Both nations pledged that they would not attack the other. With the threat of a Soviet attack from the east now gone, Hitler felt free to carry out his plan.

On September 1, 1939, German forces attacked Poland. Two days later, Britain and France declared war on Germany. World War II had begun. The war was truly a world war in more ways than World War I. Besides Europe, major fighting took place in North Africa, East and Southeast Asia, and on many islands in the Pacific. Britain and France, and later the United States and Soviet Union were the major Allies. They opposed the Axis—Germany and Italy, which were later joined by Japan. Eventually, however, the war involved 49 nations on the Allies' side and 11 as members of the Axis.

The Early Fighting   By mid-1940 German forces had conquered France and much of northern Europe. Encouraged by Hitler's success, Italy then entered the war by attacking Greece and Egypt. By mid-1941, Italy and Germany also controlled the Balkans and most of North Africa. With the United States and the Soviet Union officially neutral, only Great Britain remained to resist the Axis Powers.

In late 1940 Hitler launched a weeks-long air assault on Britain, preparing for a land invasion of that nation. The German air raids caused great destruction on the ground. But the British air force was able to keep control of the skies over Britain. This forced Hitler to cancel the invasion. Instead, in June 1941 he broke his 1939 agreement with Stalin and invaded the Soviet Union. German forces pushed deep into the Soviet Union before its army finally stopped their advance at the city of Stalingrad in September 1942.

genocide the planned and systematic extermination of an entire racial, ethnic, political, or culture group

Everywhere that German armies conquered, Jews, Gypsies, and other groups the Nazis considered dangerous or inferior were rounded up and held in prison camps. In 1941 Hitler ordered the killing of such prisoners. Eventually the Nazis systematically murdered some 6 million Jews and others in Germany and elsewhere in a **genocide** known as the Holocaust.

As German forces conquered Europe, Japan sought control of the conquered nations' colonies in Asia. In mid-1941 Japanese troops occupied French Indochina—today the nations of Cambodia, Laos, and Vietnam. Japan next eyed the Dutch East Indies and British Malaya. The colonies of this region offered a rich source of raw materials for Japan's industries. Concerned about further Japanese imperialism, Britain and the United States banned exports of oil and other vital goods to Japan. Japan responded on December 7, 1941 by attacking the U.S. naval base at Pearl Harbor in Hawaii. Japanese land forces then invaded Malaya, the East Indies, and the American-controlled Philippine Islands.

Defeating the Axis Powers   The attack on Pearl Harbor brought the United States directly into the war against Germany and Italy as well. With U.S. involvement, the war's tide began to turn against the Axis. In November 1942, a British-American force landed in North Africa and began driving the Axis forces back. That same month, the Soviet Red Army was able to surround the Germans attacking Stalingrad. They surrendered in February 1943, and other German forces were soon in retreat across the Soviet Union. Meanwhile, the Axis army in North Africa surrendered in May 1943.

The Allies saw similar success in the Pacific. In June 1942, U.S. forces turned back an attack on Midway Island and inflicted heavy

All eight battleships anchored at Pearl Harbor were destroyed when Japanese military forces attacked Pearl Harbor on December 7, 1941. From left to right, this photo shows three stricken U.S. battleships: USS *West Virginia*, severely damaged; USS *Tennessee,* damaged; and USS *Arizona,* sunk.

losses on the Japanese navy. After the Battle of Midway, Japan was on the defensive for the rest of the war. In August, U.S. forces began a campaign to retake islands captured by the Japanese.

In June 1943 American and British forces began bombing Germany. In July they invaded Italy. The Italian army soon surrendered, but German troops in Italy continued to fight until April 1945. In the meantime, defending Italy weakened Hitler's ability to the Soviet Red Army's advances in the east. The strain on German military resources grew even greater when Allied troops invaded France in June 1944. They slowly pushed German forces back. By early 1945 Allied forces were advancing into Germany from both east and west. On April 25, 1945, U.S. and Red Army troops met at the Elbe River in central Germany. On May 7 Germany surrendered.

The war in Europe was over, but Japan continued to fight. Allied forces in the Pacific captured island after island as they advanced toward Japan. By November 1944, they were close enough for U.S. warplanes to begin bombing Japan itself. In the spring of 1945, American troops captured two key islands—Iwo Jima and Okinawa. Control of these islands put the Allies in position to invade Japan. Planning for the invasion began. But an invasion was not needed. Instead, the United States used a secret new weapon to end the war. In August, U.S. planes dropped two atomic bombs on the cities of Hiroshima and Nagasaki. Both cities were destroyed. More than 100,000 people were killed in the two blasts. (Thousand more died later from the bombs' radiation.) The horrible devastation of these attacks convinced Japan's leaders to surrender, bringing World War II to an end on August 14, 1945.

The United States ended fighting with Japan by dropping two atomic bombs in 1945. This photo was taken from the plane that dropped the atomic bomb on the city of Nagasaki.

Costs and Consequences   The destruction brought by World War II far exceeded the destruction of World War I. Estimates of the number of lives lost run as high as 60 million. More than 25 percent of these dead were **civilians,** including the nearly 6 million Jews slaughtered in the Nazi Holocaust. Millions more were forced from their homes. Europe lay in ruins. Its economy and that of Japan were destroyed.

U.S. military forces occupied Japan following the war and helped the Japanese create a democratic government. Army General Douglas MacArthur remained in control until Japan adopted a new constitution in 1947. Germany suffered a similar but harsher fate. It was divided into four military zones, each occupied by U.S., French, British, or Soviet troops. In 1949 the U.S., French, and British zones were united to form the democratic nation of West Germany (officially called the Federal Republic of Germany). The Soviet zone became East Germany (officially the German Democratic Republic) and was ruled by a communist government. Although it was not the Allies' intent, Germany would remain divided for about the next 40 years.

civilian someone who is not an active member of a police or military force

18.6 The Postwar World

As Germany's defeat became certain, Allied leaders met at the Yalta Conference in February 1945 to plan for the peace. They agreed that the Eastern European nations freed from the Germans by the Red Army would have democratic governments. Soviet leader Stalin, however, later ignored this pledge. Communist governments were installed in those nations and remained under Soviet control. This division of Europe marked the beginning of the Cold War—a nearly 50-year political and military rivalry between the United States and Soviet Union and their allies.

Asia After World War II Japan's defeat ended its control of Korea. The peninsula was divided into a southern zone occupied by U.S. forces and a northern zone, which Soviet troops had invaded near the end of the war. In 1948 these zones became the nations of South Korea and North Korea.

In China, conflict between the nationalists and communists was suspended during World War II, as both groups fought the Japanese. After the war, however, the civil war resumed. By 1949, the nationalists had been defeated and the communist People's Republic of China was established. The nationalists fled to the island of Taiwan and set up a rival government.

World War II also strengthened independence movements in South and Southeast Asia. Indians demanded independence when the war ended in return for helping the British fight Japan. Independence was delayed, however, by differences between India's Hindu and Muslim religious groups. Finally, in 1947, British India was divided into two countries. Pakistan was established as a Muslim homeland, while India remained a predominantly Hindu nation.

The peoples of Southeast Asia believed that their resistance of the Japanese had earned them the right to independence. The United States granted the Philippines independence in 1946. Britain and the Netherlands followed with independence for Burma (now Myanmar) and the Dutch East Indies (which became Indonesia) in 1948 and 1949. The French were unwilling to do the same for Indochina, however. The Vietnamese revolted against continued French rule. The French withdrew in 1954, allowing the nations of Laos and Cambodia to be created. Vietnam was divided, like Korea, into a communist North and a noncommunist South Vietnam.

This photo shows Jewish immigrants from Europe raising the Israeli flag on a kibbutz (cooperative farm) in 1949. The United Nations established Israel as a Jewish homeland in 1948.

The Middle East and Africa France also tried to hold on to control in the Middle East and North Africa. Only after uprisings by Arab nationalists did France grant Syria and Lebanon full independence in 1946. British and Soviet forces had occupied Iran during the war. American pressure caused the Soviets to withdraw, but Iran remained under British influence until the 1950s.

Elsewhere in the Middle East, Jewish survivors of the Holocaust who had migrated there during and after the war joined existing communities in the Jewish homeland. These Jews revolted against British rule in 1946. In 1948, in accordance with a United Nations plan, Israel declared its independence as a Jewish state. Neighboring Arab states immediately invaded to destroy it. Tensions between Israel and Arab governments remain high today.

The success of Arab nationalism in Syria and Lebanon inspired the peoples of Algeria, Morocco, and Tunisia in North Africa to also revolt against the French in the 1950s. Their independence would prove more difficult to achieve, however. Independence would also be delayed for the peoples of the rest of Africa who remained under European rule.

Summary

In this lesson, you read about how imperialism and nationalist competition among nations led to two devastating World Wars in the first half of the 20th century.

Cultural Interactions Communism caused unrest as revolution during World War I installed it in Russia and its supporters attempted to spread it to other parts of the world. An extreme form of nationalism called fascism arose in Europe between the world wars, resulting in authoritarian governments, suppression of human rights, and threats to world peace.

Political Systems Competition for colonies among the world powers was an underlying cause of World War I. Nationalism within the Austro-Hungarian Empire was the immediate cause of the war. Nationalism expressed through fascism and militarism after the war soon led to World War II. That war sparked nationalism within the Allies' empires as colonial peoples who fought against the Axis demanded their freedom.

Economic Systems European nations and Japan sought control over areas that could provide raw materials for their industries and markets for their goods. These efforts caused competition among the imperial powers, and aggression, expansion, and conflict in Africa and Asia that were contributing factors to World Wars I and II.

Human-Environment Interaction The fighting in World War I, from 1914 to 1918, and World War II, from 1939 to 1945, caused massive destruction in Europe and Asia. Cities were destroyed, millions of people were killed, and millions more were displaced from their lands.

World War I

Why did the Great War last so long and bring about so much change?

19.1 Introduction

Before dawn comes the signal for yet another attack. Joined by thousands of others, the young soldier climbs out of the trench to charge the German trenches a few hundred yards away. As rockets and flares light up the **no-man's land** between the two armies, shells burst overhead. Pieces of jagged metal cut down the charging troops. Mines buried in the ground explode, hurling mud, iron, and men into the air. Then rifles and machine guns open up from the German trenches. The bullets fly by like raindrops in the wind. Barbed wire is everywhere. If the soldier gets caught in it, he will almost certainly be killed by the gunfire before he can free himself.

Men are falling all around him, but the soldier cannot help them. "Onward!" his officers command. Finally, the charging troops are in the enemy trenches. The German defenders surrender and are taken prisoner. This attack has been a success. But daybreak reveals the victory's terrible cost. The ground is littered with bodies as far as the eye can see. It is a sight that the young soldier will never forget.

This scene in France in 1918 was typical of the fighting in World War I. Entrenched armies aided by aircraft, artillery, and poison gas attacked and counterattacked, again and again, trying to push each other back. Some battles lasted for months, resulting in hundreds of thousands[2] of casualties, and causing battlefields to look like the surface of the moon. It is little wonder that what was called the Great War, and what we call World War I, became known to those who witnessed its horrors as "the war to end all wars."

Themes

Political Systems Cooperation and rivalries among nations were causes of World War I and shaped the peace that followed the war.

Economic Systems The long and widespread war drained the resources of nations on both the winning and losing sides.

Human-Environment Interaction Geography and new technology helped make World War I a deadly and destructive conflict.

◀ World War I battles often caused utter devastation to the landscape and left battlefields looking like the surface of the moon.

19.2 Rivalries Lead To War

In 1914, the Great Powers of Europe—Russia, Prussia, Austria, Great Britain, and France—had enjoyed that status for over a century. However, the power relationships between these nations had changed. In 1814, Prussia was the smallest of the Great Powers. By 1914, Germany, the nation Prussia created in 1871 after defeating the Austrian Empire and France in war, had become the strongest. Between 1871 and 1913, Germany surpassed Britain to become Europe's leading industrial power. These developments dramatically altered the balance of power in Europe.

European Relations and Rivalries   Following its 1871 defeat, the Austrian Empire reorganized as Austria-Hungary, and accepted Germany's leadership in Central Europe. France's defeat in 1871 caused it to lose status, as well as territory to the new German nation. The French resented both results. Germany was surrounded by potential enemies. Tensions with France continued, and German leaders were suspicious of Russia to the east. These concerns caused Germany to use its new industrial might to build a powerful army and navy.

In the late 1800s, however, Russia was expanding in Asia. Not until its defeat by Japan in the Russo-Japanese War of 1904–1905 did Russia refocus on European affairs. Even then, Russia was less interested in Germany than it was in the Balkan Peninsula in southeast Europe, much of which was under Turkish control as part of the Ottoman Empire.

Great Britain also was largely uninvolved in Europe in the late 1800s. Britain's main focus was on preserving its vast, worldwide empire. As long as a balance of power existed in Europe, the British had little interest in events there. By about 1900, however, developments on the continent were arousing Britain's concern. The British viewed Russia's expansion in Asia as a possible threat to their control of India. Germany's naval buildup was also serious. Britain's naval supremacy was vital to protecting its empire in a time when communication and trade still relied mainly on the sea. Britain responded to the German buildup by increasing the size of its own navy.

France began trying to match the 600,000-man German army, even though its population was only about two-thirds of Germany's 68 million. Russia, with a population nearly triple the size of Germany, faced no such challenge. In fact, its army of 1.3 million was of great concern to the Germans.

By 1914, Germany had surpassed Britain as the leading industrial power in Europe. Germany's increasing industrial strength destabilized Europe's balance of power.

Shifting Alliances   Germany was a monarchy, but its affairs were led by its first chancellor, Otto von Bismarck, until 1890. Bismarck's foreign policy was shaped by his goal to protect Germany from the two potential enemies on its borders—France and Russia. He reduced the threat from Russia in 1881 by forming an alliance with Russia and Austria-Hungary called the Three Emperors' Alliance. The following year, to protect Germany against France, Germany formed an alliance with Italy and Austria-Hungary. Together these countries formed the Triple Alliance. These alliances hurt France by depriving it of possible allies.

When the Three Emperors' League dissolved due to tensions between Russia and Austria-Hungary, Bismarck kept France isolated by forming a separate German-Russian alliance called the Reinsurance Treaty. However, a new kaiser (the German title for emperor), Wilhelm II, took the throne in 1888. Kaiser Wilhelm and other German leaders were more interested in creating an overseas empire. To help achieve this goal, Germany began strengthening its navy. Bismarck was forced to resign and the Reinsurance Treaty was allowed to expire. These developments increased tensions with both Russia and Great Britain.

France took advantage of the Reinsurance Treaty's end by forming an alliance with Russia in 1894. The French also provided money and other assistance to help Russia build railroads and modernize its army. Britain's growing concerns about Germany prompted it to join with France and Russia in 1907 to create the Triple Entente.

The Great Powers were now aligned in two rival alliances. Should a member of either alliance become involved in a conflict, the other members were pledged to support it. In addition, fighting between any members of the Triple Alliance and Triple Entente would pull the other four nations into war. The alliance system made it possible for a minor dispute to produce war throughout Europe. In 1914, in the Balkans, this possibility became reality.

Unrest in the Balkans   The growing tension between Germany and Russia mainly resulted from Germany's support of Austria-Hungary in its rivalry with Russia for control of the Balkan Peninsula. Balkan peoples sought their freedom as Ottoman power declined. The Great Powers recognized the independence of Serbia in 1878 and put Austria-Hungary in charge of Bosnia-Herzegovina—a multi-ethnic region of Croats, Turks, and Serbs on Serbia's border. Russia quickly formed close ties with Serbia and took on the role of Serbia's protector.

Russia, France, and Great Britain formed the Triple Entente in 1907. Here the pact is represented by a soldier from each country holding his nation's flag.

Many Serbs believed that Bosnia-Herzegovina should be part of Serbia. Russia supported this goal, hoping to weaken Austria-Hungary and increase its own influence in the Balkans. Russia also supported Serbia in two short Balkan Wars in 1912 and 1913. The first war ended Ottoman rule on the peninsula, and the second war divided the former Ottoman lands among the Balkan nations. Serbia doubled in size as a result.

This development heightened tensions with Austria-Hungary, which feared that Serbian expansion would stir nationalism and unrest among the empire's ethnic minority groups. In fact, organizations in Serbia, supported by leaders in Serbia's government, had been doing just that since Austria-Hungary officially annexed Bosnia-Herzegovina in 1908. In June 1914, an act of Serbian nationalism led to the murder of the heir to the Austro-Hungarian throne. Gavrilo Princip, a Bosnian Serb who had been trained by a Serbian secret terrorist organization called the Black Hand, shot and killed Archduke Franz Ferdinand in the Bosnian city of Sarajevo.

The Rush to War   Austria-Hungary saw Franz Ferdinand's assassination as a chance to crush Serbian nationalism. After making sure it had Germany's support, it made a series of harsh demands on Serbia. Austrian leaders expected Serbia to reject these demands, which would give Austria-Hungary an excuse for war. When Serbia agreed to most of them, Austria-Hungary declared war on Serbia anyway on July 28, 1914.

Russia, which was pledged to protect Serbia, began to mobilize, or ready its army and other resources, for war. On July 31, Germany gave Russia 24 hours to halt its mobilization. The Germans also demanded that France pledge **neutrality** in the event of war between Germany and Russia. When these demands were ignored, Germany declared war on Russia on August 1, and two days later declared war on France. Because of the alliance systems, nearly all of Europe was at war within two weeks.

Many Europeans greeted the outbreak of war in August 1914 with a wave of patriotic confidence and celebration. They believed that their side would be victorious in just a few months. Few could have predicted or imagined just how long and terrible this war would be.

The outbreak of war in August 1914 was greeted with enthusiasm and patriotism. Crowds in Paris celebrated France's declaration of war. This same scene played out in all the capitals of Europe. No one anticipated the horrors that were to come.

19.3 Fighting the Great War

When the fighting began in 1914, German leaders had been planning for such a war for more than a decade. The Schlieffen Plan called for Germany to defeat France in the west, knocking it out of the war before Russia could mobilize its huge army in the east. However, in the late 1800s, France had heavily fortified its border with Germany. A quick victory required bypassing these defenses by invading France from the north, through neutral Belgium, with an overwhelming force. When Belgium refused to let German troops enter its territory, Germany attacked it on August 4. Outraged by this violation of Belgium's neutrality, Great Britain declared war on Germany later that day.

European Alliances Before 1914

Triple Entente
Triple Alliance

0   250   500 miles
0   250   500 kilometers
Lambert Azimuthal Equal-Area Projection

In World War I the Allied and Central Powers faced off against each other. This map focuses on the action in Europe, but fighting extended throughout the world.

Britain's declaration of war against Germany meant that the entire British empire was at war. Britain's action made the conflict a true "world war." Hoping to gain Germany's colonies in Asia, Japan declared war on Germany on August 23, 1914. In November, the Ottoman Empire officially entered the war on the side of Germany and Austria-Hungary to form what became known as the Central Powers. They were joined by Serbia's Balkan rival Bulgaria in 1915. Britain, France, Russia, and their partners were known as the Allied Powers, or simply the Allies. Italy, which remained neutral when war broke out, joined the Allies in 1915.

Stalemate on the Western Front

The Schlieffen Plan might have worked if German leaders had not decided to transfer some forces back to Germany. However, they worried that Russia might mobilize its army faster than expected and attack Germany from the east. So a large number of troops returned to Germany to protect it. This allowed French and British forces to stop the German advance from Belgium at the Marne River, just short of Paris, in early September.

The Battle of the Marne denied Germany its goal of quickly knocking France out of the war. However, the invasion gave Germany control of part of France. The German army dug in and prepared to defend the territory it had captured. Unable to drive the Germans out, the British and French also dug trenches to defend against further attacks.

On the Western Front, the Allied and Central Powers both built an elaborate network of defensive trenches. Trench warfare on the Western Front caused great destruction, but fighting eventually reached a stalemate.

stalemate a situation in which progress by either side in a contest or dispute is blocked by the other side; a draw or deadlock

New modern weapons such as the large British artillery gun shown here contributed to the shocking destruction of World War I.

Over time, each side extended its trenches, trying to get a geographic advantage over the other. By November, a network of trenches stretched 400 miles, from the English Channel to Switzerland. This area of the fighting became known as the Western Front.

For the next three years, the Western Front was a brutal killing field as each side tried, with little success, to push the other back. For example, repeated Allied attacks on German trenches in one region of France in February and March 1915 gained only 500 yards of ground, and cost the lives of 50,000 men. In February 1916, German troops tried to break the **stalemate** by smashing through the French defenses at the town of Verdun. In June, Allied forces launched a similar assault on German lines along the Somme River. The Battle of Verdun and the Battle of the Somme each lasted for months. Nearly 2 million men were killed or wounded. Neither attack succeeded.

A New Kind of War The terrible slaughter on the Western Front and elsewhere in World War I resulted from mixing of new technology with old tactics. By the early 1900s, all European armies had rifles that could hit a target with deadly accuracy from over a quarter-mile away. The machine gun, perfected in the late 1800s, could fire 600 bullets a minute to a range of more than a half-mile. The range and accuracy of artillery was also much improved. The biggest guns could hurl an explosive shell 25 miles. Advancing troops could come under fire long before they could even see their enemy.

Such weaponry, when combined with trenches protected by entanglements of barbed wire (invented in the 1870s), gave defenders a major advantage. However, many military leaders viewed war as a test of courage and will. For example, the main offensive tactic of the French army was the infantry charge. Commanders on both sides believed that such methods could succeed if enough men were willing to die. One 1917 battle, in which the French army lost 130,000 men in 10 days, ended when troops refused to make yet another attack.

Other weapons were new to World War I, not just improvements of earlier versions. Tanks, which first appeared at the Battle of the Somme, could help troops move forward by tearing through barbed wire defenses and rolling over enemy trenches. In 1915 Germany began using poison gas. Its first use drove panicked troops from their defenses as the clouds of gas settled in their trenches. Armies on both sides were soon lobbing gas at each other in artillery shells. The airplane was another new weapon in World War I. The first planes were used to spy on the enemy. By 1917 they were directing artillery fire and dropping bombs on military and civilian targets.

The Eastern Front   Trench warfare was less widespread on the Eastern Front—the name given to the battle zones of Eastern Europe. However, the fighting there was just as bloody. In August 1914 the French begged Russia to take pressure off the Western Front by invading Germany. The Russian army was not ready to fight, but in late August it attacked anyway. A large Russian force was almost completely destroyed at the city of Tannenberg, just inside Germany's eastern border. Of 150,000 Russian troops, some 130,000 were killed, wounded, or taken prisoner.

Despite its size, the Russian army proved no match for the better equipped Germans. While the Austrians were conquering Serbia (1915) and Romania (1916), German forces advanced deep into Russia. In 1917, the huge number of lives and resources lost caused Russia's government to collapse. Months of unrest followed until, in December, a new government signed a peace agreement with the Central Powers, and pulled Russia out of the war.

The Fighting Elsewhere   In early 1915, a naval force landed French, British, and colonial troops at Gallipoli, a peninsula in the European part of present-day Turkey. The goal was to capture Constantinople, the Ottoman Empire's capital, and gain access to the Black Sea. This would provide a sea route to Russia to provide supplies that it desperately needed. However, the invaders met strong Turkish defenses. A stalemate quickly developed. In December, after suffering more than 200,000 casualties, the Allies withdrew in defeat from Gallipoli. Turkish losses were even greater, a total of about 250,000.

The Allies had little early success invading other parts of the Ottoman Empire. In April 1916, the Turks defeated a force of British colonial troops from India. However, that summer an Arab uprising against Turkish rule drove the Ottomans out of much of the Arabian Peninsula. In December 1917, the British captured Jerusalem.

The Turks' war effort was also troubled by other unrest. Russia had long been stirring up nationalism among the nearly 2 million Armenians living in Anatolia (a part of present-day Turkey). Ethnic tensions already were high when Armenian volunteers from the Russian Empire joined Russian troops in invading the Ottoman Empire in early 1915. Fearing disloyalty in their own Armenian population, Ottoman leaders ordered that nearly all the empire's Armenians be rounded up and forced into prison camps in Syria. As many as 600,000 people starved to death or were killed by Turkish troops and police in what is known as the Armenian genocide.

The Allied powers attempted to capture the Gallipoli Peninsula in Turkey from the Ottomans. In this picture, Allied troops land on the beach. Eventually, the Allies were defeated by a strong Turkish defense.

inflation a rise in prices caused by an increase in the supply of money and a resulting decline in its value

rationing limiting the amount of something that people are allowed to have when there is not enough for everyone to have as much as they want

propaganda ideas, allegations, and other information that is spread deliberately to further a cause or damage an opposing cause, and that is often exaggerated or false

The war caused shortages of food and other goods, and many countries began programs of rationing. This poster promotes obedience to rationing policies by appealing to Canadian patriotism.

Other fighting in World War I occurred elsewhere, on both land and sea. Japan and Britain seized German-held islands in the Pacific. In Africa, some 12,000 African soldiers defended German East Africa against 130,000 Allied troops for three years until finally being forced to surrender in November 1918. But the fighting in these and other places had little effect on the war's outcome. By 1917, it was clear that the victory in the Great War would be decided on Europe's Western Front.

The War at Home   The unexpected and long war in 1914 severely strained the resources of nations on both sides. When the fighting began, Austria-Hungary had enough cash reserves to pay for only three weeks of fighting. Other nations' circumstances were not much better. Nearly half of Britain's economy—and more than one-third of Germany's—depended on foreign trade, much of it with the other nations of Europe. But trade was difficult in the midst of such a war. This was especially true for Britain and Germany when each began a naval blockade of the other. Warships on each side also captured or sank their enemies' merchant ships on the high seas.

As the war continued and nations had difficulty paying its costs, many just printed more paper money. This led to **inflation**, which created hardships at home, especially for the poor. In Italy, for example, prices increased 700 percent during the war.

Shortages of food, fuel, and raw materials also developed. The German and British governments took greater control over industry and began **rationing** food and other goods. The governments of Russia and Austria-Hungary were less efficient, however, and shortages there soon became severe. German scientists developed artificial substitutes for some needed goods, such as sugar, rubber, and textiles. But even in Germany, clothing was scarce by 1916, and in cities, people simply did not have enough to eat. By 1917, food riots and strikes happened with increasing frequency.

Even before the war, all the Great Powers, except Britain, required young men to serve in the army as active-duty troops and then as reserves afterward. Heavy battlefield losses led Britain to begin requiring military service from men age 18 to 41 in 1916, while Germany made men of all ages eligible to be called. The high loss of life, combined with the wartime shortages, caused growing unrest in nations on both sides. Britain and Germany, in particular, used **propaganda** to boost morale and keep the public behind the war. However, by 1917, peace movements existed in every Great Power—including France, where German forces remained entrenched on the Western Front.

19.4 The Tide Turns

Within weeks of going to war in 1914, the British began a naval blockade of Germany to cut off its overseas trade. Great Britain declared the entire North Sea a war zone where British warships could stop merchant ships and seize any cargoes bound for Germany. In February 1915 Germany responded by establishing a blockade of Britain. The German navy was still no match for the British navy. So Germany turned to a new technology—the submarine, or U-boat (from the German word *Unterseeboot,* meaning "undersea boat").

Unlike warships that operate on the surface, submarines are not equipped to capture ships or seize their cargoes. Instead, Germany enforced its blockade by announcing that its U-boats would, without warning, torpedo and sink Allied and other merchant ships approaching Great Britain. This policy eventually brought the United States into the war.

The United States and World War I   When war broke out in Europe, the United States remained neutral. Although the nation had close historical and cultural ties with Great Britain, it had a large German-American population too. In addition, most Americans were not eager to get involved in what they viewed as a European dispute. Many American companies also saw the war as an opportunity to sell supplies to both sides.

Tensions with Britain increased when British warships seized American goods bound for Germany. However, the German blockade of Britain had more serious consequences. In May 1915, a U-boat sank the British passenger ship *Lusitania,* which was also carrying 173 tons of ammunition from New York to London. More than a thousand passengers, including 128 Americans, lost their lives. Public outrage, combined with the sinking of two more passenger ships later that year, brought U.S.-German relations to the breaking point. To avoid war, Germany promised that its U-boats would warn merchant ships before sinking them, to give those on board time to launch lifeboats.

By late 1916, however, German leaders had become concerned about how much longer Germany could continue to fight. They decided to tighten their blockade, gambling that this would force Britain to surrender before the United States could enter the war. In February 1917, Germany resumed its previous policy of unrestricted submarine warfare. Furthermore, Germany made an offer of an alliance with Mexico. It promised that if Mexico went to war against the United States, Germany would reward Mexico with lands in New Mexico, Texas, and Arizona. These actions led the United States to declare war on Germany in April 1917.

The sinking of the British passenger ship *Lusitania* by German U-boats in 1915 provoked public outrage. The United States' opposition to Germany's unrestricted submarine warfare was one reason why they entered the war.

The United States' entry into World War I was the turning point of the war. Like Germany and Austria-Hungary, Britain and France were nearly exhausted by 1917. It took nearly a year for the United States to raise and train troops and to fight in Europe. But the flow of arms, food, and other supplies to Britain and France greatly increased immediately. By July 1917, U.S. warships were helping the British navy combat the German U-boat blockade.

The Fourteen Points The United States also took the lead in trying to bring the war to an early end. In January 1918, President Woodrow Wilson issued a statement of war goals called the Fourteen Points. The first five points addressed general world concerns—an end to secret agreements between nations, freedom of the seas, the removal of trade barriers, arms reduction, and a fair settlement of colonial disputes. The next eight points dealt with specific territorial issues in Europe and the Ottoman Empire. They were based on the principal of self-determination—the right of nations and peoples to control their own fate and to decide what form of government they will have. The fourteenth point called for "a general association of nations" to be formed, whose members would work together to protect all nations.

Wilson's Fourteen Points were not embraced by other Allied leaders. However, they kept their feelings private while the war continued because they needed the Americans' help. The Fourteen Points also strengthened the peace movements in Germany and Austria-Hungary, an effect Wilson had hoped for. The Fourteen Points contributed to Germany's decision to surrender in November 1918.

The War Comes to a Close Russia's withdrawal from the war at the end of 1917 allowed Germany to move troops from the Eastern to the Western Front. With more than 500,000 more soldiers now on the Western Front, German commanders hoped to defeat the British and French forces there and end the war before a large number of American troops could arrive.

In late March 1918, the Germans launched a massive attack on the British at the Second Battle of the Somme. For the next two months, they slowly pushed the British and French forces back in heavy fighting. By June, the German army was again within artillery range of Paris. Casualties on both sides were massive. The Germans lost nearly 500,000 men. British and French losses were only slightly fewer. The German army was exhausted. But the Allies were reinforced by 300,000 American troops arriving on the Western Front each month by late spring. In June some of these troops helped French forces stop the German advance at Château-Thierry.

U.S. President Woodrow Wilson hoped to bring the war to an end. He issued a statement of war goals, known as the Fourteen Points, which emphasized the right to national self-determination.

In July, after stopping yet another German attack at the Second Battle of the Marne, the Allies counterattacked. Fighting separately for the first time, the American army defeated German forces at Saint Mihiel in September 1918. Then the Americans joined British and French forces to defeat the Germans in the month-long Battle of the Argonne Forest. These defeats pushed the German army back to the border of Germany.

The other Central Powers were also collapsing. An army of Serbian, Italian, Greek, French, and British forces overwhelmed Bulgarian troops in the Balkans. Viewing the situation as hopeless, Bulgaria surrendered on September 30. Meanwhile, British and Arab forces were rapidly advancing from the east and south in the Ottoman Empire. Bulgaria's defeat exposed the empire to attack from the west as well. On October 30, the Turks surrendered. Meanwhile, Austria-Hungary, destroyed by the collapse of its army and independence movements within its own empire, also asked for peace.

By 1918, the German people were enduring terrible hardships. By late October, those hardships became unbearable as Germans lost confidence that they would be victorious in the end. Mutinies in both the army and navy led to revolts in every major German city. On November 9 the Kaiser abdicated and then fled to the Netherlands. In Berlin, the monarchy came to an end. Civilian political leaders took control and declared Germany to be a republic.

With Germany on the verge of revolution and Allied armies poised to invade, German leaders knew that only surrender could save their nation. On November 11, 1918, they signed an armistice, an agreement to stop fighting. The Allies' terms for the armistice were stiff. Germany had to turn over much of its military equipment to the Allies and return all of its troops to German soil. The Allies prevented Germany from being able to continue the fight, but they would not occupy Germany itself. At 11:00 a.m. on November 11, the "war to end all wars" was finally over.

The War's Costs The costs to both sides in World War I were staggering. Of the 65 million men who fought in the war, some 8.5 million were killed and another 21 million wounded—many of them crippled for life. Germany and Russia each lost 1.7 million soldiers, followed by Austria-Hungary and France with more than 1.2 million dead. Great Britain and its empire suffered some 900,000 dead.

The war's civilian casualties are impossible to determine. However, the fighting left large parts of France, Belgium, and other places in Europe in ruins. The cost of this destruction has been estimated at $37 billion. To this must be added the $200 billion cost of fighting the war. Both figures were huge sums for the time. The social and economic effects of the loss of millions of lives cannot be calculated. However, in a number of European nations, an entire generation of young men had been nearly wiped out.

The war caused great suffering and death for civilians as well as soldiers. Farmers in the Somme district of France were forced to plow their fields without horses or cattle. Retreating German soldiers had taken all of their livestock.

When President Wilson arrived in Paris for peace negotiations in 1919, he received a hero's welcome. Many Europeans believed his Fourteen Points plan could help create a lasting peace.

19.5 Peace and Its Aftermath

World War I had an enormous impact on the rest of the twentieth century. The centuries-old Austrian and Ottoman empires were gone. Germany, Austria-Hungary, and Russia were no longer major powers, and France was determined to ensure that Germany would never be one again. Their place in the world order was taken by the United States and a rising power in the Pacific—Japan.

The Paris Peace Conference In January 1919, an international conference began at Paris, France, to set the terms of the peace. Twenty-seven nations were represented. However, the conference was dominated by the leaders of the most powerful Allies. Called the "Big Four," they were Prime Minister David Lloyd George of Great Britain, French premier Georges Clemenceau (kle-mahn-SOH), Italy's premier Vittorio Orlando, and President Woodrow Wilson of the United States.

The defeated Central Powers had no part in the peace negotiations, nor did Russia. Although Russia had been an Allied Power, the Big Four distrusted its new communist government. Over the next 20 months, treaties with Germany (June 1919), Austria (September 1919), Bulgaria (November 1919), Hungary (June 1920), and Turkey (August 1920) were concluded at locations around Paris.

The Treaty of Versailles The treaty with Germany was called the Treaty of Versailles. Its contents were determined by negotiations between Wilson, Clemenceau, and Lloyd George. The negotiations were often tense. Wilson's Fourteen Points had made him a hero among Europeans who were tired of war. However, the other Allies had made secret agreements that were at odds with Wilson's goals for the peace. "Mr. Wilson bores me with his Fourteen Points," Clemenceau declared. "Why, God Almighty has only Ten!"

Clemenceau, whose nickname was "the tiger," wanted Germany crushed so that it would never again be a threat in Europe. He demanded German territory for France and that Germany pay reparations—compensation for the wrongs and damage it had done. Britain's Lloyd George had more moderate views. He did not want Germany so weak that it could not trade with Britain. However, he also hoped to divide up Germany's colonies and wanted Germany to pay reparations.

Expecting a treaty based on Wilson's vision of a just peace, German leaders were shocked by what they were forced to sign. The Treaty of Versailles reduced Germany's size and population by about 10 percent. The Alsace-Lorraine region, which Germany had taken from the French in 1871, was returned to France. In the east, land was stripped away to give the Poles their own nation again. In addition, East Prussia was separated from the rest of Germany by a corridor of land given to Poland so that Poland would have access to the Baltic Sea.

The Treaty of Versailles also limited Germany's armed forces to a small navy and a 100,000-man army with no offensive weapons. German troops were banned from the Rhineland, an industrial area of Germany along its new border with France. The treaty put Rhineland's resource-rich Saar region under international control for 15 years and gave France control of the Saar's coal mines. In addition, Germany lost all of its overseas colonies.

Finally, the treaty required Germany to accept responsibility for starting the war and to pay the Allies for the damage and losses they had suffered. The amount of these reparations was later set at $33 billion (about $402 billion today). The reparations payments put even greater strains on a German economy that had been nearly destroyed by the war. The German people were especially outraged by this part of the treaty.

In this photo, German delegates listen to a speech by the French premier Georges Clemenceau at the Palace of Versailles, where peace negotiations took place. France wanted Germany to be punished severely so it could never again threaten Europe.

The Other Central Powers and Russia   Austria-Hungary fared badly too. The Allies broke up its empire along ethnic lines. A northern region largely populated by Czechs was linked with the Slovaks in the east to form Czechoslovakia. The empire's Slovene, Serb, and Croat peoples were joined with Serbia to form the new nation of Yugoslavia. Romania and Italy also gained territory, although the Italians felt that their gains were not nearly enough. The land that remained became the separate nations of Austria and Hungary. Bulgaria, another Central Power, lost territory to Yugoslavia and Greece. The Austrian army was limited to 30,000 men, while Hungary's army was limited to 35,000 men. The treaty with Bulgaria allowed it an army of 20,000.

The Allies also dissolved the Ottoman Empire. Perhaps more than anywhere else, secret wartime agreements among the Allies shaped the peace with the Ottomans. Britain and France took over most of the Arab areas of the Ottoman Empire and created borders that shaped the modern map of Southwest Asia. Greece and Italy received parts Turkey itself, while other parts came under British and French control.

This settlement led to revolution in Turkey. Enraged Turkish nationalists rejected the treaty and their government for signing it. They overthrew the Ottoman ruler, forced the Italians and French out of Turkey, and defeated a Greek army sent to enforce the treaty. A new treaty with the Allies restored the peace in 1923. It also recognized Turkey's new government and independence.

Russia was the only Allied Power to lose territory from World War I, and of all the Great Powers, its losses were the greatest. Following its revolution and withdrawal from the war in 1917, Russia was too weak to hold on to parts of its empire. When Finland and the Baltic states of Estonia, Latvia, and Lithuania revolted, the other Allies recognized their independence. However, Russia's greatest loss of territory was to Poland, one of the nations the Allies created at the Paris Peace Conference. The Big Four also gave Romania a small amount of Russian territory.

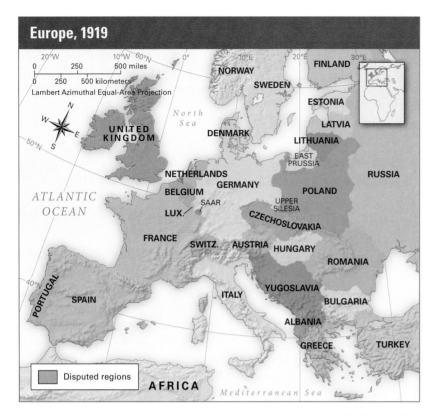

Europe, 1919

20°W   10°W 60°N   0°   10°E   20°E   30°E

0   250   500 miles
0   250   500 kilometers
Lambert Azimuthal Equal-Area Projection

NORWAY

FINLAND

SWEDEN

ESTONIA

LATVIA

LITHUANIA

UNITED KINGDOM

DENMARK

North Sea

EAST PRUSSIA

NETHERLANDS

RUSSIA

GERMANY

POLAND

BELGIUM

ATLANTIC OCEAN

LUX.

SAAR

UPPER SILESIA

CZECHOSLOVAKIA

FRANCE

SWITZ.   AUSTRIA   HUNGARY

ROMANIA

PORTUGAL

SPAIN

ITALY

YUGOSLAVIA

BULGARIA

ALBANIA

GREECE   TURKEY

Mediterranean Sea

AFRICA

■ Disputed regions

Which nations won more territory after the war? Which nations lost territory? Which nations were created that had not existed in Europe before?

aggressor a person or country that attacks first, without being provoked

mandate an authorization or order given to a lesser authority by a superior one; a territory governed under such an authorization or order from the League of Nations

The League of Nations

The Paris Peace Conference entrusted its greatest hopes for peace to the international organization Wilson had called for in his Fourteen Points. Established in the Treaty of Versailles, it was called the League of Nations. It consisted of three bodies: an assembly of representatives of all member nations, a council of representatives from the main Allied Powers (plus other nations on a rotating basis), and an executive office headed by a secretary general. The League would work closely with another new organization, the Permanent Court of International Justice (also called the "world court"), to settle disputes between nations. In addition, the League relied on collective security—joint action by member nations against an **aggressor**—to keep the peace.

The League of Nations also gave the Allies a way to take over German and Ottoman possessions in Africa and the Middle East without formally annexing them. Instead, these territories became **mandates** under League supervision. The League then assigned a member nation to govern each mandate with the goal of leading it to independence. This system allowed the Allies to control these lands despite their pledge that gaining colonies was not a goal in the peace settlement.

The Postwar Era   The death, destruction, and disillusionment brought by World War I shook western society to its core. The war caused many people to reject the long-held belief in human progress first expressed by the Enlightenment. Much of the art and literature of the 1920s reflected this change in attitude. American writers Gertrude Stein and Ernest Hemingway referred to the young men and women who came of age after the war as the "lost generation." Hemingway captured their attitudes in his 1926 novel *The Sun Also Rises*. Another Hemingway novel, *A Farewell to Arms* (1929), expressed dissatisfaction with life that was common in the 1920s.

The horrors of the war inspired an abstract art movement in Europe called Surrealism. Artists, like Spanish painter Salvador Dali, mixed images in ways that present the viewer with a world that makes no sense. Human forms painted by Pablo Picasso, another Spanish artist, were so distorted that they looked like monsters.

The "war to end all wars" created a public attitude, especially in Great Britain and the United States, that in the future, war must be avoided at all costs. The United States Senate expressed this attitude when it refused to approve the Treaty of Versailles and rejected U.S. membership in the League of Nations. U.S. Senators feared that the collective security requirements of the League of Nations would draw the United States into other wars. But Americans sought to preserve the peace in other ways. For example, the Washington Naval Conference in 1921 resulted in an agreement by the major powers to reduce the size of their navies. In 1928 U.S. and French officials drew up an agreement that outlawed war as an instrument of foreign policy. The Kellogg-Briand Pact was signed by more than 60 nations.

The absence of the United States from the League of Nations seriously weakened the organization's influence and prestige. More significant was the lack of power that the League of Nations had to enforce its will. Its real power lay in the hands of its member states, who had to decide if and when to take action to secure the peace.

This lack of power would have serious consequences in the near future. The peace settlement had left nations on both sides of the war dissatisfied. Germany felt betrayed and desired revenge. Japan and Italy had territorial ambitions that remained unfulfilled. All three nations would soon be engaged in changing their situation. The League of Nations would prove powerless to keep the world at peace.

This political cartoon shows weary American troops returning from Europe while John Bull, representing Britain, calls for more. Americans feared that joining the League of Nations would draw them into more foreign conflicts.

Summary

In this lesson, you learned about World War I, which was fought from August 1914 to November 1918. The war and its outcome changed the world in many ways.

Political Systems Germany felt surrounded by potential enemies, so it entered into alliances with other nations to protect itself. Germany's rivals entered into alliances as well. This network of opposing alliances turned a regional dispute into a major war. After the war, a defeated Germany was harshly punished and the empires of its allies were destroyed.

Economic Systems Neither side was prepared for a long war. Germany and Britain blockaded each other to cut off imports of supplies. Nations rationed goods, but the fighting eventually depleted their resources. Hardships at home caused unrest and peace movements to develop, especially in Germany and Austria-Hungary. The United States' entry into the war in 1917 provided the resources that the Allies needed for victory.

Human-Environment Interaction The fighting in World War I took place in Europe, the Middle East, and Africa. On Europe's Western Front entrenched armies battled for years, unsuccessfully trying to push each other back. There, and on the war's other fronts, modern weapons combined with traditional battlefield tactics to produce a tremendous loss of human life.

The Russian Revolution

What changes did the Russian Revolution bring about within Russia and in world affairs?

20.1 Introduction

Czar Nicholas II was at the front in February 1917, rallying his troops in World War I, when word arrived of a strike in Petrograd. (Russia's capital city, St. Petersburg, was renamed Petrograd in 1914.) The czar's aides in Petrograd assured him that the incident was minor and would end when the bitterly cold weather sent the protestors home. Instead, the strike spread, filling the streets with thousands of angry men and women. The Duma, Russia's legislature, wrote to the czar that the situation was serious.

Czar Nicholas turned to the army to restore order. When it could not, he decided to return to the capital to deal with the crisis. However, the Duma knew what had to be done. Duma members met the czar's train as it neared the city. They told Nicholas that the only way to restore order was for him to step down as czar. He tried to abdicate, or formally give up power, in favor of his brother, Mikhail. When Mikhail refused to take the throne, Russia's monarchy came to an end.

Within days, news of these events reached exiled Russian revolutionary Vladimir Ilich Lenin in Switzerland. He quickly contacted German officials for permission to travel through Germany on his return to Russia. Germany and Russia were wartime enemies, but the Germans were eager to grant Lenin's request. He openly opposed the war and would end Russia's involvement in it if he came to power there. The Germans offered him safe train passage and money to support his revolutionary activities.

Traveling in secret at night, Lenin arrived in Russia in early April. There he would take control of a revolution that changed not only Russia, but also the world.

Themes

Political Systems Russia's monarchy was ended by revolution in 1917 and was replaced by a communist government.

Economic Systems As a result of the Russian Revolution, socialism replaced capitalism in the former Russian Empire.

Social Structures The Russian Revolution radically changed the structure of Russian society.

◀ Lenin returns to Russia by train, April 1917

entrepreneur a person who takes a financial risk by starting a business

Russia was slow to industrialize, so by 1900 around 80 percent of Russians were still rural peasants living in severe poverty. Although serfdom had been abolished in 1861, this did nothing to ease the poverty of most Russians. The poor conditions faced by the peasantry made them much more likely to support revolution.

20.2 Russia Under the Czars

The overthrow of Nicholas II in 1917 ended more than 300 years of czarist rule in Russia. Russian czars were autocrats—that is, they held unlimited power to rule. While most European nations, over time, had gradually limited the power of their monarchs, Russia's czars continued to govern without being controlled by a constitution until the early twentieth century.

Russia also lagged behind the rest of Europe in social and economic development. The Industrial Revolution came late to Russia. By 1900 Russia's economy was still based mainly on agriculture. About 20 percent of the nation's farmland consisted of large estates owned by wealthy nobles. Some 80 percent of Russians were rural peasants who farmed small tracts of land and lived in grinding poverty. Peasants who moved to cities to work in Russia's developing industries often scrimped and saved to send money back home.

However, industrialization and city growth did provide opportunities for **entrepreneurs,** managers, and engineers. Along with other educated professionals, these Russians created a new social class—Russia's first middle class. Like the nation's wealthy nobles, these middle-class Russians chafed at their lack of power in government. Combined with the discontent of millions of impoverished peasants and urban workers, this situation made Russia ripe for revolution.

The Beginnings of Unrest   The unrest that would end in the Russian Revolution of 1917 began in the mid-1800s. At that time, most Russian peasants were still serfs—peasants tied to the nobles' land in a feudal system that the rest of Europe had abandoned long ago. Czar Alexander II, who came to the throne in 1855, saw danger in continuing this system. "It is better to abolish serfdom from above," he told Moscow's nobles in 1856, "than to wait until the serfs begin to liberate themselves from below."

The Crimean War finally convinced Czar Alexander II to liberate the serfs. In this war, Russia was defeated by the forces of Great Britain, France, and the Ottoman Turks. This defeat revealed how advanced the western European nations were in comparison to Russia. It also proved to the czar that Russia must reform itself to stay competitive with the more advanced Western nations. One significant reform was to liberate the serfs.

Many peasants were disappointed by emancipation. They expected that freedom would include being granted the land that they and their ancestors had farmed for centuries. Instead, those who received land had to pay for it.

Emancipation also caused discontent among the nobles. Although they were paid for land that went to the peasants, they lost its use for future income. Some nobles went **bankrupt** as a result. Others sold all their land and moved to cities where they built factories and started other businesses.

The nobles were also upset by their lack of political power. They pressured Alexander II for a national assembly to represent the wealthy and educated members of Russian society. The czar rejected this reform. Instead, he created a system of regional assemblies empowered to deal only with local issues, such as road construction and education. All classes, including the peasants, had a voice in these assemblies and in electing their members, though in practice they were controlled by the nobility.

Revolutionary Movements

Alexander II launched other reforms as well. He made changes in the education system that gave more people an opportunity to attend school. Alexander also relaxed laws that made speaking against the government a crime. These two reforms encouraged public discussion of political and social issues. Much of this discussion was highly critical of the government. It inspired revolutionary groups to form that sought to overthrow the government. These organizations drew their membership from the "intelligentsia"—the term Russians used to describe well-educated citizens who had a strong interest in politics and society. Most members of the intelligentsia were not revolutionaries, but it was from this group that the revolutionaries came. The most radical of them called for **socialism** and an end to czarist rule.

At first, the revolutionaries viewed the peasantry as the best source for creating change. Most peasants lived in villages organized into communes, in which all members owned the land jointly. From time to time, this land was redistributed according to each family's need. In 1873 and 1874, radical university students went into the country-side to rouse the peasants to revolt. However, most peasants did not understand the students' message or were not interested in it. Others resented educated young people from the cities telling them what to do. Police arrested hundreds of these students. They were imprisoned or sent to live in remote parts of the empire.

The students' failure caused great changes in the revolutionary movement. First, it split the movement into three groups. One group continued to rely on peasants as the source of revolutionary action. A second group began to focus on urban factory workers instead. The third group completely gave up on the people and turned to terrorism to spark change. Finally, the government crackdown which started with the students eventually drove all the groups **underground**.

bankrupt reduced to a state of financial ruin

socialism an economic system in which a nation's land, natural resources, industries, and other means of production are owned collectively or are controlled by the state

underground operating secretly, especially against a ruling power

Czar Alexander II was assassinated in 1881 by a left-wing terrorist group known as the People's Will. This group came to believe that terrorist acts were the best way to force political reform and bring about the overthrow of the czarist autocracy. The czar was killed by a bomb thrown by a member of the People's Will as he drove through the streets of St. Petersburg.

The Last Czars The terrorist group achieved its main goal in 1881 with the assassination of Alexander II. But instead of weakening the government, the czar's death had the opposite effect. His successor, Alexander III, greatly reduced educational opportunities, weakened the regional assemblies, and tried to bring the peasants' communes under closer control. He also stepped up censorship and the surveillance of revolutionary groups. These and other repressive measures kept the revolutionaries in check for the next 20 years.

Discontent increased again after Alexander III died in 1894 and was succeeded by his son, Nicholas II. Nicholas inspired neither the fear nor the respect that his father had commanded. He had few political ideas beyond protecting his power as czar. He angered moderate reformers by calling their goals "senseless dreams." Meanwhile, rapid changes in Russia were creating conditions for the growth of more radical movements and reforms.

20.3 Moving Toward Revolution

Nicholas II ruled a Russia that was vastly different from the society Czar Alexander II had inherited less than 40 years earlier. Russia's population doubled between 1850 and 1900—the fastest growth rate of all the Great Powers of Europe. The pace of urban and industrial growth was also fast. Russia had some 1.4 million factory workers in 1890 and 3.1 million in 1913. If all non-agricultural workers are counted, Russia's working class totaled 15 million by 1913—four times its size in 1860.

Most industrial workers had once been peasants. Despite their migration to cities, most workers stayed in touch with their villages in the countryside. Life for these recent migrants was both different and difficult. However, like their rural brethren, most lived in grinding poverty. Both women and men worked 12 to 14 hours a day for low pay, often in harsh, unsafe, or unhealthy conditions. Housing was equally bad. Families often shared unclean and overcrowded rented rooms with other families or single workers.

If Russia's peasants were discontented, its industrial workers were even more so. Industrial workers had no avenues to seek change, and the government blocked their efforts to create them. Many workers came to believe that a change of government was required before their conditions could improve. In addition, most industries were concentrated in a small number of places—especially in St. Petersburg and Moscow. The high numbers of workers in these locations gave workers a political strength far beyond their small percentage of Russia's total population. To some revolutionary leaders, these factors made industrial workers a great potential source of revolution.

The Rise of Political Parties   By the early 1900s, Russia's revolutionary and reform movements had evolved into formal, organized political parties. Since Russia was an autocracy, political parties were outlawed and had to operate in secret at first. However, they became legal in 1905.

The Socialist Revolutionary Party was founded in 1901. It called for the czar's overthrow and the seizure and redistribution of all land to the peasants. Its members believed that Russian society should be based on the type of socialism and equality found in peasant communes.

The other major revolutionary party was the Russian Social Democratic Workers' Party, or Social Democrats. Founded in 1898, the Social Democrats believed that Russia's future lay with industrialization and a society built around the industrial working class. Their views were based on the theories of the radical nineteenth-century political thinker Karl Marx. However, the Social Democrats differed over how to apply Marx's ideas to bring about a socialist revolution in Russia. This dispute split the party in 1903. One group, led by Lenin, took the name Bolsheviks, from the Russian word for "majority." Several other groups that were by no means united became known as the Mensheviks, from the Russian word for "minority."

In 1905, reformers who were opposed to both socialism and revolution formed the Constitutional Democratic Party—also known as the Kadets. The Kadets were Russia's main moderate political party through the revolutions of 1905 and 1917, and the civil war that followed.

The socialist philosophy of the Russian Social Democratic Workers' Party was based on the ideas of the 19th century thinkers Karl Marx and Friedrich Engels. In 1903, a dispute over how to best apply Marxist ideas in Russia split the party into two factions. Lenin led the Bolshevik faction. Here Lenin speaks at an unveiling of a sculpture of Marx and Engels in 1918.

Marxism and Leninism   Karl Marx believed that in industrial societies a class of owners, which he called the bourgeoisie [boorzh-wah-ZEE], took advantage of the working class or proletariat [proh-luh-TAYR-ee-uht] in order to make profits. He predicted that when workers had been driven deep into poverty as a result of this system, they would revolt and establish a socialist state. Over time, a classless society would emerge in which people would live cooperatively without a need for government. Marx called this final stage of revolution *communism*.

Marx's theories became known as Marxism. Russia's Mensheviks thought that the revolution they wanted would follow this pattern. Lenin held a different view. He believed that pure Marxism did not apply to Russia because its industrialization was more recent and its workers were unlike the proletariat of industrial nations such as England or Germany. Lenin argued that Russian workers did not yet have the class consciousness they needed to launch a revolution. He claimed that a group of professional revolutionaries from the intelligentsia would have to lead Russia's proletariat to revolution instead. This adaptation of Marxism is called Leninism. Lenin shaped the Bolshevik Party around these views.

The Revolution of 1905   Russia's humiliating defeat in its war with Japan in 1904 and 1905 added to a growing discontent with the czar's rule. Peasant groups, industrial workers, the intelligentsia, and non-Russian nationalists within the empire were all seeking a voice in the government. Moderate reformers and others called for the creation of a national legislature elected by the people.

In January 1905, a huge throng of St. Petersburg workers marched on the czar's palace to present him with a long list of demands. The peaceful march was met by troops who opened fire. About 130 protestors were killed in what came to be known as Bloody Sunday. News of this event was soon followed by news of Japan's crushing defeat of Russian forces in battles on land and sea. The empire erupted in uproar. Widespread strikes took place. Peasants began seizing land or other property from landowners. Nationalists in Finland, Poland, and other non-Russian parts of the empire rose in revolt. Units of the army and navy mutinied.

Workers in Russia's industrial centers formed councils called *soviets*. Each soviet consisted of elected delegates from all the factories and workshops in the city or town. The soviets organized strikes and negotiated with employers and police. Some even helped run their city or town during the crisis.

In 1905, Russian troops opened fire into a crowd of peaceful protesters in St. Petersburg, killing 130 people. The massacre came to be known as Bloody Sunday. This event, along with news of Russia's defeat in the Russo-Japanese war, sparked the Revolution of 1905.

Czar Nicholas II allowed for the election of the first Duma in 1906, but this concession did nothing to diminish opposition to the monarchy. This American political cartoon from 1906 shows the czar threatened from two sides, by both discontent within the Duma and anarchist groups.

Reform, Repression, and Continued Unrest   In October 1905, Nicholas II finally gave in. He reluctantly agreed to allow an elected national legislature, called the Duma, to accept a written constitution, and to grant the people basic **civil liberties**. However, these actions did not end the unrest. In December, the Moscow soviet launched an armed revolt. It was crushed by the army with great loss of life. Bands of the czar's supporters, who opposed the reforms, attacked Jews, university students, and known radical leaders. Terrorists from the Socialist Revolutionary Party murdered hundreds of police officers and other government officials.

Meanwhile, Nicholas tried to pull back on the reforms he had granted and to crack down on those who threatened his power. The first Duma was elected in March 1906. Although it was controlled by the Kadets, it still proved too radical for the czar. When he and the Duma deadlocked over a constitution and other proposed reforms, he dissolved it and called new elections. The second Duma contained a large number of members from revolutionary parties. So Nicholas dissolved that Duma, too, and changed the election laws to give the lower classes less power and more power to the nobles. That produced a third Duma in 1907 that was more to his liking—as was the fourth Duma, elected in 1912.

At the same time, the czar continued to rely on the police to help him keep control. Police spies became members of soviets, political parties, and other organizations. Thousands of suspected radicals and others were arrested. Many of them were imprisoned or executed. Some revolutionaries left the country to avoid arrest. Among them was Lenin, who fled Russia in 1907. He did not return until 1917.

The government also launched a program to give every peasant his own land. Nicholas hoped to weaken the communes, turn peasants into successful small farmers, and increase the peasants' loyalty to the czar. This was perhaps the most genuine and successful of Nicholas's reforms. However, it came too late. It would have required decades to achieve, and the monarchy would survive for just a few more years.

civil liberties personal freedoms that are protected by law from the actions of a government

20.4 The Bolsheviks Take Control

The reforms and crackdowns that followed the Revolution of 1905 slowed peasant disturbances, strikes, and other protests. For a time, a degree of calm returned to the empire. However, the complaints of the industrial working class had not been addressed, and tensions remained high. After 1912, violent strikes took place with increasing frequency across the empire. Many of them were efforts to improve workers' conditions. Strikers expressed the view that their goals could only be achieved with the overthrow of the monarchy.

The outbreak of World War I in 1914 greatly influenced the coming of the revolution of 1917, as well as the course the revolution took, its outcome, and the government that emerged. Russia was poorly prepared for the war, and it put an enormous strain on Russian society. Nearly 15 million men were called to military service. Of these, nearly 6 million had been killed, wounded, or captured by 1917.

Most Russians supported the war at first, and the violent strikes initially subsided. Patriotic fervor soon faded, however, as the Russian army suffered defeats and economic hardships developed at home. By 1915, war protests appeared in every social class. The protests increased in 1916, as the call-up of millions of peasants into the army reduced the food supply. The high costs of fighting the war caused prices to rise, while workers' wages remained low. By late 1916, conditions on the home front had become grim. Worker and peasant opposition to the war and the government grew even stronger. Most upper- and middle-class Russians continued to support the war itself, but they became increasingly critical of the government.

The demonstrations in Petrograd that began the February Revolution had widespread support. They were sparked by female factory workers, and male workers soon joined. Students, teachers, soldiers, and members of the middle class took to the streets as well. Here, demonstrators burn a portrait of the czar.

The February Revolution

The Russian Revolution of 1917 was actually two revolutions. The first, called the February Revolution, toppled a 400-year-old monarchy and established a democracy. The second, called the October Revolution or the Bolshevik Revolution, brought even more drastic change to Russia.

The February Revolution began in Petrograd (formerly St. Petersburg) on February 23, 1917, when women factory workers, angered over the food shortages, protested having to stand in line for bread. They called on men at nearby factories to join them. Within days, nearly all workers in Petrograd were on strike.

They were joined by students and members of the city's middle class. Troops called out to end the demonstrations refused to do so. Instead, many soldiers joined the protests. Meanwhile, the uprising spread to cities and army units across the empire.

Nicholas, who was away at World War I's Eastern Front, responded to the crisis by dissolving the Duma. However, it refused to disband. Instead it formed a temporary government, called the Provisional Government, to rule Russia until a democratic assembly could be elected to create a new, permanent system of government. Russia's top military commanders decided to support the Provisional Government in the hope that it could end the unrest that was hurting Russia's war effort. Having lost control of his army, his government, and his people, Nicholas gave up the throne.

Dual Power   The Provisional Government tried to rule for the entire nation, but most of its members were from the middle class. Working class Russians instead placed their loyalty in the Petrograd Soviet, and in similar councils, called *soviets*, that quickly sprang up in other cities. In the summer of 1917, the leaders of these local soviets united to form the All-Russian Soviet in Petrograd.

The All-Russian Soviet and the local soviets became a sort of second government for Russia. When they disagreed with the Provisional Government, they passed laws and issued orders on their own. This system of "dual power" contributed to the chaos that developed, as peasants seized land, soldiers deserted, and ethnic minorities demanded self-rule.

In September 1917, Bolsheviks gained control of the Petrograd Soviet. In October, they succeeded in overthrowing the Provisional Government. This is a painting of the meeting on October 26, 1917, in which the Bolshevik-dominated Soviet government installed Lenin as chairman.

The October Revolution   In April, Bolshevik leader Lenin returned to Russia after 10 years in exile. He immediately called for the soviets to overthrow the Provisional Government. However, the Mensheviks and other less radical revolutionaries controlled most soviets. The Bolsheviks were in the minority. When Bolshevik workers and soldiers took to the streets of Petrograd in July 1917, the Petrograd Soviet refused to support them. Government troops easily ended the uprising.

Events soon turned in the Bolsheviks' favor. By mid-August, the government's war offensive was going badly and shortages of food and other goods had become severe. An increasing number of Russians supported transferring all government to the soviets. "All Power to the Soviets!" became their cry. This caused Russia's more conservative elements, like the Kadets, to call for extreme measures.

Key Events in the Russian Revolution

February 23, 1917
February Revolution begins. Protests begin in Petrograd and spread throughout the empire.

March 2, 1917
Czar Nicholas II gives up the throne. Provisional Government takes over as Russia's official government.

June 3, 1917
Local soviets unite to form the All-Russian Soviet in Petrograd.

July 17, 1917
Bolshevik uprising fails in Petrograd.

September 1917
Bolsheviks begin to gain control of soviets.

October 25, 1917
October Revolution takes place. Bolsheviks overthrow Provisional Government and take power.

December 15, 1917
Bolsheviks withdraw Russia from World War I.

December 15, 1917
Bolsheviks form Red Army. Russia engulfed in civil war.

The government sent troops to seize the Petrograd Soviet. The attack collapsed, however, when Soviet members told the soldiers that they were being used to put the upper classes back in control. In September, the Bolsheviks began gaining majorities in some soviets, including the Petrograd Soviet, the country's most important. They decided that the time was right to seize power.

Lenin decided to overthrow the Provisional Government when the All-Russia Congress of Soviets met in Petrograd on October 25. This plan made the revolt look like a takeover by all the soviets instead of the act of a single political party. During the night of October 24, Bolshevik soldiers quietly took control of bridges, telegraph offices, railroad stations, and other key points in the city. The next morning Lenin announced that the government had been overthrown and that the Congress of Soviets had taken power. By the end of the day, the Provisional Government had surrendered.

On October 26, 1917, the Congress of Soviets voted to approve the Bolsheviks' actions and formed a leadership council to head the new government. It put Lenin in charge and named Bolsheviks to other key posts. At Lenin's request, the Congress passed decrees giving all private land to the peasants and giving workers control of their factories. A second revolution had taken place with hardly a shot being fired, and Lenin had turned the people's demand for "All Power to the Soviets" into a Bolshevik government.

Civil War The Bolsheviks moved quickly to solidify their power. They reaffirmed censorship of the press, created a new secret police force to deal with those who opposed them, and ended Russia's participation in the Great War. They also had to deal with the democratic elections the people had been promised after the February Revolution. The Bolsheviks controlled only Petrograd, Moscow, and some other industrial regions, so Lenin only reluctantly agreed to let the elections take place. Less than 25 percent of the delegates elected to the new national assembly were Bolsheviks. Rather then share power with other parties, Lenin forced the assembly to disband. This plunged Russia into a complicated, three-year civil war.

The Bolsheviks formed an army, called the Red Army, in February 1918. In Europe, the color red historically symbolized socialist revolution. In March they changed the name of their party to the Communist Party. The communists, or "Reds," were opposed by anticommunist forces called the "Whites." The Whites included Russians who wanted to restore the monarchy, supporters of the Provisional Government and capitalist democracy, and some Mensheviks and Socialist Revolutionaries. Peasant forces, called the "Greens," fought to keep their lands free of both Red and White control.

This Bolshevik propaganda poster from 1919 is entitled "Beat the Whites with the Red Wedge." It uses the visual language of avant-garde modernism to convey a simple but powerful message about the Russian Civil War. What is represented by the white circle? By the red wedge?

The Whites were aided by the Allies—mainly the United States, Britain, and France—who provided troops and supplies. The Allies did this in part because they did not want Russia to pull out of World War I. But they also did this because they feared that the communists would spread their revolution if they were not defeated. Indeed, Lenin formed an organization called the Comintern in 1919 to organize and aid communist parties in other nations. However, the White armies were hopelessly divided by both geography and the causes for which they were fighting. These factors weakened the Whites and helped lead to their defeat.

The Red Army also had to deal with nationalist movements in non-Russian parts of the former empire. Rather than granting these regions complete independence, the communists established six self-governing Soviet republics. By 1922, they had defeated the Whites and the Greens and joined these republics with Russia to form the Union of Soviet Socialist Republics (also known as the Soviet Union and USSR).

War Communism and the Red Terror   The civil war caused Lenin to introduce an economic policy called war communism. The government took over all private businesses and industries and dictated what was to be produced. Workers, who understood communism to mean that they would control the means of production, resisted with frequent strikes. In the countryside, the peasants were forced to provide grain and other produce so that Russia's cities and the army could be fed. Armed bands of party members and Red Army troops were sent to villages to collect this food. Groups of unhappy peasants rose in revolt.

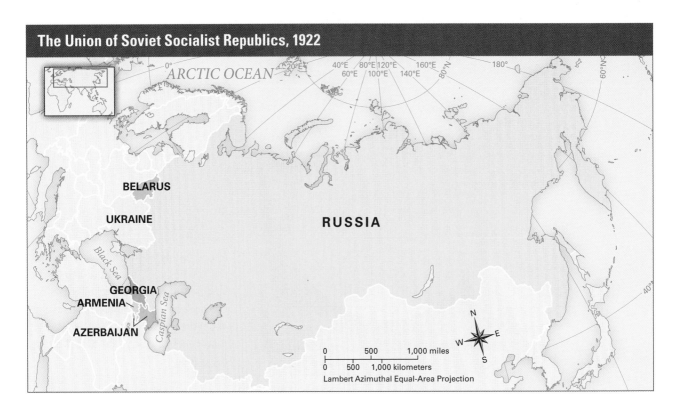

The Red Army dealt with nationalist movements in non-Russian parts of the former empire by granting some autonomy to these regions. However, they did not grant them independent statehood. Rather, they joined together six self-governing republics to create the Union of Soviet Socialist Republics (USSR) in 1922.

Faced with such unrest as well as civil war, the communists used extreme measures to stay in power. They called these measures the Red Terror. Lenin ordered the secret police to arrest any person suspected of being an enemy of the revolution. Potential enemies included nobles, religious leaders, merchants, former government officials, noncommunist revolutionaries, and other members of the educated middle class. Striking workers and peasants who resisted war communism also faced harsh punishments.

The police were permitted to execute anyone they arrested. It is estimated that as many as 300,000 persons met this fate. They included the czar and his entire family, whom Lenin ordered to be killed in July 1918. Thousands of other "enemies" were held in prisons or under harsh conditions in prison camps, where many more died. Lenin was motivated by his firm belief that the only way the revolution would survive was if the Bolsheviks retained control.

As part of Lenin's War Communism policy, peasants were forced to provide food to the Red Army. The government also took charge of all food distribution. This resulted in severe food shortages. In this 1919 image, starving people collapse on the street.

New Policies and New Leadership

In 1921, Lenin replaced war communism with the New Economic Policy, or NEP. The civil war had ended in victory for the Reds, but the peasant revolts continued. Lenin realized that the Bolshevik Revolution could not survive if the countryside opposed it. The NEP relaxed the extreme policies of war communism. Taxes replaced the requirement that peasants provide the government with food. Farm products could now be freely bought, sold, and traded. Communications, transportation, and major industries such as mining, oil, and steel remained under government control. However, other businesses could be privately owned and operated for profit.

As Lenin was reshaping Soviet communism, his health was beginning to fail. His death in 1924 set off a power struggle in the Communist Party. Over the next four years, party secretary Joseph Stalin outmaneuvered and eventually ousted his rivals. By 1928, he was securely in power.

Lenin's tomb, shown here, is situated in Red Square, at the center of the capital city of Moscow. After Lenin's death in 1924, the Soviet government decided to preserve Lenin's body so that their national hero could be honored by future generations. The body was embalmed, and it remains on public display in the mausoleum to this day.

Summary

In this lesson, you learned about the origins, causes, development, and phases of the Russian Revolution of 1917, and the changes it brought to Russia's government, economy, and society.

Political Systems The conditions that led to the Russian Revolution arose in the mid and late 1800s. Russia's czars resisted giving up power in the face of growing discontent. The reforms they did make increased Russians' desire for greater change. The revolution that eventually resulted had two phases. The first ended the monarchy and replaced it with a government that represented the upper and middle classes. The second phase, which brought more radical reformers to power, drew its support from the working class.

Economic Systems Russian industry was growing rapidly by the early 1900s, but most Russians remained involved in agriculture. Wealth was unevenly divided. The few nobles and other Russians who owned large estates and businesses were well off, while the rural peasant masses and urban industrial workers lived in great poverty. The Bolshevik Revolution established a system in which the government controlled production in the hope of redistributing the wealth and bettering workers' lives.

Social Structures Russian society historically consisted of a small class of nobles and a huge peasant class. Industrialization in the late 1800s helped to create an educated middle class as well as an industrial working class that was closely linked to the rural peasantry. The Bolshevik Revolution made society more level by elevating the status and power of the working class while destroying Russia's upper and middle classes.

Foreign Influences and Political Revolutions in the Americas

What were the causes and effects of political unrest in Latin America in the 19th and 20th centuries?

21.1 Introduction

It was still dark that morning of September 16, 1810, when Father Miguel Hidalgo rang the bells of his church in the rural village of Dolores to summon his Indian and mestizo, or mixed-race, parishioners. "My children!" he shouted to the crowd. "Will you free yourselves?" This call to action launched Mexico's 11-year fight for freedom from Spanish rule. Father Hidalgo's famous cry, known as the "Grito de Dolores," is still reenacted every year throughout Mexico on September 15, the eve of Mexico's Independence Day.

So it was on September 15, 1910, when dignitaries from around the world gathered in Mexico City to celebrate the 100th anniversary of Mexico's independence and the 80th birthday of its long-time authoritarian leader Porfirio Díaz (pohr-FEE-ree-oh DEE-ahz). Díaz spared no expense on the lavish, month-long event. Its cost was greater than his country's entire education budget.

Díaz arranged for a costly exhibit of Spanish art in a new building specially constructed to display it. The building also housed a theater, and an elaborate, one-of-a-kind stained glass curtain was created for the occasion by the famous designer Louis Tiffany. At one grand ball, Díaz provided 20 train carloads of imported French champagne. It was served by European waiters or by Mexicans who looked European. Díaz wished to portray Mexico as the land of Cortés, not the land of Montezuma. He had the city's poor, who were overwhelmingly Indian and mestizo, rounded up to keep them out of sight.

In his 30th year of rule, Díaz seemed to be at the height of his power. Few could have imagined that in just a few months he would be overthrown in what became one of the greatest political and social revolutions of the 20th century. The Mexican Revolution of 1910 would upset the political and social status quo throughout Latin America.

Themes

Political Systems Latin American governments were unstable in this era as liberal and conservative elites, often backed by the military, struggled for control.

Economic Systems Largely rural resource-based and export-based economies grew and changed in response to global economic conditions.

Social Structures Vast disparities between social classes created tensions and helped to trigger unrest and political change.

◀ A statue commemorating Father Hidalgo's famous "Grito de Dolores"

Porfirio Díaz, the authoritarian leader of Mexico who rose to power in 1877, was an example of a Latin American caudillo. Díaz was a mestizo of humble origin, but he ruled with the support of the upper class as well as the army.

oligarchy a form of government in which a small group holds all the power to rule

elite a group of persons who occupy a privileged position in society, often due to birth and/or education and who have power and influence

21.2 Continuity and Change

The revolutions in Latin America in the early 1800s brought independence from Spanish and Portuguese control, but they changed very little else. The social structure of the new nations remained essentially intact. The new nations adopted constitutions based on U.S. and European models. These new constitutions promised representative government and equality. However, Latin America did not have much of a democratic tradition. In practice, most nations became **oligarchies** ruled by upper-class citizens of European descent. The majority of people had little or no voice in government.

The decades that followed independence from Europe were marked by instability and unrest. Much of it involved disputes between *caudillos*. Caudillos were army generals or powerful civilian leaders backed by armed groups of followers. Not all caudillos came from the upper classes. Some had very humble backgrounds. However, they usually ruled with upper-class support. In return, caudillos protected their supporters' wealth and property.

Caudillos, Conservatives, and Liberals   A few caudillos actually brought order to their nations. For example, Juan Manuel de Rosas ruled Argentina as dictator from 1835 to 1852. He was supported by ranchers from his area and a force of *gauchos* (cowboys). His brutal tactics allowed him to maintain stability. He was able to defeat attempts by caudillos from other regions to overthrow him.

More often, however, caudillos and dictators brought political instability. They usually did not have the support of most of the people. Some were elected with the support of only the upper classes. Others seized power through force. Mexico had 48 governments between 1825 and 1855. Chile had 30 between 1823 and 1830.

In most Latin American countries, two competing groups struggled for power. These groups were usually known as liberals and conservatives. Both groups were made of **elites** of European descent. They shared the goals of protecting their property and keeping their own class in power.

The conservative elite worked to preserve the old colonial culture. Conservatives generally opposed modernization and economic development. In general, the conservative elite consisted of large landowners.

In Latin America, there was a stark contrast between the living standards of the upper classes and those of everyday people. Elites lived in colonial mansions, such as the one pictured here, while the poor lived in squalor. Despite independence from Spain, the conservative elite worked to maintain the old hierarchical colonial culture.

The liberal elite tended to be wealthy merchants and professionals. They claimed to support the Enlightenment ideal of rights and freedom for all people. However, they also believed that the common people were not ready to exercise most rights and freedoms wisely. Liberals therefore supported powerful governments. They thought this was the best way to modernize society and prepare the people for freedom and equality. This approach often produced dictatorships. They sacrificed people's rights in the name of "progress."

Throughout the 1800s, liberals and conservatives competed for control of government in many countries. Argentina, Colombia, Uruguay, and Venezuela experienced long periods of unrest. In the 1880s, conservatives emerged victorious in Argentina, Bolivia, Brazil, Colombia, and Paraguay. In Venezuela, unrest continued until a military dictator took over in 1908.

Elsewhere in South America, the liberals gradually gained control. By World War I, they had replaced conservative governments in Argentina, Bolivia, and Paraguay.

Economic and Social Trends Latin American economies in the 1800s were based on the export of agricultural products and other raw materials. Americans and Europeans bought coffee and sugar from Brazil. Cattle and sheep from Argentina and Uruguay supplied meat to Great Britain. Rubber from Brazil, wool from Argentina, and copper and nitrates from mines in Chile and Peru provided raw materials for European industries.

Many countries began developing their infrastructure in the mid-1800s to meet demand for their raw materials. Governments and business people built roads and railroads to bring goods to cities on the coast. They expanded and modernized harbors. Merchant ships switched from sail to steam. Foreign investors financed most improvements. Foreign banks often made loans to Latin American governments or business people to pay for such projects. In many cases, foreigners owned local railroads, mines, ranches, and plantations.

At first, most investment was European—and mainly British. However, by the early 1900s, the United States had replaced Britain as the biggest investor in Latin America.

The growth of industry in the United States and Europe in the late 1800s and early 1900s brought rapid growth to Latin American economies. By World War I, the region was exporting 18 percent of the world's grain, 38 percent of its sugar, and 62 percent of its coffee, cocoa, and tea. Many Latin American elites became rich as a result. The masses, however, did not benefit as much.

Other changes also took place as Latin American economies developed. In rural regions, Indians and other peasants were forced off their land as ranches and plantations grew. Some became hired hands. Others moved to cities to find jobs. Factories appeared to process agricultural products for export. In Mexico City, hundreds of new factories opened. Manufacturing also sprang up in countries like Chile and Brazil.

As workers left the countryside for jobs in factories, urban populations grew quickly in some Latin American countries. São Paulo, Brazil, increased from 35,000 people in 1883 to 350,000 by 1907. Rio de Janeiro's population doubled to one million between 1890 and 1920. By the mid-1900s, about 40 percent of Latin Americans lived in urban areas. However, in less developed countries like Bolivia, Ecuador, Paraguay, and Peru the population remained largely rural.

As cities grew, an urban middle class emerged. Economic growth attracted large numbers of immigrants from Europe. Argentina and Brazil received the most European immigrants. Immigrant workers organized Latin America's first labor unions. This kind of social and economic change and the example of a revolution in Mexico would bring even greater unrest to South America in the 20th century.

As cities grew, workers left the countryside for jobs in urban centers. In this photo, you can see porters at work in La Paz, Bolivia, in 1920. Despite the growth of La Paz in this period, Bolivia remained one of the least developed countries in Latin America.

The Dominican Republic and Haiti   The Dominican Republic and Haiti share the island of Hispaniola. Both experienced unrest throughout most of the 19th century. Starting in 1822, Haiti ruled the Dominican Republic. In 1844 the Dominicans drove the Haitians out. From 1844 to 1899, the Dominican Republic was ruled by a series of caudillos. Most of them opposed democracy. They all borrowed heavily from foreign banks. Eventually all were forced from power. Haiti had 20 rulers between 1843 and 1915. Nearly all of them were assassinated or overthrown. Despite the political instability, U.S. and European businesses continued to make major investments in both nations.

By 1905 Haiti and the Dominican Republic were in serious financial trouble due to heavy borrowing and political corruption. U.S. officials feared that Germany or some other European power might take over one or both countries to collect on unpaid debts. In 1905, the United States took control of both countries' **customs** operations. It used the money collected to pay each country's **creditors**. U.S. President Theodore Roosevelt justified this action by stating, "Chronic wrongdoing, or an impotence which results in a general loosening of the ties of civilized society, may . . . ultimately require intervention by . . . the United States . . . to the exercise of an international police power."

This policy statement became known as the Roosevelt Corollary. It was used by later U.S. presidents to justify other interventions in Latin America. Following renewed unrest, U.S. troops occupied Haiti in 1915 and the Dominican Republic in 1916. The Dominican Republic remained under U.S. control until 1924, and Haiti until 1934. In both countries the Americans built roads, schools, and health clinics. They also improved sewer, water, and communications systems.

U.S. troops trained and armed national guards in each country. These groups often sought power after the United States left. As a result, Haiti underwent frequent military rebellions and coups. In 1957 François "Papa Doc" Duvalier (frahn-SWAH doo-vahl-YAY) began a long and feared dictatorship. In the Dominican Republic, the military put General Rafael Trujillo (rah-fay-EL troo-HEE-yoh) in power in 1930. His 31-year rule became one of the cruelest dictatorships of modern times.

customs taxes that must be paid to the government on goods brought in from other countries

creditor a person or company to whom money is owed

In 1905, the United States intervened in Haiti and the Dominican Republic to ensure that their debts were paid to foreign powers. This political cartoon shows President Theodore Roosevelt policing the Caribbean Sea. The boat in the foreground reads "debt collector," a role the United States felt it was justified in playing in Latin America.

THE BIG STICK IN THE CARIBBEAN SEA

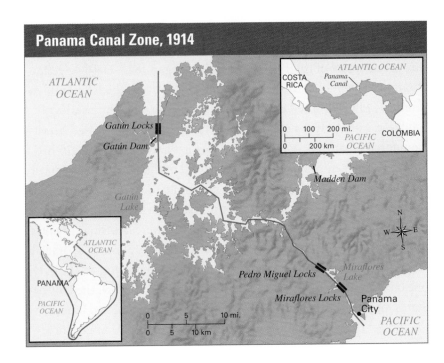

Panama Canal Zone, 1914

ATLANTIC OCEAN

Gatún Locks
Gatún Dam
Gatún Lake

COSTA RICA
Panama Canal
ATLANTIC OCEAN
PACIFIC OCEAN
COLOMBIA
0 100 200 mi.
0 200 km

Madden Dam

PANAMA
ATLANTIC OCEAN
PACIFIC OCEAN

Pedro Miguel Locks
Miraflores Lake
Miraflores Locks
Panama City
PACIFIC OCEAN

0 5 10 mi.
0 5 10 km

In addition to providing a more direct route to Asia, the Panama Canal greatly reduced the distance for ships travelling between the east and west coasts of the United States. Before, ships had to take the long route all the way around South America, as shown at the bottom left of this map. Because the canal was of such strategic and commercial importance, the United States intervened several times in Panamanian politics to ensure their continued control of it.

Panama In the late 1800s, Europeans and Americans began seeking a shortcut across Central America to create a more direct trade route with Asia. A French company began digging a canal across Panama in the 1880s, but it ran out of money. In 1902, it offered to sell the project to the United States. However, the government of Colombia (to which Panama belonged) refused to approve the deal. The French then encouraged a group of Panamanians who wanted independence from Colombia to rebel. President Roosevelt aided the revolt. In 1903, the new government of Panama gave the United States control of the Canal Zone. This was a 10-mile strip of land along the canal route. Construction resumed the next year, and the Panama Canal opened in 1914.

The canal gave the United States a major interest in Panamanian politics. Unrest in Panama led U.S. troops to intervene several times between 1908 and 1925. Panamanian nationalism grew during the 1930s. This resulted in the election of two successive anti-American presidents. The second was overthrown in 1941. The new president turned his nation's defense over to the United States. U.S. troops occupied Panama until massive public protests forced them to leave in 1947.

Nicaragua Conservative rule in Nicaragua brought stability from 1857 to 1893. In 1893 the liberal General José Zelaya (hoh-ZEH zeh-LAH-yah) came to power. He established a brutal dictatorship that lasted 16 years. During that time, Zelaya opened Nicaragua to foreign investment. New roads, railroads, and seaports were constructed. Banana and coffee exports increased. By the early 1900s, Americans controlled the country's banana and coffee industries.

In 1909, Zelaya invited German and Japanese investors to build a canal across his country to compete with the canal the Americans were building in Panama. The United States responded by sending 400 Marines to help the conservatives overthrow him. U.S. military troops were stationed in Nicaragua from 1912 until 1933. They helped to keep several conservative presidents in power. They also armed and trained a Nicaraguan National Guard to keep the peace after they left.

In 1936, the National Guard commander General Anastasio Somoza (ah-nah-STAH-see-oh soh-MOH-zah) overthrew Nicaragua's elected president. After a rigged election, he became president himself. He used the National Guard to create a brutal dictatorship that lasted until he was assassinated in 1956.

General Anastasio Somoza (left) overthrew Nicaragua's elected president in 1936 and established a dictatorship that lasted for 20 years. He is shown being received by the U.S. Speaker of the House, during his 1939 tour of the United States.

Other Nations in Central America   Clashes between liberals and conservatives also divided Guatemala, Honduras, and El Salvador. All experienced violent dictatorships during the first half of the 20th century. These dictators protected U.S. financial interests. In return, they received money and support. Only Costa Rica avoided this fate. In 1889 it held the first entirely free and fair presidential election in all of Central America. Costa Rica became the region's only stable democracy.

Summary

In this lesson, you learned about the causes and effects of political unrest in Latin American nations during the 1800s and 1900s.

Political Systems   Liberal and conservative elites competed for control of government. Both groups favored strong leaders who could protect private property and control the pace of change. This often meant military or civilian dictators who came to power with a group's backing, either through rigged elections or by violent means.

Economic Systems   Most Latin American economies were based on the export of agricultural products—such as coffee, sugar, and bananas—as well as natural resources such as copper and oil. Growth and development was largely accomplished through foreign investment and loans. Early industry centered on processing raw materials for export. Later, the Great Depression caused some countries to begin manufacturing for the home market, as imported goods became scarce or too expensive.

Social Structures   Initially society consisted of a wealthy upper-class minority and a mass population of poor, often landless rural peasants. As cities and industry grew, an urban middle class and working class developed. Governments used repression and reform to keep workers and peasants under control. Over time, however, the middle class began to challenge the elites for political power.

North Africa and the Middle East

How did European colonialism lay the groundwork for the emergence of the modern Middle East?

22.1 Introduction

In July 1915, as World War I raged in Europe, Sir Henry McMahon, Great Britain's High Commissioner in Egypt, received an intriguing letter. The emir, or commander, of Mecca, a man named Hussein ibn Ali (hoo-SAYN ib-NAH-lee) offered to launch an Arab revolt against the Ottoman Empire in return for British support for an independent Arab nation after the war.

The Ottoman Empire had entered the war in 1914 on the side of the Central Powers. Mehmed V, the Ottoman sultan and caliph (head religious leader) claimed that the Allies were intent on destroying Muslim rule and that the war was a fight for the survival of Islam. The Ottoman declaration of war was designed to unify the empire's Muslims. In part, it arose from the desire of the Ottoman rulers to make sure they kept the loyalty of the empire's Arabs, who spoke a different language from the Ottoman rulers. In 1915, the Ottomans began arresting and publically executing Arab leaders suspected of disloyalty. Rather than strengthening Muslim unity, the Ottoman actions caused Arabs like Hussein to reach out to the Ottomans' enemy, Great Britain.

The prospect of an alliance with someone of Hussein's stature and prestige excited British leaders. McMahon's superiors instructed him to write back to Sharif Hussein, and the two men exchanged a series of letters. Hussein agreed to denounce the Ottomans as enemies of Islam and to lead an armed rebellion. The British pledged to provide funds, weapons, and supplies for the revolt. They also agreed to an independent Arab state after the war, although the exact borders of that country were left vague. But history did not turn out quite as Hussein hoped.

The Hussein-McMahon letters are famous today. They form the basis for a huge controversy over whether the British broke promises they made to Arabs about the future of the Middle East. The debate contains the roots of tensions that still challenge the Middle East today.

Themes

Cultural Interaction Religious tensions played a major role in shaping events in the Middle East before and after World War I.

Political Systems The decline and end of the Ottoman Empire aroused the conflicting forces of nationalism and imperialism in both North Africa and the Middle East.

Hussein ibn Ali helped lead an Arab revolt in 1916, as had been agreed in the Hussein-McMahon letters.

The first Ottoman sultans were descendents of Osman I, who founded the empire in the early 14th century. Osman's son, Orhan I, expanded the Ottoman principality into a powerful state. Here Orhan I presides over the Ottoman court.

millet communities of non-Muslim people organized according to religion, in which minority groups held a limited amount of power to rule themselves

22.2 The Ottoman Empire

By the early 20th century, the Ottoman Empire had been in existence for six centuries. At its height in the late 1600s, it reached into Eastern Europe almost to Vienna and across North Africa to the Atlantic Ocean. Much of the Middle East (also called Southwest Asia) was also under Ottoman control. The Ottoman sultans ruled over a multi-ethnic empire in which the people spoke many languages and practiced many religions.

Tensions with Neighboring Peoples   The Ottoman Empire shared some of its borders with the Safavid Empire, which was ruled by the Persians. The Safavid Empire included present-day Iran, eastern Iraq, and western Afghanistan. The border between the two empires changed over time and was a source of conflict for more than a century. However, the rivalry between the Ottomans and Safavids was more than geographical. It was also based on their religious beliefs. Safavid leaders made the Shi'a branch of Islam their empire's official religion. This development increased tensions with the Ottoman Empire, where the Sunni branch of Islam was the majority religion.

Ottoman Organization and Government   The overall head of the Ottoman Empire was the sultan. The early sultans were descendants of Osman I, the ruler of a region in what is now northwest Turkey. In the early 1300s, Osman began conquering nearby territory and established the Ottoman Empire. The name *Ottoman* is derived from Osman's name.

As the empire expanded, the sultans relied on armies that were brought together by members of the elite living around the empire. The sultans rewarded them for their service by giving them the revenues of specific regions in the empire. Unlike European feudalism, these military leaders had no rights over the communities or political control over the areas.

In order to allow each of the religious groups to practice their own laws, the Ottomans established the millet system. Each **millet** was headed by a religious leader and had limited power to set its own rules under the overall supervision of the Ottoman administration. The millets supervised marriage, divorce, and baptism according to their own laws, so that Christians and Jews did not have to obey Muslim laws. Nonetheless, Muslims, Christians, and Jews lived in the same communities and sold their goods in the same markets, despite intermittent ethnic and religious conflict.

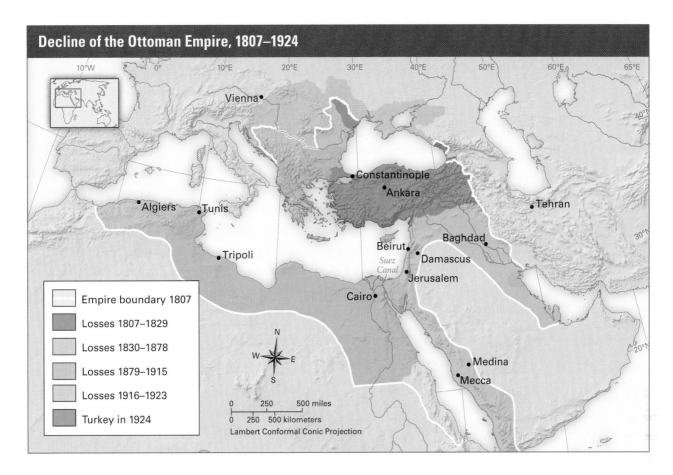

Decline of the Ottoman Empire, 1807–1924

Legend:
- Empire boundary 1807
- Losses 1807–1829
- Losses 1830–1878
- Losses 1879–1915
- Losses 1916–1923
- Turkey in 1924

0   250   500 miles
0   250   500 kilometers
Lambert Conformal Conic Projection

Map labels: Vienna, Constantinople, Ankara, Tehran, Algiers, Tunis, Tripoli, Beirut, Baghdad, Suez Canal, Damascus, Jerusalem, Cairo, Medina, Mecca

The Long Decline   Historians have offered many possible explanations for the decline of the Ottoman Empire. Some claim that the sultans became less powerful. Others argue that there were economic reasons for the decline, beginning when Europeans reached the New World and brought back huge amounts of silver. Since the Ottomans used silver-based currency, the inflation that resulted left the empire without enough funding to continue to grow. Some thinkers inside the empire argued that the problem was that they had strayed too much from the laws of Islam, and that returning to the faith would reinvigorate the empire. Other Ottoman thinkers claimed the problem was that the empire had not changed enough with the times.

In 1683, the Ottomans tried but failed to capture the European city of Vienna, located in Austria. This defeat exposed the empire's military weakness. It also encouraged Austria, Russia, and other European powers to fight several wars with the Turks between 1710 and 1812, taking much of the empire's European territory. Austria and Russia also worked to stir up unrest among the empire's non-Muslim peoples.

In the 1800s, the Ottoman Empire became caught up in the rivalries of Europe's Great Powers as they competed for colonies and spheres of influence. Russian and British aid helped the Ottomans drive French forces out of Egypt in 1801. Six years later, however, it was France that helped them resist a British invasion of Egypt.

At its height in the late 1600s, the Ottoman Empire reached almost to Vienna in Europe and across North Africa to the Atlantic Ocean. The empire slowly declined over time, losing most of its territory in the 19th and early 20th centuries. By 1924, what remained of Ottoman territory became the republic of Turkey.

With British, French, and Russian help, Greece ended Ottoman rule and gained independence in 1832. Yet in the 1830s, Great Britain and Russia also helped the Ottomans defeat Muhammad Ali, the viceroy of Egypt, after he rebelled and seized the region of Greater Syria.

"In my cabinet there are two opinions about Turkey," Russia's Czar Nicholas I told British leaders in 1844. "One is that she is dying; the other is that she is already dead." Britain's policy, however, was to preserve the Ottoman Empire. The British believed that doing this would help maintain the balance of power in Europe. However, completion of the Suez Canal in Egypt in 1869 gradually brought a change in British policy. The canal became a vital transportation link between Britain and its colony of India. To help the British protect the canal, the sultan allowed them to take over the island of Cyprus in 1878. Four years later, following France's occupation of nearby Tunisia, Britain took control of Egypt itself.

The Young Turks were a revolutionary group that succeeded in overthrowing the Ottoman sultan in 1909. Whereas the Ottoman Empire had been multi-ethnic, the Young Turks put a new emphasis on Turkish ethnic nationalism, which angered Arabs within the empire.

The End of an Empire

By the late 1800s, most of the Ottomans' European empire was gone. So was Ottoman control over most of North Africa. Reformers proposed creating a constitutional democracy and combining the remaining provinces into a unified Turkish state. The sultan agreed to a constitution in 1876. However, he soon cancelled it and ruled as an autocrat for the next 30 years.

In 1909, a nationalist group called the Young Turks overthrew the sultan and replaced him with his brother. The new sultan allowed the constitution to be implemented. The Young Turks also strengthened ties with Germany in an effort to modernize, westernize, and industrialize the empire. These policies drew the empire onto the losing side in World War I. They also aroused Arab nationalism. In 1916, an Arab army helped Britain to defeat the Ottoman Empire. In October 1918, the Ottoman government surrendered. The Allies dissolved the empire and placed its territories under their control.

22.3 Turkey and Iran

In a series of agreements made during World War I, the Allies planned for the division of the Ottoman Empire once the Central Powers had been defeated. By this time much of North Africa was already under European control. Great Britain and France now took over the empire's Arab provinces as well.

In December 1918, Allied forces entered Constantinople (now called Istanbul), the Ottoman capital, and took the sultan into custody. They began carrying out plans for changes in Asia Minor, the peninsula between the Black and Mediterranean Seas that the Turks viewed as their homeland. An eastern region was stripped away to create a separate nation for the Armenians, who had suffered horribly during World War I under Ottoman rule. Greek forces seized other territory. Much of the rest of Asia Minor came under British, Italian, and French influence or control.

The Birth of Turkey The sultan had little choice but to accept these developments. Other Turks would not, and widespread revolts broke out. The sultan sent the Turkish war hero General Mustafa Kemal to urge cooperation with the Allies. Instead, Kemal helped organize the resistance. In 1919, a nationalist gathering led by Kemal called for all of Asia Minor to be included in an independent Turkish state. When the Ottoman parliament supported this demand, the occupying Allied forces dissolved it and arrested nationalist leaders.

In 1920, the nationalists formed another parliament, with Kemal at its head, in the city of Ankara. Called the Grand National Assembly (GNA), it declared itself the government of a new nation called Turkey. It also declared that the sultan's government was controlled by infidels and that Muslims had a duty to resist the foreign occupation.

By late 1922, Turkish nationalist forces had pushed the Greeks out of Asia Minor. France and Italy had also withdrawn their troops and the sultan had fled. In 1923, the Allies signed a new peace treaty with the nationalist government. The treaty recognized Turkey's independence and new borders. The GNA declared Turkey to be a republic and elected Mustafa Kemal as its first president.

Mustafa Kemal Atatürk is pictured here (center, in light-colored hat) with fellow nationalists, all wearing the traditional fez style of hat. However, Atatürk would soon ban the fez as part of his program to modernize and westernize Turkey.

Kemal quickly launched a series of reforms to modernize and westernize Turkey. Islamic law was discarded and religious courts were abolished. Parts of the German, Italian, and Swiss legal systems were adopted in their place. Women gained civil rights and the right to vote. Calling on people to become "modern," Kemal banned men from wearing the fez, a traditional Turkish hat. He required government workers to wear Western-style clothing. The Latin alphabet replaced Arabic script for writing the Turkish language. Kemal traveled throughout the country with a chalkboard teaching people the new writing. All Turks were required to take **surnames**. The GNA gave Kemal the name Atatürk, which means "Father of the Turks." Today he is Turkey's greatest national hero.

Atatürk controlled Turkey's government until his death in 1938. By then the threat of another major war was developing in Europe. Although some pro-German and anti-Russian feelings existed, Turkey remained neutral through most of World War II. It declared war on Germany just weeks before the Germans surrendered. This allowed Turkey to take part in creating the United Nations, the world organization founded in 1945.

World War II brought change to Turkey, despite its neutrality. The war encouraged industrial growth. In addition, the Allies' victory encouraged the growth of Turkish democracy. Political parties arose to challenge the one-party system under which Atatürk had ruled. Threats from the Soviet Union caused the United States to begin providing economic and military aid in 1947. This relationship drew Turkey even closer to the West.

surname the family name common to the members of a family

In 1906, widespread protests forced the Persian shah to adopt a constitution. This photo depicts one such demonstration, when 12,000 men assembled on the grounds of the British Embassy and demanded a parliament and constitutional government in Persia.

Persia Becomes Iran   By the late 1800s, Great Britain and Russia had become involved in the internal affairs of Persia, an ancient country ruled by a series of shahs between 1797 and 1896. Russia carved out a sphere of influence in the north, while Great Britain did so along the Persian Gulf. The British pressured Persia to open the nation to foreign trade and investment. Manufacturing suffered as Persia became a source of cheap raw materials and a market for Western industrial goods.

Persia's merchants objected to the favored treatment that European businesses received. They called for political and legal reforms. Shiite clerics supported the merchants and the protests they organized. The unrest that resulted showed the growing power of religious leaders and the merchant class. In 1906, widespread demonstrations and strikes finally forced the shah to agree to a constitution and a national legislature called the Majles (MAHJ-less).

The Majles took a strong stand against European involvement in Persia. It also passed laws granting freedom of speech and the press. The Majles established **secular** schools, including some for girls. These reforms caused tensions with some Muslim clerics. The shah, who also opposed the Majles, shut it down in 1908. Civil war followed, but Russia intervened and ended the war in 1911. Russia withdrew its troops when World War I broke out in 1914. Although Persia declared neutrality, it became a battleground in the war.

At the end of World War I, Great Britain was the only European power left in Persia. In 1921, Britain gave in to international pressure and also withdrew. However, the British supported army officer Reza Khan in taking control of Persia's government. He deposed the shah in 1925. Crowning himself Reza Shah Pahlavi, he began the Pahlavi dynasty, which held power until its overthrow in Iran's Islamic Revolution of 1979.

Reza Shah launched a broad program of reforms to create a modern state. He changed the country's name from Persia to Iran, the ancient name of the original settlement. The system of secular schools was expanded and Iran's first western-style university opened in Tehran. The status of women changed and the requirement that women wear veils ended. In addition, women were encouraged to enter the work force.

To promote economic growth, the shah built roads, completed a railroad across Iran, and opened state-owned factories that produced basic consumer needs such as textiles and canned goods. Because he distrusted the British and Russians, he expanded trade by developing ties with Nazi Germany. By World War II, Germany was Iran's largest trading partner. Nevertheless, Reza Shah declared Iran neutral when the war began in 1939.

Despite his reforms, Reza Shah was an **autocrat**. He controlled the Majles and silenced the press. He also jailed, exiled, or executed his opponents, including some religious leaders. In 1941, the Allies used his ties with Germany as an excuse to invade Iran and replace him. They forced the shah to step down, and they replaced him with his young son Mohammad Reza Shah Pahlavi.

Reza Shah Pahlavi allowed the Allies to move war supplies through Iran to help the Soviet Union resist a German invasion. The new shah did not yet wield the same power over Iranian politics, and many political parties formed, including a pro-Soviet communist party. Instability and unrest developed as these parties competed for power after World War II. Iran's internal politics were further complicated by Soviet, British, and American competition for control of the nation's oil resources. Concerns about communism also continued to involve Great Britain and the United States in Iranian affairs.

secular having no religious or spiritual basis; not pertaining to or connected with religion

autocrat a person who rules with unlimited authority

Reza Shah Pahlavi helped modernize Iran, but he also ruled as an autocrat. He is shown here in 1931, sitting on the Peacock Throne, a traditional symbol of Persian monarchy. During World War II, the Allies forced Reza Shah to step down and replaced him with his son, who did not command as much political power.

22.4 The French Mandate

Even as World War I raged on, imperial powers were seeking ways to benefit afterward. Expecting that the Ottoman Empire would not survive the war, Great Britain and France made secret plans to divide much of it between themselves. They signed a secret treaty called the Sykes-Picot Agreement in May 1916. This agreement recognized French and British claims in different parts of Greater Syria. It also granted Great Britain control of Iraq.

This secret agreement came just weeks after Britain promised Hussein ibn Ali, the emir of Mecca, an independent Arab state in return for Arab help against the Ottomans in the war. Unaware of the secret treaty, Hussein launched his Arab revolt in June 1916 by attacking Ottoman troops defending Mecca. Within months, most of the Hejaz was in Arab hands. Hussein's son Faisal ibn Hussein commanded the Arab forces. Faisal led his troops into the Syrian city of Damascus shortly before the Ottomans' surrender in October 1918.

An Independent Greater Syria   With the war over, Faisal acted on the pledge the British had made to his father and formed a government.

After the Ottoman Empire was defeated in World War I, the League of Nations granted France and Britain mandates to control their former territories. The areas that would become Lebanon and Syria were under French control, while the British controlled the regions of Palestine, Transjordan, and Iraq.

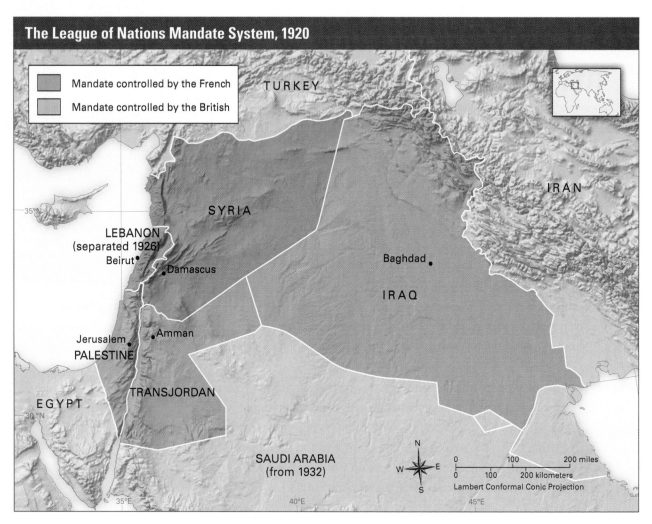

The League of Nations Mandate System, 1920

- Mandate controlled by the French
- Mandate controlled by the British

TURKEY

IRAN

SYRIA

LEBANON
(separated 1926)
Beirut
Damascus

Baghdad

IRAQ

Jerusalem
Amman
PALESTINE

TRANSJORDAN

EGYPT

SAUDI ARABIA
(from 1932)

0   100   200 miles
0   100   200 kilometers
Lambert Conformal Conic Projection

In March 1920, a Syrian national congress meeting in Damascus proclaimed Greater Syria to be an independent nation and named Faisal as king. The Allies, however, refused to recognize this action. Instead, at the San Remo Conference in April 1920, Allied leaders decided to divide Greater Syria. Largely following the Sykes-Picot Agreement, they handed the northern region over to France under the mandate system created by the new League of Nations. The southern region—including the geographic area commonly referred to as Palestine—became a British mandate.

Arabs reacted to this development with anger and frustration. When Arab nationalists urged defiance, French troops in Beirut marched on Damascus, defeated King Faisal's army, and drove him from power in July 1920. The independent Arab state of Greater Syria vanished after just five months of existence.

Syria and Lebanon   Under the League of Nations' rules, the mandate system required Great Britain and France to promote economic development in their mandates and to prepare them for self-government. The British and French took different approaches to achieving these goals. Britain ruled by controlling Arab leaders that it placed in power. France's rule was more direct and resulted from a desire for long-term French control.

France sent large numbers of French officials, supported by an occupying army, to govern its mandate. They gave Muslim Arab leaders only limited opportunities to practice self-government. These policies were largely driven by three factors: concern for the Christian minority, which France had long pledged to protect; French investments in railroads, ports, and other economic activities made during the Ottoman Empire; and France's rivalry with Britain for power in the Middle East.

The French organized their mandate into several governing districts based on cultural and religious differences. However, this division did not weaken Arab nationalism. Many minorities wanted a free and united Greater Syria too. That became clear in 1925 when a minority group called the Druze rebelled against French rule. They were soon joined by Arab nationalists from across the region in a revolt that took two years to put down.

Major changes followed the Druze Revolt. In 1926, the French separated Lebanon from the rest of the mandate and gave it a constitution and limited self-government. The constitution required that the three largest religious groups in Lebanon—Christians, Shi'a Muslims, and Sunni Muslims—share power. Lebanon's president was to be Christian, its prime minister a Sunni, and the head of its legislature a Shiite. But Lebanon did not have total self-government. The French governor retained the right to **veto** actions of Lebanon's government.

The Druze are a minority religious sect from the region of Greater Syria. In 1925, they led a rebellion against French rule. This photo shows the great losses suffered by Druze soldiers as they unsuccessfully defended the city of Rashaya from French legionnaires.

veto to prohibit or refuse to approve

The French Mandate government improved and expanded Lebanon's education system. The schoolboys pictured here attended school in Ras-el-Matn, Lebanon. Today Lebanon has one of the highest literacy rates in the Middle East, in part due to the legacy of the French Mandate.

In 1928, France allowed Arabs in the rest of its mandate to form a limited government too. The government had an elected legislature controlled by Arab nationalists, and it wrote a constitution, approved by the French governor only after removing references to a united Arab state. In 1936, Arab leaders and French officials negotiated a treaty allowing limited independence for a nation to be called Syria. This was a much smaller nation than the united Arab state of Greater Syria that had existed briefly after World War I. The Syrian legislature approved the treaty, but France never did. In 1939, Syria's elected government resigned and the constitution was suspended.

War and Independence   Syria and Lebanon followed nearly identical paths to gain independence during World War II. After Germany occupied France in 1940, Hitler allowed the French to form a pro-Nazi government called the Vichy government. France's former government leaders fled to Great Britain. They became what was called the Free French government.

Vichy officials took over France's Middle East mandate. However, they were driven out in 1941 by British, Arab, and Free French forces. The Free French officials who replaced them promised that independence would soon follow. The Free French allowed new elections in Syria and Lebanon in 1943. The elections again put the nationalists in power. Both governments passed laws and took other actions to end French rule. The French responded by arresting the leaders of Lebanon's government. In Syria, French troops tried to restore control.

The British pressured Free French leaders to accept Lebanon's **autonomy** in 1943 and Syria's in 1945. However, the French refused to remove their troops. France's other wartime Allies—the United States and Soviet Union—recognized both nations' independence in 1944, which increased the pressure on France to withdraw. In 1946, the last French troops left Syria and Lebanon. British forces also withdrew, leaving both nations finally free.

The Legacy of French Rule   While ruling their mandate, the French had made many improvements. They built roads, promoted improved agricultural practices, expanded education, and improved public health and education. The French enlarged the harbor in Beirut, a major trading port, and they improved public utilities in Damascus and other ancient cities. However, more than two decades of French rule had left many Arabs bitter.

In Syria, French policies prevented development of a strong system of democratic self-government. Lebanon was somewhat better prepared for autonomy. However, the system of government the French created there ensured the development of religion-based struggles for power. These legacies would shape the future of both nations.

The British statesman Arthur Balfour was influenced by Zionist leaders to support a Jewish homeland in Palestine, and in 1917 he authored the Balfour Declaration. In 1926, Balfour (center, holding hat) visited Palestine, where he was enthusiastically welcomed by the Jewish population.

22.5 The British Mandates

In the secret Sykes-Picot Agreement of 1916, Great Britain and France decided that the region of Palestine should be handled differently than the rest of Greater Syria. Three world religions— Judaism, Christianity, and Islam—considered its ancient city of Jerusalem holy. Palestine also contained many other places that were sacred to one or more of these faiths. The British and French agreed that, for this reason, it should be under international rule. However, the British wanted to control the area because they believed its proximity to Egypt would help protect the Suez Canal.

In 1917, Britain issued the Balfour Declaration, announcing its support for "the establishment in Palestine of a national home for the Jewish people." The declaration also pledged that "nothing shall be done which may prejudice the civil and religious rights of existing non-Jewish communities in Palestine."

The Balfour Declaration reflected the growth of Zionism, a nationalist movement that called for Europe's Jews to move to their ancient homeland. In part, this statement was designed to rouse support among American and European Jews for the Allies' war effort—especially in Russia, where calls to withdraw from World War I were increasing. In part, this statement was an expression of genuine understanding and support for Zionism.

The other Allied powers endorsed the Balfour Declaration. The San Remo Conference abandoned the plan for international control in Palestine and made it a solely British mandate. This Mandate for Palestine included area between the Jordan River and the Mediterranean Sea and a larger region to the east, which was later called Transjordan. The special situation in the area west of the Jordan River, ultimately caused Britain to govern each region separately.

Transjordan Becomes a Nation

Statehood for Transjordan was achieved fairly smoothly. In 1921, British authorities appointed Abdullah ibn al-Hussein emir of Transjordan. Abdullah was another son of Sharif Hussein and the brother of Faisal. The Bedouin tribes who lived in the region were willing to accept Abdullah as their ruler, which would help to unify Transjordan as a nation. Giving Abdullah his own country also encouraged him not to oppose France's overthrow of Faisal as king of Greater Syria.

In 1923, Great Britain proclaimed Transjordan a nation preparing for independence under protection of the British. Technically it remained part of the Mandate for Palestine. That relationship was clarified by a treaty five years later that gave the British control of Transjordan's finances, foreign policy, and army. Britain relaxed these controls slightly in 1936 to allow Transjordan to establish relations with other Arab countries.

In 1921, British authorities met with Abdullah ibn al-Hussein (second from left) at his camp in the city of Amman, where they appointed him emir of Transjordan. He would later become king after Transjordan gained full independence.

The British provided financial aid to improve Transjordan's roads, communications, education, and other public services. This aid also built a strong army, led by British officers, which Abdullah used to keep the area's Bedouin tribes under control. Part of this army, a force called the Arab Legion, helped the British drive the Vichy French from Syria and a pro-Nazi ruler from Iraq during World War II. Six months after the war ended, another treaty with Britain gave Transjordan full independence, and Abdullah named himself king. In 1949, Transjordan officially became the Hashemite Kingdom of Jordan, or simply Jordan.

Zionist a person who supports the right for Jews to return to and create a state in their ancient homeland

Tensions Over Palestine

Growing anti-Semitism in Europe in the late 1800s strengthened the **Zionist** movement. After the Russian Revolution of 1905, persecution caused thousands of young Russian Jews to flee to Palestine. There they joined the small number of Jews who had lived in the area since it was a Jewish kingdom millennia before. By World War I, Palestine's Jewish population numbered 85,000—compared to 535,000 Muslims and 70,000 Christians, most of whom were Arabs.

Over time Arab opposition to Jewish immigration grew. At first, Arabs viewed Jewish immigration with only mild concern. Some even felt that Jewish immigration would help the area modernize. In 1919, Syrian leader Faisal agreed to support Jewish settlement in Palestine. But his acceptance was based on the condition that the Allies recognize Greater Syria's independence.

The British gained control over Palestine in 1917 and remained in control there for the next 30 years. British officials tried to keep peace between Arabs and Jews and to involve both groups in the Mandate's economic development. Both goals proved difficult to achieve. Meetings of Arab leaders rejected the Balfour Declaration in 1920 and again in 1921, and anti-Zionist riots broke out in Palestine. In 1922, however, the League of Nations recognized the Jewish historical connection with Palestine. It authorized Britain to establish a Jewish homeland "while ensuring that the rights and position of other sections of the population are not prejudiced [damaged]."

Jewish immigration slowly increased after World War I. In the 1920s and 1930s, Jewish and Arab populations grew by roughly the same amount. Since the Jewish population was smaller, this equal growth resulted in Jews becoming a larger percentage of the population. This increased Arab opposition to the growing Jewish presence.

By 1933, nearly 240,000 Jews lived in the Palestine Mandate—about 20 percent of the population. The Zionists were determined to settle as many Jews there and to buy as much land as they could. Palestinian Arabs were equally determined to slow both developments and to stop them if possible. The British, whose task it was to prepare the Palestine Mandate for self-rule, found themselves caught in the middle of this conflict.

This illustration honors the vision of Theodore Herzl, who founded the modern Zionist movement in the 19th century. Herzl, a Hungarian Jew, believed that Jews could escape the persecution they faced in Europe only by returning to their ancient homeland.

The British created a workable government, made transportation improvements, and brought water and electricity to cities and towns throughout the region. Jewish leaders believed it was in their best interests to cooperate with the British. Arabs generally opposed British rule because of its support of Zionism and tensions between powerful Palestinian Arab families weakened Arab unity. As a result, the Jewish population often seemed to benefit more economically from British policies than the Arabs did.

Hitler's rise to power in Germany brought a huge wave of mostly German Jewish immigration to the Palestine Mandate in the 1930s. This influx of Jewish immigrants alarmed Palestinian Arabs, who launched a major uprising in 1936. Arab workers went on strike, and militias attacked Jewish settlements and British military outposts. Britain sent 20,000 troops and finally put down the revolt in 1939. Meanwhile, the Zionists armed a Jewish militia force to protect themselves from these attacks that grew to 15,000.

In reaction to increased Jewish immigration, Palestinian Arabs organized an uprising in 1936. Here, Palestinian Arabs in the town of Abou Ghosh pledge themselves to the cause of preventing Jewish settlement in Palestine.

The Palestinian Revolt forced Britain to change its policies. British leaders feared that if war came in Europe, they would not be able to also deal with Arab unrest in the Palestine Mandate. In 1937, British leaders proposed dividing the Mandate into separate independent Jewish and Arab states. Arab leaders stated they would not accept any Jewish state. Zionist leaders stated they could not accept the proposal without negotiations over the borders. With tensions growing sharply in Europe in 1939, Britain withdrew its support for a Jewish homeland. The British promised that the Palestine Mandate would become an independent Arab state within 10 years. They also restricted the right of Jews to purchase land and limited Jewish immigration to 75,000 over the next 5 years and pledged that the Palestinian Arabs would set the limit after that.

The British announcement came as reports of the Holocaust, the Nazi effort to murder all of Europe's Jews, were beginning to be made known. Jewish leaders in the Mandate were shocked and furious. However, there was little they could do at the time and many Zionists volunteered to help Britain's war effort despite the restrictions.

As the war neared an end, however, radical Zionist leaders launched a guerrilla campaign against British rule. Assassinations, kidnappings, bombings, sabotage, and some acts of terrorism followed. The vast majority of Zionists, including the leadership, condemned terrorism and worked to stop it, for example, by reporting terrorist suspects to the British.

Meanwhile, the United States pressured Great Britain to let some 100,000 Holocaust survivors into the Palestine Mandate. Arabs responded to this development with additional violence. By 1947 the British had had enough. They turned to the newly formed United Nations to find a solution.

Iraq and Independence   Like other Arabs, Iraqis expected independence after the Ottomans' defeat in World War I. Instead, Iraq became a British mandate. When Arab nationalists resisted the French mandate in Syria in 1920, Iraqis also rose in revolt. As French forces deposed Faisal, the Arabs' new king in Syria and brought an end to the independent Greater Syria, British troops put down the rebellion in Iraq.

After putting down the rebellion, Great Britain tried to reach a settlement with Iraqi nationalists. The British offered to make Faisal king of Iraq and to create an Arab government under the British mandate. Faisal accepted, with two conditions. He wanted the people to offer him the throne, and he wanted the mandate replaced by a treaty of alliance. Faisal's selection as king was confirmed by a **plebiscite** in 1921. The next year the mandate was replaced by a treaty of alliance with Great Britain.

The constitution Iraq adopted in 1924 created a constitutional monarchy with a national legislature and parliamentary government. New treaties in 1926 and 1927 changed the Iraqi-British relationship, but nationalists continued to call for full independence. Britain finally announced that this would take place in 1932. Just before surrendering control, Britain set Iraq's border with the British **protectorate** of Kuwait. This action was never approved by the government of free Iraq, however, and this would lead to future border disputes.

Faisal's death in 1933 set off a power struggle among Iraq's political leaders. His son took the throne, but instability followed. In 1936, the army took over and controlled Iraq's government until 1941. During this period, Iraq enjoyed economic growth. Oil had been discovered in 1927. By the mid-1930s oil revenues were financing new railroads, schools, and irrigation projects. Oil also played an important role in Iraq's foreign relations, especially during World War II and afterward.

When World War II broke out, Iraq remained neutral, despite its treaties with Great Britain. Iraq's neutral position changed after Germany conquered France. Expecting the Allies to lose the war, nationalist leaders urged Iraq to free the Palestine and Syria Mandates from the British and French. Some called for an alliance with Germany and opened negotiations with the Axis Powers. Britain responded in 1941 by invading Iraq and putting a pro-British government back in power.

plebiscite a direct "yes" or "no" vote by the people of a country on a matter of national importance

protectorate a relationship of control between two nations, in which the stronger one provides larger services and protection, while the weaker makes many basic decisions

The British carried out a coup in Iraq in 1941 to secure a government more in line with their interests. This aroused short-lived and unsuccessful opposition. In this photograph, Iraqi tribal warriors gather to attack British positions.

22.6 The Arabian Peninsula

In contrast to events in the British and French mandates, Arabs on the Arabian Peninsula remained free from European control. Like Turkey, the nation of Saudi Arabia was shaped by the vision of its creator, Ibn Saud (IB-uhn sah-OOD). However, while Kemal Atatürk created a secular Turkey, Ibn Saud built his state around the teachings of Wahhabi Islam. Ibn Saud was the only Arab leader who was truly independent of the western powers between World Wars I and II.

Allegiance to Wahhabism, an austere form of Islam, set the kingdom of Saudi Arabia apart from its neighbors. Starting around 1750, the Saudis fought for control of the Arabian Peninsula. This illustration depicts a Saudi battle with the Ottomans in 1818.

The Kingdom of Saudi Arabia The first Saudi state arose about 1750, when local ruler Muhammad ibn Saud joined with Islamic religious reformer Muhammad ibn 'Abd al-Wahhab to form a kingdom. The kingdom rose and fell several times over the next 150 years as Saudi rulers fought other Arab families, Egypt, and the Ottoman Empire for control on the peninsula.

In 1902, the Saudi ruler Ibn Saud recaptured Riyadh, the kingdom's traditional capital, from a rival Arab leader and reestablished the Al Saud dynasty. By the end of World War I, he controlled most of the central peninsula. However, he worried that the British might oppose his further expansion. These suspicions grew when Britain put members of a rival Arab family—Abdullah and Faisal, the sons of Sharif Hussein ibn Ali, the ruler of the Hejaz—on the thrones in Transjordan and Iraq.

Ibn Saud addressed this concern in 1924, when he led a force into the Hejaz, seized the Muslim holy cities of Mecca and Medina, and drove Hussein from power. Ibn Saud then negotiated treaties to set his country's borders with Transjordan and Iraq. In 1927, Britain recognized him as king in return for his pledge to respect the British protectorates on the peninsula. In 1932, he united the territories he ruled to form the Kingdom of Saudi Arabia. Ibn Saud became known as King Saud.

King Saud used his powerful personal leadership, religious values, negotiating skills, and marriage alliances to turn warring tribal factions into a strong, centralized government. His marriage alliances produced 37 sons. Along with other family members, they eventually took important roles in government. A large royal family developed that saw its welfare and that of Saudi Arabia as identical. The early years were difficult, however, because the kingdom was very poor.

At first, the annual Muslim *hajj,* or pilgrimage, to Mecca was the kingdom's main source of **revenue**. The Great Depression of the 1930s caused a decline in the number of people making the pilgrimage, thus shrinking Saudi Arabia's income. A greater source of income arose in 1938 when an American company discovered oil in Saudi Arabia. World War II delayed the start of production, but large numbers of foreign oil workers began arriving after 1944. The Saudi government joined with several American oil companies to form Aramco (the Arabian American Oil Company) to manage production and share the wealth.

The Persian Gulf Emirates   Several regions along the Persian Gulf did not become part of Saudi expansion because they were British protectorates. They are known today as the United Arab Emirates (UAE) and the nations of Qatar, Bahrain, Oman, and Kuwait. Great Britain became interested in this region in the early 1800s, largely from a desire to protect its routes to India from Arab pirates.

The British also did not want the Ottomans or any other of the Great Powers to create spheres of influence in the Persian Gulf. They worried that some of the 10 tribal families who ruled these regions might be pressured into turning over territory to an outside power. Between 1820 and 1916, the British concluded treaties with the *sheikh,* or tribal and family leader, in each region. Each treaty recognized the sheikh's control within certain borders and stated that those borders could not be changed without Britain's consent. In return, Britain promised to protect the sheikhdom.

hajj in Islam, the pilgrimage to Mecca that is prescribed as a religious duty for Muslims

revenue money that a government receives from taxes and other sources and uses to operate and provide public services

In 1944, Saudi Arabia joined with American oil companies to extract and distribute the region's petroleum. As a result, the United States became the most influential foreign power in Saudi Arabia. Here, King Ibn Saud (center) meets with President Franklin Roosevelt (right).

One result of these treaties was that they changed traditional tribal relationships. Tribal boundaries became clearer and tribal alliances became thought of in terms of land ownership. This became important when oil was discovered in Kuwait and Qatar in the late 1930s (and much later elsewhere). When foreign oil companies arrived to search for oil, they looked for the "owner" of the land. According to the British treaties, this meant the sheikh and his family. When oil production began, both became rich. Following Arab tradition, they distributed much of their new wealth to the region they controlled. At first this meant gifts for friends and food for anyone who needed it. Eventually, however, it paid for schools, hospitals, and roads in the sheikhdom.

Changing Control in Yemen The British captured Yemen's port city of Aden in 1839. They gradually spread their control east along the Gulf of Aden. To the north, they came into conflict with the Ottoman Empire, which controlled the Hejaz along the Red Sea. In 1904, a treaty set the border between the two regions. North Yemen became independent at the end of World War I, when Turkish forces withdrew. South Yemen remained under British control. In 1937, Aden became a British colony. In the rest of South Yemen, the British negotiated peace among some 1,400 tribes and clans who had fought over the territory for decades and made it a British protectorate.

Oil was discovered in Kuwait in the late 1930s. It became an enormous source of wealth, which the sheik used to develop the state's schools, hospitals, and roads. This photo shows Kuwaiti men filling up new imported American cars at a modern gas station. As might be expected, gas was very inexpensive in Kuwait.

22.7 Colonialism in North Africa

By 1900, the power the Ottomans once had over North Africa was long gone. European imperialism began chipping away at that part of the empire in the 1830s and continued throughout the century. Only Morocco, which had successfully resisted Ottoman conquest, escaped European colonial rule. Nevertheless, it could not escape the Europeans' battle for influence and control in the region.

Morocco's location at the Strait of Gibraltar, which connects the Atlantic Ocean and the Mediterranean Sea, made it attractive to several European nations. France showed a strong interest as early as 1830. In the early 1900s, both France and Spain established spheres of influence there. In 1912, these spheres of influence became French and Spanish protectorates and remained so for the next 44 years.

France and the Barbary States   The Mediterranean coast of North Africa extending west from Egypt was known in the early 1800s as the Barbary Coast. The four Muslim states that shared this coastline—Morocco, Algiers, Tunis, and Tripoli—were known as the Barbary States. Both names refer to the Berbers, a people indigenous to the area who had converted to Islam.

Pirates were a constant threat to traders along the Mediterranean coast. In 1827, France sent a government official to Algiers to discuss the situation. The Ottoman viceroy became angry and struck the Frenchman with a fly swatter. This insult provided the excuse for France to invade Algiers in 1830, bringing an end to three centuries of Ottoman control.

More than 40 years of unrest followed as thousands of Europeans poured in. They settled on Algerians' land and took advantage of the native peoples. Frequent rebellions resulted. French troops brutally put down these revolts, seizing even more land and relocating its population to less desirable areas. When the fighting finally ended in the 1870s, nearly a third of native Algerians had died from disease, starvation, or warfare.

Although Tunis was officially a province of the Ottoman Empire in the 1830s, in reality it was an autonomous state. When the Ottomans overthrew the viceroy of neighboring Tripoli and reestablished direct control, Tunis turned for help to the French in Algiers. France responded with decades of military and financial aid. However, mismanagement, corruption, and unrest plagued Tunisian rulers. By 1869, Tunis was bankrupt and in debt to European banks. France forced Tunis to become a French protectorate in 1881. Although the Tunisian ruler remained in place, a French governor held all the real power.

In 1827, the French ambassador Pierre Duval was sent to discuss the problem of piracy along the Mediterranean coast with the Ottoman viceroy Hussein ibn El Hussein. However, the meeting did not go well. In a fit of anger, Hussein struck the French ambassador with a fly-swatting fan. France used this incident as a pretext to invade Algiers in 1830.

This photograph shows life in Tunis in 1899. Tunis became a French protectorate in 1881, and the French contributed a lot to Tunisian development. However, French interference also aroused Tunisian nationalism.

The French strengthened the Tunisian finances, established modern communications, and developed mining and agriculture. But these improvements were not enough to dampen Tunisian nationalism. In the early 1900s, a group of French-educated Tunisians formed the Young Tunisians, a political party that called for less French control. A French crackdown drove the party's leaders underground. They emerged again after World War I to lead a Tunisian nationalist movement.

A nationalist movement also arose in Algeria. About 173,000 Algerians served in the French army during World War I. Hundreds of thousands of others worked in factories in France. There they enjoyed a higher standard of living than they had at home. They also learned of democratic principles that French officials had long refused to apply to the Muslim majority in Algeria. Algerian soldiers who served with French forces in the Middle East were inspired by Arab nationalism. However, French officials and Algeria's European settlers opposed reforms to give Algerians political power and equal rights.

By the 1930s many Algerians were supporting nationalist leaders who called for violent resistance to French rule. Tunisian nationalism also took a more radical turn. A demand for a constitution in the 1920s was answered by French troops and only minor reforms. French attempts to suppress a growing Tunisian independence movement in the 1930s only led to its spread and to greater unrest.

When World War II began, some Tunisian nationalist leaders were exiled to France. The Nazis released them after France fell and tried to gain their support. When Axis forces entered Tunisia, they were allowed to return home. There they joined the Tunisian ruler in forming a nationalist government. When the Free French regained control in 1943, this government was removed. After the war, Arab independence in the French mandate in the Middle East forced France to allow a nationalist government in Tunisia. During this period, the Tunisian independence movement continued to grow.

Algerian soldiers arrive in France during World War I. Hundreds of thousands of Algerians served in the French army or worked in French factories during the war. In France, Algerians were exposed to standards of living and political rights that they had been denied at home.

Algeria was not invaded by Axis troops. However, Axis radio broadcasts beamed into Algeria promised Muslims a better world after the war. The Free French responded in 1943 by offering French citizenship to some groups of Algerian Muslims. However, this limited reform did not change Algerian public opinion. In 1945, French authorities fired on peaceful demonstrators who were displaying Algerian nationalist flags. Thousands of Muslims were killed as French forces put down the violent uprising that followed. This event became the first battle in Algeria's long war for independence that began in the 1950s.

Italian Colonialism Italy gained a sphere of influence in Tripoli in the mid-1800s. By the early 1900s, Italian businesses had important commercial interests there. When the Ottomans failed to agree to demands to protect those interests, Italian troops invaded Tripoli and occupied it in 1911. Although they quickly defeated its Ottoman defenders, the native population proved harder to subdue. Years of

Italian troops enter Tripoli in 1911. Italy seized Tripoli from the Ottomans to protect Italian businesses and commercial interests they had established in the region.

warfare followed before Italy finally gained control. Meanwhile, it spent huge sums of money building towns, roads, and agricultural colonies for Italian settlers. In 1934, Italy united the region to form a colony called Libya.

Allied troops drove Italian and other Axis forces out of Libya during World War II. The British and French each governed part of Libya until 1951, when the United Nations granted it independence.

martial law military control of an area in place of civilian authorities; usually authorized by a government in emergencies when local law enforcement agencies cannot maintain public order and safety

The British in Egypt   In 1859 the Ottoman viceroy of Egypt authorized a French company to dig a canal across the strip of land that separates the Mediterranean and Red Seas. The Egyptian government had part-ownership of the Suez Canal, which opened in 1869. The canal cut the distance between Great Britain and India in half. When heavy debts forced Egypt to sell its share in 1875, the British government bought it and became the canal's largest single owner. By 1881, more than 80 percent of the traffic through the canal was British.

In 1879, Egypt's debt problems caused the European powers to demand that the viceroy be removed. The Ottoman sultan appointed a new viceroy. However, Egyptian nationalists, angered over the Europeans' influence, rose in revolt. British troops invaded Egypt in 1882 to protect the Suez Canal and put down the rebellion. They remained for 74 years. The occupation made Egypt part of the British Empire. It was not a colony because officially the viceroy's government continued to rule. However, the real power in Egypt was a British governor called an "agent," backed by British troops.

The British put Egypt's financial problems in order. They cut spending, paid the debt, and used what money remained on agriculture and railroads. Education received little attention. This policy upset many Egyptians. They were also angered by the number of British in important government jobs, which denied Egyptians the opportunity to gain experience in self-rule.

In the early 1900s, Egypt's nationalists began calling on the British to get out. Instead, when the Ottoman Empire joined the Central Powers in 1914, Britain made Egypt a protectorate and placed it under **martial law**. Egypt's Legislative Assembly was suspended and nationalist leaders were temporarily silenced. Thousands of Egyptians were forced into work supporting the British war effort.

The Wafd, an Egyptian nationalist party, formed in 1918, and remained a powerful political force in Egypt until the end of World War II. This 1936 photograph shows a gathering of Wafd members.

Egyptian nationalism emerged from the war even stronger. A nationalist political party called the Wafd formed in 1918 to seek independence. It quickly became a powerful political force. Britain's arrest of Wafd leaders in 1919 set off weeks of strikes, demonstrations, rioting, and acts of sabotage across Egypt. British troops crushed what Egyptians call the 1919 Revolution. Hoping to head off further trouble, Britain ended its protectorate and declared Egypt independent in 1922.

A constitution was written and a legislature elected. An Egyptian king, Fu'ād I, took the throne. Little else changed, however. British troops remained in Egypt and the power struggle continued until World War II. This time the struggle was among the British, the Wafd, and the king.

The Wafd controlled Egypt's legislature until the mid-1930s. Both the king and the British worked to break its power. In 1925 and again in 1928 Fu'ād dissolved the legislature and ruled alone. He also encouraged the formation of other political parties. Meanwhile, the British lured the Wafd into supporting an unfavorable treaty. When Fu'ād died in 1935, his son Farouk took the throne and signed the Wafd-backed treaty. Although the treaty reduced British control, it still did not give Egypt full independence. Many Egyptians blamed the Wafd. Some began to support newer, more radical nationalist groups like the Muslim Brotherhood and Young Egypt. The Wafd lost control of Egypt's legislature in the elections of 1936.

The Wafd returned to power, with British support, during World War II. Early Axis victories in Europe increasingly convinced Egyptians that Germany would win the war. Many were pleased at this prospect because of their dislike for the British. Some groups, such as Young Egypt, openly supported the Nazis. The British were determined to prevent Egyptian cooperation with Germany. In 1942, as German troops advanced on Egypt, Britain ordered King Farouk to form a Wafd-controlled government. New elections at the end of the war ended the Wafd's power and the party split into competing groups. Popular support swung toward organizations like the Muslim Brotherhood, which continued to push for the end of British control.

Summary

In this lesson, you learned about imperialism in North Africa and the Middle East and changes that took place there in the first half of the 20th century.

Cultural Interaction The Ottoman Empire's subjects enjoyed religious freedom, but tensions often existed among religious groups because of mutual intolerance. The sultan failed to unite the empire's Muslims against the Allies in World War I. After the Ottoman empire's breakup, the Turks formed a secular government.

Political Systems As the Ottoman Empire declined, Great Britain and France took advantage of its weakness to control large parts of North Africa and the Middle East. Their presence was met with growing nationalism. By the end of World War II, Turkey, Syria, Lebanon, Jordan and Iraq had all established their own governments. However, except for Saudi Arabia, the rest of the Middle East and all of North Africa remained under Western control.

The Rise of Fascism and Totalitarian States

What accounted for the rise of totalitarian states after World War I?

23.1 Introduction

"The world must be made safe for democracy," President Woodrow Wilson declared as the United States entered World War I in 1917. However, the Central Powers' defeat did not produce that result. Hopes for democracy were soon crushed by the disappointing peace that followed—a peace in which even some of the war's winners felt more like losers.

Anger seethed on the losing side as well. Resentment was most prominent among the Germans, who suffered from the harsh terms of the Treaty of Versailles peace settlement. While bitterness festered, nations also struggled to rebuild war-torn economies.

As a result, the peace of the 1920s was a troubled one, marked by instability within nations and between them. Unrest intensified in the 1930s, as the Great Depression that began in the United States spread around the world. The hard times that followed, when added to tensions that already existed, caused people in some countries to support autocratic leaders who promised order, prosperity, and a better future. To many, the sacrifice of freedom these leaders demanded seemed a fair price to pay for the benefits they offered. Dictatorships developed in Germany, Italy, the Soviet Union, Hungary, Portugal, Poland, Romania, and elsewhere.

> ### Themes
>
> **Cultural Interaction** Fascism was an ideology that placed patriotism, loyalty to strong leaders, and the welfare of the state above the rights and freedoms of its citizens.
>
> **Political Systems** The political and economic disorder that resulted from World War I and the Great Depression helped communism and fascism to spread and totalitarian dictators to gain power.
>
> **Economic Systems** Under both fascism and communism, many economic activities are tightly controlled by the government.

◀ A crowd of Blackshirts gather to celebrate the seventh anniversary of Facism in Italy.

23.2 Italy Under Mussolini

Italy took a position of neutrality when World War I began. However, secret and sometimes vague offers of territory in Europe, Africa, and Asia Minor lured Italy to join the Allies against the Central Powers in 1915. The war proved highly unpopular among Italian troops—who were mostly peasants forced to fight for a cause they did not understand. Thousands of factory workers at home, compelled to work under military discipline, also opposed the war. By war's end, bread riots, strikes, and other antiwar protests required troops to restore order. In addition, the peace settlement gave Italy less territory than Italian leaders expected.

Post-War Problems and Unrest Italy's small gains from the war came at great cost. Some 600,000 Italians were killed and another 950,000 were wounded. Money the government had printed to pay for the war caused disastrous inflation. By 1920, the lira (Italy's unit of currency) was worth only a sixth as much as before the war. Prices soared and savings lost value as a result. Meanwhile, unemployment rose as the government cancelled orders for wartime goods. Adding to the economic crisis, jobless workers had to compete with returning soldiers for whatever work was available.

Strikes became widespread as unions demanded higher wages. Food shortages developed as farm workers went on strike. Other strikes paralyzed railroads and mail delivery. Massive rioting and industrial strikes plagued many of Italy's urban regions. In rural areas, peasants seized land from large landowners. Socialists and radical Catholic reformers led much of this unrest, although the two groups opposed and distrusted each other.

By 1920, the Socialist Party held the largest number of seats in Italy's parliament. Catholic reformers also had formed a political party called the Popular Party. Together, the two parties controlled the national government and almost half of Italy's city governments. Some socialists called for a revolution like Russia's 1917 Bolshevik Revolution. In 1921, radical socialists formed the Italian Communist Party.

Many Italians were greatly alarmed by these developments. Bands of war veterans, nationalists, students, and others attacked socialist reformers, destroyed socialist newspapers and labor union offices, and broke up strikes. Wealthy landowners and industrialists, who opposed socialism, gave money to help these groups operate. A war veteran and former socialist named Benito Mussolini led one of these right-wing antisocialist groups.

In this 1918 Italian poster, a woman representing Italy guides a returning soldier toward the factories. The slogan on the poster states, "Work, the new duty." However, the prospects for employment after the war were dismal for both unemployed workers and war veterans.

The Rise of Mussolini After holding various jobs, including two as a schoolteacher, Mussolini became the editor of Italy's leading socialist newspaper in 1912. However, he resigned from this job after deciding to support Italy's entrance into World War I and he was then expelled from the Socialist Party. Others who supported his pro-war views gave him the money to start a new paper, *Il Popolo d'Italia* (The Italian People). After he was wounded in the war, Mussolini returned to his newspaper. Claiming to speak for soldiers and workers, he used the newspaper to attack socialists as unpatriotic traitors. He suggested that a dictator was needed who could deal with Italy's social and economic problems effectively.

In early 1919, Mussolini organized a new political movement. At first, his followers numbered fewer than 200. They were a mix of war veterans, former socialists, revolutionaries, and other discontented persons. Mussolini called them the *fascio di combattimento* (fighting band). The name arose from the *fasces*—bundles of birch rods bound with strips of leather—that were symbols of authority in ancient Rome. They illustrated the idea of strength through unity and give the term **fascism** its name.

Mussolini's group was based in Milan, a city in northern Italy. Similar groups arose in other cities. These groups operated independently, but they took their inspiration from the ideas, words, and actions of Benito Mussolini. Each group included "action squads" that patrolled their cities, attacking organizations of socialists, communists, **republicans,** Catholics, and trade unionists. These armed bands soon controlled many rural areas as well. They were named the Blackshirts for the shirts that were part of their uniform.

Mussolini organized his followers into a political party in 1921. Surrounded by black-shirted supporters, he inspired crowds at fascist rallies with his grand gestures and dramatic speaking style. His facts were often wrong and his attacks often misdirected, but crowds became caught up in the anger, strength, and resolve he projected. Backed by industrialists, large landowners, shopkeepers, and other members of the urban middle class, the number of fascists grew from less than 1,000 in 1920 to more than 250,000 by mid-1922. Fascists captured 35 seats in Italy's parliament in the 1921 elections and became part of the ruling **coalition**.

Mussolini Takes Power Mussolini had little respect for Italy's democratic government, which he regarded as weak and ineffective. At a rally of 40,000 party members in October 1922 he declared, "Either the government will be given to us, or we will seize it by marching on Rome." A few days later, as 25,000 Blackshirts marched toward Rome, Italy's prime minister prepared to call out the army to crush them. However, the king, fearing an army revolt or civil war, instead appointed Mussolini prime minister and asked him to form a new government.

Benito Mussolini ruled Italy from 1922 to 1943. He was able to garner and maintain support through his passionate—albeit factually inaccurate—speeches and dramatic gesticulations.

fascism a political philosophy or totalitarian system marked by strong central authority and that places the nation, and often a race, above individual rights and freedoms

republican a person who believes in a system of government in which the people exercise power through elected representatives

coalition a temporary union of political parties, usually, in a parliamentary system, in order to form a government; a joining of separate forces to accomplish a common goal

This image depicts the signing of the Lateran Treaty in 1929. This treaty, signed by Cardinal Gasparri and Mussolini, declared Vatican City as an independent state and compelled the Pope to align with fascism.

For the next 18 months, Mussolini headed a coalition government while he gradually concentrated power in his own hands. He made his Blackshirts into Italy's national militia. Mussolini also pushed a law through the legislature that allowed the Fascists to secure a majority in parliament in 1924. When the leader of the Socialist Party declared that the elections were a fraud, he was murdered by a Fascist thug with connections to Mussolini's government. The opposition parties quit parliament in protest. With the opposition gone, Mussolini began reshaping Italy into a **totalitarian** state. A law passed by the Fascist parliament in December 1925 effectively made him a dictator and he took the title of *Il Duce* (the Leader).

Only the Catholic Church, headquartered at the Vatican in Rome, remained free of Fascist rule. Mussolini cleverly gained the Church's cooperation in 1929 by signing a treaty with the Pope. The treaty made Vatican City an independent state. It also recognized marriage laws of the Catholic Church as Italian state law, and allowed the Church to provide religious education in Italian schools. Catholic officials were persuaded to accept Fascist rule in order to preserve these benefits.

Life Under Fascist Rule   "Fascism denies that the majority, by the simple fact that it is a majority, can direct human society," Mussolini declared. "[I]t denies that numbers alone can govern by means of a periodical consultation"—that is, elections. Thus, elections were abolished. Local mayors and town councils were replaced by appointed officials. Opposition parties and labor unions were dissolved, and Fascist thugs killed some of their leaders.

"[A]ll individuals or groups are relative, only to be conceived of in their relation to the State," Mussolini wrote to explain fascism in 1932. This part of fascist philosophy meant an end to basic individual rights and freedoms. Freedom of speech and the right to assemble disappeared. The press was tightly **censored,** as were two new forms of media—motion pictures and radio. Slogans such as "Mussolini is always right" and "Believe! Obey! Fight!" covered public buildings and schools. New textbooks reflecting the Fascist view of the world appeared in classrooms. Parents were strongly pressured to enroll their children in Fascist youth groups. Control was carried out by the army and police—and through a huge network of spies and secret police. Special courts were set up to try anyone who opposed fascism or *Il Duce.* Thousands of Italians were imprisoned or sent to live on remote islands.

Many Italians, especially among the middle class, accepted these changes. Tired of strikes, riots, and other chaos, they were willing to submit to dictatorship if Mussolini could restore order and economic prosperity.

totalitarian a governing system in which a ruling elite holds all power and controls all aspects of society, allowing no opposition and often maintaining power with the use of terror and secret police

censor to examine something in order to remove parts of it that are considered objectionable

The Corporate State In 1926, Mussolini began to manage Italy's economy according to a principle called **corporatism**. The workers in an industry became part of a government-supervised organization called a corporation. The industry's employers also had a corporation. In 1934, a government decree joined these groups to create corporations of both workers and owners for 22 major industries. The businesses in these corporations remained privately owned. However, within each corporation, representatives of workers, owners, and the government set prices, wages, and hours of labor.

This program helped Italy develop modern and efficient steel, power, chemical, and other industries, which helped the nation to weather the Great Depression. The huge public works programs Mussolini launched in the 1930s also helped Italy combat the Depression. Thousands of unemployed workers found jobs building roads, draining swamps, and building new towns on the reclaimed land.

Mussolini's social and economic programs won him the admiration of those who had become disappointed in liberalism and democracy. Many hailed him as a genius for his success in transforming his divided and demoralized nation. By the late 1930s, however, his foreign policy was causing many people in Italy and elsewhere to change their opinions about him.

corporatism the organization of a society into industrial and professional corporations which exercise control over individuals subject to them and serve as units of political representation.

Mussolini's Foreign Policy Mussolini was among those who felt betrayed by the Allies when they divided the German and Ottoman empires after World War I. Italy was largely denied any new territories in Africa and the Middle East. Mussolini told Italians that he would rectify this disappointment and restore Italy to the glory days of the ancient Roman Empire. He began to fulfill this pledge in 1935 by invading the East African nation of Ethiopia. In Ethiopia, the Italian army acted with great brutality. They carried out massacres and used poison gas, which horrified the rest of Europe. His aid to fascist forces in a civil war in Spain cost him even more international support. It also began to arouse opposition at home.

As other European leaders turned on Mussolini, he drew closer to another fascist dictator—Germany's Adolf Hitler. In 1939, he allied Italy with Germany in a treaty called the Pact of Steel—an alliance that led to Italy's disastrous involvement in World War II. Military disaster in World War II eventually led to Mussolini's overthrow in 1943 and his death at the hands of the Italian people in 1945.

Here, Adolf Hitler and Mussolini inspects the Blackshirts. Both men presided over fascist governments, and both held resentment against other European countries, which helped the two dictators form an alliance. This alliance would become official after the two signed the Pact of Steel in 1939.

Increasing discontent among the Germans led to instability in the republic and inspired radical groups such as the Freikorps. This German poster asks men with weapons to join the Freikorps in order to protect the Fatherland.

23.3 Hitler and Nazi Germany

As Italy moved toward fascism after World War I, Germany moved toward democracy—at least at first. In November 1918, two days before Germany's surrender in World War I, the German emperor fled the country and German leaders formed a republic. A National Assembly was elected to write a new constitution. The assembly met in early 1919 in the city of Weimar (VY-mahr).

The constitution that emerged was remarkably democratic. The head of government would not be a monarch, but a president elected by the people. Women gained the right to vote—a right that did not yet exist in the United States. Finally, the constitution granted everyone, including radicals who opposed democracy, the right to spread their views.

The new government of Germany was called the Weimar Republic, after the city where the new constitution had been written. Even after the government relocated to Germany's capital Berlin in the spring of 1920, the name stuck.

Instability and Unrest   The Weimar Republic was in trouble from the beginning. One huge problem it faced was that some of its leaders had signed the hated Treaty of Versailles in June 1919. The treaty stripped Germany of its overseas empire and took territory from Germany itself. It forced Germany to sign a "war guilt" clause, in which Germany had to accept responsibility for starting the war. It also required Germany to pay billions of dollars in reparations for the harm the war had caused. Many Germans viewed the leaders who signed the treaty as traitors. Some began to question if the leaders of the new republic were responsible for Germany's defeat on the battlefield as well. These attitudes undermined the political legitimacy of the Weimar Republic from its very beginning.

In addition to facing huge payments for war damages, Germany suffered other hardships after the war. Peace did not bring a return to economic prosperity. Food shortages continued and unemployment remained high. The country was racked by strikes, street violence, and threats of revolution from both the right and the left. Organized armed groups known as *Freikorps* sprang up. Led by former army officers, their ranks included ex-soldiers, unemployed workers, and general malcontents. Most were intensely nationalistic and radically right-wing. In March 1920, one of these bands briefly seized control of the government, hoping to restore the monarchy. The **coup** (koo) collapsed when communists and socialists called a general strike that paralyzed Berlin.

Germans' discontent with the republic was demonstrated when in the first elections, held in June 1920, the Weimar government lost its majority. More than 25 percent of the members elected to the Reichstag, Germany's parliament, wanted to abolish the constitution. No group ever again held a majority of the seats. A series of unstable

coup a sudden, violent overthrow of an existing government by a small group

political coalitions tried to rule. More than a dozen coalition governments were formed by 1930. None of them was able to take effective action on major problems.

Trying to stimulate the economy, win public support, and deal with their massive war debt, the government printed huge amounts of money. Runaway inflation resulted. In 1920, a U.S. dollar was worth 40 German marks. Two years later, it was equal to 18,000 marks. By mid-1923, the mark was losing value with astonishing speed. In one instance, the price of a loaf of bread rose from 20,000 marks to 5 million marks in one day. By the end of 1923, inflation had spiraled so out of control that one U.S. dollar equaled 4.2 trillion German marks. Wheelbarrows were needed to carry enough money to pay for daily purchases. A lifetime's worth of savings could no longer even buy the most basic necessities. The finances of people living on fixed incomes were utterly devastated.

The chaos caused by out of control inflation inspired radicalism in German society, on both the left and the right. Communists saw the opportunity for a Bolshevik-style revolution. Freikorps forces put down left-wing revolts throughout Germany. In Munich, Adolf Hitler, the leader of the right-wing National Socialist German Workers' Party, also saw opportunity in the unrest caused by the economic crisis.

In an attempt to boost the German economy, the government began printing more money. However, the excessive amount of bills made the German mark practically worthless. Instead of spending money on necessities, this woman finds the paper currency more useful as fuel for a stove.

Hitler and the Nazis   Like Mussolini, Hitler served in World War I. He was born and raised in Austria but moved to Munich, Germany, in 1913. After the war broke out, he volunteered for the German army. He served throughout the war but was eventually wounded. He was recovering in a hospital when Germany surrendered. Hitler was disappointed and enraged over the war's outcome. He viewed the German leaders who signed the surrender and the Treaty of Versailles as criminals.

After his discharge from the hospital, Hitler returned to Munich in 1919. He soon joined the small, right-wing German Workers' Party, which had been founded in the city earlier that year. In 1920, the party changed its name to the National Socialist German Workers' Party, also known as the Nazi Party. The word *Nazi* was derived from the German words for *National Socialist*.

Hitler worked hard to increase party membership. Munich was home to large numbers of unhappy war veterans and people who opposed the Weimar Republic. Some 30,000 Freikorps members lived in the region. Hitler brought many of them into the party. The Nazis rewarded his efforts by making him their leader in 1921. One of his first acts was to form the party's Freikorps members into a private army. They became the SA (from the German term for *Storm Division*), or Brownshirts for the uniform they wore. Like Mussolini's Blackshirts they provided security at rallies, marched in parades, and terrorized communists and other enemies of the party.

Hitler also created a 25-point **platform** for the Nazi Party It called for Germany's rejection of the Treaty of Versailles and the expansion of German territory to include all German-speaking peoples. Other goals included the denial of citizenship and political power to those who were not ethnically German—and especially to Jews. Hitler proclaimed that Germans were superior to all other people and that Germany's problems were the fault of its two greatest enemies, communists and Jews. He condemned the Weimar government for failing to solve Germany's problems and pledged to restore Germany to greatness by creating a Third Reich— a third German Empire to replace the one stripped by the Allies.

This message appealed to many unemployed ex-soldiers, small farmers, and members of the lower middle class. By 1923, the Nazi Party had about 55,000 members. Hitler decided that it was time to take action. In November 1923, a force of Brownshirts and other Nazi supporters tried to seize the Bavarian state government in Munich. Hitler expected that other groups also agitating against the Weimar government would support him. They did not, and the coup failed following a gun battle with police. Hitler was arrested and jailed for nine months. He used this time to write a book, *Mein Kampf* (My Struggle), which outlined his plans for restoring Germany to greatness.

Hitler's promise to restore Germany's greatness and his claim that Germans were superior to all other people appealed to discontented citizens. By 1923, Hitler felt confident enough to stage a coup against the Weimar government. The coup, however, was unsuccessful and resulted in Hitler's arrest.

Hitler's Rise to Power   After his release from prison in 1924, Hitler worked to rebuild the Nazi Party. He decided to take power through legal means. He would organize a national party able to gain power through elections and use propaganda to attract mass support. Nazi groups soon sprang up throughout Germany. By 1928, party membership exceeded 100,000. However, in that year's Reichstag (the German parliament) elections only 12 Nazis were elected to the 463-member parliament.

Four years later, everything had changed. The reason was the Great Depression. After the American stock market crashed in late 1929, U.S. loans to Germany stopped. The German economy depended on these loans. Unemployment rose from 8.5 percent in 1929 to 30 percent by 1932. Industrial production was cut nearly in half and German exports fell by two-thirds. Banks failed and credit dried up. As farmers went bankrupt, food shortages reappeared.

The Nazis launched an intense **propaganda** campaign. It emphasized a message that would appeal to unemployed workers, farmers, and young people eager to support the ideals of German nationalism. The Nazis said that the Treaty of Versailles, the Weimar government, communists, and Jews were responsible for the economic crisis. They promised to restore order, prosperity, and national pride to Germany. The Nazi message also appealed to middle class Germans who were being hurt by the Depression or had lost status during the 1920s. By the end of 1932, the party had more than 1.4 million members.

platform a declaration of principles on which a group of persons stands, especially the principles and polices adopted by a political party or candidate

propaganda information that is purposely spread, without regard to its accuracy, in order to gain support for a cause or to damage an opposing cause

The desperate times made voters more willing to accept the Nazis' extreme views. In the 1930 elections, the number of Nazis in the Reichstag jumped from 12 to 107. In 1932, the number reached 230. Although not a majority, the Nazis were by far the largest party in parliament. After months of delay, in January 1933 the republic's president, Paul von Hindenburg, reluctantly appointed Hitler as chancellor—the top position in the cabinet.

Hitler in Control   Once in power, Hitler moved quickly to end the republic and create a fascist totalitarian state. In March 1933, the Reichstag building was destroyed by fire. Hitler blamed the Communists and convinced President Hindenburg to authorize the Brownshirts to crush them. He also convinced the Reichstag to pass a law that gave him personal emergency powers to govern. Hitler used this law to bring Germany totally under Nazi control. All other political parties were banned. Nazis were appointed to head all state and local governments. Labor unions were dissolved and replaced with Nazi organizations. After Hindenburg died in 1934, Hitler combined the offices of president and chancellor and took the title of *Führer* (Leader).

Many early members of the Nazi party were former soldiers who had served in World War I, and the Nazi movement was militaristic in style. This Nazi campaign poster from 1932 makes an appeal for votes using the imagery of war, although Germany was at peace. It states, "We are making sacrifices for the new Germany."

Hitler also crushed all possible rivals, even those within the Nazi Party. During one night in June 1934, he had the head of the SA and many other SA commanders killed. Political opponents outside the party were also murdered. Hitler turned to the SS (*SchutzStaffel* or "Defense Corps")—elite troops who pledged personal loyalty to the Fuhrer—to be his private army.

The SS was responsible for Germany's internal security. Some units acted as police and rounded up people who the Nazis considered to be enemies of the state. Arrests, which at first focused on communists and socialists, soon extended to other groups—and especially to Jews. The SS was aided by the *Gestapo,* Nazi Germany's secret police. Gestapo officers used torture, terror, and other brutal methods to gain information.

The Nazis gradually took control of all phases of German life. Most Germans supported Nazi rule, or at least accepted it. They were tired of the instability and unrest that characterized the Weimar Republic. Many welcomed the strong and seemingly effective government the Nazis provided. Unemployment fell as jobless Germans went to work on huge public-works projects. Many found work in weapons factories as Hitler prepared to restore Germany's military power. Many Germans who opposed Nazi rule fled the country. Most of the rest were frightened into silence, hoping that Hitler would eventually be overthrown.

The Campaign Against Jews   Hitler had explained his intensely anti-Semitic views in his book, *Mein Kampf.* He wrote that Jews were "a parasite within the nation" and "a menace." He came to view them as the incarnation of evil. Within days of taking control, Hitler began his campaign against German Jews. It started with Brownshirt attacks on Jewish communities across Germany. The police did not stop the attacks. Violence against Jewish businesses and their employees caused many of them to close down. SA and SS members put up signs warning the public not to enter stores owned by Jews. Later, all Jewish businesses had to display signs indicating their Jewish ownership.

The Nazis tried to eliminate Jews from Germany's economy by limiting their ability to work. In April 1933, all Jews in government jobs were forced to resign. In January 1934, they were banned from working for any non-Jewish business. They were also banned from farming. Their land was seized and turned over to non-Jewish farmers. Limits were set on the number of Jews who could teach school or practice medicine or law. Jewish communities set up organizations to help the unemployed.

In 1935, Jews were stripped of their citizenship. Marriages between Jews and other Germans were forbidden. The law defined a Jew as anyone with more than one Jewish grandparent. Jews eventually were required to carry identity cards. Meanwhile, the Nazis encouraged and even organized steadily increasing violence against the Jewish population. The worst violence took place the night of November 9, 1938, when Nazis launched attacks on Jewish communities all across Germany. Mobs smashed their way into homes, dragged Jews out of bed, and beat them. More than 1,000 people were killed. Jewish schools, cemeteries, and synagogues were vandalized. The windows of thousands of Jewish businesses were smashed and the shops looted. The terror became known as *Kristallnacht,* "The Night of Broken Glass."

Thousands of Jews fled Germany after Hitler came to power, even though they were required to leave all their money behind. Legal emigration stopped in October 1938 when all Jews had to hand in their passports. In early 1939, Hitler stated that war would mean the "extermination of the Jewish race in Europe." The outbreak of World War II in September 1939 set Hitler's genocidal plan into motion.

During the Kristallnacht attacks, Nazis destroyed Jewish businesses, burned down synagogues, and subjected Jews to public shaming. In this photo, three Jewish women are paraded before a crowd wearing signs reading "I have been excluded from the national community." Nazis believed German Jews could never be true "Germans."

23.4 The Spanish Civil War

Although Spain was neutral in World War I, it was involved in a war in Morocco. As a result, Spain suffered from much of the same unrest that plagued Italy and Germany in the post-war years.

Morocco had become a French and Spanish protectorate in 1912. When some Moroccan tribes resisted Spanish rule, Spain sent troops to conquer them. A long and costly war resulted. Fighting continued until 1926. Meanwhile, at home, the war grew increasingly unpopular. Calls for more troops sparked riots, and disorder spread throughout Spain. Radical protesters burned churches and convents. Communist agitators, strikes, and assassinations contributed to the unrest.

General Miguel Primo de Rivera (front left) toppled the Spanish government in 1923 and ruled as a dictator. He was supported by the army and the Spanish King Alfonso XIII (front right), who remained on the throne.

Spain's king and parliament seemed incapable of either restoring order or winning the war. In 1921, the king authorized a "final" campaign for victory in Morocco. The offensive ended in a terrible massacre of Spanish troops and caused a political crisis. The crisis ended when a coup led by General Miguel Primo de Rivera toppled the government in 1923. Although the king remained on the throne, Primo de Rivera dissolved the parliament and ruled as dictator. The army, with support from conservatives wanting social order, kept him in power.

Primo de Rivera brought the Moroccan War to a successful end. His economic policies and public works programs benefitted Spain and reduced unemployment. By 1930, however, he had lost the support of the army and the king forced him to resign. But the king's years of cooperation with a dictator had cost him public support. A year later, he too stepped down, and Spain became a republic.

The Spanish Republic   A left-wing government was elected in 1931. Its main support came from the working class. Government leaders pledged to convert Spain to socialism through the democratic process. They began a series of land and labor reforms and weakened the power of the Catholic Church by putting education under state control. However, the left became divided over the pace of change. This split allowed a right-wing government supported by wealthy Spaniards and the Church to be elected in 1933. The new government reversed the reforms. Revolts broke out across Spain, which authorities quickly suppressed.

The left-wing parties united into a coalition called the Popular Front, hoping to regain control of the government. The other parties formed an opposing coalition called the National Bloc. One of its members was the Falange, a new party inspired by Italian fascism. When the Popular Front won the 1936 elections, riots and other unrest followed. The National Bloc begged the army to save Spain from socialism and communism.

Civil War and the End of the Republic In July 1936, army units in Spain rose in revolt. They were joined by General Francisco Franco, commander of the Spanish army in Morocco. Franco moved troops across the Strait of Gibraltar and invaded southeastern Spain. Another rebel general seized parts of the north. The rebels chose Franco, a hero of the Moroccan War, as their leader. Backed by the Falange, he set up a government in the northern city of Burgos. It was a fascist military dictatorship in which Franco assumed the title of *Caudillo* ("Leader").

The rebel government ruled only part of the country. The Popular Front remained in power in other regions, including many of Spain's cities. In some places, militias of workers armed by the Popular Front helped army troops overthrow their upper-class officers. These troops remained loyal to the left-wing government. A bloody, three-year civil war followed as each government tried to win control over all of Spain. Supporters of the Popular Front, the republic's elected government, took the name Republicans. The rebels called themselves Nationalists.

Because of their close connection with the fascist Falange party, the Nationalists received aid from Hitler and Mussolini. Italy sent 70,000 troops while Hitler provided warplanes and pilots. Both also supplied

Pablo Picasso created his 1937 painting, *Guernica*, in response to the brutal destruction of the Spanish town of Guernica by the Nationalist forces. The Nationalists were aided by fellow fascists Hitler and Mussolini, and Guernica was bombed by Italian and German warplanes. The painting has become a symbol of the violence and tragedy of war.

tanks and artillery and the soldiers to operate them. The Republicans were aided by some 60,000 anti-fascists, republicans, communists and other volunteers from foreign nations. About 40,000 of these foreigners fought in what were called the International Brigades, largely under communist commanders. The Soviet Union supplied the Republicans with tanks and aircraft.

Both sides used harsh methods to control unrest in the regions they ruled. However, the Nationalists were especially brutal. They pursued a deliberate policy of terror. Franco used his German air force to bomb Madrid and other population centers. In the end, his army's superiority exhausted the Republican forces. In March 1939 the Nationalists finally seized Madrid. The Republican government and some 500,000 soldiers and civilians fled across the border into France.

Franco's Spain Peace did not end the Nationalist terror. For years after, Franco continued to rule using the emergency powers he gained during the war. After World War II, hostile world opinion labeled him the "last surviving fascist dictator" and Spain remained largely isolated by the world community. Although he loosened his hold on power slightly in his final years, his dictatorship continued until his death in 1975.

23.5 Stalin and the Soviet Union

Vladimir Lenin's death in 1924 set off a power struggle for leadership of the Soviet Union. Joseph Stalin eventually won this struggle. By 1929, he had gained control of both the Communist Party and the Soviet state.

Joseph Stalin (right) was a devoted follower of Lenin (left). In 1922, when this picture was taken, he became the secretary general of the Central Committee of the Bolshevik Party. He used this position to outmaneuver his rivals and establish totalitarian rule in the Soviet Union.

Stalin's Rise to Power   Unlike most Communist leaders, Stalin was not a Russian. He was born and raised in Georgia, a region north of Turkey on the Black Sea that Russia had long controlled. He learned Russian in school and always spoke it with a distinct Georgian accent. After being expelled from school in 1899, he got involved with radicals who were working to overthrow Russia's czar. He joined the Social Democrats and when they split in 1903, he sided with the Bolsheviks and became a devoted follower of Lenin.

By 1912, Stalin had been arrested six times for revolutionary activity. He had also changed his real surname to Stalin—derived from *stal,* the Russian word for "steel." In 1912, Lenin appointed him to a leadership position on the Bolshevik Party's Central Committee. Stalin was arrested again in 1913 and exiled to Siberia. When he was allowed to return in 1917, he did not go back to Georgia. Instead he went to St. Petersburg, Russia's capital, where Czar Nicholas II had just been overthrown. Stalin played a major part in the October Revolution that finally brought the Bolsheviks to power, and in the civil war that followed.

In 1922, Stalin became the Central Committee's secretary general— the head of the branch that handled the party's daily operations. Other top Communists thought his job, with all its paperwork, was routine and boring. However, Stalin used it to influence the membership of important committees and appointments to key party positions. These tactics allowed him to build support in the party while weakening Lenin's expected successor, Leon Trotsky.

After Lenin's death, Stalin allied with two other top Communists to remove Trotsky from party leadership in 1925. He then formed another alliance to oust these allies. When he was strong enough, he used his position as secretary general to remove this second set of allies as well. Trotsky went into exile in Mexico, where Stalin had him murdered in 1940.

The Soviet Economy   Stalin continued to support the Comintern, the organization Lenin created to encourage communist revolutions around the world. However, Stalin's main goal was to make the Soviet Union a strong, modern, industrial nation. He replaced Lenin's New Economic Policy (NEP) with another approach to the economy. He set production goals for a five-year period. This policy meant a return to war communism—the **command economy** that had followed the 1917 revolution.

command economy an economic system in which government makes the decisions about what and how much will be produced

Stalin's First Five-Year Plan focused on modernizing and industrializing agriculture. This 1932 propaganda poster shows a farmer with a brand-new tractor and asks, "Are you ready for the spring sowing?" Despite lofty goals, Soviet agricultural production failed to meet the basic needs of the population, creating famine in the Ukraine.

The First Five-Year Plan focused on industry and agriculture. The authorities seized the small businesses that Lenin had allowed under the NEP. Rural peasants were forced to merge their lands to create large, state-owned farms called "collectives." Those who resisted faced attack by Russian troops. Thousands of peasants were arrested by Stalin's "political police" and executed or worked to death in concentration camps in Siberia.

By 1932 Soviet society and the economy were under great strain. Most industries were failing to meet their goals. Agricultural production was down, but production quotas were set unrealistically high. In the Ukraine, foodstuffs were taken by government agents to meet the quotas, leaving too little food to support the population. About five million Ukrainians died from starvation between 1932 and 1933.

Nevertheless, Stalin announced that the First Five-Plan had met its goals and ended it a year early. He launched the Second Five-Year Plan in 1933. That plan focused on producing goods for the people. Its goals were more realistic and industrial output increased. In 1938, a Third Five-Year Plan shifted emphasis to weapons production, as Hitler pushed Europe closer to war. Stalin's economic policies succeeded in creating an industrial economy. However, Soviet agriculture continued to show poor results.

Stalin's Reign of Terror   The failure of the First Five-Year Plan caused opposition to Stalin to grow. In 1934, he launched a terror campaign to eliminate this opposition and gain total control of the government. The assassination of a key Communist official—a rival whose death Stalin himself probably ordered—provided the excuse for the crackdown. Stalin had almost all the party's Central Committee members arrested. The arrests marked the start of what became known as the Great Purge—an effort to eliminate anyone and everyone who might be "enemies of the people."

Dozens of top Communist leaders were dragged to Moscow and placed on trial. At these very public "show trials," they were forced to confess to fictitious crimes against the Soviet Union and were sentenced to death. Stalin's former allies in the power struggle of the late 1920s were among those executed. He also executed much of his military leadership. Meanwhile Stalin's secret police quietly rounded up thousands of lower-level Communists. They included local party officials, factory managers, military officers, and government office holders. The police also arrested ordinary citizens—engineers, lawyers, teachers, writers, artists, and many others. Some of them were shot. Others were sent to concentration camps.

Just a year after the Great Purge began, more than 2 million people were being held in concentration camps. Most of these camps were located in far north Siberia near the Arctic Circle. In 1937 and 1938, the secret police set up special courts that tried people and sentenced them to death before their arrest. Hundreds of thousands were executed in this manner and were buried in secret mass graves.

By the time the Great Purge ended around 1940, nearly half of the Communist Party's 2.3 million members had been executed or had died in concentration camps. About 4.5 million members of the general public met a similar fate.

Many supporters of communism put their faith in the Soviet experiment. However, Stalin's rule proved that communism was far from an ideal solution to the problems of capitalist society. When Stalin destroyed economic and personal rights and freedoms to meet the needs of the state, communism became just another type of totalitarianism. Today, the term "Stalinism" is still used to describe brutal totalitarian rule.

The victims of Stalin's Great Purge were often sent to concentration camps in Siberia, where they were forced to perform unending forced labor. These camps were known as *gulags*.

Summary

In this lesson, you learned about the rise of totalitarian governments in the 1920s and 1930s. The years between World War I and World War II were marked by fascist and totalitarian government on an unprecedented scale.

Cultural Interaction Mussolini Hitler, Franco, and Stalin all promised to restore order to their nations and return them to greatness. None had any respect for democracy or individual freedoms. Many citizens came to agree with these leaders that a strong nation was more important than individual rights.

Political Systems In Spain, Italy, and Germany, democratic governments were unable to restore stability or prosperity after chaos caused by war. In Italy, Mussolini overthrew the government by threatening to use force. Hitler used Germany's democratic system to take power. In Spain, Franco gained power by defeating the elected government in a civil war. All three leaders used violence and terror against their people to secure their hold on power. Democracy never existed in the Soviet Union, but Stalin used similar brutality to gain total control of the ruling Communist Party and the nation.

Economic Systems Under both Mussolini and Stalin, government was involved in managing the nation's economy. Mussolini created corporations in which workers and owners were forced to cooperate in setting wage, price, and production levels that the government had to approve. In Stalin's communist state, the government owned all means of production and determined what and how much would be produced. Nazi Germany exercised less direct economic control. Both Hitler and Mussolini launched large public works programs to ease unemployment that resulted from the Great Depression. Hitler also used economic weapons and tools in his brutal campaign to persecute Germany's Jews.

World War II

Why was there another global conflict so soon after World War I?

24.1 Introduction

Two important conferences—one in the 1920s and the other in the 1930s—tried to preserve the fragile peace that existed after World War I. Both conferences failed to achieve that goal.

From November 1921 to February 1922, representatives of the United States, Great Britain, France, Japan, and five other nations met in Washington, D.C. Just as the Paris Peace Conference of 1919 hoped to bring lasting peace to Europe after World War I, the Washington Conference hoped to do the same for Asia. The delegates agreed on several treaties during their weeks in Washington. In the Nine Power Treaty, the nations pledged to respect China's territory and independence. Another treaty between the United States, Britain, France, Italy, and Japan required them to limit the size of their navies. The United States, Britain, France, and Japan also agreed to respect one another's rights to the Pacific islands and Asian territories that each possessed.

In September 1938, the prime ministers of Great Britain and France met with Italy's Benito Mussolini and German dictator Adolf Hitler at Munich, Germany. The British and French leaders feared that Hitler's actions were pushing Europe toward another war. Most recently, he had demanded parts of neighboring Czechoslovakia, which Britain and France were pledged to defend. Instead, over Czechoslovakia's objections, the two leaders signed the Munich Pact, agreeing to Hitler's demands. Hitler and British Prime Minister Neville Chamberlain also declared their desire to resolve further differences through consultation rather than war.

Cheering crowds, relieved that the threat of war had passed, welcomed Chamberlain home. Britain has achieved "peace with honor," he told them. "I believe it is peace for our time." Chamberlain's words were challenged by his rival Winston Churchill, soon to be Britain's next prime minister. "You were given the choice between war and dishonor," Churchill declared. "You chose dishonor and you will have war."

Themes

Cultural Interaction Attitudes about the superiority or inferiority of certain racial, religious, and culture groups have provoked tension, violence, and other conflict throughout history.

Political Systems The quest for world prestige and power, a need for natural resources, the desire to conquer enemies, and the wish to unite people of the same ethnic or racial heritage under one rule have all driven nations to create empires.

Economic Systems Nations have sometimes sought to obtain the raw materials and other resources they need for industrial growth by conquering or controlling other regions.

Human-Environment Interaction Advances in technology have increased the destructive effects of war on people and on the regions in which they live.

Neville Chamberlain believed that his compromise with the Germans at the Munich Conference had secured peace for Europe.

aggression the practice of making unprovoked attacks or other military encroachments on the territory of another country

militarism a belief in increasing a nation's military strength as the way to become or remain powerful; the glorification of military virtues and ideals

24.2 The Road to World War

Both Japan and Germany had a mixed history of military rule and democracy. Both also began to industrialize in the decades before World War I. However, unlike Germany, Japan lacked raw materials for its industries. Instead, it relied on a strong military to obtain them from other nations.

The Rise of Militarism in Japan In the decade after World War I, Japanese **aggression** declined. In 1920, Japan helped form the League of Nations. It also joined many other nations in signing the Kellogg-Briand Pact, a 1928 agreement that condemned war. Civilians gained more power in Japan's government, although the nation's emperor continued to play a strong role. New political parties developed and calls were made to extend the right to vote to all people.

Not all Japanese were happy with these trends. Some objected to Japan's agreement to the treaty signed at the Washington Conference, which limited Japan's navy to three-fifths the size of the U.S. and British navies. Many Japanese also were concerned about events at home, such as the rise of communism and socialism and other disruptive influences of Western culture.

The worldwide economic depression of the 1930s further weakened Japan's democracy. Japanese leaders began to believe that expansion through conquest would solve Japan's economic problems. This belief moved Japan toward a policy of **militarism**. The military began to play a greater role in Japanese politics and government.

Japanese militarism was combined with extreme nationalism. Radical nationalists called for more aggressive military action abroad to acquire territory and raw materials. When Japan's prime minister tried to stop such plans, a group of naval officers killed him in 1932. Army troops carried out more political assassinations in 1936. Politicians, fearing for their lives, gave up more power to the military.

Between 1931 and 1940, Japan invaded Manchuria as well as a substantial portion of Chinese territory further south. They also seized French Indochina. When the League of Nations opposed this aggression, Japan simply withdrew from the League.

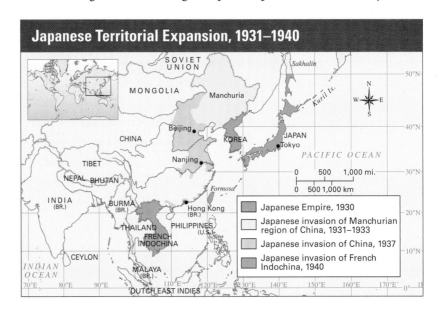

Japanese Territorial Expansion, 1931–1940

- Japanese Empire, 1930
- Japanese invasion of Manchurian region of China, 1931–1933
- Japanese invasion of China, 1937
- Japanese invasion of French Indochina, 1940

Militarists Expand Japan's Empire   Japan and other imperialist powers had long held spheres of influence in China. Japan's sphere of influence was in Manchuria, a region in northeastern China that was rich in natural resources. In 1931, Japan's army seized the entire region. When the League of Nations pressured Japan to return Manchuria to China, Japan refused and withdrew from the League. Instead, Japan turned Manchuria into an industrial and military base for its expansion into Asia.

More aggression followed as Japan grew stronger and the military gained control of its government. In 1936, Japan withdrew from the naval limitation treaty it had signed at the Washington Conference. In 1937, Japanese troops clashed with Chinese forces outside Beijing, China's capital. Japanese forces quickly took Beijing and then pushed south against sometimes fierce Chinese resistance. After capturing the city of Nanking (known today as Nanjing), Japanese soldiers went on a six-week rampage known as the Rape of Nanking. They massacred more than 100,000 Chinese civilians and brutally raped about 200,000 Chinese women.

By 1939, Japanese forces controlled most of northern and eastern China, including its main cities and industries. By 1941, Japan had added French Indochina to its Asian empire to go with Formosa (now called Taiwan), Korea, large areas of China, the southern half of Sakhalin Island, and several small Pacific islands.

Testing the League of Nations   Japan's aggression tested the League of Nations. The League was intended to serve as an instrument of international law. In theory, it could impose boycotts and other economic **sanctions** or use the combined military force of its members to keep unruly nations in line. In practice, however, it was a weak organization, in part because the United States was not a member. The League failed to respond effectively to Japan's challenge.

Throughout the 1930s, Germany and Italy also tested the League's will. Like Japan, Germany pulled out of the League of Nations in 1933. At the same time, Hitler began rebuilding the German military. In 1935, he announced the formation of an air force and the start of compulsory military service. Both actions were in violation of the Treaty of Versailles. Hitler's violation of the treaty boosted his popularity in Germany.

The League of Nations lodged a formal protest, but it refused to consider sanctions against Germany. The next year, Hitler challenged France and the League by sending troops into the Rhineland, which the Treaty of Versailles had stripped from Germany and placed under international control. This was another test of the League's resolve to stand up to aggression.

> **sanction** a measure, often involving suspension of diplomatic or economic relations, taken by a nation or group of nations against another nation to pressure it to change its behavior

Italy invaded Ethiopia in 1935 as part of a quest to construct a New Roman Empire under Mussolini. The Ethiopian forces were easily overwhelmed. They appealed to the League of Nations for help, but the League's response was weak and ultimately had no effect.

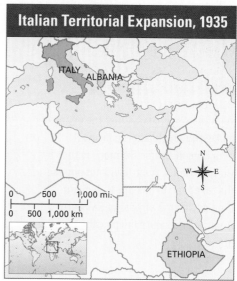

Italian Territorial Expansion, 1935

Axis Powers the name given to Italy and Germany, and later also to Japan and other German allies, during World War II

appeasement making concessions to an aggressor in order to avoid conflict

Munich Pact a settlement reached in September 1938 in which Britain and France agreed to let Germany annex part of Czechoslovakia

embargo a government order involving trade with another nation that forbids the buying or selling of something

With the Anschluss, Hitler took control of Austria and furthered his goal of uniting all ethnic Germans in the German Reich. Austria did not oppose the takeover. In this photo, jubilant crowds line the streets of Salzburg, Austria, and salute the passing German army.

Meanwhile, Mussolini began his quest to build a New Roman Empire. In October 1935, the Italian army invaded the African nation of Ethiopia. The poorly equipped Ethiopian forces could not stop the invaders. Ethiopia appealed to the League of Nations, which voted to impose economic sanctions on the aggressor. The sanctions were mild, and few League members seriously applied them. In May 1936, Italy officially annexed Ethiopia. Hitler heartily approved of the invasion. In October, he and Mussolini joined in a treaty of friendship that forged an alliance, known as the Rome–Berlin axis, between their countries. Because of this alliance, Germany and Italy were called the **Axis Powers**.

Britain and France Appease Hitler Encouraged by events in Italy and Spain, and by his own successful occupation of the Rhineland, Hitler continued his campaign of expansion. During this time, Great Britain and France did little to stop him, choosing instead to follow a policy of **appeasement**.

Hitler next set his sights on neighboring Austria, the country of his birth. At the time, Austria had an unstable government with fascist elements. Hitler pressured its leaders to join the German *Reich*, or "empire." Hitler issued an ultimatum to the Austrian chancellor: he could hand over power to the Austrian Nazis or face an invasion. He handed over power to the Nazis. Nevertheless, Hitler's army invaded anyway, crossing the border into Austria without opposition on March 12. The next day he proclaimed *Anschluss*, or "political union," with Austria. Great Britain and France remained spectators to this German expansion.

Hitler claimed that he wanted to bring all ethnically German areas in eastern Europe back into the German Reich. By signing the **Munich Pact** in September 1938, he acquired the Sudetenland, a German-speaking region of Czechoslovakia. He told Chamberlain that this would be his "last territorial demand." Just six months later, however, Hitler revealed that he wanted more than to bring all ethnic Germans into the German Reich. In March 1939, he annexed Bohemia, an ethnically Czech region. When Britain and France failed to act, Mussolini invaded nearby Albania in April 1939. It took just a few days to conquer this small nation across from Italy on the Adriatic Sea.

U.S. Neutrality Like Great Britain and France, the United States did little to thwart Japanese, German, and Italian aggression. When Mussolini invaded Ethiopia, for example, the League of Nations considered an oil **embargo** against Italy. With no fuel, the Italian army's offensive would have ground to a halt. The League asked the United States, a major oil supplier, if it would join the embargo. President Franklin D. Roosevelt refused, pointing out that he had just signed the Neutrality Act of 1935. This act prevented the United States from supplying "arms, ammunition, or implements of war" to nations in conflict. Because the law said nothing about oil, Roosevelt chose to not block oil shipments to Italy.

Congress passed additional neutrality acts in 1936 and 1937, all designed to keep the country out of conflicts brewing in Europe, such as the Spanish Civil War. Americans passionately supported this **isolationism**. Like Europeans, they recalled the horrors of World War I and wanted to avoid getting drawn into a new conflict.

isolationism a policy of limiting a nation's international relations so that it can exist in peace and harmony by itself in the world

24.3 The Return of War, 1939–1941

As Winston Churchill predicted after the Munich Conference of 1938, appeasement only made Hitler bolder. However, Germany's takeover of Bohemia in March 1939 finally caused Great Britain and France to draw a line in the sand. Hitler had been demanding the return of Danzig, an ethnically German city in the Polish Corridor that lay on the Baltic Sea. The Polish Corridor, a strip of land that cut through and divided Germany, had been created by the Treaty of Versailles to give Poland a seaport. Britain and France now warned Hitler that any aggression against Poland would result in war.

Germany Reduces the Soviet Threat   Hitler already planned to attack Poland and risk a general war in Europe. Part of his planning for this war involved the Soviet Union. He intended to eventually conquer the Soviet Union, which had vast farmlands and other resources that could fulfill Germany's quest for *Lebensraum,* or "living space." However, Hitler needed the Soviet Union to remain neutral if Britain and France went to war. The geography of such a war concerned him. The Soviet Union lay to the east of Germany. Britain and France lay to the west. Hitler did not want to fight on two fronts, east and west, at the same time. For that reason, Soviet neutrality was vital.

The Nazis and Communists despised and distrusted each other. So the world was shocked when Hitler and Soviet dictator Joseph Stalin signed a nonaggression treaty in August 1939. The pact served the interests of both leaders. Hitler no longer had to worry about going war with the Soviets before he was ready. For Stalin, the pact satisfied his desire for more power and for secure borders. In return for Stalin's pledge to not attack Germany, Hitler secretly promised him a part of Poland and a sphere of influence in Eastern Europe.

In their 1939 non-aggression treaty, Hitler promised Stalin a part of Poland, and guaranteed Russia a sphere of influence in eastern Europe. In return, Stalin pledged not to attack Germany. This political cartoon from 1939 shows Hitler and Stalin scheming to divide the world between them.

Blitzkrieg German for "lightning war," a military tactic that combined swift, massive, and highly coordinated attacks by planes, tanks, and infantry to overwhelm and quickly conquer an enemy

The War Begins   With the Soviet Union neutralized, Hitler quickly sprang into action. On September 1, 1939, Hitler announced that Germany was annexing Danzig. As he spoke, German forces were invading Poland. Two days later, France and Britain declared war on Germany.

Hitler's attack on Poland introduced a new kind of warfare—the *Blitzkrieg,* or "lightning war." It consisted of swift, massive, and highly coordinated attacks by waves of warplanes, tanks, and infantry. Communications by radio, a new technology perfected in the 1920s, allowed such attacks to be coordinated and carried out. German warplanes launched attacks on railroads, airfields, communications networks, military bases, and other strategic sites. Meanwhile, infantry, supported by tanks and artillery, pushed toward key cities and other objectives. As German planes rained bombs and bullets on the enemy, motorized infantry units quickly swept toward and around them. Then the foot soldiers moved in to finish the job.

Faced with such overwhelming force, the Polish army quickly collapsed. Two weeks after the Blitzkrieg began, Soviet troops invaded from the east. By early October, all of Poland was under German or Soviet control.

Hitler then switched his focus to the west. He moved 2 million soldiers to Germany's border with France and the Low Countries—Belgium, the Netherlands, and Luxembourg. France relied for its main defense on the Maginot Line, a string of heavily armed fortresses along the German border. Most French troops massed here, while others gathered along the border with Belgium. British forces crossed the English Channel, prepared to aid France and the Low Countries. For the next few months, not much happened. Newspapers began referring to this as the "Phony War."

Suddenly, in a series of lightning actions, Hitler struck. In April 1940, German forces launched surprise attacks on Denmark and Norway. Within a few weeks, they had conquered these two Scandinavian countries. Then on May 10, the Germans invaded the Low Countries. In 18 days, those three nations were in German hands.

Using Blitzkrieg tactics, a German army burst through Luxembourg and southern Belgium into France in just four days. Then it began a dramatic drive toward the French coast. Skirting the Maginot Line, the Germans sped westward. Hundreds of thousands of French and British troops found themselves trapped in a shrinking pocket of French countryside. They retreated toward the port of Dunkirk on the northwest coast of France. Britain sent every boat it could find across the English Channel to evacuate the soldiers. The daring rescue saved some 338,000 men.

The Blitzkrieg

Germany's blitzkrieg tactics were designed to avoid the stalemate and trench warfare of World War I. The objective was to break through enemy lines at the weakest points and then rush forward to spread fear and confusion behind the lines. Pockets of enemy resistance could then be isolated and destroyed. A blitzkrieg attack unfolded in six stages.

① German attackers identify a weak spot in the enemy's defensive line.

② Infantry troops create a smokescreen to hide the forces gathering for a breakthrough.

③ Planes bomb military and civilian targets behind the lines. Paratroopers disrupt communications and slow the movement of enemy reinforcements.

④ Tanks break through the weak spot, spreading panic among troops and civilians.

⑤ Motorized divisions move through the opening and circle back to surround the enemy forces from behind.

⑥ Infantry troops arrive to take care of any remaining areas of resistance.

Paris soon fell to the Germans as well. Mussolini took this opportunity to declare war on Great Britain and France. On June 22, France surrendered to Germany. Under the terms of the armistice, Germany occupied three fifths of the country. A **puppet government** ruled the unoccupied region. It was called Vichy France, for the town that was its capital.

The Battle of Britain   The fall of France left Great Britain to face Hitler alone. Britain's new prime minister, Winston Churchill, vowed to continue the fight. "We shall defend our island whatever the cost may be," he declared. "We shall fight on the beaches, landing grounds, in fields, in streets and on the hills. We shall never surrender."

Hitler, however, was determined to conquer Britain, the last holdout against Nazi rule. Yet he realized that Britain's navy could keep his army from crossing the English Channel. To counter that threat, Germany had to control the air. Hitler set up bases in conquered lands from France to Norway and moved some 2,500 bombers and fighter planes to them.

From these bases, German planes flew thousands of air raids over Great Britain in the summer and fall of 1940. They bombed ports, airfields, radar stations, and industrial centers. Fighter planes of the Royal Air Force (RAF) countered this onslaught in what became known as the Battle of Britain. Between July and October, the RAF had lost 915 aircraft. However, RAF pilots had downed more than 1,700 German aircraft.

Germany had great military success in the first year and a half of the war. Poland, Denmark, Norway, the Low Countries, and France all quickly fell under German control. Only England was able to successfully fend off the German war machine.

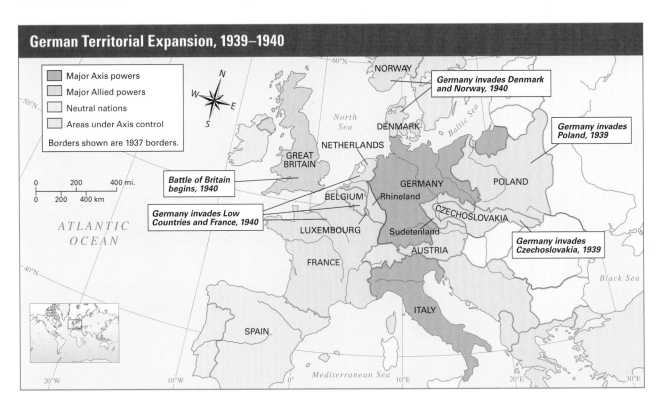

German Territorial Expansion, 1939–1940

Major Axis powers
Major Allied powers
Neutral nations
Areas under Axis control

Borders shown are 1937 borders.

0   200   400 mi.
0   200   400 km

Germany invades Denmark and Norway, 1940

Germany invades Poland, 1939

Battle of Britain begins, 1940

Germany invades Low Countries and France, 1940

Germany invades Czechoslovakia, 1939

NORWAY
North Sea
DENMARK
Baltic Sea
NETHERLANDS
GREAT BRITAIN
GERMANY
POLAND
BELGIUM   Rhineland
CZECHOSLOVAKIA
LUXEMBOURG
Sudetenland
AUSTRIA
FRANCE
ATLANTIC OCEAN
ITALY
SPAIN
Black Sea
Mediterranean Sea

In September 1940, Britain launched its first bombing raid on Berlin. After that, Hitler shifted his targets to British cities. Bombing attacks over the next several months devastated parts of London and other large cities. Londoners called this period the Blitz, a shortening of Blitzkrieg. By spring 1941, the number of raids dwindled. German industry simply could not replace the lost planes fast enough. The British had successfully defended their homeland. Their victory raised hopes that Hitler could be stopped.

Two young Royal Air Force pilots concentrate on flying their bomber. During the Battle of Britain in 1940, British RAF pilots downed so many German aircraft that German production of new planes could not keep up with the losses. Despite widespread destruction, the British successfully defended their country from the German attack.

The United States Prepares for War When war broke out in Europe, isolationism lost some of its appeal for Americans. Most wanted to help the Allies, but they did not want the United States to get involved in the fighting. Yet France and Britain needed weapons, and the Neutrality Acts banned arms sales to belligerent nations. So in November 1939, Congress passed another Neutrality Act through Congress that repealed the arms embargo. However, the new law included a "cash-and-carry" provision. Nations had to pay cash for materials and carry them away in their own ships.

After the fall of France, the United States finally began to prepare for war. Defense spending soared, as did the size of the army. In September 1940, Congress enacted the first peacetime military draft in U.S. history. Yet during the 1940 election campaign, President Roosevelt assured Americans, "Your boys are not going to be sent into any foreign wars." Still hoping to avoid war, Americans elected him to an unprecedented third term.

In December 1940, with the Battle of Britain still raging, Churchill declared that his country was nearly bankrupt. Roosevelt was determined to provide Britain "all aid short of war." He urged Congress to adopt a plan to lend, not sell, arms to Britain. This legislation, the Lend-Lease Act, passed in March 1941, but only after heated public and congressional debate.

In June 1941, Hitler broke his pact with Stalin by attacking the Soviet Union. The Soviet army retreated in the face of the invasion. With Churchill's support, the United States began sending supplies to the Soviets under the Lend-Lease Act. In August, Churchill and Roosevelt secretly met aboard warships in Canadian waters of the North Atlantic. There they prepared a declaration of post-war aims known as the **Atlantic Charter,** which later influenced the charter of the United Nations. Both agreed to not use the war to seek new territory or to make peace with the Axis separately. They also asserted the right of all peoples to self-government. Three months later, Congress voted to allow American merchant ships to arm themselves and sail to Britain.

Atlantic Charter the statement of principles and war goals reached by U.S. President Franklin D. Roosevelt and British Prime Minister Winston Churchill in 1941, which later formed the basis for the charter of the United Nations

The United States Enters the War

While war raged in Europe, Japan continued its expansion in Asia. After Hitler conquered France, Japanese troops pushed into French Indochina, in Southeast Asia. Japan also set its sights on the Dutch East Indies (now Indonesia), then colonies of German-occupied Netherlands, and on British Malaya. These regions would provide the oil, rubber, and other raw materials needed by Japanese industries.

The attack on American territory at Pearl Harbor, Hawaii, rallied American support for joining the war. This image shows the wrecked remains of the USS *Arizona* battleship, destroyed by Japanese bombs in Pearl Harbor.

Meanwhile, hoping to keep the United States out of the war, Hitler sought to expand his alliance. In September 1940, Germany, Italy, and Japan signed the Tripartite Pact, making Japan a member of the Axis Powers. The three nations agreed to provide mutual support in the event that any one of them was attacked by a country not yet in the war. The attacker they had in mind was the United States. If the United States entered the war, it would be forced to fight in both Asia and Europe. Hitler hoped that the threat of a two-front war would ensure American neutrality for a while longer. However, events caused his Japanese allies to pursue different plans.

The United States reacted strongly to Japan's actions in Indochina. In August 1941, it froze Japanese assets in the United States and banned the export of American oil and other vital resources to Japan. When efforts to peacefully obtain oil from the Dutch East Indies failed, Japanese leaders decided that war with the United States could not be avoided. In October 1941, General Hideki Tojo became prime minister of Japan, replacing a civilian leader. Tojo, an aggressive militarist, prepared the nation for war.

On December 7, 1941, Japanese aircraft carriers approached Hawaii, where the U.S. Pacific Fleet was anchored at Pearl Harbor. From these carriers, more than 300 bombers and fighter planes launched an attack on Pearl Harbor. In just over two hours, the Japanese damaged or destroyed 18 American warships and about 300 military aircraft. More than 2,400 Americans were killed and some 1,200 wounded. However, the Japanese failed to sink any American aircraft carriers, which had been out to sea during the attack. This failure would prove critical in the Pacific war that followed.

24.4 The War in Europe, 1942–1945

In late December 1941, Franklin Roosevelt and Winston Churchill met in Washington, D.C. Their purpose was to devise a strategy to help the Allies defeat the Axis Powers. They knew they could not afford to fight an offensive war on two fronts—Europe and the Pacific—at the same time. So they decided to concentrate most of their forces on first winning back Europe, while fighting only a defensive war against Japan in the Pacific.

Nazis Invade the Soviet Union and North Africa The Axis controlled much of Europe and North Africa at the start of 1942. Great Britain had saved itself but the Nazis had invaded the Soviet Union, using Blitzkrieg tactics to overcome Soviet troops massed at the border. One large German force nearly reached Moscow before the onset of winter froze it in its tracks. Another force marched toward the Soviet Union's oil-rich Caucasus region.

Oil played a key role in Axis strategy. Hitler already controlled oil fields in Romania, but he sought more oil to keep his war machine running. He also hoped to cut off Allied oil from the Middle East. But first he had to secure North Africa by pushing the British out of Egypt. In 1941, Hitler sent the Afrika Korps, a tank-based army division commanded by Erwin Rommel, to bolster the Italian army struggling against the British in North Africa. By June 1942, Rommel's force had taken much of the region and driven deep into Egypt.

Nazis Begin to Persecute the Jews Conquered nations suffered greatly under Nazi rule. Millions of Europeans were forced to work in the German arms industry. The Germans treated Russians, Poles, and other Slavs with special contempt, partly because Hitler claimed that Slavs were subhuman. The Nazis worked them to death and killed large numbers of them outright.

No group suffered under Nazi Germany more than the Jews. After Hitler came to power, he passed laws that increasingly persecuted Jews and stripped them of their rights. Many Jews tried to flee, but most countries, including the United States, refused to admit more than a token number of refugees. Hitler had long been obsessed with the "Jewish question"—how to rid Germany of Jews. As German rule expanded, more Jews came under Nazi control and the "Jewish question" grew more critical to the Nazis. In some places, the Nazis forced Jews into overcrowded **ghettos,** small sections of cities that could be walled off and guarded. Hundreds of thousands of Jews in these ghettos died from starvation and disease. In just two of the hundreds of ghettos, more than 112,000 died between 1941 and 1942 alone.

At first, the Nazi invasion of the Soviet Union was quite successful, as the Germans used brutal blitzkrieg tactics to drive further and further into Russia. However, they were stopped by the frigid Russian winter before they reached Moscow. In this 1942 photo, the German army struggles through wintry conditions outside Moscow.

ghetto a section of a city in which members of a minority group live, especially because of force or social, legal, or economic pressures

This photo taken at the Belzec extermination camp in Poland shows piles of discarded shoes that once belonged to the people murdered by the Nazis. Out of the 430,000 Jews who entered Belzec, only two survived.

Eventually, Hitler decided on what the Nazis called the "final solution"—a plan to systematically exterminate the Jews of Europe and North Africa. The slaughter began in the Soviet Union, shortly after the invasion in 1941. Mobile killing squads rounded up and murdered more than a million Soviet Jews. In early 1942, the Nazis built the first of six death camps in Poland. Jews, many from ghettos, were shipped to these camps by rail, often packed into cattle cars.

Unlike regular concentration camps, these death camps were equipped with gas chambers. Camp operators sealed groups of Jews and other prisoners inside these rooms and turned on the deadly poison gas, usually hydrogen cyanide. Pregnant women, young children, the elderly, and the sick were gassed soon as soon as they arrived. Some able-bodied prisoners were kept alive as long as they could work, often at a nearby factory. Each death camp could murder thousands of people each month. In addition to Jews, the Nazis gassed gay men and women, disabled people, and Gypsies, among others.

The Allies Debate War Strategies   When Roosevelt and Churchill met in Washington in December 1941, they had only a vague understanding of the extent of Hitler's extermination policies. Their goal was to figure out how to win the war in Europe. To do this, they had to choose from a number of possible strategies.

Invading occupied France was a possibility, because the French people would support such an invasion. Also, nearby Britain could serve as a staging area for the massing of troops and resources before the assault. But the German army had a strong presence in France that would make such an invasion extremely difficult. Some thought a direct attack on Italy made more sense. The Italian army was fairly weak, and Italy would provide a good base for securing the rest of Europe. Others wanted to launch the Allied offensive in North Africa, which was not as well defended and could serve as a gateway to Europe. But it was far from the final target, Germany, and would also test the Allies' ability to transport and supply their forces.

Great Britain's choice of strategy was clear. Already caught up in the battle for North Africa, Churchill wanted the Allies to strike there first. In contrast, Soviet leader Joseph Stalin wanted an invasion of France to take pressure off his army. The USSR, now one of the Allies, greatly needed help. Roosevelt eventually was convinced to support the British plan. In June 1942, he made the decision to invade North Africa in the fall.

Allied Gains in North Africa and Italy

In November 1942, Allied forces made sea landings in Morocco and Algeria. Led by American General Dwight D. Eisenhower, they swept east into Tunisia. The Germans quickly sent reinforcements across the Mediterranean. Meanwhile, British forces stopped Rommel and forced him out of Egypt. Rommel's Afrika Korps retreated west toward Tunisia, with the British in hot pursuit.

American soldiers did their first fighting of the war in a series of battles in the winter of 1942–1943 in Tunisia. They helped the combined Allied armies launch a final offensive in May 1943. Axis resistance collapsed in North Africa, leaving about 250,000 German and Italian soldiers in the hands of the Allies.

The Allied forces took around 250,000 German and Italian soldiers prisoner after Axis defenses collapsed during the North Africa campaign. Here, Axis prisoners are shaving and standing around in a temporary prison camp in Tunisia in May 1943.

Using North Africa as a staging area, the Allies crossed the Mediterranean into Sicily, a large island in southern Italy. The massive invasion in July 1943 met little opposition at first. Its success alarmed many Italians. Mussolini's North Africa campaign and several other failures had caused them to lose faith in *Il Duce*. The Fascist Grand Council met on July 24 and voted to restore the king and parliament to power. Mussolini resigned the next day. Italy soon surrendered to the Allies. In October it declared war on Germany.

German troops remained in Italy, however. As the Allies pushed north, the Germans battled them every step of the way. By October, the Allied army had taken about a third of the Italian peninsula, but they did not get much farther that year. A solid German defensive line completely stopped the Allies about 60 miles south of Rome, the Italian capital.

The Battle of Stalingrad   The decision to invade North Africa left the Soviet Union on its own. In June 1942, Axis troops began to push farther into Soviet territory. Hitler split his forces so they could seize the rest of the Caucasus and also take Stalingrad, a large city on the Volga River. At Stalingrad, German firebombs set most of the city ablaze, but Stalin ordered his soldiers to not retreat. By mid-September, Axis troops had a large Soviet force trapped in a strip of the city along the Volga.

Fierce street-by-street fighting followed for two months. Then, in November, the Soviet Red Army began a **counterattack,** sending its troops forward against the Nazi assault. In a few days, the Soviets had encircled the German troops. Hitler insisted that his soldiers fight to the death, which most of them did. In January 1943, the remains of Hitler's army, starving and frozen in the bitter Russian winter, surrendered. The Battle of Stalingrad cost Germany more than 200,000 troops, while more than a million Soviet soldiers died. However, the Soviet victory forced the Germans to retreat, giving up all they had gained since June 1942.

counterattack an attack made in response to an enemy's attack

The Allies bombed German cities to try to weaken civilian morale. The German city of Dresden was firebombed into absolute ruin by a combined force of British and American planes. In this image, bodies lie in the street amid the smoldering rubble of Dresden.

D-Day June 6, 1944, the day that Allied forces invaded France to free it from Nazi rule and eventually defeat Germany in World War II

Allied Bombing Campaigns   Hitler's losses in the Soviet Union left Germany with only one major source of oil—Romania. The Romanian oil fields became a prime target of Allied bombing. However, the Allies' main target in their air campaign was Germany.

American pilots typically launched daytime raids. They favored aiming at specific targets such as oil refineries, railroads, and factories with the intent of disrupting Germany's ability to supply and equip its fighting forces. By the end of the war, Germany's infrastructure and economy were in ruins.

British pilots relied mainly on saturation bombing, the rapid release of a large number of bombs over a wide area. They usually flew nighttime raids over enemy cities. The strategy behind bombing cities, with its appalling loss of life, was to destroy civilian morale and force a surrender. This tactic turned German cities like Dresden and Hamburg into rubble-strewn graveyards. However, it did not bring an early end to the war.

In August 1944, American planes dropped more than a thousand bombs on an oil-production facility in Poland. Five miles to the west stood Auschwitz, the largest Nazi death camp. Jewish organizations and others urged the United States to bomb Auschwitz. If the gas chambers or nearby rail lines were destroyed, they said, thousands of lives could be saved. American military officials denied these appeals. They said they could not afford to divert resources from military targets. Their main goal was to hasten the end of the war.

The Allies Liberate France   To meet that goal, Allies focused most of their resources in 1944 on an invasion of France. General Eisenhower directed the effort. To prepare for the invasion he gathered more than 1.5 million troops in southern England. Also at his command were some 1,200 warships, 800 troops transport ships, 4,000 landing craft, 10,000 airplanes, and hundreds of tanks. Troops would cross the English Channel by ship to Normandy, in northern France.

D-Day—the day the invasion began—came on June 6, 1944. Allied planes overhead and warships offshore provided covering fire, while landing craft delivered some 50,000 soldiers and 1,500 tanks to five Normandy beaches. German forces with well-entrenched guns put up a fierce resistance. However, by the end of the day nearly 150,000 Allied troops had come ashore and controlled a 59-mile section of the Normandy coast. Over the next few weeks the rest of the Allies' huge army followed them into France.

In July, an American army under General Omar Bradley and a British army under General Bernard Montgomery began a rapid sweep across France. In August, the Allies liberated Paris. In September, the first American troops crossed the French border into Germany.

War in Europe and North Africa, 1942–1945

Axis powers before World War II
Extent of Axis control early Nov. 1942
Allies
Neutral nations
Allied troop movements
Major battles (Allied victories)

At the start of 1942, the Axis powers controlled much of Europe and North Africa. The Allied strategy for reversing the course of the war called for massive invasions of Axis-controlled territory. Allied troop movements ultimately converged in Germany, where the Allies captured Berlin, the capital city, in May 1945.

The Horror of the Holocaust   As American, British, and other Allied troops carried out the invasion of France, the Red Army chased a retreating German force out of the Soviet Union and into Poland. The Nazis frantically tried to hide evidence of their concentration camps in Poland. They cleared out many of the forced-labor camps, marching prisoners westward and shooting any who fell behind. They also tried to dismantle some of the death camps, quickly killing the remaining prisoners. With the Soviet army closing in on Auschwitz, the Nazis crowded about 60,000 Jews and others onto freight trains and shipped them west into Germany. The survivors ended up in camps such as Buchenwald and Dachau.

Allied forces invading Germany from France stumbled upon concentration camps. These camps, though not as grim as the death camps of Poland, shocked the soldiers. They held thousands of slave laborers, starved to near death. Many of these Holocaust victims, too sick to even eat, died in the weeks after they were liberated. At Dachau, the smell of rotting flesh led American GIs to 28 railway cars packed with dead bodies. They also uncovered evidence of medical research. Nazi doctors at the camp had carried out inhumane medical experiments on more than 3,500 prisoners.

The Nazis committed crimes so reprehensible that no word existed to describe them. In 1944, a Polish Jew coined the term *genocide* to refer to the systematic killing of a racial, political, or cultural group.

Holocaust the systematic, state-sponsored, persecution and murder of Jews by the Nazis

The Nazis murdered 6 million Jews, or one-third of the world's Jewish population. An existing word that means "sacrifice by fire"—*holocaust*—was capitalized to give a name to this terrible slaughter. The **Holocaust** was the systematic, state-sponsored, persecution and murder of Jews by the Nazis. The Nazis also murdered Gypsies, Serbs, Polish intellectuals, resistance fighters from all the nations, German opponents of Nazism, gay people, Jehovah's Witnesses, disabled people, habitual criminals, and the poor.

The War in Europe Ends   When the Allies crossed from France into Germany, they met fierce resistance. By December 1944, their offensive had stalled. Hitler made plans to burst through the Allied lines in the wooded Ardennes region of Belgium, where the American forces were weakest. He launched his counteroffensive on December 16. Eight German armored divisions smashed into the surprised Americans, creating a huge bulge in the American line. Allied air support and quick action by General George Patton's Third Army forced the Germans to withdraw by mid-January. The Battle of the Bulge was the last German offensive on the western front.

By April 1945, the Red Army had fought its way through Poland and into Germany, to the outskirts of Berlin. On April 30, with advancing Soviet soldiers just half a mile from his Berlin bunker, Hitler killed himself. German forces quickly began surrendering. On May 8—Victory in Europe Day or V-E Day—the war in Europe officially ended.

This photo shows the barracks inside the Buchenwald concentration camp after the liberation of the camp by the Allies in 1945. Prisoners at the German concentration camps performed slave labor in terrible conditions, and many starved to death.

24.5 The War in Asia, 1942–1945

Japan's attack on Pearl Harbor on December 7, 1941, was the first in a series of strikes against Allied territory in the Pacific. Within hours, Japanese planes had also attacked U.S. bases in the Philippines and British forces in Hong Kong, and Japanese troops landed in Malaya. By the end of March 1942, the Japanese had captured Hong Kong and Singapore, the American islands of Guam and Wake, and the oil-rich Dutch East Indies. Japan had also invaded several larger possessions of the Allies, including the American-held Philippine Islands and the British colony of Burma.

In the Philippines, Americans and Filipinos under General Douglas MacArthur resisted a fierce Japanese onslaught. Disease and malnutrition killed many of the defenders. In March 1942, President Roosevelt ordered MacArthur to leave the islands. "I shall return," MacArthur promised the Americans and Filipinos he left behind. Two months later, Japan completed its conquest of the Philippines. On the largest island, the Japanese marched 70,000 American and Filipino defenders 63 miles up the Bataan Peninsula to a prison camp. Japanese soldiers beat and bayoneted those who could not keep up. More than 7,000 died on the brutal Bataan Death March.

The fall of Burma, in May 1942, had serious consequences. Japan controlled most of coastal China, so no supplies could reach the Chinese army by sea. It relied on British and American supplies carried in from India over the Burma Road. Now Japan had cut this lifeline. If Japan defeated China, hundreds of thousands of Japanese soldiers would be free to fight elsewhere. To help China keep fighting, the Allies set up an airborne supply route over the Himalayas.

American forces fought the Battle of the Coral Sea using planes based on aircraft carriers. In this photo, the flight deck crew of the USS *Lexington* aircraft carrier helps maneuver a Hellcat fighter plane.

The Pacific War Begins Japan's string of victories in the Pacific hurt the Allies' confidence. To boost morale, President Roosevelt asked for a strike on the Japanese home islands. Military strategists came up with a plan to fly B-25 bombers off an aircraft carrier. The B-25 could make a short takeoff. It also had the range to reach Japan and then land at Allied airfields in China.

On April 18, 1942, 16 bombers took off from the U.S. carrier *Hornet,* which had sailed to within 650 miles of Japan, to bomb Tokyo and other Japanese cities. Although the surprise attack did little damage, it thrilled Americans as much as it shocked the Japanese. Japan reacted by putting more precious resources into defending the home islands.

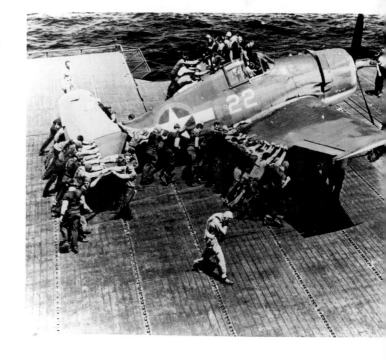

The Americans also learned of Japanese activity far to the south in the Coral Sea. The Japanese were moving into position to isolate Australia, a key ally. To stop them, the United States sent two aircraft carriers, several cruisers, and a few destroyers—all that could spared at the time—to face a larger Japanese force that included three carriers.

The resulting Battle of the Coral Sea, in early May 1942, was fought entirely by carrier-based aircraft. It was the first naval battle in history in which the enemies' warships never came within sight of each other. Japanese aircraft sank one U.S. carrier and damaged the other. American planes sank one Japanese carrier and damaged the other two. Despite the fairly even losses, the Americans gained a strategic victory and blocked Japanese expansion to the south.

The Allies Stop Japanese Expansion   The United States led the Allied forces in the Pacific and did most of the fighting. The "Europe First" approach to the war put Pacific commanders at a disadvantage. Because they had fewer ships, planes, and soldiers than the Japanese, a defensive strategy made sense. U.S. naval forces would try to contain the Japanese by stopping their expansion in the Central and South Pacific.

American forces achieved this goal at the Battle of Midway in June 1942. The Americans intercepted a Japanese message telling of plans for a major offensive. They figured out that the target was the U.S. base at Midway, a pair of islands about 1,200 miles northwest of Pearl Harbor. With this knowledge, the navy sat in wait for the Japanese fleet. When it was in striking distance, American planes from Midway and from three aircraft carriers demolished the enemy force. All four Japanese carriers and about 300 aircraft were destroyed. Japan never recovered from these losses. The Battle of Midway was its last offensive action.

Crew members have difficulty walking along the sloping deck of the USS *Yorktown* aircraft carrier, after it was hit by Japanese torpedoes at the Battle of Midway. The ship survived the onslaught, but was soon torpedoed again and sank on June 7, 1942.

The Allies Turn the Tide   After the Battle of Midway, the Allies went on the offensive. They followed a strategy of capturing Japanese-held islands using them as stepping-stones. Each captured island became a base for attacks on other islands. A tactic known as leapfrogging—bypassing or "jumping over" certain islands—allowed them to carry out this strategy with limited resources. Cut off from reinforcements and supplies, Japanese forces on the bypassed islands were left to wither.

The Allied offensive began August 1942, when 11,000 U.S. Marines invaded Guadalcanal, in the Solomon Islands northeast of Australia. After months of resistance, Japanese troops abandoned the island in February 1943. They left behind more than 25,000 dead defenders.

Despite the success of leapfrogging, many of the island invasions came at a terrible cost. Thousands of soldiers died in the jungles of Guadalcanal, New Guinea, Tarawa, and Saipan. But they kept pushing the Japanese back, closer and closer to the home islands of Japan. In October 1944, MacArthur made his triumphant return to the Philippines, where his forces would battle the Japanese until the end of the war. In August 1944, the Marines finished retaking the Mariana Islands. The Marianas campaign was a landmark victory. It gave the Allies secure bases from which U.S. B-29s could make long-range bombing raids on Japan.

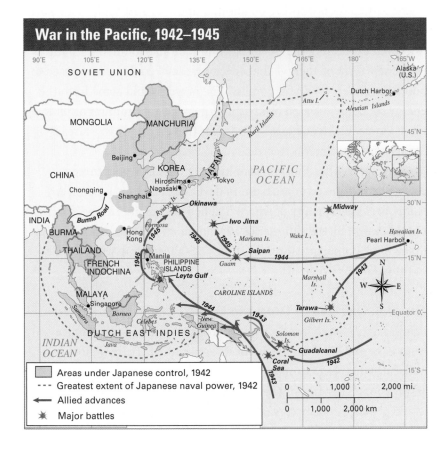

War in the Pacific, 1942–1945

The Allies began their offensive in the Pacific in August 1942 with the invasion of Guadalcanal. As the Allies captured islands, they then used these islands as bases for attacks on other islands. They gradually drove the Japanese forces back toward Japan.

The physicist J. Robert Oppenheimer was the director of the Los Alamos laboratory in New Mexico that developed the atomic bomb. Here Oppenheimer (left) stands on the charred ground at the site of the first atomic bomb test explosion with U.S. General Leslie Groves.

The Allies Push Toward Japan   The Allied push through the Pacific steadily shrank the defensive perimeter the Japanese had established around Japan. That perimeter disappeared after the Allies captured the key islands of Iwo Jima and Okinawa in early 1945. Iwo Jima's airfields provided a base for fighter planes to escort bombers over Japan. Control of Okinawa, just 310 miles south of Japan, gave Americans a staging area for an invasion of Japan itself.

On the small volcanic island of Iwo Jima, the defenders dug caves, tunnels, and concrete-lined bunkers. Three months of Allied bombardment before the February 1945 invasion did little to soften these defenses. The month-long land battle was among the bloodiest of the war. Nearly all of the 22,000 Japanese troops fought to their deaths. More than 6,800 American troops also died.

To take the much larger Okinawa, the Allies mounted a huge invasion in April 1945. More than 1,200 American and British ships, including 40 aircraft carriers, supported a force of 182,000 American troops. As on Iwo Jima, the 120,000 troops defending Okinawa fiercely resisted the invaders. The Battle of Okinawa continued for two months. It claimed the lives of some 12,000 American and more than 100,000 Japanese soldiers.

Developing the First Nuclear Weapon   The capture of Okinawa set the stage for a final invasion of Japan. However, American scientists had been working on another option. In 1939, German-born Jewish American scientist Albert Einstein had written to President Roosevelt explaining that scientists might be able to turn uranium into a new form of energy. That energy, he said, could be harnessed to build "extremely powerful bombs." The power would come from the energy suddenly released by splitting the nuclei of uranium or plutonium atoms. Einstein expressed his fear that Germany was already engaged in experiments to create such a weapon.

Three years after Einstein sent his letter, the U.S. government established a top-secret program to develop an atomic weapon. A team of scientists, many of whom had fled fascism in Europe, carried out this work. By the summer of 1945, their efforts had produced the first atomic bomb, or A-bomb. On July 16, a test bomb was exploded in the New Mexico desert.

The U.S. Decides to Drop the Bomb   New American president Harry Truman faced a difficult decision. He had taken office just weeks earlier, when President Roosevelt died. Truman now had to decide whether to drop an atomic bomb on Japan or to launch an invasion. After Iwo Jima and Okinawa, he knew an invasion would produce enormous casualties. The number of Allies killed and wounded might reach half a million, he was told.

Truman faced a stubborn enemy. American B-29s were already destroying Japan with conventional bombs, including firebombs. This bombing campaign had killed hundreds of thousands of people and turned large areas of Japan's cities, with their masses of wooden buildings, into cinders. At the same time, a naval blockade had cut off the supply of raw materials to Japan. Many of Japan's leaders realized that it could not possibly win the war. Yet the Japanese refused to accept Truman's demands for an unconditional surrender.

Some U.S. strategists believed only the shock of the still secret A-bomb would end the Japanese resistance. Others opposed it, insisting that the current bombing campaign would soon bring surrender. Some A-bomb opponents claimed that the Japanese would give up if Truman would agree to let them keep their beloved emperor. However, Truman stuck to his demand for an unconditional surrender. He warned Japan that the alternative was "prompt and utter destruction."

Two A-bombs End the War in the Pacific   On August 6, 1945, an American B-29 named *Enola Gay* dropped an atomic bomb on Hiroshima, Japan, a city of 300,000 people. Within seconds of the explosion, up to 80,000 people died. The blast's shock wave toppled nearly 60,000 structures. Hundreds of fires consumed the rest of the city. Three days later, the United States dropped a second bomb, wiping out the city of Nagasaki and instantly killing some 40,000 people. As many as 250,000 Japanese may have died from the two bombs, either directly or as the result of burns, radiation poisoning, or cancer.

The destruction of Nagasaki brought a Japanese surrender. Truman received it on August 14, Victory over Japan Day, or V-J Day. The terms of the surrender allowed the emperor to keep his office but only in a ceremonial role. In September, the Allies officially accepted the surrender aboard the American battleship *Missouri* in Tokyo Bay.

Nagasaki was reduced to complete rubble after the United States dropped an atomic bomb on the Japanese city in August 1945.

war crime a violation of internationally accepted practices related to waging war

Nuremberg Trials trials the Allies held in Nuremberg, Germany, after World War II to hold Nazi leaders and other Germans accountable for war crimes and other atrocities they committed during the war

After Japan surrendered, the American General Douglas MacArthur was put in charge of the country. The Allies did not directly govern Japan, but MacArthur was given the power to overrule any decisions made by the Japanese government.

The Cost of World War II   Millions worldwide celebrated V-J Day, which marked the end of the Second World War. But they also mourned the loss of life. As many as 60 million people died in World War II—about half of them civilians. The Soviet Union had the highest losses. Perhaps 20 million or more Soviet soldiers and civilians were killed, although an accurate count was never made. Poland was also hard hit, suffering about 6 million deaths, nearly all of them civilians. Nearly 2 million Japanese were killed and more than 4 million Germans. Britain, France, and the United States each lost several hundred thousand people.

More than 20 million Europeans were made homeless by the fighting. The huge number of dead and homeless in China and the rest of Asia will probably never be known. Nor can the cost of all the property destroyed, resources depleted, and economic activity disrupted by the war. Just the money governments paid to fight the war totaled more than a trillion dollars.

War Crimes Trials and Restructuring   The Allies made a number of demands of the Axis Powers at the end of World War II. Germany and Japan had to disarm and give up all territory they had taken. They also were temporarily occupied by Allied forces. The Allies did not want to inflict more suffering on the people of these defeated nations. However, they did want to punish those who had committed **war crimes**.

In November 1945, the Allies put 22 Nazi leaders on trial in the German city of Nuremberg. They were charged not only with war crimes but also with crimes against humanity, such as enslavement, extermination, and persecution on racial or political grounds. Judges from the United States, the Soviet Union, Great Britain, and France heard their cases. Twelve defendants were condemned to death by hanging, seven received prison terms, and three were acquitted in the **Nuremberg Trials**. Other cases followed, including convictions of officials who ran concentration camps and doctors who carried out gruesome medical experiments on prisoners.

In October 1946, a separate court in Tokyo put 28 Japanese war criminals on trial. All were found guilty. Sixteen received life sentences. Seven were sentenced to death by hanging, including Prime Minister Tojo and the general responsible for the Bataan Death March.

The Allies also set out to restructure Germany and Japan after the war. Germany was divided into four military occupation zones, one each for the United States, the USSR, France, and Britain. Berlin, which lay entirely within the Soviet zone, also was divided in four parts—one for each occupying power. The Americans took a different approach to postwar Japan. They put American General MacArthur in charge of the country. Allied soldiers occupied Japan, but they did not control it directly as they did in Germany. Instead, the Japanese government carried out the political reforms that MacArthur and his staff prescribed. However, MacArthur had ultimate power in Japan, and could overrule Japanese decisions as he saw fit.

After dissolving Japan's empire and disbanding its military, the Allies worked to bring democracy to Japan. Officials under MacArthur prepared a new constitution. It set up a parliamentary government, based on the British model, with a strong legislature and an independent judiciary. The emperor would only have ceremonial powers. Women as well as men could elect members of parliament, and a bill of rights ensured civil and political liberties. MacArthur also ensured that its constitution renounced the use of force as an instrument of power. Japan was restored to full **sovereignty** in 1951. However, many more years would pass before Germany regained full independence.

sovereignty freedom from external control

Summary

In this lesson, you learned about events that resulted in World War II between 1939 and 1945, the course of the fighting in Europe, North Africa, and Asia, and the war's final outcome.

Cultural Interaction As other European nations came under German control, the Nazis began a program to exterminate all Jews and other groups they viewed as inferior. By the end of the war, approximately 6 million Jews had been murdered in a systematic mass-murder campaign that became known as the Holocaust.

Political Systems After World War I, Germany rearmed and seized ethnically German territories, but German ambitions to control wider territories soon became clear. Britain and France did not resist these moves at first. When they did, Germany went to war. Soon, most of western Europe was under Nazi control. In the east, Germany invaded the Soviet Union to destroy communism and gain oil.

Economic Systems As Japan industrialized in the early 1900s, the small island nation did not have the natural resources its industries needed. To get them, Japan relied on its military to conquer other lands. In 1931, Japan began a long war to take control of China. By 1940, it was also eying Southeast Asia and the East Indies for the oil, rubber, and other raw materials these regions contained. When American leaders tried to block Japan's expansion, Japan went to war against the United States.

Human-Environment Interaction German warplanes waged a ferocious bombing campaign to conquer Britain in 1940 and 1941. Despite suffering great destruction, Britain did not fall. Soon, British and American long-range bombers were bringing similar destruction to Germany and its cities. In Asia, Allied forces captured Pacific islands ever closer to Japan and used them as bases to launch damaging air attacks on the Japanese home islands. In August 1945, American bombers dropped two tremendously powerful atomic bombs on Hiroshima and Nagasaki. Each city was almost totally destroyed. The tremendous destruction and high loss of life caused Japan to surrender, bringing World War II to an end.

Forces for Independence and Revolution in Asia

How did popular movements transform India and China after World War II?

25.1 Introduction

In April 1930, Mohandas Gandhi, a small thin man of 61, led a group of Indians to a seashore on India's west coast. There, as authorities watched, he and the others walked along the shoreline, picking up handfuls of natural sea salt. With this simple and defiant act, they intentionally broke the law. Salt was heavily taxed in British India. It was illegal to produce or sell salt without paying the tax. This deprived the great majority of Indians of needed salt because they were poor. By picking up the sea salt, Gandhi and his group were technically "producing" salt.

The authorities did not arrest Gandhi that day. However, he was arrested several weeks later after announcing a march on a nearby salt factory. The march took place anyway. On May 21, 1930, police attacked some 2,500 peaceful protesters as they approached the factory gate. The protesters did not fight back, flee, or even try to block the blows. They knew that their non-violent resistance would help draw attention to how unfairly they were being treated by the British.

Meanwhile, in nearby China, 30-year-old revolutionary leader Mao Zedong had also acted against his government. Like Gandhi, he wanted to replace a government he had once supported. However, Mao did not share Gandhi's belief in nonviolent protest. He would soon spearhead a long civil war that would cost millions of lives and make China a communist nation.

India and China have histories that are as similar as they are different. Each civilization has existed for thousands of years. Over that time, its people have experienced rule by powerful local leaders or distant emperors as well as invasion, conquest, or other domination by outsiders. By the mid-1800s, India and much of China were under European control. It is here that their histories differ. In the mid-1800s, India was a colonial possession of Great Britain, while China continued to be ruled by its emperor. In the 1900s, however, that all changed.

Themes

Cultural Interaction Religious tensions and differing ideologies have created conflict and have been forces for change throughout history.

Political Systems The spirit of nationalism has encouraged revolts, revolutions, and other unrest that have affected nations' political structures and altered their forms of government.

Human-Environment Interaction Wars and other conflicts have prompted mass migrations that changed human characteristics of regions and nations.

◀ Gandhi and his supporters protested unfair salt taxes on the Salt March.

This engraving from 1858 shows Indian rebels attacking the British artillery battery in the city of Lucknow. In 1857, sepoy soldiers who were trained and led by British officers revolted against the British. Rural peasants, maharajas, and the Indian emperor also joined the rebellion.

25.2 The British in India

The British presence in India began in 1612 when the East India Company opened a trading post on India's northwest coast. By 1690, the company had two more posts on India's east coast. Three of India's most important cities developed from these trading centers—Bombay (now Mumbai), Madras (now Chennai), and Calcutta (now Kolkata). The company bought such raw materials as a blue dye known as indigo, saltpeter (used in making gunpowder), sugar, salt, and textiles in India and took them back to Europe for sale. The French, Dutch, and Portuguese also had trading posts in India and engaged in a similar trade.

The East India Company As India's Mughal dynasty weakened in the late 1600s, the East India Company turned its trading posts into forts. Sepoys—Indian soldiers trained and led by British officers—protected these forts. The company gained the favor of the Mughal emperors, who sought to benefit from its military and naval power. Company officials also allied with local rulers and sometimes used the sepoys to settle regional power struggles.

These practices allowed the company to extend its influence far into India's interior. British victories in Europe's wars in the 1700s, which also caused Europeans in India to fight, further increased the company's power. Most of the French, Dutch, and Portuguese traders were gone by the early 1800s. By the 1850s, the East India Company was more powerful than the emperor himself and it controlled some 60 percent of India. The rest was ruled by more than 500 Muslim, Sikh, and Hindu princes called *maharajas*.

The East India Company developed a large network of Indian merchants to obtain the products the company desired. However, company officials showed little respect for India's rich and ancient culture. Instead, the British saw themselves as the bearers of civilization. English became the official language in regions the company controlled. Upper-class Indians were offered an English-style education so they might help the British deal with India's masses. Conservative Hindu and Muslim leaders resented such policies, as well as the Christian missionaries who arrived. Many Indians thought that Western culture and religion were being forced on them. Some were also troubled by the railroads and other technology the British introduced.

Tensions came to a head in 1857 when sepoys in northern India rose in revolt against their British officers. They were soon joined by rural peasants and many others unhappy with the British presence in India. The rebels also included the emperor and maharajas who had lost territory to the East India Company. Fighting went on for more than a year. Some 10,000 British troops finally put down the revolt.

The British Raj   The 1857 uprising brought the East India Company's power to an end. In August 1858, Parliament transferred the rule of India from the company to Britain's monarch. The British government pledged to respect the rights of the maharajas to the territories they ruled. More than 560 such regions remained politically independent throughout the entire 90 years of the **British Raj,** or "rule."

During the Raj, India's government became the world's largest imperial **bureaucracy**. A viceroy appointed from Britain ruled the colony. He was assisted by appointed councils that issued laws and helped to carry them out. An appointed governor in each of the colony's provinces managed district officials who formed the lower levels of the **Indian Civil Service**. These officeholders were nearly all British. Indians, including those with English educations, were rarely selected to fill these positions.

As more and more British arrived in the colony, a separate British society emerged. Although **segregation** did not officially exist under law, an informal type of segregation took hold. The British lived in their own communities and moved in social circles that were closed to Indians regardless of their education, abilities, or class.

Some Britons bought rural lands and became the landlords of the peasants who lived there. They made these peasants grow tea, coffee, and other commercial crops for export overseas instead of food for local populations. Parts of India experienced famines because of these policies. Meanwhile, Britain's industries increased their exports to India.

British Raj the 90-year period of British colonial rule in India that took place between 1858 and 1947

bureaucracy a system in which nonelected government officials are organized into specialized departments and operate according to fixed rules within a hierarchy of authority

Indian Civil Service the body of some 1,500 appointed officials who carried out day-to-day government of British India

segregation the forced separation of a race, class, or ethnic group

After the 1857 rebellion, Great Britain transferred rule of India from the East India Company to the British monarch. In 1875, the Prince of Wales completed a tour of India. In this photograph, the Prince (holding rifle) poses with his hunting party and the Bengal tiger they have killed.

tariff a tax on imported goods

Indian National Congress an organization founded in 1885 to improve the rights and status of Indians in British colonial India and a major political party in India since its independence in 1947

Many of these products were less expensive than Indian-made goods. India's traditional textile industry and other industries suffered as a result, especially because the British banned Indian textiles from their home market while allowing their relatively cheap British textiles to flood the Indian market **tariff** free. At the same time, India's natural resources were being depleted to meet the demands of British industry.

In 1885, delegates from across British India met to found the **Indian National Congress**. They were mostly Western-educated Indian lawyers, teachers, and other professionals. Nearly 75 percent were Hindus and only 2 were Muslims—a make-up that reflected the tensions between India's Hindu majority and its largest religious minority. The Congress passed resolutions demanding economic reforms and more participation by Indians in their government. These demands had popular appeal. By 1888, more than 1,200 delegates were attending the Congress's annual meetings.

The British did bring Indians into local governments in the late 1800s and onto the viceroy's legislative council. However, very few became part of the Indian Civil Service—the officials that Britain called the "steel frame" of its rule.

25.3 Independence for India

The first large-scale resistance to the British Raj occurred in response to Britain's division of Bengal into two separate provinces in 1905. Bengal was a region in northeastern India populated by 85 million people. The British had long considered the province too large to govern effectively. However, English-educated Bengalis saw the split as a destruction of their beloved homeland and an attempt to reduce Hindu power. The fact that one of the new provinces contained a Muslim majority inflamed their discontent. To protest these developments, they organized a boycott of British goods. The Indian National Congress soon spread the boycott throughout India. Nationalist protesters took to the streets in cities across India. Some of these demonstrations turned into violent riots.

The intensity of the Hindu reaction concerned India's Muslims, many of whom favored the division of Bengal. Especially troubling was the Hindus claim that Bengal was a Hindu land. To protect Muslim rights and promote loyalty to the British, Muslim elites formed the All-India Muslim League in 1906. They hoped their organization would balance the power of the Indian National Congress, which Hindus dominated.

In 1912, British officials reversed course and reunited Bengal. The action restored the power and prestige of the Indian National Congress, which had been weakened by its failure to undo the split. However, Muslim leaders felt betrayed. They began to question their support of the British and the status of Muslims in India.

India in World War I   Tensions were temporarily forgotten as World War I began in 1914. More than 300,000 troops of the British Indian Army were rushed to overseas battlefields. The British Indian Army reinforced Allied troops on Europe's Western Front and fought against Ottoman forces in the Middle East. India's maharajas volunteered men and money to the war effort. Although some Indian Muslims hesitated about waging war against the Muslim Ottoman Empire, by the war's end in 1918, some 1.3 million Indians had served on every major front.

About 1.3 million Indian soldiers served in World War I. The soldiers in this photograph served on the western front in France. Indians hoped that the British would reward their service with greater independence after the war, but they were disappointed when few changes took place.

As the fighting raged, Britain promised to make major political changes in India after the war. This led the Indian National Congress and the Muslim League to form a temporary alliance. They believed that Britain might reward India's loyalty by offering **home rule** or even complete independence and they wanted to be united in dealing with any British reforms. However, despite Britain's promises, little positive change took place. British officials returned, and they ousted Indians who had taken their place during the war. Indian soldiers, who had been treated as valuable allies during the war, became "natives" again.

Massacre at Amritsar   In 1919, the viceroy's legislative council passed a series of laws—which every Indian council member opposed—extending wartime measures that had limited personal rights and freedoms. Intended to suppress political unrest, the laws allowed the government to shut down newspapers during emergencies and to jail political activists without trial. A Congress member, Mohandas Gandhi, called for a **general strike** to protest these laws and launched a nationwide movement for its repeal.

The strongest protest came from Punjab, a northwestern province that had provided nearly half of India's combat troops during the war. In April, two nationalist leaders were arrested at a huge protest rally in the city of Amritsar. When the protesters demanded their leaders' release, British troops fired on them. Several protesters were wounded or killed. The enraged mob rioted, destroying British property and killing several Britons. The British responded by banning further public assemblies.

Despite the ban, some 10,000 unarmed Indian men, women, and children gathered in a walled square on April 13, 1919, for a peaceful protest. A British general placed soldiers at the entranceway and ordered them to fire on the crowd. There was no escaping the terror. Several minutes and some 1,650 rounds of ammunition later, nearly 400 protesters lay dead. More than 1,000 others were wounded.

home rule limited self-government over internal matters that is granted by a large political unit to a smaller one within it

general strike a work stoppage by a large portion of the entire workforce of a locality or country

Amritsar Massacre the unprovoked killing or wounding by British troops of nearly 1,500 peaceful protesters at Amritsar, Punjab in 1919

The **Amritsar Massacre** shocked all of India and raised Gandhi to leadership in the Indian National Congress. The general was removed from command, but the British did not severely punish him. Gandhi called this response a "whitewash." British leaders finally made some minor reforms that allowed Indians to be elected to provincial councils. It was not enough. The Congress adopted a policy of resistance to British rule. Millions of other Indians suddenly became nationalists. After years of patiently accepting British rule while they waited for change, they now wanted Britain out of India.

When Mohandas Gandhi found few opportunities for practicing law in India, he traveled to South Africa, where he worked for an Indian law firm. This 1903 photo shows Gandhi, seated in the center of the image, with fellow employees of the law firm. The racial prejudice Gandhi encountered in South Africa spurred him to begin a life of political activism.

Mohandas Gandhi   "I can no longer retain affection for a government so evilly manned as it is nowadays," Gandhi wrote in 1920. He made it his mission to change that situation. Gandhi's methods for resisting British rule made him one of the most influential political figures of the twentieth century.

Gandhi was born in 1869, the son of a high official in a small princely Hindu state in western India. At age 18, he went to Britain to study law. Returning to India, he found few opportunities for success as a lawyer. So in 1893, he went to work for an Indian firm in South Africa. There, his legal training and personal encounters with racial prejudice caused him to lead a long struggle to gain equal rights for South Africa's Indian minority.

Returning to India in 1914, Gandhi soon became a member of the Indian National Congress. However, he refused to take part in any anti-British activities until 1919. But the insensitive reaction of the British to the Amritsar Massacre drove him to launch a resistance movement that employed tactics he had used in South Africa.

Gandhi's *Satyagraha* Movement   In 1920, Gandhi announced a campaign of massive and widespread nonviolent resistance and noncooperation with the British. He called on Indians to boycott all British goods, businesses, schools, courts, and elections. He urged them to refuse any titles, honors, or offices the British offered—and, if all else failed, to refuse to pay British taxes. He claimed that only the total withdrawal of support for British rule would bring freedom for India.

Some Indian leaders questioned Gandhi's tactics. They declared that a violent uprising was needed. Gandhi rejected the use of violence. However, his experience in South Africa had taught him the value of being the target of it. The small Indian population in South Africa had faced a seemingly impossible task in its struggle with the powerful and oppressive white government. Yet the thousands of Indians willing to accept jail or beatings for refusing to obey laws or end strikes caused their movement to succeed. It was a terrible ordeal for them, but it had brought attention to an unjust government.

Indians were not a minority in India, of course, but its British government was just as powerful as the one in South Africa. Gandhi claimed that millions of Indians engaged in peaceful **civil disobedience** would bring Britain's colonial officials to their knees. He urged his followers to use only the weapons of *satya* (truth) and *ahisma* (nonviolence or non-injury) against their British oppressors. In time, he stopped using the term "passive resistance" to describe his strategy and adopted the more accurate *satyagraha* (truth-force) instead. For Gandhi, satyagraha blended politics with deeply-held Hindu beliefs. Many of his followers viewed him as a guru, or spiritual teacher. They called him *Mahatma*, or "Great Soul."

Gandhi's satyagraha (truth-force) movement rejected violence and urged Indians to practice nonviolent civil disobedience. This illustration shows one type of peaceful demonstration that satyagraha participants used to draw attention to their cause.

Resistance, Conflict, and Compromise   Gandhi's noncoopera-tion movement was an immediate success. Millions of Indian voters boycotted the provincial elections of 1920. Congress members who were running for seats on provincial councils withdrew their candi-dacies. By 1922, widespread civil disobedience had put some 60,000 Indians in prison. Yet British policy stayed the same. So Gandhi decided to use his most powerful weapon—a boycott on payment of taxes. However, before he could organize this final boycott, some of his followers in northern India trapped and killed 22 officers inside their police station. Shocked and disappointed by this event, he ended the noncooperation campaign.

Sensing that Gandhi was losing support, the British arrested him. During the two years he was in jail, his support did slip. Some mem-bers of Congress formed a political party that took part in the 1923 elections and called for home rule. When he regained his freedom in 1924, Gandhi found that much had changed. Radical young Congress members charged that he had betrayed the independence movement by ending the satyagraha. They were calling for armed rebellion against Britain. Worst of all, the unity between Hindus and Muslims that existed during the satyagraha had dissolved. Tired and discour-aged, Gandhi withdrew from politics.

In 1927, the British government formed a commission to sug-gest reforms for India's government. Outraged that this commis-sion contained no Indians, Gandhi returned to public life. He again became head of the Indian National Congress. In 1928, the Congress demanded the Britain grant India **dominion** status within a year. When this demand was not met, Gandhi launched a second satya-graha. Its high point was the famous **Salt March** of 1930. This protest of a minor tax on salt shocked both the British and the Congress. But it was a stroke of genius.

civil disobedience the breaking of or refusal to obey laws or other governmental commands to protest and bring attention to a perceived injustice and force change

dominion a nation within the British Empire that controls its own domestic and foreign affairs, but is tied to Britain by allegiance to the British monarch

Salt March a nonviolent campaign of civil disobedience led by Mohandas Gandhi in 1930

In this photo, Gandhi and his followers harvest sand to boil for salt, in violation of British law. The Salt March inspired civil disobedience throughout India. It also created sympathy around the world for the cause of Indian nationalism.

The Salt March began in April 1930, when Gandhi led a group of followers on a 240-mile walk from his home to the sea. Hundreds more joined the march as it passed through rural villages. Images of this frail man striding forward, staff in hand, to confront the British over a tax on a basic human need won Gandhi world-wide attention and support. The brutality of the British response to this nonviolent action, which for the first time included women, also affected world opinion.

Besides women, the second satyagraha included other groups who had not taken part in the earlier campaign. For the first time, large numbers of people in central and south India gave the movement their support. The civil disobedience inspired by the Salt March resulted in 60,000 arrests in 1931. In one three-month period in 1932, some 40,000 Indians were arrested. Many of those jailed, including Gandhi himself, remained there for up to two years. After his release, Gandhi again retired from politics and resigned from the Indian National Congress. Jawaharlal Nehru, who had been elected President of the Congress in 1929, succeeded him as its head.

Ominously, Muslims' support for Gandhi's first satyagraha was missing in his second. One reason was the riots between Hindus and Muslims that engulfed every major northern Indian city in 1924. However, Muslim leaders had also become concerned about Hindu domination of the independence movement. They worried about being shut out of any negotiations with the British that might shape the future of India's government. By 1930, some Muslims had begun to call for a separate nation for their minority community.

The Muslim League did not join these calls until 1940. It still hoped to work with the Indian National Congress to create one independent India. However, in 1935 Britain increased Indians' power in their provincial governments. In the elections that followed this reform, the Indian National Congress—which had reorganized as a political party, the Congress Party—won control of nearly every province in India. It rejected a coalition with the Muslim League as unneeded. Only two powers existed in India, Nehru said—the Congress and the British. The Muslim League responded by working hard to build its popularity and power among Muslims. By World War II, the divisions were in place that split British India after the war.

War, Partition, and Independence   In September 1939, Britain issued India's declaration of war on Germany without even consulting Indian leaders. The Congress Party's provincial governments resigned in protest. The party demanded immediate independence in return for India's support in the war. A renewed civil disobedience campaign resulted in the arrest of 20,000 Congress members by 1941.

In 1942, with Japanese troops threatening British Asia, Britain countered with an offer of independence after the war. Suspicious of British promises, Congress rejected the compromise. It began a violent campaign to drive the British from India. British troops crushed the uprising. Authorities cracked down by arresting some 60,000 more Congress members, including its entire leadership, and imprisoning them for the rest of the war.

These events delighted the Muslim League, which supported the war in every way possible. As the government's split with Congress widened, its ties with the League grew closer. The Muslim League asked the British to include a separate nation for Muslims in any plan for India's independence.

The partition of British India in 1947 resulted in mass migration as people fled their homes to settle in the state associated with their own religious group. This image from 1947 shows a homeless boy on a hill above a large refugee camp that sprung up to house dislocated migrants.

On August 15, 1947, British India became the independent nations of India and Pakistan. Some 15 million people—Hindus, Muslims, and members of other groups—fled their homes in order to be on the "right" side of the border. As many as a million others were slaughtered in the religious violence that accompanied that migration.

25.4 Reform and Revolution in China

As Indian leaders worked to reform British rule in India, Chinese reformers sought to bring change to their nation and its government. In 1850, radicals tried to end the Qing (ching) dynasty whose emperors had ruled China for more than 200 years. The resulting Taiping Rebellion turned into a long civil war. Chinese troops finally defeated the rebels in 1864. The rebellion cost some 20 million lives, according to conservative estimates, and it seriously weakened the Qing dynasty.

Reform Movements Lead to Power Struggles The Self-Strengthening Movement, which began in the 1860s, tried to establish modern industries and otherwise reform China according to Western ideas. However, conservative Qing rulers opposed China's Westernization and disliked the spheres of influence that Western nations established in China by late 1800s. However, the Qing were too weak to resist this economic imperialism. China was also too weak to prevent Japan from seizing Korea in the Sino-Japanese War of 1894–95 and taking control of part of Manchuria.

China's defeat in the Sino-Japanese War increased the calls for reform. When the emperor began to make some of these changes, he angered the conservative empress dowager (the widow of a dead emperor) Cixi (tsoo-SHEE). In 1898, Chinese officials loyal to Cixi removed the emperor. She took power and reversed his reforms.

In June 1900, Boxers murdered the German foreign minister in Beijing. Many other westerners and Chinese Christians were besieged in the city. In August, a coalition of 19,000 foreign troops arrived in Beijing to crush the Boxer forces. This Japanese print from 1900 shows allied forces driving Boxers away from the imperial palace in Beijing.

Boxer Rebellion an uprising by a secret group known as the Righteous and Harmonious Fists, called "Boxers" by Westerners, that attempted to drive all foreigners from China

regent a person who rules a country while its monarch is too young, old, or ill to rule, or is absent

Cixi supported Chinese leaders who encouraged an uprising against foreigners called the **Boxer Rebellion**. Bands of Boxers roamed the countryside in 1899 attacking Christian missionaries and destroying foreign-owned mines and other property. Many foreigners fled to Beijing, China's capital. In August 1900, some 19,000 troops sent to Beijing by Western nations defeated Chinese forces and freed the foreigners the Boxers had trapped there. The Boxers were Buddhist mystics who believed that they were immune to bullets, which proved not to be the case. A coalition of British, French, and other European forces crushed their rebellion.

After the Boxer Rebellion failed, Cixi began making some of the reforms she had reversed in 1898. However, it was too late. The Qing dynasty had been hopelessly weakened. Protests and revolts broke out across China. Cixi died in 1908. Just before her death, she had the emperor she replaced in 1898 killed by poison. This left his three-year-old nephew Puyi to be emperor. A **regent** ruled until 1912, when revolution forced Puyi from the throne. Puyi was China's last emperor. His overthrow ended 267 years of Qing rule and a form of government more than 2,000 years old.

The Revolution of 1911   Although the Boxer Rebellion failed to drive foreigners from China, it strengthened Chinese nationalism. This was especially true for young and well-educated Chinese. When the reform movement also failed, many of these Chinese came to believe that revolution was the only solution. They wanted to replace China's old ruling system with a republican form of government.

The revolutionaries were led by Sun Yat-sen, a Western-educated medical doctor from South China. Although he had no political training, Sun was troubled by the Qing rulers' resistance to modernizing China. Following China's defeat in the Sino-Japanese War, he called for a revolt in Canton (now Guangzhou), the capital of his home province. When the plot collapsed, Sun fled China. He spent the next 16 years living in Europe, Japan, and the United States. During his exile, Sun collected funds from Chinese overseas to organize several more uprisings in China. They all failed.

Another revolt occurred in 1911, when army units near Beijing rebelled against the Qing. As the revolt spread, Sun's supporters joined it. By November, 15 of China's 24 provinces had declared independence from Qing rule. Sun returned to China and was named president of a new Chinese republic. However, Yuan Shikai, the commander of China's army, was already acting as China's leader. To avoid civil war, Sun stepped aside. In February 1912, Yuan became the first president of the Republic of China.

25.5 China's Civil War

Sun Yat-sen, leader of China's 1911 revolution, is known as the father of modern China. He hoped to build a nation based on what he called the Three Principles of the People—nationalism, democracy, and socialism. However, the new republic's first president, Yuan Shikai, was mainly interested in increasing his power. To counter Yuan, Sun joined with other former revolutionaries to found a new political party—the Kuomintang (KMT) or Nationalist Party.

The Republic's Early Struggles   Elections in February 1913 gave the Nationalist Party a majority of the seats in China's new parliament. Yuan responded by having the party's leader killed. When a revolt against Yuan failed in the summer of 1913, Sun and its other leaders fled to Japan. In November, Yuan banned the Nationalists and removed its members from parliament. In 1914, he dissolved parliament and issued a new constitution that made him president for life.

Sun Yat-sen was a Western-educated doctor who led a revolutionary movement in China. He came to believe that reform within the existing system was not possible, and that China's imperial government should be overthrown and replaced with a republic.

Yuan declared China neutral when World War I began in August 1914. However, Japan, which fought for the Allies, seized the German sphere of influence in Shandong, in eastern China. Japan also forced Yuan to grant it a sphere of influence in Manchuria. When Yuan appealed to the United States and other Western powers for help, they refused to get involved.

Perhaps unwisely, Yuan chose this moment of humiliation to announce his plans to make himself emperor. Rebellions broke out all over China. Japan secretly provided arms and money to Sun and other leaders to aid these revolts. In several provinces, **warlords** declared their independence of the central government in Beijing. After Yuan fell ill and died in June 1916, alliances of warlords fought for control of that government. Sun Yat-sen and warlords in southern China organized a rival government in 1917. Its repeated efforts to control all of China plunged China into a long civil war.

> **warlord** a military leader who governs by force, usually within a limited area

Hoping to regain Shandong, both governments declared war on Germany in 1917. However, the Paris Peace Conference following World War I let Japan keep German holdings in China. Some Chinese nationalists blamed the Beijing government for this failure. On May 4, 1919, a massive student protest erupted in Beijing. The calls for change that followed became known as the May Fourth Movement. They ranged from the westernization of China to the establishment of socialism. The May Fourth Movement, along with China's split between the two rival governments, soon sent the nation down a new revolutionary path.

China's Nationalist Government   In October 1919, Sun Yat-sen restarted the Nationalist Party. He hoped that a democratic political party in the south would weaken the warlords in Beijing, which the West recognized as China's legal government. In 1921, Sun became president of China's southern government. Because of its domination by the KMT, that government became known as the Nationalist government.

Until his death in 1925, Sun devoted himself to reuniting China under Nationalist rule. However, his appeals to the Western democracies for aid were ignored. So Sun turned to the Soviet Union, which had recently achieved its own revolution. In 1923, Soviet advisers arrived to help Sun unite China. The Chinese Communist Party (CCP), founded with Soviet help by members of the May Fourth Movement in 1921, was instructed to cooperate with the KMT. CCP members joined the KMT, although they never lost their identity as Communists.

The Rise of Chiang Kai-shek   One result of Sun's cooperation with the Communists was the rise of Chiang Kai-shek as leader of China. Chiang came from a prosperous farm and merchant family in northern China. He had gone to Japan as a young man to train for a military career. There he met Chinese exiles plotting the overthrow of the Qing dynasty and became a revolutionary. When China's 1911 revolution began, he returned home to fight against the Qing.

In 1918, Chiang joined Sun Yat-sen in reorganizing the Nationalist Party. Sun sent Chiang to the Soviet Union, where he learned Western military strategy from the Red Army. Returning home, he organized the Nationalist government's National Revolutionary Army and was named its commander. In 1926, Chiang led this army north to fulfill Sun's dream of reuniting China. Chiang's army was accompanied by Soviet military advisers. He was also assisted by a KMT "propaganda corps" of Chinese Communists who stirred up unrest against the Beijing government in the regions it controlled. By 1927, much of China was in Nationalist hands.

Nationalists Versus Communists   While the Nationalist army was on what was called the Northern Expedition, serious splits took place in the KMT. With Sun gone, a struggle developed among its leaders for control of the party. Radical party members wanted to establish socialism or communism in China. They hoped to gain the support of China's poverty-stricken masses with calls for social revolution. This alarmed the party's conservative wing, which wanted only to unify China under Nationalist rule. Many KMT conservatives were well-to-do. They preferred Chinese society as it was. At the same time, the party's socialists and conservatives shared a concern over the Communists' growing power.

Chiang Kai-Shek traveled to Russia to learn Western military strategy from the Soviets. As commander of the Nationalist army, Chiang helped the Nationalists gain control of most of China by 1927.

All these issues came to a head in early 1927, when radical leaders moved the Nationalist capital from southern to northern China. The party's conservatives appealed to the leader they backed, Chiang Kai-shek. In April, he set up a rival Nationalist government in the city of Nanjing and expelled Communists from the army and the party. He also used Nationalist troops to brutally end a Communist-led general strike by workers in Shanghai. Large numbers of Communists were arrested and executed. Similar anti-Communists actions were carried out in several other Chinese cities. Those who survived fled into hiding in the countryside.

In 1928, Chiang captured Beijing and completed the Nationalists' reunification of China. A new national government was established at Nanjing, with Chiang at its head. The West quickly recognized Chiang's Nationalist government as China's legal government.

Mao Zedong hoped to lead Chinese peasants in a communist revolution. After Mao was expelled from the Nationalist Party in 1927, he organized a peasant revolt in Hunan Province. This Chinese propaganda poster shows Mao heroically leading his peasant army.

The Rise of Mao Zedong   One of the Communists who escaped to the countryside in 1927 was the head of the KMT's propaganda corps, Mao Zedong. Like Chiang Kai-shek, Mao was the son of a prosperous farmer and merchant. Although he had no formal military training, he too took part in the 1911 revolution that overthrew the Qing dynasty. After the revolution, Mao drifted about, in search of education and a profession. May 1919 found him at Beijing University, where he took part in the May Fourth Movement.

Mao helped found the CCP in 1921 and was one of the first Communists to join the KMT, where he quickly rose to a leadership position. Along with other radical KMT leaders, Mao worked to organize peasants for a communist revolution. After being expelled from the KMT in 1927, he led a peasant revolt in Hunan Province. When Nationalist forces crushed the revolt, Mao and a few hundred survivors fled into the mountains. There he helped organize a Red Army of peasants and workers that by the spring of 1928 had some 10,000 troops.

The Communists' Struggle for Power   Mao wanted to wage a **guerrilla war** from bases in the Chinese countryside. The leaders of the CCP opposed this strategy. They ordered the Red Army to attack several major cities in south-central China in hopes of inspiring a workers' revolution. No such revolution took place and the Communist forces were crushed by the Nationalist army.

The urban campaign's failure increased Mao's standing in the CCP. His followers created 15 rural bases in central China. From these areas, they seized land from wealthy landowners and gave it to the peasants. By 1931, the Red Army had grown to some 200,000 troops. Mao established the Chinese Soviet Republic in southeastern China, with himself as its head. Under his leadership, the Communists soon controlled a population of several million.

guerrilla war a form of warfare that involves surprise attacks by small groups of fighters, including harassment of the enemy and sabotage

Long March the year-long, 6,000-mile retreat of the Red Army and communist leaders from southeastern to northwestern China after their defeat by Nationalist forces in October 1934

Thousands of Chinese died in World War II as Japan tried to destroy China's will to fight in bombing campaigns. In this 1945 photo, Chinese civilians haul loads of rubble through a city destroyed by a Japanese attack.

Chiang sent four expeditions to crush Mao's government. The Red Army successfully fought them off using guerrilla warfare tactics. Finally, in late 1934, some 700,000 Nationalist troops advanced on the Communist capital. CCP leaders ordered the Red Army to directly attack this overwhelming force. The Red Army was nearly destroyed as a result. In October, Mao, other government and CCP officials, and the remains of their army broke through the Nationalist lines and fled.

Over the next 12 months they crossed 18 mountain ranges and 24 rivers in a 6,000-mile retreat that became known as the **Long March**. For the first three months, they suffered repeated attacks from Chiang's ground troops and almost constant bombardment from his warplanes. Of the 100,000 Communists who began the Long March, only 8,000 survivors arrived at their new base in northwest China in October 1935. However, the retreat allowed Mao to oust his rivals and take control of the CCP.

With the Soviet border and Japanese-held territory in northeast China nearby, Mao was able to rebuild his army without fear of attack by Nationalist forces. By 1937, it again numbered about 100,000 troops.

The Nationalists and Communists in World War II   Japan's invasion of China in 1937 brought a temporary halt to China's civil war. Nationalist and Communist leaders agreed that it was better for both armies to resist the Japanese than to continue fighting each other. An uneasy alliance was formed. However, little cooperation existed. The burden of resisting the invasion fell on the Nationalist army. By the time Japan's conquest was complete in 1939, Chiang's army had been seriously weakened. It retreated into western China, along with other Chinese who fled from Japanese rule. This region became known as Free China.

For the rest of World War II, Japan tried to bomb Free China into surrender. Thousands of soldiers and civilians died. Free China was also plagued by political disputes and corruption. The Nationalist government and its army were further weakened as a result.

Meanwhile, the Communists broke most of the Red Army into small units. These groups went behind enemy lines to fight a guerrilla war against the Japanese. By the end of the war in August 1945, the Communists had gained control over thousands of miles and some 90 million people behind Japanese lines in northern and central China. The Red Army had grown to between 500,000 and 1 million troops.

Formation of the People's Republic of China   With World War II over, conflict between China's Communists and Nationalists resumed. The situation had changed, however. The war had left the Nationalists unpopular and weak, while the Communists emerged from it much stronger. A negotiated peace between the two groups was blocked by conservatives in the KMT, who still believed in a military victory. The fighting resumed in March 1946. The Nationalists made gains at first, but the tide soon turned in the Communists' favor.

Buoyed by widespread peasant support in the countryside and supplied with weapons left behind by the Japanese, the People's Liberation Army (the Red Army's new name after the war) began to push south in 1947. By late 1948, the Nationalist position was looking increasingly hopeless. In January 1949, the Communists took Beijing without a fight. Most of China's other major cities soon passed from Nationalist to Communist control. Chiang Kai-shek abandoned mainland China, moving his government and remaining Nationalist forces to the nearby island of Formosa, which became the nation of Taiwan. He proclaimed the Taiwanese city of Taipei the temporary capital of China. On October 1, 1949, Mao Zedong announced the formation of the People's Republic of China, with its capital at Beijing. The Nationalists remained in Taiwan.

By 1945, the Red Army numbered between 500,000 and 1 million troops. In this photograph, Communists troops march on Shanghai in May 1949. The Communists took all major cities in China and drove the Nationalist army from the mainland.

Summary

In this lesson, you learned about events, conflicts, ideas, and other forces that brought great change to India and China.

Cultural Interaction Religious tensions between India's Hindu majority and its Muslim population existed throughout the British Raj. As Hindus' calls for independence from Britain grew, these tensions took on a political tone. The Muslim minority did not want to live under a Hindu-controlled government. So British divided India in 1947 to create two independent nations—a largely Hindu India and a largely Muslim Pakistan. Tensions increased in China when some Chinese tried to establish communism there. Other Chinese leaders opposed communism's principles and practices. Differences between these groups led to war between them. The Communists won this war after a long struggle, and China became a communist nation.

Political Systems In the late 1800s, Indian nationalists began pushing for a greater Indian voice in India's British colonial government. When Britain did not allow India self-government after its loyal support in World War I, a long period of unrest followed. Britain granted independence to India and Pakistan in 1947. In China, nationalists' efforts to strengthen and modernize the nation brought revolution in 1911. China functioned as a republic for a brief time before political unrest divided the country. In the 1920s, attempts to reunite China resulted in civil war. The war ended in 1949, with China unified under Communist rule.

Human-Environment Interaction As Britain prepared to divide India in 1947, many Hindus lived in regions that were going to be part of Pakistan. Many Muslims lived in what would become the nation of India, where Hindus would be a majority. As independence approached, millions of India's Muslims moved to Pakistan. Millions of Hindus relocated from Pakistan to areas that would remain part of India. Widespread violence between Hindus and Muslims encouraged this migration and accompanied it.

Era Overview: The Cold War and Beyond, 1945–Present

How did the Cold War change the world?

26.1 Introduction

In April 1945, near the end of World War II, a historic encounter took place between U.S. and Soviet troops in Germany. Although the two allies had joined forces to defeat the Nazis, the two armies had been fighting on different fronts. Now, as they moved across German territory—the American soldiers from the west and the Soviet soldiers from the east—they came face-to-face at the Elbe River in eastern Germany.

Although they were unfamiliar with each other, the Americans stood on one bank of the river and waved, while the Soviet soldiers hailed them from the other side. Spotting a small boat nearby, U.S. Lieutenant Albert L. Kotzebue and a few of his men made their way across the river. There, the soldiers embraced each other warmly. One American later recalled, "We didn't know what to expect from the Russians." But he added: "If you put an American uniform on them, they could have been American!" The following day, senior officers from the two armies met for a formal handshake and photographs in the nearby town of Torgau.

The United States and the Soviet Union had much to celebrate at the end of the war. But the good feelings of April 1945 would not last for long. Tensions soon arose over their different visions for the postwar world. Within a few years, they had become locked in a fierce struggle for power, known as the **Cold War**.

In this lesson, you will learn why and how these two great powers came into conflict. You will also learn how other nations were drawn into the Cold War, and how this conflict influenced the course of history.

Themes

Cultural Interaction During the Cold War, the United States and the Soviet Union, the two great powers of the post-war era, struggled for global domination. This struggle affected nations around the world.

Political Structures Governments and politics were shaped by Cold War realities. Nationalist movements and revolutions erupted in other countries.

Economic Structures The differing economic models of capitalism and socialism helped fuel Cold War conflict. Nations pursued different goals based on these models.

Social Structures Societies were also affected by the Cold War. Issues of social class played a role in the Cold War struggle.

Human-Environment Interaction The Cold War prompted migration in some parts of the world. New weapons technology played a key role in the conflict.

◄ American and Russian soldiers meet across a bridge on the Elbe River (top) and embrace on the streets of Torgau, Germany (bottom).

The United Nations was founded in June 1945. Here President Truman speaks at the conference in San Francisco where the UN Charter was drafted. The United States and the Soviet Union both joined this new international body, which many saw as a hopeful sign that the two powers would be able to work together in the postwar era.

26.2 The Cold War Begins

At the end of World War II, much of Europe lay in ruins. The United States, however, emerged from the war stronger than ever. The Soviet Union, with its huge land mass and abundant resources, was also poised to become a great power. Together, these two **superpowers** would dominate world affairs.

Signs of Cooperation At first there were hopeful signs that the United States and the USSR might cooperate in the postwar era. In February 1945, as the war was winding down, the "Big Three" Allied leaders—Franklin Roosevelt, Joseph Stalin, and Winston Churchill—met in the Soviet city of Yalta. There they made plans for postwar Europe. They agreed to divide Germany into four Allied occupation zones to be administered by the United States, Great Britain, France, and the Soviet Union. Berlin, the German capital, lay within the Soviet zone but would also be divided among the Allies. In addition, Stalin agreed to support free and fair elections in the liberated countries of Eastern Europe.

At Yalta, the Soviets also agreed to join the **United Nations** (UN). This international body was founded in June 1945, when 50 nations signed the UN Charter. The charter established a General Assembly of all the member-states, plus an 11-member Security Council to settle disputes. UN members agreed to promote peace, security, and international cooperation. They pledged "to save succeeding generations from the scourge of war."

U.S.-Soviet Divisions Despite these hopeful signs, deep divisions between the superpowers made lasting cooperation unlikely. These divisions were based on the two nations' differing histories and different goals for the postwar world.

Some of the differences arose from the war itself. During the war, nearly 300,000 American troops lost their lives. Aside from the attack on Pearl Harbor, however, no fighting took place on American soil. The American economy also boomed during the war because of wartime spending. In contrast, about 28 million Soviet people—soldiers and civilians— died during the war. The fighting devastated the Soviet Union and its economy. Virtually no Soviet citizen was untouched by the war.

The two superpowers also had contrasting goals and beliefs. Having been profoundly scarred by the war, the chief aim of the Soviets was to ensure their security. During the war—and throughout its history—Russia had been highly vulnerable to invasion. The Soviet state wanted to make sure it protected itself from any future attack, particularly from the west. It wanted to create a buffer zone of friendly countries in Eastern Europe.

In neighboring countries, the Soviets also wanted to promote regimes sympathetic to communism, the ideological foundation of the USSR government. Soviet leaders envisioned a communist utopia of social justice and economic equality. To achieve that goal, the government set out to reorganize the economy along socialist lines. Under socialism, the government owned all factories. The state seized private land and took charge of agricultural production, or turned land over to peasant collectives. Soviet leaders were confident communism would inevitably prevail over capitalism as ordinary workers and peasants in other nations followed the Soviet model. But they knew that this victory would not occur without a struggle.

The United States was also concerned with security. Pearl Harbor had made it clear that the United States was no longer safe from attack. It needed to defend itself against threats from abroad. A key part of its strategy was to prevent hostile powers from taking control of the countries and resources of Eurasia, as the Axis powers had tried to do during the war. To accomplish that, the United States would need to maintain a strong military presence overseas, with military bases and strong allies in Europe and Asia.

Americans believed that their system of democratic capitalism—with its ideology of individual liberty and personal freedom—would prevail over socialism. To achieve that end, the United States required the free flow of global trade, with access to resources and markets for its goods.

Given their differences, the United States and the Soviet Union were unlikely to remain allies for long. Although they both wanted a peaceful, secure world, their contrasting perspectives on how to achieve that objective put them in conflict.

This Soviet poster from 1945 promotes the role of industrial and agricultural workers in building a socialist society. Under socialism, the Soviet state owned all factories and collectivized agricultural production.

Iron Curtain the ideological barrier that divided Eastern and Western Europe during the Cold War

containment the U.S. policy of attempting to restrict Soviet power and influence around the world by preventing the spread of communism

Marshall Plan a U.S. aid plan designed to promote economic recovery in Europe after World War II

Stalin hoped that by blockading Berlin, he could force the Western powers to abandon the sections of the city they controlled after World War II. However, he did not anticipate the extraordinary airlift the Allied Powers would undertake, in which they delivered 2,323,738 tons of food, fuel, and other supplies to Berlin by airplane in what became known as the Berlin Airlift.

The Emerging Conflict   The first obvious signs of trouble appeared in Eastern Europe. Although Stalin had promised to allow Eastern European countries to decide their own fate, he soon withdrew that pledge. In Poland, Bulgaria, and Romania, he made sure that pro-Soviet governments took power. He later did the same in the rest of Eastern Europe. The Soviet-dominated countries of Eastern Europe became known as Soviet "satellites."

In response, the United States and Great Britain accused the Soviets of dividing Europe and stifling national self-determination. In a famous speech in March 1946, Winston Churchill warned of the Soviet threat. "From Stettin in the Baltic to Trieste in the Adriatic," he declared, "an iron curtain has descended across the continent." The term **Iron Curtain** came to symbolize the growing divide between East and West. From Moscow, Stalin blasted Churchill's speech as a "call to war."

Meanwhile, the United States was devising policies to counter Soviet power. Early in 1946, a U.S. official in Moscow, George Kennan, wrote a tough analysis of Soviet aims. He said that the USSR had imposed tyranny on its people and meant to do so elsewhere. The only effective response, he argued, was for the West to check, or contain, the spread of Soviet power and influence. This approach, known as **containment,** became official U.S. policy.

President Harry Truman, who had taken office after Roosevelt's death in 1945, soon acted on the containment policy. In March 1947, he called for American aid to Greece and Turkey, two countries under threat from communist elements and backed by the USSR. In a speech Truman declared, "We must assist free peoples to work out their own destinies in their own way." This support for countries seeking to resist communist influence was known as the Truman Doctrine. It became a key principle in U.S. Cold War policy.

The United States followed up with another action designed to limit Soviet power. In June 1947, Secretary of State George Marshall unveiled a financial aid plan to assist postwar recovery in Europe. This plan, known as the **Marshall Plan,** was warmly received in Western Europe. But the Soviets forbade their Eastern European satellites from participating, recognizing that U.S. aid would undermine Soviet influence. The Marshall Plan eventually provided $13 billion in aid to Western Europe, helping to promote economic growth and political stability.

The Western allies also announced plans to combine their German occupation zones into a new West German state. Angered by this move, Stalin declared a blockade of the Allied sectors of West Berlin in June 1948. Berlin was entirely within the Soviet zone, but the city had been divided into Western allied and Soviet sections. The Berlin blockade cut West Berlin off from all supplies brought in by land. Stalin hoped to starve the city into submission and force the Allies to retract their plans for West Germany. Instead, the United States organized the Berlin airlift, a massive effort to fly food and other essential goods into Berlin. The plan succeeded, and after a year Stalin lifted the blockade. Soon afterward, Germany split into two nations. The Federal Republic of Germany, commonly known as West Germany, was under Western influence. The German Democratic Republic, known as East Germany, became a Soviet satellite.

NATO a mutual defense pact formed by Western nations in 1949

The Lines Harden By 1949, the lines of the Cold War were clearly drawn. Europe was divided between the communist East and capitalist West. The two sides carried out the Cold War through economic policy, diplomatic actions, propaganda, espionage, and secret operations. Although the superpowers never engaged in a direct shooting war, the threat of violence was always present.

In 1949, the Western allies formed **NATO,** the North Atlantic Treaty Organization. This group, which included the United States, Canada, and Western European nations, was dedicated to mutual defense. Members agreed to treat an attack on one country as an attack on all.

In this photograph from 1948, British military police erect a sign to mark the boundary between the British and Russian sections of the city of Berlin. In June 1948, tensions between the Soviets and the Western allied powers resulted in Stalin blockading the allied sectors of the city.

Europe During the Cold War

NATO members
Warsaw Pact members
Nonmembers

By 1955, two opposing military alliances had formed. A majority of Western European countries had joined NATO, the North Atlantic Treaty Organization. The Soviets and the nations of Eastern Europe had formed the Warsaw Pact. The formation of these mutual defense alliances reflected increasing military tensions between East and West.

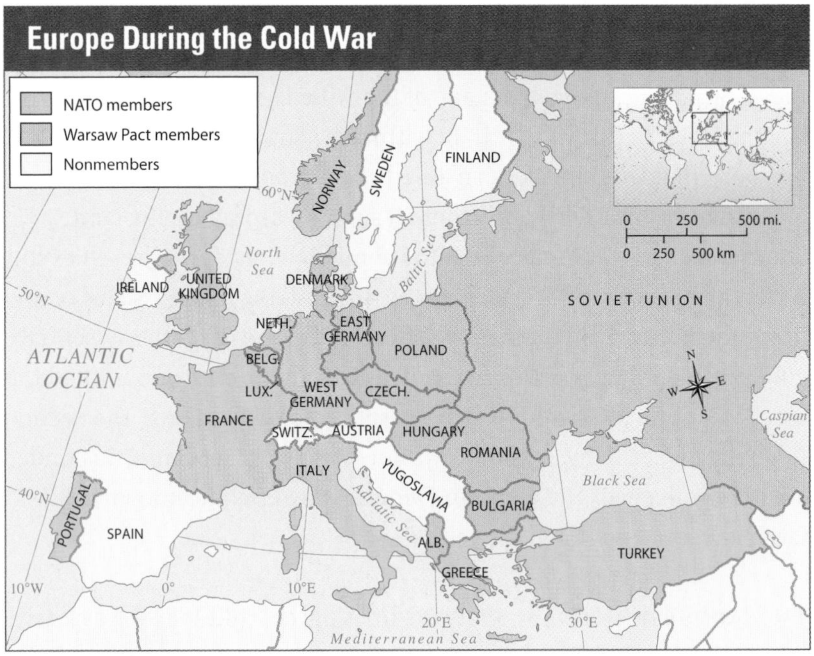

Six years later, in 1955, the Soviet Union formed its own defense alliance, the **Warsaw Pact,** which included the nations of Eastern Europe.

These mutual defense pacts revealed the rising military tensions between East and West. They also reflected the threat posed by nuclear weapons. The United States had used the atomic bomb against Japan in 1945. Four years later, the Soviet Union exploded its own atomic bomb. By the early 1950s, both superpowers had developed a more powerful nuclear device, the hydrogen bomb, or H-bomb. By the 1960s, they had created long-range missiles called intercontinental ballistic missiles, or ICBMs, which could carry nuclear warheads to targets a continent away. The superpowers had become engaged in an expensive and deadly **arms race.** This competition over weaponry stoked fears of nuclear war and raised the stakes in the superpower conflict.

The United States and Soviet Union also got involved in a space race. In 1957, the Soviet Union launched *Sputnik,* the first artificial satellite to orbit Earth. A few months later, the United States put its own satellite into space. In 1961, the Soviet Union sent the first human into orbit, followed soon after by the first American astronaut. In 1969, the United States landed the first men on the moon. The space race was another costly form of superpower competition, but it also brought important advances in science and technology.

The Cold War continued for more than 40 years. During that time, the superpowers sought to dominate each other and bring less powerful nations over to their side. The United States and the Soviet Union were not the only major players in the Cold War, however. Another important actor was China.

26.3 China's Communist Path

After World War II, China was torn by civil war. Nationalists fought with communists for control of the country. The Communists, led by Mao Zedong, eventually won. In 1949, they founded the People's Republic of China. The Nationalists fled to the island of Taiwan, where they formed their own government.

China in the Cold War   The triumph of communism in China took both the United States and the Soviet Union by surprise. They had assumed that the Nationalists would defeat Mao's forces. At first, American officials held out hope that China would reject Soviet influence and remain neutral in the Cold War. However, Mao soon sided with the Soviet Union. In February 1950, he and Stalin sealed their alliance by signing a mutual defense pact.

Communist states now ruled a vast portion of Eurasia, from Eastern Europe to the East China Sea. This made the United States and its Western allies very nervous. The balance of power in Eurasia was clearly tilting toward the communists.

Over the next few years, Mao consolidated his control over China and expanded China's borders. In 1950, Chinese forces invaded and occupied Tibet, a land with a long history of Chinese influence. China also threatened to invade Taiwan and take control of the island. The United States intervened and provided military aid and assistance to defend Taiwan and its Nationalist government.

Mao's Revolutionary Policies   Meanwhile, Mao sought to strengthen communist rule in China. He placed power in the hands of the Communist Party and began to restructure the economy based on Marxist principles. But the character of Chinese communism was different from Soviet communism. Mao and his followers believed that peasants—not urban workers—were the revolutionary class.

The first step was to organize Chinese agriculture along socialist lines. In 1950, the government passed a land reform law, breaking up large estates and distributing land to poor peasants. These small plots were soon combined into larger collective farms, which in theory would be more efficient. A few years later, the government followed the Soviet model of development by setting up even larger collective farms—called communes—where private property was abolished and production goals were set by the state. Chinese women were granted equal rights and given a greater role in production.

The government also socialized industry, putting most factories under state ownership. In 1953, it began a Five-Year Plan designed to modernize the country and to increase industrial production. The plan was a success. Industrial output doubled, with the greatest gains in steel and other heavy industries.

This Chinese poster from 1949 celebrates the triumph of the Communists, led by Mao Zedong, over the Nationalists in China. Both the United States and the Soviets were surprised by the communist victory in China.

During the Cultural Revolution, student groups known as the Red Guards were empowered by Mao to attack people who were considered anti-revolutionary. Members of Red Guard units sometimes even attacked their own teachers or parents. Here Red Guards parade their victims, who are wearing hats proclaiming their supposed crimes, on the streets of Beijing.

Cultural Revolution a period of revolutionary upheaval and political persecution in China from 1966 to 1976

But these results did not satisfy Mao. In 1958, he announced a new plan, called the "Great Leap Forward." This plan set higher targets for both agriculture and industry. Farmers were forced to work on large rural projects and create their own "backyard industries" to produce steel and other goods. The plan was a disaster. Farming suffered and food production fell sharply. By 1961, some 30 million Chinese had died of starvation— the largest famine in human history.

Shifting Course The failure of the Great Leap Forward damaged Mao's reputation, both at home and abroad. Relations with the USSR became strained after Joseph Stalin's death in 1953. Under Stalin's successor Nikita Khrushchev, the USSR rejected the murderous violence and repression that had characterized the Stalin era. Meanwhile, the Chinese continued to laud Stalin as a hero. The Soviet Union chose to distance itself further, cutting off aid to China and ending their alliance.

Mao's image also suffered in China. Facing mounting criticism, he stepped down as head of state and allowed other leaders to set policy. The government launched a program of economic reform, making investments in agriculture and industry and shutting down many state enterprises. Within a few years, the economy began to recover.

Mao regarded these new policies as a betrayal of communism, and he accused reformers of promoting capitalist values. He claimed that the Communist Party had lost touch with the people.

In 1966, Mao called on students to revive China's revolutionary spirit. Radical student groups, known as the Red Guards, took to the streets demanding a return to communist ideals. China was soon engulfed in a wave of revolutionary turmoil known as the **Cultural Revolution**. With Mao's blessing, the Red Guards persecuted or attacked anyone they considered antirevolutionary. Targets of violence included party members, government officials, artists, intellectuals, and others who were said to embrace "old" ideas. Many people were beaten or jailed, and up to a million were killed. Rival armed groups began to fight pitched battles in the streets. The country was on the verge of civil war.

Alarmed by this turmoil, Mao and other top officials stepped in to restore order. In 1968, the Red Guards were officially disbanded. The most extreme phase of the Cultural Revolution was over by the following year. However, political struggles continued until Mao's death in 1976. New leaders eventually took over and introduced reforms, but China remained a communist state.

26.4 Cold War Conflicts

Although the United States and the Soviet Union never went to war directly, Cold War tensions provoked conflicts in other parts of the world. Both superpowers competed for the loyalty and resources of the world's less-developed nations. This competition fueled civil wars and other violent struggles. The fiercest fighting took place in Korea and Vietnam, but conflicts also erupted in Latin America, the Middle East, and Africa.

War in Korea   The first major battle of the Cold War took place in Korea. The **Korean War** lasted from 1950 to 1953 and nearly caused a wider war.

At the end of World War II, Korea was liberated from Japanese control and divided in half. The Soviet Union occupied the northern half, while the United States occupied the south. By 1949, both countries had withdrawn their forces, but Korea remained divided between the communist north and noncommunist south. In June 1950, North Korea invaded the south with Soviet and Chinese backing. The United States responded immediately by sending troops to defend South Korea. It also gained support from the United Nations, which called on member-states to form a UN army to repel the invasion.

At first it appeared that North Korea would defeat the UN army. But General Douglas MacArthur, the UN commander, managed to encircle and isolate the North Korean forces. He then moved north, all the way to the Chinese border at the Yalu River.

To prevent a UN victory, China got involved. It sent 300,000 troops into North Korea and pushed the UN forces back. MacArthur called for air strikes against China, possibly with nuclear weapons. President Truman rejected the idea, fearing it could draw the Soviet Union into the war. Eventually, the fighting reached an impasse. North and South Korea returned to their 1949 borders and signed an armistice, or end to the fighting.

For a time, the Korean conflict had raised the threat of a nuclear war between the superpowers. Instead, it ended in a stalemate. Today, Korea remains divided. South Korea has prospered as a capitalist and democratic state. North Korea, on the other hand, is a strict communist dictatorship. Relations between the two Koreas remain tense.

Korean War a war from 1950 to 1953 between communist North Korea and non-communist South Korea that involved Soviet and Chinese support for the North and U.S. and UN support for the South

This picture, taken in October 1950, shows U.S. troops transporting North Korean prisoners of war. The United States sent troops to defend South Korea after communist North Korea invaded the south in June 1950.

Viet Cong communist insurgents in South Vietnam

Vietnam War the war between North and South Vietnam from the early 1950s to 1975

domino theory the belief that if Vietnam fell to the communists, the rest of Asia would fall like a row of dominoes

President Johnson believed that U.S. involvement in Vietnam had to be escalated to prevent all of Asia from falling into communist hands. In 1965, he ordered air strikes and sent in American combat troops. In this photograph from 1966, two U.S. soldiers drag away a wounded Viet Cong fighter.

The Vietnam War The next major conflict arose in Vietnam. It began as an anticolonial fight for independence, but it soon became a Cold War struggle between communist and noncommunist forces.

At the end of World War II, Vietnam was still part of the French colony of Indochina. After the war, Vietnamese nationalists—led by the communist leader Ho Chi Minh—declared independence. For eight years, French and Vietnamese forces battled in the Indochina War.

In 1954, the French were defeated. Vietnam was divided into a communist north—backed by China and the USSR—and an anti-communist south, backed by the United States. Within a few years, communist-led rebels, known as the **Viet Cong,** rose up against the southern government. The **Vietnam War** was about to begin.

The United States entered the war in stages. At first it provided South Vietnam with military aid and assistance, including military advisers. These advisers trained the South Vietnamese army and also took part in combat. By late 1963, some 17,000 U.S. advisers were on the ground in Vietnam.

In 1964, after reports of an attack on a U.S. ship off the North Vietnamese coast, President Lyndon Johnson called for an escalation of U.S. involvement. He argued that the United States had a duty to defend South Vietnam from communist aggression. "If we are driven from the field in Vietnam," Johnson declared, "then no nation can ever have the same confidence in . . . American protection." If Vietnam fell to communism, he said, other Asian nations might also fall. This idea became known as the **domino theory**.

In early 1965, the United States carried out air strikes against targets in North Vietnam. Soon after, it sent its first combat troops into Vietnam. Over the next two years, U.S. forces in the country increased rapidly. By 1969, more than half a million American soldiers were serving in Vietnam.

The United States dedicated vast military resources to the war effort. Yet despite its superior firepower, it could not achieve victory. The U.S. government faced mounting opposition at home and abroad to its war in Vietnam. In contrast, the Viet Cong were committed to fight to their last resources to drive the Americans out of Vietnam. By the early 1970s, the United States had begun to pull its troops out and shift responsibility to the army of South Vietnam.

In 1973, the last American soldiers left Vietnam. Within three years, North Vietnam had conquered the south and united the country. Many southerners fled communist rule. Most made their way to refugee camps in other parts of Southeast Asia, and later to the United States.

Like China, Vietnam eventually adopted reforms and opened up its economy. Communist officials continued to retain a tight grip on the government.

Troubles in Latin America   Latin America also became a battleground in the Cold War. Widespread poverty and sharp divisions among social classes made the region ripe for political upheaval. As in other parts of the world, communists promoted class struggle in Latin America as a means to achieve social justice and diminish economic inequalities. The United States, which had long dominated the hemisphere, remained alert to the growth of communism in the western hemisphere.

The first Cold War incident in Latin America occurred in Guatemala. In 1953, a nationalist president—Jacobo Arbenz Guzmán—began a program of land reform. He took unused land from the American-owned United Fruit Company and gave it to poor peasants. Arbenz was not a communist, but he had communist support. A year later, the United States staged a covert action to oust Arbenz and replace him with a military dictator. The Guatemalan army held power for most of the next three decades.

In Cuba, a revolution led by Fidel Castro overthrew the nation's U.S.-supported dictator, Fulgencio Batista, in 1959. Castro sided with the poor against Cuba's wealthy middle and upper classes. He soon declared his communist sympathies and made Cuba a Soviet ally. The United States responded with efforts to remove Castro from power, including a failed invasion at Cuba's Bay of Pigs in 1961.

Cold War tensions with Cuba reached their height in October 1962, during the Cuban Missile Crisis. Castro had allowed the Soviet Union to install nuclear missiles in Cuba, within striking distance of American cities. The United States placed a naval blockade around the island and demanded that the Soviets remove the missiles. It also considered a possible invasion of Cuba. For two anxious weeks, the world teetered on the brink of nuclear war. Eventually the Soviets backed down and withdrew the missiles, in return for a U.S. promise not to invade Cuba.

In 1959 Fidel Castro successfully overthrew the U.S-backed ruler of Cuba. After he took power, Castro toured the United States. Here Castro takes questions from the press upon his arrival in Washington, D.C., in April 1959. However, Castro soon allied himself with the Soviet Union.

For the next few decades, Cuba remained a source of Cold War frictions. The United States accused Castro of promoting revolution in the Americas. To halt the spread of communism, the United States used covert methods to oppose leftist influence. For example, the United States helped overthrow a democratically elected socialist government of Chile in 1973. A brutal military dictatorship ruled Chile for the next two decades.

A revolution in Nicaragua also aroused American concerns. Leftist rebels, known as the Sandinistas, toppled a U.S.-backed dictatorship in 1979. The Sandinistas' ties to Cuba and aid to rebels in neighboring El Salvador soon sparked conflict with the United States. The United States began funding a rebel army, called the Contras, to fight the Sandinistas in 1981. The Contra war inflicted great damage and undermined Sandinista rule. In 1990, the Sandinistas lost power through elections.

Tensions in the Middle East   Cold War conflict also erupted in the Middle East. Egypt was the site of the first crisis. In the early 1950s, a nationalist leader, Gamal Abdel Nasser, gained power in Egypt. To balance Western influence, Nasser accepted aid from the Soviet Union. Then, in July 1956, he seized the Suez Canal, a key waterway operated by France and Great Britain. In response, France, Britain, and Israel invaded Egypt and retook the canal. The United States, fearing a Soviet intervention, persuaded the allies to withdraw. It then increased its own presence in the Middle East to secure its oil supplies and continue its support of Israel.

Iran was another hot spot. After World War II, Iranian nationalists rose up against the pro-Western polices of the shah, Mohammad Reza Pahlavi (PAH-luh-vee). In 1951, Iran's parliament—led by Prime Minister Mohammed Mossadeq (moh-sah-DEHK)—seized a British oil company. The new government also accepted Soviet aid and forced the shah to flee the country. Fearing that Iran might become a Soviet ally, the United States carried out a **covert action**, a secret operation by the Central Intelligence Agency, or CIA. The action resulted in Mossadeq's arrest and the shah's return to power. Over the next two decades, the shah continued his efforts to modernize Iran. However, he coupled his policies of Westernization with oppressive, authoritarian measures carried out against his people by the secret police. In 1979, he was overthrown and replaced by a strict Islamic regime.

Conflicts in Sub-Saharan Africa   The Cold War also made a deep impact on sub-Saharan Africa. In the more than two decades after World War II, nearly every African nation had gained independence from colonial rule. A number of these countries were caught up in the struggle between the two superpowers.

covert action a secret political, economic, or military operation sponsored by a government and designed to support a foreign policy objective

Congo was the first flashpoint. After gaining independence from Belgium in 1960, Congo desperately needed foreign aid and assistance. Its new prime minister, Patrice Lumumba, was an ardent nationalist. When the United Nations rejected his plea for aid, he turned to the USSR for help. Fearing increased Soviet influence in Africa, the CIA worked with local army officers to overthrow Lumumba and install a new pro-American regime.

The superpowers also got involved in wars in various parts of Africa, including Angola and Ethiopia. In Angola, a civil war in the mid-1970s pitted three rebel armies against each other in a vicious struggle for power. The Soviet Union and Cuba supported one army, while the United States supported another. China also got involved. A cease-fire was only reached in 1989. In Ethiopia, the United States and Soviet Union backed opposing sides in a war with neighboring Somalia. Both countries are located in the Horn of Africa, a region of East Africa with close access to the Middle East. The superpowers' involvement in the war reflected their strategic interest in this region.

During the period from 1945 to 1990, wars around the world killed some 40 million people. Most of those conflicts were related, directly or indirectly, to the Cold War. Other factors, including the legacy of colonialism, also played a crucial role in promoting conflict. But the power struggle between the United States and the USSR exacerbated those wars and made them more deadly.

During the Cold War, the United States and the Soviet Union never went to war directly. However, they competed for allies and resources throughout the world. Their interventions, especially in the countries of the developing world, often helped fuel violent conflict.

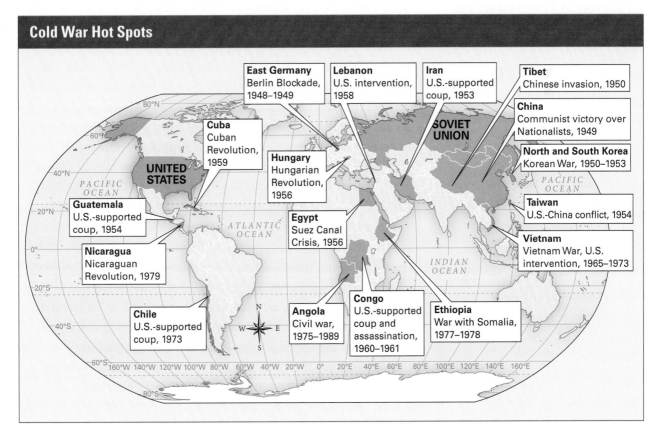

Cold War Hot Spots

26.5 The End of the Cold War

The Cold War also took a toll on the superpowers. The cost of their rivalry, both in financial and human terms, was enormous. At times it seemed that the struggle would go on forever. Eventually, however, Soviet power declined, and the Cold War came to an end.

Challenges to Soviet Power   The Soviet Union dominated Eastern Europe for more than forty years. Subjugation of these countries—known collectively as the Soviet bloc—was critical to Soviet power. At times, however, the people of Eastern Europe tried to escape Soviet domination.

In October 1956, Hungarians mounted a revolt against their government and its Soviet backers. At the time, the USSR had a new leader, Nikita Khrushchev, who had replaced Stalin after his death in 1953. Khrushchev had publicly criticized Stalin's harsh rule and called for a more humane path to communism. But this new approach did not include letting Soviet satellites leave the Soviet sphere of influence. Khrushchev ordered an invasion of Hungary to crush the rebellion. Some 20,000 Hungarians died and a new, Soviet-controlled government was installed. Twelve years later, in 1968, the Warsaw Pact nations invaded Czechoslovakia to crush another reform movement.

Meanwhile, thousands of Eastern Europeans tried to flee to a better life in the West. This migration was most evident in East Germany. By 1961, 2.6 million East Germans had fled by crossing the border between East and West Berlin and then moving on to West Germany. To stop the flow, the Soviet Union built a wall separating the two halves of the city. The Berlin Wall was up to 15 feet high and 100 miles long and included guard towers and minefields. The Berlin Wall was patrolled by soldiers who had orders to kill anyone who tried to cross. Khrushchev admitted that the wall was a "hateful thing," but he believed it was necessary to preserve communism. President Kennedy called the wall a "vivid demonstration of the failures of the communist system."

Easing Cold War Tensions   By the 1970s, Cold War tensions began to ease up. Leaders on both sides embraced the idea of **détente**, a French word that means a relaxation of tensions. Behind this effort to reduce tensions, however, was the continued threat of nuclear war.

Until the late 1960s, the United States had held the edge in the arms race. With its more advanced nuclear arsenal, the United States believed it could force the Soviet Union to back down in any serious dispute. It was even willing to go to the brink of war—a policy known as brinkmanship—to make its point. This policy was based on the notion of **deterrence,** the idea that a country will not risk war if it faces the prospect of certain destruction.

East Germany put up the Berlin Wall in 1961 to stop the flow of people crossing from East to West Berlin. In this image from 1961, a family tries to visit with relatives on the other side of the wall. The Berlin Wall became a symbol of the Cold War's division of Eastern and Western Europe.

détente the easing of Cold War tensions and hostility between East and West during the 1970s

deterrence the policy of building a weapons arsenal so deadly that no other nation will dare attack

By 1969, however, the Soviet Union had caught up in the arms race. Each side was now equally capable of destroying the other. They also realized that their huge military costs were harming their economies. As a result, both nations sought ways to curb the arms race and reduce the risk of nuclear conflict.

Détente began under U.S. President Richard Nixon. With his Soviet counterpart, Leonid Brezhnev, Nixon negotiated an important arms reduction agreement, the Strategic Arms Limitation Treaty (SALT), in 1972. This treaty limited the number of nuclear weapons each side could possess. Nixon also reached out to China, making a historic visit to Beijing in 1972.

By normalizing relations with China, Nixon hoped to reduce tensions in East Asia. But he also hoped to play China and the USSR off against each other. At the time, the two communist powers were locked in a bitter rivalry to lead the communist world. They were willing to improve relations with the United States to further their own strategic interests.

Détente continued through the 1970s. The United States and the USSR expanded trade links and increased cultural and scientific exchanges. However, continued frictions—including arms-control disputes—eventually brought détente to an end. The final blow came with the Soviet invasion of Afghanistan in 1979.

In 1972, President Nixon made a historic visit to China. Here he is touring the Great Wall of China along with First Lady Patricia Nixon. By improving U.S. relations with China, President Nixon hoped to ease tensions in East Asia. Nixon also embraced a policy of détente with the Soviet Union.

The Afghan War   Communists seized power in Afghanistan in 1978. Civil war broke out, and Muslim rebels threatened to topple the government. The Soviet Union sent in troops to occupy the country and prop up the regime. In response, the United States imposed tough sanctions on the Soviet Union, including a boycott of the 1980 Moscow Olympics. It also began supplying arms and aid to the Afghan rebels. The Cold War was back in full force.

Soviet leaders expected a quick victory in Afghanistan. But like the United States in Vietnam, the USSR soon got bogged down. They poured more money and troops into a war they could not win. The Soviet economy suffered, and thousands of Soviet soldiers lost their lives. The Afghan war undermined the power and credibility of the Soviet state. The last Soviet forces left the country in 1989.

The Soviet Decline   Afghanistan was just one of many problems afflicting the USSR by the late 1980s. In fact, the Soviet system itself was in crisis.

The main problem was economic. The state-run Soviet economy could not compete with the private enterprise system of the capitalist West. Soviet citizens had low living standards, and basic goods were in short supply. Although the Soviet people received free public services, such as health care and education, the quality of these services was often poor.

The Soviet leader Mikhail Gorbachev came to power in 1985. He led reforms within the Soviet Union and improved relations with the West. Here Gorbachev (right) poses with Vice President George H.W. Bush and President Ronald Reagan in New York during his 1988 visit to the United States.

Soviet citizens also had less personal freedom than their counterparts in the West. When they saw images of Western life, many Soviet people felt their own lives were lacking. As a result, dissatisfaction spread through Soviet society.

In 1985, however, a new Soviet leader came to power. Mikhail Gorbachev (mik-ah-IL GOR-beh-CHOF) was a dynamic reformer who was determined to change the Soviet system. Gorbachev believed that conflict between communism and capitalism was not inevitable. Like another Soviet reformer, Khrushchev, he argued that East and West could peacefully coexist, rather than pursing an endless struggle for power. He also wanted to promote "communism with a human face" by embracing universal values, such as freedom of thought and expression.

Gorbachev proposed two main avenues of reform to revive the Soviet Union. One was called *perestroika*, or restructuring. Perestroika was intended to make the Soviet economy more efficient and productive. Perestroika reduced central planning and adopted some limited free-market policies in light industry and services. For the first time since the 1920s, people were allowed to open small private businesses, such as cafes and repair shops. Gorbachev's second main reform was *glasnost*, or openness. Glasnost encouraged Soviet citizens to voice new ideas and suggest ways to improve society. The free flow of ideas was seen as essential to economic reform. Gradually, glasnost introduced greater freedom of the press and of public speech to Soviet society.

Gorbachev also sought improved relations with the West, including new arms-control agreements. U.S. President Ronald Reagan was at first skeptical. But he eventually recognized Gorbachev as a genuine reformer. The two pursued a renewed effort at arms control. Relations between the United States and Soviet Union warmed to levels that had not been seen since World War II.

Despite all reforms, however, the Soviet economy continued to decline, and Gorbachev's reputation at home suffered. His reforms, including the Soviet renunciation of interference in East European politics, unleashed a popular push for democratization across the Soviet bloc. In 1989, the countries of Eastern Europe threw off communist rule, one after the other. On November 9th the Berlin Wall came down, a powerful moment for Europe and the world. The following year, Germany was reunited. The Soviet Union itself collapsed in 1991, dissolving into 15 separate states. The Cold War was over.

After the Cold War   As the countries of the former Soviet bloc in Eastern Europe and some of the former Soviet republics moved toward democracy, China remained firmly under the control of its communist party. In 1989, China blocked political change by cracking down on pro-democracy protesters in a massacre at Beijing's Tiananmen Square. Despite continued one-party rule by the communists, China was moving toward a capitalist economy. It adopted economic reforms and built a capitalist-style economy, while maintaining political authoritarianism.

The hard-line communist government of East Germany was forced out in October 1989. On November 9, 1989, the government of East Germany opened the Berlin Wall so people could travel freely to the West. This photo shows young people climbing on top of the wall in celebration.

For more than four decades, the Cold War exerted a major influence on the world. It fueled wars, revolutions, and social unrest. It shaped political and economic systems. It promoted military expansion and the exploration of space.

With the end of the Cold War, the world entered a new, multipolar age. World events no longer hinged on the struggle between two great powers, but on the interlocking interests of many nations.

Summary

The Cold War lasted for more than four decades, from the end of World War II to the collapse of the Soviet Union in 1991. It had a major impact on the course of history.

Cultural Interactions Soviet-American rivalry took the form of a clash between the opposing belief systems of communism and capitalism. This was a political struggle for global domination expressed in terms of ideology. The Soviet Union and the United States sought to advance their beliefs and bring other nations over to their side.

Political Structures Governments during the Cold War tended to embrace the values of either communism or capitalism. Cold War politics influenced wars and revolutions around the world.

Economic Structures The economies of East and West also reflected their ideological foundations. The Western democracies built capitalist economies based on private enterprise. The communist nations of the East created socialist economies based on state and collective ownership.

Social Structures Issues of social class played a key role in the Cold War struggle. In poor parts of the world, such as Latin America, class divisions and economic inequality helped fuel social unrest and revolution.

Human-Environment Interaction The Cold War spurred migration from zones of conflict and political repression, such as Vietnam and Eastern Europe. It also promoted the development of advanced technology in many fields, including weapons systems and space travel.

LIFE

PANAMA CITY:
AT CANAL ZONE BORDER
RIOTERS HOIST FLAG
ABOVE A FLAMING CAR

JANUARY 24 · 1964 · 25¢

The Cold War and the Third World

How did the Cold War affect Third World nations?

27.1 Introduction

On January 9, 1964, a riot erupted in the Panama Canal Zone, a U.S.-controlled territory in the heart of Panama. The trouble began when Panamanian students tried to raise Panama's national flag at an American high school. American residents objected and fighting broke out. The riots continued over the next three days as thousands of Panamanians joined in. More than 20 people died in the unrest.

The riots in the Canal Zone reflected longstanding resentment of the U.S. presence in Panama. The United States had controlled the Canal Zone since 1903. A treaty signed that year gave the United States rights to the Panama Canal and the land around it "in perpetuity" (forever). Since then, the United States had viewed the canal as essential to international trade and American security.

President Lyndon Johnson blamed the riots on communist Cuba. He claimed that Cuba was "sending guns, money, and agents into Panama" to encourage revolution. For the people of Panama and the rest of Latin America, however, the riots were an expression of nationalism. They saw the Canal Zone as a symbol of American imperialism.

The riots did have one positive effect, though. The United States began negotiations to hand the canal over to Panama. It took many years, but in 1977 the United States and Panama finally signed the Panama Canal Treaties. On December 31, 1999, Panama gained full control over the canal.

The story of the Panama Canal riots is one example of the legacy of imperialism, which took on new life during the Cold War. In this lesson, you will learn more about that legacy and how it affected nations and people around the world.

Themes

Cultural Interaction A clash of ideas and beliefs occurred during the Cold War. Nations struggled with the effects of imperialism and colonial rule.

Political Structures Wars and revolutions upset old political structures. Many, but not all, were replaced by democratic governments.

Economic Structures Poor countries faced tough economic challenges. Aid from rich nations and international agencies influenced their choices.

Social Structures Social classes in poor nations suffered from deep economic inequality. Class divisions sometimes gave rise to social unrest.

Human-Environment Interaction Rich nations developed new means to obtain natural resources. Wars damaged the environment in many regions.

The unrest that broke out in Panama in 1964 was featured on the cover of the American magazine *Life*.

In the late 1960s, women in northern India were still using ancient farming techniques. Third World nations, such as India, were in less advanced stages of economic development than the industrialized West and Soviet Union.

developed country a wealthy nation with substantial industrialization

Third World the poor, less-developed nations of the world, which lay outside the two great blocs of East and West

developing country a poor nation with little or no industrialization

covert action a military operation that is carried out secretly and often outside of official channels

27.2 Challenges for Poor Nations

In the decades after World War II, many nations in Africa and Asia gained independence from European colonial rule. These new nations faced many challenges as they tried to overcome the legacy of imperialism. Their futures were affected by the Cold War, as competing superpowers sought to extend their power and influence throughout the world.

Three Worlds During the Cold War, the two sides in the superpower struggle were sometimes referred to as separate "worlds." The capitalist nations of the West were known as the First World, while the communist countries of Eastern Europe were the Second World. Both sets of countries had advanced industrial economies and great economic and political power. In economic terms, they were considered **developed countries**.

Most countries, however, fell into another category, called the **Third World**. Because these countries were in less advanced stages of economic development, they were known as **developing countries**. It was among the developing countries of the Third World that most Cold War conflicts took place.

The Third World Dilemma Many Third World nations were caught in the middle of the superpower struggle. Some had clear ties to one side, but did not fully belong to either camp. Other countries had less defined loyalties.

Many Third World countries had only recently shaken off colonial rule. Others—such as those in Latin America—had been independent for longer but were still struggling. These nations faced many problems. Most suffered from conditions of extreme poverty and social inequality. Often, a small minority of citizens held most of the wealth and power. By controlling the reins of government, this upper class was able to stifle reforms that might help the poor and benefit the nation as a whole.

In the 1950s and 1960s, however, a number of nationalist leaders emerged in the Third World. These leaders wanted to build stronger, more developed countries. They also wanted to reduce the influence of foreign powers over their affairs. At the same time, they also needed aid and assistance from wealthier nations.

If a country accepted aid from one of the superpowers, though, it risked falling under that superpower's control. It also might prompt a hostile reaction from the other side. The country could become the target of **covert actions** or other measures designed to undermine the government and remove its leader. In this way, Third World nations were often squeezed between East and West and became a battleground in the superpower conflict.

The Nonaligned Nations   A number of Third World leaders sought to distance their countries from the Cold War struggle. They tried to follow a separate path—not aligned with either East or West—that would allow them to grow and develop on their own terms. This group of countries became known as the **nonaligned nations**.

One of the main leaders of the nonaligned movement was Jawaharlal Nehru, the prime minister of India. Nehru had helped lead his country to independence from Great Britain in 1947. Now he wanted to ensure India's independence from both superpowers. Along with other nonaligned leaders—such as President Gamal Abdel Nasser of Egypt and President Sukarno of Indonesia—Nehru convened a conference at Bandung, Indonesia, in 1955. There, 29 Asian and African states condemned colonialism and asserted their freedom from restrictive Cold War alliances. In a speech, Nehru declared:

> *"If all the world were to be divided up between these two big blocs, what would be the result? The inevitable result would be war. Therefore every step that takes place in reducing that area in the world that may be called the* unaligned area *is a dangerous step."*
> —Jawaharlal Nehru, speech at the Bandung Conference, 1955

Prime Minister Jawaharlal Nehru (left) of India and President Nasser of Egypt (right) were both leaders of the nonaligned movement. They were nationalist leaders who refused to ally themselves with either side in the Cold War.

The nonaligned movement enjoyed some success. More than 110 countries eventually joined the movement, trying to chart a middle course between East and West. By remaining neutral, some nonaligned countries were able to get economic and political support from both sides. However, the movement remained weak, in part because member states quarreled with each other and failed to build a unified policy. It also faltered because the superpowers continued to exert **hegemony**—a dominating influence—over poor nations.

New Economic Patterns   The superpowers often exercised their hegemony through economic means. The United States and USSR sought to influence countries by offering foreign aid or other forms of economic assistance, but that aid often came with strings attached.

The superpowers put pressure on developing countries to adopt either socialist or capitalist economic policies. The Soviets believed that the spread of socialism would pull countries into the Soviet orbit and validate their economic model. The United States assumed that the spread of capitalism would promote U.S. influence and benefit the U.S. economy.

nonaligned nations independent Third World countries that tried to remain neutral in the Cold War struggle between East and West

hegemony a dominating influence of one country or group over another

Industries in Third World nations were often developed by foreign multinational corporations, who were able to extract huge profits. For example, the rich copper mines in the Democratic Republic of the Congo were owned and operated by a Canadian corporation. Here, a Congolese man works in a copper plant in 1971.

multinational corporation
a large company based in one country but with operations in other parts of the world

Choosing between these two economic systems was not easy for developing countries. Many hesitated to join the West because it was associated with colonial rule. In contrast, socialism held appeal because it claimed to be anti-imperialist and dedicated to social and economic equality. Nationalist leaders were also impressed with the USSR's rapid economic development. Nevertheless, poor nations did not want to lose the economic benefits the West had to offer.

Being in the capitalist bloc included access to loans from two powerful financial institutions, the World Bank and the International Monetary Fund (IMF). These institutions were created after World War II to help stabilize national economies and the world financial system. Their loans helped Europe recover from the war, although the Marshall Plan proved far more effective in that regard. In the decades that followed, the World Bank and IMF provided other nations with loans. However, in most cases the World Bank and IMF would only help capitalist nations. As such, they offered an incentive to Third World countries to join the Western world.

The superpowers also sought access to the natural resources of the developing world. Previously, colonial powers had simply taken minerals, crops, and other raw materials from their colonies as they wished. Now, in the post-colonial era, they had to find new ways to obtain those products. Both East and West offered economic rewards, such as aid or special trade deals, in return for the right to extract Third World resources.

Western access mainly occurred through large companies known as **multinational corporations**. These companies signed contracts with foreign states to make investments and do business within their territory. These contracts often benefited the companies more than the countries, however. For example, a multinational might make huge profits mining diamonds in Africa, but pay only a small fraction of those profits to the host nation.

Nevertheless, developing countries found foreign companies hard to resist because they lacked the capital, technology, or know-how to extract the resources on their own. Working with multinationals at least offered the prospect of increased trade and income. It also brought wealth to some portions of society, usually the upper classes.

27.3 Conflict in Latin America

In the decades after World War II, Latin American countries sought to join the ranks of developed nations. Some, like Brazil and Argentina, were relatively advanced, but most had social and economic problems typical of the Third World. Most countries also remained under the influence of foreign powers, particularly the United States. Latin American nationalists wanted to remove these restraints and help their countries develop. During the Cold War, these circumstances gave rise to political conflict throughout the Americas. Three notable cases involved Guatemala, Cuba, and Chile.

Reform and Repression in Guatemala In 1950, Guatemala elected a new, nationalist president, Jacobo Arbenz Guzmán. Guatemala had a long history of authoritarian rule under military strongmen. The majority of its people were Mayan Indians who suffered from extreme poverty. Arbenz set out to tackle these problems through a series of reforms.

A key change under Arbenz was land reform. Most Guatemalans were peasant farmers who owned little or no land. Arbenz took unused land from large landowners and distributed it to poor peasants. But he soon ran into trouble. Much of this land belonged to the United Fruit Company, a U.S.-based multinational that grew and exported bananas. Both United Fruit and the U.S. government protested the land takeover.

Although Arbenz was not a communist, U.S. officials accused him of being "soft" on communism. They claimed that his policies would allow the Soviets to gain a foothold in Central America. When Arbenz refused to reverse course, the United States launched a covert action to remove him from power. In 1954, it organized and funded a rebel army of Guatemalan exiles, which trained on United Fruit Company lands in neighboring Honduras. The rebel force marched on the capital and overthrew the government in a **coup d'etat** as two U.S. fighter jets provided air cover to the rebels. A military regime took over and established close ties with the United States.

The Guatemalan army remained in control of the country for most of the next three decades. During that time, Guatemala was polarized between the political extremes of the right and left.

coup d'etat the sudden overthrow of a government by violent force; from a French term meaning "blow to the state"

In the 1960s, a civil war broke out between leftist guerillas and the government. The war went on for years, costing the lives of some 200,000 people. Most of the victims were Mayan Indians killed by the army. Up to a million people fled their homes and became political refugees. Civilian rule was finally restored in 1985, and peace accords were signed in 1996. However, Guatemala today remains a fragile state.

The Cuban Revolution   Cuban nationalists also wanted to reform their country. Cuba had gained independence from Spain in 1898 after the Spanish-American War. After the war, however, the island remained under United States control. Cuba became a U.S. **protectorate**.

By the 1950s, American companies dominated the Cuban economy. They bought land and made large investments in the sugar industry. Sugar exports made Cuba one of the richest countries in Latin America, but this wealth was poorly distributed. A small, privileged class occupied the top of the social pyramid, with a sizable middle class below them. Most Cubans lived in poverty, however, and enjoyed few social or economic benefits.

As long as Cuba's leaders protected American interests, they could count on U.S. support. One leader, Fulgencio Batista, dominated Cuban politics for 25 years. Near the end of his reign in the 1950s Batista ruled as a dictator. His corrupt and brutal rule aroused strong opposition among Cuban nationalists and radicals.

One of these activists, a young lawyer named Fidel Castro, formed a small guerrilla army to overthrow Batista. The rebel forces launched hit-and-run attacks from the rugged mountains of eastern Cuba. Gradually, they gained popular support. Against all odds, Castro and his army forced Batista to flee the country. In January 1959, they entered Havana in triumph.

protectorate a nation protected and controlled by a stronger nation

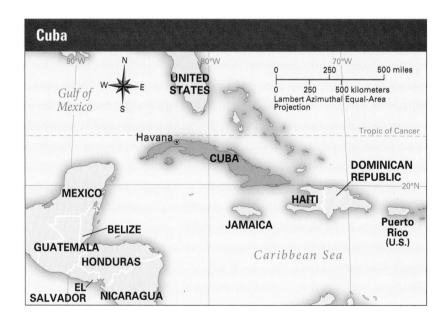

Soon after Fidel Castro took power in 1959, he allied himself with the Soviet Union. This 1960 photograph shows Castro (the bearded man in the center) and Soviet Premier Nikita Khrushchev (the bald man, also center) making their way through a crowd. Castro's relationship with the Soviets was a central reason why the United States attempted to overthrow the Castro regime.

The rebels had won, but the Cuban Revolution had just begun. Castro began to implement radical reforms, including land reform. He also asserted Cuba's independence from the United States by nationalizing American companies. This meant that the Cuban government took ownership of the companies' assets. The United States retaliated by imposing a trade **embargo** on Cuba.

Cuba then turned to the Soviet Union. Castro forged close ties with the Soviets and began to build a communist state. He established public health and education programs and raised the standard of living for most Cubans. He erased class distinctions in Cuban society, but he also restricted personal freedoms and jailed or executed his opponents. As a result, many Cubans fled the island for other parts of the Americas, especially the United States.

The United States responded by trying to overthrow the Castro regime. The CIA carried out various covert actions, including plots to assassinate Castro. In 1961, it tried to repeat the events in Guatemala seven years earlier, organizing a rebel army of Cuban exiles to invade Cuba at the Bay of Pigs. This invasion failed miserably, and Castro emerged stronger than ever.

Over the years, Cuba remained a major flashpoint in the Cold War. During the Cuban Missile Crisis of 1962, the placement of Soviet missiles in Cuba brought the world to the brink of nuclear war. Cuba also tried to spread leftist revolution in Latin America and Africa, which further aggravated tensions with the United States.

Throughout this period, Cuba relied on Soviet economic aid. That aid ended with the collapse of the Soviet Union in 1991. Since then, Cuba has struggled to keep its economy afloat. Meanwhile, the U.S. trade embargo on Cuba continues. Relations between the United States and Cuba remain difficult.

> **embargo** a government order that restricts or prohibits trade with another nation

Chile's Socialist Experiment   Conflict also arose in Chile during the Cold War. Chile had a history of democratic government that made it a model for much of Latin America. It also had a long history of foreign investment. For example, three U.S. companies controlled Chile's copper industry, the nation's largest source of income.

In 1970, Chileans elected a socialist president, Salvador Allende (ah-YEN-day). Allende promised to follow a "democratic road to socialism." With the support of Chile's congress, he nationalized the copper industry. He also took over foreign firms in other key industries.

These actions alarmed powerful people in both Chile and the United States. They feared that Chile was heading toward communism. U.S. President Richard Nixon had already tried to prevent Allende's election. Now Nixon ordered a covert operation to bring down the government. One strategy was to undermine the Chilean economy by cutting off aid and blocking loans from the World Bank and other financial institutions. As Nixon put it, the aim was to "squeeze" the economy until it "screamed."

By 1973, a combination of outside pressure and internal factors led to an economic crisis in Chile. As the economy sank, Chilean society became increasingly polarized. In September, the military launched a coup d'etat. Tanks rolled through the streets and fighter jets attacked the presidential palace. Allende died during the attack and his government was overthrown.

A military dictatorship under General Augusto Pinochet (pin-oh-CHAY) ruled Chile for the next 17 years. It brutally repressed its opposition, torturing and killing thousands of people. It also imposed drastic free market policies, an economic "shock treatment" that caused great hardship for most Chileans. Eventually the economy rebounded, however, and the nation prospered. In 1990 Pinochet stepped down, and democracy returned to Chile.

A crowd of marchers in Santiago, Chile, in support of Salvador Allende for president. Allende was a socialist, and his election in 1970 caused many in Chile and the United States to fear that Chile would become a communist state.

27.4 Wars in Indochina

Southeast Asia was an even deadlier battleground during the Cold War. In the former French colony of Indochina—Vietnam, Cambodia, and Laos—several million people died in wars and other violent conflicts. The Cold War was a major factor in these conflicts, but their roots lay in a longer history of imperialism and colonial rule.

The Vietnam War   The first French people came to Vietnam in 1612 as Catholic missionaries. Two centuries later, the French invaded the country. It took nearly three decades for France to conquer all of Vietnam, along with Cambodia and Laos. In 1887, France established the colony of French Indochina.

France ruled French Indochina in typical imperial fashion. It exploited Vietnam's economic resources, including rice, coal, minerals, and rubber. It also used the colony as a market for French goods. It made little effort to develop local industries or a skilled middle class. All the wealth of the colony went to the French and a few privileged Vietnamese. Most of the people did not benefit from colonial rule.

Nationalist revolts against the French began during the early days of the colony. By the 1930s, one of the leading groups in this struggle was the Vietnamese Communist Party, founded by Ho Chi Minh. During World War II, when Vietnam was occupied by Japan, Ho formed a broad nationalist alliance called the Viet Minh (vee-EHT MIN). After the war, the Viet Minh seized power in the northern part of the country, while the French retained control in the south. Vietnam was divided between a communist-led north and a noncommunist south.

By 1947, the two Vietnams were at war. The Viet Minh called their fight a "war of national liberation." For the French and their U.S. allies, however, it was a war against communism. The Indochina War went on until 1954, when France suffered a crucial defeat at the Battle of Dien Bien Phu and sued for peace. The peace agreement, known as the Geneva Accords, left Vietnam divided between the communist north and the non-communist south. Elections to unify the country were scheduled for 1956 but were canceled by South Vietnam because of the likelihood that the popular communist leader Ho Chi Minh would win the elections if held.

The Geneva Accords divided Vietnam into the communist north and the non-communist south. When the Viet Cong threatened South Vietnam, the United States intervened to keep South Vietnam from falling to communism. Fighting in the Vietnam War eventually also spilled over into the neighboring countries of Cambodia and Laos.

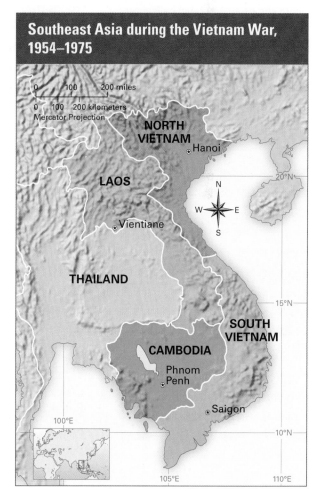

Southeast Asia during the Vietnam War, 1954–1975

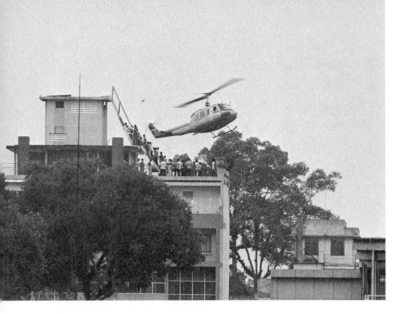

As the North Vietnamese army advanced toward the southern capital of Saigon in 1975, people feared violence from the communists. They also feared life under a communist regime, and many tried to flee. This photo shows an American helicopter picking up Vietnamese evacuees on a Saigon rooftop.

Meanwhile, the U.S.-backed government of South Vietnam became a dictatorship under Ngo Dinh Diem (NOH DIN dee-YEM). As local opposition grew, a communist rebel force—the Viet Cong—launched a guerrilla war against the government in the south. The United States responded by sending more military aid to the government of South Vietnam. By 1965, the United States was deeply involved in the Vietnam War. American troops were engaged in ground combat and U.S. planes were launching air strikes on North Vietnam.

The United States was determined to prevent South Vietnam from falling to communism. But the North Vietnamese and Viet Cong were even more determined to defend and unite their homeland. In the end, it was a war the United States could not win. Facing strong antiwar sentiments at home, the Nixon administration withdrew the last U.S. troops from Vietnam in 1973. In 1975, the north conquered the south and Vietnam was united under a communist government.

The Vietnam War had cost the lives of 58,000 American soldiers. It was much more destructive for Vietnam, however, killing as many as 2 million Vietnamese. In the years that followed, Vietnam would struggle to recover from the war.

Conflicts in Cambodia and Laos   The Vietnam War was not confined to Vietnam. It also spilled over into Cambodia and Laos, causing great death and destruction.

Cambodia gained independence from France in 1953. During the Vietnam War, it tried to remain neutral to avoid being drawn into the conflict. However, both the United States and North Vietnam violated Cambodian sovereignty by sending troops into the country. North Vietnam also gave aid and assistance to Cambodia's communist rebels, the **Khmer Rouge** (KMAYR ROOZH). In the early 1970s, the United States launched massive bombing raids on Cambodia to cripple the Khmer Rouge. These raids devastated the country, but they did not prevent a communist takeover.

In April 1975 the Khmer Rouge seized power. Their leader, Pol Pot, promptly took radical steps to transform Cambodian society. He forced people into labor camps and tried to purge all capitalist elements from the country. In the process, nearly two million people died, a fifth of the nation's population. Around a quarter million were murdered. The rest died of starvation and illness. It was one of the worst **genocides** in human history.

Khmer Rouge the communist movement in Cambodia that took power in 1975

genocide actions taken with the intent to destroy an ethnic, racial, or religious group

By this time, the Khmer Rouge and communist Vietnam had become enemies. In 1979 Vietnam overthrew Pol Pot and installed a new regime. Peace returned and Cambodia gradually recovered.

Laos also experienced great upheaval during this period. In the 1960s and 1970s, communist guerrillas—called the Pathet Lao—fought the Laotian government. Both North Vietnam and the United States intervened in this struggle, sending weapons and troops across the border. The United States also conducted air strikes in Laos and funded a "secret army" to fight the Laotian communists. When the United States pulled out of Vietnam, it also left Laos. In 1975 the Pathet Lao took over and formed a new government.

The Aftermath of War The wars in Indochina all resulted in communist victories. The domino effect—the idea that one country after another might fall to communism—had taken place but mostly as a reaction to a history of imperialism and colonial rule.

In the aftermath of war, each country worked to rebuild its national life. The challenges were enormous. The wars had shattered economies and societies, decimated populations and damaged the environment. U.S. bombing raids, for example, had destroyed forests and farmlands and left toxic chemicals in the soil and water. Unexploded bombs and land mines continued to kill or maim innocent civilians throughout the region.

Nevertheless, the countries of Indochina have all made progress in the past four decades. Cambodia has held democratic elections, while Vietnam and Laos—though still communist—allow some democratic rights. All three countries have adopted market reforms and opened up their economies to the world. They are still among the world's poorest countries and face many pressing problems, including widespread corruption. But they are actively seeking a path to economic development.

On display at a memorial are some of the remains of the nearly two million people who died under the Khmer Rouge regime. The Khmer Rouge was a Cambodian communist rebel force that took power in 1975 and carried out an appalling genocide on its own people.

27.5 Upheaval in Africa

Between 1955 and 1975, 42 African countries gained their independence. These countries carried the legacy of decades of European imperialism and colonial rule.

Africa's Colonial Legacy   When European powers carved up Africa in the late 1800s, they paid little attention to the traditional homelands of African peoples. Europeans drew borders that cut across these homelands, dividing ethnic and cultural groups and putting different groups in the same territory. After independence, most of these borders remained. New nations lacked cultural and social unity. In some cases, ethnic groups within countries fought for power.

The new African nations also faced severe economic problems. European powers had exploited the colonies for their resources and labor. They built mines and plantations to produce raw materials for export. They rarely established industries or **infrastructure** that would benefit the nations themselves.

In general, European powers failed to prepare Africans for independence. In most countries, education levels remained low. There was a shortage of trained professionals—managers, doctors, engineers, and political leaders—to build the new nations.

This colonial legacy made it hard for African nations to advance. Their economies were weak and their governments unstable. They were prone to social and political upheaval. In many cases, they relied on dictators to maintain order. Many also turned to the superpowers for political and economic support.

infrastructure the facilities or equipment required for a community or nation to function, including roads, power systems, and transportation

Nigeria's Search for Stability   Nigeria illustrates some of the challenges that faced African nations. A former British colony, Nigeria gained independence in 1960. At first its prospects looked good. It was one of the largest and richest countries in Africa. But ethnic problems soon divided the nation.

Nigeria is home to three main ethnic groups. The Hausa-Fulani, a mostly Muslim group, live in the north. The Yoruba, half of whom are Christian and half of whom are Muslim, live in the southwest. The Igbo, a mostly Catholic group, live in the southeast. After independence, these groups shared power in a federal system of government. Each group tried to gain advantage, fearing domination by the others.

The political system soon broke down. In 1966, a group of army officers—mostly Igbos—overthrew the government. A few months later, Hausa officers staged a counter-coup and toppled the new regime. Rioting erupted against the Igbos, and thousands were killed.

In 1967, the Igbo region seceded from Nigeria. It called itself the Republic of Biafra. Civil war broke out and more than a million people died, mostly from starvation. In 1970, Biafra was defeated and forcibly reincorporated back into Nigeria.

After the war, the army kept control over Nigeria for most of the next three decades. It claimed that military rule was necessary to ensure peace and prosperity. Although the army promised to return power to civilians, it repeatedly went back on that pledge.

In 1999, however, democracy was finally restored. By this time, Nigeria had become one of the world's leading oil producers. The government hoped to use oil income to develop the country, but the results were mixed. Oil revenues brought great wealth to Nigeria, but corruption also increased. Meanwhile, other sectors of the economy—including farming and manufacturing—suffered from neglect. Most Nigerians remained desperately poor. Two-thirds of the population lived on less than $1 a day. Oil also led to conflict, as residents of the Niger delta—the country's main oil region—demanded a fair share of the oil wealth. Armed groups kidnapped oil workers and attacked oil facilities.

Ethnic and religious conflicts also increased under democratic rule. Violence erupted between Muslims and Christians, especially in northern Nigeria. Thousands of people died in these riots.

Nevertheless, Nigeria has managed to remain democratic. Several free elections have taken place since the end of military rule. This record of democracy and the rule of law offers hope that Nigeria can maintain stability and move beyond the troubles of the past.

Ethnic tensions in Nigeria erupted into civil war in 1967, when the homeland of the Igbo ethnic group seceded to form the Republic of Biafra. In this photo, soldiers for the Biafran national army prepare to resist an attack by Nigerian federal troops.

South Africa's Struggle for Democracy   South Africa also faced great obstacles in its path to democratic rule. It won independence in 1910, long before most African nations. However, the end of colonial rule did not bring freedom for most South Africans.

After independence, South Africa remained under the control of its white minority. The state passed laws to deny basic rights to blacks, Asians, and mixed-race peoples, who made up four-fifths of the population. This policy continued under the Afrikaners, who gained power in 1948. The Afrikaners are people descended from the first Dutch colonists in South Africa.

apartheid the system of racial separation in South Africa, designed to create a fully segregated society

The Afrikaner government instituted a policy of **apartheid,** or racial separation. It imposed segregation throughout society, in schools, offices, parks, restaurants, and theaters. It also set up a system of ten African homelands, separate regions of the country where blacks were meant to live. Under apartheid, everyone was classified by race. Only whites were allowed to vote in national elections or hold public office at the national level. The police could arrest and detain people without trial, including anyone who opposed the government.

Many South Africans, both black and white, resisted apartheid. The strongest opposition came from the African National Congress (ANC), a group formed in 1912 to promote black rights. The ANC organized marches, strikes, and other protests. The government cracked down on these actions, killing many protesters and putting others in jail. One of those jailed was the ANC leader Nelson Mandela, who was imprisoned in 1964.

South Africa's repressive policies sparked criticism around the world. The United Nations condemned apartheid and placed an arms embargo on the country. Various countries also imposed economic sanctions on South Africa, restricting trade and investment. The United States—which relied on South Africa as a trade partner and Cold War ally—was slow to join the anti-apartheid movement. Eventually, it too called for change.

Under mounting pressure, South Africa finally agreed to reforms. The process began slowly but picked up speed under a new president, F.W. de Klerk. In 1990, de Klerk released Nelson Mandela from prison. Over the next two years, the government struck down most apartheid laws. It also announced that free, democratic elections would be held in 1994.

The policy of apartheid imposed strict racial segregation throughout South African society.

The ANC won the elections, and Nelson Mandela became the country's first black president. He promised to promote national unity and build a democratic state, with equal rights and freedom for all. In 1996, the South African parliament passed a new constitution that enshrined those principles in law.

Mandela was followed in office by two more democratically elected presidents. These leaders tried to address South Africa's many economic and social problems. They launched programs in education, housing, and other public services. Nevertheless, poverty remained a serious problem. Most South Africans struggled to meet their basic needs. Other concerns included high crime rates and the spread of the deadly disease HIV/AIDS. Despite these challenges, however, South Africa's successful transition to democracy gave hope for the future.

Black South Africans lined up to vote in 1994, the first national election in which the black majority was allowed to participate. The people elected Nelson Mandela, who became the first black president of South Africa.

Summary

In this lesson, you read about the impact of imperialism and the Cold War on developing nations. Countries emerging from colonial rule faced tough challenges during the Cold War era.

Cultural Interaction Former colonies tried to escape the legacy of imperialism. They hoped to follow their own path to national development. But they were often forced to choose between the opposing ideologies of capitalism and socialism. Many got caught up in the superpower conflict.

Political Structures Many developing countries formed democratic governments. But others turned to authoritarian rule. Political structures in some countries were affected by wars and other conflicts.

Economic Structures Most former colonies faced severe economic problems. They often turned to the superpowers for economic aid and support, but that aid often influenced the economic policies those nations could follow.

Social Structures Social classes in developing countries were marked by great economic inequality. Divisions between social classes often gave rise to unrest. Some countries, such as Cuba, tried to erase social classes entirely.

Human-Environment Interaction Developed countries often turned to former colonies for natural resources. Wars and other conflicts did great damage to natural environments. They also prompted mass migrations of people fleeing violence and oppression.

Movements Toward Independence and Democracy

How have emerging nations fared in their quest for political stability, economic growth, and democracy?

28.1 Introduction

South Korea had a tough start as a nation. Two years after gaining independence from the Japan in 1948, it went to war with its neighbor North Korea. During the ensuing war, at least 2.5 million lives were lost, but no resolution to the essential conflict was ever reached. Although an armistice was brokered in 1953, tensions with the north remained high.

In the years that followed, South Korea struggled to gain political stability. In 1961, the military seized power in a coup d'etat. The military ruled for the next three decades, restricting political freedoms and cracking down on its opponents. But the military also developed the economy, turning South Korea into an industrial powerhouse. During this period, the nation's economy grew at an average of nearly 9 percent a year. South Korea became one of the Asian Tigers, a group of four rapidly growing economies that included Singapore, Taiwan, and Hong Kong.

In 1992, democratic elections returned South Korea to civilian rule. The new leaders continued to emphasize economic growth. However, the economy stumbled during a financial crisis in the late 1990s. But it rebounded and has continued to prosper.

South Korea now has one of the largest economies in the world. Its population is highly educated and enjoys good social and economic conditions. The country has developed and modernized while retaining its cultural traditions. It has also remained democratic. Overall, South Korea is one of the great success stories among the world's postcolonial states.

Few emerging nations have fared as well as South Korea, however. This lesson presents case studies of five countries that have sought political stability and economic development in the past half-century. Most have had mixed success in their efforts to achieve autonomy, democracy, and economic growth.

Themes

Cultural Interaction Ethnic and cultural differences have made it difficult for many developing countries to unite and achieve stability.

Political Structures Emerging nations have faced challenges in forming democratic governments. Some have resorted to authoritarian rule.

Economic Structures Some countries have managed to build strong economies, while others have struggled to develop.

◀ Tradition and modernity coexist in Seoul, the capital city of South Korea.

28.2 Indonesia: A Nation of Islands

Indonesia is a large country made up of thousands of islands. It has the fourth largest population in the world. Today it is a relatively stable and prosperous nation. But it has experienced great upheaval in its path to national development.

Independence Under Sukarno In the 19th and early 20th centuries, what is now Indonesia was a Dutch colony known as the Dutch East Indies. Indonesia declared independence from the Netherlands in 1945, at the end of World War II. But the Dutch fought to hold on to their colony. They sent troops to defeat a revolution led by the nationalist leader Sukarno. In 1949, after a series of bloody battles, the Dutch finally agreed to leave.

Indonesia established a democratic government, with Sukarno as president. The new government faced many challenges. Indonesia is an **archipelago** of more than 18,000 islands. Its population includes many different ethnic and religious groups. As a result, the country was hard to unify. Rebellions broke out on several islands. The government was also unstable. Many different political parties vied for power.

By the late 1950s, Indonesia was in crisis. At that point, Sukarno moved to assert control. He declared **martial law** to quell unrest. He then established a system he called "guided democracy," which gave more power to the president and weakened the national parliament. In effect, Sukarno became a dictator. He built large monuments to glorify the state and restore national pride. He also became a leader of the nonaligned movement during the Cold War, and refused to declare allegiance to either the Eastern or Western power blocs. But he was a vocal critic of Western imperialism.

To stay in power, Sukarno relied on support from two key forces in the country: the military and the Communist Party. Sukarno's reliance on the communists raised fears among the military, though, and eventually led to his downfall.

On October 1, 1965, a group of communists kidnapped and killed six army generals. Chaos spread across Indonesia, as the military and its right-wing supporters waged a brutal crackdown on the left. An estimated half a million people died in violent attacks over the next year. Meanwhile, the military arrested Sukarno and took control of the government. In 1968, a top general, General Suharto, became president.

archipelago a group of islands

martial law temporary control of the civilian population by the police or military, often invoked during times of civil unrest

Sukarno led Indonesia to independence from the Netherlands and became the nation's first president. Later, he established dictatorial control over the country. Here Sukarno is shown visiting the United States in 1956.

Indonesia, 1949–1998

THAILAND

South China Sea

Aceh

MALAYSIA

PHILIPPINES

BRUNEI

Celebes Sea

PACIFIC OCEAN

Location of separatist violence

Sumatra

Kalimantan

Sulawesi

Papua

Equator — 0°

PAPUA NEW GUINEA

Java Sea

Maluku

N W E S

Jakarta

Java

Bali

East Timor

West Timor

10°S

0   500   1,000 miles
0   500   1,000 kilometers
Lambert Azimuthal Equal-Area Projection

INDIAN OCEAN

100°E

110°E

120°E

130°E AUSTRALIA

Suharto's New Order   Suharto promised to bring about a "New Order" in Indonesian politics. He reversed many of Sukarno's policies. He banned the Communist Party and allied Indonesia with the West. He also set out to develop the country's economy. He encouraged foreign investment to help expand trade and industry.

For the next thirty years, Suharto directed an authoritarian regime. This regime was not a typical military dictatorship. It allowed some political rights, including the right to vote in controlled elections. Most freedoms were restricted, however, including any actions that could threaten the military's hold on power. **Human rights** abuses were widespread. This was especially true in East Timor, a region that sought independence.

Suharto also allowed rampant corruption. He rewarded fellow officers, family members, and political allies with lucrative business deals. Bribery was widespread. Critics called this scheme "crony capitalism." (The term *crony* referred to the unfair practice of cronyism, in which a powerful person or group favors personal allies without regard to their qualifications.) At the same time, the country's economy also grew. Like South Korea, Indonesia became an economic success story.

In 1997, however, a financial crisis swept across East Asia. Indonesia's economy suffered, causing widespread civil unrest. In 1998, Suharto resigned and a civilian president took over.

Because the nation of Indonesia is made of thousands of islands, with many different ethnic and religious groups, it has proven hard to unify. Between 1949 and 1998, Indonesia was ruled by two authoritarian leaders. Despite authoritarian rule, separatist conflicts broke out throughout the Indonesian archipelago.

human rights rights that are regarded as belonging to all people, such as the right to life, liberty, and equality before the law, as well as freedom of religion, expression, and assembly

The Democratic Era   Since then, Indonesia has worked to strengthen its democracy. It has held democratic elections for local and national office, including the first direct presidential election in 2004. Voter turnout for these elections has been high.

Indonesia's leaders still face many problems, however. Separatist movements have continued to test the nation's unity. In 2002, East Timor won its independence after decades of violent conflict. The region of Aceh (AH-chay), on the island of Sumatra, also gained substantial political autonomy after years of struggle.

Natural disasters have also plagued Indonesia. In 2004, an earthquake off Sumatra caused a great tsunami, or tidal wave, that destroyed coastal areas of Aceh and killed more than 130,000 people. Another major earthquake struck in 2006, killing thousands more. In 2010, a volcanic eruption on Sumatra forced a mass evacuation.

Islamic extremism is another troubling issue. Indonesia has the world's largest Muslim population. For the most part, Indonesians are moderate Muslims. But the rise of terrorism by Islamic radicals has also affected Indonesia. In 2002, a bombing in a resort town on the island of Bali killed 202 people. Other terrorist attacks followed. The government has sought to identify and prosecute extremist groups. It has also sought to bolster Indonesia's tradition of religious moderation. But political violence remains a major concern.

Coastal areas of the Aceh region were destroyed by a devastating tsunami that struck on December 26, 2005. More than 130,000 people were killed.

28.3 Pakistan: Dictatorship and Democracy

Like Indonesia, Pakistan is an important **developing country** with a large Muslim population. It occupies a strategic location in South Asia, between India and Afghanistan. Since independence, it has tried to build a stable democracy. But it has spent much of its history under military rule.

After Partition   Pakistan won its independence in 1947, when the British left India. Under the partition agreement, Pakistan and India, which had both been part of British India, became separate nations. One of the main reasons for partition was the fact India's population was largely Hindu and Pakistan's population was largely Muslim. The founders of Pakistan wanted to establish an independent Muslim state. But partition caused many problems. Millions of Muslims living in India fled for Pakistan, while an equal number of Hindus and Sikhs living in the area of Pakistan moved to India. This mass migration—and the violence that accompanied it—left deep scars on both nations.

Another problem was the division of Pakistan in two parts. The two sections of the country, East and West Pakistan, were separated by more than a thousand miles of Indian territory. This separation posed a major obstacle to national unity.

Ethnic and cultural differences also divided Pakistan. West Pakistan included five major ethnic groups, along with several minor ones. Punjabis were the largest group. East Pakistan, the more populous section, was mostly Bengali. No common language, except English, united these various groups.

In addition, most of the wealth and resources of British India remained in India. Pakistan expected India to share some of this wealth after partition, but India refused. As a result, Pakistan faced great economic and political challenges.

Civilian and Military Rule   Given these problems, it was unclear whether Pakistan could survive as a nation. Its first leader, Mohammed Ali Jinnah— the father of Pakistani independence—managed to hold the nation together for a short time, but he died after a year in office. The leaders that followed were less successful.

> **developing country** a country whose economy is less industrialized and where average incomes are much lower than those of highly industrialized nations

When Pakistan gained its independence from Britain in 1947, its territory was divided into East and West Pakistan. The two regions were separated by a vast expanse of Indian territory. East Pakistan broke off to form the nation of Bangladesh in 1971. Another problem facing Pakistan was its dispute with India over the territory of Kashmir.

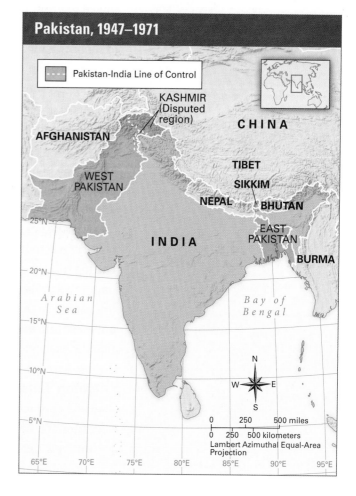

Pakistan, 1947–1971

Pakistan-India Line of Control

KASHMIR (Disputed region)

AFGHANISTAN

CHINA

WEST PAKISTAN

TIBET

SIKKIM

NEPAL   BHUTAN

INDIA

EAST PAKISTAN

BURMA

Arabian Sea

Bay of Bengal

0   250   500 miles
0   250   500 kilometers
Lambert Azimuthal Equal-Area Projection

populism a political philosophy that favors the common person's interests over those of wealthy people or business interests

exile the condition of living outside one's home country, usually for political reasons, either by choice or by order of the home country's government

al Qaeda an international terrorist organization, founded by the terrorist leader Osama bin Laden

Conflict with India added to Pakistan's problems. In 1948, Pakistani forces invaded Kashmir, a largely Muslim region claimed by both Pakistan and India. In response, the Hindu ruler of Kashmir ceded the region to India and asked for Indian support. The two sides fought to a stalemate. In 1949, the United Nations negotiated a ceasefire. Kashmir was divided along a ceasefire line, called the Line of Control. India kept most of the territory, and tensions with Pakistan continued. Two more wars followed, in 1965 and 1999. Today, Kashmir remains a conflict zone.

At the same time that Pakistan was engaged in conflict with India, it also suffered from the fact that the Pakistani state itself was becoming increasingly unstable. Disputes broke out between East and West Pakistan. In 1958, the president declared martial law. Soon after, the military took over and established a dictatorship.

The military ruled Pakistan for more than a decade. At first, many Pakistanis welcomed military rule. They hoped the army would bring order and stability. The United States also backed the Pakistani military as an ally in the Cold War. U.S. aid helped bolster the military's strength and keep it in power.

During this time, tensions between East and West Pakistan continued to grow. In 1971, East Pakistan declared independence as the new nation of Bangladesh. Civil war broke out and India sent troops to support Bangladesh. Pakistan soon surrendered. By this time the military regime had lost public support. It handed over power to a new civilian government, led by Zulfikar Ali Bhutto (BOO-toh).

Bhutto governed Pakistan for the next six years. His policies, which combined elements of socialism and **populism,** at first won him popular support. The economy eventually suffered, however, giving rise to more unrest. Bhutto was also accused of crimes against his political opponents. In 1977, the army took over again. Bhutto was arrested for his alleged crimes and later executed.

Over the next three decades, Pakistan continued its pattern of political instability. Rule shifted between military and civilian hands. During this time, Benazir Bhutto—the former leader's daughter—held power twice. She was the first woman in modern history to lead a Muslim nation. In the 1990s, however, she was charged with corruption and went into **exile.** She returned in 2007 to take part in elections. Two months later, while campaigning for office, she was assassinated.

Ongoing Tensions In 2008, the military handed over power to civilians once more. The new government faced many pressing issues. Chief among them was Pakistan's role in the fight against terrorism.

That role increased after September 11, 2001, when **al Qaeda** launched its brutal attacks against the United States that killed nearly 3,000 people at the World Trade Center, the Pentagon, and in western

Pennsylvania. In response to 9/11, Pakistan pledged support for efforts to combat terrorism. It promised to end aid to the **Taliban** in Afghanistan and to crack down on extremist groups at home. This policy sparked a violent reaction from Islamic militants. Terrorist attacks increased in Pakistan. Many Pakistanis criticized their government for helping the United States and other Western powers in the struggle against militant Islam. At the same time, the United States questioned whether Pakistan was truly committed to that struggle. Tensions between the countries were further strained in 2011 when U.S. military forces located and killed Osama bin Laden, the leader of al Qaeda, in Pakistan.

Terrorism poses serious risks to the stability of Pakistan and all of South Asia. So does the ongoing conflict with India. Pakistan has been linked to several terrorist attacks in India, including a bloody assault in the city of Mumbai in 2008. Tensions between the two nations remain high. To make matters worse, both countries possess nuclear weapons. In the past, escalating conflict has raised the threat of nuclear war. Both India and Pakistan have tried to resolve their problems through diplomacy, but a long-term solution is still not in sight.

Benazir Bhutto was the first woman in modern history to lead a Muslim nation. In this photo, Bhutto is surrounded by supporters after her party won a majority in parliament in 1988. She later became prime minister.

Taliban a radical and ultraconservative Muslim group that supported al Qaeda and ruled Afghanistan from 1996 to 2001, when U.S. forces ousted it from power

28.4 Tanzania: The Struggle for Development

The East African country of Tanzania became an independent state in the 1960s, along with many other African nations. Its first leader had a strong vision for the country. But like most African nations, Tanzania struggled to develop.

Independence and Self-Rule   The modern country of Tanzania was formed by the union of the territories of Tanganyika and Zanzibar. Tanganyika was the larger and more populous of the two. It was colonized by Germany in the late 1800s. The Germans established plantations to grow export crops such as rubber, cotton, and coffee.

After World War I, Britain took over Tanganyika under a League of Nations **mandate**. When the League dissolved after World War II, the colony became a **UN trust territory,** under the administration of the United Nations and also under British supervision. In 1961, Tanganyika gained independence in a peaceful transfer of power. The leader of the independence movement, Julius Nyerere (nee-REH-ray), became president in 1962.

Zanzibar—a group of islands off the East African coast—became a British protectorate in the late 1800s. Before that, Arab sultans had ruled the islands. The sultans continued to act as formal rulers even after the British established a protectorate over Zanzibar. Zanzibar was famed for its spices, especially cloves. In fact, the scent of cloves was said to be so strong that sailors on the Indian Ocean could smell it far out at sea.

Zanzibar gained independence in 1963. A year later, it joined with Tanganyika to form the United Republic of Tanzania. Zanzibar retained substantial autonomy, however. Although it took part in the national government, it also had its own president and legislature.

Socialism Under Nyerere   President Nyerere played a crucial role in Tanzania's development. He was an honest and respected leader who tried to serve his country's interests. Unlike many African leaders, he did not use his power for personal gain. But, as he acknowledged himself, he made many mistakes along the way.

Nyerere wanted to build a socialist society in Tanzania. He established free, public education and carried out literacy campaigns. He nationalized industries and placed farmland under collective ownership.

Julius Nyerere led the movement for Tanzanian independence. He became the country's first president in 1962. Nyerere was a respected and effective political leader. On the other hand, his socialist economic policies proved to be disastrous for the Tanzanian economy.

He made Tanzania a one-party state, though he allowed democratic rights within that system. Nyerere called his socialist program *ujamaa*, a Swahili word for "familyhood." He hoped it would ensure equality for all.

Nyerere pursued an active foreign policy. He became a leader of the nonaligned movement during the Cold War. He also helped found the Organization of African Unity, now known as the **African Union**. He supported the anti-apartheid movement in South Africa and the independence struggle in Zimbabwe. He promoted democracy in neighboring Uganda by helping to oust its brutal dictator, Idi Amin.

Nyerere's political leadership earned him widespread praise, both at home and abroad. His social policies helped overcome ethnic and regional differences and unite the country. But his economic policies were a disaster. Tanzania remained one of the poorest countries in the world. Its state-owned industries were inefficient and corrupt. In addition, most farmers opposed Nyerere's policy of collective agriculture. Individual incentive and productivity declined, and farm production collapsed. In the end, Nyerere was forced to abandon the scheme.

Despite his economic failures, Nyerere's rule helped make Tanzania one of the most politically stable countries in Africa. He was elected to four full terms in office. Then he voluntarily stepped down. In 1985, he handed power over to another elected leader.

Tanzania Today   Nyerere's successors moved toward a free-market economic system. They turned many state-owned companies over to private hands. These policies helped promote economic growth. During the 2000s, the country's **gross domestic product** (GDP) grew by around 6 percent a year. Still, Tanzania remains a poor, developing country. Living standards have not improved much for most Tanzanians.

Neyerere's successors also reformed Tanzania's political system. They allowed various political parties to take part in elections. In general, the electoral process has been peaceful and orderly. The country has had some problems with political violence, however. In 1998, al Qaeda militants bombed the U.S. embassy in the main city of Dar es Salaam. Zanzibar has also seen a rise in Islamic extremism. For the most part, though, Tanzania has maintained its political stability.

> **African Union** a group of 53 African states that works to promote peace, security, and development in Africa
>
> **gross domestic product** the total value of goods and services produced in a country in a year

On August 7, 1998, the Islamic militant group al Qaeda bombed the U.S. embassy in Tanzania. In this photo, U.S. soldiers and Tanzanian police stand guard next to debris from the blast. The attack in Dar es Salaam was accompanied by a simultaneous attack by al Qaeda on the U.S. embassy in Nairobi, Kenya.

28.5 Mexico: Stability and Change

Mexico has been an independent nation for two centuries. It has a large economy with a strong industrial base. It also has a well-established political system. Yet Mexico still faces many of the problems of a developing country, including widespread poverty and corruption.

Stability Under the PRI Mexico's modern history began with the Mexican Revolution of the early 1900s. This revolution overturned the old elitist and often repressive political order. But it also left the country in chaos. To restore order, Mexico's leaders created a new political system based on one-party rule. In 1946, this party became known as the PRI: the Institutional Revolutionary Party. The PRI brought decades of political stability to Mexico.

The PRI established what some political analysts called the "perfect dictatorship." It exercised absolute power, while preserving the rituals of democracy. Every six years, Mexico held presidential elections in which various parties took part. But the PRI always won, usually by lopsided margins. The government controlled the political process through bribery, fraud, and violence. In 1968, when students staged a mass protest in Mexico City, security forces gunned them down. Several hundred people lost their lives.

At the same time, the PRI presided over decades of steady economic growth. Analysts called it the Mexican Miracle. The government built roads, dams, schools, and power plants. It funded social welfare programs and developed the tourist industry. But corruption also grew. PRI officials enriched themselves at the public expense. Most presidents left office as wealthy men. No one seemed to mind as long as the economy kept growing.

The benefits of growth were poorly distributed, though. The upper and middle classes profited, while most Mexicans did not. The wealthy lived like their affluent counterparts in developed countries, while the poor barely survived on small farms or in urban slums. Many Mexicans chose to immigrate illegally to the United States in search of jobs and a better life.

In the 1970s, the Mexican economy got a big boost from huge oil discoveries. Mexico became the world's fifth largest oil producer. Suddenly, the country was awash in oil money. Banking on future revenues,

One problem Mexico has faced is a wide gap in the standards of living for their wealthiest and poorest citizens. The homes pictured here are both located in the Mexico City area. Some inhabitants of Mexico City have been forced to construct makeshift houses on the edge of garbage dumps. In contrast, others are able to live in very comfortable, affluent conditions.

it took out large foreign loans to finance major construction projects. Prosperity and growth looked like permanent conditions in Mexico.

In 1981, however, world oil prices collapsed. Mexico was thrown into financial crisis. It could not repay its debts to foreign banks. Building projects stalled and companies went bankrupt. The economy crashed. Mexico got **bailout** money from the United States and other international lenders. But the boom years were over. As one reporter wrote, "The greatest economic surge in modern Mexican history had turned into the worst economic crisis in six decades."

Changes in the System   Mexico gradually recovered. But in the years that followed, Mexicans grew more critical of their government.

Criticism increased after a massive earthquake struck Mexico City in 1985. The quake leveled large parts of the city and killed at least 10,000 people. When the government was slow to respond, citizen groups formed to carry out much of the relief work. This effort planted the idea of citizen action.

Mexico's political opposition began to play a more active role. In 1988, the PRI candidate for president—Carlos Salinas de Gortari—barely won office in what many saw as a fraudulent election. Opposition candidates won state elections, however. They also won enough seats in congress to challenge the PRI's long hold on power.

During his presidency, Salinas signed the **North American Free Trade Agreement** (NAFTA). This treaty between Mexico, the United States, and Canada created a free trade zone in North America. It allowed most goods to pass freely among the three countries, without **tariffs** or other trade barriers.

In 1994, just after NAFTA went into effect, rebels in the southern state of Chiapas rose up against the government. They called themselves the Zapatistas, after one of the leaders of the 1910 Mexican Revolution, Emiliano Zapata. They demanded land and rights for Mexico's peasant farmers. The government agreed to meet with the rebels, and the rebellion died down. But it had shaken the political structure.

Meanwhile, the political opposition was continuing to organize. In 1997, opposition parties won enough seats in congress to deny the PRI its majority control for the first time since its founding in 1929. A far greater shock occurred in 2000, however, when an opposition candidate—Vicente Fox Quesada—won the presidential election. The PRI honored the results and gave up power. It was the end of seven decades of control by the official party.

bailout the act of saving or rescuing something, such as a business, from financial problems

North American Free Trade Agreement (NAFTA) a 1993 treaty, signed by Mexico, the United States, and Canada, to create a free trade zone

tariff a tax on imported or exported goods

The Zapatistas staged a rebellion in the state of Chiapas, Mexico, in 1994. The rebels fought in protest of economic policies that they believed would hurt Mexico's indigenous population.

Mexico City is one of the most populous metropolitan areas in the world. Manufacturing, tourism, and finance are some of the most important industries in this bustling capital. Like Mexico as a whole, Mexico City faces its share of problems. But it also reflects Mexico's enormous potential for future development.

drug cartel a criminal organization that controls drug trafficking operations

The New Millennium Since then, Mexico has continued on its democratic path. The PRI remains an important political force, but it must compete for power with other political parties.

The Mexican economy has also continued to grow, although the gap between rich and poor remains great. Poverty in Mexico still spurs illegal immigration to the United States, but this migration has decreased in recent years due to improved social and economic conditions and a lower birth rate in Mexico. An increase in the cost and risk of migrating illegally to the United States has also helped decrease migration rates

One alarming trend, however, has been rising crime and violence related to the drug trade. For decades, Mexico has supplied illegal drugs to the U.S. market. More recently, the powerful **drug cartels** that control the trade have threatened security in Mexico. The cartels battle each other for control of the trade. They also bribe and intimidate officials. In 2006, the government declared war on the cartels. It called in the army to crack down on the drug trade. But this only led to a dramatic increase in violence.

Despite these problems, Mexico is a strong developing country. It has a highly skilled population and deep cultural traditions. Although it faces many challenges, it has enormous potential for growth and development.

28.6 Poland: An Emerging European State

During the Cold War, Poland was an ally of the Soviet Union and a key member of the Eastern bloc. At the end of the Cold War in the late 1980s, it freed itself from communist rule. Today, Poland is a democratic state with a growing market economy.

A Difficult History For much of its history, Poland was occupied or controlled by foreign powers. Its location in central Europe was an important factor. Poland lay on vital land routes between Western Europe, the Eurasian plains to the east, and the Baltic Sea to the north. As a result, invading armies often overran Polish territory.

Poland enjoyed a golden age in the 1400s and 1500s. It became a powerful kingdom—the largest in Europe—with a strong Catholic culture. But it was later carved up by Prussia, Austria, and Russia. For more than a century, Poland ceased to exist as a nation.

The 1900s brought new problems. The two world wars ravaged Poland. World War II was especially devastating. During World War II, Poland was invaded and occupied by Nazi Germany. Its population was decimated and its economy destroyed. After the war, Poland came under Soviet control.

The Rise and Fall of Communism The Soviets had promised to let Poland decide its fate after the war. Instead, they manipulated elections to make sure that Polish communists gained power. By 1947, a pro-Soviet government was in charge.

Poland's communist leaders adopted many features of Soviet rule. They established a **command economy** run by the state. They emphasized heavy industry and collective farming. They built a large secret police force to control the population. They also sought to suppress religion by cracking down on the Catholic Church.

command economy an economic system in which decisions about production and consumption are made by a powerful ruler or government

In 1978, the Polish cardinal Karol Wojtyla became Pope John Paul II. He was a Polish nationalist, and his activism contributed to the peaceful dissolution of the Soviet Union. He also traveled widely and worked for understanding among different religions. Here the pope greets a stadium of admirers in 1979, on a tour of the United States.

Solidarity a Polish union movement of the 1980s that became the major force of opposition to communist rule in Poland

These policies had limited success, however. Poland's state-run factories and farms were inefficient and unproductive. Most Polish farmers resisted collective agriculture. By the 1960s, the government had reversed its farm policy and allowed land to revert to private ownership. Most Poles also remained faithful Catholics, despite official persecution. The Catholic Church, for its part, helped keep Polish traditions alive.

Two major events further weakened communism in Poland. One was the selection in 1978 of Polish cardinal Karol Wojtyla (voy-TIH-wah) to become Pope John Paul II. The pope's visit to Poland the following year prompted an outpouring of popular support that undermined communist rule. The pope reminded Poles of their national heritage and their right to basic freedoms. As one historian noted:

> When John Paul II kissed the ground at Warsaw airport on June 2, 1979, he began the process by which communism in Poland—and ultimately everywhere else in Europe—would come to an end.
>
> —John Lewis Gaddis, *The Cold War*, 2007

Lech Walesa was the charismatic leader of the Solidarity trade union movement in Poland. His work helped weaken communist control in Poland, and he became a national hero. He was elected president of Poland in 1990.

The second major event was the birth of the **Solidarity** trade union movement in 1980. That year, workers at the Lenin Shipyard in Gdansk went on strike, demanding the right to form a union. The strike soon spread to other factories and gained national support. Under intense pressure, the government bowed to the strikers' demands and legalized unions. The strike leader, Lech Walesa (lech va-WHEN-sah), became a national hero and the head of the newly formed Solidarity trade union federation.

Although the government had legalized Solidarity, it still regarded the union movement as a threat. A year later, it declared martial law. It arrested Walesa and other union leaders. It reversed its course and banned Solidarity, although Solidarity continued to exist and organize strikes as an underground organization. In 1983, Walesa was awarded the Nobel Peace Prize. Eventually the government lifted martial law and released opposition leaders from jail. It also began talks with Solidarity.

In 1989, the government agreed to hold elections for seats in a new national parliament. Although these elections were restricted, opposition candidates backed by Solidarity won nearly all the seats open to them. The communists tried to reassert control, but they could not hold on to power. A non-communist was named prime minister. The following year, Lech Walesa was elected president.

The Polish Republic   The new democratic government overhauled Poland's political and economic structures. It declared itself a republic and replaced central planning with a market economy.

At first, Poland's transition to capitalism was difficult. The new government tried to move quickly toward a free market. It froze wages and removed price controls on consumer goods. It also ended government subsidies to industries and turned many businesses over to private hands. However, these policies caused a severe **recession,** high inflation, and rising unemployment. Many Poles criticized the government for sacrificing social needs in the rush to capitalism.

Within a few years, however, the economy had turned around. By the mid-1990s, Poland boasted one of the highest economic growth rates in Europe. Not all regions and sectors of the economy benefited equally, and the gap between rich and poor increased. Nevertheless, the growth itself was a testament to Poland's post-communist success.

Poland also continued to strengthen its democratic system. It held regular, free elections in which various parties competed for power. It also became more integrated into Europe. It joined NATO, the Western military alliance, in 1999. In 2004, it became a full member of the **European Union (EU)**. These steps were another sign of Poland's emergence as a strong, independent nation.

recession a period in which there is a decline in economic activity and prosperity

European Union an alliance of European countries begun in 1993 which was designed to advance the continent's economic integration and unify its laws and foreign policies

Summary

This lesson presented case studies of five countries that are in the process of national development. Each country faces distinct challenges, but all are seeking to achieve economic growth and political stability.

Cultural Interaction   In some countries, ethnic and cultural diversity has proved an obstacle to national unity. For example, Indonesia has found it difficult to unite its various peoples and regions in a single nation. So has Pakistan. But this problem is not universal. In Tanzania, strong leadership and wise social policy helped bring diverse peoples together.

Political Structures   Emerging nations often struggle to gain political stability. All of the countries covered in this chapter have relied on authoritarian rule at one time or another. But they have also sought to build democracy. The democratic outcomes in countries such as Mexico and Poland offer hope for the future.

Economic Structures   Building a strong economy is a challenge for most countries. In the past, all of the nations described here used state controls to promote economic growth. More recently, they have moved toward free market policies. The results have been generally positive, though poverty and income inequality remain serious problems.

Shifts of Power in the Middle East

29

Why is the Middle East a flashpoint in world affairs?

29.1 Introduction

In 1981, Egyptian President Anwar Sadat (AHN-wahr sah-DAHT) was attending a military parade in Cairo. Fighter jets roared overhead as army vehicles rolled past the reviewing stand where Sadat was seated. Suddenly, several soldiers leapt from a truck and opened fire on the president. They murdered Sadat and several other people.

Fourteen years later in 1995, Israeli Prime Minister Yitzhak Rabin (YIHT-sahk rah-BEEN) was attending a peace rally in Tel Aviv. As he was leaving, a man in the crowd pulled out a gun and shot him in the back. Rabin died shortly afterward.

These two assassinations had much in common. Although Sadat and Rabin stood on opposite sides of the Arab-Israeli conflict, they both sought peace in the Middle East. By embracing political compromise, they aroused violent opposition from extremists on both sides.

In Sadat's case, the assassins were Muslim militants who blamed him for undermining the cause of radical Islam by signing a treaty with Israel. In Rabin's case, the killer was a Jewish extremist who opposed Rabin's efforts to negotiate with the Palestinians. The death of these two leaders was a blow to those who hoped for peace and religious moderation in the Middle East, but their legacies continue. Despite popular opposition, Sadat's peace agreement with Israel survived his assassination. Rabin's commitment to a negotiated peace with Palestinians remains the official goal of the Israeli government and his memory is honored each year with a national day of mourning.

The nations of the Middle East faced many challenges in the decades after World War II. Like other developing countries, they sought to achieve political stability and economic growth. But they were unsettled by wars and political conflicts. In this lesson, you will read about some of these conflicts, and about efforts to promote peace and stability in the region.

Themes

Cultural Interaction Ethnic and religious differences have troubled the modern Middle East. Jews and Arabs have fought over land, Israel's right to exist, and questions about Palestinian statehood. Conflict has also erupted between Shi'a and Sunni Muslims.

Political Structures Many groups in the Middle East have fought to establish and strengthen independent nation-states. Political revolts and revolutions have unsettled the region.

Economic Structures Some states in the Middle East have created state-run economies on a socialist model. Oil is a key resource for many Middle Eastern economies.

Human-Environment Interaction Oil production has brought great wealth to the Middle East, but it has also caused problems.

◄ Israel and parts of Egypt, Syria, Jordan, and Saudi Arabia are visible in this satellite photograph of the Middle East.

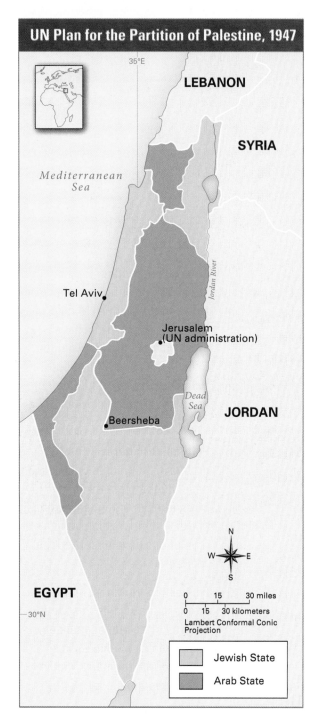

UN Plan for the Partition of Palestine, 1947

LEBANON

SYRIA

Mediterranean Sea

Tel Aviv

Jerusalem (UN administration)

Jordan River

Dead Sea

JORDAN

Beersheba

EGYPT

N W E S

| 0 | 15 | 30 miles |
| 0 | 15 | 30 kilometers |

Lambert Conformal Conic Projection

Jewish State
Arab State

The United Nations plan for the partition of Palestine created separate Jewish and Arab Palestinian states. However, complicated settlement patterns in the region resulted in fragmented, discontinuous territories. The city of Jerusalem had long been a site of conflict. The plan hoped to solve this issue by making Jerusalem a separate UN-administered territory not belonging to either state.

29.2 The Arab-Israeli Conflict

A major source of tension in the Middle East has been the Arab-Israeli dispute over land, Israel's right to exist, and questions about Palestinian statehood. In the first four decades after World War II, Israel and the Arab states fought four wars. Since then, Palestinian Arabs have continued to struggle with Israel.

The Roots of the Conflict   Both Jews and Palestinian Arabs have historic claims to the area in the eastern Mediterranean known as Palestine, which Jews call the Land of Israel. Each group considers the land its ancestral home. By the 19th century, many Jews were living outside of Palestine, in communities throughout Europe and the Middle East. In the late 19th century, Zionism, or Jewish nationalism, developed in Europe. Zionism advocated that Jews outside their ancient homeland of Israel return there. This prompted increased Jewish migration to Palestine. After World War I, the area became the British Mandate for Palestine. Jewish migration to Palestine increased and Palestinian Arabs increasingly opposed Jewish immigration with violence. The British, who controlled the Palestine Mandate, failed to come up with a solution.

During and after World War II, Jews fled Europe to escape persecution, and many settled in the Palestine Mandate. Shocked by the Holocaust, many nations backed the idea of a modern state for Jews in their historical homeland, where they would be safe from persecution. Meanwhile, violence between Jews and Palestinian Arabs increased. After the war, Britain turned the issue over to the United Nations.

In 1947, the UN approved a plan for the partition of the British Mandate for Palestine. The plan called for a "two-state solution." One state would be Jewish and the other Arab. Both sides were dissatisfied with the plan. The states were small and fragmented. Arabs would not accept any Jewish state and were upset that Jews, who made up one third of the population, would receive more than half the land. Jews were upset that more than half the land allocated for a Jewish state was arid dessert. They also felt it was unfair that their state was being reduced when 80 percent of the original Palestine Mandate had already been closed to them with the creation of Transjordan. Jerusalem, an important city to both communities, was to be under international control.

Jews ultimately supported the plan, but Palestinian Arabs and neighboring Arab states were opposed. They wanted there to be no Jewish state, but rather a single state under majority Palestinian Arab control. Although historically there had never been an independent Arab Palestinian state, by this time a distinct sense of Arab Palestinian nationalism had developed. The term "Palestine," came to refer to a state Arabs hoped to create in the region, and the label "Palestinian" came to imply an Arab ethnic identity.

On May 14, 1948, as Britain ended its Palestine Mandate and pulled out of the region, Israel declared itself an independent state in keeping with the UN plan. The following day the armies of five Arab nations—Egypt, Syria, Jordan, Lebanon, and Iraq—invaded Israel. However, these armies were poorly trained and disorganized. In contrast, Israel's forces were disciplined and ready for combat. By January 1949, Israel had won a decisive victory.

Young Jews in the city of Tel Aviv celebrate the proclamation of the new state of Israel on May 14, 1948. The next day, five Arab nations that opposed the creation of a Jewish state invaded Israel, beginning the 1948 war.

After the war, Egypt and Jordan controlled most of the land the UN had set aside for the Palestinian Arab state. The rest of the area became part of Israel. Egypt held the Gaza Strip, a small piece of land along the Mediterranean Sea. Jordan held the West Bank, a hilly region of central Palestine west of the Jordan River. There was no Palestinian state.

During the fighting, more than 700,000 Palestinians fled to nearby countries. The Palestinian refugees said they had been forced from their land, but Israel held that they had left voluntarily. It refused to let the refugees return to their homes, and their land came under the control of Israel. Palestinian Arabs who remained in Israel became citizens and today the Arab minority comprises approximately one fifth of the population of Israel. A comparable number of Jews—820,000— also became refugees as a result of the war. These Jews were persecuted and displaced from Arab states as part of the Arab rejection of Israel's right to exist. The majority—586,000— resettled in Israel.

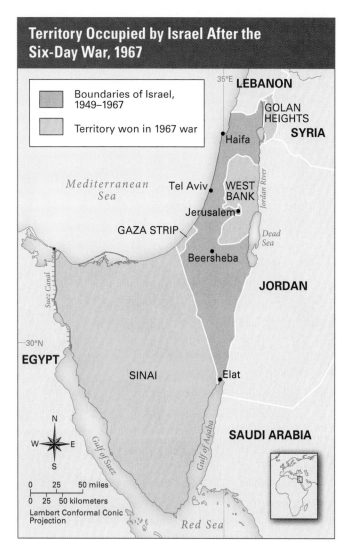

Territory Occupied by Israel After the Six-Day War, 1967

Boundaries of Israel, 1949–1967

Territory won in 1967 war

35°E — LEBANON

GOLAN HEIGHTS

SYRIA

Haifa

Mediterranean Sea

Tel Aviv

WEST BANK

Jerusalem

Jordan River

GAZA STRIP

Dead Sea

Beersheba

JORDAN

30°N

EGYPT

SINAI

Elat

Suez Canal

Gulf of Suez

Gulf of Aqaba

SAUDI ARABIA

N W E S

0   25   50 miles
0   25   50 kilometers
Lambert Conformal Conic Projection

Red Sea

In the Six-Day War of 1967, Israel quickly defeated Arab forces and occupied more territory than ever before. At the end of the war, they held land that had previously been controlled by Egypt, Jordan, and Syria. However, in 1982, the Israelis returned the Sinai Peninsula to Egypt.

Six-Day War the third Arab-Israeli war, in 1967, which resulted in a quick Israeli victory and a major expansion of Israeli territory

Intermittent Warfare   Israel and its Arab neighbors remained in a state of tension after the 1948 war. The Arab states refused to recognize the state of Israel or its right to exist. And Israel remained on guard against future attacks.

In 1956, President Nasser of Egypt seized the Suez Canal from Britain and France. This ignited tensions in the region. Additionally, Egypt began to blockade Israeli shipping, considered under international law to be an act of war. In the second Arab-Israeli war, the British and French united with Israel to invade Egypt's Sinai Peninsula in October 1956. Opposition from other nations, including the United States, forced the invaders to withdraw, however, by March 1957.

The third war—known as the **Six-Day War**—took place a decade later. After the Suez conflict, Nasser viewed Israel as a mortal threat to Arabs. In the spring of 1967, he decided to act. He sent Egyptian troops into the Sinai Peninsula and closed off the Gulf of Aqaba, which was Israel's outlet to the Red Sea. He also made military alliances with other Arab states, and publically declared his goal to destroy Israel. Israel viewed the naval blockade as an act of war and the other developments as a threat to its existence. In response to these actions and aggression from Syria, Israel acted on what it perceived as an imminent attack from its surrounding neighbors. It sent fighter jets to destroy airfields in Egypt, Syria, and Jordan and then launched lightning-fast ground attacks. In just six days, it won a resounding victory.

After the Six-Day War, Israel controlled all of the former British mandate west of the Jordan river, including the West Bank, Jerusalem, and the Gaza Strip. It also occupied the Egyptian Sinai and Syria's Golan Heights, a hill region that looks down on northern Israel. Around 200,000 more Palestinian refugees fled to Jordan. It was a humiliating defeat for the Arab states.

Six years later, in October 1973, Egypt and Syria launched the fourth Arab-Israeli war. By this time, Anwar Sadat had become the Egyptian president. He was determined to restore Egypt's power and prestige. The Arab forces began their attack during Yom Kippur, the holiest day of the Jewish calendar. They caught the Israelis off guard, pushing them back in the Sinai and down from the Golan Heights. But Israel fought back and regained territory. A UN ceasefire ended the fighting, but did not bring a formal peace.

The Struggle for Peace After the war, Egyptian President Anwar Sadat began to work for peace with Israel. In 1977, he stunned the world by visiting Jerusalem and speaking before the Israeli parliament. In that speech, he announced, "Today I tell you, and I declare it to the whole world, that we accept to live with you in permanent peace based on justice." In exchange for peace, Sadat called on Israel to respect Palestinian rights and return Arab lands taken in the 1967 war.

In 1978, Sadat and Israeli Prime Minister Menachem Begin (meh-NAH-hehm BEH-gihn) met for peace talks at Camp David, the U.S. presidential retreat in Maryland. These talks led to the **Camp David Accords**. Under this agreement, Egypt agreed to recognize Israel as a nation, and Israel agreed to return the Sinai Peninsula to Egypt. A peace treaty the following year ended three decades of war between the two nations.

Other Arab states were furious with Sadat for making peace with Israel. Three years later, Sadat was assassinated. But the Egyptian-Israeli peace continued.

Meanwhile, Palestinians took up the conflict with Israel. They resented Israel's control over the West Bank and Gaza and many felt Israel should be destroyed. The main group spearheading this cause was the **Palestine Liberation Organization** (PLO), led by Yasir Arafat (YASS-sir AH-rah-fat). The PLO waged a political campaign to win support for a Palestinian homeland. But it also engaged in armed struggle, attacking targets and committing acts of terrorism in Israel and elsewhere. Israel fought back, bombing suspected PLO strongholds. In 1982, Israel invaded Lebanon, which was in the middle of a civil war, to strike at PLO bases there. World opinion and persistent guerrilla attacks eventually forced Israel to withdraw.

Camp David Accords a 1978 peace agreement between Egypt and Israel in which Israel returned land taken from Egypt in 1967 and Egypt recognized Israel's right to exist

Palestine Liberation Organization an organization established in 1964 to represent Palestinian interests and that pledged to destroy Israel; in 1993 it agreed to peace with Israel

In 1978, Egyptian President Anwar Sadat (center) and Israeli Prime Minister Menachem Begin (right) signed the Camp David Accords. Here Sadat and Begin acknowledge applause as the Accords are announced in the U.S. Congress. However, many Arabs were angry with Sadat for making peace with the Israelis.

A masked protestor holds up a Palestinian flag and a rock during an Intifada demonstration. Palestinian youths often attacked Israeli soldiers with stones and bottles during the first Intifada popular uprisings, which began in 1987.

A new phase of the conflict began in 1987 with a popular uprising called the *Intifada*. Palestinians in the West Bank and Gaza held strikes and demonstrations to protest Israeli policies. Youths hurled stones and bottles at Israeli soldiers. The PLO helped organize the uprising and supplied Palestinians with firearms. Israeli authorities cracked down by arresting, beating, and sometimes killing protesters and suspected terrorists. The Intifada went on for six years and finally prompted peace talks between the Israelis and the Palestinians.

In 1993, a series of secret negotiations between Israel and the PLO in Oslo, Norway, produced the **Oslo Accords**. The PLO agreed to recognize Israel in return for Palestinian self-rule in portions of the West Bank and Gaza. Under the accord, a governing body called the **Palestinian Authority** would manage affairs in Palestinian-controlled areas. Many Palestinians and Israelis were unhappy with the accord, however. Both said it gave away too much to the other side. Prime Minister Rabin's role in forging the agreement led to his assassination two years later by an Israeli extremist.

After the Oslo Accord, the peace process stalled. Palestinians gained self-rule in some areas, but the handover of land was slower than expected. The PLO renounced violence, but Palestinian attacks on Israelis continued. In 1987, at the beginning of the Intifada, a Palestinian terrorist group known as Hamas was established. In the era after the Oslo Accord, this group and others launched terrorist attacks on Israel. In the fall of 2000, this violence increased during what became known as the Second Intifada. To bolster security, Israel constructed a barrier wall across the West Bank to prevent terrorists from being able to enter Israel easily. Unfortunately, the barrier isolated some Palestinian towns. Israelis also continued to build permanent settlements in the West Bank, further angering Palestinians.

Oslo Accords the agreement signed in 1993 in which the PLO recognized Israel and Israel granted Palestinian self-rule in parts of the West Bank and Gaza

Palestinian Authority the governing authority for Palestinian self-rule established through the Oslo Accord

The ultimate goal of the peace process remains a two-state solution. But five key issues continue to hinder a peace agreement. One is persuading Arabs who reject Israel's existence to recognize Israel's right to exist as a Jewish state. A second issue is Israel's control of land taken in the 1967 war. A third is the demand that Palestinian refugees and their descendants be allowed to return to land in Israel, an issue known as the "right of return." A fourth is control over Jerusalem. And a fifth issue is control over scarce water resources in the Jordan River Valley. These issues have no easy solutions. But until they are resolved, peace between Israelis and Palestinians will remain elusive.

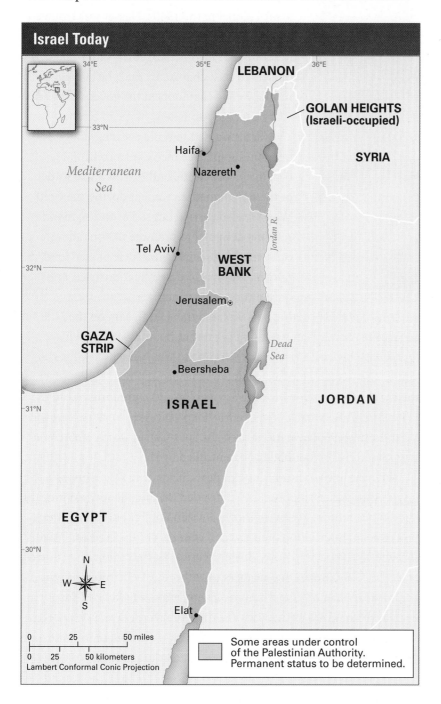

Israel Today

The map shows Israel's borders since the Sinai Peninsula was returned to Egypt. The status of the Gaza Strip and the West Bank remained in dispute at the turn of the 21st century.

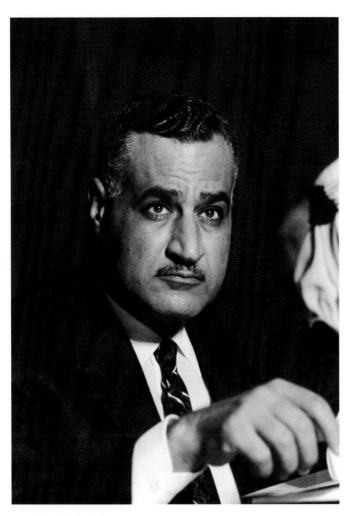

President Gamal Abdel Nasser of Egypt was one of the most influential figures in the Middle East in the years after World War II. He was an Egyptian nationalist, a pan-Arab leader, a leader of the nonaligned movement, and an outspoken critic of the West.

Suez Crisis an international incident in 1956 involving Egypt's seizure of the Suez Canal and invasions of Egypt by Israel, Britain, and France

29.3 Political Change in Egypt and Iran

Egypt and Iran play a key role in Middle Eastern affairs. Both are large, populous countries. In the decades since World War II, political changes in these countries have helped shape events in the Middle East.

Nationalism in Egypt   President Gamal Abdel Nasser and his nationalist policies defined postwar politics in Egypt. As a young army colonel in the 1940s, Nasser was troubled by political corruption and foreign influence in his country. He joined together with other army officers to seek change. In 1952, he helped lead a military coup that toppled the government. Two years later, he had taken charge of Egypt.

Nasser wanted to build a strong, independent Egypt, free of Western control. He became a vocal critic of the West and a leader of the nonaligned movement during the Cold War. He also carried out social and economic reforms designed to promote national development along socialist lines. He passed land reform, nationalized private industries, and built a state-run economy.

One of Nasser's main goals was to build a large dam on the Nile River. The Aswan Dam would help prevent flooding and provide Egypt with hydroelectric power. Hoping to win Nasser's loyalty, the United States offered loans to support this project. But Nasser angered the U.S. by forging ties with the Soviet bloc and communist China. When the United States withdrew its loans, Nasser struck back at the West. In July 1956, he nationalized the Suez Canal, which crossed Egyptian territory but had been controlled by the French and British.

Thus began the **Suez Crisis**. In part due to a blockade Egypt had imposed on Israeli shipping, Israel invaded the Sinai Peninsula. Britain and France followed with their own invasion of Egypt. These actions provoked an international outcry and charges of imperialism. Fearing that the crisis could advance Soviet interests in the region, the United States put pressure on the invaders to withdraw their troops. Egypt kept the canal, and Nasser became a hero across the Middle East.

Now recognized as the leader of the Arab world, Nasser began to promote the cause of Pan-Arabism. This was a movement to unite Arab countries around common goals. Nasser took control of the

Arab League, a group of Arab member-states founded in 1945 with British support. The league was designed to promote Arab unity while keeping Arab states in the Western orbit. Nasser sought to mold the league to his own interests.

Inspired by Nasser's leadership, Syria joined with Egypt in 1958 to form a new Arab state, the United Arab Republic (UAR). This union was a testament to Nasser's Pan-Arab vision, but it was flawed from the start. The two countries had done little to prepare for unification. Egypt—the bigger, stronger state—dominated the UAR. Syria was politically unstable and difficult to control. Many Syrians also resented Egyptian rule. In 1961, Syria pulled out of the UAR, and the union collapsed. Nasser's image as an Arab leader suffered.

Other setbacks followed. In 1962, Nasser sent Egyptian troops to fight in a civil war in Yemen. The war became a quagmire, with no end in sight. Again, Nasser's image suffered. But the biggest blow came in the Six-Day War with Israel in 1967. The Arab loss hurt Nasser's reputation in Egypt and the Arab world. He remained in office, but his power and stature were diminished. In 1970, he died of a heart attack.

The presidents who followed Nasser largely abandoned his policies. President Sadat, who took over in 1970, made peace with Israel and developed close relations with the West. Hosni Mubarak (HOHS-nee moo-BAH-rahk), who took power after Sadat's death, continued Sadat's foreign policies. He ruled Egypt with an iron hand, holding on to power for three decades until public protests finally drove him from office in 2011. His overthrow was part of the "Arab Spring," a broad, regional uprising against dictatorship that spread across the Middle East.

Arab League an organization of Arab states in the Middle East, formed in 1945 to encourage cooperation, peace, and security among member states

The Suez Canal extends across the Isthmus of Suez and connects the Red Sea and Mediterranean Sea. Egypt has controlled the Suez Canal since 1957.

In 1953, the CIA assisted Iranian conspirators in overthrowing the nationalist Mossadeq government and returning the shah to power. In this photo, Shah Mohammad Reza Pahlavi (center) returns from exile to the capital city of Tehran.

Revolution in Iran   Nationalism also surged in Iran after World War II. In 1951, the outspoken nationalist leader Mohammed Mossadeq was appointed premier, taking power from the shah of Iran. Two years later, however, Iranian conspirators aided by the CIA overthrew Mossadeq's government. Mossadeq had angered Western nations with his nationalization of British petroleum interests in Iran. The shah of Iran, Mohammad Reza Pahlavi, regained power and ruled for the next 26 years.

During the shah's reign, Iran pursued a policy of modernization and close ties with the West. The economy grew rapidly, fueled by oil revenues. The shah undertook large building projects and expanded the military. While Iran prospered, however, its people enjoyed few political rights. The shah's fearsome secret police—the SAVAK— cracked down on dissent.

Nevertheless, opposition to the shah's rule grew. Banned political groups met in secret. Members of Iran's Islamic clergy—including top Shi'a clerics, called ayatollahs—lent their voices to the opposition. They saw the shah's modernizing policies as a threat to Islamic values. One cleric in particular, Ayatollah Ruholla Khomeini (ho-may-NEE), attacked the shah's secular rule. In 1964, Khomeini was forced into exile.

By the mid-1970s, however, Iran's economy was collapsing from overspending, mismanagement, and corruption. In 1977, the shah confessed to his chief minister: "We're broke. Everything seems doomed to grind to a standstill." The minister was even more frank: "It terrifies me that one day everything will simply cave in around us."

Meanwhile, popular discontent was rising. Strikes and protests broke out. From exile, Ayatollah Khomeini called for the shah's overthrow and the creation of an Islamic state. Faced with mounting unrest, the shah lost control. In January 1979, he left Iran for medical treatments and never returned. Millions of Iranians flooded the streets in joyous celebration. Khomeini returned from exile to a hero's welcome and soon took over as Iran's supreme leader.

The **Iranian Revolution** had just begun, however. The new regime established a strict Islamic **theocracy**. It imposed Islamic law in the courts and Islamic teachings in the schools. It enforced a Muslim code of conduct in public places. Women lost many of their civil rights. Critics of the regime were arrested or executed.

Iranian Revolution the overthrow of the shah of Iran in 1979 and the creation of an Islamic state

theocracy a state governed by religious leaders

Khomeini hoped to spread the Islamic revolution to other Muslim countries, which he believed were governed by corrupt, un-Islamic leaders. He also voiced a strong hatred for the United States, a country that had long supported the shah. In October 1979, the United States allowed the shah to enter the country for medical treatment. Soon after, Iranian militants seized the U.S. embassy in Tehran, the Iranian capital city. They took dozens of Americans hostage and held them for more than a year. The Iran hostage crisis finally came to an end in January 1981.

By that time, war had broken out between Iraq and Iran. Iraq was led by Sunni Muslims, but the majority of the population was Shi'a. The vast majority of Iranians were also Shi'a. Iraqi leaders, fearing that the Iranian Revolution might spark a Shi'a uprising in their own country, invaded Iran in 1980. The war went on for eight brutal years, ending in a stalemate and ceasefire in 1988.

Since then, Iran has remained a volatile presence in the Middle East. It has embraced the Palestinian struggle against Israel. It has also supported Lebanon's Hezbollah guerillas, a Shi'a group that regularly attacked Israel. The United States has accused Iran of supporting terrorism and seeking to develop nuclear weapons. Iran has rejected these charges and had accused the United States and other Western nations of trying to block its legitimate rise to power.

Ayatollah Khomeini waves to a crowd of supporters upon his return to Iran in 1979. Khomeini was an Islamic cleric who called for the overthrow of the shah and oversaw the transformation of Iran into a strict Islamic theocracy. He was Iran's ultimate political and religious authority until his death in 1989.

29.4 Oil and Power in the Persian Gulf

Iran and Iraq are both part of the Persian Gulf region. This region has played a major part in world events over the past several decades, in large part because of oil. The countries of the Persian Gulf—which include Iran, Iraq, Saudi Arabia and a number of smaller Persian Gulf states—possess a major share of the world's oil reserves. Oil has brought great wealth and many benefits to the region, but it has also contributed to conflict.

The Oil States Oil production began in the Middle East in the early 1900s, but it was only after World War II that the region became a major oil producer. By 1960, Middle Eastern countries were supplying 25 percent of the oil in the non-communist world. A decade later, they were supplying half. The great majority of that oil came from the Persian Gulf region.

Iran and Iraq were the first important oil producers in the Gulf. But they were soon eclipsed by Saudi Arabia, which was home to some of

Beginning in the years after World War II, states of the Persian Gulf region became key suppliers of oil to the rest of the world. Oil has also played a central role in conflicts in the region.

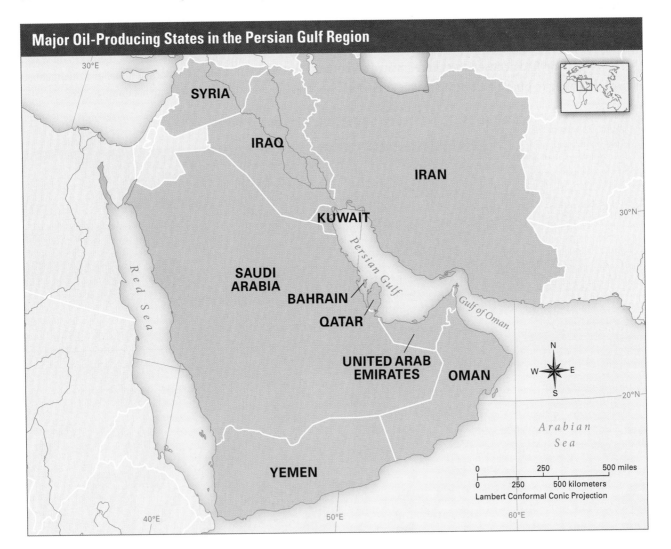

Major Oil-Producing States in the Persian Gulf Region

the largest oil fields in the world. Other Gulf nations, such as Kuwait and the United Arab Emirates (UAE), also became key producers.

At first, Western oil companies controlled all production in the region. Over time, however, Gulf nations managed to gain increased control over their oil resources. They did this by forming their own oil companies and working together to negotiate new contracts with foreign firms.

In 1960, major oil producers formed the **Organization of Petroleum Exporting Countries** (OPEC). The first five members of OPEC were Iraq, Iran, Kuwait, Saudi Arabia, and Venezuela. Eventually, other oil producers joined the group. OPEC members worked to regulate oil prices and production levels and to gain a larger share of oil revenues.

A major turning point occurred in 1973, during the fourth Arab-Israeli War. To support the Arab cause and put pressure on Western countries, Arab members of OPEC placed an embargo on oil exports to countries supporting Israel. The **Arab oil embargo,** which lasted for six months, caused oil shortages in the West and a sharp rise in prices. This action brought Arab oil states increased income and greater power and influence.

The Gulf nations used much of their new oil wealth for national development. They built roads, schools, airports, power plants, and other infrastructure that helped transform and modernize their societies. Economic growth was most evident among the states of the Arabian Peninsula, which changed radically over the course of a few decades. Saudi Arabia became a financial superpower, while the UAE boasted one of the highest standards of living in the world.

Oil wealth also had some negative effects, however. Some countries became overly dependent on oil income. A fall in oil prices could have a severe impact on the economy. Oil states imported many workers from other parts of the world, but these workers had few rights and lived as second-class citizens. In addition, some countries, such as Iran, used oil revenues to buy weapons and expand their military. This military buildup fueled tensions in the region.

Iraq Under Saddam Hussein   One country that sought to expand its regional power was Iraq. With increased oil revenues, Iraq built a powerful army and began to seek a larger role in the Middle East.

The architect of these changes was the Iraqi dictator Saddam Hussein. Saddam Hussein rose to power as a member of the Baath Party, a Pan-Arab socialist movement that took charge of Iraq in the late 1960s. Within a few years, he had become the dominant force in the Baath regime.

Organization of Petroleum Exporting Countries (OPEC) an association of major oil producing nations, founded in 1960 with the aim of gaining control over oil prices and production

Arab oil embargo a halt in oil exports from Arab countries to the West, which began during the 1973 Arab-Israeli War and lasted for six months

Saddam Hussein ruled Iraq as a brutal strongman for nearly three decades. Saddam Hussein used his country's oil wealth to build a powerful army, which he used in wars of aggression against the neighboring countries of Iran and Kuwait.

Though he was not yet president, Saddam Hussein was the strongman who controlled the government and set its policies. In 1972, for example, he nationalized the oil industry, boosting oil revenues and enhancing his own power. He also tried to negotiate peace with the Kurds, a large ethnic group in northern Iraq that had been fighting the government for years. His efforts failed, however, and the conflict continued.

In 1979, Saddam Hussein became president. His first task was to secure his grip on power. The main threat came from revolutionary Iran, which had called for the overthrow of the Iraqi government. Saddam Hussein believed that Iran was weak, and that a victory in war would boost his reputation in the Arab world. In September 1980, he invaded Iran.

Saddam Hussein expected to win a quick victory, but he was sorely mistaken. Although the Iraqi army enjoyed early success, Iran rallied and regained lost ground. The Iran-Iraq War entered years of stalemate, and the death toll mounted. Toward the end of the war, Iraq used chemical weapons on the Iranians and on its own Kurdish population in northern Iraq. The losses were horrific. By 1988, when the two countries declared a ceasefire, nearly a million people had been killed or injured. The economic damage to both countries was enormous.

The Persian Gulf War   Saddam Hussein's efforts to defeat Iran had failed, and Iraq's economy was near collapse. But he still had a huge army, and his ambitions were undiminished. Two years later, he launched another invasion to recoup his losses and restore his image. This time his action would prompt a strong international response.

On August 2, 1990, Iraq invaded the small Persian Gulf nation of Kuwait and quickly captured its capital, Kuwait City. Iraq had long claimed Kuwait as part of Iraq. Saddam Hussein also wanted to seize Kuwait's oil and other assets. He did not expect the world to come to Kuwait's aid. But again, he was badly mistaken.

In 1991, a coalition of forces led by the United States drove the Iraqi army out of Kuwait. Here an American soldier stands on a destroyed tank, as oil wells ignited by retreating Iraqi forces burn in the background.

The UN Security Council imposed sanctions on Iraq, blocking its foreign trade and freezing its foreign assets. Saudi Arabia, which feared that Iraq might try to seize its oil fields as well, called on foreign countries to repel the Iraqi invasion. Under U.S. leadership, a coalition of forces from various countries—including Britain, France, and several Middle Eastern nations—was assembled to force Iraq out of Kuwait.

Saddam Hussein was given a deadline of January 15, 1991 to withdraw from Kuwait, but he refused. The following day, the **Persian Gulf War** began with a massive aerial attack on Iraq and its forces in Kuwait. Five weeks later, the ground war began. Coalition forces swept through Kuwait and into southern Iraq, encountering little resistance. In just four days, the fighting was over. Iraq agreed to a ceasefire and abandoned its claim to Kuwait.

Despite a crushing defeat and ongoing sanctions, Saddam Hussein's regime survived. When Iraq's Kurdish and Shi'a populations rose up in revolt soon after the war, Saddam Hussein carried out a brutal campaign of repression. More than 100,000 people were killed.

Saddam Hussein held on to power until 2003, when a second invasion of Iraq by U.S.-led coalition forces overthrew his dictatorship. Iraq established a new, democratic government. But violence continued as Iraqi insurgents battled U.S. troops and government forces in a drawn-out war that involved the United States until late 2011.

Persian Gulf War a 1991 conflict between Iraq and a coalition of international forces, led by the United States, following Iraq's invasion of Kuwait

Summary

In this lesson, you read about events in the Middle East after World War II. Middle Eastern states faced conflict in their efforts to develop their economies and build stronger nations.

Cultural Interaction The conflict between Jews and Arabs in the Middle East was in part caused by the different goals of the two groups. Shi'a and Sunni Muslims have also clashed, particularly in Iran and Iraq.

Political Structures Nationalism surged in the Middle East after World War II. Leaders such as President Nasser of Egypt tried to make their countries strong and independent. Political revolts and revolutions arose throughout the region. Iraq became a dictatorship. After a revolution, Iran was governed by an Islamic theocracy.

Economic Structures Some Middle Eastern countries adopted socialist policies to aid development. They nationalized private businesses and built state-run industries. Oil became a key economic factor after World War II, particularly in the Persian Gulf region. Oil revenues helped some countries develop and modernize.

Human-Environment Interaction Oil development has had significant effects on the Middle East. Workers have migrated into the region to take jobs in the oil industry. Countries have also fought over oil resources.

Contemporary Global Issues

What are key challenges facing the world in the 21st century?

30.1 Introduction

In 1958, China under Mao Zedong launched the Great Leap Forward. This program aimed at advancing the country's economy by taking advantage of China's population of nearly 650 million people. It called for the intensive use of human labor, rather than heavy machinery, as a means of industrializing.

The program set high goals for the production of grain to feed China's workforce and increase exports. To achieve these goals, the government moved Chinese peasants onto huge collective farms. The government thought that the collectivization of farming could vastly increase China's agricultural output. However, collectivization had the opposite effect. Collectivization disrupted rural life, causing a huge drop in grain production. Combined with the natural disasters of droughts and floods, the effect on China was catastrophic. Between 1959 and 1962, some 20 million Chinese died, mostly of starvation.

In spite of having a wealth of resources, the Chinese economy only limped along. Politically, China isolated itself from the international community.

Starting in the 1970s, however, China undertook reforms. It reversed old policies and moved toward a market-oriented economy, with a robust private sector. By 2001, only the United States had a larger economy. China also carved out a role for itself on the world political stage. For example, it sought and gained a prestigious seat on the Security Council of the United Nations.

China's success, however, generated new problems. Rapid economic expansion led to severe environmental damage. A rising population, which reached 1.34 billion in 2010, tested China's ability to provide jobs for the young people and migrants from the countryside who were flooding the labor market. China's struggles are not unique. Population growth, resource management, economic development, and the search for peace and security are global issues that all countries must deal with in the 21st century.

> ## Themes
>
> **Cultural Interaction** Dominant cultures spread their ideas, values, technologies, and styles of life around the globe.
>
> **Political Structures** Governments have become more democratic over time.
>
> **Economic Structures** Capitalism has become the dominant economic system in the modern world.
>
> **Social Structures** A country's population and how it is distributed affects family size and composition as well as people's general well-being.
>
> **Human-Environment Interaction** A country's store of natural resources and how they are managed can have profound effects on its economy.

◀ This multistory shopping mall is located in Chengdu, China.

By 2011, world population had soared to 7 billion. Here, London commuters make their way through the Liverpool Street railway station. In 2010, the population of the metropolitan area of London was nearly 8 million people.

birthrate the number of births divided by the population during a given period, often expressed as births per 1,000 people in a given year

death rate the number of deaths divided by the population during a given period

life expectancy the average number of years people live within a given population

total fertility rate the average number of children women would give birth to in their lifetime if the current birthrate did not change

30.2 Changes in World Population

In 1960, the world's population reached 3 billion. By 2011, it had soared to about 7 billion. How high will it go? Some demographers, or experts in the study of human populations, believe that the number of people on planet Earth will level off sometime in the 21st century. The population will continue to rise in some countries as it falls in others. In either case, changes in world population will likely have profound effects.

Population Change The world population will continue to rise as long as more people are born each year than die. It will fall when, and if, the reverse becomes true. The rise or fall of the population in any one country, city, or other defined area has a somewhat different basis. Four factors determine how a population changes in a given area. They are births, deaths, immigration (migration into), and emigration (migration out of). Births and immigration add to the population. Deaths and emigration subtract from it.

Countries with a high birthrate can gain population quickly, especially if the death rate is low. **Birthrate** is the number of births divided by the population during a given period. It is often expressed as births per 1,000 people in a year. **Death rate** is the number of deaths per 1,000 people in a year.

Related to the death rate is another concept, life expectancy. **Life expectancy** is the average number of years people live within a given population. Like the birth and death rates, this figure varies from country to country. In Afghanistan in 2010 a newborn baby had a life expectancy of around 47 years. A baby born in France had a life expectancy of around 80 years. Factors that affect life expectancy include disease, nutrition, sanitation, and access to medical care.

Related to the birthrate is the **total fertility rate** (TFR). The TFR is the average number of children women would give birth to in their lifetimes if the current birthrate did not change. In many of the countries of Europe, East Asia, and North America the fertility rate has remained fairly low for decades. Generally, women in those countries give birth, on average, to two or fewer children in their lifetimes. In some of those countries, such as the United States, immigration keeps the population higher than it would otherwise be.

Population Distribution   Demographers also study population distribution, or how a population breaks down into categories. One category a demographer may analyze is population distribution by geography. More people may live in one area of a country than in another. Demographers determine differences by measuring how densely various areas are populated. The number of people in a given land area is that area's **population density**.

The population of urban areas is much denser than that of rural areas. Today, urbanization—the process of forming and expanding towns and cities—is increasing. In 2008, for the first time, most of the world's people lived in cities. The percentage of people living in urban areas could grow to 70 percent by 2050.

Rural-to-urban migration has been a fact of life since the Industrial Revolution. Industries tend to locate in urban areas, where they have ready access to supplies, transportation, and labor. People migrate to cities, in large part, because that is where the jobs are. This is true in India, where some of the most densely populated cities in the world are located. One Indian city, Mumbai, has about 11,500 people per square mile. The American city of Chicago, in contrast, has a density of about 585 people per square mile.

Population distribution can also be examined in terms of gender. At its simplest, this involves counting how much of a country's population is male and how much is female. But demographers study gender statistics for many other reasons. They can use gender statistics to measure the status of men and women in a society. They look for unfairness in jobs, education, health care, politics, and other spheres of life. Where they find a lack of equality, demographers can urge the government to search for ways to close the gender gap.

Another way that population is distributed is by age. Age data can reveal the size of a country's youth population, its working-age population, and its elderly population. Too many young people can place a burden on parents and schools. Too few young people might lead to a future shortage of workers, which could limit economic growth. Too many elderly might place a strain on health-care and other social support systems.

Population Challenges   In the late 1960s, the world experienced a population explosion. Between 1960 and 1999, the population doubled, from 3 billion to 6 billion. Demographers thought that dealing with this enormous growth would be the main population challenge facing humans in the future. In the 1990s, however, the growth rate began to slow. The population was still expanding, but at a less extreme pace.

> **population density** the number of people in a given land area

India has some of the most densely populated cities in the world. In some Indian cities, many people live in crowded slums, such as this Mumbai neighborhood.

developing country a poorer country whose economy is less industrialized than those of highly developed countries

genocide actions taken with the intent to destroy an ethnic, racial, or religious group

In 2010, the world's birthrate was 20 and the death rate was 8. That gap explains why the population of the world continues to increase. What it fails to show, however, is that the birthrate has been declining for several decades, as has the fertility rate. The death rate has also been falling, but not as rapidly. If these trends continue, annual births and deaths will one day be equal. The world's population will stabilize. Nevertheless, today, individual countries still face serious population challenges.

One basic challenge some nations face is simply having too many people. Birth and fertility rates remain high in many **developing countries**. The nations of the developing world have less industrialized economies than those of highly developed regions such as Europe. Their people, in general, have lower incomes and lower standards of living.

Developing countries often lack the resources to support their growing populations. China faced this problem as early as the 1950s. It could not grow enough food to feed its people. In 1979, China instituted a one-child policy to try to limit the population. This drastic program of birth control required Chinese couples to limit their families to a single child. The one-child policy has slowed China's growth rate, but it has created another problem. The one child in a family may be the sole caregiver of his or her aging parents and grandparents.

The problem of taking care of an aging population may, in fact, be the main demographic challenge of the 21st century. Over the past 50 years, women have been giving birth to fewer children on average, and improvements in agriculture and public health have allowed people to live longer. These trends have created an increasingly elderly population in many developed countries, such as Japan and Germany. Meanwhile, many developing countries, such as Rwanda, are still dealing with the challenges of a growing population.

Rwanda The recent history of Rwanda has made it difficult to limit population growth. In 1990, tensions between this Central African nation's two main ethnic groups, the Hutus and the Tutsis, sparked a civil war. In 1994, the governing Hutus perpetrated a **genocide**—the systematic killing of people from a particular ethnic, racial, or religious group—wiping out three quarters of the Tutsi population.

Because so many Rwandans had died in the war, many parents felt a need to have many children. But despite the death toll of the recent conflict, Rwanda still had too many people. Its limited natural resources could not support them all. For this reason, Rwanda's government made family planning a priority in an attempt to control the number of children in a family. It recognized that limiting population growth was a key to ending poverty and to developing the economy.

Efforts to limit population growth in Rwanda have been largely unsuccessful. In 2011, the population was increasing at one of the fastest rates in the world. As a result, Rwanda is a very youthful country.

It instituted programs aimed at helping parents freely and responsibly determine the number of children that they could support and limit their family size.

Rwanda's population density in 2011 was the highest of any country on the sub-Saharan African continent. The rate at which Rwanda's population was increasing was among the highest in the world.

Japan and Germany   Two developed countries, Japan and Germany, face a different kind of demographic challenge. The people of Japan and Germany are not producing enough children to support an expanding elderly population. Children, in time, become workers. By paying taxes, workers contribute to the social programs upon which many retired people depend. Children also become parents and have children of their own. Countries with very low birthrates face the challenge of an aging—and even a falling—population. Demographers have projected that Japan's population will drop from 127 million in 2010 to 95 million in 2050. Germany faces the same situation.

The Germans and the Japanese have considered ways of dealing with their aging populations. They include encouraging people to have more children, raising the retirement age to keep people working, and adding more women to the work force. But the most controversial answer is immigration. Plenty of young workers from developing countries are willing to move to Germany or Japan. However, many Germans and Japanese have opposed immigration. One reason is national identity. Immigrants, they fear, might alter what it means to be "German" or "Japanese." A further barrier in Japan is the language, which is difficult for foreign workers to learn.

An age-sex graph, also known as a population pyramid, displays a population's age and sex composition. These pyramids show the populations of Rwanda and Japan in 2011. The graph for Rwanda, with its wide base and narrow top, is typical of a young population. In contrast, the shape of Japan's graph reflects an aging population. The birthrate in Japan is low, and a larger percentage of people survive into old age.

Population Pyramids for Rwanda and Japan

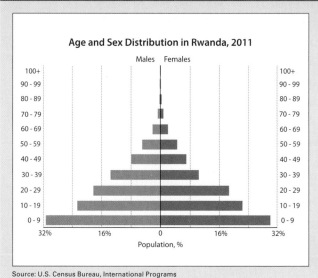

Age and Sex Distribution in Rwanda, 2011

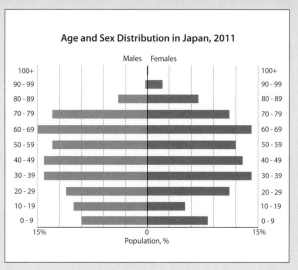

Age and Sex Distribution in Japan, 2011

Source: U.S. Census Bureau, International Programs

A worker does the dirty work of operating an oil drill. In the 20th century, industrialized countries came to rely heavily on petroleum as an energy source. Once oil is extracted from the ground, it is used up forever. Because of this, oil is classified as a nonrenewable resource.

natural resource any naturally occurring material that people find useful or valuable

30.3 Managing Natural Resources

The conditions of life vary greatly from one country to another. Some people are able to enjoy prosperity. Others are forced to merely seek survival from one day to the next. The difference between these groups is often their access to resources. One of the key challenges of the 21st century is how to manage Earth's natural resources in a way that helps all humans thrive—while limiting their negative impact on the environment.

The Three Forms of Natural Resources   Natural resources are naturally occurring materials that people find useful. They include water, soil, trees, minerals, and fossil fuels. They come in three basic forms.

Some natural resources are renewable. Unless human activities destroy them, they will replenish themselves in time. For example, a new forest will grow up after its trees have been harvested for timber.

Some natural resources are nonrenewable. Fossil fuels, such as coal, oil, and natural gas, took millions of years to form. But once humans use them, they are effectively gone forever.

Flow resources, the third form, have similar properties to renewable resources, except that they can be used only when and where they occur. They include sunlight, wind, and flowing water. Each serves as a source of energy—often called alternative, clean, or green energy.

Location of Earth's Natural Resources   Nearly every substance on Earth, and within Earth's crust, is a potential natural resource. At any one time, however, humans value certain resources more than others. Wood was once the resource of choice for use as fuel. The arrival of steam power during the Industrial Revolution cut back on the value of wood and increased the value of coal. In the 20th century, industrial countries came to rely more on petroleum, or oil. Some other form of energy may one day replace oil.

The location of resources affects where people settle and helps determine their activities. Deposits of coal or oil or gold attract people and industries whose aim is to extract those resources. Towns and cities grow up along rivers or other sources of fresh water. Farmers migrate to areas with fertile soil.

Today, fossil fuels and certain minerals are among the most highly valued natural resources. The largest reserves of oil and natural gas are found in the Middle East. The largest quantities of gold come from China, the United States, Australia, South Africa, and Russia. The most productive diamond mines are located in Australia, the Democratic Republic of the Congo, Russia, and South Africa. A relative newcomer to the list of high-value minerals is tantalum, a key metal used in computers and mobile phones. It is mined in Australia, Brazil, and Canada.

Humans have always needed water. Today, supplies of fresh water are distributed fairly evenly across the globe. However, in the desert regions of Africa, the Middle East, Australia, China, and the United States, water is scarce. In other places, drinking water is polluted or limited by drought.

Land is also an indispensable resource. People live on it. They grow crops and graze animals on it. Some of the most productive farmland is in the United States, China, Brazil, India, Mexico, and Russia. Forested land covers vast areas in Russia, Brazil, Canada, the United States, and China.

How Resources Are Developed, Distributed, and Consumed

Some of the wealthiest countries in the world are those with a large quantity of highly valued, but scarce, natural resources. China, for example, controls more than 90 percent of the world's supply of rare-earth minerals. These elements have been called "21st-century gold" because of the key role that they play in wind turbines, fuel cells, compact fluorescent light bulbs, and high-tech weaponry. Another country, Saudi Arabia, has more than a fifth of the world's known oil reserves.

To take advantage of its resources, a country must have the technology and organization to develop and distribute them. Saudi Arabia, for example, has developed advanced technology for oil exploration, drilling, extraction, and transport. It has also designed a reliable system for marketing its product to refiners, who turn crude oil into gasoline and other products.

The major oil refiners, like many of the world's largest businesses, are **multinational corporations**. They have facilities—offices, factories, stores, warehouses—in multiple nations. Nearly all of these huge companies are based in the United States, Japan, or Western Europe. They include automakers, banks, retailers, and fast-food chains. Multinational corporations play a leading role in the global network of resource production, distribution, and consumption.

Unlike oil, land is a natural resource that occurs throughout the world. Land, if fertile, can be developed to produce food. Many countries have fertile land, but not all fertile land is equally productive. Through the mid-1900s, many poor countries in Asia and elsewhere experienced periodic famines. Their traditional farming methods could not produce enough food to feed growing populations. They needed help further developing their land.

Starting in the 1960s, with the aid of Western nations, Asia underwent a "Green Revolution." Farmers turned from manual to mechanized agriculture. They applied chemical fertilizers and pesticides. They planted high-yielding varieties of rice, wheat, and other crops. As a result, between 1970 and 1995, their production of cereals more than doubled. Incomes also soared, pulling many people in Asia out of poverty.

multinational corporation a company with facilities in more than one country

China controls a vast majority of the world's supply of rare-earth minerals. The region of Inner Mongolia, where this rare-earth mining facility is located, is an especially rich source. However, mining has stripped the landscape bare and polluted the environment with toxic waste.

The refusal of Arab countries to export oil to the United States in the early 1970s led to an oil crisis. Oil prices shot up, and gas was in short supply. Gas stations had to shut when they ran out of fuel. When stations did open, long lines of cars would form as customers waited to purchase the available gas.

Worldwide, the poverty rate among developing countries has been decreasing. As people in these countries gradually escape poverty, they consume more resources. They increase demand for non-local and imported goods, such as refrigerators, televisions, and cars. Today, developed countries consume most of Earth's resources by far. But rising demand from developing countries may lead to more intense competition—and conflict.

Competition for Resources   Competition for vital resources such as oil and water has already led to international disputes. In 1960, five major oil producers—Saudi Arabia, Iran, Iraq, Kuwait, and Venezuela—founded the Organization of the Petroleum Exporting Countries, or OPEC. Their goal was to coordinate their oil policies in order to keep prices high. In 1973, Arab countries placed an embargo, or ban, on the United States to punish it for supporting Israel when Egypt and Syria invaded. The embargo led to much higher prices in the United States and severe shortages of gasoline and heating oil.

In 1980, Iraq invaded Iran in part to try to take possession of its rich oil fields. Eight years of bitter fighting ended in a ceasefire. Just two years later, in 1990, Iraq invaded another of its OPEC partners, Kuwait, and captured its oil fields. In what was called the Persian Gulf War, a coalition of countries led by the United States quickly forced Iraq out of Kuwait. The demand for oil, not only from developed, industrial countries but also from the developing world will likely continue to rise. This will only intensify the competition for this scarce, nonrenewable natural resource.

In desert regions, the basic need for water can also lead to conflict. Civilizations would likely not have arisen and prospered in arid lands, such as Mesopotamia and Egypt, without their being located near rivers. Water was, and still is, the key to producing enough food for a population. Today, especially in times of drought, countries in the former lands of Mesopotamia regularly squabble over rights to the waters of the Tigris and Euphrates rivers. But in Egypt, a potential clash over the Nile River involves not just its African neighbors but also distant—and much wealthier—states.

Before its waters reach Egypt, the Nile flows north through the fertile plains of Ethiopia and Sudan. Saudi Arabia, South Korea, China, and India have all obtained large tracts of land there for farming. They use the land to grow grain, which they ship home to feed their own people. Growing this grain takes a lot of water out of the Nile. This could eventually severely reduce the flow of the Nile through Egypt, which relies on the river to irrigate its own grain crops. Water shortages could one day lead to a food crisis in Egypt—and set off conflict in northeastern Africa.

Human Impact on the Environment   In 1970, Americans celebrated the first Earth Day, a day for raising awareness of environmental issues. At the time, air and water pollution were widespread in the United States. Automobiles and factories spewed poisonous gases into the air. Cities fouled nearby waters with sewage and chemicals. Pesticides and fertilizers seeped into rivers and streams. Humans were ruining their environment and damaging their own health.

Similar problems in other countries prompted people around the world to become much more aware of the need to protect the environment. Earth Day has become an international event. As a result of this increased awareness, air and water are cleaner now, but much remains to be done.

One ongoing environmental concern is global climate change. Many scientists consider it the key environmental challenge of the 21st century. They note that Earth's average temperature is rising. These scientists warn that global warming could alter climates enough to lead to a number of problems. They think that melting glaciers and polar ice sheets will cause sea levels to rise, flooding low-lying coastal plains and submerging some islands. Extreme weather events, such as floods, droughts, and hurricanes, will become more common. The yield of certain crops, such as rice and cereals, will drop, especially in tropical regions.

Most climate scientists believe that human activities, especially the burning of fossil fuels, play a significant role in climate change. These activities, they say, have introduced large amounts of carbon dioxide and other gases into the atmosphere since the start of the Industrial Revolution. There the gases act like a greenhouse, holding in the sun's heat and raising the temperature on Earth. This **greenhouse effect,** they argue, is a major cause of climate change. They warn that humans must cut back on the gases that produce the greenhouse effect or face dire consequences.

Some scientists, however, dispute that the earth is warming. Others believe that the warming of Earth is caused by natural climate cycles and not by human activities. Still, the present consensus of most of the scientific community is that global warming is a real, human-made phenomenon.

greenhouse effect the trapping of the sun's heat in the lower atmosphere, caused by the presence of carbon dioxide and other gases

By the late 1960s, concern about pollution and the destruction of the environment by industry was increasing, especially in the United States. American environmentalists organized Earth Day to increase awareness of the need to protect the environment. This photo shows a gathering in New York City on the first Earth Day, April 22, 1970.

Consumer goods are shipped around the world cheaply and efficiently using cargo ships. Goods are loaded into large metal shipping containers, which are made to a standardized size for ease of handling in ports across the globe. Here cranes help unload a cargo ship filled with shipping containers in the port of Stone Town, Tanzania.

30.4 Patterns of Global Economic Interaction

Global interaction is not a new phenomenon. By 1600, European states were carrying on a brisk trade with lands all over the world. However, the patterns of interaction have changed. More than ever before, modern countries depend on one another. They do not just trade—they form trading partnerships. They rely on the same communications and transportation systems. They are served by the same multinational corporations. Their economies are, in effect, intertwined.

globalization the process of increasing the interdependence of the world's economies

common market a group formed by countries within a geographical area with the goal of eliminating taxes on trade goods and allowing the free movement of labor and capital among its members

Economic Interdependence   The process of increasing the interdependence of the world's economies is called **globalization**. In a fully globalized world, goods and services, money, and information would flow freely across national boundaries. The world's borders will most likely never be completely open, but the process has begun. Today, multinational corporations buy and sell goods whose parts often come from several different countries. Multinational banks fund international economic exchanges. Information travels across borders via the Internet and other high-speed communications networks.

Globalization has resulted largely from a quest for free trade. After World War II, the United States and many European nations came to believe that free and open trade would benefit world economies and help prevent future conflicts among nations. The United States, especially, promoted free trade as a strategy for helping European economies recover from the war and as a way to keep nations out of the Soviet Union's sphere of influence. In 1951, six countries in Europe formed the European Coal and Steel Community to create a common market for those two products. A **common market** is a grouping of countries that promotes lower trade barriers among its members. Through the years, the European Coal and Steel Community expanded, and it added a political dimension to its goal of unifying the continent economically. Today, it is known as the European Union (EU).

European success at stimulating trade sparked other moves toward free trade. In 1994, the North American Free Trade Agreement (NAFTA) went into effect. Under NAFTA, the United States, Canada, and Mexico agreed to create their own common market. Their purpose was to get rid of trade barriers, especially tariffs, on goods and services traveling from one of the three countries to another. The United States has since negotiated free trade agreements with more than a dozen other countries.

Similar agreements have blossomed among countries all over the globe, often with the help of the World Trade Organization (WTO). Founded in 1995, the WTO is an international organization run by more than 150 member-nations. Its main goal is to reduce trade barriers throughout the world. It does so by offering a forum for countries to negotiate trade agreements and providing a set of rules to guide international trade. If a trade dispute arises, the WTO will help settle it.

Trade agreements tie countries together in a dependent relationship. A key requirement for such an agreement is that all participants must be able to profit from that relationship. They do so, in part, by making the most of their comparative advantage.

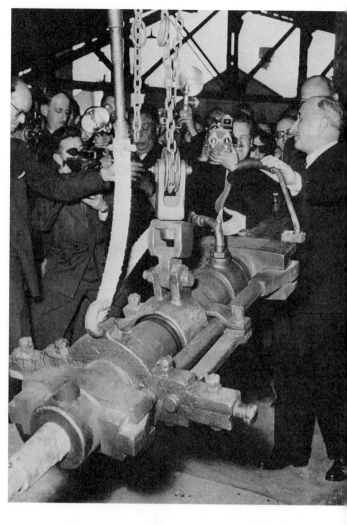

In this 1953 photo, the French politician Jean Monnet presides over the ceremonial opening of the European Coal and Steel Community in a Luxembourg steel factory. Monnet was a leader in establishing the ECSC common market in the years after World War II.

Comparative Advantage   A strong driver of free trade is an economic theory known as **comparative advantage**. The theory states that a country that can produce a good more efficiently than others has an advantage compared with its competitors. A country might derive an advantage from its geographic location, fertile farmland, mineral wealth, or highly educated workforce.

Free trade agreements reflect the real-life application of this theory. They allow countries to sell their trading partners the goods and services that they can produce more cheaply, and to buy from their partners goods and services that they need but cannot produce as cheaply.

From the 1800s well into the 1900s, industrialized countries grew wealthy from selling manufactured products. They could produce finished goods more cheaply and efficiently than less developed countries. But they relied on those countries for raw materials. Britain, for example, had a comparative advantage over Egypt in the production of textiles. Egypt, though, could produce cotton more efficiently than Britain. When those two countries engaged in trade, each made the most of its comparative advantage.

comparative advantage the theory that in international trade, countries should specialize in the goods that they are most efficient at producing

A country's comparative advantage can shift over time. Through most of the 1900s, Brazil, India, and China, like most of the world's less developed countries, were poor. They contributed raw materials to the world economy, but little else. Today, each of those countries has become much more competitive in global trade. Along with Russia, they are known as the BRIC economies (from the first letter of each country's name). They have been singled out for their potential to become economic powerhouses in the coming years.

For much of its history, Brazil contributed raw materials to the world market, but recently Brazil has become competitive in the global trade of manufactured goods. This factory in Recife, Brazil, produces textiles.

Many developing countries have found that they have a comparative advantage in human resources, or labor. Wages paid there are often much lower than in developed countries. For this reason, they have attracted labor-intensive service and factory work once performed in the West and Japan. Today, for example, many poor but well-educated, English-speaking people in India work at call centers. By telephone, they handle sales and customer support for numerous American and British companies. In China, factory workers produce goods found in stores throughout the world.

The evolution of the corporation played a role in the globalization of labor. The classic multinational corporation was based in one country—mainly in the United States, Western Europe, or Japan. It did business in other countries through subsidiaries, or companies that it controlled. Government policies in a base country often helped corporations but also restricted their business practices. These policies generally encouraged corporations to keep jobs in the home country.

The 1990s and early 2000s saw a rise in mergers between companies based in different countries. The resulting global corporations essentially decoupled themselves from any one nation's resources—and their often restrictive government policies. Global corporations made business decisions based on their own priorities. One consequence was the **outsourcing,** or sending abroad, of jobs from developed to less developed countries. There the low cost of labor reduced the cost of production. Today, corporations outsource not only unskilled but also skilled jobs. A computer sold in the United States, for example, may be designed by engineers in India and assembled by technicians in Mexico.

outsource contract out or send offshore

Distribution of Wealth and Resources In spite of the economic impact of job losses, the developed nations are still the wealthiest nations of the world, at least for now. With generally high wages and standards of living, their citizens consume most of the world's goods, by far. In the process they use up a large percentage of the world's oil, metals, and other natural resources.

Many people in developing countries would like to enjoy the same standards of living as developed countries. This helps explain migration patterns. Each year, hundreds of thousands of workers head for North America, Western Europe, Japan, Australia, and elsewhere in search of a better life. Many of them send part of their earnings back to their families in their home country. That flow of cash, known as remittances, provides important economic support to households and to governments in many of those countries. In 2009, remittances worldwide topped $400 billion.

Impact of Globalization One criticism of globalization is that it has not closed the gap in standards of living between developed and developing countries. Another is that it forces developing countries to link their economies with the rest of the world even if they do not have the resources to compete successfully. As a result, critics say, those countries focus on the global marketplace and end up ignoring the needs of people locally. They also give up some of their sovereignty to powerful multinational corporations, which make economic decisions that can have a huge impact on a country.

Others insist that globalization has actually helped close the economic gap between developing and developed countries. The outsourcing of jobs, they argue, gives a welcome boost to developing economies. Workers in China and India, for example, can now afford consumer goods such as televisions and cars. To narrow the unequal distribution of wealth and resources, supporters of globalization insist that developing countries should be encouraged to pursue free-trade policies. In 2000, the Secretary General of the United Nations agreed, saying:

> *The main losers in today's very unequal world are not those who are too much exposed to globalization. They are those who have been left out.*
> —Kofi Annan, speaking at a United Nations convention, February 2000

Critics argue that globalization hurts local economies. The Korean Peasants League, pictured here at an anti-World Trade Organization protest in 2005, is a militant anti-globalization group. They argue that free trade policies harm the interests of local Korean farmers.

Globalization includes more than just the exchange of goods. New ideas and inventions have always spread from region to region, but with globalization, scientific knowledge, medical advances, and new technology all pass easily across modern borders. Part of the reason for this is the information revolution. As countries build advanced communications systems, they connect themselves more effectively with the world.

Another result of this connectedness is the globalization of culture through a process of cultural diffusion. Today, in a world of global commerce, nearly any product can be sold nearly anywhere. But the developed world dominates global commerce. It also dominates the mass media—television, radio, movies, and the Internet. Through these channels, goods as well as ideas and values can flow. They can alter local cultures, changing the foods people eat, the way people dress, and even the way they think. With globalization, some cultural shift is inevitable. But nobody is sure what the impact will be or how globalization will affect traditional cultures.

Globalization has increased cultural connectedness and the free exchange of ideas and styles. One example of this is the China Central Television Headquarters building, pictured here. It was designed by the innovative Dutch architect Rem Koolhaas, but was constructed in Beijing, China, and has become a visual symbol of modern Beijing.

30.5 Conflict, Cooperation, and Security

The Cold War ended in 1991 with the breakup of the Soviet Union. Throughout the world, people looked forward to a time of peace and security. Globalization did encourage cooperation—economic and political—among nations, but the world continued to be plagued by violent conflict.

Ethnic Violence   Many countries have more than one ethnic group living within its borders. Each group may have its own language, religion, or customs. In some of these countries, the clash of different cultures has led to extreme levels of bloodshed. Northern Ireland, Cambodia, Bosnia, Rwanda, and Sudan all have a recent history of ethnic violence.

Northern Ireland is part of the United Kingdom. It split off from the rest of Ireland in the 1920s because it had a Protestant majority loyal to Great Britain while the rest of Ireland was majority Catholic. In the decades that followed, Northern Ireland's Protestant majority used its political power and control of institutions to oppress the Roman Catholic minority. The Catholics fought for their rights, often using terror tactics such as bombings. The Protestants fought back, and the violence escalated. Thousands of British troops were sent to the region to try to restore order. Only in the late 1990s was a lasting peace achieved, through a series of negotiations and compromises.

Cambodia experienced ethnic violence on an even more destructive scale. In 1975, after years of civil war, Cambodia fell into the hands of the guerrilla fighters of the Khmer Rouge. The Khmer Rouge was a radical communist political group. From 1975 to 1979, it engaged in an extreme campaign to destroy its enemies. Those supposed enemies included the wealthy, the educated, and the members of nearly every ethnic minority in the country. First the Khmer Rouge emptied the cities, sending most of Cambodia's urban population into the countryside to work the fields as forced labor. Many died from exhaustion, starvation, or disease. Mass executions of "class enemies" and ethnic minorities followed. This genocide resulted in the deaths of more than 1.5 million Cambodians.

Bosnia also experienced the horrors of ethnic violence. Bosnia and Herzegovina (or, simply, Bosnia) became a province of Yugoslavia in 1946. Ethnic tensions among its Serb, Croat, and Muslim populations boiled over into civil war in 1992, when Bosnia declared its independence from Yugoslavia. Bosnian Serbs opposed separation from Yugoslavia. In the war that followed the Serbs pursued a policy of **ethnic cleansing,** a brutal—but ultimately failed—attempt to expel all Muslims from Bosnia by force. Their tactics included rape and mass murder.

Those same tactics also appeared in the genocide that afflicted the African nation of Rwanda. Beginning in the early 1990s, rebels from the Tutsi ethnic group fought for power against the governing Hutu ethnic group, who far outnumbered them. A peace accord reached in 1993 was shattered that same year when the extremist nationalist Hutus began a killing spree. In a 100-day period, the extremist Hutus slaughtered some 800,000 people throughout the country. The victims were Tutsi men, women, and children and some moderate Hutus. Tutsi forces later defeated the Hutus and ended the genocide.

In Sudan, ethnic conflict pitted the governing Arab Muslims of the north against a small minority of African Christians and followers of native religions in the south. The southern Sudanese had long complained of mistreatment by the government. Starting in the mid-1980s, defiant southerners launched a guerrilla war aimed at liberating their region from the north. The warfare left some 2 million Sudanese dead. In 2005, a peace treaty opened the door to self-rule. In 2011, the southern region became the independent nation of South Sudan.

Northern Ireland experienced violence between Protestants and Catholics beginning in the 1960s and lasting until the late 1990s. Here Catholic youths throw stones during a riot in Belfast, the capital of Northern Ireland, in 1970.

ethnic cleansing forced removal from a given territory of persons of another ethnic or religious group

Two wounded refugees flee Rwanda, which was devastated by ethnic conflict and genocide in 1993.

terrorist one who carries out unlawful violence against civilian targets in order to instill fear and advance political goals

Lingering Sources of Tension and Conflict The splitting of Sudan did not bring peace. Violent clashes between feuding ethnic groups continued elsewhere in Sudan, namely in the western region of Darfur where non-Arab tribes face vicious attacks from government-supported militias. To a lesser degree problems continue in South Sudan itself. Ethnic discord in this region of Africa is just one of several lingering sources of tension and conflict in the 21st-century world. Another is instability in the Middle East.

The Middle East today is home to about a dozen states with a majority Muslim population. Israel, a Jewish state in this otherwise Muslim region of the world, has long faced hostility from its neighbors. Two ongoing sources of conflict have been rejection of Israel's right to exist and Israel's control of areas that the largely Muslim Palestinian Arabs want for their own state.

Another source of instability in the Middle East is the presence of radical Islamic terrorist organizations. The United States became a target of radical Muslim **terrorists** on September 11, 2001. The 9/11 attacks on the twin towers of the World Trade Center in New York City and on the Pentagon killed nearly 3,000 people and led to a global "war on terror." The war began with a U.S.-led invasion of Afghanistan. That was where Osama bin Laden, the mastermind of the 9/11 attacks, had based his terrorist organization, known as al Qaeda.

U.S. troops intended to find Osama bin Laden and destroy al Qaeda. Ten years later, in neighboring Pakistan, an American assault force finally located and killed bin Laden. By that time, al Qaeda's strength had been steadily reduced. However, as American troops prepared to withdraw from

On September 11, 2001, radical Muslim terrorists flew commercial jet aircrafts into each of the towers of the World Trade Center in New York City, collapsing both towers. The Pentagon was also targeted in this coordinated attack. In total, nearly 3,000 people were killed.

Afghanistan, the country remained unstable, its future uncertain.

In 2003, the United States also invaded Iraq. The U.S. government had intelligence that led them to believe that Iraqi leader Saddam Hussein was stockpiling weapons of mass destruction (WMD). The goal of the invasion was to find and destroy those weapons, whether chemical, biological, or nuclear. Over time, troops did uncover a few aged chemical weapons but no significant stores of WMD. Soon after invading Iraq, U.S. forces drove Saddam Hussein from power. However, the Iraq War turned out to be a long and costly struggle against remnants of Saddam Hussein's regime and various Muslim militias and extremist groups, including al Qaeda.

In early 2010, Iraqis elected a national government. The United States formally ended its military operation in Iraq in late 2011 after nearly nine years of war. Nearly 4,500 U.S. troops were killed in Iraq and more than 30,000 were wounded. Estimates of Iraqi civilian deaths were in the tens of thousands.

Some extremist groups in the Iraq War received military training and arms from Iran. In the early 2000s, this Islamic republic steadily gained power and influence in the Middle East. Many in the West feared that Iran was seeking to develop nuclear weapons. The Iranians, however, insisted that their nuclear program had only the peaceful goal of producing nuclear power.

In 1999, tensions in Kashmir led to open conflict between India and Pakistan. In this photo, Pakistani soldiers aim an artillery gun across the Line of Control, the boundary that separates the Indian and Pakistani-controlled sections of Kashmir.

Two countries to the east of Iran—Pakistan and India—do possess nuclear weapons. What makes this a worrisome situation is that these South Asian countries are fierce rivals. A major source of tension between them is the region of Kashmir. Kashmir lies east of Pakistan and north of India. About 48 percent of Kashmir is under Indian occupation and 35 percent is occupied by Pakistan, with the remaining territory under control of China. Like Pakistan but unlike India, Kashmir's population is mainly Muslim. Pakistani troops have, on occasion, moved into Indian Kashmir in support of those who want to separate from India. Their actions led to wars in 1965 and 1999. Violence in the region has claimed more than 40,000 lives, and Kashmir continues to be a potential flashpoint in relations between India and Pakistan.

The Struggle for Democracy   In the 1970s and 1980s, authoritarian rule seemed to be yielding steadily to democracy. From South Korea to South Africa, from Czechoslovakia to Chile, dictatorships gave way to democracies. By and large, these regime changes did not come about through violent revolution. The causes were complex. They included rising levels of education and prosperity, increasing

In April 2011, protesters filled Tahrir Square in the Egyptian capital city of Cairo. The popular uprising brought about the resignation of the Egyptian president Hosni Mubarak and was a central event in what came to be known as the Arab Spring.

Arab Spring name for the popular upheavals that swept Arab countries of North Africa and the Middle East in 2011

demands for human rights, and pressure for political change. Unpopular policies instituted to deal with a failing economy helped undermine many authoritarian governments as well.

By the late 1980s, even the Soviet Union found itself struggling to maintain communist rule. Its unproductive system of collective farming had led to food shortages. Its huge military budget had sapped the economy of resources. Economic reforms (*perestroika*) and political reforms (*glasnost*) ultimately led to a fairly peaceful transition to capitalism and democracy.

In the early years of the 21st century, progress toward democratization continued. It centered on North Africa and the Middle East, where strong rulers kept their people oppressed. Activists in these countries had long sought democratic reforms, but authoritarian government persisted. Then, in 2011, a remarkable series of popular revolts swept this largely Arab Muslim region. Together, they became known as the **Arab Spring**.

The first uprising occurred in the North African country of Tunisia. Starting in December 2010, Tunisians, many of them young and unemployed, took to the streets to protest the lack of jobs, high food prices, poverty, and government corruption. In mid-January 2011, the growing demonstrations caused Tunisia's president to flee the country.

Tunisia's outburst of democratic action triggered other revolts. By the end of January 2011, pro-democracy demonstrations broke out in several Egyptian cities. In April 2011, massive, largely peaceful protests in the capital city of Cairo led to a dismantling of the government and the arrest of Egypt's president, Hosni Mubarak. In Egypt, as in Tunisia, social media played a key role. Activists used Facebook and Twitter posts to help organize and spread information about the uprising.

Demonstrations also took place in Algeria, Yemen, Lebanon, Iran, Bahrain, Syria, and elsewhere. The level of violence varied. In Libya, anti-government actions took the form of an armed rebellion. With the help of NATO air strikes, the rebel army managed to gain control of the country in August and oust the Libyan dictator, Muammar al-Gaddafi. He was killed shortly after his capture by the opposition.

Antigovernment unrest in Syria began in early 2011. Syria's dictatorship government, led by Bashar al-Assad, responded with military force. The government sent out troops and tanks in a sustained effort to suppress the rebellion. The United States, France, Germany, and the United Kingdom called on Assad to step down, but the crackdown continued into 2012. By early 2012, more than 7,000 Syrians had died.

The future of democratizing countries is uncertain. Throwing off authoritarian rule is not easy. Neither is replacing it with a democratic government. Countries in transition to democracy, however, do not need to go it alone. Just as NATO supported Libyan freedom fighters, other global organizations stand ready to help in the transition to democratic rule. The United Nations made clear its intention to promote justice, human rights, and political security in the region. The World Bank and the International Monetary Fund (IMF) promised aid as a way of encouraging economic security and stability.

Summary

In this lesson, you read about global issues that affect the contemporary world. These include changes in world population, the challenge of managing natural resources, patterns of global interaction, and issues stemming from conflict between and within nations.

Cultural Interaction Today, foods, goods, new technologies, and scientific and medical advances all cross international borders with ease. As a result, nations and corporations that dominate global commerce and mass media are able to spread their cultural ideas and values worldwide.

Political Structures Throughout the modern world, dictatorship is giving way to democracy. From the fall of communism in the Soviet Union to the democratization movement known as the Arab Spring, people have demanded political and economic reforms that promise to give them more individual freedom and a better life.

Economic Structures A majority of nations have decided that capitalism offers the best route to economic growth and a higher standard of living. Even Communist China has made the radical shift from a communist economic system to a market-oriented one.

Social Structures Earth's overall population is rising, but in some developed countries it is falling. Those countries must find ways to support their aging population. Much higher birthrates in the developing world result in larger families and a younger population. These countries often lack the natural resources to support a growing population.

Human-Environment Interaction The development, distribution, and consumption of Earth's natural resources vary from one country to the next. How those resources are managed can have a profound effect on the environment and on people's standard of living. Industrial development has had a negative impact on the environment. Starting in the 1970s an environmental movement arose which increased awareness of the problem. Many scientists today believe that the biggest problem facing the environment is global climate change.

Resources

The Strahov Library in Prague, Czech Republic, has thousands of books, prints, and manuscripts that date from the ninth to the eighteenth century.

Physical Features of the World

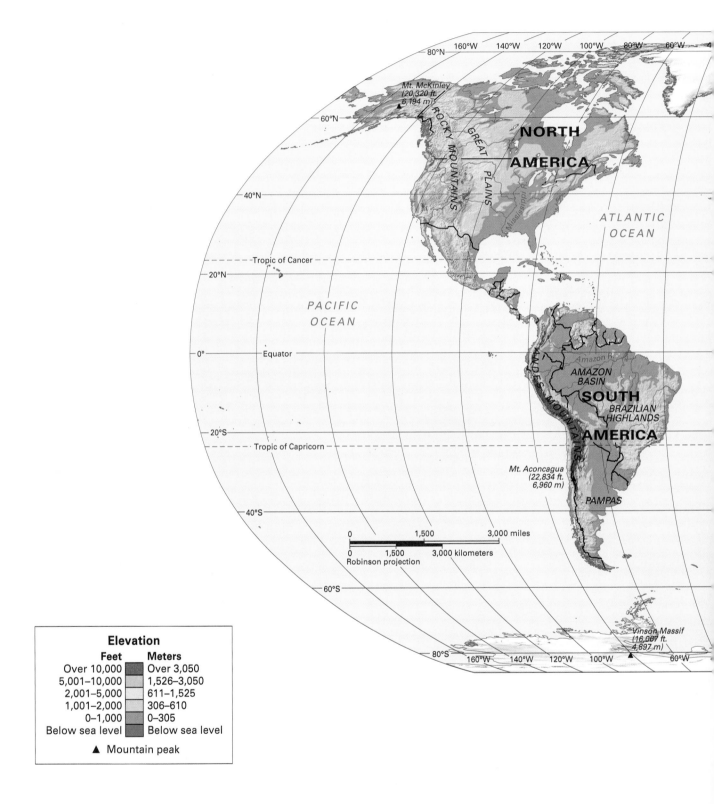

Elevation

Feet		Meters
Over 10,000		Over 3,050
5,001–10,000		1,526–3,050
2,001–5,000		611–1,525
1,001–2,000		306–610
0–1,000		0–305
Below sea level		Below sea level

▲ Mountain peak

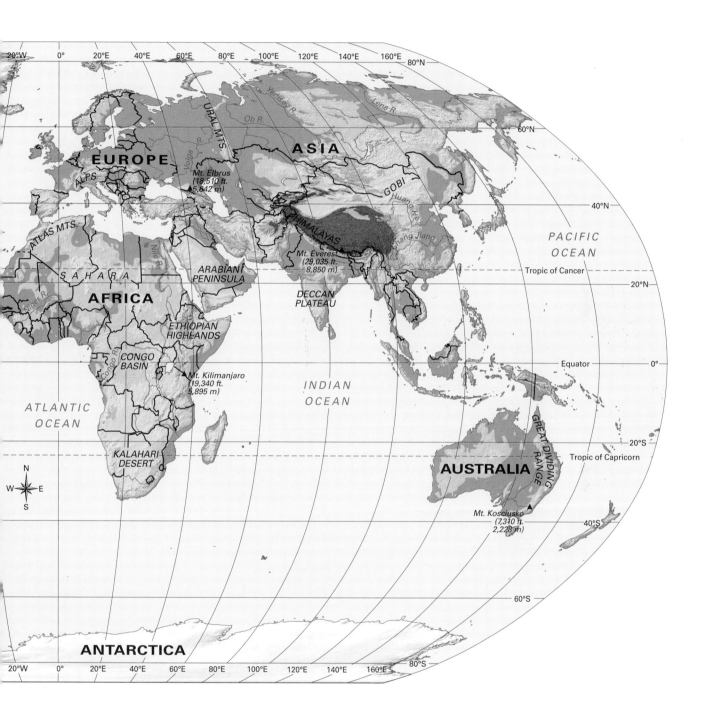

20°W 0° 20°E 40°E 60°E 80°E 100°E 120°E 140°E 160°E 80°N

60°N

EUROPE

ALPS

ASIA

URAL MTS.

Volga R.

Ob R.

Yenisey R.

Lena R.

Mt. Elbrus
(18,510 ft.
5,642 m)

40°N

GOBI

Huang He

Nile R.

ATLAS MTS.

S A H A R A

ARABIAN
PENINSULA

HIMALAYAS

Chang Jiang

PACIFIC
OCEAN

Mt. Everest
(29,035 ft.
8,850 m)

Tropic of Cancer

20°N

AFRICA

Niger R.

DECCAN
PLATEAU

ETHIOPIAN
HIGHLANDS

CONGO
BASIN

Congo R.

Mt. Kilimanjaro
(19,340 ft.
5,895 m)

INDIAN
OCEAN

Equator

0°

ATLANTIC
OCEAN

KALAHARI
DESERT

AUSTRALIA

GREAT DIVIDING RANGE

20°S

Tropic of Capricorn

N
W   E
S

Mt. Kosciusko
(7,310 ft.
2,228 m)

40°S

60°S

ANTARCTICA

20°W 0° 20°E 40°E 60°E 80°E 100°E 120°E 140°E 160°E 80°S

Political Boundaries of the World

THE BAHAMAS
DOMINICAN REPUBLIC
HAITI
CUBA
Puerto Rico (U.S.)
ST. KITTS AND NEVIS
JAMAICA
ANTIGUA AND BARBUDA
BELIZE
Guadeloupe (FR.)
DOMINICA
HONDURAS
Martinique (FR.)
ST. VINCENT AND
GUATEMALA
ST. LUCIA
THE GRENADINES
EL SALVADOR
NICARAGUA
BARBADOS
GRENADA
COSTA RICA
TRINIDAD AND TOBAGO
VENEZUELA
GUYANA
PANAMA
SURINAME
COLOMBIA
French Guiana (F

CANADA

Alaska (U.S.)

Greenla
(DEN

UNITED STATES

ATLANTIC
OCEAN

MEXICO

Hawaii
(U.S.)

Tropic of Cancer

PACIFIC
OCEAN

Galápagos Is.
(EC.)
ECUADOR

Equator

BRAZIL

PERU

SAMOA

BOLIVIA

TONGA

PARAGUAY

Easter I.
(CHILE)

CHILE

URUGUAY

ARGENTINA

| 0 | 1,500 | 3,000 mi. |
| 0 | 1,500 | 3,000 km |

Falkland
Is.

Robinson projection

Abbreviations	
ALB.	ALBANIA
AUS.	AUSTRIA
BEL.	BELGIUM
B.H.	BOSNIA and HERZEGOVINA
CR.	CROATIA
CZ. REP.	CZECH REPUBLIC
DEN.	DENMARK
HUNG.	HUNGARY
KOS.	KOSOVO
LUX.	LUXEMBOURG
MAC.	MACEDONIA
MONT.	MONTENEGRO
NETH.	NETHERLANDS
SERB.	SERBIA
SLK.	SLOVAKIA
SLO.	SLOVENIA
SWITZ.	SWITZERLAND

- Independent nations are printed in bold capital letters: **FRANCE**.
- Nations whose independence or governing rule is in dispute are printed in bold type: **Taiwan**.
- Territories, provinces, and the like governed by an independent nation are printed in bold type, with an abbreviation for the ruling nation: **French Guiana (FR.)**.
- Areas whose governing rule is in dispute are printed in nonbold type: Falkland Islands.
- Areas that are part of an independent nation but geographically separated from it are printed in nonbold type, with an abbreviation for the ruling nation: Hawaii (U.S.).

Physical Features of North America

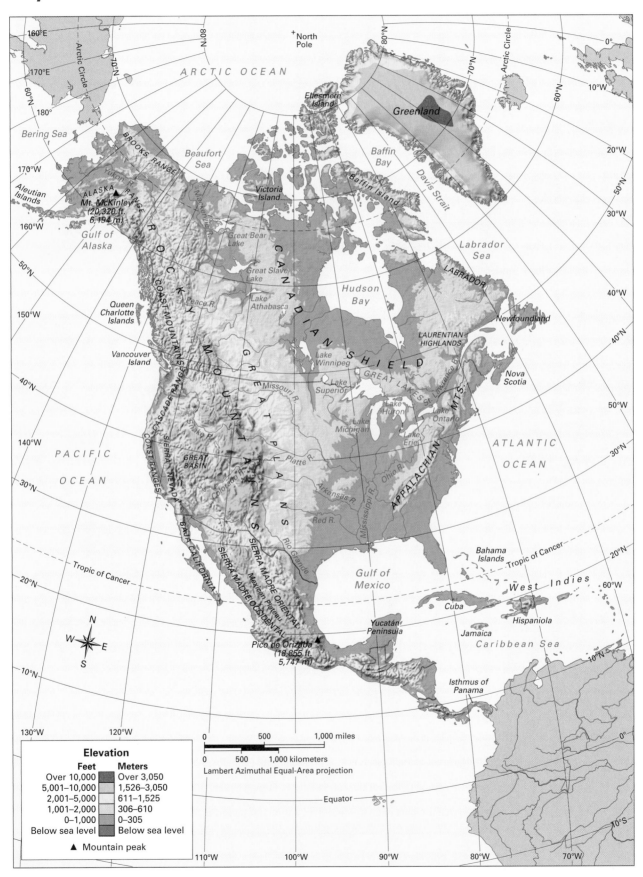

Elevation

Feet	Meters
Over 10,000	Over 3,050
5,001–10,000	1,526–3,050
2,001–5,000	611–1,525
1,001–2,000	306–610
0–1,000	0–305
Below sea level	Below sea level

▲ Mountain peak

0   500   1,000 miles
0   500   1,000 kilometers
Lambert Azimuthal Equal-Area projection

Political Boundaries of North America

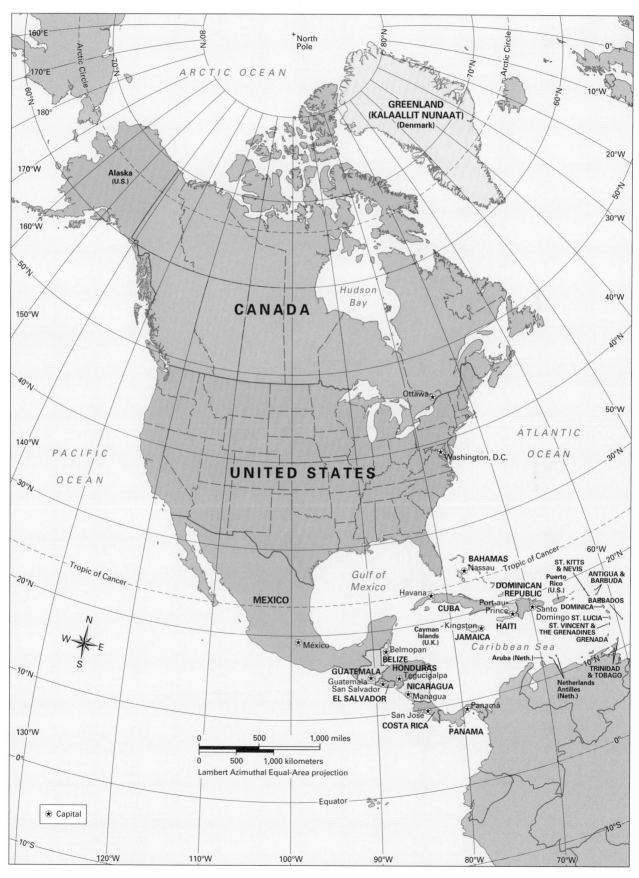

ARCTIC OCEAN

North Pole

GREENLAND (KALAALLIT NUNAAT) (Denmark)

Alaska (U.S.)

CANADA

Hudson Bay

UNITED STATES

Ottawa ⊛

Washington, D.C. ⊛

PACIFIC OCEAN

ATLANTIC OCEAN

Tropic of Cancer

MEXICO

Gulf of Mexico

BAHAMAS
Nassau ⊛   Tropic of Cancer

ST. KITTS & NEVIS

Puerto Rico (U.S.)

ANTIGUA & BARBUDA

Havana ⊛
CUBA

DOMINICAN REPUBLIC

BARBADOS

Port-au-Prince ⊛
Santo Domingo ⊛   DOMINICA

Cayman Islands (U.K.)

Kingston ⊛
JAMAICA

HAITI

ST. LUCIA
ST. VINCENT & THE GRENADINES
GRENADA

México ⊛

Belmopan ⊛
BELIZE

Caribbean Sea

Aruba (Neth.)

TRINIDAD & TOBAGO

GUATEMALA
Guatemala ⊛
San Salvador ⊛
EL SALVADOR

HONDURAS
Tegucigalpa ⊛

NICARAGUA
Managua ⊛

Netherlands Antilles (Neth.)

Panamá ⊛

San José ⊛
COSTA RICA

PANAMA

0   500   1,000 miles
0   500   1,000 kilometers
Lambert Azimuthal Equal-Area projection

Equator

⊛ Capital

Physical Features of South America

Caribbean Sea

ATLANTIC OCEAN

LLANOS

GUIANA HIGHLANDS

Orinoco R.

AMAZON BASIN

Amazon R.

Equator

Galápagos Islands

PACIFIC OCEAN

ANDES MOUNTAINS

Lake Titicaca

ATACAMA DESERT

ANDES MOUNTAINS

GRAN CHACO

BRAZILIAN HIGHLANDS

São Francisco R.

Iguazú Falls

Tropic of Capricorn

Mt. Aconcagua (22,835 ft. 6,960 m)

Paraná R.

Uruguay R.

PAMPAS

N
W   E
S

ATLANTIC OCEAN

PATAGONIA

Laguna del Carbón (-344 ft. -105 m)

Strait of Magellan

Tierra del Fuego

Falkland Islands

Cape Horn

| | 500 | 1,000 miles |
| 0 | 500 | 1,000 kilometers |

Lambert Azimuthal Equal-Area projection

Elevation

Feet	Meters
Over 10,000	Over 3,050
5,001–10,000	1,526–3,050
2,001–5,000	611–1,525
1,001–2,000	306–610
0–1,000	0–305
Below sea level	Below sea level

▲ Mountain peak

Political Boundaries of South America

Caribbean Sea

ATLANTIC OCEAN

Caracas ★

VENEZUELA

Georgetown ★
GUYANA
Paramaribo ★
Cayenne ★
SURINAME
French Guiana (Fr.)

Bogotá ★

COLOMBIA

Equator

Galápagos Islands (Ecuador)

★ Quito

ECUADOR

Equator

PERU

BRAZIL

Lima ★

PACIFIC OCEAN

La Paz ★

BOLIVIA

Brasília ★

★ Sucre

Tropic of Capricorn

PARAGUAY

Asunción ★

Tropic of Capricorn

CHILE

ARGENTINA

N
W ✦ E
S

Santiago ★

URUGUAY

Buenos Aires ★
Montevideo ★

ATLANTIC OCEAN

0   500   1,000 miles
0   500   1,000 kilometers
Lambert Azimuthal Equal-Area projection

★ Capital

Falkland Islands (U.K.)

Physical Features of Europe and Russia

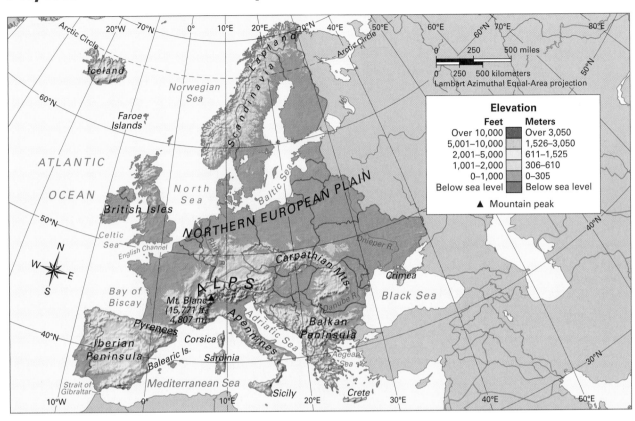

Elevation

Feet		Meters
Over 10,000		Over 3,050
5,001–10,000		1,526–3,050
2,001–5,000		611–1,525
1,001–2,000		306–610
0–1,000		0–305
Below sea level		Below sea level

▲ Mountain peak

Lambert Azimuthal Equal-Area projection

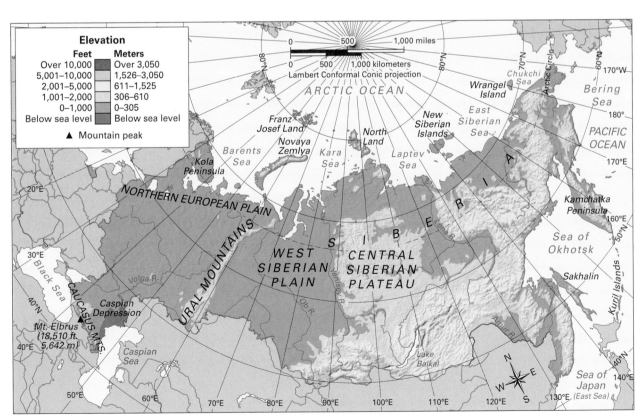

Elevation

Feet		Meters
Over 10,000		Over 3,050
5,001–10,000		1,526–3,050
2,001–5,000		611–1,525
1,001–2,000		306–610
0–1,000		0–305
Below sea level		Below sea level

▲ Mountain peak

Lambert Conformal Conic projection

Political Boundaries of Europe and Russia

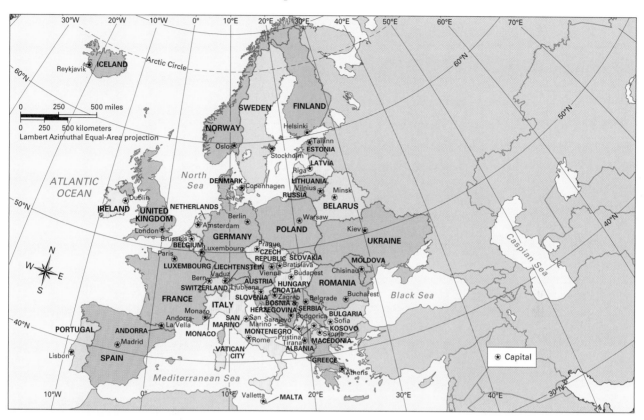

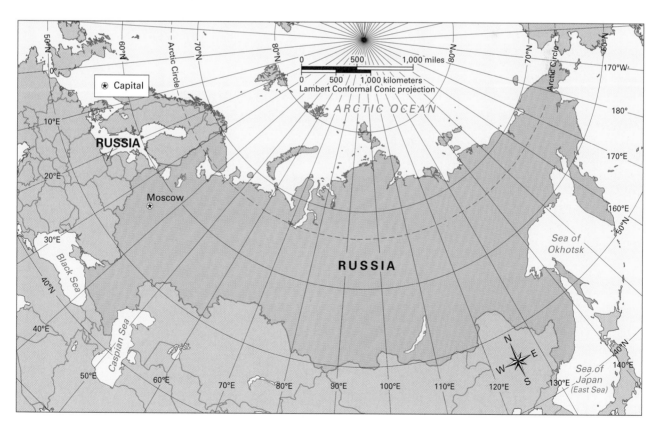

Physical Features of Africa

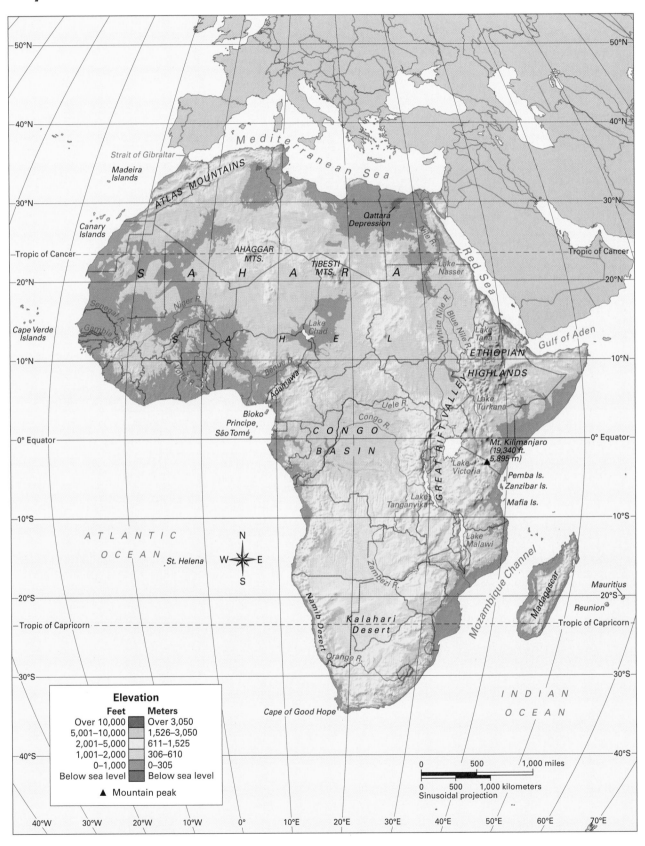

50°N · 40°N · 30°N · Tropic of Cancer · 20°N · 10°N · 0° Equator · 10°S · 20°S · Tropic of Capricorn · 30°S · 40°S

Strait of Gibraltar
Madeira Islands
ATLAS MOUNTAINS
Mediterranean Sea
Canary Islands
Qattara Depression
Tropic of Cancer
AHAGGAR MTS.
TIBESTI MTS.
S   A   H   A   R   A
Nile R.
Lake Nasser
Red Sea
Senegal R.
Niger R.
Cape Verde Islands
Gambia R.
S   A   H   E   L
Lake Chad
White Nile R.
Blue Nile R.
Lake Tana
Gulf of Aden
Volta R.
Benue R.
Adamawa
ETHIOPIAN
HIGHLANDS
Bioko
Principe
São Tomé
Uele R.
Congo R.
C O N G O
B A S I N
GREAT RIFT VALLEY
Lake Turkana
Mt. Kilimanjaro
(19,340 ft.
5,895 m)
Lake Victoria
Pemba Is.
Zanzibar Is.
Mafia Is.
Lake Tanganyika
ATLANTIC
OCEAN
St. Helena
Lake Malawi
Madagascar
Mauritius
Reunion
Mozambique Channel
Namib Desert
Zambezi R.
Kalahari Desert
Orange R.
Cape of Good Hope
INDIAN
OCEAN

N
W   E
S

Elevation

Feet	Meters
Over 10,000	Over 3,050
5,001–10,000	1,526–3,050
2,001–5,000	611–1,525
1,001–2,000	306–610
0–1,000	0–305
Below sea level	Below sea level

▲ Mountain peak

0   500   1,000 miles
0   500   1,000 kilometers
Sinusoidal projection

40°W · 30°W · 20°W · 10°W · 0° · 10°E · 20°E · 30°E · 40°E · 50°E · 60°E · 70°E

Political Boundaries of Africa

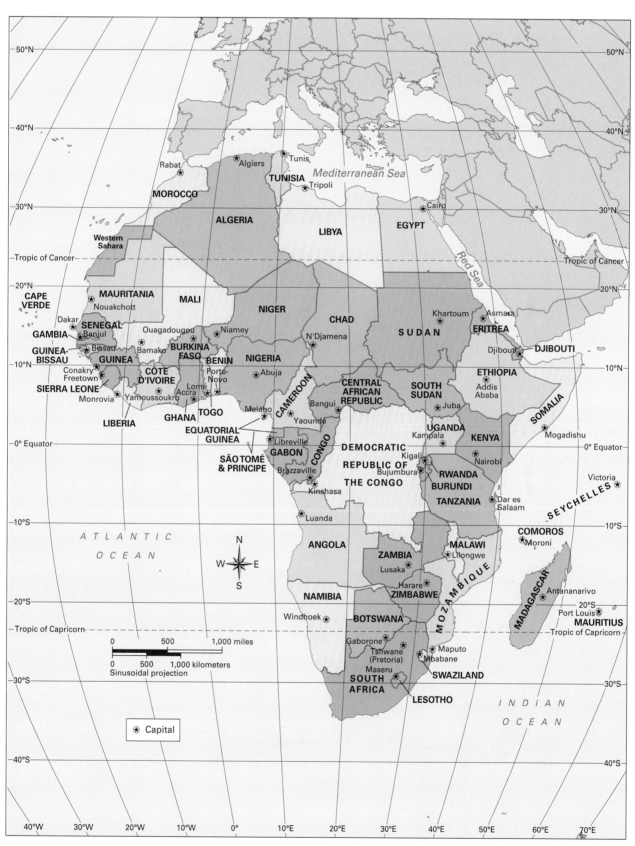

Physical Features of Southwest and Central Asia

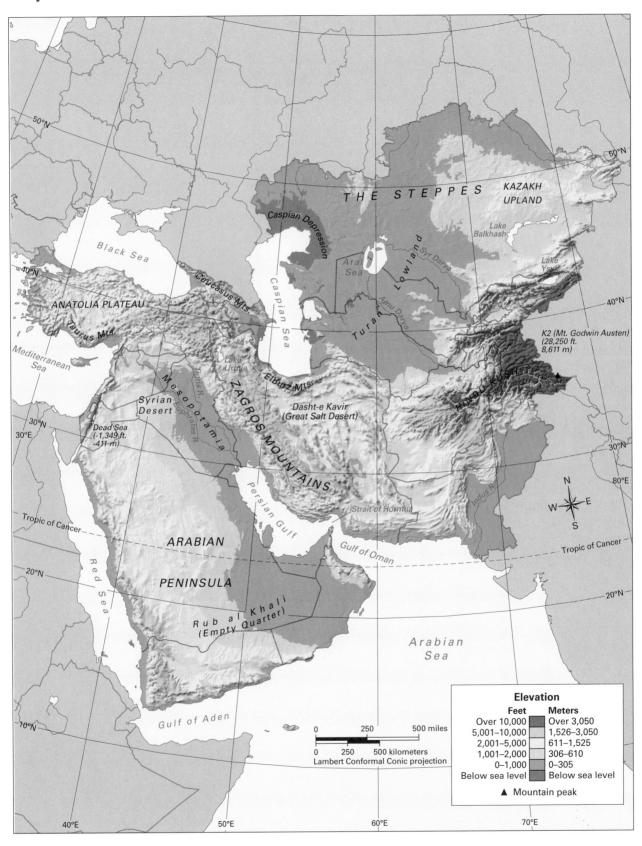

THE STEPPES

KAZAKH UPLAND

Caspian Depression

Black Sea

Lake Balkhash

Aral Sea

Turan Lowland

Syr Darya

Lake Ysyk

Caucasus Mts.

Caspian Sea

Amu Darya

ANATOLIA PLATEAU

Taurus Mts.

Elburz Mts.

K2 (Mt. Godwin Austen)
(28,250 ft.
8,611 m)

Mediterranean Sea

Lake Urmia

Dasht-e Kavir
(Great Salt Desert)

HINDU KUSH

Syrian Desert

Tigris R.

Euphrates R.

Mesopotamia

ZAGROS MOUNTAINS

Dead Sea
(-1,349 ft.
-411 m)

Indus R.

Persian Gulf

Strait of Hormuz

Tropic of Cancer

ARABIAN

Gulf of Oman

Tropic of Cancer

Red Sea

PENINSULA

Rub al Khali
(Empty Quarter)

Arabian Sea

Gulf of Aden

Elevation	
Feet	**Meters**
Over 10,000	Over 3,050
5,001–10,000	1,526–3,050
2,001–5,000	611–1,525
1,001–2,000	306–610
0–1,000	0–305
Below sea level	Below sea level

▲ Mountain peak

0   250   500 miles

0   250   500 kilometers
Lambert Conformal Conic projection

50°N · 50°N · 40°N · 40°N · 30°N · 30°N · 20°N · 10°N

30°E · 40°E · 50°E · 60°E · 70°E · 80°E

Political Boundaries of Southwest and Central Asia

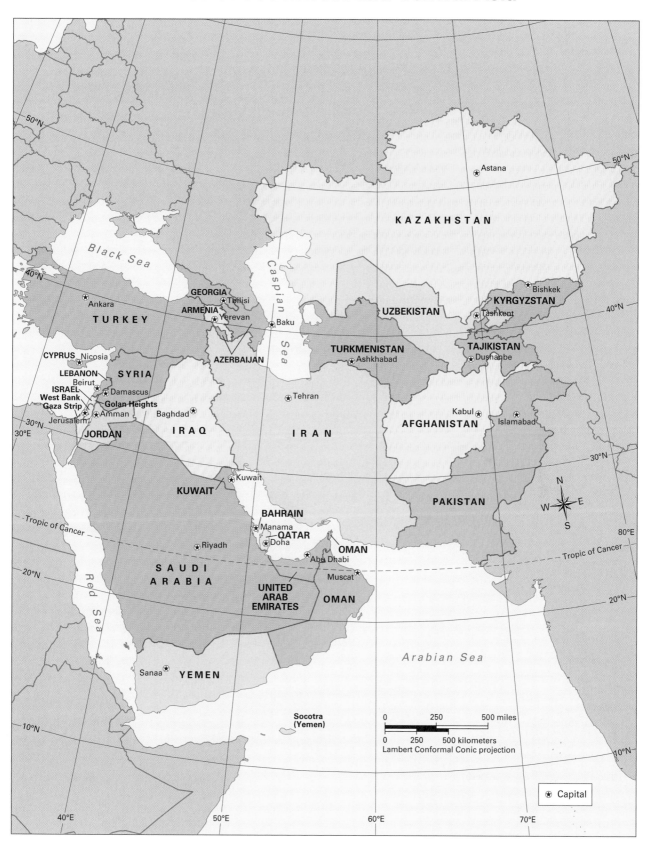

Black Sea

Caspian Sea

50°N

40°N

40°N

30°N

20°N

10°N

30°E

40°E

50°E

60°E

70°E

80°E

Tropic of Cancer

Tropic of Cancer

Red Sea

Arabian Sea

KAZAKHSTAN
⊛ Astana

Ankara ⊛

TURKEY

GEORGIA
⊛ Tbilisi
ARMENIA
⊛ Yerevan
⊛ Baku

AZERBAIJAN

UZBEKISTAN
⊛ Tashkent

Bishkek ⊛
KYRGYZSTAN

TURKMENISTAN
⊛ Ashkhabad

TAJIKISTAN
⊛ Dushanbe

CYPRUS Nicosia ⊛
LEBANON
Beirut ⊛
ISRAEL ⊛ Damascus
West Bank
Gaza Strip Golan Heights
Jerusalem ⊛ ⊛ Amman

SYRIA

Baghdad ⊛

IRAQ

⊛ Tehran

IRAN

Kabul ⊛
Islamabad ⊛

AFGHANISTAN

PAKISTAN

JORDAN

⊛ Kuwait

KUWAIT

BAHRAIN
⊛ Manama
QATAR
⊛ Doha

Riyadh ⊛

SAUDI
ARABIA

UNITED
ARAB
EMIRATES

⊛ Abu Dhabi

OMAN

Muscat ⊛

OMAN

N
W ⊛ E
S

Sanaa ⊛ YEMEN

Socotra
(Yemen)

0		250		500 miles

0	250	500 kilometers

Lambert Conformal Conic projection

⊛ Capital

Physical Features of South Asia, East Asia, and Southeast Asia

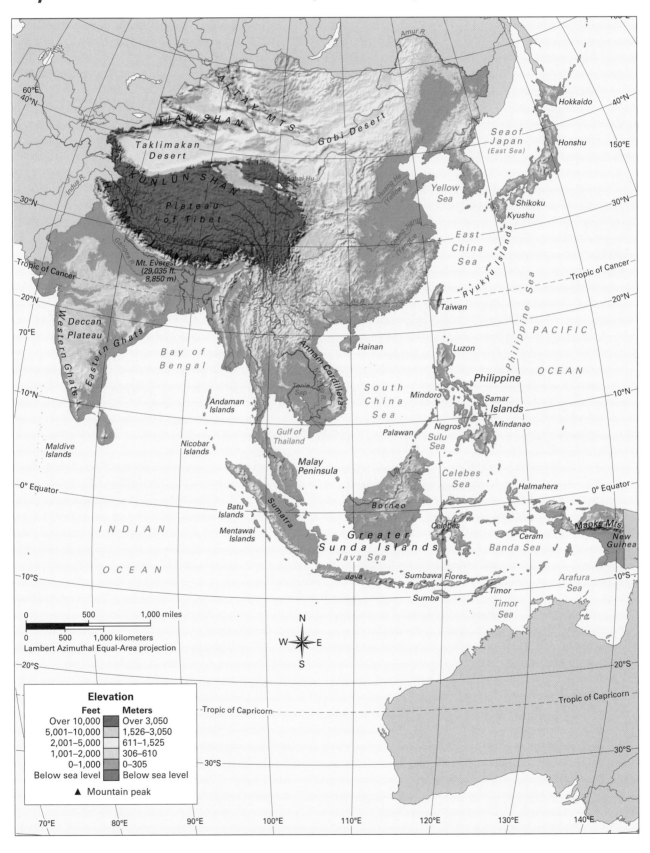

Elevation

Feet	Meters	
Over 10,000	Over 3,050	
5,001–10,000	1,526–3,050	
2,001–5,000	611–1,525	
1,001–2,000	306–610	
0–1,000	0–305	
Below sea level	Below sea level	

▲ Mountain peak

0   500   1,000 miles

0   500   1,000 kilometers

Lambert Azimuthal Equal-Area projection

Political Boundaries of South Asia, East Asia, and Southeast Asia

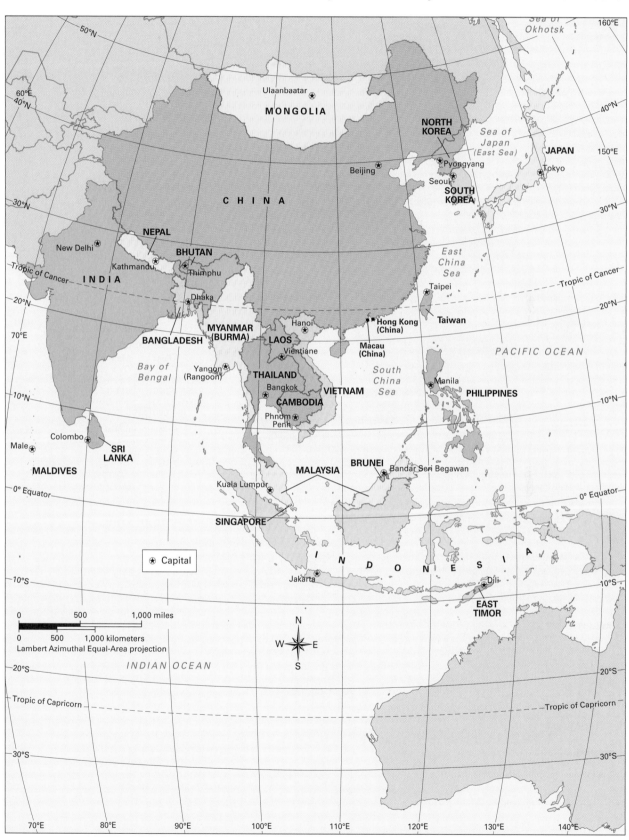

Physical Features of Oceania and Antarctica

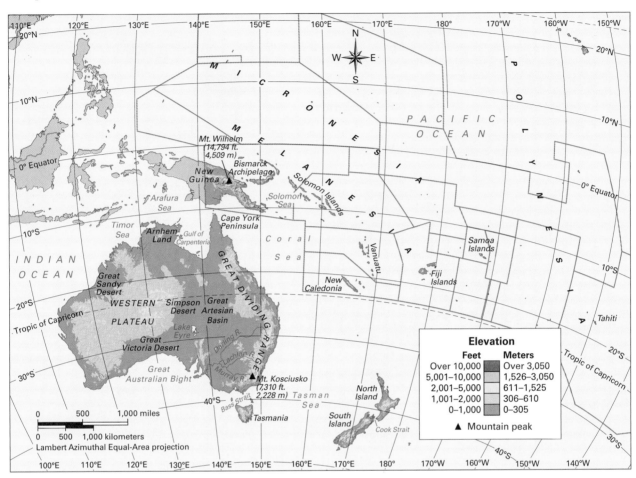

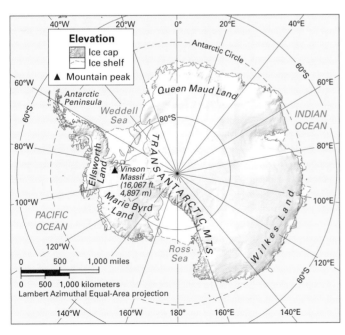

Political Boundaries of Oceania and Antarctica

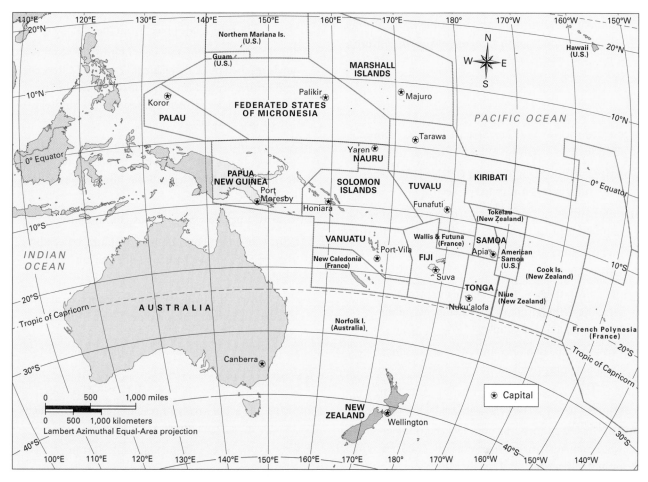

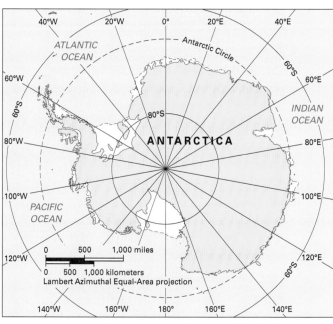

Glossary

Some words in this book have been respelled to help you pronounce them. Respelled words have been adapted from *Merriam-Webster's Collegiate Dictionary, Eleventh Edition; The American Heritage Dictionary of the English Language, Fourth Edition;* and *Random House Dictionary.*

A

absolute monarch a hereditary ruler whose power is unlimited

absolutism a system of rule in which a monarch or other ruler enjoys unlimited power

African Union a group of 53 African states that works to promote peace, security, and development in Africa

Afro-Eurasia the vast region made up of Africa, Europe, and Asia

aggression the practice of making unprovoked attacks or other military encroachments on the territory of another country

aggressor a person or country that attacks first, without being provoked

al Qaeda an international terrorist organization, founded by the terrorist leader Osama bin Laden

Amritsar Massacre the unprovoked killing or wounding by British troops of nearly 1,500 peaceful protesters at Amritsar, Punjab in 1919

apartheid the system of racial separation in South Africa, designed to create a fully segregated society

apostles the twelve followers of Jesus, designated to spread his message

appeasement making concessions to an aggressor in order to avoid conflict; the policy of giving in to the demands of a potential enemy in order to avoid conflict

Arab League an organization of Arab states in the Middle East, formed in 1945 to encourage cooperation, peace, and security among member states

Arab oil embargo a halt in oil exports from Arab countries to the West, which began during the 1973 Arab-Israeli War and lasted for six months

Arab Spring name for the popular upheavals that swept Arab countries of North Africa and the Middle East in 2011

archipelago a group of islands

aristocracy a ruling class of noble families

arms race a competition to achieve weapons superiority

artifact a human-made object from the past

Atlantic Charter the statement of principles and war goals reached by U.S. President Franklin D. Roosevelt and British Prime Minister Winston Churchill in 1941, which later formed the basis for the charter of the United Nations

authoritarian relating to or favoring a concentration of power in a leader or leaders who are not responsible to the people and which calls for blind submission to authority

autocrat a person who rules with unlimited authority

autonomy control over one's own affairs, especially the right of self-government; self government; independence

Axis Powers the name given to Italy and Germany, and later also to Japan and other German allies, during World War II

B

bailout the act of saving or rescuing something, such as a business, from financial problems

bankrupt reduced to a state of financial ruin

Bessemer process a relatively inexpensive method for converting iron to steel by using a blast of air to remove carbon from molten iron

bias a personal preference or prejudice

birthrate the number of births divided by the population during a given period, often expressed as births per 1,000 people in a given year

Blitzkrieg German for "lightening war," a military tactic that combined swift, massive and highly coordinated attacks by planes, tanks, and infantry to overwhelm and quickly conquer an enemy

Boxer Rebellion an uprising by a secret group known as the Righteous and Harmonious Fists, called "Boxers" by Westerners, that attempted to drive all foreigners from China

boyars Russia's landowning nobility

British Raj the 90-year period of British colonial rule in India that took place between 1858 and 1947

bubonic plague a deadly bacteria responsible for the Black Death of the 1300s; transmitted by fleas living on infected rats

bureaucracy a complex system of officials and workers who manage the activities of a government; a system in which nonelected government officials are organized into specialized departments and operate according to fixed rules within a hierarchy of authority

Byzantine Empire the name for the eastern Roman Empire, located at the crossroads of Europe and Asia; it lasted from about 500 to 1453 C.E.

C

caliph a spiritual and political leader of the Muslims

Camp David Accords a 1978 peace agreement between Egypt and Israel in which Israel returned land taken from Egypt in 1967 and Egypt recognized Israel's right to exist

capital the tools, machines, and buildings used to produce goods and services; wealth in the form of money or of resources that are used to produce other goods

capitalism an economic system, based on the premise of self-interest, in which all resources are privately owned and markets determine how those resources are distributed

caste a hereditary social class in Hindu society

censor to examine something in order to remove parts of it that are considered objectionable

chronology a sequence of events in time

city-state a political unit consisting of an independent city and the lands surrounding it

civil disobedience the breaking of or refusal to obey laws or other governmental commands to protest and bring attention to a perceived injustice and force change

civil liberties personal freedoms that are protected by law from the actions of a government

civil service examination a test given to qualify candidates for positions in the government

civil service the bureaucracy of government officials

civilian someone who is not an active member of a police or military force

civilization a highly organized and complex society

coalition a temporary union of political parties, usually, in a parliamentary system, in order to form a government; a joining of separate forces to accomplish a common goal

Cold War the struggle for power that took place between the United States and the Soviet Union in the decades after World War II

Columbian Exchange the transfer of plants, animals, and diseases between the eastern and western hemispheres

command economy an economic system in which decisions about production and consumption are made by a powerful ruler or government

Commercial Revolution the rapid expansion of trade and commerce that transformed Europe, starting in the 16th century

common market a group formed by countries within a geographical area with the goal of eliminating taxes on trade goods and allowing the free movement of labor and capital among its members

comparative advantage the theory that in international trade, countries should specialize in the goods that they are most efficient at producing

concession a special economic privilege granted to a foreign power

conquistador Spanish conqueror of the Americas

conservative favoring the maintenance of existing institutions and traditional values

Constantinople the city on the eastern edge of Europe, which Constantine made the capital of the Roman Empire in 330 C.E.

constitutionalism a political theory calling for government according to fundamental laws and principles

containment the U.S. policy of attempting to restrict Soviet power and influence around the world by preventing the spread of communism

corporatism the organization of a society into industrial and professional corporations which exercise control over individuals subject to them and serve as units of political representation

Counter-Reformation a movement to revive and defend Catholicism in response to the Reformation

counterattack an attack made in response to an enemy's attack

coup d'etat the sudden overthrow of a government by violent force; from a French term meaning "blow to the state"

coup a sudden, violent overthrow of an existing government by a small group

covenant a sacred agreement

covert action a secret political, economic, or military operation sponsored by a government and designed to support a foreign policy objective

creditor a person or company to whom money is owed

Crusades Christian campaigns to retake the holy lands from Muslims

cultural diffusion the spread of cultural traits from one society or place to another; the spread of ideas, inventions, or other cultural elements from one society to another

Cultural Revolution a period of revolutionary upheaval and political persecution in China from 1966 to 1976

culture the shared beliefs, practices, and traditions of a group

customs taxes that must be paid to the government on goods brought in from other countries

czar a Russian emperor

D

D-Day June 6, 1944, the day that Allied forces invaded France to free it from Nazi rule and eventually defeat Germany in World War II

daimyo feudal lords in Japan

Dar al-Islam lands under Muslim rule, where Islam can be practiced freely

death rate the number of deaths divided by the population during a given period

denomination a religious group or movement within a larger religion sharing a common interpretation of that religion

despot an absolute ruler

détente the easing of Cold War tensions and hostility between East and West during the 1970s

deterrence the policy of building a weapons arsenal so deadly that no other nation will dare attack

developed country a wealthy nation with substantial industrialization

developing country a poor nation with little or no industrialization, whose economy is less industrialized than those highly developed, highly industrialized countries and where the average incomes are much lower than those of highly industrialized nations

dharma a belief found in Hinduism and other Indian traditions that a person has a duty or obligation to live an honorable life

dialect a regional variety of a language

dictatorship a nation or government in which total control is in the hands of one all-powerful ruler

direct democracy rule by the people, carried out through direct participation in government

divine right the notion that a ruler's power is derived from God and cannot be questioned

domestic system a pre-industrial system of manufacturing in which workers crafted products in their homes using raw materials supplied by merchants

domestication a biological process in which the physical characteristics of wild plants and animals change as a result of human intervention

dominion a nation within the British Empire that controls its own domestic and foreign affairs, but is tied to Britain by allegiance to the British monarch

domino theory the belief that if Vietnam fell to the communists, the rest of Asia would fall like a row of dominoes

drug cartel a criminal organization that controls drug trafficking operations

dynasty a line or series of rulers descended from one family

E

Eastern Orthodox Church a Christian religion that developed out of early Christianity in the Byzantine Empire

economic imperialism the domination of one nation by another nation—and companies within it—that is economically more powerful

elite a group of persons who occupy a privileged position in society, often due to birth and/or education and who have power and influence

embargo a government order involving trade with another nation that forbids the buying or selling of something; a government order that restricts or prohibits trade with another nation

emperor the political leader of a territory containing several countries or groups of people

empire a large political unit in which a number of different lands or peoples are governed by a single ruler

enclosure the repossession and fencing-in by landowners of formerly common lands, often for the purpose of commercial farming

Enlightenment an intellectual 18th-century movement that sought to apply scientific methods to the study of society and government

entrepreneur a person who takes a financial risk by starting a business

epidemic an outbreak of disease that spreads rapidly

ethnic cleansing forced removal from a given territory of persons of another ethnic or religious group

European Union an alliance of European countries begun in 1993 which was designed to advance the continent's economic integration and unify its laws and foreign policies

evidence information in various forms used by historians to reconstruct the past

excommunication expulsion from a church or religious community

exile the condition of living outside one's home country, usually for political reasons, either by choice or by order of the home country's government

F

factory system an industrial system of manufacturing in which workers, raw materials, and machinery are gathered under the same roof

fascism a political philosophy or system marked by strong central authority and that places the nation, and often a race, above individual rights and freedoms

filial piety respect shown by children to their parents

G

gender roles customs relating to the position of men and women in society

general strike a work stoppage by a large portion of the entire workforce of a locality or country

genocide actions taken with the intent to destroy an ethnic, racial, or religious group; the planned and systematic extermination of an entire racial, ethnic, political, or culture group

geocentric theory the idea that Earth is the center of the solar system or universe

Ghana a medieval civilization and empire in West Africa

ghetto a section of a city in which members of a minority group live, especially because of force or social, legal, or economic pressures

globalization the process by which the regions, peoples, and economies of the world are becoming increasingly interconnected; the process of increasing the interdependence of the world's economies

glyph a symbol for a word, idea, or sound in a hieroglyphic system of writing

Great Dying the devastation of American Indian populations by diseases brought over from Europe

greenhouse effect the trapping of the sun's heat in the lower atmosphere, caused by the presence of carbon dioxide and other gases

gross domestic product the total value of goods and services produced in a country in a year

guerrilla war a form of warfare that involves surprise attacks by small groups of fighters, including harassment of the enemy and sabotage; an approach to warfare that relies on mobility, hit-and-run tactics, and the element of surprise to harass a larger, stronger opponent

gunpowder revolution the military advances that resulted from the development of gunpowder weaponry

H

habeas corpus the legal concept that an accused person cannot be jailed indefinitely without being charged with a crime

haiku short Japanese verse of 17 syllables

hajj in Islam, the pilgrimage to Mecca that is prescribed as a religious duty for Muslims

hegemony a dominating influence of one country or group over another; indirect social, political, or economic influence exerted by a dominant state

heliocentric theory the idea that the sun is the center of the solar system, with Earth and the other planets revolving around it

heresy holding religious beliefs that contradict the teachings of the church

heretic a person who holds beliefs that are contrary to a set of religious teachings

hierarchy a ranking of groups of people according to their importance, status, or power

Holocaust the systematic, state-sponsored, persecution and murder of Jews by the Nazis

home rule limited self-government over internal matters that is granted by a large political unit to a smaller one within it

human rights rights that are regarded as belonging to all people, such as the right to life, liberty, and equality before the law, as well as freedom of religion, expression, and assembly

humanism a Renaissance philosophy emphasizing the worth of the individual and balancing religious faith with secular learning

Hundred Years' War a series of battles fought between France and England from 1337 to 1453

hunter-gatherer a human who subsists by hunting wild animals and gathering wild plants

I

ideology a set of basic ideas, beliefs, and values that form the basis of a social, economic, or political philosophy or program

imperial belonging or related to an emperor

imperialism a policy in which a state takes political and economic control of areas beyond its borders; extending a nation's power and influence by gaining control over territory through political or military means

Indian Civil Service the body of some 1,500 appointed officials who carried out day-to-day government of British India

Indian National Congress an organization founded in 1885 to improve the rights and status of Indians in British colonial India and a major political party in India since its independence in 1947

indulgence an official church pardon that relieved Catholics from punishment for sins

Industrialization the process of converting from an agricultural society to one in which large-scale production dominates

Industrial Revolution beginning in the late 1700s, a period in which mechanical power replaced muscle power for the production of goods.

inflation a rise in prices caused by an increase in the supply of money and a resulting decline in its value

infrastructure large-scale transportation, communication, and other systems that support economic activity

infrastructure the facilities or equipment required for a community or nation to function, including roads, power systems, and transportation

interchangeable parts parts that can be swapped for one another in the assembling of a product, because they have been precisely cut and shaped to be identical

interregional involving or linking two or more regions; referring to a land area covering two or more regions

Iranian Revolution the overthrow of the shah of Iran in 1979 and the creation of an Islamic state

Iron Curtain the ideological barrier that divided Eastern and Western Europe during the Cold War

isolationism a policy of limiting a nation's international relations so that it can exist in peace and harmony by itself in the world

J

janissary slave soldier in the Ottoman Empire, usually Christian

Jewish Diaspora the spread of the Jewish people outside their homeland, beginning about 586 B.C.E.

K

kabuki a style of Japanese theater

karma a belief found in Hinduism and other Indian traditions that the good and evil done in a past life determines the nature of that person's next life

khan Mongol tribal leader

Khmer Rouge the communist movement in Cambodia that took power in 1975

kinship family relationship, either by birth, marriage, or adoption

Korean War a war from 1950 to 1953 between communist North Korea and non-communist South Korea that involved Soviet and Chinese support for the North and U.S. and UN support for the South

L

labor union an organization formed by workers to represent them in negotiations with employers concerning employment issues

liberal favoring individual political and economic freedom, with limits on state power

liberalism a political ideology favoring individual political and economic freedom, with limits on state power

life expectancy the average number of years people live within a given population

Long March the year-long, 6,000-mile retreat of the Red Army and communist leaders from southeastern to northwestern China after their defeat by Nationalist forces in October 1934

M

Magna Carta a written legal agreement signed in 1215 that limited the English monarch's power

Mandate of Heaven the Chinese belief or idea that a ruler's power stemmed from divine authority or came from divine approval

mandate an authorization or order given to a lesser authority by a superior one; a territory governed under such an authorization or order from the League of Nations; specifically, a former German or Turkish colony given over by the League of Nations to France and Britain to administer after World War I

Marshall Plan a U.S. aid plan designed to promote economic recovery in Europe after World War II

martial law temporary military control of an area in place of civilian authorities; usually authorized by a government in emergencies when local law enforcement agencies cannot maintain public order and safety and often invoked during times of civil unrest

mass production the high-volume, low-cost manufacture of identical items through the use of specialization and interchangeable parts

matrilineal a family line traced through the mother

mercantilism an economic philosophy that favored self-sufficiency, called for stockpiling gold and silver, encouraged exports, and discouraged imports

meritocracy a system in which advancement is based on individual ability or achievement and not on birth rights; rule by officials of proven merit

Mesoamerica a region of pre-Columbian culture stretching from central Mexico through northern Central America

mestizos persons of mixed European and Native American ancestry

middleman person who provides a service that links two people or groups

militarism a belief in increasing a nation's military strength as the way to become or remain powerful; the glorification of military virtues and ideals; the predominance of the armed forces in making and carrying out the policies of a nation; the glorification of military preparedness and armed strength

millennium a period of 1,000 years

millet communities of non-Muslim people organized according to religion, in which minority groups held a limited amount of power to rule themselves

Model Parliament a governing body created by King Edward I that included some commoners, Church officials, and nobles

monopoly complete control by one firm of the production and/or the supply of a good

monotheism belief in one God

Monroe Doctrine a United States foreign policy focused on keeping European powers from controlling any Latin American nation

multinational corporation a company with facilities in more than one country; a large company based in one country but with operations in other parts of the world

Munich Pact a settlement reached in September 1938 in which Britain and France agreed to let Germany annex part of Czechoslovakia

N

nation-state a politically independent state whose people have a common culture and nationality

nationalism pride and devotion to one's nation; also, the idea that a people with a common language, culture, and history should have its own nation-state

nationalize to transfer something from private ownership to ownership by the government

NATO a mutual defense pact formed by Western nations in 1949

natural resource any naturally occurring material that people find useful or valuable

natural rights rights that belong to people "by nature," simply because they are human beings.

neutrality the position of not favoring or supporting either side in a dispute

nirvana an ideal state of happiness and peace, attained through enlightenment

no-man's land an unoccupied area between opposing armies

nonaligned nations independent Third World countries that tried to remain neutral in the Cold War struggle between East and West

North American Free Trade Agreement (NAFTA) a 1993 treaty, signed by Mexico, the United States, and Canada, to create a free trade zone

Nuremberg Trials trials the Allies held in Nuremberg, Germany, after World War II to hold Nazi leaders and other Germans accountable for war crimes and other atrocities they committed during the war

O

oligarchy a form of government in which a small group holds all the power to rule

Organization of Petroleum Exporting Countries (OPEC) an association of major oil producing nations, founded in 1960 with the aim of gaining control over oil prices and production

Orthodox Christianity the religion of the Eastern Orthodox Church, which split from Catholicism during the Byzantine Empire

Oslo Accords the agreement signed in 1993 in which the PLO recognized Israel and Israel granted Palestinian self-rule in parts of the West Bank and Gaza

outsource contract out or send offshore

P

Palestine Liberation Organization an organization established in 1964 to represent Palestinian interests and that pledged to destroy Israel; in 1993 it agreed to peace with Israel

Palestinian Authority the governing authority for Palestinian self-rule established through the Oslo Accord

partition divide a region into separate political units

pastoral nomad member of a group whose economy revolves around its herd of domesticated animals, with which the group periodically moves to find new grazing land

patriarch in the Eastern Orthodox Church, the bishop of an important city

Pax Mongolica the state of peace that existed in Eurasia under Mongol rule

periodization the division of history into periods of time

Persian Gulf War a 1991 conflict between Iraq and a coalition of international forces, led by the United States, following Iraq's invasion of Kuwait

perspective a painting or drawing technique that gives the appearance of depth on a flat surface

pictograph a drawing that stands for a word, phrase, or name

platform a declaration of principles on which a group of persons stands, especially the principles and polices adopted by a political party or candidate

plebiscite a direct "yes" or "no" vote by the people of a country on a matter of national importance

point of view a person's way of thinking about a subject

political revolution a seizure of government by people intent on replacing the existing political system

polytheism the worship of multiple gods

popular sovereignty the doctrine that the people are the source of all political power wielded by the state

population density the number of people in a given land area

populism a political philosophy that favors the common person's interests over those of wealthy people or business interests

primary source a historical record or document produced by an eyewitness or other observer who lived during the time period in question

productivity the amount of goods or services that result for each unit of required resources used (output per unit of input)

propaganda ideas, allegations, and other information that is spread deliberately and purposely, without regard to its accuracy, to further and gain support for a cause or damage an opposing cause, and that is often exaggerated or false

protectorate a nation protected and controlled by a stronger nation; a relationship in which the protection and partial control of one nation is held by another, more powerful nation and in which the stronger one provides larger services and protection, while the weaker makes many basic decisions

Protestant a Christian who separated from the Catholic Church during the Reformation; today, any member of a Christian church founded on the principles of the Reformation

puppet government a government that is appointed by and whose actions are controlled by an outside authority

Q

Qur'an the holy book of Islam

R

racist based on prejudices related to racial differences

rationing limiting the amount of something that people are allowed to have when there is not enough for everyone to have as much as they want

recession a period in which there is a decline in economic activity and prosperity

Reformation a reform movement of the 16th and 17th centuries that split the Catholic Church and gave birth to the Protestant religion

regent a person who rules a country while its monarch is too young, old, or ill to rule, or is absent

Renaissance a flowering of culture, based on classical Greek and Roman ideas, that began in Italy in around 1300 and later spread throughout Europe

republic a system of government in which the people rule through representatives who govern according to law

republican a person who believes in a system of government in which the people exercise power through elected representatives

republicanism belief in a form of government marked by separation of powers and representation of the people through elected officials

Resurrection in Christian belief, Jesus's rise from the dead

revenue income used to fund a nation's expenses; money that a government receives from taxes and other sources and uses to operate and provide public services

Roosevelt Corollary an extension of the Monroe Doctrine declaring that the United States would police unstable Latin American debtor nations; also known as the Big Stick Policy

rule of law the idea that all citizens, even the most powerful, are subject to the law

S

Salt March a nonviolent campaign of civil disobedience led by Mohandas Gandhi in 1930

samurai Japanese warriors

sanction a measure, often involving suspension of diplomatic or economic relations, taken by a nation or group of nations against another nation to pressure it to change its behavior

scientific method a method of investigation involving observation and theory to test scientific assumptions

Scientific Revolution a shift in thinking about the study of nature and the natural world that began in the mid-1500s and moved beyond traditional religious teachings

secondary source a record or document referring to past events but not produced at the time

secular having no religious or spiritual basis; not pertaining to or connected with religion; non-religious; related to concerns of the world; worldly

sedentary settled; nonmigratory

segregation the forced separation of a race, class, or ethnic group

separation of powers the division of powers among branches of government

serf a peasant farmer bound to the land with no political representation of social rights

Shi'a a minority branch of Islam that maintains loyalty to the caliph Ali and his descendants

shogun military ruler in feudal Japan

Six-Day War the third Arab-Israeli war, in 1967, which resulted in a quick Israeli victory and a major expansion of Israeli territory

social contract an agreement in which people give power to a government in return for its protections

socialism an economic system in which a nation's land, natural resources, industries, and other means of production are owned collectively or are controlled by the state

solar year the time it takes Earth to travel once around the sun

Solidarity a Polish union movement of the 1980s that became the major force of opposition to communist rule in Poland

sovereign self-governing and independent

sovereignty freedom from external control

spatial frames different geographic perspectives that historians apply to world events

sphere of influence an area within which the political and economic interests of one nation are more important than those of other nations; a territory that a foreign state claims to control in another country

stalemate a situation in which progress by either side in a contest or dispute is blocked by the other side; a draw or deadlock

stele a vertical stone slab or pillar with carvings or inscriptions

strike a form of protest in which workers refuse to work; an agreement among workers to stop working in order to force an employer to improve wages, hours, benefits, or working conditions

Suez Crisis an international incident in 1956 involving Egypt's seizure of the Suez Canal and invasions of Egypt by Israel, Britain, and France

Sufis a mystical form of Islam in which believers seek direct personal experience of God, often through prayer and meditations

Sunnah the example set by Muhammad for how Muslims should live

Sunni the majority branch of Islam, which accepted the rule of the Umayyad and Abbasid caliphates

superpower an extremely powerful nation, one of a very few dominant states in an era when the world is divided politically into these states and their satellites

surname the family name common to the members of a family

suspension bridge a bridge held up by cables anchored at each end

T

Taliban a radical and ultraconservative Muslim group that supported al Qaeda and ruled Afghanistan from 1996 to 2001, when U.S. forces ousted it from power

tariff a tax on imported or exported goods

terrorist one who carries out unlawful violence against civilian targets in order to instill fear and advance political goals

theocracy a state governed by religious leaders

Torah Judaism's most sacred text, consisting of the first five books of the Hebrew Bible

total fertility rate the average number of children women would give birth to in their lifetime if the current birthrate did not change

totalitarian a governing system in which a ruling elite holds all power and controls all aspects of society, allowing no opposition and often maintaining power with the use of terror and secret police

trans-Saharan trade trade between peoples north and south of the Sahara

trephination a type of surgery in which a hole is made in the skull

triangular trade a colonial pattern of trade that involved the transport of slaves from Africa to the Americas, sugar and other products from the Americas to Europe, and manufactured goods from Europe to Africa

tribute payment or respect offered by a less powerful state to a more powerful state

U

UN trust territory former mandates placed under United Nations administration after World War II

underground operating secretly, especially against a ruling power

unemployment insurance money paid by governments to workers who cannot find jobs

United Nations an international organization founded in 1945 to promote peace, security, and cooperation among the world's nations

universal standards ideas or values, such as human rights, that are said to apply to all people

urbanization the process of turning a rural area or village into a town or city

V

vernacular the native language of a people, region, or country

veto to prohibit or refuse to approve

Viet Cong communist insurgents in South Vietnam

Vietnam War the war between North and South Vietnam from the early 1950s to 1975

W

war crime a violation of internationally accepted practices related to waging war

warlord a military leader operating outside the control of the government; a military leader who governs by force, usually within a limited area

Warsaw Pact a 1955 defense pact between the USSR and Eastern European nations

westernization the spread of ideas and values originating in Europe and the Western world

world religion a religion practiced in various parts of the world, beyond its land of origin

Z

Zionist a person who supports the right for Jews to return to and create a state in their ancient homeland

Index

Page numbers in bold type indicate definitions. Page numbers followed by the letter "c" indicate a chart, graph or table. Page numbers followed by the letter "m" indicate a map.

B

Baath Party, 451

Babur, 131

Babylonian Exile, 33

Bacon, Francis, 154

Baghdad (Muslim Empire), 58

Bahrain, 325, 472

bailouts, **433**

Balfour Declaration, 319, 321, 322

Balkans
  Austria-Hungary's desire for, 251
  Islam's influence in, 39
  Ottoman Empire, as part of, 116, 127, 129
  pre-WWI, 252, 253, 267–268
  Russia's desire for, 252, 253, 268
  in WWII, 260

Bangladesh, 428

banking system, 224

bankruptcy, **283**

baptism, 36

Barbary States. *See also specific country*
  France and, 327–329

Bastille, 203

Bataan Death March, 370–371

Batista, Fulgencio, 304, 399, 412

Battle of Adowa, 242

Battle of the Argonne Forest, 275

Battle of Britain, 356–357

Battle of the Bulge, 364

Battle of Concord, 198, 199

Battle of the Coral Sea, 366

Battle of Crécy, 71, 72

Battle of Dien Bien Phu, 415

Battle of Lepanto, 130

Battle of Lexington, 198, 199

Battle of Marne, 269
  Second Battle, 275

Battle of Midway, 261, 366

Battle of Omdurman, 231, 233, 242

Battle of Orléans, 72

Battle of Saratoga, 200

Battle of Somme, 270
  Second Battle, 274

Battle of Stalingrad, 361

Battle of Verdun, 270

Battle of Yorktown, 200

Battuta, Ibn, 95

Battuta's caravan, 95

Bay of Pigs, 399, 413

B-25 bombers, 365

Becket, Thomas, 68

Begin, Israeli P.M. Menachem, 443

Belgium
  claiming of Congo Basin, 240
  as Flanders (in the Renaissance), 148
  Industrial Revolution, 218, 226
  in WWI, 269, 275
  in WWII, 354, 364

Berlin blockade, 393

Berlin Wall, 402

Bessemer process, **219**

Bhutto, Benazir, 428

Bhutto, Zulfikar Ali, 428

Biafra, Republic of, 419

bias, **3**

big business, 224

"big picture" view of history, 1, 3, 7

Big Stick Policy, 243

Bill of Rights, 181, 201, 202

bin Laden, Osama, 470

birthrate, **456,** 458

Bismarck, Otto von, 267

Black Death. *See* bubonic plague

Black Hand, 268

Blackshirts, 335, 336

Blitz, the, 357

Blitzkrieg ("lightning war"), **354,** 355

Bloody Sunday, 286

Boccaccio, Giovanni, 147

bodhi tree, 42

Boers, 239

Bolívar, Simón, 183, 209

Bolivia, 209. *See also* Latin America
  in the 18th/early 20th centuries, 297, 298, 302, 303

Bolshevik Party, 286

Bolsheviks, 285, 289, 345
  Revolution of 1917. *See* Russian Revolution of 1917
  after the Revolution of 1905, 288

Bombay (now Mumbai), 374

Bonampak murals, 103

Bonaparte, Napoleon, 182, 183, 204, 205, 208

Bosnia, ethnic violence in, 468, 469

Bosnia-Herzegovina

post-Ottoman Empire, 252
  pre-WWI, 267–268

Boston Tea Party, 198

bourgeoisie, 286

Boxer Rebellion, 186, 212–213, 250, 382

boyars, **140**

Bradley, U.S. General Omar, 362

Brahman, 41

Brahmins, 40

Brazil. *See also* Latin America
  in the 18th/early 20th centuries, 297, 298, 302, 303
  independence movements, 183
  Portuguese colonization of, 168
  post-WWII, 411
  revolutions in the 1800s, 210
  slave trade, 169
  sugar, 168

brazilwood, 168

Brezhnev, Leonid, 403

BRIC economies, 466

Britain. *See* Great Britain

British East India Company, 194, 236

British Enlightenment, 155–156

British Guiana, 244

British Honduras, 244

British Mandate for Palestine, 440, 441

British Raj, 236, **375–376**

Brownshirts, 339, 340, 342

Bruegel, Pieter, 149

bubonic plague, **62,** 65, 67, **69,** 160
  feudalism's decline and, 69–71
  impact of, 70–71
  spread of, 69, 70m

Buchenwald, 363

Buddha, 42

Buddhism, 31
  beliefs of, 43
  development of, 42
  Han Dynasty, 27
  influence of, 44
  Mauryan Empire, 28
  origins of, 42
  regional variations of, 48–49
  spread of, 43–44, 44m, 123
  Xuanzang, 51

buildings. *See* architecture

bureaucracy, **85, 116, 161, 375**
  Ottoman Empire, 128

détente, **402,** 403

deterrence, **402**

developed countries, **408**

developing countries/nations, **408, 427, 458**

    comparative advantage of, 466

devshirme, 129

dharma, 28, **41**

dialects, **103**

diamonds in Africa, 239, 410

Dias, Bartolomeu, 164

Díaz, Porfirio, 295, 299–301

di Cavour, Camillo, 206

Dickens, Charles, 191

dictators/dictatorships, **255.** *See also specific dictator*

    after World War I, 255–257

difference, 5

"different cultures" model, 1

Diocletian, Roman Emperor, 26, 53

direct democracy, **24**

diseases. *See also specific disease*

    Colombian Exchange, spread from, 121

    environmental factors, 65

    Native Americans, death of, 114, 121–122, 168

    Roman Empire, 53

    slavery voyages, 170

    urbanization and, 227

Divine Comedy, The (Alighieri), 147

divine right, **115**

"dome of heaven," 79

domestication, **14**

domestic system, **221**

Dominican Republic

    independence for, 304

    in the 19th/early 20th centuries, 305

    U.S. imperialism in, 244

dominion, **379**

domino theory, **398**

drastic, **106**

Dresden, 362

drug cartels, **434**

    in Mexico, 434

Druze Revolt, 317

Duma(s), 287, 289

Dürer, Albrecht, 149

Dutch East India Company, 173, 176

Dutch East Indies, 424

    independence for, 262

Duvalier, François "Papa Doc," 305

dynasty, **20, 86**

E

Eannes, Gil, 159

Earth Day, 463

Eastern Han, 27

Eastern Orthodox Church, 75, **78**

    arts, 79

    hierarchy in, 79

    liturgy of, 79

    prayer, 79

    role, in Byzantine Empire, 78

East Germany, 261, 393, 402

East India Companies, 176, 374–375

    British East India Company, 194, 236

    Dutch East India Company, 173, 176

East Pakistan, 427, 428

East Timor, 426

economic imperialism, **250**

economic structures/systems, 6

    ancient societies, 9, 29

    Byzantine Empire, 75, 81

    Cold War, 389, 405, 407, 421

    collapsing/expanding empires (300–1500 C.E.), 51, 65

    contemporary global issues, 455, 473

    developing countries, 423, 437

    Enlightenment, 145, 157

    Eurasia empires (1400–1800), 126, 142

    fascism and totalitarianism, 333, 347

    feudal period, 67, 73

    First Global Age (1400–1800), 109, 125, 159, 177

    Ghana, Kingdom of, 91, 99

    global achievements/crises, 247, 263

    Imperial China, 83, 89

    imperialism, 231, 245

    Industrial Revolution, 179, 185, 215, 229

    laissez-faire policies, 228

    Latin America (19th c./early 20th c.), 295, 307

    Middle East, 439, 453

    political revolutions, 197, 213

    religion and, 31, 49

Renaissance, 145, 157

Russian Revolution of 1917, 281, 293

Scientific Revolution, 145, 157

World War I (WWI), 265, 279

World War II (WWII), 349, 371

Ecuador, 298, 302. *See also* Latin America

education

    Confucianism, beliefs of, 46

    in Cuba (late 19th c./early 20th c.), 304

    in Cuba (under Castro), 413

    in czarist Russia, 283, 284

    in Egypt under British rule, 330

    Enlightenment, impact of, 157

    globalization, impact of, 472

    in India under British rule, 194, 374

    industrialization, impact of, 191, 226

    Islamic law and, 39

    in Lebanon (under French rule), 318

    in Meiji Japan, 211

    Mexican Revolution, impact of, 300, 303

    Ming scholar-officials, 89

    printing press, impact of, 145

    religious influences, 39, 48, 336

    in the Renaissance, 146

    Song dynasty, 87

    South Africa, post-apartheid, 421

    Soviet crisis in, 403

    after the Spanish Civil War, 343

    in Tanzania under Nyerere's rule, 430

    in Transjordan, 320

    Western imperialism, impact of, 245

Edward I, King of England, 69

efficiency experts, 225

Egypt

    ancient Egypt, 20–21

    British in, 330–331

    democratic movements in, 472

    hieroglyphics, 21

    independence in 1922

    nationalism in, 330–331, 446–447

    pre-WWII, 330–331

    in WWII, 331

Eightfold Path, 43

Einstein, Albert, 368

elite, **296**

Notes

Chapter 2

24, Pericles: "Thucydides (c. 460/455-c. 399 BCE): Pericles' Funeral Oration from the Peloponnesian War (Book 2.34-46)," at Ancient History Sourcebook, www.fordham.edu/Halsall/ancient/asbook.asp.

Chapter 4

58, Yakut, *Geographical Encyclopedia:* William Stearns Davis, ed., *Readings in Ancient History: Illustrative Extracts from the Sources*, 2 Vols. (Boston: Allyn and Bacon, 1912–13), Vol. II: *Rome and the West.* **61, Genghis Khan's grandson:** Felipe Fernández-Armesto, *Civilizations* (Free Press, 2001). **62, Marco Polo:** Jack Weatherford, *Genghis Kahn and the Making of the Modern World* (Crown, 2004).

Chapter 6

76, French soldier (Geoffroi de Villehardouin): Charles Diehl, *Byzantium: Greatness and Decline*, trans. Naomi Walford (New Brunswick, NJ: Rutgers University Press, 1957). **78, Procopius:** Procopius, *The Secret History*, trans. Richard Atwater (New York: Cosimo, 1927).

Chapter 7

83, Emperor Han Wu Di: Herbert Allen Giles, ed. and trans., *Gems of Chinese Literature* (B. Quaritch, 1884), at www.books.google.com.

Chapter 8

92: Arab historian: A. Adu Boahen and Alvin M. Josephy, *The Horizon History of Africa*, Vol. 1 (New York: American Heritage, 1971).

Chapter 10

117, Giles Fletcher: *The European Emergence: TimeFrame AD 1500–1800* (Time-Life, 1989). **119, Guatemala colonist:** Peter Winn, *Americas* (Pantheon, 1992). **119, Spanish conquistador:** Charles C. Mann, *1491* (Vintage, 2006). **121–122, Eyewitness to Great Dying in Peru:** Charles C. Mann, *1491* (Vintage, 2006). **122, Bernardino de Sahagún:** Bernardino de Sahagún, *General History of the Things of New Spain*, quoted in Charles C. Mann, *1491* (Vintage, 2006). **122, Charles C. Mann on Great Dying:** Charles C. Mann, *1491* (Vintage, 2006).

Chapter 11

128, Babur: Rhoads Murphey, *A History of Asia* (HarperCollins, 1992), also in Stanley Wolpert, *A New History of India* (Oxford, 2009). **130, Indian on Mughal decline:** Rhoads Murphey, *A History of Asia* (HarperCollins, 1992). **131, Ming emperor Zhu Yuanzhang:** Patricia Buckley Ebrey, ed., *Chinese Civilization and Society: A Sourcebook* (The Free Press, 1981). **133, Emperor Qianlong:** Rhoads Murphey, *A History of Asia* (HarperCollins, 1992).

Chapter 12

147, Niccolò Machiavelli: Stephen Thompson, ed., *The Renaissance* (Greenhaven, 2000). **150, Martin Luther:** Stephen Thompson, ed., *The Renaissance* (Greenhaven, 2000). **154, Francis Bacon:** J.M. Roberts, *History of the World* (New York: Penguin, 1990). **155, René Descartes:** René Descartes, *Discourse on the Method for Reasoning Well and for Seeking Truth in the Sciences* (1637), at http://records.viu.ca/~johnstoi/descartes/descartes1.htm#t6. **156, Adam Smith:** Adam Smith, *An Inquiry into the Nature and Causes of the Wealth of Nations* (London: Methuen and Co., Ltd., 1904).

Chapter 13

165, Christopher Columbus: David Boyle, *Toward the Setting Sun: Columbus, Cabot, Vespucci, and the Race for America* (New York: Walker & Company, 2008). **165, Pope:** Treaty of Tordesillas, translated in Frances Gardiner Davenport, *European Treaties Bearing on the History of the United States and its Dependencies to 1648* (1917, Carnegie Institution). **167, King Philip IV of Spain:** Stanley J. Stein and Barbara H. Stein, *Silver, Trade, and War: Spain and America in the Making of Early Modern Europe* (Baltimore: The Johns Hopkins University Press, 2000). **176, John Locke:** John Locke, *Some Considerations of the Consequences of the Lowering of Interest, and Raising the Value of Money. In a Letter Sent to a Member of Parliament, 1691*, at Electronic Text Center, University of Virginia Library, http://etext.virginia.edu/toc/modeng/public/LocCons.html.

Chapter 14

181, Patrick Henry: Mayo W. Hazeltine, ed., *Masterpieces of Eloquence: Famous Orations of Great World Leaders From Early Greece to the Present Time* (New York: P. F. Collier and Son, 1905). **185, Napoleon:** Teich Mikuláš and Roy Porter, eds., *The National Question in Europe in Historical Context* (Cambridge, United Kingdom: Cambridge University Press, 1993). **191, Charles Dickens:** Charles Dickens, *Hard Times (*London: Chapman and Hall, 1858). **194, Karl Marx:** Marxists, "The Future Results of British Rule in India," at Works of Karl Marx 1853, http://www.marxists.org/archive/marx/works/1853/07/22.htm.

Chapter 15

197, Thomas Paine: Thomas Paine, "Thoughts on the Present State of American Affairs," *Common Sense*, at University of Virginia Library, Electronic Text Center, http://etext.virginia.edu/toc/modeng/public/PaiComm.html. **199, Benjamin Franklin:** *The Pennsylvania Magazine of History and Biography*, Volume 45 (Philadelphia: Historical Society of Pennsylvania, 1921). **200, Thomas Paine:** Jack A. Goldstone, ed., *The Encyclopedia of Political Revolutions* (Washington, D.C.: Congressional Quarterly). **203, Declaration of the Rights of Man and of the Citizen:** Wickham Legg, ed., *Select Documents Illustrative of the History of the French Revolution* (Oxford: Clarendon Press, 1905), translation by TCI. **204, Olympia de Gouge:** Micheline R. Ishay, *The History of Human Rights: From Ancient Times to the Globalization Era* (Berkeley and Los Angeles: University of California Press, 2004, 2008).

Chapter 16

225, Sir John Barnard Byles: Sir John Barnard Byles, *Sophisms of Free-Trade and Popular Political Economy Examined* (Philadelphia, PA: Henry Carey Baird, 1872). **228, Adam Smith:** Adam Smith, *An Inquiry into the Nature and Causes of the Wealth of Nations*, Edwin Cannan, ed. 1904 (London: Methuen, 1904/1776), at Library of Economics and Liberty, www.econlib.org.

Chapter 17
231, Winston Churchill: Winston Churchill, *The River War: An Historical Account of the Reconquest of the Soudan* (London: Longmans, Green, 1899), at Internet Modern History Sourcebook, http://www.fordham.edu/halsall/mod/1898churchill-omdurman.html. **233, Jules Ferry:** Robert Aldrich, ed., *The Age of Empires* (London: Thames & Hudson, 2007). **234, Rudyand Kipling:** Rudyard Kipling, "The White Man's Burden," *McClure's Magazine*, vol. XII, No. 4, February 1899. **235, Sir James Stephen:** Ian Copland, *The Burden of Empire: Perspectives on Imperialism and Colonialis*m (South Melbourne, Australia: Oxford University Press, 1990).

Chapter 18
247, Archduke Franz Ferdinand: Memoir of Count Franz von Harrach, at www.firstworldwar.com/source/harrachmemoir.htm. **248, Bernhard von Bulow:** Bernhard von Bülow, "Hammer and Anvil Speech before the Reichstag, December 11, 1899 (English translation; excerpts)," at the World War I Document Archive, ed., Richard Hacken, Brigham Young University Library, wwi.lib.byu.edu.

Chapter 19
276, Georges Clemenceau: Dixon Wecter, *The Hero in America: A Chronicle of Hero-worship* (New York, Charles Scribner's Sons, 1941), at www.bookrags.com/quotes/Georges_Clemenceau. **Chapter 19 Lesson Presentation at www.teachtci.com:** Erich Maria Remarque, *All Quiet on the Western Front* (New York: Little, Brown and Company, 1929). Copyright © 1929 and 1930 by Little, Brown and Company; copyright renewed © 1957 and 1958 by Erich Maria Remarque. Reprinted by Permission of the Estate of Erich Maria Remarque.

Chapter 20
282, Czar Alexander II: "Russia," *Encyclopædia Britannica, Encyclopædia Britannica Online,* Encyclopædia Britannica Inc., 2012, www.britannica.com/EBchecked/topic/513251/Russia.

Chapter 21
305, Theodore Roosevelt: Albert Shaw, *The American Monthly Review of Reviews,* Volume 31 (New York: The Review of Reviews Co., 1905).

Chapter 22
312, Czar Nicholas I: Edward S. Creasy, *History of the Ottoman Turks, with a new introduction by Zeine N. Zeine* (Beirut: Khayats, 1961). **319, Balfour Declaration:** Baron Noel-Buxton, *Oppressed Peoples and the League of Nations* (London: J.M. Dent and Sons, 1922). **321, League of Nations:** Charles Herbert Levermore and Denys Peter Myers, *Yearbook of the League of Nations,* Volume 1 (New York: Brooklyn Daily Eagle, 1921).

Chapter 23
336, Benito Mussolini: Internet History Sourcebooks, Fordham University, www.fordham.edu/Halsall/mod/mussolini-fascism.asp. **342, Adolf Hitler:** "Adolf Hitler," *Encyclopædia Britannica, Encyclopædia Britannica Online,* Encyclopædia Britannica Inc., 2012, www.britannica.com. **342, Adolf Hitler:** Martin Goodman, ed., Jeremy Cohen and David Sorkin, associate eds., *The Oxford Handbook of Jewish Studies* (Oxford University Press: New York, 2002).

Chapter 24
349, Neville Chamberlain: Neville Chamberlain's "Peace For Our Time" speech, at Eurodocs, ed., Richard Hacken, Brigham Young University Library, www.lib.byu.edu/estu/eurodocs. **349, Winston Churchill:** Carlo D'Este, *Warlord: A Life of Winston Churchill at War,* (New York, Harper Collins, 2009). **352: Adolph Hitler:** "Nazis Take Czechoslovakia," Triumph of Hitler, The History Place, www.historyplace.org. **356, Winston Churchill:** Carlo D'Este, *Warlord: A Life of Winston Churchill at War,* (New York, Harper Collins, 2009). **Franklin Roosevelt:** "President and Public Pressure: For a Redress of Grievances," at The White House Historical Association, www.whitehousehistory.org. **368, Albert Einstein:** "Einstein's First Letter to Roosevelt," Albert Einstein's Letters to President Franklin Delano Roosevelt, at Hypertextbook,www.hypertextbook.com. **369, Harry Truman:** Stephens Walker, *Shockwave: Countdown to Hiroshima* (New York: HarperCollins, 2005).

Chapter 25
379, Mohandas Gandhi: *Non-cooperation: Recent Speeches and Writings of Mahatma Gandhi* (Madras, India; Ganesh and Co., 1920).

Chapter 26
389, American soldier: John Lewis Gaddis, *The Cold War: A New History* (New York: Penguin, 2005). **391, United Nations charter:** United Nations, at www.un.org. **392, Winston Churchill:** Walter LaFeber, *America, Russia, and the Cold War* (Hoboken, New Jersey: John Wiley, 1967) **392, Joseph Stalin:** Walter LaFeber, *America, Russia, and the Cold War* (Hoboken, New Jersey: John Wiley, 1967) **392, Harry Truman:** John Lewis Gaddis, *The Cold War: A New History* (New York: Penguin, 2005). **398, Lyndon Johnson:** John Lewis Gaddis, *The Cold War: A New History* (New York: Penguin, 2005). **402, John F. Kennedy:** John Lewis Gaddis, *The Cold War: A New History* (New York: Penguin, 2005). **407, Lyndon Johnson:** Ronald E. Powaski, *The Cold War* (Oxford: Oxford University Press, 1998).

Chapter 27
409, Jawaharlal Nehru: "Prime Minister Nehru: Speech to Bandung Conference Political Committee, 1955," at Internet Modern History Sourcebook, Fordham University, www.fordham.edu/halsall/mod/modsbook.asp. **414, Richard Nixon:** Thomas E. Skidmore and Peter H. Smith, *Modern Latin America* (Oxford: Oxford University Press, 1989).

Chapter 28
433, reporter on Mexican economy: Jonathan Kandell, *La Capital: The Biography of Mexico City* (New York: Random House, 1988).

Chapter 29
443, Anwar Sadat: "President Anwar Sadat's Address to the Israeli Knesset," at ibiblio: The Public's Library and Digital Archive, www.ibiblio.org. **448, Mohammad Reza Pahlavi:** Mehran Kamrava, *The Modern Middle East, A Political History since the First World War* (Berkeley and Los Angeles: University of California Press, 2005).

Credits

Chapter 13
158: Library of Congress, Geography and Map Division 160: Scala/Art Resource, NY 161: Scphoto48/Dreamstime.com 163: Bettmann/CORBIS 164: Tiziano Casalta/Dreamstime.com 165: North Wind Picture Archives/Alamy 166: The Granger Collection, NYC 167: North Wind Picture Archives/Alamy 168: The Granger Collection, NYC 169: The Art Archive 170: North Wind Picture Archives/Alamy 171: Lschirmbeck/Dreamstime.com 172: The Art Archive/Maritiem Museum Prins Hendrik Rotterdam/Gianni Dagli Orti 173: PjrStudio/Alamy 174: Mary Evans Picture Library/Alamy 175: Georgios Kollidas/Dreamstime.com 176: Mary Evans Picture Library/Alamy

Chapter 14
178: Tetra Images/Alamy 180: Library of Congress 181: North Wind Picture Archives/Alamy 182: Mary Evans Picture Library/Alamy 183: Getty Images 184: Everett Collection Inc/Alamy 185T: The Art Archive/Museo del Risorgimento Brescia/Gianni Dagli Orti 185B: The Art Archive 186: Mary Evans Picture Library/Alamy 187: North Wind Picture Archives/Alamy 188: The Francis Frith Collection/Art Resource, NY 189: Duncan Walker. iStockphoto 190: Nicku/Dreamstime.com 191: Library of Congress 192: The Art Archive/Maritiem Museum Prins Hendrik Rotterdam/Gianni Dagli Orti 193: The Art Archive 194: The Print Collector/Alamy

Chapter 15
196: Library of Congress 198: Library of Congress 199: Library of Congress 200: Library of Congress 201: Jon Helgason/Dreamstime.com 202: Giraudon/Bridgeman 203: Mary Evans Picture Library/Alamy 204: The Granger Collection, NYC 205: The Art Archive/SuperStock 206: ZU_09\iStockphoto 207: The Granger Collection, NYC 208: The Art Archive/Museo Historico Nacional Buenos Aires/Gianni Dagli Orti 209: Getty Images 210: The Art Archive/Museo Nacional Bogota/Gianni Dagli Orti 211: Library of Congress 212: Library of Congress 213: Library of Congress

Chapter 16
214: Rob Rayworth/Alamy 216: Steven Wynn/iStockphoto 217: David Taylor-hughes/Dreamstime.com 218: David Bukach/iStockphoto 219: Library of Congress 220: The Art Archive/Bibliothèque des Arts Décoratifs Paris/Collection Dagli Ort 221: Classic Image/Alamy 222: Ivy Close Images/Alamy 223: Idanbury/Dreamstime.com 224: Library of Congress 225: Lordprice Collection/Alamy 226: The Art Archive/Conservatoire des Arts et Métiers Paris/Marc Charmet 227: Duncan Walker/iStockphoto 228: The Granger Collection, NYC 229: Sampete/Dreamstime.com

Chapter 17
230: The Granger Collection, NYC 232: Hulton-Deutsch Collection/Corbis 233: Lebrecht Music and Arts Photo Library/Alamy 234: Library of Congress 235: Stapleton Collection/Corbis 236: Getty Images 237: Library of Congress 238: Library of Congress 239: Hulton-Deutsch Collection/CORBIS 240: Library of Congress 242: Library of Congress 243: Library of Congress 244: Library of Congress 245: Library of Congress

Chapter 18
246: Art Archive, The/SuperStock 249: De Agostini/Getty Images 250: Library of Congress 251: Bettmann/Corbis 252: Library of Congress 253: Bettmann/Corbis 254: Popperfoto/Getty Images 255: Everett Collection/SuperStock 256: De Agostini/SuperStock 257: Library of Congress 258: Fox Photos/Getty Images 259: graficart.net/Alamy 260: Library of Congress 261: Library of Congress 262: Getty Images

Chapter 19
264: Library of Congress 266: Private Collection/The Bridgeman Art Library International 267: akg-images/Alamy 268: Musee de la Ville de Paris, Musee Carnavalet, Paris, France/Archives Charmet/The Bridgeman Art Library International 270T: Bettmann/CORBIS 270B: Library of Congress 271: INTERFOTO/Alamy 272: Library of Congress 273: Archive Images/Alamy 274: Library of Congress 275: Library of Congress 276: The Art Archive/National Archives Washington DC 277: Everett Collection/SuperStock 279: Library of Congress

Chapter 20
280: The Granger Collection, NYC 282: The Art Archive/Culver Pictures 284: DIZ Muenchen GmbH, Sueddeutsche Zeitung Photo/Alamy 285: Rue des Archives/The Granger Collection 286: RIA Novosti 287: Mary Evans Picture Library/Alamy 288: The Granger Collection, NYC 289: Heritage Images/Corbis 291: The Granger Collection, NYC 292: The Stapleton Collection 293: rusm/iStockphoto

Chapter 21
294: Bpperry/Dreamstime.com 296: Library of Congress 297: Library of Congress 298: Library of Congress 299: Library of Congress 300: Library of Congress 301: Library of Congress 302: INTERFOTO/Alamy 303: Dmitri Kessel/Time Life Pictures/Getty Images 304: Library of Congress 305: The Granger Collection, NYC 307: Library of Congress

Chapter 22
308: The Granger Collection, NYC 310: Universal Images Group/SuperStock 312: The Granger Collection, NYC 313: INTERFOTO/Alamy 314: Photos 12/Alamy 315: Hulton-Deutsch Collection/CORBIS 317: Bettmann/CORBIS 318: Library of Congress 319: Library of Congress 320: Library of Congress 321: The Granger Collection, NYC 322: Library of Congress 323: ullstein bild/The Granger Collection 324: The Print Collector/Alamy 325: Bettmann/CORBIS 326: Bettmann/CORBIS 327: Private Collection/Archives Charmet/The Bridgeman Art Library International 328: Library of Congress 329T: Library of Congress 329B: Library of Congress 330: Keystone-France/Gamma-Keystone via Getty Images